# Open-Source Technologies for Maximizing the Creation, Deployment, and Use of Digital Resources and Information

Shalin Hai-Jew
*Kansas State University, USA*

Information Science
**REFERENCE**

| | |
|---|---|
| Managing Director: | Lindsay Johnston |
| Editorial Director: | Joel Gamon |
| Book Production Manager: | Jennifer Romanchak |
| Publishing Systems Analyst: | Adrienne Freeland |
| Development Editor: | Austin DeMarco |
| Assistant Acquisitions Editor: | Kayla Wolfe |
| Typesetter: | Nicole Sparano |
| Cover Design: | Nick Newcomer |

Published in the United States of America by
Information Science Reference (an imprint of IGI Global)
701 E. Chocolate Avenue
Hershey PA 17033
Tel: 717-533-8845
Fax: 717-533-8661
E-mail: cust@igi-global.com
Web site: http://www.igi-global.com

Library of Congress Cataloging-in-Publication Data

Open-source technologies for maximizing the creation, deployment, and use of digital resources and information / Shalin Hai-Jew, editor.
    p. cm.
Includes bibliographical references and index.
Summary: "This book highlights the global importance of open-source technologies in higher and general education by exploring a variety of issues related to open-source in education, such as its practical underpinnings, requisite cultural competence in global open-source, strategies for employing open-source in online learning and research, the design of an open-source networking laboratory, and other endeavors"--Provided by publisher.
ISBN 978-1-4666-2205-0 (hardcover) -- ISBN 978-1-4666-2206-7 (ebook) -- ISBN 978-1-4666-2207-4 (print & perpetual access) 1. Educational technology. 2. Open source software. 3. Digital communications. I. Hai-Jew, Shalin.
LB1028.3.O5547 2013
371.33--dc23
                        2012020188

British Cataloguing in Publication Data
A Cataloguing in Publication record for this book is available from the British Library.

All work contributed to this book is new, previously-unpublished material. The views expressed in this book are those of the authors, but not necessarily of the publisher.

*This is for R. Max*

# Editorial Advisory Board

# Table of Contents

## Section 1
## Foundations to Open Source Development

## Section 2
## Open Source Development in Higher Education Practice

**Section 3**
**Open Source in the Wide World**

**Section 4**
**Developing the User "Installed Base" for Open Source Resources**

# Detailed Table of Contents

### Section 1
### Foundations to Open Source Development

Open source software and the open source movement have changed how users access the Internet and produced equality of access for the global community. Despite the access to free software and code sharing for the public and corporate users, open source users remain unaware of cultural competency standards for all its users and designers. The research on cultural competence is conspicuously absent. This chapter defines open source cultural competence as an ethical and equity imperative for open source systems and the communities served by this free, accessible software. A theoretical framework for integrating cultural competence into open source technology is presented, one that emphasizes cultural competency best practices. Future implications for integrating cultural competence into open source technology are highlighted.

As the open source paradigm is influencing the modern economic world, an increasing number of scientific disciplines use the open working model in knowledge production process. The contemporary research field requires a new shift towards the constantly evolving digital age where collaboration and exchange of information is growing. The shift from traditional research models to open science may be the starting point for scientific innovation. This work presents the case of open scientific research as an analogy to the open source software movement and uses a case study from the Geo-Information technology sector.

The open educational movement is primarily about facilitating a philosophical view: the idea that universal access to quality education should be a global priority. Open educational courses are byproducts of the implementation of this philosophy. Unfortunately, the principles that are fueling the open educational movement are in direct opposition to the typical culture found in higher education institutions in the United States. The lack of awareness of or indifference to these cultural differences can hinder the integration of open educational resources. Successful integration of open educational courses into degreed programs requires an acknowledgement of the cultural dissonance that may result as well as a systematic plan for addressing it. This chapter highlights some of these cultural differences and outlines a framework for addressing them.

**Chapter 4**

Members of the private and public liberal arts colleges can play a special role in generating a coherent new paradigm for the undergraduate science education of Black American and Latino students—the two cohort populations in universities across the country that currently are not only the fastest growing, but also the greatest rates of attrition. The task at hand has potential significance in this new century beyond home institutions because students must be prepared to live in a world where technology is leveling the playing field and where the United States can no longer rely solely on the inherited teaching methods of the past to remain preeminent in science. Therefore, it is imperative that institutions of higher education develop strategies and interventions that engage students of color and help them achieve degrees in the STEM fields (science, technology, engineering, and mathematics). One approach, discussed in this chapter, is to create open source digital learning communities, that is, identities where knowledge can be constructed and disseminated through learning modalities that stimulate student engagement and persistence to graduation.

**Chapter 5**

Using a game theory model to analyze whether a content developer should pursue publishing with an open-source or proprietary publisher, this work describes a strategy for those content developers working in higher education in terms of an articulated strategy for publishing. This research also suggests the high costs of publishing for content developers and proposes ways for open-source publishers to attract and maintain talent for open-source publishing in socio-technical spaces. This chapter offers fresh insights on the uses of game theory to model stakeholder motivations and payoffs, and from there articulate basic strategies; in line with game theory, this model also suggests directions and hypotheses for future research in open-source academic publishing.

**Section 2**
**Open Source Development in Higher Education Practice**

**Chapter 6**

This chapter considers a virtualized open source networking lab to support Web based IT education. It discusses the difficulties in teaching networking related IT courses online. The discussion leads to the solution of virtualized open source technology. The chapter also examines some strategies in developing an open source virtual networking lab for hands-on practice in networking related IT courses. It then presents a case study on the use of an open source virtual networking lab in e-learning.

Digital educational resources are an increasingly visible and important component of the online learning environment. Concurrently, many organizations are faced with limited financial resources with which to provide their materials to the learners. In order to continue delivering materials but reduce the total cost of delivery organizations can implement free and open source technologies for digital educational resource deployment. Open source software and free online services, properly employed, can enhance organizational effectiveness while also reducing organizational expense.

Faculty, administrators, and staff at institutions of higher education are singularly well poised to create open-source digital learning contents. Creating open-source digital learning contents seems to fit with a university's mission and the education paradigm of sharing knowledge and training up others to move a domain field forward. Indeed, they have contributed to many open-source endeavors. While individual open-source development endeavors may require a relatively light investment by colleges and universities, the work of building open-source resources involves significant planning in order to support the endeavor in an organized way on a campus. This chapter introduces some of the known challenges and methods to building open-source resources for online learning in the higher education environment in the US.

Distance Education in India has come a long way since the launch of correspondence courses in 1962 at the Delhi University. There have been many changes over the period of time, and thus, a transition was observed from print based correspondence courses to media supported distance education. With the advent of technology, expansion of telephone network, and lowering of tariff, there has been expansion of e-learning services, web based education, and mobile learning. Currently there are around 600 conventional (face-to-face) universities in India serving around 1.2 billion students. Starting with one Open University in 1982, now we have 15 open universities. There are single mode and dual mode distance education institutions. These provide instructions from print based to technology enabled means. All these developments transformed the teaching learning. Many of the institutions followed Open Educational Resources and Open Source movement. Reasons are varied for adopting open source. With the purpose to reduce the costs on software development, freedom to improve the software and freedom to redistribute to help neighbours has made individuals, institutions, and governments support open source. In this chapter, the author examines some of the initiatives of Open Source in the field of higher, open and distance education in India.

## Section 3
## Open Source in the Wide World

Rising costs, combined with an increasing lack of flexibility of commercial course management technology tools such as uLearn and Blackboard, have prompted educators to consider other options. New advances in free and open source software, webware, and hardware are becoming attractive alternatives for educators and school systems due to decreased funding. These innovative digital tools hold promise to help educators overcome a variety of impediments to teaching and learning in the 21st century such as fostering student motivation. In the context of second/foreign language learning, the author seeks to present various technologies to P-16 educators that can be used for student oral language assessment. The author provides an overview of the obstacles language teachers must overcome in order to teach more effectively, as well as a synopsis of various options with which language instructors may not be familiar. Afterwards, findings from empirical research comparing the use of digital technology for the measurement of student speaking proficiency to the more conventional face-to-face method are presented. Student and instructor perceptions of using free and open source software are discussed, and the chapter concludes with a discussion of challenges that can appear when changes in assessment methods take place as well as avenues for future research.

Rabies is the deadliest infectious disease known to humans and animals and yet is almost always preventable even after an exposure has occurred. The lack of educational awareness is a major reason why over 55,000 people die of the disease every year. The Global Alliance for Rabies Control, in association with international partners in the field of public health, initiated new educational initiatives aimed at increasing global awareness for those living at daily risk of exposure to rabies. Three of the open source educational initiatives are described in this chapter, including: World Rabies Day; the establishment of a freely accessible scientifically accurate education bank; and hosting global webinars that connect public health experts interested in reducing the burden of rabies in their regions.

This chapter focuses on the how the advent of Web 2.0 has influenced the role of webmaster and given rise to the wiki master. In section 1, the author provides an overview of the role of webmaster and how a Web 2.0 mindset began to exert an influence on the duties of this individual. The section concludes with the rise of collaborative Web technologies, specifically Wikis. Section 2 describes the evolution of the wiki master and provides a distinction from its predecessor. The specific roles of a wiki master are described in detail here. Section 3 provides a case study-type overview of the wiki master at ELATEwiki. org. Section 4 provides more detail by looking a typical day in the life of the wiki master at ELATEwiki. Conclusive remarks are provided in the final section of this chapter.

## Chapter 13

A core form of the international sharing of research and analysis is done through articles, both those presented in live conferences and those published in any number of journals. Interactive articles integrate various elements to the basic text: hyperlinks; immersive simulations; electronic games; data sets; knowledge collections; digital photographs; multimedia; integrated wikis and blogs; and other aspects. These value-added pieces that build exploration, experience, and interactivity, are enabled by current authoring tools and Web servers and open-source contents. Enriched articles often encourage return engagements, and their open-source publishing often leads to greater levels of citations and readership. These enable the design of a work for multiple audiences, with opt-in sections for different levels of readers, for example. Interaction enables opportunities for more reflection, recursiveness, and understanding a topic from multiple angles and different levels of abstraction. Interactive articles tend to appear in open-source (or at least open-access) publications online, which enables access by wider reading publics and machine-searchability and often wider citations.

## Chapter 14

Although the subject of educational games has become a massive area of study, this chapter will present a small overview of what an instructor/facilitator should know and comprehend so as to start to put together an educational game. Through understanding of the components, structure, and utilization of various resources (such as open-source materials), the creation of an educational game is achievable to all.

## Section 4
## Developing the User "Installed Base" for Open Source Resources

## Chapter 15

This chapter surveys recent and continuing trends in software tools for preparation of open courseware, in particular audiovisual lecture materials, documentaries and tutorials, and derivative materials. It begins by presenting a catalog of tools ranging from open source wikis and custom content management systems to desktop video production. Next, it reviews techniques for preparation of lecture materials consisting of five specific learning technologies: animation of concepts and problem solutions; explanation of code; video walkthroughs of system documentation; software demonstrations; and creation of materials for instructor preparation and technology transfer. Accompanying the description of each technology and the review of its state of practice is a discussion of the goals and assessment criteria for deployed courseware that uses those tools and techniques. Holistic uses of these technologies are then analyzed via case studies in three domains: artificial intelligence, computer graphics, and enterprise information systems. An exploration of technology transfer to college and university-level instructors in the information sciences then follows. Finally, effective practices for encouraging adoption and dissemination of lecture materials are then surveyed, starting with comprehensive, well-established open courseware projects that adapt pre-existing content and continuing through recent large-scale online courses aimed at audiences of tens to hundreds of thousands.

The educational use of digital technologies such as mobile devices, computers, and the Internet are progressively replacing pens, books, and the physical spaces known as libraries. Both online synchronous and asynchronous learning modes are emerging as part of the learning styles used with children physically attending schools. Consequently schools and school districts deploy various sorts of software applications to meet the range of teaching, learning, and management functions they perform. As leaders of schools, principals have heightened responsibilities concerning the philosophical directions of schools, as well as aligning the uses of technologies across all facets of their organizations. Set against the backdrop of Australian experiences, this chapter sets out to canvas some of the less considered factors that ought to be taken into account when schools select software applications. Gaining congruence between school philosophies and the technologies used, often-time means open source software ought to be a preferable solution to closed, proprietary software. This argument is justified from pedagogical and management perspectives. Furthermore, it is argued that making informed decisions before adopting the use of a particular technology requires that school leaders understand the educational and technical demands of that technology, and also have a socially-critical understanding of technologies in education and in society more generally. Finally, it is argued that if school principals are willing to consider open source software solutions, the options for teaching and learning with technologies and the strategies for managing the infrastructure of the school in robust and cost effective ways, opens up.

# Chapter 17

Those who work in instructional technologies and design have long been turning to the usages of open-source resources (learning / course management systems, software tools and apps, authoring tools, digital learning objects, simulations, games, and virtual spaces) for online learning—for many reasons—their easy availability (through download), the often-free price-tag, the popularity of open-source resources among learners, and the savings in terms of development (not maintenance) costs. This chapter examines the selective adoption of open-source resources for online learning and the practical considerations that inform this decision.

# Preface

## INTRODUCTION

"Open source" approaches to the world of content development and sharing is highly contested. A majority of business models in the world require high-level control of all intellectual property (IP) and the need to develop and produce in proprietary ways. Without this regime, the global economy could not function. Research and development (R&D), which is expensive to fund, is highly protected, and employees work for such companies after having signed various non-disclosure and non-compete agreements. Certainly, there is a role for maintaining secrets and ensuring that these are not lost to leakage, espionage, or inadvertent sharing.

The role of "open source," though, has its place. Open source refers the transparency of released code for all to view and access. It refers to the collaborative building of a shared product for the benefit of a larger populace—often without user cost (but with outsized contributions by the open source developers and sponsoring organizations). Open source refers to projects that are designed and developed under the auspices of the general public, without necessarily having a commercial patron or sponsor; it can also refer to projects that are collaborations between open source developers and commercial entities with an interest in a particular product.

Theoretically, it may push out the productivity of a society—by affecting the Pareto efficiency curve (a conceptualization that represents the cumulative output of a society given limited resources and the societal strategies for the allocation of resources). This curve is conceptually achieved when no one may be better off without making someone else worse off. This assumes that all resources are used in the maximal ways possible—with excess unallocated resources—in a kind of zero sum situation. Another conceptualization of the production possibility curve looks at a society's investments as butter (civilian expenditures) and guns (defense expenditures). There are trade-offs between choices in a nation-state's allocations. Open source, if it captures wide popularity, has a potential to push out the production possibility curve for both guns and butter because of the nature of innovations. New technologies and methods of work may benefit multiple aspects of a society.

Open source refers to any number of digital contents (software, authoring tools, digital learning objects, photos, video, audio, and other objects) released to the public through a fairly new brand of copyright release. On another level, open source manifests as an idealistic social movement of open-sharing. Given the interdependence required between developers and users and other stakeholders, open source creates social cohesions (and divisions) in electronic spaces.

## Some Enablers of Open Source Development

In a competitive profit-driven market, open source enables parallel development tracks of digital resources that would not be produced otherwise. At core, the broad phenomena of open source development and sharing fulfill basic structural needs in human productivity. Open source combines both for-profit and non-profit endeavors in shared projects that benefit users and bring something to market much faster than it would otherwise. Such endeavors also enable the creation of digital resources that would not exist otherwise. The effects of such open source also set standards for proprietary products and has been argued to make the de facto price of a good "free" in a rush to the lowest cost object.

Open source endeavors tap the so-called wisdom of the crowd on the one hand particularly for general by-product sorts of contributions. Then, too, this taps those with unique skill sets in particular domains. Subject matter experts, in-betweeners, and novices may collaborate around shared virtual development endeavors in distributed communities of practice, which benefit these groups with new learning and innovations. These endeavors provide informal ways for people to develop their respective talents and to broaden their skill sets. The benefits of sharing in open source spaces may benefit people's development of individual interests as well as their professional development. Open source development projects and sites may provide opportunities for self-discovery and collaborative learning—as an incubator for talent.

The creation of open source resources also enables the expression of altruistic impulses and endeavors so that the work of many may benefit the larger global environment. (Research suggests that the developers are a very productive elite minority who carry an undue work load. This phenomenon is depicted in a power curve, but the users of their efforts are many.) In a world with plenty of information hierarchies (consider the numerous databases that require payment for access), and elite access to higher education (access to the means of production for high-end knowledge), this is one of haves and have-nots. World demographics suggest that there are many youth coming of age who will not have access to university educations, and open source learning resources may be part of a larger solution for such social needs as education. To maximize the uses of time and the development of human talent, such open source works may enable people to achieve part of their full potential. Open source learning offers greater paths of entry to various types of learning, both formal and informal.

Finally, open source also enables the fostering of user communities based around particular technologies or resources. The building and maintenance of such communities strengthens the work of the developers by offering the insights of a group of users who may provide feedback, documentation, and bug finds that strengthen the overall work. The mixing of developer and user communities around particular resources enable the forging of human connections and ties over distance and their shared expressiveness with each other. While there is an assumption that "free-riding" cannot continue forever as a sustainable model of interaction, it is probable that some will never transition from such status to developer and contributor status. Users can contribute by their mere usage of the tool, resource, or contents.

For all the goodwill in the world, these talents and energies would not be so easy to tap if it were not for the affordances of various Web 2.0 and other collaborative technologies. Further, it may be helpful to consider that if one had to pay for some of these open source works, one would likely not have sufficient funds to cover the actual costs of development. Human expertise is expensive to develop, and it is expensive to deploy.

## Open Source Technologies

What has enabled these broad phenomena of open source development and sharing, and virtual community building, has been a harnessing of the connectivity of the Web and the Internet with a broad range of technologies. There are collaborative work sites which enable individuals to coordinate their work and the submittal of that work (such as open source technology platforms to develop open journals, publications, and books; collaborative work sites that enable web conferencing, texting, mutual annotations of shared work, and work archival such as learning / course management systems and other integrative work spaces). These systems enable project leaders to track people's contributions and to authenticate identities and histories. There are digital libraries and repositories (and referatories) that enable peer-to-peer sharing of resources (like audio, video, photos, multimedia, learning objects, software code, and digital collections, among others). General collaborative tools—like web conferencing tools, instant messaging tools, text messaging, voice over IP calling, micro-blogging, blogging, and wikis—may be used to harness people's creativity and to encourage collaboration. These technologies are broadly scalable and may be applied to various circumstances for various types of problem-solving and co-development. Digital resources, by their nature, also do not degrade across multiple uses of the same resource, or in the economics parlance, non-rival goods. Once the marginal investment has been made in the resource, the making and distribution of future copies is economically negligible.

## Beyond Computer Code Development

While code developers opened the way with open source licensure and various software programs (operating system, server software, learning management systems, authoring tools, editing tools, games, simulations, and others), other parts of society are beginning to follow suit. Lawyers have established broad-based licensure releases. In higher education, there is the sharing of open-courseware with full university curriculums shared in zipped files; high-end digital learning objects; games and simulations; and other digital resources. There are open source learning communities. There are massively open online courses with open-sharing of live learning.

## An Afterthought or Byproduct

The broader public has taken to sharing the products of their creative labors in terms of various types of art. People share photos that they take on trips. They use their web cams to capture themselves sharing various talents and ideas. Others blog about various interests and types of expertise. In a sense, open source has become a people's movement—based on a groundswell of sharing and interpersonal relating, some shared values of egalitarianism and fair access and quality. Citizens offer informal reportage—first-person narrations, videos, audio, and other resources. For many, this is the low-hanging fruit, the product of moment-by-moment inspirations. People share their skills, digital objects, information, and beliefs and attitudes. In general, these objects are not monetized, and even if they are, sharing such resources is not particularly lucrative.

This suggests a challenge in terms of creating communities that encourage the development of quality information—not misinformation, not irrelevant information, and not environmental "noise."

The phenomenon of open source allows plenty of levels of access and types of expertise. In wikis, whole communities of individuals will self-monitor and self-correct each other. They will conduct roll-backs to erase others' insights if they do not meet particular standards. Elitist collaborations are for those who enter by invitation and who then collaborate around limited challenges.

## More Formal Open Source Sharing

Large companies have funded co-shared open source development in order to sell hardware platforms or software. However, beyond proprietary and commercial interests, there may be more formal open source development for the purposes of public relations (such as universities that share open course-ware). Universities are also supporting open source publications and digital learning objects to show their commitment to e-learning quality and their concerns for the larger learning of the society. Some non-profit organizations support the creation of open source development as an afterthought or workplace byproduct. Some consciously fit this model into the business discipline of the organization—particularly on information that has broad appeal and interest and the potential for broad social good (such as public health, foreign language learning, financial management, environmentalism, and other topics). For those who want to create open source contents from their work places, it's critical that they have the necessary political cover and resources to pursue such work.

Some open source publishers have both a commercial wing and an open source one. The commercial division puts out published works and articles in repository formats—for subscription. However, they also have public sites that offer open source books in digital format for free download. The open source channel offers other ways for information to be shared, and they may drive traffic to the commercial side of the publishing house. Open source channels may help raise the profile of a publisher as well.

## Starting out as Open Source Object Users

While some acculturate to open source as developers, others begin first as open source resource users. These are individuals who may peruse open source encyclopedias; download open source images; learn from open source columns; play open source games; edit through open source editing tools; and use a variety of digital tools made available through open source means. They benefit off of others' expertise and largesse. What open source users may take away from these learning objects is manifold. They may learn something about others or a particular phenomenon. They may be entertained.

There have been professional attempts to ride the publicity wave and to create viral enthusiasms through word-of-mouth. There are contrived multimedia games. There are "grassroots" endeavors that turn out to be "turfgrass" (artificial) instead. Numerous professionals have interests in reaching out to the general public in order to affect their choices and behaviors. Open source may be one channel to reach potential users.

Even if information wants to be free, not all of it will flow through open source channels into public spaces. Proprietary information will not be released into public because of the compromise in competitive advantage if anything is leaked. Research and development (R&D) data or anything that can be monetized will be protected. Anything that may compromise security will be carefully protected, potentially embargoed into perpetuity. And yet, to generally have an impact on the larger public, resources and information have to flow outward to the public, so there is plenty of pressure pushing outward. There is space for protectionism, but there has to be space for sharing as well.

As open source production becomes more main stream, there has been a shift in cultures. It's not just information and contents that are easily created and disseminated; rather, these also consist of more high-end middle works between the massive software projects and the incidental digital artifacts from people's lives. Such works will take more investments of time and complexity to create. They will require specific skill sets and expertise. To find an audience, such objects need to be shaped for particular delivery, and they have to be sent through the proper channels to find their audiences. Audiences have to be created and nurtured. Within this open source ecology, people all have their mixed and individual roles. They are users and developers. They may dabble in public relations or project management or research, but they may be expert in development or scripting work. People combine skill sets on various ad hoc teams in open source.

While this phenomenon of open source started out in a liberal democratic political context, this meme and practice goes well beyond such conceptualizations. At the core, this is about human collaborations for the benefit of themselves and others. It is about making education and information more broadly available to others. It is about more fair access to digital resources. The hopes of many are riding on this phenomenon. Even those in private industry have R&D and other projects that tap into open source development and product lines. One example would be the widespread cultivation of app developers for many makers of tablet devices.

## The Need for Open Source Quality

The superficial culture around open source might suggest that the masses prefer sensationalistic experiences that go viral. There may be a sense of value to prolific creativity, regardless of quality—just to get hits on a name. There might seem to be a value to gimmickry to drive traffic. And yet, quietly, underneath all the buzz and hype, there are open source collections of valuable information and destination sites that are the ones that define the state-of-the-domain-field. These are the spaces that offer actual and unique informational value and further transference of value to learning uses for others. These are the spaces that will be long-lived and will optimally offer continuing value. These are the spaces of particular interest in this book. While the Internet enables Long Tail diversity and specialization, the core audience still has foundational open source needs that are in the mainstream, and these are the users that most developers will target.

Fundamentally, open source quality may mean a variety of things—depending on the open source contents. One general feature may be the importance of accurate labeling or metadata or annotation. Digital objects require a clear sense of origins. Automated information captures such as the exact latitude and longitude of an image capture may be done automatically by a digital camera or sensor device. Others endeavors will require human interventions to capture the information to properly identify and label objects. For example, a photo may show people in a physical space, but without further explanations, their context and the relevance of their gathering may not be clear. Other quality features of open source objects may involve fidelity and authenticity particularly for photo-realistic imagery. Common practices here suggest that there should be objective size indicators of an object. This focus on authenticity also assumes a kind of non-manipulation, such as not "jumping" color (a common practice in commercial media post-production). Another quality feature may involve the informational value or uniqueness of the information. (For all the hundreds of millions of open source images available online, there are numerous other requirements for specific images that go unfulfilled.) For open source digital learning objects, the learning value of the resource may be important, which suggests proper instructional design, development, and delivery. Depending on the types of digital objects, there may be varying objective quality standards that will be defined by the professional practitioners in the field and the users in the field.

The concept of formalizing open source contributions suggests that content developers have to be accountable for their creations and the effects (to a degree) of their works in the larger environment. This has to be achieved without the super-structure of a workplace or financial incentives, but possibly within the guidelines of applicable laws. Peer evaluations and reputation offer some leverage to create quality, but these still vary in effectiveness—particularly when people who create such contents may be using pseudonyms or handles that may separate themselves from the work that they actually do. Some open source endeavors are fly-by-night. Currently, the development supply chains for open source goods lack a formalism that might ensure a professional-level of follow-through and quality management. However, a popular understanding is that too much formalism may squelch the culture of open source and the good will and talent which fuels the endeavors.

## Text Objectives

Initially, the conceptualization and ambition for the text was to touch on a range of issues. Foremost, this was to highlight ways to design virtual spaces to enhance the creation of quality open source contents. This would entail the design of technologies but also the virtual leadership and coordination needed to actualize such endeavors. Another objective was to study the motivations of those who create open source contents, with the idea that their contributions may be better elicited and facilitated. There was the understanding that virtual communities may be harnessed to nurture open source creativity. I wanted this book to examine the hierarchy of open source resources and information available and the process of how such digital collections are collected and often curated (directly or indirectly) for quality. Then I also focused on the user community—the ways that such users are cultivated and maintained, and then, too, how they actually find and vet open source learning resources and integrate and use them. As a subcategory of open source development, mixed open source endeavors combine both for-profit investments and good-will development. Finally, I also wanted a focus on the role of open source in higher education (and informal and self-discovery learning and education) and the affordances there. There were hopes that others would propose ideas that would break the anticipated areas of interest. At the far edges, some proposed topics in the draft outline included possible works on open source legal structures. Another thread involved open source resources for K-12 learning.

As it has turned out, *Open Source Technologies for Maximizing the Creation, Deployment, and Use of Digital Resources and Information* has touched on all of these factors but in varying degrees. This is to be expected. Whatever the initial plans and no matter how wide the solicitations for writing, authors necessarily have to write from their own professional and personal experiences. Nothing can truly be written to order. These initial manuscript objectives may still, in a sense, serve as a general approach to what may be explored. The contributions of the authors in this collection point the way to fresh directions in this area as well. These ideas will be discussed further on in this introduction.

## AN OVERVIEW OF THE CHAPTER CONTENTS

This book is organized in four different sections. The first, "Section 1: Foundations to Open source Development" sets a baseline of understandings about open source, based on theory and analysis. "Section 2: Open source Development in Higher Education Practice" highlights in-world experiences with open source development and live education projects. "Section 3: Open source in the Wide World" focuses on global-level open source projects with objectives that go well beyond the ivory tower. "Section 4: Developing the User 'Installed Base' for Open source Resources" provides perspectives on the users of open source and the work of meeting their needs.

"Section 1: Foundations to Open source Development" offers a mix of challenges and new understandings about open source in education. More specifically, in the opening chapter "A Model of Cultural Competence in Open source Systems," Dr. Doris Carroll challenges those working in open source to build with cultural competencies in mind for greater accessibility of open source resources and communities. In Dr. Dimitris Kavroudakis' "Open Source Approach to Contemporary Research: The Case of Geo-Information Technology," he examines the influence of the open source paradigm in research and knowledge creation, with a specific focus on the geo-information technology area. In Dr. Yolanda Debose Columbus's "Facilitating the Integration of Open Educational Courses," she describes the cultural adaptation work necessary to integrate open educational resources into higher education programs and offers a framework to enable that process.

Dr. Gladys Palma de Schrynemakers, in Chapter 4, "Creating a Digital Learning Community for Undergraduate Minority Science Majors," argues for increased use of open source resources to create virtual communities to improve learning for minority science majors. In Chapter 5, "Analyzing the Competitive Dynamics in Open Source Publishing Using Game Theory," Dr. Shalin Hai-Jew analyzes the dynamics in open source publishing and the competition between such publishers and proprietary ones—using a game theoretic model.

"Section 2: Open Source Development in Higher Education Practice" focuses on some applied cases of development. Dr. Lee Chao highlights the work of setting up an open source virtualized networking lab in Chapter 6, "Virtualized Open Source Networking Lab" to enhance information technology (IT) education. Dr. Jason Caudill, in "Deploying Digital Educational Resources with Free and Open Source Technologies" highlights the importance of open source resources in the constrained budgetary environment of higher education. In Chapter 8, "Building Open Source Resources for Online Learning in a Higher Education Environment," Dr. Hai-Jew argues for the co-creation of open source learning objects and resources in higher education, which is a center of online learning and digital learning object creation. Sue Polyson Evans, CEO and co-founder of SoftChalk, LLC, has contributed a sidebar Q&A on the SoftChalk Cloud repository. Dr. Ramesh C. Sharma provides a high-level overview of some of the open source endeavors in India in Chapter 9: "Open Source for Higher Conventional and Open Education in India."

In "Section 3: Open Source in the Wide World," Dr. Peter B. Swanson describes the uses of economical digital tools to measure the foreign language proficiencies of second-language learners, in "Measuring Language Learners' Speaking Proficiency in a Second Language Using Economical Digital Tools." Peter Costa and Dr. Deborah J. Briggs, in Chapter 11, "Open Source Educational Initiatives to Improve Awareness of Rabies Prevention," describes innovative uses of open source technologies to disseminate critical and life-saving information in the global push for rabies control. Dr. Roger W. McHaney, in "The Web 2.0 Mandate for a Transition from Webmaster to Wiki Master," describes his evolution in thinking and practice in serving as the wiki master for the E-Learning and Teaching Exchange wiki (ELATEwiki). In Chapter 13, "Creating Open Source Interactive Articles for the Wider Publics," Dr. Hai-Jew describes a new and interactive form of immersive digital articles in open source journals using a range of technologies. Brent A. Anders, in Chapter 14 "Creating a Video Based Education Game: A How-To Guide," provides insights on an open source global public health game that was created for dissemination to a wide audience.

Finally, in "Section 4: Developing the User 'Installed Base' for Open Source Resources" focuses on the criticality of meeting the needs of users of open source resources. Dr. William H. Hsu, in Chapter 15: "Creating Open Source Lecture Materials: A Guide to Trends, Technologies, and Approaches in Information Sciences," offers a professor's view of how open source resources enhance the work of education in the information sciences in this engaging qualitative meta-analysis informed by firsthand professional experiences. Dr. Kathryn Moyle eloquently discusses the importance of providing options for school principals in opting in to open source resources in "Aligning Practice and Philosophy: Opening up Options for School Leaders." Finally, Dr. Hai-Jew describes the analytical work that goes into "Selectively Employing Open Source Resources for Online Learning" in Chapter 17.

## The Future of Open Source

Every publishing project involves plenty of learning. This was so in this case as well. I have learned that it does take plenty of design in socio-technical spaces and virtual leadership and nurturance to enable the development of quality open source resources and information. Such work also happens in the context of talented peers; good work does not happen in a vacuum. Open source content developers work hard to share and distribute innovations. The users of open source contents also contribute much to the process in terms of development work as well as support for the developers. The non-profit organizations, companies, and institutions of higher education that support open source content development are critical players in proving the political and resource spaces to achieve important open source work.

Still, the core players are the subject matter experts (SMEs) who are willing to spend their time, talent, and treasure in generous ways with the general public—to make the world a better and more sharing place.

*Shalin Hai-Jew*
*Kansas State University, USA*

# Acknowledgment

In academic publishing, the differences between proprietary publishing and open-source are negligible for the editors and writers, who earn quite nominal sums in terms of royalties, in most cases. Still, I wondered if the culture of open-source may sometimes be antithetical to proprietary publishing, which may have explained some of the challenges in soliciting work—beyond the typical difficulties of asking others to invest so much effort into the research and writing. This manuscript went past deadline by about half a year. I hope that this final manuscript has made the extra wait worth it.

The authors of this text contributed fresh insights in their chapters. They persisted through a long editorial process. They peer-reviewed each other's works and responded with discernment and candor. I am thankful for each of their chapters. Steven Saltzberg of SoftChalk, LLC, enabled the inclusion of Sue Polyson Evan's sidebar on the SoftChalk Cloud repository. I am deeply grateful for his excellent work in facilitating that.

I am grateful to the advisory committee who served as volunteers for this publishing effort, with no compensation. Each contributed some helpful work reaching out to potential contributors, and several even put their shoulders into the effort and wrote well-received chapters. I am thankful for their discipline to enable them to come through every time. Dr. Rosemary Talab offered fresh critiques and insights on several chapters.

A hearty thanks goes to the editorial board (who are listed in alphabetical order). They generously lent use of their professional names and credibility to this project. Many also provided excellent editorial feedback on the chapter drafts for the respective authors. Others even put in the hard work to write full chapters (that also went through double-blind editorial peer review).

Mary Lou Forward, *OCW Consortium, USA*

Jason Maseberg-Tomlinson, *Kansas State University, USA*

Roger W. McHaney, *Kansas State University, USA*

Ramesh C. Sharma, *OER Foundation, New Zealand & Defense Unit of Indira Gandhi National Open University (IGNOU), India*

The many excellent folks at IGI Global kept this project on track. In particular, Hannah Abelbeck provided some much-needed informational support at a critical period and helped shepherd this project to completion. She offered flexibility and direction at critical moments. I am glad that this publisher takes chances with the projects they support, and they offer plenty of editorial support and direction. Without them, *Open-Source Technologies for Maximizing the Creation, Deployment and Use of Digital Resources and Information* would not see the light of publishing day.

# Section 1
# Foundations to Open Source Development

# Chapter 1
# A Model of Cultural Competence in Open Source Systems

**Doris Wright Carroll**
*Kansas State University, USA*

## ABSTRACT

*Open source software and the open source movement have changed how users access the Internet and produced equality of access for the global community. Despite the access to free software and code sharing for the public and corporate users, open source users remain unaware of cultural competency standards for all its users and designers. The research on cultural competence is conspicuously absent. This chapter defines open source cultural competence as an ethical and equity imperative for open source systems and the communities served by this free, accessible software. A theoretical framework for integrating cultural competence into open source technology is presented, one that emphasizes cultural competency best practices. Future implications for integrating cultural competence into open source technology are highlighted.*

## INTRODUCTION

Open source software (OSS) and the open access movements have changed the playing field for Internet open source software design, and web-based technology since 1998. Open source software is defined simply as software that is available for downloading from the Internet for free (Quint-Rapoport, 2010). Open source software, or OSS, refers to groups of programs that allow the free use of the software and further the code sharing for the public in general and for corporate users of the software (Choi, Kim, & Yu, 2009).

DOI: 10.4018/978-1-4666-2205-0.ch001

Despite its dynamic and innovative approaches, open source technology has failed to define guidelines or standards for cultural competence in open source software. Moreover, the research literature regarding cultural competency for those who use, design, and write source code for this technology is virtually nonexistent. While open access advocates have noted potential benefits for developing nations (Cockerill & Knols, 2008; Chan & Costa, 2005), there remains skepticism about the long-range benefits of open source software's for developing nations and underrepresented groups.

Now is the ideal time for OSS users, global communities, developers, and source code writers to tackle cultural competency and embrace these competencies openly and honestly. For these reasons, and still others yet to be invented, open source professionals and university faculty must blog and dialogue together to discuss cultural competency within open source systems.

The purpose of this chapter is to define and articulate cultural competency within open source systems. The cultural communication and technical skills, awareness, and content knowledge that users and designers must have in order to practice in a culturally competent manner are identified within an ethical practice framework.

## Cultural Competence

Cultural competence is a complex, psychosocial and socio-cultural process of cultural awareness, content knowledge, and applied or practice skills. It is as an active, developmental, and ongoing process, one that is aspirational rather than achieved (Sue & Sue (2008). While psychologists and other social scientists have examined the role of these socio-cultural variables for more than forty years, few have considered their impact on the ways that humans interface with, make sense of, and benefit from web-based technologies including the Internet, YouTube, Face book, and open source software. Multicultural researchers and

theorists never envisioned cultural competence defined outside the context of human-to-human interface, and they never conceived of an ethical standard of competence within the reality of a virtual world as experienced through an Avatar. So, this notion of cultural competence between humans and their technology is new, novel, and [likely] controversial.

Sue and Torino (2005) defined cultural competence within a counseling context as:

*Cultural competence is the ability to engage in actions or create conditions that maximize the optimal development of client and client systems. Multicultural counseling competence is defined as the counselor's acquisition of awareness, knowledge, and skills needed to function effectively in a pluralistic democratic society (ability to communicate, interact, negotiate, and intervene on behalf of clients from diverse backgrounds), and on an organizational/societal level, advocating effectively to develop new theories, practices, policies and organizational structures that are more responsive to all groups (p. 17-18).*

The culturally competent professional works toward achieving several primary goals. First, a culturally competent professional is aware of his/her own personal assumptions about human behavior, values, biases, preconceptions, personal limitations, and so forth. Second, the culturally competent professional is one who actively attempts to understand the worldview, values, and assumptions about human behavior. Third, a culturally competent helping professional is one who is in the process of accurately developing and practicing appropriate relevant, and sensitive interventions (Sue, Arrendondo, & McDavis, 1992).

These goals make it clear that cultural competence is an active, developmental, and ongoing process of change. Counseling and mental health professions have articulated the attributes, awareness, skills, and behavioral changes necessary to effect cultural competence in three broadly defined areas: (1) awareness, (2) competence knowledge, and (3) skills, behaviors or actions (D.W. Sue, 1992; D. W. Sue et. al. (1998). These psychosocial, content, and behavioral principles have relevance to and viability for open source communities, source code designers, and individual users in significant and meaningful ways (Sue & Sue 2008).

## Open Source Cultural Competencies

This discussion of cultural competencies within open source systems begins with a practical definition and recognition of its relevance in a web-based online environment. Four elements are critical to the development of cultural competence within an open source setting. Taken together, these elements extend and expand Sue and Torino's (2005) definition by attending to the unique structural elements of open source design, its technologies, and accessibility to constituent groups including source code designers, individual users, and global cultural communities. These elements include: (1) design, (2) content knowledge, (3) communication, and (4) inclusiveness.

## Design

Writing and distributing source code has socio-cultural elements in the creation, development, and distribution of source code to users and constituent communities. Socio-cultural source code elements are not understood fully, and yet they are believed to influence how code is written and most assuredly shape its distribution. It includes any and all technical, structural, and socio-cultural mechanisms used to write and distribute source code. As an ethical imperative or standard of practice, it is characterized as a set of practices of creating software – good software- that was freely and publically accessible, albeit privately owned (Kelty, 2008, p. 1).

## Knowledge

Knowledge as an element of open source includes, but is not limited, to recognizing and defining the cultural competency body of content knowledge in open source technology and among open source communities. It involves the recognition of cultural knowledge about open source users globally, both the culture-specific knowledge about a particular ethnic, racial, gendered, or nation group, and the cultural specific information about their accessibility and use.

This element is extended to include culture-specific knowledge about women and their accessibility to and use of, and participation in writing source code. It includes gendered knowledge about open source accessibility and the recognition of gendered biases, particularly in source code design.

Lastly, knowledge can involve the recognition about the intersectionality of cultural, race, ethnicity, gender, and national group with regard to access to and use of open source software. This recognition of intersectionality implies that users have specific information regarding how users construct cultural meaning overall, and specifically, how they construct multicultural content about open source software and open source communities.

## Communication

This element regards the various technical and human communication mechanisms through which open source users and their communities access, receive, retrieve, and store information, and how they engage one another in open source systems. Cultural competence in communication can be extended to include the specific language mechanisms of access, and the nature of collaboration and other forms of engagement.

## Inclusiveness

This element regards an active commitment to promoting access across open source communities, independent of privilege, power, or economic capacity to contribute. Fours essential components blend together to form the construct of inclusiveness: (A) globalization, (B) recognition of indigenous culture, (C) language access and accommodation, and (D) disability access/accommodation.

A.  Globalization refers to the commitment that open source code and software are distributed across the entire globe to its broadest user audience. It is a proactive awareness.

B.  The recognition of indigenous communities within a nation state involves an active process of respect and recognition of their right to collaboration and communication with equal access to other communities in open source.

C.  Language access and accommodation involves the recognition of and willingness to communicate within a language that is appropriate for the ever-changing culture-specific open source community. It is the recognition of language privilege, or preference for English as the preferred mode of communication over other languages. It embodies the cognitive process of realization that not everyone communicates online in English. It respects and affirms the diversity of languages necessary for a successful and effective open source community. Moreover, language access applies to source code designers and speaks to their willingness to write source code in ways that will allow the greatest number of designers to use and translate it for a growing audience of open source users and communities.

D.  Disability accommodation refers to the specific recognition and content knowledge about the best ways to write source code to accommodate a variety of disability including, but not limited to visually impaired, hearing impaired, persons with learning disabilities, and other cognitive, affective, emotional, visual, and auditory disabilities that would impair users from participating fully in open source communities.

Taken together, these four elements are morphed to form the construct known as inclusiveness, which is the fourth variable critical to understanding cultural competency in open source. These cultural ingredients are significant factors in the establishment and maintenance of cultural competency within open source systems and among users and source code designers. These constructs provide a strong foundation from which open source users can build cultural competency statements for their global communities. Beginning that process of building cultural competencies requires that OSS communities take an honest and open look at themselves as a cultural community of users and source code writers.

## OSS as Crooked Room

Socio-cultural factors are believed to influence open source members' preconceptions about open source technology, its power and privilege. It shapes how members are recognized within open source communities and how they construct personal meaning about their participation.

Political scientist and MSNBC ® commentator, Melissa V. Harris-Perry (2011) reconstructed the concept of "crooked room" to explain the distorted experiences of African American women in the United States who are bombarded with [and distracted by] degrading images. The crooked room phenomenon was an outcome discovered during the classic field dependence studies by Witkin, Moore, Goodenough and Cox (1977). Women must deconstruct those negative images and reconstruct them into a healthier, less patriarchal manner. For African American women, the dilemma is one of recognition – of identity, difference, and citizenship.

Recognition is a useful framework for understanding interconnections between individuals and groups within the open source movement. She argues that the central issue of recognition, i.e. accurate recognition, for marginalized and stigmatized groups, is that these individuals want recognition for their group, but they desire recognition of their distinctiveness from their group (Harris-Perry, 2011, p. 39).

Individuals from socio-cultural, socio-economic, gendered, and impoverished communities hold to the implicit promise that OSS will provide recognition for their groups. Thus, recognition for members in open source communities is constructed with an eye toward increasing their power globally in open source technology and among open source communities, known more intimately as the *recursive public* (Kelty, 2008).

## Recursive Publics

We begin the conversation by considering the early origins of OSS social constructivists whom anthropologist Christopher Kelty (2008) referred to as the *recursive public*. "[I]t is a collective independent of other forms of constituted power and is capable of speaking to existing forms of power through the production of actually existing alternatives" (p. 3). They exist independent of, and as a check on, constituted forms of power, including markets and corporations. This reality means that geeks and others can [and should] make comparisons among the two that allow everyone to understand the changing relations of power and knowledge. Recursive publics are a collective body, with a mission, structure, measurable outcomes, and

a conscience – all requisites in a civilized [and largely demographic] society (Kelty, 2008).

Concerned with both moral and technical order, recursive publics face a dual conflicting reality which implies both technology- i.e. the hardware, software, networks, and protocols- and best practice or ethical standards, i.e. moral order, which articulates the proper order for collective political power and market, or commercial actions. Regarding the latter, the moral order involves how should the economy and society be ordered collectively for the good of the "public." (p. 28).

Despite its well-meaning moral order, recursive publics are nonetheless "tilted in the crooked room." They want recognition as a legitimate and moral body for the open source movement. Yet, as an open source body, they themselves have failed to recognize the socio-cultural, socio–political, gendered, and socio-racial issues that influence access, inclusion, and equitability within open source. Without an understanding of cultural competence, the recursive public falls short of achieving these requisite goals.

Thus, the recursive publics remain tilted in the room, not because they do not have the resources to straighten the perceptual tilt, but rather, they have failed to consider the socio-cultural, socio-racial, and gendered realities of open source access [or lack thereof]. They have failed to recognize the power that is afforded them by the nature of their recursive position. Recursive publics are not craving recognition, like [b]lack women in American society who were disenfranchised and out of power. To the contrary, recursive publics remain crooked in the room because of their naivety and reluctance to examine the social-political, gendered, and socio-cultural elements of the open source movement in general, and to give these societal elements the same importance as been afforded such issues as freedom of access and freedom to use copyleft licenses.

The only way to correct the *tilt* is for the recursive public to take ownership of and aquire the leadership to embrace cultural competency in open source systems and across the entire open source movement.

How do they straighten the crooked room? The answer is clear. First, the recursive public must admit its own 'privilege" in its current practices. Second, it must give legitimacy to a new recognition – that of the public's voice of diversity, inclusion, and difference, through cultural competency. As an ethical imperative and a standard of practice, it must forever be embedded in source code, and then translated through our communication to all within open source systems- those with advantage [and power], and those with no power.

## OPEN SOURCE CULTURAL COMPETENCY STANDARDS

In support of this achievable goal, four cultural competency standards are described and articulated below. These standards are adapted from psychological, mental health, and social science practice standards, and are modified here to provide a conceptual framework for open source cultural competency within the open source movement and are presented in Table 1.

### Awareness

The cultural competence of awareness represents an active cognitive shift from uninformed and naïve about cultural differences and cultural cues in the open source environment along a continuum toward increasingly sophisticated professional and cultural self-awareness. Mental health professionals over that last forty years have researched and dissected this dimension extensively. In multicultural counseling and therapy, a culturally competent professional is one who is actively] involved in the process of becoming aware of one's own assumptions about human behavior, including values, biases, preconceptions, personal limitations, and so on (Sue & Sue, 2008).

For open source systems, cultural awareness is realized in seven distinct ways.

1. Individuals are transformed from being naïve and unaware to having an active awareness and sensitivity to one's own cultural background and heritage and to valuing and respecting differences as presented in OSS environments.
2. Aware of own cultural values and biases about cultural or nation groups, and how they may affect the individuals, communities, or constituent groups who use, access, design for, or make use of OSS.
3. Comfortable with expressing differences between OSS groups and individuals in terms of race, gender, national identity, cultural background, and other socio-demographic variables.
4. Sensitive to socio-cultural and socio-political variables that may challenge their ease of access to OSS.
5. Aware of issues of socio-political variables such as privilege, power, and colonialism that places one group in favor in accessing or using OSS services and technologies.
6. Awareness of gendered issues within open source communities.
7. Awareness of intersection of culture, race, and gender access issues across time and countries.

Each element is presented in such a way that permits the user, designer, or learner to construct his or her own personal meaning for each dimension, thereby becoming "geek-friendly" in applying cultural competency constructs to OSS.

### Knowledge

Knowledge, or content knowledge, refers to the cultural content knowledge unique to OSS. In most instances, this knowledge is new content, i.e. cultural content, about an OSS cohort or global

*Table 1. Cultural competence in open source systems (Adapted from: Sue, Arrendondo, & McDavis, 1992; and Sue, Carter, Casas, Fouad, Ivey, Jensen, & LaFromboise, et al., 1998)*

| 1. Awareness | 2. Knowledge | 3. Skills and Practice | 4. Advocacy |
|---|---|---|---|
| Individuals are transformed from being naïve and unaware to having an active awareness and sensitivity to one's own cultural background and heritage and to valuing and respecting differences as presented in OSS environments. | Knowledgeable and informed about the various culturally diverse groups who use, access, design, and otherwise take advantage of OSS to educate and inform their communities. | Able to disseminate and distribute OSS resources to a global community in a fair, equitable, and inclusive manner. | Challenges privilege within OSS communities as presented by preconceptions about global consumers. |
| Aware of own cultural values and biases about cultural or nation groups, and how they may affect the individuals, communities, or constituent groups who use, access, design for, or make use of OSS. | Knowledgeable about the socio-political system's operation globally with respect to its treatment of marginalized groups globally and their access to open source software, technology, and other resources. | | Challenges the notion that OSS perpetuates systemic colonialism and technological imperialism. |
| Comfortable with expressing differences between OSS groups and individuals in terms of race, gender, national identity, cultural background, and other socio-demographic variables. | Knowledgeable about the cultural aspects of source software design. | Able to communicate with OSS individual users and communities in a culture-specific manner using language that is appropriate to and respectful of cultural group differences. | Challenges male gendered privilege in writing code and active participation in open source communities. |
| Sensitive to socio-cultural and socio-political variables that may challenge their ease of access to OSS. | | | Promotes collaboration across multicultural and multilingual communities, esp. second language collaborations. |
| Aware of issues of socio-political variables such as privilege, power, and colonialism that places one group in favor in accessing or using OSS services and technologies. | Knowledgeable about the systemic, institutional, and nationalistic barriers that prevent diverse client groups from using OSS resources equitably. | Able to design and share source code with users in ways that affirm and value the cultural and gender group differences of individual users and communities in a fair, equitable, and inclusive manner. | Recognizes and deconstructs coding biases, especially those based on race, culture, gender, nationalism, or linguistic differences. |
| Awareness of gendered access issues. | Knowledgeable about the cultural specific aspects of the distribution and dissemination of OSS resources to a global community in a fair, equitable, and inclusive manner. | Able to write code that accommodates cultural variations in usage and access. | |
| Awareness of intersection of culture, race, and gender access issues across time and countries. | | | |

group or community. Most of the time, such content knowledge is a cognitive process of acquisition, storage, and retrieval of a new cultural cognitive mapping structure about OSS. Five ingredients are essential in this cognitive domain.

For open source systems, cultural content and knowledge is realized in five (5) distinct ways.

1. Knowledgeable and informed about the various culturally diverse groups who use, access, design, and otherwise take advantage of OSS to educate and inform their communities.

2. Knowledgeable about the sociopolitical system's operation globally with respect to its treatment of marginalized groups globally and their access to open source software, technology, and other resources.

3. Knowledgeable about the cultural aspects of source software design.

4. Knowledgeable about the systemic, institutional, and nationalistic barriers that prevent diverse client groups from using OSS resources equitably.
5. Knowledgeable about the cultural specific aspects of the distribution and dissemination of OSS resources to a global community in a fair, equitable, and inclusive manner.

OSS users are charged to show evidence of culture-specific knowledge about groups who use OSS and its surrounding socio-cultural and socio-racial political system. They are charged to have culture-specific information about each cultural group involved with OSS and be informed about the culture-specific aspect of OSS software design. Moreover, OSS members should be familiar with the culture-specific systemic, institutional, and nationalistic barriers that prevent OSS from simple transfer to OSS resource protocols to a larger constituent base. Lastly, OSS members should become knowledgeable about the cultural specific aspects of the distribution and dissemination of OSS resources to a global community in a fair, equitable, and inclusive manner.

## Skills and Practice

This cultural competency regards behavioral and best practice indicators of cultural proficiency in open source systems. It demonstrates active and visible evidence of cultural competency. Four standards are noted in this competency standard.

1. Able to disseminate and distribute OSS resources to a global community in a fair, equitable, and inclusive manner.
2. Able to communicate with OSS individual users and communities in a culture-specific manner using language that is appropriate to and respectful of cultural group differences.
3. Able to design and share source code with users who affirm and value cultural and gender group differences of individual users

and communities in a fair, equitable, and inclusive manner.
4. Able to write code that accommodates cultural variations in usage and access.

## Advocacy

Advocacy is an affirmative construct that involves a user's affirmation and commitment to share culture-specific source code elements with others in the open source community. Born from social justice practice in the social sciences (Sue & Sue, 2008), advocacy involves a set of actions that promote equity, access, and cultural competency with open source systems and technologies, and among open source users and their communities. It implies a proactive commitment to write code that accommodates cultural variations in use and access. Second, it challenges notions of open source privilege as presented by preconceptions about global users and their capacity to contribute to the OSS community.

It challenges the OSS practices that contribute to systemic colonialism and technological imperialism.

Finally, advocacy seeks to deconstruct [cross-cultural] coding biases. It promotes collaboration, especially those involving global and second language collaborations.

## Recommendations for Growth

Given the tremendous growth with the open source movement, the need to establish cultural competency is urgent. It is time for the open source movement to embrace cultural competency and, by doing so, fulfill its mission to promote free, open access to Internet and web technology. But, what can open source users, code designers, and members of the open source global community do to move toward cultural competency Three simple, yet significant recommendations to enhance cultural competency in open source systems are proffered below.

1.  Reframe the Berlin Declaration statement and rewrite the Open source Definition, to include cultural competency standards that inform the open source communities with culture-specific knowledge. The Berlin Declaration mission statement is an ideal place to include a cultural competence standard. It says, "We define open access as a comprehensive source of human knowledge and cultural heritage that has been approved by the scientific community" (p. 1). The cultural heritage language notation here is an ideal place to further elaborate this mission statement with cultural competency or social justice statements or standards.

The Open source Definition (OSD), created by the Open source Initiative (OSI) provides practice standard guidelines for open source users and communities. OSD makes clear there should be no discrimination against persons or groups [Standard 5] or against fields of endeavor [Standard 6]. These guidelines are strengthened by the inclusion of cultural competency standards that will benefit all members within open source communities.

2.  Elaborate and expand the culture-specific issues related to writing source code. This recommendation requires that source code must now recognize culture-specific issues that influence how source code is written and interpreted by OSS members. The time now is ideal to ask source code writers to consider what is cultural competence and to articulate it into behavioral standards.

3.  Elaborate and expand understanding of the culture-specific access elements. To date, there has been little attention to making sense of the ways in which culture influences how members access open source software and how they use culture in their constructions of open source communities. These elements might be understood implicitly. However,

there is a need to articulate culture-specific behavioral standards for open source access.

While these recommendations are simple, they are not without challenges and obstacles. These simple suggestions urge the open source community to take responsibility [and accountability] for eradicating faulty cultural preconceptions, misconceptions, and biases. It means, for example, the recursive public must recognize and realize the gendered nature of OSS as a first step toward increasing women's participation in source code design.

The Berlin Declaration is a strong, affirmative document that advocates for equity in the advancement of scientific knowledge, but it has yet to finish its work in realizing cultural heritage. It is a technical and economic advancement document through which extraordinary partnerships have been realized. However, it has not recognized nor addressed the implicit and explicit race and gender biases, nor has its members acknowledged its own power and privilege. These challenges are inevitable socio-political and socio-racial constructions that have to be recognized and eradicated before all members in the open source communities can have true open access.

## CONCLUSION

Cultural competency is an essential component of open access to technology, and it is critical to the sustainability of the open source movement. For this reason, it must be recognized and accounted for openly and honestly if the movement is to move forward toward its primary mission to disseminate scientific, technical, and academic knowledge to a diverse global community.

This chapter has introduced and defined cultural competency within open source systems and articulated a working framework for understanding its roles for users, source code designers, and others within this global community. The future of the open source movement intersects with cultural competency, and other socio-political, socio-racial, and socio-cultural variables. This conversation must continue globally throughout all open sources communities. The outcome of this ongoing examination about cultural competency leads to an open, accessible, and diverse open source community, one that will inform the world community for years to come.

## REFERENCES

*Berlin Declaration on Open Access to Knowledge in the Sciences and Humanities*. (2003). Retrieved from http://oa.mpg.de/openaccess-berlin/berlin-declaration.html

Chan, L., & Costa, S. (2005). Participation in the global knowledge commons: Challenges and opportunities for research dissemination in developing countries. *New Library World, 106*(3/4), 141–163. doi:10.1108/03074800510587354

Choi, C. J., Kim, S. W., & Yu, S. (2009). Global ethics of collective internet governance: Intrinsic motivation and open source software. *Journal of Business Ethics, 90*, 523–531. doi:10.1007/s10551-009-0057-5

Cockerill, M. J., & Knols, B. G. J. (2008). Open access to research for the developing world. *Issues in Science and Technology, 24*(2), 65–69.

Harris-Perry, M. (2011). *Sister citizen: Shame, stereotype, and racism in America*. New Haven, CT: Yale University Press.

Kelty, C. (2008). *Two bits. The cultural significance of free software*. Durham, NC: Duke University Press.

*Open Source Initiative*. (n.d.). Retrieved from http://www.opensource.org/

Quint-Rapoport, M. (2010). *Open source in higher education: A situational analysis of the open journal systems software project*. Doctoral dissertation, Toronto, Canada, University of Graduate Department of Theory and Policy Studies in Education University of Toronto.

Sue, D. W., Arrendondo, P., & McDavis, R. J. (1992). Multicultural competencies/standards: A call to the profession. *Journal of Counseling and Development, 70*(4), 477–486. doi:10.1002/j.1556-6676.1992.tb01642.x

Sue, D. W., Carter, R. T., Casas, J. M., Fouad, N. A., Ivey, A. E., & Jensen, M. (1998). *Multicultural counseling competencies: Individual and organizational development*. Thousand Oaks, CA: Sage.

Sue, D. W., & Sue, D. (2008). *Counseling the culturally diverse: Theory and practice* (5th ed.). Hoboken, NJ: Wiley.

Sue, D. W., & Torino, G. C. (2005). Racial-cultural competence: Awareness, knowledge, and skills. In Carter, R. T. (Ed.), *Handbook of racial-cultural psychology and counseling* (pp. 3–18). Hoboken, NJ: Wiley.

Witkin, H. A., Moore, C. A., Goodenough, D. R., & Cox, P. W. (1977). Field-dependent and field-independent cognitive styles and their educational implications. *Review of Educational Research, 47*(1), 1–64. Retrieved from http://www.jstor.org/stable/1169967

# Chapter 2
# Open Source Approach to Contemporary Research:
## The Case of Geo-Information Technology

**Dimitris Kavroudakis**
*University of the Aegean, Greece*

## ABSTRACT

*As the open source paradigm is influencing the modern economic world, an increasing number of scientific disciplines use the open working model in knowledge production process. The contemporary research field requires a new shift towards the constantly evolving digital age where collaboration and exchange of information is growing. The shift from traditional research models to open science may be the starting point for scientific innovation. This work presents the case of open scientific research as an analogy to the open source software movement and uses a case study from the Geo-Information technology sector.*

## 1. INTRODUCTION

Contemporary academic research environment is evolving rapidly, adapting to modern scientific challenges. Complexity of modern scientific topics requires advanced approaches to handle and analyze rich and dynamic data. Additionally, the structural and methodological research work-flow is becoming even more complex as

the scientific approaches require more methods, types of analysis and data. The challenges of modern academic research environment include data compatibility and data management issues. Furthermore, methodological and work-flow transparency is considered a "good-practice" as it is easier to document, debug and expand. Open source methodology is considered to be a viable and reliable approach mainly due to reliability,

DOI: 10.4018/978-1-4666-2205-0.ch002

scalability, cost effectiveness, and performance issues. Additionally, open source software and collaboration approaches, offer valuable tools in a fast growing information age. Freedoms of open source software, such as redistribution and re-calibration of software source code, are particularly attractive to modern scientific labs.

Open source methodology is suitable for the contemporary academic research environment. The transparent and flexible work-flow model is ideal for a highly competitive environment such as modern research lab. The reliability of software tools and the scalability of processes is necessary to such environments and can be very cost effective alternative solutions to modern non-transparent proprietary software. The incorporation of collaboration software to a modern scientific environment offers fast data and information exchange and can cope with the rapidly evolving arena of scientific research. Finally, data-related issues such as data interchange formats and open source data-management-logic, offer adaptability of data to a number of working environments. Everyday researchers worldwide are lowering the barriers to collaboration and communication, especially with the increase of internet infrastructure. Not only is software being "open sourced," but so is hardware and scientific research itself. Many researchers are going beyond passively being open and they are actively seeking participation and creating communities to refine their research. The aim of this text is to illustrate the suitability and comparative advantage of open source working model, in contemporary academic research environment and in geographical science with the example of OpenStreetMap.

## 2. OPEN MODEL OF KNOWLEDGE PRODUCTION

Open source as a term refers to the availability of the source code of a software. Computer software is made of source code which is compiled and generates an executable software. The term "open

source" indicates that the source code is freely available to everyone. Open Source Software (OSS) is licensed in one of the approved OSS licensing agreements that guides the rights and freedoms of the user and the developer. Today there are more than thirty open source licenses recognized by the Open Source Initiative (OSI 2011) and the Free Software Foundation (FSF 2011), which offer a number of legal rights. On the other hand proprietary software refers to the material that does not offer the source code of the application. And are products of mainly closed and concentrated model of production which includes the use proprietorial capital resources. The development circle of the software is centralized and managed by the company which owns the copyrights

Open source production uses a distinctive development and distribution model and it may also be part of a proprietary material. The product may also have two licenses which offer a flexible scheme to the end user to choose the one which best suits his needs. Open source material is sometimes confused with *public domain material* or *shareware* or *freeware*. This is not always true as the term open source refers to the freedom of the end-user and is not related with the price of the software. The "openness" of the term refers to the liberty of the user and not the price. The open source licenses give the user freedom to run the program, to study the code and adapt it, to redistribute copies and improve it.

Those freedoms characterize the development and use of open source material such as software and provide the necessary framework of action for future licensing. Each of the above freedoms has some benefits for the end-user and the community. The freedoms focus on computer software products, but can be also applied to other "open source" processes such as knowledge production process and research. Knowledge production process can be any research and development process in an academic institution, at a research center or in a proprietary environment.

The reason behind the fast spread of open source production model is due to a number of advantages over other production models such as: standards, flexibility, value customers, innovation, quality and choice. More specific, technology and knowledge which is build on true open standards that are consistent and compatible overtime with other technologies is more competitive than other as it offers compatibility (Krechmer 2005, Chen et al. 2006). Ability to customize the production process according to the needs of the product is a valuable ability which makes open source production very competitive. Furthermore, customers of open source material pay for what they really need as the "product" is highly customizable and can feed their needs. The speed of development circles of open development processes is very competitive and the quality is constantly increasing as the number of involved entities is increasing.

The open working model is based on new working activities such as collaboration which is becoming increasingly popular (Patel et al. 2011). Collaboration between individuals from around the world is constantly increasing as the means of collaboration evolve enabling faster exchange of information. The new ecosystem of tools that help towards sharing and exchanging of information include social networking, wikis, forum, chat, video-conferences, document sharing etc. Those "bridges" between supply and demand of knowledge is sometimes very constructive and produces remarkable collaborative products. One such example is Wikipedia which is a peer production on-line encyclopedia. It includes a concurrent production of knowledge by a vast number of readers and editors in order to produce the bigger encyclopedia over the Internet. This collaborative production system is leading the way in open source production as it illustrates the power and flexibility of this type of production but on the same time it faces some serious skepticism such as validity of the information and is vulnerable to information vandalism. The solution to those threads is the coordinated and targeted editing of

the material by a centralized group of individuals who is ensuring greater accuracy and integrity of the information used. The vandalism thread can be monitored by advanced software which flags strange activity and inappropriate behavior and informs the moderators/ administrators. This example of peer production is leading the way in the open source development and is used as an example of coordinative production with community driven aspects.

The open source movement has proven itself in the software world to be a highly efficient and innovative model for software development. Many of the products created by Open Source communities are leading their field such as Linux for operating system and Apache Web server for internet web servers. Today more than ever before this model of production is increasingly introduced in software development and other research environments and fields. Another term which is common in open source model of production is transparency which is different to openness in production. A transparent project in not necessary an open source project. Transparency refers to the ability of the community to examine the internal structures, information and communication of a project. This involves a published road-map, schedule, deliverables, aims and objectives as well as a public bug tracking system for reporting and reviewing defects. Additionally a transparent project includes published design documentation access to communication archive. The term "free" is often misconstrued in terms of FOSS. Developed by Richard Stallman, "free" means the ability to do whatever you wish with FOSS software (Stallman 2004). The licenses implemented to achieve this require that any code created under the license must be freely available to anyone who wants it and a small charge may be involved to cover distribution costs so in essence FOSS is no "free as in beer."

Open source movement is based on the sharing of information and knowledge. The open source production is a different model than the typical proprietary model in the sense that a part or all of the "product" is open, and accessible by others. This is fundamentally different from the "closed" production process where the production of a product is the responsibility of a company which controls the direction and the future of the product.

The production which is open for everyone to participate under certain conditions is called "commons-based peer production." This is a new model of economic production in which the creative energy of a big community is co-ordinated into large meaningful projects. The technological advances of home computers and internet infrastructure are aiding the collaboration and exchange of information in this type of production. In most cases, there is lack of traditional hierarchical organization structure and financial compensation. It is a socio-economic system of production that is emerging in the digitally evolving networked world. The term "commons-based peer production" is coined by Harvard Law School Professor Yochai Benkler (Benkler et al. 2006) and has been used as a basic conception in various recent scientific works (Staring et al. 2008, Kallinikos 2009, Andreev et al. 2010, Tsiavos et al. 2010). Some of the core principles of the idea of commons based peer production is the radical decentralization of intelligence in communications network and the centrality of information. Due to this type of production the *information-network economy* has evolved, and some of the examples of this notion are: free software production and open source Operating Systems production (GNU Linux), which heavily make use of the internet infrastructure to form groups and teams for the coordinated production of various digital products with high market value. Sharing resources, information, ideas and data enables the decentralized peer-production which is highly flexible to changes (either in human resources or technological changes) and offers the output to a widely distributed audience. This productive synergy speeds up the understanding and implementation of complex systems and problems and offers flex-

ibility, speed and error-free production. The term "commons-based" refers to lack of proprietary input. The inputs and outputs of the production are available to everyone to use, study, alter and redistribute. The term "peer production" refers to the decentralized model of production and the lack of hierarchical system. Collaboration is not managed by any single individual but is the outcome of all contributors involved. Collaboration of scientists and contribution of information is very common in scientific projects. Knowledge production is a complex process which requires complementary works to collaborative in order to produce knowledge. The start of a scientific project is usually the end-point of one or more other scientific projects.

## 3. OPEN RESEARCH

Research is one of the leading factors of economic growth as it provides knowledge and know-how to the industry and the market in general. Academic research is the research which takes place under an academic institution such as Universities and Colleges. Research produces knowledge as for example the production line of a factory produces cars. The "car factory" example is commonly used as a parallelism to facilitate the discussion and examination of knowledge production process which is a process of transforming raw inputs to meaningful advanced products. As the open working model is revolutionizing the working environment, research activity is influenced by open research movement which supports the open working model in research activity. There have been calls lately in numerous social institutions for greater openness. Those calls ask for increased transparency for processes and information flow. Scientific knowledge discovery is different as there has been an ideology of openness since the 17th century. Nevertheless this scientific openness has been subject to restrictions William Eamon's (1994). The nature of science has changed the last three centuries as the open/closed model depends on the institution and the scientific group characteristics. The term science is used very broadly, and it can refer to a body of knowledge, or useful means of developing practical techniques, or the human institution in which the knowledge and techniques are generated, or to all of these at once.

The work of Kuhn (1962) is an analytical illustration of scientific history over the years. This is a work which discusses topics such as scientific doubt and ideas as well as theory acceptance. This historiography of science is a good manuscript for the foundation of scientific production, knowledge management and paradigm shift. Another notable manuscript about knowledge and new ideas of production is the work by Christensen (1997). Christensen analyses new ideas of production and companies dealing with new innovative products and how can those production models survive a highly competitive landscape. Christensen discusses how disruptive technologies have developed in the IT industry and identifies six steps in the emergence of disruptive technologies. One of the most notable manuscripts of the open source production field, is the Cathedral And The Bazaar by Raymond (Raymond 1999). Raymond's work focuses on two distinctive models of open source production with respect to source code availability between production phases. This manuscript is a highly influential essay in open source community as it forms the starting point for the use of Bazaar style production where the source code and the knowledge required for the production of a software is fully available to anyone interested, over the internet. This type of production has boosted the production of many open source software such as Mozilla's projects such as Firefox (McHugh 2005) and Thunderbird (Mozilla 2011).

According to Cottey (2009), there are four levels of openness in science. This is a classification shows the spectrum from completely secret to radically open research. The first three levels are already established. Steps towards the fourth kind have been taken in the last few years, but there is still room for improvement. The levels are secret science, restricted science, circumspect science and open science. *Secret Science* is the category, where even the existence of the project is concealed, and nobody (beyond the scientific team and the supervisors, knows about the project and its inputs-outputs). *Restricted Science* is the one where the outputs of the project and the publication of the results is subject to limitations in respect of timing and level of detail. Most commercial and applied government/military science belongs to this category. *Circumspect Science* is the scientific exploration where the scientists publish their findings when the project is complete, but till then are quite 'close'. This is the most common type of academic projects today, when there are no specific restrictions from a proprietary source. Finally open science, refers to scientific projects with a radical kind of openness both in terms of findings but also in terms of structure, methodology and flow of information.

Research activity is a knowledge production process and as such has its own production models. Two of the most distinct models of production are the centralized and decentralized models. The centralized model of production uses a central facility (factory building) to house the line of production. This production process is using "in-house" capital such as: machines, workers, storage, electricity etc, from the start (design of the product) to the end (shipping to the retail shop). The production may also take place in other premises but the copyrights and the ownership of the product belong to the enterprise behind the production. On the other hand the decentralized model of production refers to the open model of production where each party uses material to create a specific part of the product. This model of production uses a central facility to organize the fragmented processes of production. Each party produces a small part that is not the actual end-product.

Open source production mostly uses decentralized methodology of production as it utilizes a community of participants who are responsible for the production of a part of the end-product. Scientific software is the software for research purposes in an institution and in some cases consists of highly specialized modules.

Sometimes, the arsenal of scientific tools does not include one unique utility (software or hardware) that is used for the production of knowledge from the first to the last part of the research. This type of tool is rare as the methodological approach changes overtime and the scientific demands vary between projects. On the other hand, scientific tools are a group of tools, loosely joined to a work-flow. Each part is responsible for its own input and output and it is the researcher's responsibility to prepare a viable work-flow with the currently available tools. The selection of the correct scientific tools is crucial as it may determine the extent, accuracy, and flexibility of the research and the outputs.

The availability of reliable open source software for scientific research is vital as it facilitates knowledge production and provides the research unit with material that has comparative advantages over proprietary software. Those advantages are community development, customization and cost. The existence of a vibrant community which supports and develops a software, is a comparative advantage. The community contributes to the development and the support. Community development adds extra value to the product because a number of programmers from around the world are willing and able to participate towards the design and implementation of the software. The community support is the process during which problem solving takes place on-line with collaboration technologies such as: wiki, forum, or blog. This relatively cheap product support adds extra value as it consists of a great diversity of people from around the world, speaking various languages and willing to solve users problems. The customization ability of a software, is a comparative advantage as it provides great flexibility to the end user. As software tools do not necessary have all those small modifications that are needed

from all users, the ability to modify and extend the abilities of a software, makes it more flexible than its competitors. Finally, the cost of development and support of an open source software is relatively smaller than the proprietary. The use of open source development methodologies and the cultivation of an on-line community, offers relatively cheap alternatives. The smaller cost is not associated with poor quality as price of a software does not necessary reflects the quality and capabilities of that tool.

The four main freedoms of open source software can also used to show the suitability of open working model in research environment. More specifically, the freedom to run the program, for any purpose offers to modern scientists the opportunity to use the available tools and methods anywhere without license restrictions which may limit the number of machines or concurrent users. The freedom to study how the program works and change it to make it do what you wish enables the modern scientist to have access to the source code of the software used, and alter it according to the needs of the research. This makes the software particularly flexible as it can suit the needs of a research project. The freedom to redistribute copies so you can help your neighbor encourages the redistribution of scientific tools to aid other research clusters. This is a helpful point as it enables the tools exchange and can help other scientists reproduce the results of research without the need to buy costly software. Finally the freedom to distribute copies of your modified versions to others gives the scientific community an opportunity to benefit from the alterations made to the tool-set. This contributes towards the spread of effective scientific software as more scientists will use it.

Open research tools with the above freedoms are used in open research activity. Open research refers to the research activity which is using open source model of production in knowledge discovery process. Open research as a broader term includes the use of open methodology and data to produce results that will also be open to the public. The openness in research refers to method, data and collaboration. Methodological transparency enables openness in the method used for research activity. The data openness refers to the availability and re-use of scientific data, or the idea that primary scientific data should be available to anyone without restrictions from copyright, patents, or other mechanisms of control. Finally collaboration refers to the ability to exchange information between scientists for scientific reasons. The tools and methods of scientific exploration must be conceptually and operationally reproducible. The methodological approaches used include underlying theoretical assumptions that are reproducible in principle. Small systems can be reproduced in practice but as systems extend and become more complex, calculations that are reproducible in principle, become non-reproducible in practice without public access to the code, data and meta-data of the research. It is therefore imperative that tools and methods of advanced scientific research be available in open source licenses for other scientists to study.

Reproduction in research is based on collaboration of researchers. This is a key concept in academic environment as it forms the basis of knowledge production. Collaboration is vital in a research environment as it enables the exchange of ideas, methods, data and results to facilitate the knowledge production. Due to the type and size of the modern scientific topics, collaboration can provide data and materials exchange that would have cost to the research facility. Innovative approaches are needed to facilitate open research activities so that we can build upon, rather than recreate information. This will save time and financial sources and will aid towards the rapid evolution of modern academic findings. Academic publishing in science is a well proven practice that promotes sharing of findings. The sharing of more information than just the findings will enable to fully understand the methodology and the workflow of information in order to produce the results.

This is valuable in order not to replicate the same research activity and the constructively use the results of other researches as basis for the development of new knowledge. Scientific publishing is a well established method of recognition in the scientific world. The publication of scientific work in various forms (journals, conferences, reposts etc) is a way of measuring the professional credibility and activity of a scientist. This has its roots back in 16th century, with *virtuosi* competing over mathematical puzzles, scientific challenges, and other tests of talent and knowledge. In open source science as in open source software world, the recognition is measured with the contribution of a scientist to the production of knowledge and the participation on the relevant debate on the field. The open source paradigm, discussed earlier, can also be implemented to scientific research and academic environment. Nevertheless this implementation may also face some challenges. One of those challenges is the existence of economical norms limiting or prohibiting the sharing of methods, data and results. A private company investing in scientific research may protect the output of the research as this may be a valuable asset which will generate profit in the future. This is especially common in health sciences research where the research process is time consuming and the output may have a very high market value. As the open source community is constantly growing, the number of actively participating entities will reach a point where the research of costly topics will be doable. In other words, it is a matter of time until reaching a point where this type of open collaborative research may be doable by the open source community because the critical mass of participants reach a number big enough for quality research. A second challenge in open source scientific process is the "problem of the lowest hanging fruit." This refers to a peculiarity of the open source model of production where the actively participating individuals tend to focus on relatively easy topics and develop applications they find interesting. This enthusiasm targeting only specific applications creates a number of developing projects which depend only on the enthusiasm and joy of the programmers. Sometimes, at a later stage, when the enthusiasm and the joy is lost, the project tend to decay and eventually get discontinued if there is no other participant willing and able to participate. This type of problems will eventually disappear especially as the internet infrastructure is evolving and more individuals have access to information and knowledge. The community of active participants will grow and create a critical mass participation that will soon span all the possible computational and scientific topics. Of course new topics will still be unexplored and there will be the need for new applications and software, but it will be a matter of time until the critical mass of individuals start working on the subject.

## 4. THE CASE OF GEO-INFORMATION TECHNOLOGY

A discipline which has been influenced by the open research movement is the geo-information scientific field which includes disciplines using spatially aware data. Geographical sciences focus on the analysis of human and physical phenomenon. It has a number of tools and methods and deals not only with in-site observation but also with computational models and digital maps. As with any other modern scientific field, geography has a computational section, which focuses on computer modeling of spatial events and cartography. There are a number of software for spatial analysis of data and digital mapping. Geo-information technology includes Geographical information Systems (GIS), location based services and remote sensing. This sector of information technology is a key technology for developing nations with a vast range of applications in areas such as environment protection and management, agricultural production, location based products and services (health, GPS, navigation), and research.

The influence of open research to geographical sciences is mainly in the areas of tools, and datasets. There are a number of reasons for a scientist to choose to work with open source GIS instead of using a proprietary GIS system. The first reason for choosing open source GIS is the comparative advantage of knowing more than just the interface of the software and the marketable skills an open source software offers. Using open source GIS one knows the fundamentals of spatial data management and characteristics rather than button memorization. In this ever-changing job market it is a benefit to have a good idea about the internal structure of the software and its components. Open source knowledge becomes an increasingly necessary job skill as employees are more flexible in software use and have a deeper knowledge of data and methods. Additionally the low costs of buying learning and using open source GIS software makes this technology very competitive and offer an excellent alternative for research centers and scientists. Another advantage of working with open source GIS software is the openness of the data format which increases the portability of the data over time and the exchange of data formats with other similar applications. A possible pitfall of the current state of the open source GIS ecosystem is the numerous loosely connected libraries and tools with high learning curve which are not part of a main centralized library project but are individually developed and need to run separately. The plethora of options and tools is sometimes a problem as new scientists do not know which tool to choose and why.

As with any other software sector, there are a number of proprietary and open source geographical software. The open source GIS software has a vibrant community of programmers and users that contributes towards the development of fully functional professional GIS software. The open source GIS, as an open source product have some freedoms which make them valuable for research and professional environment. More specific, the scientist has the opportunity to use the available tools and methods for any purpose, without worrying for the purpose or the consequences of the use. This is a very important freedom as generally, research tools are licensed with strong licenses without permitting derived works or excluding scientific fields. Next, modern scientists have access to the source code of the geographical software, and alter it according to the needs of the research. This makes the software particularly flexible as it can suit the needs of strange and peculiar research project enabling the addition of extra features and the adoption of new standards. Furthermore, it can be freely redistributed to aid other research clusters. This is a helpful point as it enables the tools exchange and can help other scientists obtain a copy of the scientific tool. This makes the publication of research easier as the scientists include the software as well and avoid the costly proprietary software that someone would have to buy in order to evaluate the duplicate the research. Finally, the freedom of improvement and distribution provides the scientific community the ability to include the alteration of a tool-set to a new product. This new package will include corrections modifications and alterations that are proposed by the researchers. This freedom also offers the distribution of this new package in order to offer the chance to other researchers to use the updated/altered GIS software. This is a very good practice as it helps towards the spread of effective scientific software as more scientists will use it and redistribute it. In other terms if an updated/altered version of the software is helpful, more scientists will use it and redistribute it.

As with other open source fields, open geo-information technologies share data and methodology. The motives for sharing vary according to the entity and the type of material shared. The most common motives for sharing geographical data and methods are: necessity, reciprocity, reputation and profit. More specific necessity refers to organizations and users exchange data or methods in order to meet necessary legal requirements and laws by government. This applies to administrative

boundaries and catchment areas of services such as police and ambulance navigation, fire stations placements and similar needs. Reciprocity motive refers to situations when users or organizations exchange data for cooperation in order to pursue common goals/benefits. This may as well be the production of a common product or service and the collaborative research project between research agencies. Furthermore, in some cases entities share spatial data in order to improve or alter their public image, reputation or prestige in the community. This is very common nowadays as open source online communities appreciate individuals or agencies that share data and methods. Finally users or organizations choose to publicly share spatial data in order to facilitate the use, penetration or evolution of other products or use it as a basis for other profitable complementary operations. A typical example is the complementary relationship between GPS devices and map data. The use of the one requires the existence of the other. Consequently the availability of maps and GPS data, simplifies the use of GPS devices and increases sales and profit.

In geo-information science, users and organizations share data and methods. Methods include specialized know-how of converting, altering and reproduce data and meta-data of spatial information. Spatial data are the chunks of spatially aware information useful for mapping and analysis. Their exchange is easier than before as internet technologies enable fast and reliable sharing and exchange. The types of spatial data exchanged are community, proprietary and personal data. Community data are the ones that many users collect and connect/link them together to form a repository of collective spatial information. Proprietary spatial data are the data that have been collected and processed from a company holding exclusive rights and takes decisions upon data's license and format. The personal data are the ones that individual users collect, analyze and decide upon its format and license.

There are a number of advantages for sharing spatial data and methodology. Initially, more errors can be fixed and the efficiency of a method increases, as the number of active users of a dataset or a methodology increases. Also, as data exchange practice evolves, the quantity of collected data increases. The introduction of web sharing platforms and data compression, increases the details and quantity of spatial data shared between users and organizations. Next, the public availability of various spatial datasets and methods aids the research of spatial topics and contributes towards the development of spatially aware products and services. Furthermore, the availability of various spatially aware datasets, and the use of open protocols and file formats, facilitates the linkage of information between multidisciplinary datasets and cross-tabulations which produce new interconnected data. Finally, the availability and transparency of a spatial methodology, stimulates public participation and contribution of many entities towards the fine tuning of processes and methods which gradually creates an efficient work-flow which has been checked by the open source community.

There are a number of projects which focus on the sharing and exchange of spatially aware data. One of the most notable is the OpenStreet-Map project.

The OpenStreetMap project is one of the best known examples of volunteered web Geographic Information system. It started in 2004 and has been successful in providing free high quality spatial data. It is an example of collaborative open source geo-information project. It consist of a big collaborative geographic database with an associate website for upload, rendering and editing geographic data. In brief, this project aims to develop a free alternative to Google Map with maps and data without copyright restrictions. Its spatial database includes a constantly increasing number of features such as roads, land use information as well as points of interest (POI) and location / routes of various services. Anyone can contribute new data to the main map or edit the existing data. The working model of OpenStreetMap is relatively simple. It provides an open web platform for uploading and editing geographical data. The user may upload raw uncorrected sources of GPS data. Those tracks can then be used as a basis for the digitizing (vectorizing) of roads and networks which form the actual data of OpenStreetMap. Additionally there are a number of other basis data used as a background layer to digitize on top of them. Those include free Ordnance Survey data and historical maps out of copyright. Those are use only as a reference and the digitized vector roads and networks may be edited by other users as well. In other words, users participate in the creation of a map from raw or historical data sources. The OpenStreetMap project is a collaborative wiki and the owners of the data are the contributors with the Creative Commons Attribution/ShareAlike license (CC-BY-SA 2.0) (Commons 2003). The OpenStreetMap Foundation (OpenStreetMap Foundation 2011) is a foundation which protects, supports, and promotes the development of the project and is not controlling the future direction of it.

Figure 1 depicts the overall structure of the OpenStreetMap work-flow. Users import raw captured data to the system and at the same time editors fix or alter spatial data. The main map of OpenStreetMap is constantly updated in order to use the latest edits and additions. Finally there is a number of derived products that can be extracted from the spatial database of the project to be used for other reasons. Those are mainly spatial data of points, lines and areas representing points of interests (towns, cities, banks, hospitals etc), roads or paths and land use or borders respectively.

As with other open source projects, the communication between the participants is essential. The community of participants and editors is large and spreads across many counties (Figure 2). Some of the contact channels are mailing lists, IRC and forums. Internet infrastructure helps by providing different types of communication chan-

*Figure 1. Structure of the work-flow of OpenStreetMap*

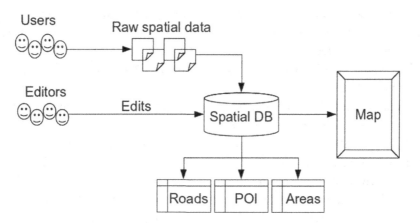

*Figure 2. OpenStreetMap usage statistics for February 2011*

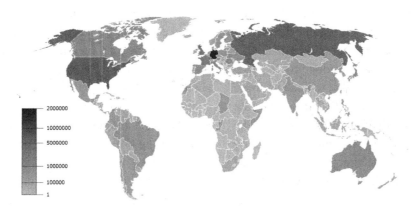

nels. A project such as this one wouldn't be possible in the past without internet infrastructure and content sharing.

The reason for the development of OpenStreetMap is that geodata is expensive and difficult to order and use. This is especially true for vector data and orienteering map data. Additionally those spatial data are not standardized, and the only "free" alternatives (e.g. Google Maps) are proprietary. Existing data are not free and open and those restrictions limit the use of the data. Additionally, commercial geodata may be old and a static snapshot of a geographical area. In the contrary, OpenStreetMap data are dynamic as anyone can edit them anytime, following the possible changes in geographical space. The project's

main map consists of nodes, ways, areas, and tags (annotations). The tags of various data on the map, consists of a small number of options for maximum flexibility. This enables flexibility as new users can easily start editing the map and secondly it enables the simple categorization of features such as roads, areas, and cities/towns. Some examples of tags for linear ways (roads) are the "type" which can take values from the set of: highway, motorway, primary, secondary, footpath, cycle-path. Other tags are: "max-speed" and "one-way" which are Boolean and determine if the road is "one-way."

The data of OpenStreetMap can be extracted, downloaded and used by anyone without limitations in the type and form of the use. This feature is potentially useful to research and development sector as these geographical data would be relatively expensive to buy and difficult to use in other applications due to license restrictions and incompatibility. OpenStreetMap data can be easily selected according to any tag (types of land, points of interest etc), extracted to common file formats and used for scientific purposes without any limitations. This increases syntactic and semantic interoperability of the data, and contributes towards a community driven sharing of geographical data and methodology. Interoperability is a key concept in open working model as it enables the inter-exchange of information between actors and assures the over-time usage of the data in different technical environments. The majority of the data is collected by non experts and volunteers without specialized experience in geographical data. This has given rise to concerns surrounding the spatial data quality. For the project to become more widely used, some measures of quality of the data are required. This will allow data users to make informed choices towards reducing or absorbing possible uncertainty or accuracy issues. In the case of OpenStreetMap project, the quality of the data refers to the extent the map represents real space. The work of Mooney et al. (2010) uses a methodology to measure the quality of OpenStreetMap data. Each time a user successfully edit a feature, a new version of that feature is created. Under this model it is possible to trace the spatio-temporal evolution of geographical features of an area. Figure 3 depicts the evolution of the boundaries

of a forest polygon in Exeter UK after 55 editing attempts. The first version of the boundary (left part) is very generalized, and the final version (right part) is very detailed. This shows that data integrity evolve as more users edit the data. The number of editors is highly connected to the quality of the spatial data in OpenStreetMap project.

The time is an issue in collaborative work such as OpenStreetMap. In the above example of boundary evolution the final version (55th edit attempt) is two years later than the original boundary. In some cases this is a problem as there is a need for accurate up to date data. Eventually OpenStreetMap project will reach a mature stage where a big part of the world map or at least the more interesting features of the world will have been edited and corrected to an acceptable level. This may be long time from now, but eventually will happen as the number of users and editors increases exponentially. The need for accurate and free geographical data forces more and more individuals and agencies to contribute to OpenStreetMap project. Accuracy of OpenStreetMap map cannot be guaranteed. Then again, few spatial proprietary products guarantee the quality and accuracy of the final product. The main idea of a wiki-style project is that users contribute with data that may not always be accurate but on the other hand other users focus on the management and fine tuning of the data. The process is continues and due to the nature of the data (spatial data), each user is mainly focusing on data from the geographical area of his/her residence. This

*Figure 3. The evolution of the boundary's detail after 55 edits*

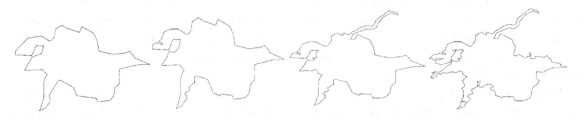

creates a decentralized net of edits that spans over the world map. A full editing history backups is stored for each user and data which makes the editing even easier to track.

The idea behind this wiki-style of managing information is somehow similar to Wikipedia where the content is becoming more and more accurate as more users and editors contribute small pieces of work. This is the power of the community and crowd-sourcing which makes projects such as OpenStreetMap competitive and promising to other alternatives. The growing number of users in the project enables the crowd-sourcing of the editing and evaluating the quality and accuracy of the data. Tasks that traditionally would have been done by a small group of employees can now be done collaboratively by a huge number of users in the community. This helps towards the fine tuning of the small errors that would be impossible to spot and prevents possible collaborative-data-vandalism, as more and more users check for possible errors or peculiarities in data. The increasing number of OpenStreetMap contributors, assure the constantly increasing quantity and quality of the data to a certain extent. The crowd-sourcing aspect of the project illustrates the ability of open research to create relatively big projects and deliver products and results that would require a great number of financial resources.

## 5. CONCLUSION

In a networked economy changes in production and management of data influence a number of sectors. When a new paradigm is established in a sector of economy, it may trigger debates about its implementation to other fields as well. The open source movement is a well established model of production which is influencing not only the computer industry but as an analogy, a number of other sectors such as geo-information sector. The established methods and practices in scientific research are constantly questi5.oned especially in a fast growing networked world. There is need for openness in various scientific practices and the sharing of information as this may trigger increase in scientific knowledge production because it supports even more the "building upon" process and the complementarity of knowledge. Geographical science is one of those scientific fields where open working model has revolutionized the structure and type of work both in the market and the research sector. Community driven process and sharing of data and methods along with open source software, brings new type of work-flow and services in the geo-information sector. Nevertheless, there is still room for improvement especially in the ecosystem of loosely combined libraries and the plethora of data transformation tools. However, the future of open source geo-information science is bright especially with the latest developments of internet infrastructure and the trend of openness in data and processes. Innovative approaches and new business models such as the ones described in this chapter are needed to facilitate open research so that can build upon, rather than recreate information. Collaboration, sharing and methodological transparency are some of the terms that play important role in the modern scientific arena and may determine the future nature of science. There is still room for improvement in the current established scientific working model, but the later developments of new technologies and the booming of worldwide web enable the evolution of new approaches and methods in information management and knowledge production process.

## REFERENCES

Andreev, P., Feller, J., Finnegan, P., & Moretz, J. (2010). *Conceptualizing the commons-based peer production of software: An activity theoretic analysis*.

Benkler, Y., & Nissenbaum, H. (2006). Commons based peer production and virtue. *Journal of Political Philosophy*, *14*(4), 394–419. doi:10.1111/j.1467-9760.2006.00235.x

Chen, P. Y., & Forman, C. (2006). Compatibility in an environment with open standards. *Management Information Systems Quarterly*, (n.d), 30.

Christensen, C. M. (1997). *The innovator's dilemma: When new technologies cause great firms to fail*. Harvard Business Press.

Cottey, A. (2009). Open science - An outline. Retrieved July 27, 2011, from http://www.uea.ac.uk/~c013/open_science/open_science.html

Creative Commons. (2003). *Creative Commons license*.

Eamon, W. (1994). *Science and the secrets of nature*. Princeton, NJ: Princeton University Press.

FSF. (2011). *Free Software Foundation*. Retrieved June 21, 2011, from http://www.fsf.org/

Kallinikos, J. (2009). *Panel: Regulation and governance in commons-based peer (social) production*.

Krechmer, K. (2005). *The meaning of open standards*.

Kuhn, T. S. (1962). *The structure of scientific revolutions*. Chicago, IL: University of Chicago Press.

McHugh, J. (2005). The Firefox explosion. *Wired*, *13*(02), 92(7).

Mooney, P., Corcoran, P., & Winstanley, A. (2010). *The effects of crowdsourcing on quality in OpenStreetMap*. Retrieved August 2, 2011, from http://na-srv-1dv.nuim.ie/stratag/index.php

Mozilla. (2011). *Mozilla Thunderbird*. Retrieved July 12, 2011, from http://www.mozilla.org/en-US/thunderbird/

OpenStreetMap Foundation. (2011). *OSMF-OpenStreetMap Foundation website*. Retrieved from http://www.osmfoundation.org/wiki/Main_Page

OSI. (2011). *Open Source Initiative portal*. Retrieved from http://www.opensource.org/

Patel, H., Pettitt, M., & Wilson, J. R. (2011). Factors of collaborative working: A framework for a collaboration model. *Applied Ergonomics*, *43*(1).

Raymond, E. S. (1999). *The cathedral and the bazaar*. New York, NY: O'Reilly Media, Inc.

Stallman, R. M. (2004). *GNU general public license*. Free Software Foundation, Inc.

Staring, K., & Titlestad, O. H. (2008). *Development as a free software: Extending commons based peer production to the south*.

Tsiavos, P., & Whitley, E. (2010). *Open sourcing regulation: The development of the Creative Commons licenses as a form of commons based peer production*.

## KEY TERMS AND DEFINITIONS

**Centralized Production:** Production of services or goods where a centralized party handles the inflows and outflows of capita sources (information, data, financial).

**Collaboration Work:** Together on a common enterprise of project and join forces with another party.

**Commons-Based Peer Production:** Commons-based peer production is a term coined by Harvard Law School professor Yochai Benkler to describe a new model of economic production in which the creative energy of large numbers of people is coordinated (usually with the aid of the Internet) into large meaningful projects mostly.

**Crowd Sourcing:** Crowdsourcing is the act of outsourcing tasks traditionally performed by an employee or contractor to a large group of people or community (a crowd) through an open call.

**Data Sharing:** Data sharing is the practice of making data used for scholarly research available to other investigators. Many funding agencies institutions and publication venues have policies regarding data sharing because transparency and openness are considered by many to be part of the scientific method.

**Decentralized Production:** Production type where smaller parts of a product are produced outside the centralized party.

**Geography:** Study of the earth's surface includes people's responses to topography and climate and soil and vegetation.

**Geo-Information Science:** Scientific area focusing on spatial information about features or attributes.

**Gift Economy:** In the social sciences a gift economy (or gift culture) is a society where valuable goods and services are regularly given without any explicit agreement for immediate or future rewards (i.e. no formal quid pro quo exists).

**Open Source:** Open source describes practices in production and development that promote access to the end product's source materials. Some consider open source a philosophy others consider it a pragmatic methodology.

**Open Working Model:** A model of production where access to methods and data is available to the public.

**OpenStreetMap:** OpenStreetMap (OSM) is a collaborative project to create a free editable map of the world.

**Proprietary Software:** Proprietary software is computer software licensed under exclusive legal right of its owner. The purchaser or licensee is given the right to use the software under certain conditions but restricted from other uses such as modification further distribution or reverse engineering.

**Public Domain:** Property rights that are held by the public at large.

**Scientific Research:** Research into questions posed by scientific theories and hypotheses.

**Scientific Software:** Computer software or just software is the collection of computer programs and related data that provide the instructions telling a computer what to do. The term was coined to contrast to the old term hardware (meaning physical devices).

**Spatial Data:** Data that define a location. These are in the form of graphic primitives that are usually either points lines polygons or pixels.

**Spatial Database:** A spatial database is a database that is optimized to store and query data related to objects in space including points lines and polygons.

**Wikipedia:** Wikipedia is a free web-based collaborative multilingual encyclopedia project supported by the non-profit Wikimedia Foundation and it consists of about 16 million articles.

**Working Transparency:** Transparency of information and data exchange during the working process.

# Chapter 3
# Facilitating the Integration of Open Educational Courses

**Yolanda Debose Columbus**
*University of North Texas at Dallas, USA*

## ABSTRACT

*The open educational movement is primarily about facilitating a philosophical view: the idea that universal access to quality education should be a global priority. Open educational courses are byproducts of the implementation of this philosophy. Unfortunately, the principles that are fueling the open educational movement are in direct opposition to the typical culture found in higher education institutions in the United States. The lack of awareness of or indifference to these cultural differences can hinder the integration of open educational resources. Successful integration of open educational courses into degreed programs requires an acknowledgement of the cultural dissonance that may result as well as a systematic plan for addressing it. This chapter highlights some of these cultural differences and outlines a framework for addressing them.*

## INTRODUCTION

Higher education institutions across the globe have mission statements that tout their commitment to providing a high-quality education to more citizens at a lower cost. Unfortunately, in the United States a post-secondary education is often only available to those who manage to pay the increasing cost (Auguste, et. al., 2010). Open educational resources seemingly present a low-cost solution to this complex and widespread problem (Open Educational Resources [OER] Commons, 2012). As a result, many institutions are developing open educational resources or integrating them into supplemental instruction. However, very few are integrating open educational courses into degreed programs (Ackerman & Zellner, 2012). Due in large part to the culture ingrained in higher education and the paradigm shift required to integrate open educational courses.

DOI: 10.4018/978-1-4666-2205-0.ch003

The culture of most higher education institution supports and rewards faculty autonomy and control. For example, copyright and intellectual property rights policies protect rights of course developers and restrict access and use of educational resources (Smith, 2009). Conversely, the open educational movement promotes universal access. The movement centers on the idea that educational resources should be free; specifically, educators should be free to reuse, revise, remix, and redistribute educational resources (Hilton et al., 2010).

Successful integration of open educational courses into degreed programs requires a paradigm shift for many administrators, faculty members, and support staff. This chapter describes a framework for acknowledging and addressing higher education institutions' cultural conflict with the open educational movement's key principles. The intended audience is key administrators who believe open educational courses are a viable solution. The goal of the framework is to outline a structure for addressing the cultural dissonance that may arise with the integration of open educational courses into degreed programs.

## BACKGROUND

In 'Winning by degrees' McKinsey & Company, report that the United States' post-secondary education system is not producing enough graduates to sustain its' current economic growth (Auguste, et. al., 2010). In order to produce, the needed number of graduates the education system would need to produce approximately 23% more graduates each year. The top producing institutions are improving their degree productivity by increasing cost efficiencies. One of the five strategies these institutions employ is extensive course redesign.

McKinsey & Company described the strategies and tactics employed by the 8 of the top producing post-secondary institutions. Some of these tactics are contrary to the typical behaviors practiced and expected in four-year post-secondary institutions. For instance, Rio Salado and Western Governor's employ a large number of part-time instructor or course mentors and centralized course development (Auguste, et., al., 2010). At four-year post-secondary institutions, the number of part-time faculty members are typical minimal and course development is traditionally left in the hands of the faculty members. Hence, many administrators are looking for other innovative ways to implement extensive course redesign. As a result of the mainstream media coverage and seemingly low cost, open educational courses seem to be a viable option. To date no institutions have integrated open educational courses into degreed program (Ackerman & Zellenr, 2012).

The open educational movement is well funded and supported. The announcement of MIT's OpenCourseWare (OCW) initiative in 2000 is generally considered the catalyst that spurred the open educational movement (Smith, 2009). Since MIT's creation of the OCW Consortium, the movement has gained momentum and popularity.

By 2005, the open educational movement was in full swing. Creative Commons and the OER Commons were created. Over 250 universities had joined MIT's OCW Consortium (2012), and many organizations became committed to developing, providing, and facilitating access to open educational resources. Currently, many well-established and highly regarded organizations are working on projects to promote the movement, such as the Open Learning Initiative by Carnegie Mellon, the Open Educational Resource Initiative by the Hewlett Foundation, and edX by Harvard and MIT.

What is notably absent in these initiatives is a focus on the utilization of open educational resources in degreed programs. This is in part due to the culture of higher education institutions. Course development is most often faculty driven. Hence, key administrators are not aware of how many open educational resources are used in courses. This trend highlights one cultural behavior in higher education institutions that may conflict with the open educational movement. The integration of open educational resources will significantly impact faculty members' practices as well as their professional identities. So, key administrators must acknowledge and address the potential cultural conflicts.

## THE NEXT STEP IN THE OPEN EDUCATIONAL MOVEMENT

The next step for the open educational movement is integrating entire courses rather than just components of courses (e.g. videos) into degreed programs. Administrators interested in this step see it as a potential way to replicate the successes of some highly productive institutions such as Rio Salado, Westerns Governors, and BYU – Idaho (Auguste, et. al, 2010). These institutions increased cost efficiencies through extensive course redesign. The greatest opposition to the integration of open educational courses in degreed programs is the apathy to the cultural implications for higher education (Ackerman & Zellner, 2012).

The development of institutional polices for governing the integration of open educational courses may reveal certain cultural inconsistencies that lay dormant in higher education. For instance, collaboration on research projects is expected. These expectations are often documented in faculty handbooks and rewarded during tenure review. Conversely, course development and expectations regarding course development are often not well-defined in the faculty workload and not rewarded during tenure review. When expectations are defined for course development, collaboration is often not a part of the policy or mandate.

Headlines neglect to discuss the potential conflict between higher education institutions' cultures and the open educational movement's philosophy. Instead they focus on the possibility presented by open educational resources. As a result, headlines tend to fuel an excitement in non-academic circles. Taxpayers, parents, and business leaders wonder why public institutions are not utilizing open educational resources, particularly when some of the best schools in the nations are creating them. Hence, governments and external stakeholders have initiated conversations with key administrators regarding the possibility of integrating open educational resources into degreed programs. These conversations focus on strategy and implementation rather than the challenges posed by the organizational culture. This focus on strategy and implementation rather than culture can be attributed to the intangible essence of culture. Culture is hidden in the beliefs, values, and principles that govern decisions and is revealed through the behaviors of the group. Behaviors can only be accurately explained and framed by those who have experience with similar cultures.

Although culture is not at the forefront of the discussions or in the headlines, it cannot be ignored or discounted. The culture of each higher education institution is unique. Higher education institutes are comprised of groups of employees such as faculty, administrators, and staff. The power and influence of these groups within each institution are different, and the philosophical views held within each of these groups are often contradictory. Integrating open educational resources may add to this cultural dissonance. Hence, planning for and addressing cultural dissonance is paramount to the successful integration of open educational resources.

### Open Educational Movement Ideas

The open educational movement is driven by the needs and rights of learners. It is based on the idea that knowledge is socially constructed and therefore should be collectively owned (UNESCO, 2002). Learners and educators should be free to reuse, revise, remix, and redistribute resources (Hilton et al., 2010). Over the past decade, these learner-driven philosophical views have blossomed. The *2010 Horizon Report* proposed that the entrance of open educational resources into mainstream teaching was fueled by a new and different ideal—the aim of supporting the expression of student choice about when and how to learn (Johnson et al., 2010).

## Culture of Higher Education Institutions

Culture provides meaning and context for individuals in an organization (Bergquist & Pawlak, 2007). Culture is based on beliefs, values, and principles and is revealed through behaviors. For instance, faculty members exert and maintain a certain amount of ownership and control over course development. They are encouraged and expected to develop or select learning outcomes, instructional content, instructional activities, and assessments. These behaviors reveal that post-secondary institutions value faculty autonomy and believe in faculty members' expertise. The behaviors reflect organizational culture.

The organizational culture serves to reduce organizational anxiety (Bergquist & Pawlak, 2007). Understanding organizational culture can provide acute understanding about beliefs, values, principles, and potential anxieties. This is particularly important when attempting to implement complex and cutting-edge projects such as the integration of open educational courses into degreed programs. An organizational culture can be defined by using Tierney's (1988) six attributes to help categorize it into Bergquist and Pawlak's (2007) six cultures.

Tierney's (1988) framework provides a structure for investigating organizational culture. He defines organizational culture using 6 attributes. Each of the 6 attributes can be defined by answering specific questions

1.  **Environment:** How does the organization define its environment? What is the attitude toward the environment?

2.  **Mission:** How is it defined? How is it articulated? Is it used as a basis for decisions? How much agreement is there?

3.  **Socialization:** How do new members become socialized? How is it articulated? What do we need to know to survive/excel in this organization?

4.  **Information:** What constitutes information? Who has it? How is it disseminated?

5.  **Strategy:** How are decisions arrived at? Which strategy is used? Who makes decisions? What is the penalty for bad decisions?

6.  **Leadership:** What does the organization expect from its leaders? Who are the leaders? Are there formal and informal leaders?

The definition of these six attributes for any organization can then be used to categorize the culture according to six cultures (Bergquist & Pawlak, 2007). In any given institution, each culture is present at varying degrees which culture primarily governs daily activities depends on the given employees' role within the organization. Each culture is defined based on beliefs values, beliefs, and the primary purpose of the institution.

1.  **Collegial Culture:** Values faculty research and culture; primary purpose of institution is the generation, interpretation, and dissemination of knowledge.

2.  **Managerial Culture:** Values fiscal responsibility and effective management; primary purpose of institution is building specific knowledge, skills, and attitudes in students.

3.  **Developmental Culture:** Values personal openness and service; primary purpose of institution is the facilitating the development of potential among students, faculty, administrators, and staff.

4.  **Advocacy Culture:** Values confrontation and fairness; primary purpose of institution as sharing existing or developing new social attitudes and structures.

5. **Virtual Culture:** Values global perspective of open, shared, responsive educational systems; primary purpose of the institution is linking educational resources to global and technological resources.

6. **Tangible Culture:** Values predictability of a value-based, face-to-face education in an owned physical location; primary purpose of the institution is honoring and reintegration of learning from a local perspective.

## Conflict: OE Ideals vs. Higher Education Culture

To date, the limited integration of open educational resources into courses has allowed the differences between open educational movement philosophy and post-secondary institutions' cultures to lay dormant. Projects focused on integrating entire open educational courses rather than components may upset the status quo and force institutions to address these conflicts.

Some aspects of post-secondary institutions' culture conflict with the fundamentals of the open educational movement. For instance, the open educational movement promotes universal access and use. Conversely, intellectual property right policies in post-secondary institutions promote limited access and use. Some aspects of post-secondary institution will also conflict with and/or open educational movement supports learners making decisions about course scheduling and availability. Conversely, course offerings and schedules in post-secondary institutions are driven by federal financial aid regulations, state funding schedules, and/or faculty member's availability.

Each institution's culture is unique and distinct. The culture of the institution that develops an open educational course will be different from the adopting institution. Culture influences behaviors and decisions. There is a prevalence of cultural differences within and across institutions. Hence, careful examination of culture and the potential impact is a critical apart to successful integration of open educational courses into degreed programs.

Integrating open educational courses into degreed programs requires a revision of the typical course development process. Administrators and faculty members' roles and responsibilities in course development are distinct. Faculty members construct the student learning outcomes, develop or find the instructional content, construct the instructional activities, and construct the assessments. Faculty members determine if they want or how closely they work with instructional technologists, instructional designers, or instructional consultants. Administrators typically do not interfere with the method or process used to construct courses. Administrators' roles and responsibilities are confined to items outside of the course, such as examining faculty members' and students' credentials, assessing the achievement of learning outcomes, and evaluating students' satisfaction of the course. The course development process is faculty driven, not learner driven. Course development is the faculty members' domain and a part of their professional identity.

The integration of open educational courses threatens the professional identity of faculty members. Some administrators and external stakeholders have proposed using entire courses or implementing competency-based learning to assess students who complete these courses, both of which infringe upon the autonomy that faculty members' value. Furthermore, integration brings into question the role of a faculty member, particularly in teaching-focused institutions. Faculty members are often the resident experts in the content area, and they select instructional content based on this expertise (Ackerman & Zellner, 2012). They are most likely to use only parts of open educational courses, such as videos, to supplement their instructional activities, rather than use entire courses.

## SOLUTIONS AND RECOMMENDATIONS

The framework for integrating open educational resources into degreed programs begins with acknowledging and systematically planning how to address the conflicting philosophical views. Shifting the paradigm in higher education from a focus on protecting the creator to a focus on benefitting the recipients requires systematic forethought and follow-through. Getting a clear understanding of the organizational culture requires purposeful conversations and interactions with a variety of stakeholders. Additionally, facilitating change requires respect and trust from a variety of stakeholders. Stakeholder social capital provides a framework to plan and facilitate these interactions and build relationships.

## Stakeholder Social Capital

Stakeholder social capital integrates stakeholder theory and social capital theory. Stakeholders are the various groups and individuals who can impact or are impacted by the achievements of an organization (Freeman, 1984). Social capital is the goodwill or the respect, trust, and acceptance available to an individual or organization (Adler & Kwon, 2002). Stakeholder social capital is the goodwill available to the leaders from the various stakeholder groups (Maak, 2007).

In higher education institutions, internal stakeholders are typically administrators, faculty members, support staff, and current students. Integrating open educational courses into degreed programs is most often a centralized effort, led by administrators. For the purpose of this chapter, the term *executive leaders* refers to administrators, and the term *stakeholders* refers to faculty members and support staff.

Integrating open educational courses into a degreed program is a new endeavor, and hence there are some inherent risks. Stakeholders who participate risk losing such things as credibility with colleagues, marketability with other institutions, and autonomy. Hence, convincing stakeholders to commit to this new focus requires executive leaders to systematically and purposefully acquire and maintain the respect, trust, and acceptance of stakeholders.

Stakeholder social capital theory exposes one way for approaching this challenge. Stakeholder social capital is impacted by the network structure of executive leaders. Network structure refers to the size, diversity, and density of relationships (Franke, 2005). The network size refers to the number of people in the network. The larger the network is, the more likely the goodwill required to implement a decision exists and can be accessed. Density refers to the degree of interconnections among members of a network. The greater the degree of interconnections among network members, the more exclusive the network. Diversity refers to the degree of heterogeneity among members of the network. The less the degree of heterogeneity among network members, the greater the opportunity for accessing goodwill that is not readily available to executive leadership (see Figure 1). Since integrating open educational resources into degreed programs poses significant and varied risk to different stakeholders, executive leaders will need to leverage goodwill at a number of levels in the organization with a variety of people. Hence, executive leaders should maintain large networks with minimal density and great diversity.

Focusing on developing relationships with a large number of people takes considerable time and effort. Time constraints, limited resources, or number of potential stakeholders may hinder this effort. Executive leaders as a whole should strategically assign stakeholders to specific leaders, and the assignments should be reviewed regularly. At any given time, the executive leadership team must be aware of the strategic goals, the critical success factors, and the primary threats to success. This information can guide executive leadership team decisions regarding which relationships to cultivate, the best way to communicate, and which tasks to prioritize.

*Figure 1. Image of stakeholder social capital*

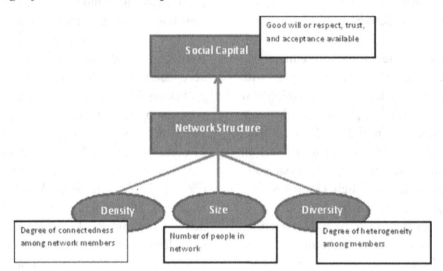

## Applying Stakeholder Social Capital: An Example

For illustration purposes, let's assume that the academic executive leaders at my institution have agreed to a pilot study. The goal of the pilot project is to integrate open educational courses into the university's four most popular programs. Based on the solution outlined previously, the first step is to build stakeholder social capital.

Academic executive leaders at my institution include the provost, associate provost, deans, associate deans, program chairs, and two directors. It is not necessary for all of the academic executive leaders to be a part of the project team, as the four most popular programs are in two colleges. Thus, the associate deans of those colleges and I will form the executive leadership team for the project.

The executive leadership team for the project will meet regularly to discuss progress, concerns, and risks. I will act as the project manager. As such, I will create the project plan, the deliverables, and the deadlines and will coordinate meetings with the project advisory board.

During the initial project leadership team meeting, we will develop a plan to establish the appropriate network structure—a network comprised of a large number of people who are minimally connected and diverse. We will start by specifying faculty members and support staff that will be most significantly impacted by converting the programs. After specifying the faculty members and support staff, we will determine which ones should be members of the project advisory board. Each of the stakeholders not on the project advisory board will be assigned to one of the project executive leaders. We will meet with our assigned stakeholders informally and regularly. Discussions during the meetings with stakeholders will be guided by Tierney's (1988) six attributes.

## FUTURE RESEARCH DIRECTIONS

The University Leadership Council concluded in its June 2012 report that there is a lack of research on the integration of open educational courses into degreed programs (Ackerman & Zellner, 2012). The movement and trends in open educational resources suggest that there is a prime opportunity for institutions to fill this niche.

## CONCLUSION

Discussions about integrating open educational resources often do not address the unique culture of higher education institutions. This is unfortunate because the culture of the institution plays a critical part in the integration of open educational courses into degreed programs. The lack of awareness or acknowledgment of the cultural implications is an oversight that must be addressed by key administrators.

## REFERENCES

Ackerman, B., & Zellner, K. S. (2012). *Integrating external open courseware into degreed programs: Assessing costs, benefits, and strategies.* Washington, DC: University Leadership Council, Education Advisory Board.

Adler, P. S., & Kwon, S. (2002). Social capital: Prospects for a new concept. *Academy of Management Review, 27,* 17–40.

Auguste, B. G., Cota, A., Jayaram, K., & Laboissière, M. (2010). *Winning by degrees: The strategies of highly productive higher-education institutions.* Washington, DC: McKinsey and Company.

Bergquist, W., & Pawlak, K. (2007). *Engaging the six cultures of the academy.* San Francisco, CA: Jossey-Bass.

Commons, O. E. R. (2012). *About OER Commons.* Retrieved from http://www.oercommons.org

Franke, S. (2005). *Measurement of social capital reference document for public policy research, development, and education.* Ottawa, Canada: Government of Canada.

Freeman, R. E. (1984). *Strategic management: A stakeholder approach.* Boston, MA: Pitman.

Hilton, J., Wiley, D., Stein, J., & Johnson, A. (2010). The four R's of openness and ALMS analysis frameworks for open educational resources. *Open Learning: The Journal of Open and Distance Learning, 25*(1), 37–44. doi:10.1080/02680510903482132

Johnson, L., Levine, A., Smith, R., & Stone, S. (2010). *The 2010 horizon report.* Austin, TX: New Media Consortium.

Maak, T. (2007). Responsible leadership, stakeholder engagement, and the emergence of social capital. *Journal of Business Ethics, 74,* 329–343. doi:10.1007/s10551-007-9510-5

OpenCourseWare Consortium. (2012). *Consortium members.* Retrieved from http://www. ocw-consortium.org/members/consortium-members.html

Smith, M. S. (2009). Open educational. *Science, 323,* 89–93. doi:10.1126/science.1168018

Tierney, W. (1988). Organizational culture in higher education. *The Journal of Higher Education, 59,* 2–21. doi:10.2307/1981868

UNESCO. (2002). *Forum on the impact of open courseware for higher education in developing countries: Final report.* Retrieved from http://wcet.info/resources/publications/unescofinalreport.pdf

# Chapter 4
# Creating a Digital Learning Community for Undergraduate Minority Science Majors

**Gladys Palma de Schrynemakers**
*Long Island University, Brooklyn Campus, USA*

## ABSTRACT

*Over the last three-decades, educators and policymakers have been alarmed about the state of American education and whether the Unites States can continue to lead the world in innovation. At risk is the performance of our students and their ability to be competitive in today's increasingly complex and challenging global environment. Clearly, while the importance of education in a global society vis-à-vis the welfare of a nation needs no defense, we must understand through real life experiences how complexity and competitiveness inform the global world.*

## INTRODUCTION

Thomas Friedman, writing in his illuminating book, *The World is Flat*, (p.8) takes a far-reaching and well-documented look at the global arena in terms of being leveled or flattened:

*The world [is] being flattened. Clearly, it is now possible for more people than ever to collaborate and compete in real time with more other people on more different kinds of work from more different corners of the planet and on a more equal footing than at any previous time in the history of the world—using computers, e-mail, networks, teleconferencing, and dynamic new software.*

DOI: 10.4018/978-1-4666-2205-0.ch004

The implications of this leveling threaten to intensify what many stakeholders already perceive as an unprecedented decline in education in the United States. For example, in a world where information is universally available, third world societies that have historically relied on the technology produced in the industrialized world now have almost immediate access to these technological capabilities. In a flat world, the rate of modernization increases significantly and homogeneously; as a result there is an acceleration in global competition that threatens the preeminence of our innovative capability.

The crisis in the academic environment is nowhere more evident or acute than in the areas of science, mathematics, and technology, which, for the most part, secured economic success and growth in the United States since the industrial revolution. Experts have reported an unbroken decline in the effectiveness U.S. science education, so much so that President Obama responded by outlining a program—Educate to Innovate—that would develop an environment that was receptive to science education and reverse the decline. In a speech delivered in 2009 (cited in the Boston Globe), the President put forth the following solution to strengthen education opportunities in the sciences and return credibility to higher education:

The key to meeting [ the country's] challenges—to improving our health and well-being, to harnessing clean energy, to protecting our security, and succeeding in the global economy—will be reaffirming and strengthening America's role as the world's engine of scientific discovery and technological innovation. And that leadership tomorrow depends on how we educate our students today, especially in those fields that hold the promise of producing future innovations and innovators. And that's why education in math and science is so important."

Creating a responsive climate for science education in twenty-first century will require that we become more creative and flexible as the ethnic and racial landscape of America changes with respect to the minority populations that will be streaming into the educational pipeline. *Population Profile*, a Census Bureau report, projects that the Black population in the U.S. will grow to over 20 million by 2030 and double to 62 million by 2050. The demographics for Hispanics also predict significant increases, e.g., a doubling from 1990 to 31 million by 2015 and a four-fold increase by the middle of this century. Furthermore, the Hispanic-origin population will make up 45 percent of the Nation's population growth from 2010 to 2030 and 60 percent from 2030 to 2050. These statistics would be reassuring if these emerging populations were (1) succeeding in school and (2) successfully entering and obtaining degrees in higher education; unfortunately, the educational pipeline for Blacks and Hispanics is fractured and leaky at best, and those that manage to enter into higher education rarely leave with a degree. The tragedy of minority attrition is painfully apparent in the numbers of those select few who choose to pursue degrees in the sciences, mathematics, and technology. Even for those who succeed, the trajectory is almost never a smooth or seamless one. For example, the American Council on Education reported in *Increasing the Success of Minority Students in Science and Technology* (2006) that although minority students entered into Science, Technology, Engineering, and Mathematics (STEM) majors at the approximately the same percentage as white and Asian counterparts their completion rates were significantly lower. Over the next decade and well into this new century, our nation will be challenged not only to fill the vacancies in the job market created by attrition and an aging workforce, but also to produce credible workers to fill the burgeoning field of science across wide-ranging venues. How well we respond to the realities of worldwide society and economy will determine if we can continue to lead the world in innovation. The choices we make in educational policies and practices must be aimed at nurturing young people, particularly in Black and Hispanic communities, and encouraging them to think about science as a professional option. It is vital, therefore, to craft a broad framework and comprehensive strategy wherein a synergy evolves between the learning environment and the educational philosophy that can be applied to meeting the strategic goals of our nation.

Obviously, many of the inherited methods of the past can no longer be relied upon to address these emerging and historical issues; however, a return to the *basics* may just be the bold initiative that is called for. Perkins (1991) describes the three basic goals of education, namely, retention, understanding, and active use of knowledge and skills, which, while not new to the educational arena, are the fundamental elements of the constructivist theory of learning. Also, important constructivists like Dewey, Piaget, Bandura, and Vygotsky and more recently Bruner and Gardner have made significant contributions to understanding how students retain and comprehend information and then apply that knowledge and skill set. In what follows, the author argues that the creation of an open-source learning community—built on the foundation of the constructivist philosophy and experience—for 21st students will help them get the most of their educational experience and broaden and secure this nation's future. A digital learning community, designed to allow students to take ownership of their learning, in part, through social media and digital content, is not only consistent with Perkin's goals, but also could help to improve student engagement. Focusing on active student learning and engagement may also address the unique challenges faced by minority student populations in the STEM majors.

The chapter will map out the current educational landscape of minorities in the STEM areas, including the issues that have an impact on student persistence and success and those that are that directly related to student learning. Moreover, an approach outlining the fundamental elements of building and implementing an open source digital learning community for STEM students

will be presented, comprising student learning goals, examples of assignments, and resources.

## EDUCATIONAL LANDSCAPE

Improving access to and success in higher education for minority populations will require an understanding of the unique challenges and unique responses for those confronting significant obstacles to matriculating in STEM fields. An investment of time and effort and resources by universities will be needed to focus on how the values, trends, and real life experiences of minority students can be tailored to create programs that focus on the important links between science and success in preparing the nation's workforce in the twenty-first century. However, anyone viewing the current educational landscape must be worried by the thought-provoking assessment of the American Council of Education (ACE, 2011) concerning the next college-age generation of students of color:

The younger generation in the United States no longer achieves a much higher level of education than its predecessors. As of 2009, 37.8 percent of U.S. adults aged 25 to 29 had obtained at least an associate degree, only marginally higher than adults aged 30 and older (35.1 percent). Only two groups, Asian Americans and whites, made notable gains over their elders (65.6 percent versus 54.2 percent, and 44.9 percent versus 38.5 percent, respectively). No gains were observed for African Americans and Hispanics (24.7 percent versus 25.0 percent, and 17.9 percent versus 17.9 percent, respectively).

These statistics become even more alarming when matched with data reported by the Census Bureau Report (2010) that—taking into account migration and fertility rates—Latinos will be the fastest growing population in the United States through 2050; moreover, during these ensuing decades, as reported by the ACE, this growing population will not necessarily be interested in education. The bad news continues: "Lower rates of degree attainment among certain minority groups continue. African Americans and Hispanics continue to be significantly less likely to earn a bachelor's degree in six years than either whites or Asian Americans." (ACE, 2006, p.2) The same report also highlights that "The racial /ethnic composition of higher education is similar to the larger national population, except for Hispanics who were underrepresented in higher education, comprising only 6 percent of the student population, as compared with 10 percent of the national population."(p.3) The crisis for Latinos in higher education must be addressed before it materializes by instituting an effective plan that focuses on better representation and persistence, while for African Americans, the focus must be on persistence. Given the anticipated demographic trends for current minority populations within an emerging global arena that values increased educational and professional preparation, universities, along with governments, must encourage and energize young people to achieve their full academic and career potential. And we must respond to these new realities now, not later.

## Persistence of Minority Students

As noted earlier, the problematic persistence rates of African Americans and Latinos in higher education are even more pronounced for those underrepresented cohorts in STEM majors. For example, the American Council on Education (2006) reports that, for both these groups, persistence remains below average in STEM fields. When all the components are analyzed, we find a troubling scenario, that is, one in which fewer and fewer minority students are entering and staying in STEM majors, even as the demographics for those groups clearly point to increases that are rising faster than their non-minority counterparts. Equally distressing are the data that show the United States has the highest attrition rates among Latinos and African Americans.

Although persistence of minority students in STEM majors maybe studied using a number of relevant parameters—including family income, number of hours worked, and related social factors—for the purposes of this chapter it will be viewed through the lenses of student preparedness and academic engagement. We will also focus on how creating a digital learning environment will help these students develop the knowledge, skills, and values to persist and earn a baccalaureate to prepare them for life as a scientist.

## College Readiness and Academic Engagement

It is instructive to begin with a working definition of *a college-ready student*: an individual who "is able to understand what is expected in a college course, can cope with the content knowledge that is presented, and can take away from the course key intellectual lessons and dispositions the course was designed to convey and develop." (Conley, 2007 p. 6) The definition is far more cogent than simply a student being able to receive a passing grade on his/her exams and ultimately in the course; more to the point, it centers on understanding content in the broader and deeper context of constructing and connecting knowledge. Below, Conley (2007) presents the key components of the college ready student in a conceptualized figure referred to as the "Facet of College Readiness," wherein cognitive strategies, content, behaviors, and contextual awareness are positioned within a *levels of organizational* structure, where each key nucleus provides a foundation for the next nuclear component. (see Figure 1)

Conley's "Key Cognitive Strategies" are consistent with similar approaches like those of constructivists like Dewey, who have also presented cognitive development theories about linkages that might be attributed to constructing knowledge that do not simply rely on memorizing or stringing together information for one class. Conley's recognizes that implicit to cognitive

*Figure 1. Conley's key cognitive strategies*

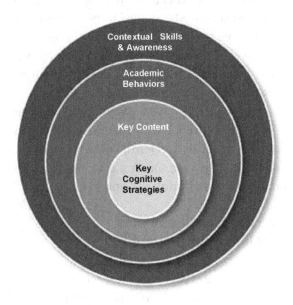

achievements are intellectual openness; inquisitiveness; analysis; reasoning, argumentation, and proof; interpretation; precision and accuracy; and problem solving. Common to all constructivists is the belief that students build their own knowledge, so it is not surprising that Conley' strategies are very similar to Benjamin Bloom's (1956) three domains of leaning: Cognitive (knowledge), Affective (Attitude), and Psychomotor (Skills). Both models, for example, agree on how the student learning environment is critical for learning content and exhibiting learning behavior and how both then can be applied in other learning arenas. With this understanding, education is not limited to learning only but is consequently converted into a fostering, nurturing, and cultivating process, where critical thinking thrives and does not collapse into remedial learning exercises. Equally important is keeping the process in mind so that we can construct education into a shaping, forming, molding activity, whose synergy will contribute to a standard form of social activity. (Dewey, 1916)

It is my contention that student persistence and student achievement can and often do result from educational environments that reinforce and reward student engagement, especially in programs that foster both creativity and open-mindedness—inside and outside the classroom. The problem is not what constitutes student engagement per se. Rather, it is with the emphasis of engagement minority undergraduates encounter in most classes and whether the courses encourage students to explore methods and opportunities of discovery. The exposure to an engaging curriculum of different levels of difficulty and complexity requires the active participation of all stakeholders, that is, student and teacher. Each must be involved in serious ongoing dialogues about learning, writing, critical thinking, and intellectual growth if we wish to have a sustained impact on making higher education an effective developmental experience and an important resource for minority populations.

The National Survey of Student Engagement (NSSE), administered by Indiana University Center for Postsecondary Research, is a well-respected survey instrument used by a large number of institutions across the United States to measure student learning experiences, in and outside the classroom. The instrument uses five measures as indicators of student engagement and is administered to freshmen and seniors. (NSSE refers to these indicators of engagement as Institutional Benchmarks.)

- **Academic Challenge:** Student coming prepared for class, the number of written papers, coursework that emphasizes analysis and theory, etc.
- **Active and Collaborative Learning:** Class discussions, making class presentations, experiential learning, group projects, etc.
- **Student-Faculty Interactions:** Students learn how to think about and solve problems by interacting with faculty members.
- **Enriching Educational Experiences:** Internships, research, and community service opportunities which provide stu-

dents with a way to integrate and apply knowledge.

- **Supportive Campus Environment:** Support structures that assist students in addressing academic and social issues.

In their broadest contexts, the aforementioned benchmarks are essentials of effective institutions that wish to provide a first-rate education and graduate truly educated people. The implications of meeting these benchmarks are much more far-reaching for institutions serving large populations of students of color, significant numbers of who find themselves ill-equipped for college work as first-generation collegians with English language learning issues. The essentials in NSSE can be used as a blueprint to build learning communities, which underlie much of the contemporary reform in higher education and focus on improving student engagement as the foundation for strategic efforts aimed at persistence and retention.

What I propose is needed to emphasize acquisition of knowledge and specific skills required of students persisting to graduation is a learning environment framework, where faculty, students, and staff work collaboratively on a primary focus: improving the possibilities for minorities to earn a baccalaureate by building learning communities that provide holistic support so they can discover what is to be learned in real and unmistakable ways. Certainly, this intellectual community has to include a digital component because technology is a cogent force, shaping how students live and learn in this new century. What is more, the logic of creating a digital social learning network is persuasive, since many students are comfortable in and knowledgeable about digital social networking, through Twitter, Facebook, etc. A digital learning community in many ways is an ideal venue to address several aspects of student engagement found in NSSE. For example, students who participate in a digital learning community often are presented with complex texts to read and write about and are asked to reflect about

the piece with class peers or analyze other digital resources provided by the instructor or found on the web. Being able to chat with their classmates about the reading helps them to learn how others understand the assignment or being able to chat with the instructor offers further clarification about the readings—activities that would prove difficult, if not impossible, in the traditional teaching milieu. In fact, the digital learning community provides a forum for multiple interactions and points of connection, not only with the material, but among students and between students and faculty. These collaborative interactions result in a synergy that allows students not only to construct knowledge beyond what is simply fed to them via traditional classroom instruction, but also to combine that knowledge into more than one perspective on something. So, in the digital community, students begin to accept responsibility for their positions and to reflect on other likelihoods in making choices; that is, they become active learners and feel that they are worthy contributors in their educational endeavor.

Learning opportunities in the digital community provide preferences for diverse students to be engaged learners in a frame of reference that is enabling and consistent with their learning styles and could therefore possibly serve as a complement to critical thinking and personal development. On the other hand, strict adherence to traditional teaching strategies has proved to be less effective in having students experiment with ideas and share their problems and successes—thus making persistence to graduation less likely. For example, two factors that contribute to introductory STEM course attrition in the first two college years are lecture-based courses and lack of interactive learning pedagogies. (Gasiewski, Eagan, Garcia, Hurtado, Chang, 2011) To be sure, classroom learning that is augmented by a digital medium not only serves to make course content real, but also improves other academic skills, e.g., reading and formal writing and helps to nurture learning bonds between students and their instructor. Such connections are particularly important in STEM courses, where the material is often complex and difficult to read and understand. The digital learning community allows faculty to buttress classroom learning with other learning opportunities that students can access any time of day.

## ELEMENTS OF CREATING AN OPEN SOURCE DIGITAL ONLINE COMMUNITY

Given our experience, we educators should not underestimate the importance of using technology to create learning communities that provide faculty and research mentors with substantive ways to teach more effectively by engaging students in a format they usually have experience with and find easy to use. If done properly, students will learn more material and be more competent. Clearly, students today live a digital existence, where they routinely share—and yes, even experience—their lives through digital media, as a favorite story of mine will demonstrate: some time ago, several of my students shared with me in class their experience watching a television show together and communicating through text messaging. I was confused at first, and this prompted me to ask if all ten were in the same room watching a soccer game and discussing what was going on by texting each other! I was astonished to hear that the answer was yes—because it required of me a frame of mind that was hard to achieve. Then and there, I knew I needed to consider rethinking and reshaping for my own sake and my student's how to reengage twenty-first century collegians through more immediate and concrete strategies that are consistent with their traditions of learning: videotaping daily occurrences and posting the videos on Youtube or Facebook. My students agreed that this was how they communicated about their lives and how they stayed connected to friends and family close by and far away. More importantly, this was how they stayed connected

to what was happening in their lives, the city, and yes, the world. When I asked them how they found out about national or world news, many said they "googled" this information. No one mentioned newspapers or magazines, but instead referenced particular topics by participating in blogs. Through this informational exchange, I began to value the ways my students perceived and functioned in the world and to realize that it was important for me not to remain fixed and committed to the teaching traditions I encountered as a student and used in the classroom. Their learning experience was dynamic, i.e., one of digital texts, moving images, and instant information, not the pedagogical inertia that too often finds a place in the academy today. This is relevant to the discussion at hand because my students are primarily minority first generation collegians, speaking over 20 languages and enrolled as majors in Biology, Chemistry, Pharmacy, Nursing, and other allied health professions.

For students in the 21st century, the world's information is a touch away, and our students are engaged and connected to that world through technology, so it is critical to teaching and learning that faculty be adept at handling information and knowledge in contemporary ways and integrating those practices in the classroom; equally important, if our aim is to engage students in their learning, we must design our courses with these insights in mind. Mark Taylor (2010), in his eye-opening work, Crisis on Campus: A Bold Plan for Reforming Our Colleges and Universities, wrote, "The liberal arts expose students to different ways of understanding the world and acting in it. Moreover, critical thinking cultivates the skills necessary for making responsible decisions that change lives of individuals and transform the world. Such reflection has never been more important than in this era of media frenzy and information overload." (p.49) Taylor's words cannot and should not be limited just to the liberal arts but applied to all fields, since all students are exposed to the same information overload. In my judgment, such exposure will require the development of digital learning environments—ones that are familiar to students and include open source technology and where they can grasp what is to be learned—like Moodle or PbWorks, for example. Open source educational technology provides educators with digital modes similar to those used in social networking, making them "user" friendly and allowing students to concentrate on content as opposed to learning technology that they will not be able to apply outside of the classroom. Open source parallels what NSSE describes as elements of student engagement and what Conley's "Key Cognitive Strategies" regards as a cohesive and connected learning environment for students.

In fact, the use of Open Source technology with cognitive strategies in a blended learning environment has a strong potential for engaging students, helping them to achieve their educational goals, and facilitating their persistence to graduation. Such interconnections between technology and pedagogical strategies can be powerful tools in helping diverse students achieve academic success:

*Some emerging research suggests that engagement may have compensatory effects for at-risk students, including low income, first generation, and students of color. These findings suggest that seeking ways to channel student energy toward educationally effective activities would be use, especially for those who start college with two or more "risk" factors. (Kuh, et al., 2006.p. 48)*

The dilemma we encounter is in actually creating a digital learning environment where students become engaged as committed participants in their own learning and thereafter develop and hone their cognitive skills. We have to start afresh and reform our undergraduate curriculum and "create environments and experiences that bring students to discover and construct knowledge for themselves, to make students members of communities of learning that make discoveries and

solve problems." (Barr & Tagg, 1995, p. 16) With this understanding—that a learning community engages students in constructing their own knowledge—we must direct our insight and energy to constructing effective pedagogical strategies for promoting digital media as a vehicle for presenting materials and assignments. Peter Honebein (1996) presents a possible approach for effective pedagogy in an open source environment in which he outlines the following conditions

1. **Provide students with the experience to construct their own knowledge.** This is a challenging notion for most faculty, since they are asking students to decide what methods are to be used to learn a subject. For example, as part of my course, students are asked to visit the American Museum of Natural History and select an artifact and then to present it as part of an exhibit room, where they are free to design their presentations as they see fit. The only requirement is the presentation must include narrative about the artifact, e.g., country of origin, culture, and usage. All students include their presentations as part of an exhibit. Students can be creative in their presentations, including music and dance from the culture and time period of their artifacts and can fashion original stories about the artifacts.

2. **Provide experience in and appreciation for multiple perspectives.** Assignments like the one mentioned in goal 1 allow students to experience different cultures through new and interesting ways. By designing an appropriate setting for presenting the cultural artifact, students are exposed to and learn about the culture, history, customs, and practices. Students are required to consider the virtual presentations of their classmates, which may assist them in better understanding their own artifacts, even as it allows them to reflect on the other presentations and cultures.

3. **Embed learning in realistic and relevant contexts (an essential part of constructive theory).** This is an issue that is particularly evident in mathematics and science courses, where students are rarely, if ever, provided with the relevant connections among the sciences. Scientists themselves admit to this critical disconnect. For example, in Natalie Angier's text, The Cannon (2007), Andrew Knoll, a professor of natural history at Harvard University, concluded that "the average adult American today knows less biology than an average ten-year old living in the Amazon, or than the average American of two hundred years ago" (p.22). Angier proceeds to interview a number of noted scientists in the all the aforementioned fields and all point to the same problem with science education, namely, the disconnect that exists between the material and real and relevant situations.

4. **Encourage ownership and voice in the learning process.** Students in a learning environment are able to design and construct their own projects and communicate with classmates through multiple mediums, which stimulate goal-directed exploration and engagement in social, educational, and ethical problems. Students can also become architects of their own learning as learning grows to be a part of their personal topography. Gone are the days of John Locke's concept of education, where students are considered to be blank slates that professors fill with knowledge.

5. **Embed learning in social experience.** First types of learning are normally guided by one's social experiences, which encompass all kinds of connections with the world; for example, children learn their first language during immersion in social learning experiences. One of the author's first forays into open source was Elgg, which is often referred to as a "social networking framework."

True to its name, Elgg allows students to function in a social networking milieu as an alternative portfolio system that "follows a constructivist paradigm, allowing the user to completely control and manage [her] e-portfolio" (Tosh & Werdmuller, 2004, p.2).

6. **Encourage the use of multiple modes of representation.** With open-source, students have the capability of presenting information in many ways. For example, in my Reality Television course, final projects varied widely, from the creation of theme songs for reality television shows to videotaped try-outs to "Who Wants to be a Millionaire," to the creation of a show based on Spoken Word. Moreover, the range and creativity of modes of presentation challenged students to find real connections and applications to the theoretical foundations in every project.

7. **Encourage self-awareness in the knowledge construction process.** This particular goal really permeates throughout the entire student experience. As students interact with each other, they are able to reflect about their experiences and their learning and become conscious of the learning process because they are in control of their learning. "Human beings are most likely to learn deeply when they are trying to solve problems or answer questions that they have come to regard as important, intriguing, or beautiful"(Bain& Zimmerman, 2009. p. 11)

Peter Honebein's (1996) vision for open source pedagogy defined some of the basic approaches to conceptualizing a digital learning community at LIU/Brooklyn with the clear intention of engaging minority undergraduate science students in a world that is ever changing, where certainty and permanence are mere illusions. Using federal funding from the predominately Black Institutions program, I and faculty from our Chemistry and Biology Departments created project QUSET (Quality Undergraduate Expanded Science Training) to address directly the shortage of disadvantaged minorities in the STEM (science, technology, engineering, and mathematics) fields. Our aim was to offer a comprehensive range of services and activities that supported and strengthened the skills and academic experiences of minority students and, in addition, to create a resource center and informational Website for other STEM students at this institution and for the public at large. The first objective of Project QUEST was to create a heuristic educational science program for undergraduates that would optimize their skills in the life sciences and assist them in finding careers in the STEM fields. And the second was to create a digital learning community where students could develop critical thinking, literacy, and written communication skills in a scientific context. An essential component of Project QUEST was to run weekly academic seminars for students, where the approaches for an effective digital learning community were put in place. Project QUEST students Scholars participated in weekly Academic Seminars of 1 ½ hours duration, designed to develop literacy, technological, critical thinking skills, and scientific competencies and scheduled once a week for ten weeks during each academic semester. The seminars had specific student learning goals and objectives, outlined below.

## Overall Learning Goals

- **Critical Thinking:** Students will have the ability to identify, reflect upon, evaluate, integrate, and apply different types of information and knowledge to form independent judgments. Students experience writing and other critical thinking processes as a way to learn.
- **Complexity:** Students will be exposed to an approach to understanding scientific knowledge that distinguishes between ambiguity and nuance and clarity and precision.

- **Communication:** Students will be required to communicate scientific concepts, experiments, etc. effectively through writing protocols and oral presentations; moreover, they will be asked to contextualize their own ideas and those of others using rhetorical analysis, logical reasoning, and information literacy.

## Learning Objectives

- Read and write with a critical point of view that demonstrates greater depth of thought and a more thorough understanding of the rhetorical situation (Learning Goals: Critical Thinking, Complexity, Communication)
- Write research-based essays that contain well-supported arguable theses and that demonstrate personal engagement and clear purpose (Learning Goals: Critical Thinking, Complexity, Communication; Meta-Goal: Intentional Learning)
- Locate and select and appropriately use and cite evidence that is ample, credible, and smoothly integrated into an intellectually argument (Learning Goals: Complexity, Communication; Meta-Goal: Information Literacy)
- Analyze the rhetorical differences, both constraints and possibilities, of different modes of presentation (Learning Goals: Critical Thinking, Complexity; Meta-Goal: Intentional Learning)
- Reflect more deeply upon the writing process as a mode of thinking and learning that can be specific to scientific range of writing and thinking tasks (Learning Goals: Critical Thinking, Complexity; Meta-Goal: Intentional Learning)

## Overall Scientific Goals

- QUEST Scholars would gain instructive overview of the fundamental principles and subjects of entry-level biology, chemistry, and mathematics courses.
- QUEST Scholars would gain knowledge and experiences in basic methodologies in science used to conduct scientific research, including instruction on the use of instrumentation and the perfection of and quantitative analytical skills.
- QUEST Scholars would develop critical thinking and communication skills, both oral and written, for purpose of conveying scientific information to both professional scientists and the lay public.
- QUEST Scholars would develop intellectual independence, scientific literacy, and an appreciation for the connections between biological science and society.

Objectives were based on specific scientific context in biology, chemistry, and mathematics.

## STRUCTURE OF ACADEMIC SEMINARS

### Faculty Mentors

Faculty Mentors from Biology, Chemistry, and Mathematics met with the QUEST Project instructional resource staff three times a semester, during which the mentors, QUEST Coordinator, and resource staff proposed specific entry-level, discipline-based topics to be included over the course of the semester for student instruction. Also, at these meetings, faculty will provide recommendations for software, course materials, and other resources that will assist the instructional resource staff plan sessions for students.

## Instructional Resources Staff

Student Mentors (SM) were recruited from the Writing Center and the Academic Reinforcement Center, after which the SM and QUEST Coordinator will jointly meet once a week for an hour to plan academic seminars. Three of those meetings will include Faculty Mentors. SM will be compensated for 4 hours a week (1 hour planning, 1.5 hour session, 1.5 planning sessions).

Therefore, all the elements described in the Project QUEST Academic Seminar occurred faced- to-face with students, but the critical piece, the students' learning and connection to the material, was deposited in the Project QUEST digital learning community. All of the components outlined in Project QUEST emanated from a deliberate plan to create a learning environment that would engage students inside and outside the classroom. To accomplish this, we depended heavily on evidence in support of student preparedness and engagement supported in a constructivist framework and reinforced by concomitant technology. The construction of these learning experiences closely follows Kolb's (1981) continuum of learning cycle, where learning advances students from concrete concepts to participatory experiences, after which they begin to abstract and conceptualize complex and conflicting ideas. The digital experience exhibited is one that often creates intellectual communities that reflect this cycle, as illustrated in this diagram (p. 235). (see Figure 2)

## Examples from Project QUEST's Digital Learning Community

Below, Rosenthal (1996) argues, not surprisingly, for the importance of writing as a springboard for elevating the ability of students to think like scientists, more so for English Language Learners (ELL). I join Rosenthal in stating with confidence that writing instruction ought to be fixed to science education; however, I would also advocate that all

*Figure 2. Experiential learning model*

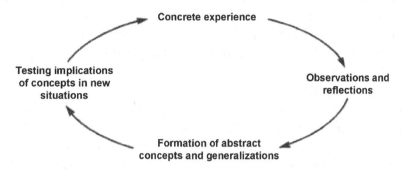

science majors be required to take a formal course in scientific writing and that science departments adopt a writing across the science curriculum program for their students.

Writing to learn science helps students clarify their thoughts, relate new information presented in class to previous knowledge, and can provide the instructor with feedback on what students do and do not understand. It helps students overcome a variety of barriers to learning such as difficulties with comprehending the text or making sense of their lecture notes. [ELL] students stand to gain even more from this opportunity to practice writing informally in English. (p.108)

With this in mind, we required Project QUEST students to read and write about topics in science in a weekly regimen. The readings ranged from traditional scientific research to historical theories, to present research dilemmas. The intent was to engage them in reading, writing, and critical reflection as a means of strengthening their academic skills through a digital medium. What follows—samples of student work from the QUEST Academic Seminars—is cogent evidence, I believe, for the value of digital learning communities in science education. (The student texts are not expurgated and therefore reflect student thinking and writing in its original form.)

For this exercise, students were asked to read a rather complex historical article in *Scientific American* (Gingerich, 1982) that reported on how cosmological theories proposed in the sixteenth century were received by scientists and the members of the Catholic Church—all heavily invested in and proponents of a geocentric cosmology. Students were given a digital prompt and had to respond using the text to support their positions.

## Digital Prompt

Galileo challenged an existing scientific model within a specific political climate. The state used this model to justify its own authority. How did Galileo's theory threaten the established religious, scientific, social and political order? What was the crucial difference between Copernicus' and Galileo's model?

## Student One Response

Galileo challenged an existing scientific model within a specific political climate. The state used this model to justify its own authority. How did Galileo's theory threaten the established religious, science, social, and political order? What was the crucial difference between Copernicus' and Galileo's model?

When Galileo advocated heliocentrism, the same theory that Copernicus first innovated, it had shocked the public, church and state. Galileo was blatant enough to withstand a trial to argue for his defense of this newly incepted scientific theory. Science was seen as a evil of deviation from the established religious texts. In terms of everyone interpretation of Galileo, with a background in physics and astronomy, it was seemed as a philosophy, stemmed from personal beliefs and bias that lead to Galileo to believe such rational theory of heliocentrism. Astronomy and physics nor mathematics are any materials that covered in the bible. It was developed by men and used by men to obtain a more exact definition of life. If Galileo, a devoted Christian would deft the sacred text, it would make anyone to believe that they can over empower to dethrone the existence of church and state.

The differences between Copernicus's model and Galileo model is that Galileo model was substantiated with the usage of microscope to validate this findings and calculation of gravity more than Copernicus model. The physics of Galileo gave the heliocentric model a more viable solution since it can predict the time that Earth, or any planet based upon their mass would revolve around the sun. Galileo used detail of Venus revolving the Sun, and the dark spots observed at the far end of the planet. Galileo wanted to use the argument deductively, one premise is true of Venus is in a planetary system that is heliocentric, the other premise using logic can provide a valid conclusion to pave way for planetary system is heliocentric.

## Student Two Response

Galileo Galilei challenged the Bible's claim that the earth was at the center of the universe. He claimed, like Copernicus, that the universe was heliocentric, or that the sun was the center of the universe and the rest of the planets revolved around it. In turn, Galileo was trialed for heresy since "There was widespread agreement that the truth resided not in astronomy but in the Bible" (Gingerich 134)" during that time. Galileo not only challenged the church's religious teachings, but he also combatted the scientific, social and political structure of his time. By doing so, he paved the way for a new analytical way of thinking in which he based his conclusions on

researched topics, instead of using the Bible to support his claims. Galileo's method is known as the "hypothetico-deductive method", where one tests a hypothesis and continues to test it until it becomes more and more convincing (Gingerich 137). His new method of thinking influenced other scientists to not rely solely on beliefs passed down to them, but to question and find answers to their questions themselves.

Galileo challenged Roman Catholic religious beliefs by contradicting the structure of the universe depicted in the Bible. His work was condemned by the church for it undermined the teaching the church had been preaching to its followers for years. It was difficult for the church to accept Galileo's claim because it threatened their power. As a leading power figure, the Roman Catholic Church could not afford to be outwitted by a mere astronomer. Interestingly enough, it became quite obvious that the church's qualm with Galileo was not so much due to his theory, but on his method of arriving at the theory. Gingerich states,

*"the Copernican system was not really the issue... The battleground was the method itself, the route to sure knowledge of the world, the question of whether The Book of Nature could in any way rival the inerrant Book of Scripture as an avenue to truth" (Gingerich, 137).*

Gingerich describes Galileo's method of analytical thinking as "the route of sure knowledge of the world" which emphasizes that for years, the church's followers were led blindly by their religious leaders following the religious teaching in the Bible. The concern of the church was not Galileo's heliocentric claim, but that if proven wrong by one man, its followers would question the validity of the church and all of its teachings.

Due to the social climate of the time, Galileo's teachings were more prone to criticism by the church. The church was suffering from opposition that began in the 1500s. During the time of the Reformation, Copernicus made his heliocentric claim, but it was not deemed heresy by the church since the church had greater concerns, such as Martin Luther's condemning the church for indulgences in 1517. Luther's opposition to the church proved to have a lasting effect on the church's efforts to regain the trust of its people. In 1542, Pope Paul III passed the Holy Roman and Universal Inquisition. In the 1570s, the Index of Prohibited Books was passed, which listed texts deemed inappropriate by the church, and lastly, in 1616, Galileo published *The Starry Messenger*, which restated the heliocentric theory. Galileo's mistake was that he chose to speak out about his theory during a time when the church was seeking to regain its power and image (The Counter-Reformation), so that any claim that opposed the church would spark instant scrutiny by the church.

The major difference between Copernicus' and Galileo's model is that Copernicus' model was never deemed heresy, for he presented it during a time when the church had other matters on its mind. Unfortunately for Galileo, he spoke up during a stressful climate for the church. This, in turn, worked against him and he was censored. The power remained at the hands of the church and the church did everything it could to make sure that it remained that way. Nevertheless, we now know that Galileo's claim was correct. It was his method of hypothetical and analytical thinking which set the path for how scientists and researchers come about concluding their works.

### Student Response to Student Two

Wow, I must say just by reading your prompt, the reading is a bit clearer to me. I'm not sure how many times you read through it, but it seems you've fully grasped the concept of the reading. I guess I'll have to read it through another time, but your take on the difference between Copernicus and Galileo's model is pretty much legit, though I didn't think along those lines. Very interesting. However, I was wondering why you didn't make

reference to the difference in reasoning the two used; if you didn't see that as a big deal or fairly significant?

### Student Three Response

Galileo's theory was based off of Copernicus' model of the solar system, which had the sun as the center of the galaxy and the earth in orbit. This model of the solar system was dangerous to the stability of society because it offended the position the church, a governing and influential entity, had on the matter. According to the church and its theologians, the bible told how the solar system was set. Galileo interpreted the very scriptures the church held against his theory to argue his theory. This was dangerous because it undermined the authority and experience of many priest and theologians across multiple generations, both before and after Galileo's time.

One of Galileo's major driving forces in his research was to be the first to discover the truth. Along with the Copernican system, scientists and the church were also reviewing the Ptolemaic arrangement and the Tychonic plan. Galileo found himself racing other scientist to find the true layout of the solar system. This proved to produce a very hostile environment for Galileo, the church, and fellow scientists.

The main difference of Galileo's theory and Copernicus' theory was that Copernicus' theory was based off of hypothetical, where as Galileo used his observation to back up his claims. Copernicus expressed his Idea of the solar system as a hypothetical theory so that it wouldn't cause trouble, where as Galileo started with hypothetico-deductive reasoning, based off of grounded observations, and becomes more convincing each time it passes a test successfully. This is exemplified by Galileo observing of Venus' waning phases which was only expressed and explained by the Copernican system.

The next prompt has student write about an article that highlights how undergraduate research enhances and better prepares and helps sustain interest of students interested in the sciences.

## Digital Prompt

1. This Study affirms that research based undergraduate programs encourage and facilitate post graduate education in the sciences. Does Quest provide similar benefits? How have you benefitted?
2. Evaluate how this article supports its claim. How could more research further substantiate the findings? What follow up would you recommend?

## Student One Response

No one can underestimate the importance of research, which is an instrumental and valuable experience to anyone especially at an important juncture while in an undergraduate phase. After reading the article about the research of correlation between science major undergraduates and educational research science related opportunity, i am more inclined to believe this is the modern trend of the young science major undergraduates today. Everywhere in universities and colleges, science major has had a demographic whether is computer science, medical or industrial. The precedence of science has prompted science students to do research to investigate if their field of study is their lifelong passion and get preparation before they graduate. To question 1, research experience is a gain, because you can take so much from the concepts of doing research and understanding the abilities you may need to acquire to better be acquainted to a science field career. You will be far off understanding what it takes to improve in area of weaknesses to get better. To question 2, As far as statistics of doing research and not doing research done by talented students is concerned, I am not convinced by the case study

due to inconclusive evidence of the demographics of imbalance of men to women ratio, ethnic backgrounds, typical age, and what university/college they attend to. To question 3, It depends on the individual's interest if research is suitable and valuable. If minority gets the chance to be selected for an undergraduate research program, then it's more likely incline to pursue a scientific career due to the exposure to the training. Minority or ethnic related based questions has no bearing for individuals who might choose the pathway to a scientific career. Crucial questions about how research helps respondents to decide a major, is the specificity. Men and women are on the opposite of the spectrum in terms of choosing research fields, while more men chose physics, engineering, and computer sciences opposed to women dominated in the answers of biology, biochemistry and neurobiology.

## Response from Seminar Mentor

Thank you for your extremely valuable comments here, which as you see, generated quite a lot of thoughtful response. Yes, let's absolutely explore in today's seminar what is to be done when data seem incomplete and the interpretation of those data inadequate. Where does the problem originate, in the methodology (the collection of the sample), or somewhere else, pointing to a larger systemic issue?

## *Student's Response to Seminar Mentor*

*Does Quest provide similar benefits? How have you benefited?*

As a Quest student for three approximate semesters, I have to say that Quest has opened me the opportunity for the interest to explore internship and other enrichment opportunities such as private tutoring with the best instructors and faculty in their respective subjects. With Quest, I was able to secure my first scientific research internship at Brookhaven National Laboratory in January 2010. Quest has allowed me to expand my learning not just in classrooms but in top advanced facilities and organizations that place students on the right path to secure their main objective of becoming scientists.

*Evaluate how this article supports its claim. How could more research further substantiate the findings? What follow-up would you recommend?*

This research can sure up its findings by investigating the locations of research universities that undergraduates are partaking in this study. This article uses an ambiguous survey that takes a random sample of undergraduate population in becoming a valid data for results are not credulous. This survey must be extended for further evaluation and monitoring for any sudden undergraduates change of plans or this study is completely a one and done deal. In one particular moment, an undergraduate can change its mind of pursuing a whole new different career.

## A Student Responding to Student One's Post

I cannot help but support your interpretation that some parts of this study was lacking results. It neglected providing data on the success of undergraduates who did not participate in REU programs. How do we know that research experience is what made undergraduates succeed? Maybe undergraduates who did not have any research experience were just as successful as those who did not. Nevertheless, it is inarguable that many benefits are obtained from having undergraduate research experience, such as the benefits you mentioned above.

The samples of student writing presented in this chapter were written during the first semester of college, when participating QUEST students also regularly attended seminars, read traditional and

*Figure 3. LIU data: Graduation and persistence of first-time Bachelor's degree seeking students (Fall 2005)*

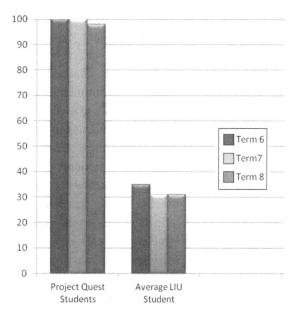

historical research articles, and viewed excerpts from TED Talks (Technology, Entertainment, and Design). The latter is a non-profit organization that started in 1984 and holds an annual conference and presents leading global figures that use engaging visual media to lecture on complex topics. The lectures are digitalized and can be accessed by students who wish to learn from experts.

Project QUEST had two important consequences: first, faculty participants began thinking more about how students learn and how curriculums constructed in a context of engagement can improve persistence in minority student populations and second, stakeholders recognized that learning community activities that routinely include reading and writing exercises have a salutary effect on critical thinking and overall student learning. What was also telling about the impact of this effort was the persistence data of QUEST students. All in all, QUEST students performed significantly better than their counterparts vis-à-vis persistence to graduation. (see Figure 3)

The improvement in persistence is significant, particularly when you consider that the persistence for students not receiving QUEST support is almost 70% less than the QUEST students. As we all know, grants come and go, but what LIU/Brooklyn did in initiating and implement this particular program was to create an interdisciplinary committee of faculty and administrators to study gateway courses in English, mathematics, and the sciences. The committee has already made doable recommendations, whose impact on student learning venues will develop in students the capacities and skills necessary to succeed in college. New advisement practices have been implemented to enroll students in classes that better support their learning needs; pre-college summer literacy programs with interdisciplinary readings have been implemented with digital learning components; and a faculty development project centered on reading-across-the-disciplines has been instituted. All of these projects are efforts designed to improve student engagement and persistence in a predominately minority campus; equally important, they are efforts to improve institutional effectiveness.

Simply put, if the United States wishes to remain preeminent in the new global arena of the twenty-first century, it will need its institutions of higher learning to make a special effort to ensure that the growing wave of minority students who enroll in science programs find a welcoming environment. This means that the curriculum has to be shaped not only by the knowledge of the learner, but also in an environment familiar to the learner—one that is more and more embedded in digital media. I am convinced that we can no longer exclusively rely on the traditional ways of teaching our students, that we must use their strengths and diversity to help them succeed in the world of science, and that we must design and implement curriculums that help students construct knowledge through dialogue.

## REFERENCES

Anderson, E., & Dongbin, K. (2006). Increasing the Success of Minority Students in Science and Technology. In *The unfinished agenda: Ensuring success for students of color, Mo. 4*. Washington, DC: American Council on Education.

Angier, N. (2007). *The canon: A whirligig tour of the beautiful basics in science*. New York, NY: Mariner Book.

Bain, K., & Zimmerman, J. (2009). Understanding great teaching. *Peer Review: Emerging Trends and Key Debates in Undergraduate Education, 11*(2), 9–12.

Barr, R., & Tagg, J. (1995). From teaching to learning—A new paradigm for undergraduate education. *Change, 27*(6), 12–26.

Bloom, B. S. (Ed.). Engelhart, M. D., Furst, E. J., Hill, W. H., & Krathwohl, D. R. (1956). *Taxonomy of educational objectives: The classification of educational goals. Handbook 1: Cognitive domain*. New York, NY: David McKay

Conley, D. T. (2007). *Redefining college readiness*. Eugene, OR: Educational Policy Improvement Center.

Cordova, D. (2010, June 10). Diversity as an educational imperative for the 21st century. Association for Professional Administrators of CSTEP and STEP. Retrieved December 12, 2011, from http://www.apacs.org/events/DCordovaKNPresentation2010.pdf

Dewey, J. (1916). *Democracy and education*, Columbia University. Retrieved February 22, 2012, from http://www.ilt.columbia.edu/publications/Projects/digitexts/dewey/d_e/chapter02.html

Dewey, J., & Dewey, E. (1962). *Schools of tomorrow*. New York, NY: E.P. Dutton. (Original work published 1915)

Foon, R. (2009, November 23rd). Obama highlights science education. *Boston Globe*. Retrieved December 20, 2011, from http://www.boston.com/news/politics/politicalintelligence/2009/11/obama_highlight_4.html

Friedman, T. (2005). *The world is flat*. New York, NY: Farrar, Straus and Giroux.

Gasiewski, J., Eagan, K., Garcia, G., Hurtado, S., & Chang, M. (2011). *From gatekeeping to engagement: A multicontextual, mixed method study of student academic engagement in introductory STEM courses*. Retrieved from http://heri.ucla.edu/nih/?c=presentations

Gingerich, O. (1982). The Galileo affair. *Scientific American, 247*(119), 127.

Honebein, P. (1996). Seven goals for the designing of constructivist learning environments. In Wilson, B. (Ed.), *Constructivists learning environments* (pp. 11–24). Educational Technology Publications.

Kolb, D. A. (1981). Learning styles and disciplinary differences. In Chickering, A. W. (Eds.), *The modern american college*. San Francisco, CA: Jossey Bass.

Kuh, G., Kinzie, J., Buckley, J., Bridges, B., & Hayek, J. (2006). *What matters to student success: A review of the literature*. Retrieved from http://nces.ed.gov/npec/pdf/kuh_Team_Report.pdf

Liu, Y. (2010). Social media tools as a learning resource. *Journal of Educational Technology Development and Exchange, 3*(1), 101–114.

Maikish, A. (2006). Moodle: A free, easy, and constructivist online learning tool. *Technology and Schools, 13*(3), 24–28.

Meiklejohn, A. (1932). *The experimental college*. New York, NY: Harper and Brothers.

Morning, A. (2008). Reconstructing race in science and society: Biology textbooks: 1952-2002. *American Journal of Sociology, 114*, 106–137. doi:10.1086/592206

National Academy of Sciences, National Academy of Engineering and Institute of Medicine of the National Academies. (2010). *Expanding underrepresented minority representation. Committee on Underrepresented Groups and the Expansion of the Science and Engineering Workforce Pipeline*. Washington, DC: The National Academies Press.

Perkins, D. N. (2001). Technology meets constructivism: Do they make a marriage? *Educational Technology*, (May): 18–23.

Rosenthal, J. W. (1996). *Teaching science to language minority students*. Clevedon, UK: Multilingual Matters Ltd.

Schroeder, U., & Spannagel, C. (2006). Supporting the active learning process. *International Journal on E-Learning, 5*(2), 245–264.

Taylor, M. (2010). *Crisis on campus: A bold plan for reforming our colleges and universities*. Alfred A. Knopf.

Tosh, D., & Werdmuller, B. (2004). *E-portfolios and weblogs: One vision for ePortfolio development*. Retrieved September 21, 2006, from http://www.eradc.org/papers/ePortfolio_Weblog.pdf

U.S. Census Bureau. (2001). *Population profile of the United States* Retrieved January 2, 2012, from http://www.census.gov/population/www/pop-profile/natproj.html

U.S. Census Bureau. (2012, February 25). *2010 census brief*. Retrieved February 25, 2012, from http://www.census.gov/prod/cen2010/briefs/c2010br-01.pdf

Weller, M. (2007). The open source option. In *Virtual learning environments: Using, choosing, and developing your VLE* (pp. 96–110). London, UK: Routledge.

Wessa, P. (2009). How reproducible research leads to non-rote learning within socially constructivist statistics education. *Electronic Journal of e-Learning, 7*(2), 173-182.

Young, K. (2011). *Minorities in higher education, 24*th *status report*. Washington, DC: American Council on Education.

Chapter 5

# Analyzing the Competitive Dynamics in Open–Source Publishing Using Game Theory

**Shalin Hai-Jew**
*Kansas State University, USA*

## ABSTRACT

*Using a game theory model to analyze whether a content developer should pursue publishing with an open-source or proprietary publisher, this work describes a strategy for those content developers working in higher education in terms of an articulated strategy for publishing. This research also suggests the high costs of publishing for content developers and proposes ways for open-source publishers to attract and maintain talent for open-source publishing in socio-technical spaces. This chapter offers fresh insights on the uses of game theory to model stakeholder motivations and payoffs, and from there articulate basic strategies; in line with game theory, this model also suggests directions and hypotheses for future research in open-source academic publishing.*

## INTRODUCTION

*The longevity and success of an OSS (open source software) project is strongly dependent on the community that provides an infrastructure for developers, users, and potential developers to collaborate with each other. -Bianca Shibuya and Tetsuo Tamai, "Understanding the Process of Participating in Open Source Communities" (2009, p. 1)*

In a time of economic scarcity and constrained budgets, those in higher education still have to seek ways to achieve high quality teaching and learning. One tactic involves the uses of open-source digital resources that are available free-of-charge and often editable / revisable. This open-source social movement has resulted in a variety of digital contents that are licensed for free and open-use by others. The freedoms spelled out in the open-source movement related to software include four basic levels of freedom (to summarize):

DOI: 10.4018/978-1-4666-2205-0.ch005

1. The freedom to run a program for any purpose
2. The freedom to study how a program works and to adapt it to local needs
3. The freedom to distribute copies of a program to help out others
4. The freedom to improve the program and to release the improvements to the public, to the benefit of the whole community (Stallman, 1986)

Over time, various types of open-source licensing schemes have been defined for the piecemeal releases of aspects of copyright related to open-source contents, including Creative Commons licensure. These have defined the terms of individual or group use, user-development, content revision, terms-of-future-sharing (especially of revisions), and transfer. Most of these have limited or absolutely restricted any commercial usage.

In higher education, some of the open-source resources deployed include the following: open courseware (whole course curriculums); open-source technologies (wikis, blogs, repositories, learning/course management systems, hard-drive erasers, video processing software, and others); open-source e-books and flexbooks (open-source e-books); open-source repositories, referatories, and open-access (works marked with proper meta data and made machine-findable for easy federated searches across databases)/open-source (open use within certain strictures) digital libraries (with curated collections); databases; electronic portfolios (eportfolios); and image-, video- and audio-sharing sites. Ideally, open-source may offer one channel for cost savings; however, this assumes that there are healthy and functioning virtual communities gathered around shared open-source endeavors. Brown and Adler (2008) argue that open education—through the sharing of open courseware and open-source digital learning objects and publications—will enable people who do not have direct access to a formal education to actually acquire one, particularly since demographically speaking, some 100 million youth will need to be educated but have nowhere to go for studies. The more informal learning route through open education may ensure that they have the education and skills to enable them to compete and function in the world.

There are histories of virtual communities forming around large collaborative projects in software development (for Linux, Apache, Mozilla Firefox, and others), but those open-source coordinated developer communities do not yet seem to exist broadly in open-source academic publishing except in pockets. The closest sorts of equivalent communities exist in some open-source periodical and book publishing endeavors, with editorial leadership and the shepherding of projects through to the publication phases. In terms of digital learning objects, there are open-courseware methods of collecting pre-existent courses; repositories and referatories for accepting collections of digital resources; and open-source encyclopedias for free-will contributions. However, these projects do not structure or commission the work. They often merely receive and house the open-source objects. There is no direct collaborative way for people to understand where the needs are in terms of open-source development.

In that light, it would be helpful to model open-source academic publishing and how it competes in the commercial and proprietary publishing environment. The modeling of this environment may lead to some ideas on how to originate, develop, evolve, and grow such socio-technical communities for the development of quality open-source resources for academic purposes.

Software developer Raymond, in "The Cathedral and the Bazaar," described two software development models, with the "cathedral" representing elitist and exclusivist development and hidden software codes, vs. the "bazaar," representing egalitarian and inclusivist approaches to development and open / transparent software codes. Originally, the debate was between the efficacy of a closed vs. open innovation model, or a private investor vs. social production model.

One of Raymond's core observations is that with a sufficient number of people analyzing a thing, all basic "bugs" or problems can be solved. These two approaches represent two different models of harnessing human innovation. The first approach is the more traditionalist market economy approach which suggests that developers put in the initial investment with the hope of a financial reward later down the line. The latter harnesses both intrinsic and extrinsic motivations of developers and pays developers back in renown. However, the latter is also known as an "involuntary altruism game," and it's less costly for content developers to let someone else develop the code or contents and then to free-ride (Baldwin & Clark, 2006, p. 5)

The first model benefits larger society by the level of innovations and broad mainstream distributions that are offered by industry. It is often more tied into the existing legal structures. The latter one offers overall lower-cost benefits to a broader spectrum of society; even those who may not be able to afford the costs of commercial products may use these products. These latter digital goods tend to be created with a level of code transparency which may not be available with the proprietary goods of the first.

The rewards of the first model for content developers include wages and possibly patents, but their intellectual property belongs to the company. Whether or not their ideas ever show up in a commercial product depends on the decisions of their respective employers. The latter offers a greater flexibility for content developers to initiate, develop, and continue projects based on their own interests because of their non-reliance on organizational funding to ensure that the project goes forward. This lowers the marginal costs of the development because the developer does not receive the typical financial rewards of workplaces. The developers are bearing most of their own costs—and often the costs of maintaining the open-source communities. In terms of a market sector, if the proprietary companies are

profitable, they will dominate in terms of market share. If not, then the default goes to the open-source community, which reduces profits for the proprietary fields (Saint-Paul, 2003). Both for-profit businesses and open-source endeavors have relatively high failure rates, the first because of cash-flow issues (with some half of new companies failing in the first year and eighty percent failing by the fifth year) and the latter generally because of content developer abandonment (with commitments in the matter of months on some researched open-source projects).

For-profit companies will work with open-source entities on shared projects because of the reality of complementary goods, or those which entail the uses of other complementary products for usage (such as electronic games and the electronic platforms on which they're played). Fosfuri, Giarratana, and Luzzi (2008) studied press information about open source software products released between 1995 – 2003 and found three main findings: "(a) firms with large stocks of software patents are more likely to release OSS (open-source software) products; (b) firms with large stocks of software trademarks are less likely to release OSS products; (c) firms with large stocks of hardware trademarks are more likely to release OSS products" (p. 292). In other words, firms with intellectual property bound up in legal protections will have a strategy to release open source software products, but not those with public branding through trademarks of various sources. Those with plenty of hardware trademarks are more likely to release open source software products, which may indicate the complementarity of open-source applications and software to enable the sales of the hardware, or vice versa. The private collective innovation model can benefit from and benefit the open-source movement. The open-source movement can benefit from some of the resources and professional expertise of the proprietary commercial companies. This cooperative and semi-interdependent melding also enables for-profit companies to integrate some of the "disruptiveness" of the open-source movement—through the mutual benefit.

Lerner and Tirole show that open-source projects tend to be loosely structured, with plenty of choices by the various numbers of content developers. In a loosely coupled and informal organizational structure, content developers may choose the projects they pursue, and they may often define the channels through which their works will be distributed, and they may often even dictate the intellectual property licensing terms. While early efforts at open-source were ad hoc, informal, and poorly regulated, since then, more laws and rights releases (sometimes known informally as "copyleft" vs. "copyright") have been created to protect this phenomena and work of open-source endeavors. Developers incur the costs of time, the foregoing of direct monetary compensation, and the opportunity costs of other tasks not done.

In the short-term, they may enhance their skill set and job performance. They may get future job offers. They also get ego gratification (Lerner & Tirole, "The scope of open-source licensing…" 2005, p. 30). There, too, is the power of "audience," which enables them to send costly signals of high-trust competence, according to Lerner, Pathak, and Tirole (2006):

*Economic theory suggests that long-term incentives for working on an open source project are stronger under three conditions: 1) the more visible the performance to the relevant audience (peers, labor market and venture capital community); 2) the higher the impact of effort on performance; and 3) the more informative the performance about talent (for example, Holmstr6m, 1999).[6] The first condition gives rise to what economists call "strategic complementarities." To have an "audience," programmers will want to work on software projects that will attract a large number of other programmers. (p. 114)*

Open-access articles, those that are labeled for easy discoverability across multiple digital repositories for effective federated searches, do attract a wider range of readers and have a greater research impact—based on an empirical study of citations of open-access articles vs. those published in a proprietary way (Antelman, 2004). However, the loose coordination means that work may be duplicative and therefore wasteful of people's efforts (Lerner & Tirole, "The economics of technology sharing…, 2005, p. 107). The transparency of the source coding enables customization of the product by heterogeneous users (p. 109), assuming the skill set of coding expertise to edit the underlying code. That very transparency may also enable malicious hackers to may read the open code and hack the system (p. 110), so there are some downside security risks.

Open-source has long been considered disruptive of the larger economic context. It is said to challenge current power structures. It may change pricing. It up-ends some commercial assumptions of human labor. If the proprietary companies are profitable, they will dominate. If not, then the default goes to the open-source community, which reduces profits for the proprietary fields (Saint-Paul, 2003, as cited in Lerner & Tirole, "The economics of technology sharing," 2005, p. 112). The complexity of this situation means that there will be multiple equilibria for the various stakeholders / players. Multiple equilibria suggest that there may be a variety of competitive strategies to maximize gains, which implies variance.

For all the potential benefits, though, there are some residual negative implications of open-source. Lewis has called open-source creation a "strategy of the weak" by start-ups and niche competitors who want to take away market share from the strong. He writes, "With few exceptions, open source software has never crossed the chasm into the mainstream without first becoming a commercial product sold by a commercial enterprise"

(Lewis, 1999, p. 125). Since 1999, though, this movement has gained much more credence. Open-source creations have been labeled different types of cultural production and artistic endeavors and communications exchanges—and certain products which cannot be "provisioned efficiently by markets alone" (Benkler, 2004, p. 348).

For the socio-technical "virtual communities" that evolve around the creation of digital contents through open-source means, it makes sense that the distributed community would be built around innovating the larger issues through a meritocracy-based leadership and community "herding." While open-source has been criticized as inefficient by some authors, such communities thrive only with actual measureable progress. Such developer communities are described as horizontal (vs. corporate vertical) ones. These have also been termed "visible work communities," which reveal internal meritocracies. Some research has found that the productivity of such communities fall along the lines of a power law, with a few contributing the majority of the contents and then the contributor power law curve falling off exponentially. Some have critiqued just how inclusive open-source is though, with only an estimated 2% of contributors to open-source software being women (Mahmod, Yusof, & Dahalin, 2010). This low percentage may well be a further reflection of the relatively low and declining numbers of females in the computer science field.

## A REVIEW OF THE LITERATURE

Open-source software was invented in 1998 by a small group of those working in high technology. This approach to open-source development of works has focused around information goods—in digital form. The re-usability of digital contents has enabled the creation of contents that may be re-used in multiple contexts without a degradation of the user experience. The affordances of the Internet and World Wide Web (WWW) enable the near-free storage and distribution of most digital contents. Benkler (2004) has written about open-source creation of contents. He shows how digital goods are shareable (or "non-excludable" from those who did not contribute but who still enjoy the benefits of the digital good) and non-rivalrous (able to be used by many simultaneously without diminishing the good) ones. Once a thing has been created, the bulk of its cost has already been absorbed, and to share, exchange, host, and deliver that content has mild or near-non-existent transactional costs. Benkler describes sharing as a "modality of production," with much less of the traditional physical-capital constraints of innovation and sharing. This conceptualization results in a positive social aggregate payoff or a social optimization of resources. (In any collective action problem situation, though, there are many who will fall into inaction and merely free-ride others work.)

Harhoff, Henkel, and von Hippel (2003) suggest that there are market inefficiencies in the current intellectual property regimes, namely, that the patenting process and other ways that innovators may access royalties is expensive, inefficient, and sometimes ineffectual. For some innovators, it may make sense to share their findings in the sense of going open-source, or going with uncompensated spillovers. Licensing itself is "not a particularly effective means for capturing royalty income" (Harhoff, Henkel, & von Hippel, 2003, p. 1754). The high costs of patenting (monetarily and with time) are a deterrent (p. 1755). And most intellectual property is not concealable into the long-term. That's not to say that revealing innovations is all positive: "Negative effects from free revealing are associated with any advantage this action provides to free-riding competitors relative to the innovator," the authors write (2003, p. 1757). The authors' model shows some of the simple aspects of stakeholders—as the innovator (user 1), the manufacturer, and then the potential user (user 2). If the discounted profits yielded by the traditionalist system are outweighed by going open-source, this rationalist model assumes that the innovator will pursue this latter route. This model changes depending also on if the manufacturer adds value to the innovation, but sharing with a manufacturer always means non-exclusive benefits from the innovation (shared royalties with the manufacturer). The authors also consider whether both users might innovate and then reveal or not reveal their innovations to the manufacturers. In a sense, open-source is about removing the middle-person or manufacturer.

Not all digital or informational goods would fall equally valuably under this open-source model. Open-source approaches seem to benefit the making of public goods for public users and for the making and sharing of so-called cultural objects. Certain innovations are dominated by certain innovation structures. High-value private information generally is not released through open-source channels but rather through proprietary ones.

## SOME MOTIVATIONS OF OPEN-SOURCE CONTENT DEVELOPERS

Developers who create open-source contents are both simultaneous owners and non-owners. Their signing over of particular release rights for their contents means that they are forgoing certain types of potential future profit. Their initial investments into the work—mean that they will lose out on certain opportunity costs, time costs, effort costs, and investments of funds and equipment (in some cases). Such endeavors are not free of risk or costs. Not all endeavors will bear fruit.

Based on rational choice theory, research suggests that content developers are building open-source contents based on a mix of intrinsic (internal) and extrinsic (external) motives. Intrinsic motivations may be to enhance the public good by contributing to others; this is an essentially altruistic motive. Benefits (positive spillover effects) to a particular knowledge-based field has found

that open-science, for example, leads to greater absorptive capacity of scientists (Lerner & Tirole, 2000, p. 4), with higher R&D productivity. Labor economics approaches suggest that measureable rewards may accrue that enhance future earnings or job opportunities or other benefits related to "career concerns" (Lerner & Tirole, 2000, p. 3). The expected utility of the publicity earned by open-source developers may mean measureable rewards down the line even though the publicity is ephemeral, transitory, and intangible. Hann, Roberts, Slaughter, and Fielding (2004) found that human capital in the form of project contribution did not lead to increased wages, but the credentials earned through open-source merit-based ranking systems led to significantly increased wages—because such contributions may be an indicator of productive capacity (p. 1). Such content creation may reflect also on the workplace, as having the flexible absorptive capacity to accommodate new ideas and practices.

Polanski describes open source projects as "networks of developers, distributors and end-users of non-proprietary created knowledge goods" (2007, p. 1). He summarizes the importance of intrinsic and extrinsic motivations for individuals to participate in an open-source project. Using a centipede approach, he argues an economic pattern underlying open-source contents, and he suggests that there is a maximum sustainable cost in the open-source mode. Using a rational actor approach, he suggests that if a potential developer or distributor or user has an anticipated negative payoff (a negative expected utility), then there is a disincentive to proceed or continue. He uses an algorithm to model this.

In a market production (economy) model, a creation's value comes in the later stages when the developers try to recoup their original investment. The proprietary license is not able to "sustain sequential knowledge production" in some cases for projects that are "convex and modular" because of the cost-dominance in that model—whereas open-source production may enable this based on volunteer work (theoretically). Innovations are necessarily time-dependent and sequential, with new innovations being built over the earlier work—so there is no time invariant assumption. The sequencing of aggregating cost along with proprietary costs mean that the innovations will not continue indefinitely but will be constrained by various mechanisms in the environment. The subgame perfection or strategy profile for certain types of projects then defaults to open-source endeavors (in terms of a backwards induction approach that looks at plausible selections of choices at every decision node and assuming a finite set of moves in this game and working backwards from the terminal nodes). In an open-source and voluntary context, the conceptualization of that created content and work is affected by ex-post open licensing. This is seen as more pro-social in the long run, and in a sense, different types of innovations may emerge from this model (vs. market production of some knowledge goods). To encourage quality, peer review is encouraged—in a practice that is commonly used for quality assurance in academic, open-source, and professional/proprietary practices.

Those who create for open-source do not want their work to benefit a commercial entity. Commercial misappropriation (or usurpation of the open-source work for others' financial benefit / free-riding) is described as a threat to the integrity of the open-source endeavor. Nov and Kuk (2008) suggest that an open-source community may maintain healthy participation by its members if it controls the outputs from external appropriation—or the monetizing (or accrual of rewards) by an outside party. The authors write:

*The findings suggest that perceived justice of the open source license terms, and intrinsic motivations are both negatively related with effort withdrawal intentions. Moreover, we find that the effect of the fairness personality trait on effort withdrawal is stronger for individuals who are low in perceived justice and weaker for individuals high in justice. (Nov & Kuk, 2008, p. 2850)*

People will tend to engage more the more they feel that the open source licensing terms are just. Individuals with the fairness personality trait with a strong sense of justice will tend to have less of an effort towards withdrawal from the open-source community. This paper suggests that people volunteer because of intrinsic rewards of expressing "altruistic and humanitarian concerns for others." They also contribute in order to socialize with their peers or to fulfill prior social relations (Hahn, Moon, & Zhang, 2006). They are willing to take a marginal private loss in order to contribute to a much larger public gain—so the marginal social gain far outweighs the smaller marginal private gain (or loss). These open-source contributions enable positive externalities, such as "positive feedback," and the resulting contributions of some may inspire others to also contribute through the open-source option. Further, such work may promote career development. Through open-source contributions, a protective element keeps the ego safe from "negative features of the self" and reduces guilt for being more fortunate than others (Nov & Kuk, 2008, p. 2850).

Using a variety of licensing structures (attribution / non-attribution; commercial / non-commercial; allowing derivative works or not), the developers and owners of open-source contents may distribute their contents selectively in the market—and will save others from having to invest a certain amount of costs for development. Giving away secret innovations with monetary value may not make sense in open-source contexts, but attaining patents itself is expensive, rife with uncertainty, and may not be the best strategy in getting an innovation in the world or for attaining royalties (there are inefficiencies in the current intellectual property regime for some types of innovations); there are relative benefits to secrecy in some cases and relative benefits of secrecy in free revealing in others (Harhoff, Henkel, & von Hippel, 2003, pp. 1758 – 1759). Pursuing publication in a commercial resource may involve prohibitively high levels of competition. Publishing in the conference notes of a professional conference often is expensive—not only in terms of time but the attendant costs of conference attendance.

## DEVELOPING AN OPEN-SOURCE USER COMMUNITY

While free, such open-source contents still have to win an audience. The Technology Acceptance Model (TAM), created by Davis and Bagozzi, has been used to describe how people adopt open-source and other types of technologies; the digital contents or technologies have to pass a test of perceived usefulness and ease of use ("Technology acceptance model"). Those who integrate open-source technology systems have to ensure that a product aligns with actual needs and fit within the organization's culture and technological systems.

Open-source and open-access digital libraries make their resources available in a variety of ways. Some offer free and open software that may be used for the archival of self-submitted author works. Others offer unqualified (immediate and full entrée) access to the journals and articles. Some offer dual-mode access—with both a print subscription and an electronic open-access version of a journal. Others offer delayed open access, with subscribers getting access to information for a period of time before it is released to the public. Others require an author fee to support open-access to their works. (For some academic publications, these fees may range in the hundreds to over a thousand dollars per article.) A partial open-access model means that some articles of a journal are available through open-access, but fees are charged by the piece for others. A per-capita approach enables open access to various countries based on a percentage of the per-capital income, in a sliding scale approach. Others only enable abstracts to be published. And finally, institutional members provide funds in a cooperative approach to enable open access (Willinsky, 2003).

Chief information officers (CIOs) are said to be leery of free and open source software because of concerns regarding "legal issues, costs and support" along with quality ("performance, reliability, scalability") and low information about the product (Riesco & Navón, 2006, p. 107). Van Rooij (2011) looked at data from a 2009 survey instrument that went out to chief information officers and chief academic officers of various public, private, private non-profit, and private for-profit institutions of higher education in the US—based on a list of 900 names from the Higher Education Publications, Inc. list. The survey was built off a 2006 baseline survey to assess the cultural openness to using open-source software. This research examined the US higher-education adoption landscape of open-source and the adoption of policies and procedures to ease that process (van Rooij, 2011, p. 1173). The software mentioned included the following: authoring tools, learning / course management systems, online collaborative teams / communities of practice, student portfolios, faculty portfolios, testing / assessment tools, and computer assisted instruction (CAI) tools. Various systems were also examined: campus operating systems, campus portals, CMS/LMS, digital repositories, library systems, and administrative / enterprise resource planning (ERP) systems.

Van Rooij found that open source software was gaining traction for both teaching and learning, particularly with campus-wide deployments of open-source software (OSS) learning management systems in the 2006–2009 period. "Student engagement and support of active learning" are dominant drivers of OSS adoption for chief academic officers, while the reduction of software licensing fees was a main motivator for chief information officers. Both groups were concerned about the total cost of ownership of systems. Van Rooij writes:

*Institutions have made great strides in developing formal policies and procedures around the adoption of new technologies, particularly in the areas of security, compliance with the appropriate Federal and state regulations (e.g., FERPA, Section 508), and around ownership of intellectual property developed by faculty (p. 1178).*

Wiley (2007) took this idea further and suggested that universities might well themselves be expected to support open educational resources as content creators and distributors as part of their social contracts with the public. Daniel, Kanwar, and Uvalic-Trumbic (2006) suggest that there are six stakeholder groups with an interest in shifting higher education to serve the four billion "at the bottom of the world's economic pyramid"; these include "governments, higher education institutions/providers, student bodies, quality assurance and accreditation groups, academic-recognition organizations, and professional bodies" (p. 1). These changes are occurring in a time when universities have been engaging in "an unprecedented surge in patenting" amidst accusations that they are the "new patent trolls" (Lemley, 2008, p. 611), which may suggest a dichotomizing of information—with some going open-source and public, and yet others going the protected patent route (for new funding streams and university self-funding in a time of declining public revenues).

These works do show that the culture in higher education is supportive of using open-source software, particularly in resource-poor situations. The political convergence around open-source is a part of the "authorizing environment" for leaders and enables the putting into place of policies and practices for open-source adoption. There does seem to be a market for open-source adoption, and this may imply respect for faculty and content developers who create open-source contents for this academic environment. This survey also showed that the administrators were willing to go open-source for mission-critical systems such as learning / course management systems (L/CMSes)…which says something about their perception of the dependability of the open-source software.

Donnellan, Fitzgerald, Lake, and Sturdy (2005) describe the importance of knowledge management through digital means and showcase three knowledge management solutions: D-Space (by MIT), Data Centric KMS, and Lotus Notes. The first two are open-source, and the third is proprietary. The authors compare the development status, platform, requirements, email linkage, metadata, costs, and customization abilities for each of the three. They note that the informal service community helps level the competitive playing field for smaller players. They highlight the importance of evolving whatever system it is that an organization uses for its knowledge management. Knowledge management is not static but about building a community of users, the authors point out.

In this new landscape, proprietary publishers are those who attract and cultivate talent. They bring together editors, subject matter experts (SMEs), and authors, and they support their work by offering a range of editing, revision, publishing, distribution, and marketing and sales services. Open-source publishers also attract talent. They use peer reviewers and subject matter experts to vet contents. In general, open-source publishers often have less overhead than proprietary publishers and have varying standards for the acceptance of contents for publication. Finally, there are also endeavors that are shared by proprietary and open-source publishers—such as publications that may be open-source but are sponsored by for-profits.

## GAME THEORY

Historically, game theory originated from economics and used mathematics to represent interdependent decisions in a particular social context (Morrow, 1994, p. 1). Over the years, this approach has been used in a variety of fields to depict strategic situations and to inform decision-making in such competitive and incomplete-information contexts. Game theory models underlie computer simulations of political, ecological, business, economical, and other contexts in part for predictive analytics. Some practical applications of game theory are to add mathematical precision to arguments (by quantizing them) and proposing hypotheses to be tested in the real world using empirical evidence. A range of tools used in basic game theory will be applied in this chapter and will be defined as they are mentioned. One large caveat to the predictiveness of any sort of modeling is that forecast errors multiply often exponentially as one moves further from a particular moment in time (Taleb, 2010, p. 162).

## A PROPOSED GAME THEORETIC MODEL OF OPEN-SOURCE ACADEMIC PUBLISHING

To create a model of open-source academic publishing, it was important to first define some of the real-world aspects. In many ways, the stakeholders (whether proprietary, open-source, and / or mixed) in publishing work in a non-cooperative environment, with most of them making independent self-concerned decisions. However, there is room for mutual benefit and project-by-project cooperation because sometimes their interests collide. For example, proprietary publishers comb the open-source literature to scout talent, and vice versa. Both types of publishers benefit from technological innovations that may originate with the other. The developer or author is the core creator of innovations in this system, and his / her / their choices about whether to go with proprietary or open-source affect the domain field. Given the complexity of play, there are a number of rationalizable strategies without a defined Nash Equilibrium, or rather, there may be multiple Nash Equilibria in this "game." (Nash Equilibriums / Equilibria may be understood as the optimal or "best replies" between one player in response to another. A Nash Equiibrium is a state of play in which neither player wants to unilaterally defect—so their highest expected util-

ity is achieved in the particular Nash Equilibrium state-of-play.) Sequential Bayesian equilibrium (with changing strategies as behaviors and new information come in) may also affect how each of the various stakeholders "play" at each decision juncture. Some essential approaches to game theory modeling follow:

An open-source publisher will attract a certain amount of talent. They will win some publications and acolytes, and they will lose others. To keep followers over time, they will have to continue adding value to the various contributors and resource users. Open-source has theoretically infinite capacity (server space) for electronic publishing. While some open-source publishers have print equivalencies, they usually will charge for the print versions.

A commercial (proprietary) publisher will attract a certain type of developer and may also attract some open-source developers who can meet the standards of commercial publishers and who have some followers who find appeal in their work. The commercial publisher will be more elitist in part because of their greater expense and their limited capacity.

The market share between commercial and open-source may remain static unless one has some sort of competitive advantage over the other. It is assumed generally that commercial publications will attract more high-end talents...and that open-source will attract more general practitioners.

### Small-Scale Modular Projects

This model works for small open-source projects in the sense that developers work on small-scale projects. These dynamics would differ for large-scale open-source projects like the development of open-source software. That circumstance will involve different game dynamics, motivations, stakeholders, and so on. Those projects would involve more challenges with defect handling and quality control, project documentation, coordination of work, and other group and leadership elements.

## One Pure Dominant Strategy

There are no dominated (always losing or always with lower payoffs) strategies to avoid except to not-create and to not-try-to-publish which is a sure non-publication. In other words, non-engagement is the dominated strategy. However, a non-effort entails no cost, and it's clear that creating contents involves a sunk effort investment and time / energy cost—not to mention the costs of going through the submission process. The rest of the strategies (of engagement with publishers—whether open-source or proprietary) all allow some potential for future gains albeit with a requirement of developer investment. (In the real world, this is not to suggest that there are many who do not play the dominated strategy. The effort needed to attempt to publish is disheartening to many.)

## A Nash Equilibrium View for Content Developers

In this sense, here is where the main players will play to: A content developer will play a diversification strategy and publish in both venues and will use both venues to maximize his / her "utils" (utilities or units of relative satisfaction, in economic theories). Publishing in each track is complementary to the other, and there are potential complementary benefits. (A core assumption of this model is that the content developer is creating contents that meet a publishing threshold for acceptance, whether the publisher is a proprietary, open-source, or mixed publisher.)

## CRITICAL STAKEHOLDER VIEWS AND SIGNALING COMMUNICATIONS

The centrality of the content developer (writer, researcher, and others) for both the proprietary publisher and the open-source one drives the model. To begin, then, the developer begins the chain of events that may or may not lead to publi-cation. Here, the developer's "chain of beliefs" is important to affect his / her / their decision-making. A "chain of belief" refers to the understandings that the general content developer has about the probability of successful publishing—based on the moves and actions of the publisher. These belief sets are continually updated as new information emerges from the situation.

The signaling—"costly signaling" ("burned money"), or "cheap talk" or "babbling talk" (costless messaging)—will affect each side's different beliefs and so affect their motivations to action. For a content developer, imposing costs on the self is a way of costly signaling, and that extra cost may be a commitment to invest a high level of work and revision work into a creation. In face-to-face interactions, the communications may be both explicit and implicit [what Boranić (1979) calls "silent information," or what may be termed today micro-expressions and other nuanced communicative interactions]; in electronically mediated communications, the signaling is generally purposive and explicit. It rises above the noise and conveys valuable meaning.

## General Content Developer's Chain of Beliefs

- Wants to publish regularly (on par with his/her professional field) (quantity) as evidence of professional productivity (with publishing a contributory, sufficient, and necessary cause for tenure progression).
- Wants to contribute to the world through an area of expertise (quality).
- Wants to maintain professional reputation and personal name brand.
- Wants to protect internal ego against harm (e.g. rejection or embarrassment) and to maintain encouragement for future initiatives and risk-taking.
- Wants to maintain personal / interpersonal reputation.

- Wants to outcompete some colleagues (but publication is generally non-exclusive—two competitors can appear in the same publication).
- Wants to promote a career and avoid career risks—simultaneously.
- Competes for "positional goods" that enhance social prestige and income-earning.
- Wants to minimize opportunity costs (what one cannot do because one is investing time in trying to write and publish).
- Wants to maintain healthy professional relationships.
- Wants to create a name, body of work, and legacy for posterity.
- May make decisions based on familiarity; professional relationships, and relative ease-of-effort.
- Feels social accountability to colleagues and the larger community but may have varying accountability to various publishers depending on prior interactions.
- Works in an environment of incomplete information and so has to garner substituted information in lieu of actual knowledge (based on experiences, the directions and policies for publishing, the writings of those who have published, and ruminating on meta-meta analysis about others' motives, strategies, and needs); must constantly evolve "beliefs" for accuracy. Choices will evolve over time, with changing best responses, so there is no defined dominant pure strategy.
- Has varying "chains of beliefs".

## Not Always a Unitary Actor in Decision / Action

- Wants to collaborate with some colleagues (some cooperative strategies).
- May be affected by writing and content-creation partners.

## Implications of the Game

- Must have a diversification strategy or publish both in commercial and open-source channels (which may be seen as complementary channels).
- Must have a sustaining strategy to keep up personal productivity (based on idiosyncratic needs, ego sustainment, imagination sustainment, and continuing learning).
- Must strive for long-term archival and memory of one's work for posterity (in terms of findability / discoverability).
- The subgame perfection (SGP) move at every juncture is to push forward towards publication with either a proprietary or an open-source publisher but not a vanity press. Each move is towards a lesser loss than would be incurred from stopping. To stop pressing forward means a sure loss and the disappearance of the value of the sunk costs; to press forward is to increase the chance of possibly publishing. This is true even if a work has been rejected before. The literature is full of anecdotes of master works which were rejected numerous times before finding a publisher, and of individual experiences where persistence ultimately paid off in terms of publication. In a sense, the declination of a manuscript is in the hands of the editors and the peer reviewers—and not really in the hands of the content developer. If a developer experiences a number of declinations from a source, then that may be sufficient clue to pursue other venues.

For the developer, there is no true payoff until the manuscript acquires the quality imprimatur of peer review and reaches a wider audience. A simplified payoff table of the model follows. At the top is the publishing by invitation—by a proprietary commercial publisher or an open-source publisher. This is a rarity. The work still has to go into the writing, but the writing has essentially a guaranteed slot because the work was solicited.

## PAYOFFS OF THE MODEL

In order to activate the model, it is important to use a series of payoffs for various outcomes. At the top-paying terminal nodes, +10 is listed for having a manuscript accepted by a proprietary or commercial open-source publisher through a "by invitation" arrangement. Such arrangements mean little in the way of editorial constraint. Here, the reputation of the author opens the doors. The +8 payoff refers to publication by a commercial or open-source publisher initial review or peer review, with no additional changes required. The +6 specifies publication after the cost of requested revision is invested by the author. The +4 is the payoff for the experience of submitting a work to a publisher who chooses not to publish the work—but which results in assistive feedback that may help the author improve the work. A content developer who self-publishes on a vanity site earned a payoff of +2. For the simplicity of the model, 0 is the set point where an author has invested time and effort to write a work (whether he or she decides to submit it for publication),

but there are professional gains in the learning experience of the writing—so the stasis point is 0: -4 for the work invested and +4 for the payback in professional development.

In the negative payoffs category, a -2 is earned from failure to fully complete the planned work; -4 for the work completely written but not sent out; -6 for the work sent out but no response, -8 for a rejection with or without critique (which is a dead loss), and a -10 for a submittal that results in professional reputation damage of the author. Table 1, "A Projected Payoffs Table for a Content Developer," lists various potential payoffs for various interactions between content developers and either commercial or open-source publishers.

On a purely numerical basis, the optimal scenario for a developer here is 10, and the worst is a -10 where there was an investment but no return, and even a negative kind of "blowback" where there is harm to reputation. Per the conventions of game theory, the payoff values are set somewhat arbitrarily to represent relationships and perceived "utils." These are used to test or "proof" the model, and adjustments may be made in the future. The point here is not to fully necessarily represent real-world reality but to arrive at hypotheses that may be tested both for the model and for the reality that is alluded to behind the model. (A model

*Table 1. A projected payoffs table for a content developer*

| +10 | Publication by proprietary commercial or open-source publisher (by invitation) |
|---|---|
| +8 | Publication by commercial publisher / publication by open-source publisher (acceptance after initial review or peer review with no additional changes required) |
| +6 | Publication by commercial publisher / publication by open-source publisher after revision |
| +4 | Assistive feedback from the publisher or peer review group, and leads from publishers, but no publication |
| +2 | Self-publication on a "vanity" site |
| 0 | (Assumed sunk costs in initial work investment or -4 in work but +4 in professional development and learning) |
| -2 | Failure to complete planned work |
| -4 | Work written but not sent out |
| -6 | Work sent out but no responses |
| -8 | Rejection with or without critique |
| -10 | Reputation damage from the manuscript submittal |

is extrapolated from the world, but a model is always necessarily limited in terms of its depictions, whether dynamic or static.)

The risk profiles of individual players will affect how they proceed with publishing. Machina (1987) famously showed how there are factors beyond expected utility of a decision that affect human decision-making. One of his main findings was that individuals have different risk profiles towards particular endeavors, with some who are more risk-averse and others more risk-acceptant. Further, he found that as rewards and costs became more extreme in a situation, the indifference curves started to skew, with more extreme preferences for security or risk in some gambles (or "lottery games") per the Allais paradox (1953). How an issue is framed or depicted also can change people's preferences, whether they are conceptualizing a protective (insurance) or risk-taking (lottery) approach.

An invited publication is the closest to a "sure thing," which means a probability of 1. All the other potential outcomes, with their weighted outputs are percentages, as represented in the tables. Angelsen does show that for some who are risk-averse, in a condition of individual choice under uncertainty, they will strive for as close to probabilistic certainty as possible (1993).

To do rough calculations of the expected utility of going with an open-source or proprietary publisher, the following shows various output values. One assumption is that the sunk costs of

effort (-4) are off-balanced by the learning gains (+4), with the assumption that topic pursued has professional merit. This examines the expected utility of going with an Open Source Submission, represented as (OSS).

To spell out the information: The expected utility of an open-source submission EU(OSS) is equal to the sum of the following: the probability of outright acceptance (p)(OA), the probability of conditional acceptance (p)(CA), the probability of peer review with rejection (p)(PRR), the probability of an outright declination (p)(OD), and the probability of a non-response (p)(NR). The payoffs of each of these outcomes may be positive or negative in light of whether they're a gain or a cost to the content developer.

Table 2, "The Expected Utility of a Content Developer Going with an Open-Source Submission," shows an expected utility of -2.4. This means that there will likely be a loss in terms of the overall payoffs. The system is not set up with any sort of guaranteed success. The high costs of the work mean that content developers already begin with sunk costs.

$$EU(OSS) = (p)(OA) + (p)(CA) + (p)(PRR) + (p)(OD) + (p)(NR) =$$

An expected utility of -2.4 shows that the author is working against some challenging odds and tough expectations in the publishing cycle. The competition is steep. The work involves much

*Table 2. The expected utility of a content developer going with an open-source submission*

| EU(OSS) | (.1)(8) | (.2)(6) | (.2)(-1) | (.4)(-8) | (.1)(-10) | |
|---|---|---|---|---|---|---|
| | Outright acceptance | Conditional acceptance (assumption of -2 because of additional work, but the overall benefit of 8) | Peer review with rejection (-5 rejection, initial +4 in peer review learning off-set for -1) | Outright declination | Harm to reputation | |
| | .8 | 1.2 | -.2 | -3.2 | -1 | Expected utility -2.4 |

up-front effort and preparation, which is not even reflected in this formula. Those investments are assumed. That said, once the work is done, it doesn't mean that the expenditures are complete; rather, the submission process entails continuing investments of work.

Likewise, the same formula may be applied to a proprietary submission but with a different weighting of the probabilities, given the more elitist cathedral (vs. bazaar) approach of proprietary publishers.

$$EU(PS) = (p)(OA) + (p)(CA) + (p)(PRR) + (p)(OD) + (p)(NR) =$$

The following table deals with the expected utility of submitting a manuscript to a proprietary publisher (symbolically represented as "PS" for Proprietary Submission). This formula shows clearly tougher odds. Table 3, "The Expected Utility of a Content Developer Going with a Proprietary Submission," shows an expected utility of -3.8. This is a higher loss than going with an open-source publisher.

The assumptions of the proprietary submission are that there are nominally lowered chances of either outright acceptance or a non-response. Editorial oversight often means higher expectations of the manuscript quality. The same professionalism often means a professional response, at least by proprietary academic publishers. Another core assumption is that the rewards and outputs are the same moving through the model, but with more challenging probabilities—because of the costs that proprietary publishers face in moving a written work through the publication process and into production, marketing, and delivery. What is not directly addressed here are the changing personal author preferences (and those of his / her authorizing environment), which may change the value or weighting of the choices here. Further, the risk acceptance or risk aversion of the content developers will affect the preference weighting of the various pursuits within this game model

The equations suggest that EU(OSS) > EU(PS), so OSS P PS.

Open-source submission is preferable to proprietary submission, broadly speaking.

The fact that both equations result in negative payoffs suggests that submitting to either open-source or proprietary journals is a disincentive. Anecdotally, this may be borne out by the low percentage of professionals who pursue academic publications. It is highly likely though that more complex calculations that take into effect long-term gains, such as the employment benefits cited above, may alter the directions of the payoffs into positive territory. In game theory, this is the concept of the "shadow of the future." Another possibility is that those who publish accept the costs of doing business in either open-source or proprietary publications. Another further explanation is that some people in some jobs may have

*Table 3. The expected utility of a content developer going with a proprietary submission*

| EU(PS) | (.05)(8) | (.1)(6) | (.3)(-1) | (.5)(-8) | (.05)(-10) | |
|---|---|---|---|---|---|---|
| | Outright acceptance | Conditional acceptance (assumption of -2 because of additional work, but the overall benefit of 8) | Peer review with rejection (-5 rejection, initial +4 in peer review learning off-set for -1) | Outright declination | Harm to reputation | |
| | .4 | .6 | -.3 | -4 | -.5 | Expected utility -3.8 |

to publish in order to earn grants and to groom their professional reputations, and the costs are merely accepted.

Between open-source and proprietary publishing, the expected utility of open-source publishing is less costly than for proprietary publishing. What might this reality suggest?

First, if there is a lower cost to publish in open-source, ceteris paribus, then new researchers and writers may enter the competitive publishing industry by going to open-source publications. Those new researchers who are at universities will have to select the open-source publications with high reputations in the field. Not all publishing is equivalent. This may suggest that this market will settle into a kind of frozen state as defined by Lewin's force-field theory, in which competing entities play to a state of competitive stasis until another game-changing appears. Proprietary publishers and open-source ones will each define their niches, with some overlapping at the margins. Both will recruit content developer talents, and the field, too, will settle out.

Second, for open-source publishers who run socio-technical spaces (like repositories, referatories, and periodicals), they may work harder on the chokepoints and challenges that writers, researchers, and content developers may face. They may more consciously nourish productivity and even professional camaraderie to smooth the process. Those who participate in such open-source communities may also better weight the odds towards each other's professional growth.

## The Open-Source Socio-Technical Publishing Site Strategist

The main strategies for an open-source socio-technical space for academic publishing would generally likely follow this strategy.

## Solicits Relevant Information and Contents (in a Knowledge Economy)

* Pursue the publication of new, original, and relevant information. Publications are one-offs, and they are zero-sum (even when information is versioned). The objects are "modular" and stand-alone. They are non-rival goods, so that one person's use of a product does not preclude another's use of the same. This is a core nature of digital goods (digital rights management notwithstanding).
* Maintains a public profile to attract new members and to maintain current members.
* Incubates and supports real innovation in the community; discourages emulation and any sort of dishonest work; discourages intellectual property (IP) theft.
* Maintains high standards of the domain field for the inclusion of information.
* Maintains regular quality contributions to encourage return-users (academic, professional, non-profit, government, and private individuals)to the site. Solicits materials from various fields to capture relevant contents.
* Avoids over-publishing so as not to have excessive materials or to strain human attention.

## Grows and Sustains the Virtual Community

* Protects developer and user reputations by ensuring that credit follows each individual developer (accurately).
* Includes the novices to experts in the horizontal self-manufacturer community.
* Maintains contributor loyalty against the incursions of commercial entities as well as other open-source publishers.

- Maintains satisfied stakeholders, which include the following groups: developers, users, and others (to ensure the community sustains itself).
- Maintains institutional memory of contributors and community history.
- Maintains long-term "forever" (into perpetuity) archival and preservation of digital works for reference and crediting even with the "slow fires" of technological obsolescence and file corruptibility.
- Extols, showcases, and embodies the principles and values. Avoids contravening the principles of open-source and shareability.
- Maintains constructive relationships with competitor open-source repositories and publishers.
- Must be "right sized" for the particular functionality for the manageability of projects, technologies, resources, and relationships.

## Resources (Financials, Legal, Human Resources, and Technological)

- Must find some funding sources to maintain the basic infrastructure for stability.
- Must maintain a legal underpinning for work to protect its resources and interests.
- Must attract and keep core volunteer (human resources) talent.
- Must be scalable based on the needs of the community (able to ramp up or down).

## Technological Functionality

- Manages multimedia and multiple types of files with various types of multi-device access.
- Maintains security of membership records; accessibility; information assurance; and robustness and availability.
- Protects against hostile incursions.

- Must adapt to the needs of the community and larger user groups.

Figure 1, "Dynamics in Open-Source (vs. Proprietary) Publishing," highlights the various stakeholders in open-source publishing. This game model is described in extensive form in order to capture some of the vicissitudes of what may happen with a manuscript submittal. This model progresses from left-to-right and is represented in decision time rather than strict chronological time. This figure shows various antecedent decisions that must be made for participation in open-source publishing and the varying values that go into those decisions. In this node-link structure, all actions are purposive and strategic, within a rational choice underpinning all decisions. This does not assume perfect knowledge, and it does assume constraints in the environment. Various decision-points highlight the choices before the content developers and their choices of where to apply their talent. Proprietary publishers represent the incumbents in publishing with long histories of defining information domains, but there is also indication of blended and hybrid publishing endeavors (in which the proprietary and open source entities cooperate for shared endeavors). This model shows that for human resourcing to occur effectively in open-source publications, there has to be value-added for content developers and the uses of personal relationships and ties to enable the work to move forward. The math above does show, though, that this model does not depict a positive out payoff for the content developers in either path given the costs, and so this model suggests that rewards have to be conceptualized in longitudinal ways that must be depicted beyond the limitations of this game theory model.

## An Extended Model

To represent the above in a simple game tree, let's assume that when an open-source publisher publishes a work that the publisher gets a payoff

*Figure 1. Dynamics in open-source (vs. proprietary) publishing*

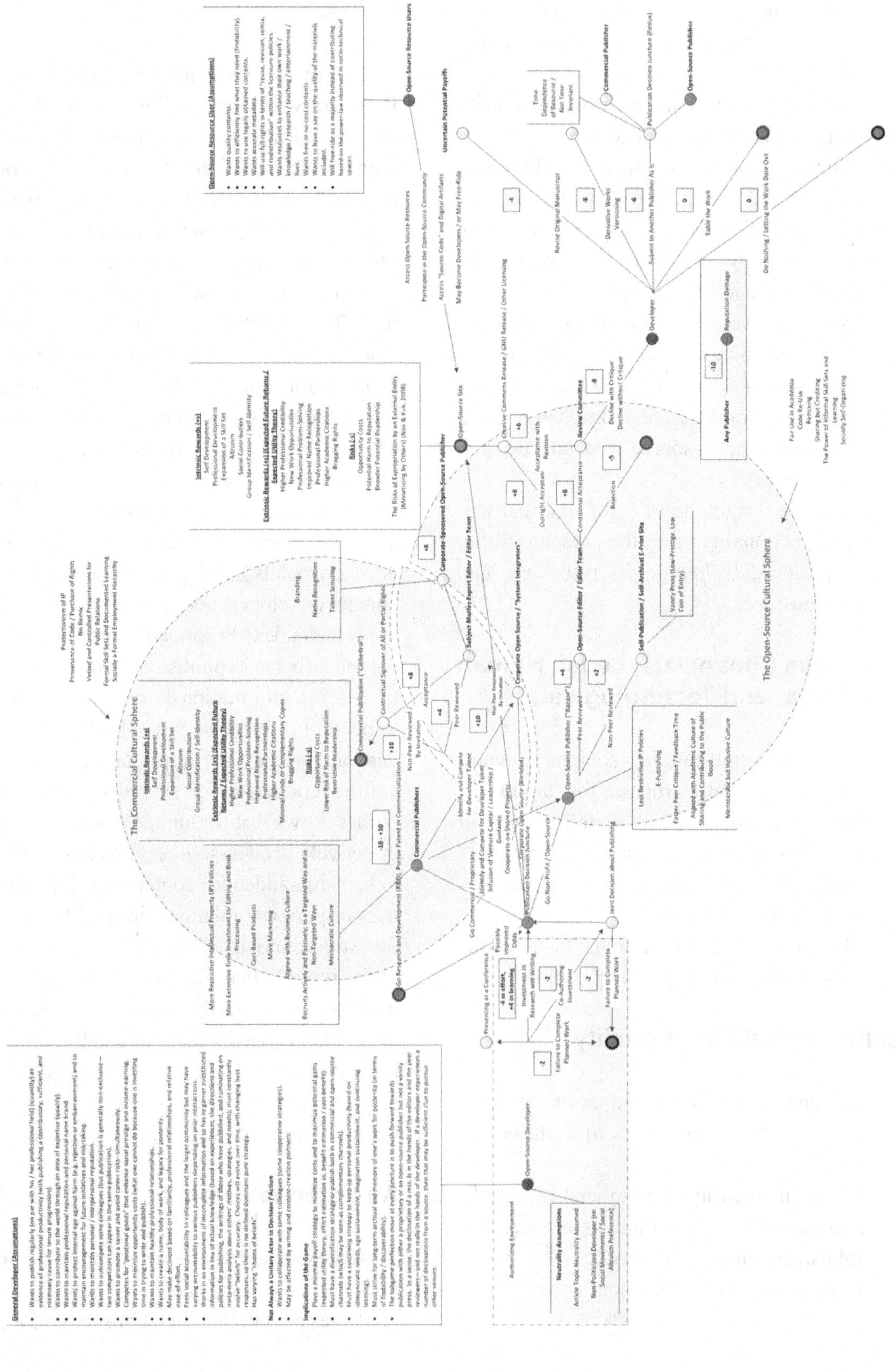

of 10. And if an open-source publisher rejects a work, it gets a payoff of -5 to represent the loss of its effort at culling talent but +5 because it is protecting its brand equity by accepting works that fit certain standards as decided by subject matter experts (SMEs) in the field. That leaves it with a total payoff of 0. Figure 2, "An Open-Source Content Developer Game Tree," shows the first player as the content developer. The second player is the open-source publisher. Each player has a decision to be made at every stage.

A basic backwards induction analysis would suggest that neither the content developer nor the publisher gains if the developer withholds the work or the publisher chooses not to publish. Both approaches incur fairly severe losses—one in effort for the content developer and one in reputation for the open-source publisher (which may be seen as not welcoming). The negative impression left by a rejection of a work may sour a professional relationship sufficiently that a content developer would be discouraged from further submitting work to a publisher. The Nash Equi-

librium in the game tree suggests that (S; P1) is the point that the various players will play to, for an expected utility / payoff of (8, 10). This backwards induction suggests that the threat of an open-source publisher rejecting a work may be seen as a non-credible threat because of the cost to the professional relationship, but in reality, rejecting a manuscript is not anomalous in a publishing situation. The model does show that there is a preference towards publishing. It may be understood that all stakeholders have something on the line when a work is submitted for consideration by a publisher.

## A Strategic or Normal Model

Strategic (or normal) models examine the various payoffs for certain courses of action. The assumption is that individuals are motivated by the expected payoffs of their actions. The game tree may be expressed as the following tables, equations, and strategy sets.

The strategy sets would be as follows:

*Figure 2. An open-source content developer game tree*

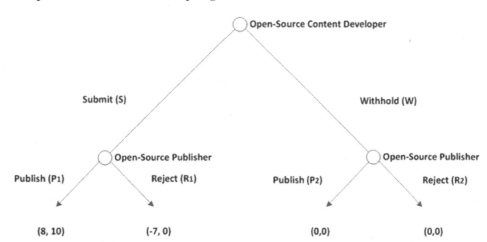

Open-Source Content Developer Strategy Sets:

S, W (submit or withhold)

Open-Source Publisher Strategy Sets:

(P1 | S, P2 | W), (R1 | S, R2 | W),

(P1 | S, R2 | W), (R1 | S, P2 | W)

Another expression of this would be as follows—in terms of a strategy payoffs table. Table 4, "A Payoffs Table for All Strategy Sets for an Open-Source Publisher," shows the interaction effects between a content developer and an open-source publisher, depending on whether the developer submits or withholds the submission, and then whether the open-source publishes or rejects the submission.

The Nash Equilibrium states are highlighted, with the open-source content developer submitting the manuscript, and the open-source publisher publishing the work for a net gain $(S; P_1)$. Another Nash is if the open-source content developer withholds a work, and the open-source publisher rejects the work $(W; R2)$

Expressed another way, though, the antecedent assumption that a manuscript may be offered is lessened based on the assumptions. For this model, let's assume that the probability of being published is about 40% and the probability of being rejected is about 60%. (Note: These are generous probabilities. In many publications, the probability of acceptance can be as low as 1/3000 or worse.) Table 5, "A Payoff Matrix of a Two-Player, Two-Strategy Game between Developers and Publishers," shows the expected payoffs based on the decisions by the Content Developer and the Publisher.

Based on the payoff matrix, the Nash Equilibrium strategy sets are as follows: (Submit; Publish) (Withhold; Reject). In other words, the open-source content developer could submit a work and have it published. That is one Nash Equilibrium. Another is for the open-source content developer to withhold a work and for the open-source publisher to reject the work as well.

While the expected utility for the content developer to go with an open-source publisher is slightly preferable to going with a proprietary publisher per the equations above, the benefit of submitting vs. not shows a preference for generally not submitting because of the point representations for the work involved.

*Table 4. A payoffs table for all strategy sets for an open-source publisher*

| Open-Source Publisher | | | | |
|---|---|---|---|---|
| | **P1, P2** | **R1, R2** | **P1, R2** | **R2, P2** |
| **Open-Source Content Developer** | | | | |
| **Submit** | **8, 10** | -7, 0 | **8, 10** | -7, 0 |
| **Withhold** | 0,0 | **0,0** | 0,0 | **0,0** |

*Table 5. A payoff matrix of a two-player, two-strategy game between content developers and publishers*

| Open-Source Publisher | | |
|---|---|---|
| **Open-Source Content Developer** | **Publish** | **Reject** |
| **Submit** | 8, 10 | -7, 0 |
| **Withhold** | 0,0 | 0,0 |

EU(Open-Source Content Developer) (Submitting)

= .4(8) + (.6)(-7) = 3.2 + -4.2 = -1.

EU(Open-Source Content Developer) (Withholding) = 0.

0 > -1, so W > S, so W P S.

If the probabilities of getting published are even lower, then the likelihood of a submittal would even be lower given the negative payoff.

In this table, the open-source content developer does not have a clear dominant strategy because 8 > 0, but -7 < 0 for the Submit (S) strategy, and the Withhold (W) strategy results in 0 < 8, but 0 > 7. For the open-source publisher, to Publish (P) results in 10 > 0, but 0 = 0. To reject, 0 < 10, but 0 = 0. So its weakly dominant strategy is to publish. In an iterated dominance analysis, it can be argued that a Nash Equilibrium may be (Submit; Publish) or (S; P) or (8; 10).

Most critically, it is important to realize that this is a cooperative game, with coordination and communications between the players in an environment of relative trust and mutual shared interests (to forward the field; to promote careers; to support and protect the work of organizations, among others). While there are some shared conjectures and understandings, there will likely be a diversity of motivations and incentives. Even so, this cooperation may extend to fellow content developers who are competing for limited spaces in various publications. Their works may complement and enhance each other's. They may work together on shared projects and therefore share bylines. They may cite each other's works in their respective publications. Further, this may be conceptualized as a repeated finite game (which eventually becomes "cyclical"). This game structure suggests that the repetition of interactions would encourage cooperation between the various players. The selfishness model of one-off

games no longer applies in this new repeated game conceptualization. There may even be asserted an infinite (∞) sort of non-ending game where none of the players know when the relationship will end. There is room for constructive interactions throughout the lifespan of the interactions—with an unknown end-point. (In game theory, in the classic Prisoner's Dilemma structure which models so many human interactions, a known end-point is a major motivation for one side or the other to "defect" in order to get a "temptation" payoff—instead of cooperating effectively with the other side. Said another way, cooperation will unravel from the terminal stage based on backwards induction.) Such a game may be theoretically infinite and continuing. After all, even with a certain number of successful co-publications, there is not an artificial limit on future collaborations—particularly if the publishers, editors, and content creators have a constructive working relationship.

On the other hand, one can also treat any engagement in publishing as a one-off, a one-time limited play, or an all-or-nothing. Individuals who want to see publishing as a pure competition may well model that, too, and likely find a Nash Equilibrium to model such a scenario, where cooperation is not a factor. There is space in this conceptualization to accept this view as well as one of the states of play. At this extreme, content developers (as individuals or as team members or organizations) may be in a race for credit and the grant moneys and fame that may come with establishing first-discoverer status. In this case, there is little room for cooperation, and the financial and reputational stakes are sufficiently high as to induce high competition.

Figure 3, "A Repeated Finite Game as a Cycle...Which Leads to Cooperation," highlights this iterated phenomenon in game theory that would suggest that the various stakeholders in this aspect of academic publishing may arrive at an equilibrium of mutual gain and mutual cooperation as this is played over time. In repeated (vs. single-shot) games, players have to consider how

*Figure 3. A repeated finite game as a cycle...which leads to cooperation*

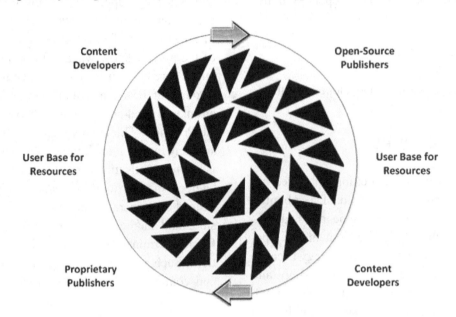

current actions affect future actions of other players—in terms of his or her reputation. Reputation then affects the constraints on players in terms of potentially negative behaviors.

As the various stakeholders learn about each other—the publishers about content developers' capabilities, the content developers learning about the publishers' standards and editorial approaches—they may find various points-of-shared interest and mutuality. They may find ways to coordinate endeavors that may limit risk—such as the uses of a query letter by a developer—to head off potential development that may not lead to a publication. In other words, they may condition their actions based on the behaviors of others. Another cooperative efficiency may involve policy changes by various publishers to enhance the odds of content developers publishing successfully. The idea of co-learning may work the other way, too—in the sense that certain publishers know which content developers not to work with, and that certain content developers know

which publishers to avoid. This is where reputation is critical in continuing iterated games. Where cooperation is not possible, it does not make strategic sense to pursue those options. In a sense, this game is about optimizing the payoffs for players where it makes sense. Such "markets" would not exist without mutual rewards surpluses that incentivize the interaction.

Another conceptualization could describe this relationship between content developers and open-source publishers as a kind of bargaining game. The content has a particular value today, but it has diminishing (or theoretically rising, but this latter conceptualization is rare) value over time or a "discount value" into the future (represented as "delta" or "$\delta$"). In game theory, two entities would not come together to bargain unless there was a "surplus" value in their collaboration, represented as "v"; "v" (value) is value-added and brings more rewards to both entities than each could achieve alone (known as the "best alternative to a negotiated agreement" or "BATNA"). The basis for the cooperation between the content provider and the publisher then is over how the surplus payoff will be divided. The more iterations of negotiation, the more declining value there is in the interaction, given the "impatience" and the declining value of a delayed agreement (Dixit, Skeath, & Reiley, 2009, p. 704). Based on game theory research, each side can figure out the optimal Nash Equilibrium play and optimal payoff in such iterated bargaining games and could theoretically come to agreement at the beginning at the outer edge of the efficiency curve (in terms of possible optimal surplus payoffs), and with a sense of fairness for both sides—which could encourage further cooperation and good faith bargaining (bargaining in candor and without inaccurate signaling, and without reneging on agreements) into the future.

## Mechanism Design to Address the "Agency" Problem

In a sense, the open-source publishing environment with the various content developers fits a classic principal-agent model. Here, the "principal" or publisher is the less-informed player; the "agent" or content developer is the more-informed player. This "agency" problem may be mitigated in a number of ways. What types of "private information" may be relevant here? As a subject matter expert (SME), a content developer may know the state-of-the-field and what ideas are most critical and in-demand (and therefore, more valuable). A content developer may know about any weaknesses in his / her work. He / she may know about prior offers or rejections on the work; critiques by others; feedback from potential prior editors, and potential rewards at play. He / she also knows the workplace situation and incentive structures for motivating the publishing.

## Screening for "Agent / Player Types" and Differentiated Products

The less-informed principal though can set up the mechanism design to encourage the content developer to self-reveal some of the relevant private information. One tool would be a screening mechanism, which will force content developers to self-reveal or self-identify what "type" they are. They self-identify as more hard-working if they pursue a more challenging track for publishing, for example. One track may be a features one which requires content developers to go through substantial peer editing / editorial vetting and revisions. Principals (the publishers) may also add barriers to the submittal of features by publicizing and adhering to certain quality standards or length standards. Using such mechanisms may encourage those with high-end works to submit but discourage those with poor works. Another lesser track may focus on shorter pieces that do not have to be vetted but which are opinion pieces and which mean less status. Another track may be an open-publishing one without any sort of gate-keeping. Content developers may self-select into the various tracks based on what they know about their own works and the works' histories. How "agents" differentiate their products by selecting the rigor they would undergo for various publications is yet another indicator. For example, a multi-year study that has been written up may be submitted to the most competitive publication in the field, whereas a light feature piece may only be submitted to a much less-competitive publication. From a constructivist perspective, the ongoing interactions between the principal and agents create a situation of mutual recognition of each other's types. How agents engage with the principals and the various structures (which elicit certain response types) should reveal something about the agents and their true identities.

## External Rewards and Signaling Motivations

A principal must set the rewards sufficiently high so as not to trigger the "incentive-compatibility constraint"—or the higher costs for those who want to publish a feature and must invest more work in order to achieve that. They also are bounded by the "participation constraint", which is the price paid by those who are submitting non-features. If those are set too low and the cost of submitting a work as a feature too high, then the principal may not achieve participation. To lower the costs of investment by content developers, a principal may support incremental investments—maybe first working with content developers who submit queries, then article outlines, and then a draft; with each new iteration, there is more of a commitment, but if the work is not headed in a direction that is suitable for the publication, then the work may be ended with less than the full cost of development work. Or the work may be versioned to appear in a lesser part of the publisher's holdings.

Perverse incentives in the game mechanism designed by the publishers (the principals) may encourage content developers (agents) to engage in "moral hazards." One moral hazard may be plagiarism—or the usurping of another's intellectual property—if there is insufficient editorial oversight. Another common moral hazard may occur when a content developer offers a work for consideration by multiple publishers. Multiple submissions mean that a publisher may go through the costly work of vetting manuscripts only to have the work appear in a different publication—before any sort of contract is signed. In this scenario, the publisher has lost on the review investment in the particular work and has not added to its own holdings or reputation. An open-source publisher that encourages multiple submissions, then, may have set up a "perverse incentive" to encourage behaviors that are counter to its own interests and also which may encourage morally hazardous behavior by the agent. In economic theory, a moral hazard situation occurs when an entity behaves negligently because it is partially shielded from the full risk of its actions by structural mechanisms or perverse incentives. Here, the developer does not necessarily have to take on the full consequences of its actions.

Ideally, this rewards structure will encourage a so-called separating equilibrium in which content developers self-identify into their various types. They are rewarded for properly signaling who they are, which enables screening to occur effectively. By contrast, a pooling equilibrium is one in which all content developers all send out the same messaging and do not differentiate. Those who have high quality manuscripts do not particularly present any differently than those who have poor or weak manuscripts. Those who have ideological sympathies with open-source may not necessarily manifest any differently than those who do not have those sympathies. [Weber (2004) describes the ideological underpinnings of open-source in the following way: "…a libertarian reverie, a perfect meritocracy, a utopian gift culture that celebrates an economics of abundance instead of scarcity, a virtual or electronic existence proof of communitarian ideals, a political movement aimed at replacing obsolete nineteenth-century capitalism structures with new 'relations of production' more suited to the Information Age" (p. 7).] This latter pooling of types means that there is poor informational signaling by the agents in the environment—which is not in the interests of the principals who cannot separate out individuals by type.

## A Systems View

From an external perspective, the open-source system is one with game players with limited rationality, incomplete information, and an incentive structure that may not necessarily encourage accurate signaling and screening. Siegfried (2006) describes how the "temperature" in a system may be used as an analogy in game theory. A heated or high temperature means that the molecules in a system (game players) may be found in different configurations. Siegfried writes:

*Temperature, in other words, represents a quantification of irrationality. In a gas, higher temperatures mean there's a higher chance that the molecules are not in the arrangement that minimizes their energy. With game players, higher temperature means a greater chance that they won't be maximizing their payoff. (p. 213).*

In other words, in a hot environment, the game players push for self-discovery of the various possibilities through exploration and expend energy in doing so. This irrational and undirected exploration entails energy costs. In a cool or low-temperature system, there is much less experimentation in terms of strategy pursuit, and it makes more sense for game players to coolly consider the available possibilities and proceed rationally—given the information that is available. In an environment where no information is available, that is depicted as one in which there is "maximum entropy" (or "maximum ignorance") or disorder. With information about the environment comes some degree of order. This analysis suggests some approaches that make be used by the "principals" in this system.

## Closing the Gap between Proprietary and Open-Source Publishing

Several factors are necessary to close the gap between open-source academic publishing and proprietary publishing. Foremost is the prestige gap (or "standing") between publishing in a proprietary publication vs. an open-source one. The criticality of peer review in selecting out quality publications is one important aspect in publication. Second, as proprietary presses remove financial rewards to writers—with ever-dwindling royalties (and no advances in many cases), the preferability for the open-source option will increase. Lastly, the benefits of reaching a wider open-source audience may well off-set the payoff of going commercial.

An open-source publisher would do well then to publicly signal not only welcome to content developers, a set of standards balanced against open consideration for submissions, and the wideness of the audience that will have access to the contents. The public signal should be conveyed as a costly signal through regular follow-through on the messages—by acting on that sense of welcome, by maintaining high publishing standards while being open about a broad range of possible publications, and while reaching out to a wide installed user base of users for recruitment.

In classical game theoretic conceptualizations, people are said not to contribute because of "pluralistic ignorance" or the lack of awareness of what is happening and how to help. Social scientists have pointed to the "diffusion of responsibility" or that sense that others will take care of a situation and that the individual does not have a direct responsibility. Both pluralistic ignorance and the diffusion of responsibility may be mitigated by open-source editors who provide the necessary information about needs, the coordination for collaborative actions, and the other work to ensure that individuals are called out to share their expertise in areas of actual need. There is a special need for such coordination in the development of open-source learning objects in terms of a "pull" demand situation vs. the supply-side provision of goods as academic content providers choose to offer.

An insight on environments in which there are no credible commitments on any side would suggest that potential payoffs are less motivating, and rather, players will go with the risk-dominant strategy (or "playing it safe," to use a colloquialism) (Kandori, Mailath, & Rob, 1993). There is an interest in protecting against losses, and the potential payoffs then are less motivating for such players. This may lead to a non-Nash Equilibrium situation of stasis or non-movement or passivity.

This model assumes that all frontline practitioners in the field have something original and valuable to contribute to the larger community. Their non-expression or silence is considered a potential loss to the larger community.

If the larger academic open-source publishing community is resilient and open to consideration of works that have been rejected, and if it offers a wider range of potential pathways for publication, it will offer multiple possible paths for showcasing content developer work and therefore will offer more opportunities for open-source content developers. More opportunities also will change the cost-benefit calculations for content developers because they have wider potential markets for their work and ways to reach a potential user base.

## Testing the Open-Source Publishing (Game-Theoretic) Model

To test the draft model, it would be important to observe the articles published in one venue or the other and to measure how much those articles are or are not game changers in the field. Where authors choose to present work serve as costly signals of their professional commitments. It would also help to assess the relative prestige and reputations of the various published writers and the venues their works appear in. Further, it would be important to observe the use cases for various content developers: What are content developers' experiences with proprietary, open-source, and mixed publishers? What encourages developers to continue being productive professionally? What sorts of services, supports, and virtual communities do content developers expect from proprietary and open-source publishers?

What sorts of tools in socio-technical spaces enhance the work's efficiencies, and which do not? Koch (2007) has used a non-parametric data envelopment analysis (DEA) approach to analyze 30 open-source software projects from SourceForge.net and found that most tools had a negative relationship to project efficiency, for

example, and more exploration of that may be helpful. He did find that open-source project efficiencies were quite high overall.

Further, how beneficial are the various publishers to the content users? What are content users' (individuals and organizations) experiences with proprietary, open-source, and mixed publishers / distributors? What are their preferred channels for acquiring academic publications? What services do they expect? How much of a voice do they want in the development of contents? How many play multiple roles—including that of content developers?

Researchers may also analyze various open-source publishers and their experiences. What strategies do they use to maintain their communities? How do they encourage the virtual communities to learn new information? How do they encourage innovation? How do they strive to ensure that there is new information and innovative work achieved by the community? What types of leadership may be observed in one open-source publication vs. another? How does that virtual leadership evolve over time? How can such groups avoid the inefficiencies observed in some open-source situations?

The actual model itself may be further refined—to include further factors that identify longer-term future benefits that may come from short-term investments (or losses). While models should be parsimonious to be effective, the decision-structure for content developers would benefit from a clearer sense of long-term motivations and incentives. Ensuring that these payoffs are addressed in the theoretical structure would ensure that the model is more complete and may mean positive instead of negative payoffs for publishing—whether the publisher is proprietary or open-source. Certainly, if one is to observe the academic research world, the investments are made into publishing and in soliciting and maintaining readers. To understand the plausibility of this state of the world, it will be important to consider longer-term payoffs like signaling in the employment market and other factors. Further, there may be a particular mixed strategies approach that may be discoverable based on an optimal probability mix (p-mix) between open-source and proprietary publishing or between a set of moves (at a decision node), given the content developer's beliefs and the underlying real-world conditions.

Further, who are the game players? What are some complicating factors in their decision-making? What about personal temperament and risk profiles and how those affect the various open-source and proprietary publishing endeavors? Are there different optimal probability mixes (p-mixes) of strategies for players who are risk-inclined, risk-neutral, or risk-averse? When are there optimal deviations from a particular Nash Equilibrium strategy? Do the various players of such publishing games set up punishment structures as well—for those who try to publish with poor quality work? What is the role of long-term memory in such an environment? Are there cultural differences between different publishing ecosystems in different contexts? If so, what? Are there social networks at play in terms of publishing—based on lines of social connections and interconnections? How do such publishing social networks and communities evolve? And how can they be supported and nourished? How may the individual creative content-developer nodes be nourished and encouraged? Is there a way to ensure that the payoffs are sufficiently great in the system to encourage greater contributions and risk-taking?

Lastly, it is helpful to introduce a deep caveat to the potential effectiveness of game theory in considering non-linearities or far outlier events that are not reflected in the Gaussian bell curve, per Taleb's (2010) writings on "black swan" events. Every framework of analysis has its insights and its limitations. As such, game theory is used here to evoke some of the dynamics of open-source publishing and how it may be made more competitive. However, that insight is one factor of myriad realities.

## The Tentative Future of Open-Source

Open-source distribution methods do align with the distributive capabilities of the Internet and WWW. This approach is more accommodative of a world with a growing number of people eligible and hungry for higher education learning. This open-source approach draws in people (content developers) desiring to contribute, and those who are willing to benefit from the positive externalities of using shared informational goods. In this spirit, this chapter offers insights on how to develop socio-technical spaces to support open-source development and sharing, and it suggests an important integration of open-source publishing in the life of a content developer.

## CONCLUSION

The application of a game-theoretic model to explore the incentive structures of open-source publishers and content developers breaks new ground. This approach suggests ways for principals (open-source publishers) to encourage rational decision-making by the content developers in the system through "cooling" the system and off-setting informational asymmetries with data and outreach and creating rewards. A model is never purely theoretical, and this one was informed from decades-long observations of both proprietary and open-source publishing. A game-theoretic model is necessarily a simplification of reality, but it optimally should shed some light on the real-world experiences in open-source publishing as a system in competition with proprietary publishing.

## ACKNOWLEDGMENT

I am grateful to the various editors that I've worked with through the years who have helped me continuously hone my craft, and that work continues to this day. The work of editors is never easy, whether their ultimate answer is the binary yes or no. I have learned plenty from both responses and the critiques in between the initial query and the finalized responses. A model has to originate from lived experiences and observations to model the world as closely as possible. Without those years of striving, this conceptualization would not have been possible. Thanks to Dr. Amanda Murdie, for her introduction to game theory in her graduate-level political science course. It's only now in retrospect that I realize how ambitious your course was—and I appreciate that—particularly that reach for impossible things. This is for R. Max, for whom strategy comes very naturally. I am grateful to Dr. Ramesh Sharma for his particularly incisive insights on the rough draft of this chapter.

# REFERENCES

Angelsen, A. (1993). *Individual choice under uncertainty.* Working paper. Bergen, Norway: Chr. Michelsen Institute: Development Studies and Human Rights.

Antelman, K. (2004). Do open-access articles have a greater research impact? *College & Research Libraries, 65*(5), 372–382. Retrieved September 9, 2011, from http://crl.acrl.org/content/65/5/372

Baldwin, C. Y., & Clark, K. B. (2006). The architecture of participation: Does code architecture mitigate free riding in the open source development model? *Management Science, 52*(7), 1116–1127. doi:10.1287/mnsc.1060.0546

Benkler, Y. (2004). Sharing nicely: On shareable goods and the emergency of sharing as a modality of economic production. *The Yale Law Journal, 114*(2), 273–358. doi:10.2307/4135731

Boranić, M. (1979). Silent information. *Journal of Medical Ethics, 5,* 80–82. doi:10.1136/jme.5.2.80

Brown, J. S., & Adler, R. P. (2008, January). February). Minds on fire: Open education, the Long Tail, and Learning 2.0. *EDUCAUSE Review, 43*(1).

Daniel, J., Kanwar, A., & Uvalic-Trumbic, S. (2006). A tectonic shift in global higher education. *Change: The Magazine of Higher Learning, 38*(4), 16–23. doi:10.3200/CHNG.38.4.16-23

Dixit, A., Skeath, S., & Reiley, D. (2009). Games of strategy, 3rd ed. New York, NY: W.W. Norton & Company. 704.

Donnellan, B., Fitzgerald, B., Lake, B., & Sturdy, J. (2005). Implementing an open source knowledge base. *IEEE Software, 22*(6), 92–95. doi:10.1109/MS.2005.155

Fosfuri, A., Giarratana, M. S., & Luzzi, A. (2008). The penguin has entered the building: The commercialization of open source software products. *Organization Science, 192,* 292–378. doi:10.1287/orsc.1070.0321

Hahn, J., Moon, J. Y., & Zhang, C. (2006). Impact of social ties on open source project team formation. In Damiani, E., Fitzgerald, B., Scacchi, W., Scotto, M., & Succi, G. (Eds.), *Open source systems* (pp. 307–317). Boston, MA: Springer. doi:10.1007/0-387-34226-5_31

Hann, I.-H., Roberts, J., Slaughter, S., & Fielding, R. (2004). An empirical analysis of economic returns to open source participation. *2004 Annual Meeting of the American Economic Association, San Diego, "Economics of Open Source Software"* (pp. 1–39).

Harhoff, D., & Henkel, J., & von Hippel. (2003). Profiting from voluntary information spillovers: How users benefit by freely revealing their innovations. *Research Policy, 32,* 1753–1769. doi:10.1016/S0048-7333(03)00061-1

Kandori, M., Mailath, G. J., & Rob, R. (1993). Learning, mutation, and long run equilibria in games. *Econometrics, 61*(1), 29–56. doi:10.2307/2951777

Koch, S. (2007). Exploring the effects of coordination and communication tools on the efficiency of open source projects using data envelopment analysis. In Feller, J., Fitzgerald, B., Scacchi, W., & Stilitti, A. (Eds.), *Open source development, adoption and innovation* (pp. 97–108). Boston, MA: Springer. doi:10.1007/978-0-387-72486-7_8

Lemley, M. A. (2008). *Are universities patent trolls?* (pp. 611 – 631). Retrieved September 10, 2011, from http://law.fordham.edu/publications/article.ihtml?pubID=200&id=2732

Lerner, J., Pathak, P. A., & Tirole, J. (2006). The dynamics of open-source contributors. *The Roots of Innovation, 96*(2), 114–118.

Lerner, J., & Tirole, J. (2000). *The simple economics of open source.* Harvard Business School. Retrieved September 2, 2011, from http://www.people.hbs.edu/jlerner/simple.pdf

Lerner, J., & Tirole, J. (2005). The economics of technology sharing: Open source and beyond. *The Journal of Economic Perspectives, 19*(2), 99–120. doi:10.1257/0895330054048678

Lerner, J., & Tirole, J. (2005). The scope of open source licensing. *The Journal of Law, Economics, & Organization, 19*(2). Retrieved October 5, 2011, from http://jleo.oxfordjournals.org/content/21/1/20.full.pdf+html

Lewis, T. (1999, February). The open source acid test. *IEEE Computer: Binary Critic,* 124 – 127.

Machina, M. J. (1987). Choice under uncertainty: Problems solved and unsolved. *The Journal of Economic Perspectives, 1*(1), 121–154.

Mahmod, M., Yusof, S. A. M., & Dahalin, Z. M. (2010). Women contributions to open source software innovation: A social constructivist perspective. 2010 International Symposium on Information Technology, (pp. 1433–1438).

Morrow, J. D. (1994). *Game theory for political scientists.* Princeton, NJ: Princeton University Press.

Nov, O., & Kuk, G. (2008). Open source content contributors' response to free-riding: The effect of personality and context. *Computers in Human Behavior, 24,* 2848–2861. doi:10.1016/j.chb.2008.04.009

Polanski, A. (2007). Is the general public licence (sic) a rational choice? *The Journal of Industrial Economics, 66*(4), 691–714. doi:10.1111/j.1467-6451.2007.00326.x

Raymond, E. S. (2003). The cathedral and the bazaar. *First Monday,* 1-45. Retrieved December 28, 2010, from http://131.193.153.231/www/issues/issue3_3/aymond/index.html

Riesco, N. B., & Navón, J. C. (2006). Enterprise applications: Taking the open source option seriously. In Avison, D., Elliott, S., Krogstie, J., & Pries-Heje, J. (Eds.), *The past and future of information systems: 1976 – 2006 and beyond* (pp. 107–118). Boston, MA: Springer.

Saint-Paul, G. (2003). Growth effects of non-proprietary innovation. *Journal of the European Economic Association: Papers and Proceedings, 1*(2-3), 429–439. doi:10.1162/154247603322391062

Shibuya, B., & Tamai, T. (2009). Understanding the process of participating in open source communities. *Proceedings of FLOSS '09,* Vancouver, Canada, IEEE, (pp. 1 – 6).

Siegfried, T. (2006). *A beautiful math: John Nash, game theory, and the modern quest for a code of nature* (p. 213). Washington, DC: Joseph Henry Press.

Stallman, R. (1986). What is the Free Software Foundation? *GNU's (GNUs Not Unix). Bulletin, 1*(1), 7–8.

Taleb, N. N. (2010). *The black swan: The impact of the highly improbable.* New York, NY: Random House. (Original work published 2007)

Technology acceptance model. (n.d.). *Wikipedia.* Retrieved July 10, 2011, from http://en.wikipedia.org/wiki/Technology_acceptance_model

Van Rooij, S. W. (2011). Higher education sub-cultures and open source adoption. *Computers & Education*, *57*, 1171–1183. doi:10.1016/j.compedu.2011.01.006

Weber, S. (2004). *The success of open source*. Cambridge, MA: Harvard University Press.

Wiley, D. (2007). *On the sustainability of open educational resource initiatives in higher education*, (pp. 1 – 21). Paper commissioned by the OECD's Centre for Educational Research and Innovation (CERI).

Willinsky, J. (2003). The nine flavours of open access scholarly publishing. *E-Medicine*, *49*(3), 263–267.

## KEY TERMS AND DEFINITIONS

**Asymmetric Information:** A state of being in which some players or stakeholders have differential amounts of relevant information.

**Backwards Induction (or Rollback Equilibrium):** A type of analysis in game theory in which every step of a game is played back to identify the subgame perfect states of play for each player at each node (in order to eliminate "non-credible threats" or implausible series of plays).

**Best Reply:** The optimal response of one player to another's action at each point of play (each turn-taking).

**Chain of Beliefs:** The cumulative and sequential collection of understandings by a player in a game model.

**Culture:** A system of common practices within certain social groups.

**Decision Node:** A point at which a player has to make a decision.

**Dominant Strategies:** The courses of action/play which result in the optimal payoffs for a player in a game.

**Dominated Strategies:** The courses of action/play which result in the poorer payoffs for a player in a game.

**Expected Utility Theory:** A set of concepts which suggest that people tend to be motivated into action by the outcomes that they expect from taking a certain action.

**Extrinsic Motivation:** The external rewards which drive human behaviors, including moneys.

**Force-Field Theory:** The concept by K. Lewin that the present (and any moment in time) is arrived at as a result of competing forces that then arrive at the moment's equilibria or a temporary freeze point.

**Game Table (Game Matrix):** A strategic or normal form of a game which shows the expected payoffs for various plays by each of the players to compare payoffs and resulting likely strategies.

**Game Tree:** A strategic tree that shows the sequence of play, the players, their expected payoffs, and other information to depict a full game scenario.

**Incentive-Compatibility Constraint:** The threshold at which an agent or "content developer" may choose not to participate in a game designed by the principal or open-source publisher because the costs imposed are much higher than the next threshold down (such as an unedited inclusion of a work in an open-source publication); the expected utility of acting in a way consistent with the principal's desires has to be at least equal to the payoffs of other courses of actions that the agent may take (in terms of defecting from the desired path of the principal).

**Incomplete Information:** The state of not having fully defined calculations at every decision node, which results in an imperfectly defined game.

**Information Set:** A combination of nodes from which a player in a game must make a decision without knowing what the prior player played (and so not knowing the actual full range of choices available with any certitude—because the player is not sure which node he or she is at when he or she makes a decision).

**Intrinsic Motivation:** The internal rewards which drive human behaviors, including altruism.

**Mechanism Design:** The creating of an incentives / disincentives situation in which a principal strives to elicit constructive actions from an agent in a situation where the principal has less information than the agent about the so-called "state of the world".

**Mixed Strategy:** A combination of randomized strategies that one side in a game may play to leave the other side indifferent between his/ her own choices; a probability mix (p-mix) is the definition of the percentages that one strategy or the other should be played for a particular player.

**Moral Hazard:** An often unintended situation in mechanism design in which an entity acts less responsibly because it is somehow shielded from the full risks of his/ her / their actions (a concept from economic theory).

**Nash Equilibrium:** A state of play where all players optimize based on a set strategy from which none would be motivated to unilaterally defect (with the assumption that all players are aware of each other's payoffs and strategies).

**Open Source:** The contract-based licensed release of digital contents for freer usage of intellectual property goods often without need for any royalty payments.

**Open-Access:** Works made broadly available and machine-findable through the proper use of metadata for easy federated searches across databases.

**Participation Constraint:** The threshold at which a potential content developer may not wish to participate with an open-source publisher.

**Payoff:** The expected result of arriving at a particular point by playing a certain strategy in a strategy tree.

**Perverse Incentive:** An (often unintended) aspect of a rewards structure that may encourage undesirable and morally hazardous behavior.

**Preferences:** The preferred payoffs, expressions, and other desires of the players which affect the strategy of play.

**Principal-Agent Model:** A situation in which a principal, or the less informed player, designs incentives through a mechanism design to motivate the agent, or the more informed player, to participate constructively in the situation (through proper incentives and punishments mechanisms).

**Proprietary:** All ownership rights protected under intellectual property law.

**Rational Choice Theory:** A body of concepts that are based on the idea that people maximize their preferences (which may be variant) given the limitations of the situation and their information and their abilities.

**Referatory:** A collection of links which are identified with metadata and which point to various resources hosted at various sites on the Web.

**Repository:** A collection of digital contents on a database.

**Risk profile:** The risk propensity or aversion of the player.

**Rollback Equilibrium:** Backwards induction analysis of play in a game tree.

**Solved Game:** A game in which all the players' decisions are mapped clearly, and there are Nash equilibria as well as subgame perfect equilibria (which shows decision strategies through backwards induction to eliminate non-credible threats).

**State of the World:** A particular real-world circumstance at a particular time period; a state of play in a certain period.

**Terminal Node:** The resulting payoff node in a strategy tree.

**Subgame Perfect (SGP):** A state of Nash Equilibrium that also passes a backward induction check for whether there are any implausible sequences of play; this subgame perfect (SGP) analysis may only be done on a strategic game tree that does not contain an "info set."

# Section 2
# Open Source Development in Higher Education Practice

# Chapter 6
# Virtualized Open Source Networking Lab

**Lee Chao**
*University of Houston-Victoria, USA*

## ABSTRACT

*This chapter considers a virtualized open source networking lab to support Web based IT education. It discusses the difficulties in teaching networking related IT courses online. The discussion leads to the solution of virtualized open source technology. The chapter also examines some strategies in developing an open source virtual networking lab for hands-on practice in networking related IT courses. It then presents a case study on the use of an open source virtual networking lab in e-learning.*

## INTRODUCTION

Meeting the hands-on requirements from networking related IT courses is challenging since a networking course in the IT curriculum has its own special needs. This kind of course has to reconfigure the operating system; therefore, it is difficult to share the computer lab used by a networking course with other courses. It is also difficult to set up a networking lab online or in a cloud computing environment because the reconfiguration of the network may cause the remote access to fail. Moreover, there are some serious security concerns about sharing the same network on campus since the students in a networking course are given the administrator's privilege. In addition, the fast development of new technologies requires computer labs to be updated frequently.

Networking labs are necessary for learning networking theories and concepts. Network system development and management is a subject that highly depends on hands-on skills. When creating a computing curriculum, it is strongly recommended by IEEE/ACM IT (IEEE/ACM,

DOI: 10.4018/978-1-4666-2205-0.ch006

2008) that the undergraduate networking courses should be backed by networking labs for hands-on practice. As described above, it requires great effort to construct networking labs. A networking lab needs its own space, network infrastructure, hardware and software. It requires extra protection and sophisticated technical support. The expense on developing and managing a networking lab is usually much higher than other types of computer labs. Due to the shortage of funding, manpower, and knowledge, developing and managing a networking lab is a burden to many higher education institutions, especially those small universities that have a limited budget. The use of open source software and the virtual technology gives some relief to the burden. The goal of this chapter is to demonstrate how to integrate the construction of an online networking lab with open source products and virtualization techniques.

This chapter starts by providing the background information about open source software in constructing networking labs. It will also give an overview about open source and free virtualization tools. Then, this chapter will discuss strategies in developing an open source virtualized networking lab. By following the strategies, a case study will illustrate the implementation of a networking lab with open source products. Through the case study, this chapter will describe the networking lab design, implementation, and evaluation. It will emphasize the use of open source products to meet the requirements of networking related IT courses.

## BACKGROUND

Constructing networking labs often requires tremendous effort. It needs a careful design of a network's infrastructure to meet the requirements by networking related courses. It also requires experience and hands-on skills for troubleshooting. Similar to the development of many IT projects, designing network infrastructure includes the planning, designing, and implementing phases. For example, Kapadia (1999) describes the design for the network infrastructure at Purdue University where a demand-based network computing system was implemented for reducing duplication of effort. For developing network infrastructure for large universities, Penrod and Harbor (2000) provide a case study to illustrate how to plan and implement the network systems. The case study discusses the issues related to the planning and creation of an IT governance structure. Penrod and Harbor (2000) illustrate some organization structures that can overcome barriers while implementing an e-learning system.

The construction of a network system requires the knowledge about network devices and network protocols. The book by Teare and Paquet (2005) discusses network hardware devices such as routers, network interface cards, switches, and bridges. Teare and Paquet (2005) explain how these devices are used in an enterprise-level network design and implementation process. As described by Olifer and Olifer (2006), network protocols are used to control and manage the communication over a network. The network protocol plays an important role for network security, performance, and management. For network management, various tools have been developed for managing networks. Many of these tools are open source products included in the Linux operating system (Maxwell, 2000). In the area of network management for e-learning, issues related to management of networked education in higher education are discussed by Uys (2001).

For many education institutions, especially those in rural areas, developing and managing a networking lab can be a challenging task. Since a networking lab cannot be shared by other IT courses due to the reconfiguration of its network infrastructure, it costs a lot more to support a networking lab. As calculated by Gerdes and Tilley (2007), a physical networking lab can cost as much as $150,000. Also, a networking lab can cause serious security concerns because the students are given the network administrator's privilege. Facing the challenges, researchers have been trying to develop various solutions to overcome the difficulties. As early as 1998, Goyal, Lai, Jain, and Durresi (1998) developed a software based simulation environment that enabled students to experiment with various networking protocols. In dealing with network security problems, Kneale, Horta, and Box (2004) proposed a virtual reality solution which moved the network laboratory into virtual reality. In their solution, the virtual network was built to link the offices in a virtual building. As the Web became one of the main methods for knowledge delivery, Casado, Watson, & Mckeown (2005) presented a virtual network system which could be remotely accessible through the Internet via the VNC technology. From the research studies mentioned above and more, virtualization seems to be the way to resolve the high cost and security problems in constructing a networking lab.

Using the virtual technology can significantly reduce the network management workload. Correia and Watson (2006) showed that the virtual network created in their labs was easy to maintain and could reduce the lab hardware cost. In the book edited by Preston (2004), researchers discussed the curriculum, behavior, and experience in virtualized teaching and learning. Recently, the use of virtualization technology in teaching has been attracting the attention of researchers. The research conducted by the University of Birmingham (2009) used the virtual technology for problem based learning. Chao (2009) discussed the use of open source software in teaching and learning.

For virtualization of a networking lab, there are three main virtualization products, VMware, Microsoft Hyper-V, and Xen, available on the market. The free and very popular VMware (VMWare, 2009) provides VMware Sever for creating virtual machines and VMware Player to run virtual machines. Open source operating systems can be installed on the VMware virtual machines as guest operating systems. These two free packages are adequate for the needs of networking lab virtualization. Microsoft Hyper-V is the technology for windows server virtualization (Microsoft, 2009). It is bundled with Windows Server 2008. One may find that it is difficult to host the Linux operating system on Hyper-V although Hyper-V allows Linux to use the drivers developed for devices only run on Windows operating systems. Xen is an open source technology that allows multiple operating systems to run on the same host computer running on a UNIX like operating system (Citrix Systems, 2009) such as Linux. In addition to these three main virtualization packages, there are dozens of other virtualization packages that can be used to create and run virtual machines for virtualized networking labs.

Due to their affordability, flexibility, and availability, open source products have long been used in networking. Open source network operating systems, network protocols, and network management tools are widely used by education institutions to support IT education. The most well-known open source operating system is the Linux operating system. By comparing it with commercial operating systems such as Apple Macintosh and Microsoft Windows, Hoagland, Brewer, and Hoogendyk (2002) consider Linux to be more suitable for higher education institutions as the education budgets continue to diminish. They also point out that the Linux operating system is more flexible so that it can be modified to serve the needs of teaching and research. Most of the important network protocols are in fact open source. One of the well-known open source network protocols is Lightweight Directory Access Protocol (LDAP). Through LDAP, an enterprise can implement centralized authentication. The open source tool dealing with LDAP is OpenLDAP. Jackiewicz's (2004) book discusses OpenLDAP in detail. There are various open source network management tools, and they can be used for network troubleshooting, analyzing, and monitoring. There are also many open source tools designed for managing network security. Some of the well-known open network management tools are Wireshark (formerly known as Ethereal) which is an open source network protocol analysis tool (Wireshark, 2011), Nagios which is an open source network monitor tool (Nagios, 2011), and Nessus which is an open source network vulnerability scanner (Nessus, 2011).

Research on using open source software in IT education has been done for many years. There are many university-wide IT infrastructures that are implemented with open source products. Wright et al. (2007) reported that they designed and implemented an open source computer lab to support the IT courses listed in SIGITE Computing Curricula at the University of California. Open source software is also often used by instructors to teach specific IT courses. For example, McAndrew (2008) from Victoria University at Australia used open source computer algebra systems software to teach a cryptography course. McAndrew (2008) concluded that, for teaching cryptography, the open source software can match or can be even better in some way than the commercial computer algebra software. Issues related to the deployment of open source computer labs are also studied by researchers. Corbesero (2006) presented a quick and inexpensive way to set up an open source computer lab which can be used effectively by a single computer science course in a dedicated mode.

As described above, the combination of virtualization and open source products can be a doable approach for the construction of networking labs which are remotely accessible through the Internet. This chapter will focus on the virtualized networking lab implemented with open source or free products. It will start with networking lab design strategies. After that, through a case study, this chapter will introduce some open source networking tools and illustrate how networking courses can be taught with a virtualized open source networking lab.

## NETWORKING LABORATORY DESIGN AND PLANNING

Based on the solution development theory or the similar ADDIE model commonly used in the instructional design theory, the construction of a networking lab normally goes through five phases, Analyze-Design-Develop-Implement-Evaluate (Dick, Carey, & Carey, 2004). This section discusses the first two phases, analyzing the requirements of the networking lab and designing the networking lab to meet the requirements.

The first phase is collecting requirement information for the networking lab. For networking related courses, there is a need of IT infrastructure to support hands-on practice on the networking content covered by the courses. The course contents in networking related courses usually cover the following topics:

- Network operating systems including both server and client operating systems,
- Network protocols including the protocols used in each layer of a network architecture,
- Network technologies including the network media and devices,
- Network subnetting and IP addressing,
- Network services including DHCP, DNS, Routing, Resource Sharing, Internet, and Remote Access,
- Network security and network management,
- Wireless and mobile networks,

These courses also require students to perform duties usually done by a network manager, security manager, or system manager. Hands-on practice in these courses requires students to re-configure operating systems and networks; this means that the networks and servers used for hands-on practice in the networking courses should not be shared with other types of IT courses. The hands-on practice on the course contents requires students to perform operations on network servers as well as network based application software through the Internet.

In addition to supporting the hands-on practice on the content included in the networking curriculum, open source products can also be used for lab management. They can be used to accomplish the following tasks.

- **Network Monitoring:** The open source tools are used to monitor network traffic. The networking lab managers are able to identify network problems with the collected information.
- **Network Troubleshooting:** With the open source network management tools, a networking lab manager can analyze the collected information for possible solutions to network problems. These tools can provide guidelines for fixing the problems.
- **Network Security:** With the open source network security management tools, students can detect network security vulnerabilities and enforce security measures. These tools can also be used to detect hacker intrusion, configure firewall properties, download and install anti-virus upgrades and patches, and so on.
- **Remote Access:** The open source remote access tools allow students to remotely access the network server and clients for network management. With these tools, the students can also manage user authentication for remote access.
- **Management Reporting:** Some of the open source network management tools also include a reporting function. Students can use these tools to write reports about network faults, analyses of observation data, and changes that have been done to fix problems.

In general, open source network management tools provide an inexpensive, easy to use, and flexible option for managing an online teaching/learning system. Based on the specific requirements by a networking lab, the goal of the network-

ing lab design is to meet the requirements listed above and to improve the affordability, flexibility, security, and availability of the networking lab. As described in the Background, the combination of virtualization and the open source approach has the potential to achieve this goal. In the following, let us take a closer look at the technologies that can be used to achieve the design goal.

To cover the course contents listed above, the networking lab needs to be equipped with the open source Linux operating system. One of the popular Linux distributions is Ubuntu Linux which includes the server, desktop, and mobile editions. With the Ubuntu server operating system, students can perform operations such as setting up network services, enforcing network security, managing the network, creating subnets, assigning IP addresses, constructing Wi-Fi access points, utilizing network protocols, and configuring network devices. The Ubuntu desktop operating system can be used to serve as the network service client, enforcing network security, configuring IP addresses, communicating with Wi-Fi accessing points, and so on. The mobile edition of the Ubuntu operating system can be used to test mobile devices, communicate over 3G mobile networks, and develop mobile applications. As an open source operating system, Ubuntu Linux also includes many stand-alone open source network management tools developed by third parties. In addition to those open source network management tools included in the Linux operating system, many open source network management packages can be downloaded from the Internet. The Linux operating system is also used to host open source application software such as Apache HTTP Server for Web development, Postfix for creating e-mail servers, MySQL for developing and managing database systems, and PHP for developing Web applications. The open source application software can be used to support other courses in the IT curriculum. Instructors and students can also customize the source code of the Linux operating system to develop some specific projects on top of the Linux operating system. The Linux operating system also supports remote access tools such as Virtual Network Computing (VNC). With VNC, students are able to remotely access the networking lab from anywhere and at anytime.

Although open source products are good for teaching and learning, they may, however, have some disadvantages when they are not used properly in business processes. The main disadvantage of open source products is the lack of marketing effort. The general public may not be familiar with them. For example, the Linux operating system only has a small portion of the PC market share even though it is free and competitive with Windows operating systems. People often perceive the Linux operating system as not easy to use. Lack of support from open source product vendors is another disadvantage. Most of Linux support comes from Linux user communities. Even though the support from the communities is often adequate, it may require some well trained technicians to search for solutions from the different communities. The general public is not used to finding answers from the Linux user communities. Another disadvantage is the lack of consistency among different Linux distributors. Linux operating systems from different Linux distributors do not exactly match each other. These Linux operating systems have different GUI interfaces and include different application software. This may confuse some users. Also, due to the small market share, it may take some time for hardware vendors to write drivers for the Linux operating system. This makes the Linux operating system less able to take advantage of newly released hardware. Things are improving. Major Linux operating system distributors such as Red Hat and SUSE have been providing support packages to their customers. As Android which is the operating system that uses the Linux kernel becomes the number one operating system for smart phones, it will help the general public reduce the anxiety about the Linux operating system.

While the Linux operating system can be used to cover most of the course contents of networking related courses, virtualization software can be used to improve security, availability, and flexibility. Virtualization is the process of using software to implement hardware such as hard drives, memory, or network interface cards (Smith & Nair, 2005). With the virtualization software, one can create a virtual machine which is the software implementation of a computer. The use of a virtual machine is similar to the use of a physical computer. One can install the Linux operating system and application software on a virtual machine. On the other hand, as a piece of software, a virtual machine can be hosted by a physical computer. Like most of the software, while running on the host computer, the virtual machine uses some of the physical memory and hard drive of the host computer. When a host computer has enough memory and hard drive space, multiple virtual machines can run simultaneously on the host computer. These virtual machines can also form a local network which is a desired feature for a networking class.

Therefore, instead of purchasing new computers and network equipment, a networking lab can be constructed with a set of virtual machines forming a network to meet the requirements of a networking related IT course. With the virtual technology, it is not necessary to construct physical computer labs on campus. Virtual machines can be created and run on a server linked to the campus network or simplify hosted by the server created on a public cloud such as Amazon or IBM Blue cloud (Chao, 2011). The cost on classrooms, lab facilities, and IT service staff can all be significantly reduced. The use of a virtual networking lab can further improve the affordability of a networking lab.

Such a constructed virtual network can be configured so that it is isolated from the university's network to reduce security risk. These virtual machines can run independently from the host computer and pose no security risk to the host computer. Students can get the administrative privilege for virtual machines but not the administrative privilege for the host computer. By doing so, the university's internal network can be well protected.

In addition to improving the security of a networking lab, the availability is also improved by virtualizing the networking lab. The virtual machines can be so configured that they are securely accessible through the Internet. Nowadays, Web based IT classes use online computer labs for hands-on practice. With the virtual networking lab, multiple users can log on to the same virtual machine at the same time from different locations. This feature of the virtual networking lab allows students to collaborate on their projects and allows instructors to help students troubleshoot misconfigurations during hands-on practice.

The use of virtual networking labs can also improve flexibility. The virtual machines can be configured specially for each IT course so that there will be no conflict with other courses. For example, the virtual machines can be configured differently for the courses Network Design and Network Security. In such a way, the configuration of the firewall in a Network Security class will not prevent the IP addressing in the Network Design class and vice versa. With the virtual machines, the lab preparation for a new semester can be easier. Instated of installing hardware and software, instructors can configure the virtual machines to meet the hands-on practice requirements and make enough copies based on class enrollment. The lab maintenance can be significantly simplified. During the hands-on practice, it is inevitable that a student may crash a computer system due to a wrong configuration. Instead of restoring the original system or reinstalling the original operating system and application software, an instructor can simply make a copy of an existing virtual machine to help the student back on track.

The disadvantage of virtualization is that the performance of virtual machines is, in general, slower than physical machines. However, it is not a real problem for most of the lab activities since most of the projects in the lab are small projects.

On the selection of virtualization software for networking lab construction, one may consider the VMWare Server and the open source Xen Server. One of the interesting features of Xen is its Xen Cloud Platform (XCP) (Xen, 2011), which is open source software to build private and public clouds. XCP allows cloud providers to host services and data centers by combining the Xen hypervisor with enhanced security, storage and network virtualization technologies. XCP allows one to import and export virtual appliances in the Open Virtual Machine Format. Various network and virtualization tools are available at XCP for potential customers to experiment with. On the other hand, although Xen Sever is free, the development tools may not. The cost can add up quickly. The virtual machines hosted on Xen can perform close to the native performance of the host computer since Xen can adjust its usage of host computer's resources to achieve better performance. When the host computer is busy, Xen will adjust itself to use less host computer's resources. The free software VMware Server is another choice. It is easy to use and has better fault tolerance. To run the virtual machines created with VMware Server, one can download the free VMware Player. VMware supports an interesting technology called PC-over-IP. It compresses the entire PC's resources and save them to a data center. When needed, the PC's resources can be transmitted to the user over a TCP/IP network to thin-client devices. At a thin-client device, it is decompressed and made ready for use.

## CASE STUDY: NETWORKING LAB FOR NETWORK MANAGEMENT

The case study illustrates the Analyze-Design-Develop-Implement-Evaluate approach in detail. The online networking lab development process basically fits in this model. Although a networking course may include many topics, this case study considers the development of a networking lab for the management of users and network resources, which is the content normally covered in the network management course.

## Requirement Analysis

In an enterprise, the user account and network resource information is saved in a directory which is similar to a database. A directory is usually hosted by a server computer called domain controller. When a user is trying to log on to a computer or a network device with the user name and password, the computer or the network device will forward the user name and password to a domain controller where the user's authentication information is stored in the directory. If the logon information provided by the user matches the authentication information, the user is allowed to log on to the computer or network device. The Network Management course requires a networking lab for students to configure the directory on the server side for the clients to access the directory remotely from client computers for user authentication.

## Design

Our first task at this phrase is to specify the protocol package for centralized authentication. The protocol used for centralized authentication is Lightweight Directory Access Protocol (LDAP) which is a client-server protocol for delivering the authentication information. LDAP is a simplified version of X.500 Directory Access Protocol (DAP). LDAP is an open source protocol, so it is possible to be adopted by other application software for user authentication. Therefore, networks of some commercial companies such as Windows and Novell also support the LDAP service. In the

following discussion, several commonly used LDAP management packages will be described.

There are three major open source LDAP management tools, OpenLDAP, Fedora DS, and Sun OpenDS. OpenLDAP can work with many different databases as its backend for data storage. It can also work with virtual databases as the backend. It is possible for OpenLDAP to handle a large authentication database containing 150 million entries. OpenLDAP can transfer over 22,000 queries/second or 4,800 updates/second (Chu, 2006). It is also compatible with the next generation Internet protocol version 6 (Ipv6). When used for user and network resource authentication, OpenLDAP is fast, reliable, scalable, and easy to configure. The OpenLDAP package can be installed on both server and client sides to handle different tasks. Due to these features, OpenLDAP is a suitable package for an enterprise or organization to implement its centralized authentication service.

Fedora DS (Fedora Directory Server) is also an enterprise-level open source LDAP server offered by the Linux distributor Red Hat. It is a full-featured open source directory service package, which provides the centralized management of users, computers, and network resources for large companies. Another feature of Fedora DS is that it can simplify the tasks of directory service management. Fedora DS can also improve security and performance. Therefore, Fedora DS is used by many large enterprises and organizations around the world.

Another well-known open source LDAP package is Sun OpenDS, which is a directory service tool. Sun OpenDS is a Java based open source directory server, so it is able to provide directory related services such as directory proxy, virtual directory, namespace distribution and data synchronization. Initially, it is developed by Sun Microsystems. Later, it has been adopted by many developers and other interested parties around the world. Since Java code can be executed on a wide range of platforms without recompiling, Sun OpenDS is suitable for developers to create new components for open source projects.

Since the OpenLDAP package is easy to install in Ubuntu Linux, the case study presented in this chapter will use OpenLDAP for illustration purposes. Our next task is to design the networking lab for supporting the configuration of OpenLDAP.

To support hands-on activities on OpenLDAP, the networking lab will be designed to meet the requirements of the hands-practice. The networking lab design includes logical design and physical design. The logical design is the blue print of the online networking lab project. It represents the future networking lab with icons, symbols, and technical terms. During the logical design, the requirements for the networking lab are translated to technical terms and the technologies will be specified for the lab project. The logical design can be done with computer software to create a logical design diagram. In our case study, the networking lab is designed for the enrollment of 25 students. For the hands-on practice on LDAP, each student needs two virtual machines, one is used as the LDAP server and the other is used as the LDAP client. A subnet should be created to connect the LDAP server and LDAP client for each student. The following diagram represents the design of our networking lab.

As Figure 1 indicates, each student has two virtual machines connected with the subnet 192.168.y.x, where y is the student number and x is number assigned to each virtual machine. There will be a total of 50 virtual machines created on the host server. When a student is trying to log on to his or her virtual machines through the Internet, he/she will first access the proxy server. If the authentication is successful, the student will be able to log on to the proxy server. From there, the connection request will be forwarded to the virtual machines assigned to the student. By using these virtual machines, the student can perform the hands-on practice required by the Network Management course.

The physical design specifies the physical components of the project. During the physical design, the designer needs to specify the operating system of the virtual machines, the way these virtual machines to be linked so that they can form a network, the security measures to be enforced on these virtual machines, the remote access mechanisms, the user account management scheme, and the configuration of the physical host server.

*Figure 1. Networking lab design*

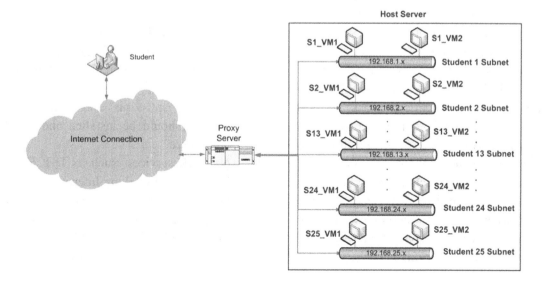

As described earlier, the open source Ubuntu Linux server edition will be used as the operating system for the server virtual machines. The Ubuntu Linux Desktop edition will be used as the operating system for the client virtual machines. The OpenLDAP package should be installed on both the server and client virtual machines. It can be downloaded directly from the Internet by students during the hands-on practice. Each virtual machine can be configured to have 1GB RAM and 15GB hard drive space if the GUI desktop is used in the hands-on practice. Without the GUI desktop, the virtual machines will take much smaller RAM and hard drive space. When the host server is powerful enough, the GUI desktop should be installed for the students who do not have experience with Linux.

The network interface cards of the two virtual machines assigned to each student are configured so that they are able to ping each other. The network cards should also be configured so that the virtual machines can communicate with the host computer. The host server is so configured that it serves as a network address translation (NAT) server which allows the virtual machines to access the Internet.

The Proxy Server can be implemented with a piece of network equipment, or a computer with the server operating system, or simply the software installed on the host server. In this case study, the open source software Squid Transparent Proxy will be downloaded and installed on the Ubuntu Linux Server edition to implement the Proxy Server. The Internet accessible external IP address will be given by the university's IT service department. Apache2 utilities will be installed and configured for carrying out the authentication task. The host configuration file will be configured to support the internal network 192.168.0.0/24 and allow the http to access the local network.

To host 50 virtual machines configured with 1GB RAM and 15GB hard drive space, it is recommended that the host server should have 32GB RAM and 1TB hard drive space. When the virtual machines are running simultaneously, they will adjust the computing resources to best use the computing resources of the host server. The host server can be installed with the Ubuntu server edition to run the virtual machines and to host a software-based proxy server. The host server needs at least two network interface cards, one for connecting to the Internet and one for connecting the private network with the ID 192.168.0.0.

To remotely access the host server, a student may download the remote accessing software such as Putty or Virtual Network Computing (VNC) if the GUI desktop is used for the lab activities. Students can install the VNC software on their personal computers with Linux or Windows operating system. Or, they can install the light version of VNC on their Smartphones so that they can do their lab assignments through a Wi-Fi wireless network, or a 3G or 4G telecommunication network. On the server side, the host server should be configured to allow the Putty or VNC client to remotely access the server. Once, logged on to the host server, a student can use the Ubuntu remote desktop service to access the virtual machines.

## Development

The third phase of the project is the development of the networking lab. During the development phase, the host server is configured to handle the following tasks.

- The host server will be physically installed and wired to the university's network.
- The Proxy Server software will be downloaded and configured according to the design.
- Firewall, anti-virus and other security patches should be installed and properly configured.
- Network services, such as DHCP, DNS, NAT, and Networking Interface Cards will be configured so that it can communicate with the university's network and allow the virtual machines to access the Internet.

- Based on the design of the virtual networking lab, the virtual machines will be created on the host server.
- Two virtual machine images used as the prototype will be created on the host server, one for the server and one for the client. Ubuntu Linux server and desktop operating systems and the required network protocols will be installed on these virtual machine images respectively.
- Depending on the enrollment, we will generate enough virtual machines with those two virtual machine images mentioned in the previous task. When making copies, we will make sure that each virtual machine has its own virtual hardware address.
- Both the instructor and students should be given the administrator's privilege for the virtual machines assigned to them.
- Configure the server and client virtual machines so that they are connected through a local private network.
- Based the enrollment, the instructor and student accounts will be created on the host server for remote access.
- Make sure that the VNC server is configured to allow remote access and make sure that the security key and VNC client software are available to students for download.

As described above, the development of a virtual networking lab takes much less effort than the development of a physical networking lab with 50 computers and network equipment. Once the networking lab is developed, the next phase is the implementation phase.

## Implementation

The tasks in the implementation phase include testing and deployment of the networking lab. In this phase the teaching materials are also created for the hands-on practice. The testing process may involve the testing of the host server, virtual machines, network protocols, security measures, as well as remote access. Before making the networking lab available to the students, the instructor should be invited to test his/her teaching materials in the networking lab. For testing the remote access, student accounts should be used to log on to the host server from an off-campus location and perform some of the lab activities on the virtual machines. If it is allowed, the instructor should test simultaneous multiple logons from different locations. The testing result should be recorded for future reference. If necessary, further adjustment should be done for the networking lab based on the testing result. After testing, the virtual computer lab is ready to be deployed for teaching and learning.

Successful deployment of the networking lab requires training and technical support. First, there should be some instructions on remote logon. The instruction on installing and configuring the VNC client should be available to the instructor and students. The instructor should be trained on how to use the networking lab, how to deploy the teaching materials to the networking lab, and so forth. The training can be carried out through face-to-face seminars or through the Webcasts. The technical support team should be organized to help the instructor and students with troubleshooting. As the semester moves along, the lab manual for the hands-on practice should be available to the students. Carefully written hands-on practice instructions can save the instructor a lot of time in troubleshooting. Since the students are not familiar with the online networking lab, hands-on practice instructions should be step-by-step and include screenshots for each step. As described in the design phase, one of the requirements for the networking lab is that it should be able to support the hands-on practice on centralized authentication with LDAP.

The lab manual should start with the introduction of directory service and LDAP. The centralized authentication is carried out with the directory service. A directory is constructed on a tree structure and is often built based on a geographic and/or organizational structure. The URL of an enterprise or a university is placed on the top level of the tree structure. The lower level entries are used to represent the units under the organization such as campuses, colleges, departments, groups, and offices. The lowest level entries will be users, computer systems, and other network resources such as network storage devices. When entries are created on the tree structure, the related data contents are grouped to form a schema. Each entry in a directory has a unique name called Distinguished Name (DN) and has a set of attributes which describe the data content of the entry. A DN consists of Relative Distinguished Name (RDN) which is constructed with the attributes' names. For example, a DN can have the following format.

DN: cn=[user name],ou=cis,dc=campus,dc=edu

where DN consists of two RDNs, the attributes Common Name cn = user name, Organizational Unit ou=cis. The Domain Content dc = campus is the parent DN. The higher level parent DN is dc = edu.

One of the directory's tasks is to quickly respond to the authentication requests from clients. LDAP is the network protocol to carry out the task. An LDAP process starts from the request by a client program. LDAP then creates a connection from the client to the LDAP server. Carried by the protocol TCP/IP suite, the request is sent to the LDAP server. Based on the authentication request and search criteria set by the client, the server searches for, validates, or updates the information in the directory. Then, the server sends its response back to the client via LDAP. To protect the data content carried by LDAP, the communication can be done through an SSL tunnel. After the authentication operation requested by the client is completed, LDAP closes the connection.

The hands-on activities may include the configuration of an LDAP server virtual machine, run a stand-alone LDAP daemon (slapd), populate the directory with user account information, and secure LDAP transactions with the SSL protocol. In the end, the students should be able to access the LDAP server virtual machine from the client virtual machine.

Before starting the confirmation of the LDAP server, the students will be instructed to test the network connection between the server and client virtual machines. Each student should make sure that the server and client machines can ping each other. The students should also make sure that the DNS is configured properly so that the virtual machines can access the Internet.

The first task of this lab is to install and configure the LDAP server. If not already installed, the following commands will be used to download and install the LDAP daemon (slapd) and LDAP utilities.

```
sudo apt-get update
sudo apt-get install slapd ldap-utils
```

During the installation, the students need to specify the administrator's name, password, and the LDAP server's IP address.

After the LDAP server and the utility tools are installed, the LDAP server should be so configured that the LDAP clients can communicate with it. The configuration starts with the following command.

```
sudo dpkg-reconfigure slapd
```

During the configuration, each student needs to specify the DNS domain name and the organization name. These names should be pre-defined by the instructor and assigned to the students. After the LDAP daemon (slapd) is configured, the students need to edit the configuration file, /etc/ldap/ldap.conf, by using the following command.

```
sudo gedit /etc/ldap.conf
```

The students need to specify the LDAP-SERVER_IP and set the bind_policy to soft. After the file /etc/ldap.conf is configured, make a copy to the folder /etc/ldap/. Now, the students should run the auth-client-config script by executing the following commands.

```
sudo auth-client-config -t nss -p lac_ldap
sudo pam-auth-update ldap
```

Once the configuration is completed, restart the LDAP daemon (slapd) with the following command.

```
sudo /etc/init.d/slapd restart
```

After the daemon is restarted, test the LDAP server with the command ldapsearch which is the tool used to find the ldap entries stored in the LDAP directory. As we may expect, there are not many entries in the LDAP directory.

The next task of the lab is to add some entries to the LDAP directory. The students can either manually add entries or migrate the entries in the Linux authentication files such as /etc/passwd and /etc/group to the LDAP directory. In this lab activity, a new account studenta is added to the LDAP directory.

The third step is to download and configure the LDAP package on a client machine. Similar to the configuration of the LDAP server, the students need to specify the LDAP server IP address and the DNS domain name.

The last step is to test the LDAP server for user authentication. If the LDAP server is configured properly, the students should be able to log on to the LDAP server from a client virtual machine with the user name studenta even though the studenta account is not set on the client virtual machine.

In this hands-on practice, the students will learn about LDAP based user authentication. They will configure the LDAP server and populate it with the information from the existing system databases. The centralized authentication allows the users whose accounts have been created on the LDAP server machine to log on to any computers in within the same network.

## Evaluation

The last phase of the networking lab project is the evaluation phase. The purpose of evaluation is to find out the impact of the networking lab and lab based teaching materials on the students. The evaluation is used to find answers for questions such as:

- If the students understand the content covered by the Network Management course,
- If the students' hands-on skills have been improved, and
- If the students' learning behaviors have been changed due to the use of the online networking lab.

The result of the evaluation will help the educators to improve their teaching. It is also used to assess the affordability, flexibility, security, and availability of the networking lab, and to identify the areas for further improvement. The evaluation of the networking lab should be so designed that it can examine if the networking lab has met the requirements identified in the analysis phase.

Since the case study has been completed, to evaluate the effect of the networking lab and its impact on the students learning, a brief post class survey has been distributed to the students who participated in the Network Management course. The Network Management course covers the content of centralized authentication. Table 1 summarizes the result of the survey. The questions selected from the survey are related to the topics such as centralized authentication, students' attitude towards the hands-on practice, and the networking lab in this case study.

The survey result indicates that the majority of the students understands the LDAP concept and is able to set up the centralized service with OpenLDAP. The students' attitudes towards the hands-on practice are very positive. 100% of the students consider the hands-on skills very important or important. Most of the students (96% of

*Table 1. Survey result*

| Survey Result | | |
| --- | --- | --- |
| I understand how LDAP works | | |
| Agree | Neutral | Disagree |
| 88% | 8% | 4% |
| I know how to set up a centralized authentication service. | | |
| Agree | Neutral | Disagree |
| 84% | 12% | 4% |
| What is your experience with the open source virtual online networking lab? | | |
| Like | OK | Don't Like |
| 72% | 24% | 4% |
| Does the class have adequate hands-on practice? | | |
| Too Much | Just Right | Not Enough |
| 8% | 80% | 12% |
| Does the class add extra workload for you? | | |
| Yes | About the Same | No |
| 56% | 32% | 12% |
| When comparing with this class, what type of class do you wish to take? | | |
| With more hands-on | Similar to this one | With less hands-on |
| 48% | 44% | 8% |
| What is your opinion about the importance of hands-on skills? | | |
| Very Important | Important | Not Important |
| 76% | 24% | 0% |
| Are you able to use the learned hands-on skills in your job and study? | | |
| Yes | Maybe | No |
| 54% | 42% | 4% |

the students) are able to or may be able to use the learned hands-on skills in their work and study. 96% of the students like or are OK with the open source virtual online networking lab. On the other hand, 56% of the students think that the class with the hands-on networking lab adds extra workload for them. An interesting observation is that, despite the heavier workload, 92% of the students are still willing to take a class similar to this one or a class with even more hands-on practice. It shows that the hands-on practice has motivated the students to work harder. The survey also shows that a few students got behind in their

work. Due to the extra workload, it is hard for these students to catch up in a lab based learning environment. Additional tutoring service may be helpful in the future.

## CONCLUSION

Teaching networking online is always a challenge to educators due to the requirements of hands-on practice. The construction of a networking lab is expensive, time consuming, and vulnerable to the university' network system. This chapter presents a solution based on the open source products and the virtualization technology. With the open source software and virtualization, this study finds that the affordability, availability, security, and flexibility can be significantly improved. Through a case study, this chapter illustrates the development of a networking lab with Linux and other open source software to support the hands-on activities required by the Network Management course. By following the Analyze-Design-Develop-Implement-Evaluate model, an open source based online virtual networking lab is designed and implemented to teach centralized authentication with the OpenLDAP package. Since networking related topics are the components of the IT education curriculum, the solution described in this chapter is meaningful to all the education institutions that offer IT education. Conducting hands-on practice in the open source virtual networking lab can better prepare our IT students to join the IT workforce.

# REFERENCES

Casado, M., Watson, G., & McKeown, N. (2005). Reconfigurable networking hardware: A classroom tool. In *13th Symposium on High Performance Interconnects (HOTI'05)* (pp.151-157).

Chao, L. (2009). *Utilizing open source tools for online teaching and learning: Applying Linux technologies*. Hershey, PA: IGI Publishing. doi:10.4018/978-1-60566-376-0

Chao, L. (2011). Development of virtual computer lab with public cloud. In P. Kommers, J. P. Zhang, T. Issa, & P. Isaias (Eds.), *Proceedings of IADIS International Conference on Internet Technologies & Society 2011* (pp. 217-220). Shanghai, China.

Chu, H. (2006). *OpenLDAP 2.4 highlights features of the upcoming release*. Retrieved October 30, 2011, from http://www.openldap.org/pub/hyc/LDAPcon2007.pdf

Citrix Systems. (2009). *Xen*. Retrieved December 15, 2011, from http://www.xen.org

Corbesero, S. (2006). Rapid and inexpensive lab deployment using open source software. *Journal of Computing Sciences in Colleges, 22*(2), 228–234.

Correia, E., & Watson, R. (2006). VMware as a practical learning tool. In Sarkar, N. (Ed.), *Tools for teaching computer networking and hardware concepts* (pp. 338–354). Hershey, PA: Idea Group Inc. doi:10.4018/978-1-59140-735-5.ch018

Dick, W. O., Carey, L., & Carey, J. O. (2004). *Systematic design of instruction* (6th ed.). Upper Saddle River, NJ: Allyn & Bacon.

Gerdes, J., & Tilley, S. (2007). A conceptual overview of the virtual networking laboratory. In *SIGITE'07* (pp. 75-82).

Goyal, R., Lai, S., Jain, R., & Durresi, A. (1998). Laboratories for data communications and computer networks. In *1998 FIE Conference* (pp. 1113-1119).

Hoagland, D., Brewer, S. D., & Hoogendyk, T. A. (2002). *Linux in higher education: Two applications that improve student learning*. Paper presented at the Massachusetts Education Computing Conference (MECC), West Barnstable, MA.

IEEE/ACM. (2008). *IT 2008, Curriculum guidelines for undergraduate degree programs in information technology* (Final Draft). Retrieved January 16, 2009, from http://www.acm.org//education/curricula/IT2008%20Curriculum.pdf

Jackiewicz, T. (2004). *Deploying OpenLDAP*. New York, NY: Apress.

Kapadia, N. H. (1999). *On the design of a demand-based network computing system: The Purdue network computing hubs*. PhD thesis, School of Electrical and Computer Engineering, Purdue University.

Kneale, B., Horta, A. Y., & Box, L. (2004). Velnet: Virtual environment for learning networking. In *Proceedings of the Sixth Conference on Australasian Computing Education, Vol. 30* (pp. 161-169).

Maxwell, S. (2000). *Red Hat Linux network management tools*. New York, NY: McGraw-Hill.

McAndrew, A. (2008). Teaching cryptography with open-source software. *Special Interest Group Computer Science Education, 40*(1), 325–330.

Microsoft. (2009). *Virtualization*. Retrieved December 6, 2011, from http://www.microsoft.com/virtualization/default.mspx

Nagios. (2011). *Nagios*. Retrieved November 30, 2011, from http://www.nagios.org

Nessus. (2011). *Tenable network security*. Retrieved November 30, 2011, from http://www.nessus.org/nessus

Olifer, N., & Olifer, V. (2006). *Computer networks: Principles, technologies and protocols for network design*. San Francisco, CA: John Wiley & Sons.

Penrod, J. I., & Harbor, A. F. (2000). Designing and implementing a learning organization-oriented information technology planning and management process. In Petrides, L. A. (Ed.), *Case studies on information technology in higher education: Implications for policy and practice* (pp. 7–19). Hershey, PA: IGI Publishing. doi:10.4018/978-1-878289-74-2.ch001

Preston, D. S. (Ed.). (2004). *Virtual learning and higher education*. New York, NY: Rodopi.

Smith, D. E., & Nair, R. (2005). The architecture of virtual machines. *Computer, 38*(5), 32–38. doi:10.1109/MC.2005.173

Teare, D., & Paquet, C. (2005). *Campus network design fundamentals*. Indianapolis, IN: Cisco Press.

University of Birmingham. (2009). *Developing a virtual teaching and learning centre for problem based learning*. Retrieved August 1, 2009, from http://www.education.bham.ac.uk/research/projects1/pbl/index.shtml

Uys, P. (2001). Networked educational management: Transforming educational management in a networked institute. In C. Montgomerie & J. Viteli (Eds.), *Proceedings of World Conference on Educational Multimedia, Hypermedia and Telecommunications 2001* (pp. 1917-1923). Chesapeake, VA: AACE.

VMWare. (2009). *VMWare*. Retrieved December 6, 2011, from http://www.vmware.com

Wireshark. (2011). *The world's foremost network protocol analyzer*. Retrieved November 30, 2011, from http://www.wireshark.org

Wright, J., Carpin, S., Cerpa, A., & Gavilan, G. (2007). *An open source teaching and learning facility for computer science and engineering education* (pp. 368–373). FECS.

Xen. (2011). *Xen Cloud Platform project*. Retrieved November 30, 2011, from http://xen.org/products/cloudxen.html

# Chapter 7
# Deploying Digital Educational Resources with Free and Open Source Technologies

**Jason G. Caudill**
*Carson-Newman College, USA*

## ABSTRACT

*Digital educational resources are an increasingly visible and important component of the online learning environment. Concurrently, many organizations are faced with limited financial resources with which to provide their materials to the learners. In order to continue delivering materials but reduce the total cost of delivery organizations can implement free and open source technologies for digital educational resource deployment. Open source software and free online services, properly employed, can enhance organizational effectiveness while also reducing organizational expense.*

## BACKGROUND

As education of all types, traditional, blended, and fully online, incorporates more digital resources into the learning environment the need for efficient and effective distribution of these resources to learners becomes increasingly important. This need for improved and expanded resource provision is, unfortunately, coupled with decreasing availability of funds for many educational organizations not only in the United States but also around the world. Compounding the financial exigencies faced by organizations are increasing financial pressures on consumers of educational products.

One potential solution to many of these issues is the use of open technologies. Many people recognize that open source software is available for free, but to be open source a program has to not only be distributed without license fees but also make its source code, the programming that makes the application function, freely available

DOI: 10.4018/978-1-4666-2205-0.ch007

(Bessen, 2005). Bretthauer (2002) explains that, "Since 1998, the open source movement has become a revolution in software development. However, the 'revolution' in this rapidly changing field can actually trace its roots back at least 30 years" (p 5). The growth of open source does seem to be accelerating. Fitzgerald (2006) stated that, "Indeed, a type of Moore's Law effect seems to be taking place as the amount of open source software available increases dramatically every 12 months or so" (p 587).

Paudel et. al. (2010) explore the value of open source technologies to developing economies, highlighting their value based on total cost of ownership, quality, and freedom. They also cite education specifically, saying that, "Education is one field where the institutions can use Open Source software to directly save money, which can be further spent on fields like research" (Paudel, Harlalka, & Shrestha, 2010, p 8). Tong (2004) explores a list of reasons that free and open source software is used in education: lower costs, reliability, performance and security, build long-term capacity, open philosophy, encourage innovations, alternative to illegal copying, possibility of localization, and learning from source code.

Open source certainly has a valuable place in the educational community and as a resource is growing and changing as quickly as education. Both are rooted in the rapidly expanding accessibility of affordable technology and Internet access that is driving so many other factors in society. Bringing the two together to support digital media deployment is simply the next step in a long progression of technology integration into the educational environment.

## INTRODUCTION

This chapter will focus on ways in which digital resources can be deployed to learners via free and open source technologies. Open source software products have been available for many years and digital media tools have grown in both availability and sophistication. Because of this growth the creation of digital learning objects has become more accessible. Such objects, however, only have value if they are used for an educational purpose.

There are many ways in which digital media can be disseminated today through free and open source resources. Open source learning management systems (LMSs) provide organizations with opportunities to post digital media online in an instructional format without the burden of paying high license and support fees to commercial LMSs. These open source LMS solutions provide an outlet to the digital media creation process that begins with the software used to create the digital media objects. An LMS not only gives educators the opportunity to disseminate their educational media, but also multiple methods to provide learners with inputs and active discussion of the material.

To share materials with a broader audience, including other educators, there are the still-emerging practices of OpenCourseWare (OCW) and open educational resources (OER). OCW is the sharing of course information, ranging from just a syllabus and notes to full video-captured lectures, freely to anyone with an Internet connection. OER is a similar practice, although OER sharing often involves just particular educational objects independent of an overall course design. Both practices offer learners access to materials for their own improvement, but the more important contribution may be as a base for other educators to create their own courses.

By providing base materials for other instructional environments OCW and OER take digital media objects and utilize them for both local and global audiences. As such, learning objects created locally with open source software, and possibly used locally in an open source LMS, can be freely available to the whole world. From start to finish, this process gives educators the opportunity to share material at every level with free solutions.

Another increasingly popular option for digital dissemination of educational resources is social media. YouTube, Facebook, Twitter, and other technologies are all finding places in the modern virtual classroom. Not only are vast amounts of already created content available, but these resources are also particularly useful for providing media access to learners without requiring the organization to carry the heavy data load on their own servers. An emerging, related open source technology is OpenMeetings, a teleconferencing system that interacts with not only Facebook but also with multiple LMS platforms. This adds synchronous meeting capabilities and recording capacity to the creation and deployment toolboxes.

## ISSUES FOR DIGITAL EDUCATIONAL RESOURCE DEPLOYMENT

The development of digital educational resources can be an expensive activity. The volume of multimedia has been shown to be the single most significant cost factor for online programs past the initial offering of a course (Whalen and Wright, 1999). The labor hours required for digital media creation are a major component of the overall cost, but the tools and hosting costs can be substantial as well. While the development of resources is beyond the scope of this work the deployment of resources already developed is at the heart of the discussion.

For institutions or individuals who have developed digital educational resources the issue becomes how to best share those resources and how to do so effectively at a minimum cost. Several different factors impact what needs to be done. The scale of the sharing, ranging from just a select group of learners to the world at large, will dictate what kind of system is needed.

This system type is also impacted by issues such as copyrights. In an environment of increasing sensitivity to how media is distributed the protection of intellectual property is a critical

issue to any sharing. Even if certain media falls under educational use licensing there are still requirements to limit access to the material to the educational environment. Doing this requires that access limits in the form of invitation-only access, password-protected access, or other security measures are available.

In order to address these multiple issues several different categories of open technologies will be addressed. All of the services presented here are available at no cost to the users but all provide different features and will be best suited to different environments.

## OPEN TECHNOLOGIES FOR RESOURCE DEPLOYMENT

### Open Source Learning Management Systems

One of the most capital-intensive digital education resources today is the LMS. Initial set-up fees are often high, and maintenance and support contracts can also consume large amounts of money. Compounding this cost are incremental upgrade costs for which the institutions often have no choice; a provider changes versions and stops supporting the one currently in place. Adding to the already considerable challenge is a growing consolidation of LMS providers which means fewer options and less competition.

Even with these considerable challenges having a good LMS available is critical to learning environments in higher education today. Even traditional, face-to-face courses can benefit from having an LMS presence and online and blended environments are difficult, if not impossible, to manage without one. With respect to digital educational resource deployment the LMS is the central hub from which all online activity will take place. In order to mitigate the high cost of commercial systems some open source alternatives will be discussed.

Aydin and Tirkes (2010) discuss that as distance learning technologies are adopted by more institutions of learning and business organizations, "…along with the advantages, installation and support costs appear to be a disadvantage compared to a traditional learning environment. These disadvantages can be reduced to a great extent by the use of open source software…" p. 593. For LMS applications there are currently two leaders, Moodle and Sakai. While there are many other open source LMS options available, just nine of which are Docebo, eFront, Dokeos, Claroline, ATutor, ILIAS, OLAT, .LRN, openlms, and Ganesha (Sampson, 2008), the focus here will be on those that are most frequently encountered. Going forward, however, it may be interesting to watch the development of Google's entry into the free LMS arena with their product, CloudCourse. Just launched in 2010 it is too early to tell what impact the system will have but Google has proven to be a powerful force in online services and may become influential in LMS design.

In choosing any LMS, open source or commercial, the focus should be on functionality and the ability of the system to meet the needs of the organization. Aydin and Tirkes (2010) provide one example of a list of such considerations:

- Compatibility and the ability to work with other LMS,
- Content management ability such as Electronic filing and file management,
- How the learning content is created and managed as a "learning object",
- Reusability of the content (Content compatibility like Scorm, AIIC, IMS),
- Rapid content creation, distribution, integration and authoring tools,
- Support for the tools using in content creation such as (Dreamweaver, Flash, Word, PowerPoint),
- Performance and extendability of the environment,
- Multi-Language Support.

While the above list is far from comprehensive it does highlight many of the major considerations for what an LMS should be able to do for an organization. This leads to an important point in the selection and use of open source software; regardless of how inexpensive the product may be it is of no value if it does not perform. Thus, even in an environment of limited resources cost cannot be the sole factor, functionality must also be considered.

In terms of cost, adopters of an open source LMS must understand that while they do not have a fee for access to the application itself there are still costs associated with operating any type of system. Wang, Blue, and Plourde, (2010) discovered this in their case study of the University of Delaware's shift to Sakai as the campus LMS.

Although all interviewees acknowledged that cost was an issue when considering open source systems versus commercial products, it wasn't a key factor. The cost saved by not paying commercial product licenses by adopting FOSS is likely spent on the salaries and benefits of people who maintain and support FOSS. As one interviewee noted, 'You don't actually save money by going to open source, because basically whatever you don't spend on licensing, you are going to spend internally on people.' (Wang, Blue, & Plourde, pp 34-35, 2010).

The exact costs of any LMS implementation will of course vary by institution and situation. It is unlikely that one can say that universally there are no cost savings to an open source LMS, but it can be said with certainty that such a system is not entirely without cost. What those costs are, and what the resultant benefits may be of those costs, are what ultimately decide the success of a project.

With a cost-benefit model in mind, what is the real advantage of open source systems? Beyond the lack of license fees for the product open source users derive a variety of benefits. To frame this, a definition of open source software is necessary. To be truly open source, an application must provide users with unrestricted access to the applications' source code; the programming that makes the application work. Giving such access to users means that those with the necessary skills can modify, improve, and repair open source applications themselves. This provides great freedom to those using such applications and also allows for a community of developers to engage in the development and redevelopment of the application.

Such community engagement is another advantage to utilizing open source applications. Because a potentially limitless number of developers can take part in the development process popular open source applications often advance and have faults repaired much more quickly than many commercial applications. This means that new features, integration with third-party applications, and other aspects of system customization are much more accessible when using open-source products. For an organization interested in agility this can be a critical advantage.

Focusing on Moodle and Sakai, particularly with an emphasis on digital educational resource deployment, both offer many options. Moodle's recent upgrade to version 2.0+ has placed an emphasis on improving media integration. Some of the new features added in the most recent version include Flash HD video support, Flash video embedding, HTML 5 support, a customizable MP3 player, and better integration with YouTube videos. These new features are in addition to existing multimedia functionality in Moodle which already included support for a full dozen media formats (http://docs.moodle.org/20/en/Multimedia_plugins). Also available inside the Moodle environment are more traditional learning object creation and sharing technologies such as discussion boards and wikis.

Outside of Moodle there is a potentially powerful new option for adding interactivity to the Moodle environment. An open source teleconferencing application, OpenMeetings, is available with a plugin to integrate the conference directly into a Moodle classroom. While technically a

separate application, OpenMeetings is an open source, server-based application that can enhance both the creation and sharing of digital educational resources. A more in-depth discussion of this technology will be provided later.

Sakai takes a unique approach to media integration in that Sakai resources can begin with the creation of a webpage within the system (https://sites.google.com/a/ithaca.edu/sakai/video/embed-av). With a webpage created media of virtually any type can then be embedded in the page and accessed inside the Sakai environment. This approach offers great flexibility but is, from a technical standpoint, a more complicated way for users to post content. Regardless of what method is employed for multimedia posting training and development for faculty will be key to the use of such advanced features.

## OPENCOURSEWARE AND OPEN EDUCATIONAL RESOURCES

### Definition and Background

While an LMS is often limited to an internal audience for a particular institution there is a growing movement to disseminate digital educational resources to a worldwide audience, making such materials available to anyone with access to the Internet. There are two complimentary, but different, technologies gaining acceptance today; OpenCourseWare (OCW) and Open Educational Resources (OER). Both are open by design, accessible from anywhere at no fee, and are excellent examples of how educators are finding new and innovative ways to reach those who want to learn.

The difference between OCW and OER is a small but important one. OER is the broader of the two categories. Hylen (2005) defines OER as, "Open Educational Resources are digitised materials offered freely and openly for educators, students and self-learners to use and re-use for teaching, learning and research" (p. 1). OCW is similar, but more narrowly defined. The Open-CourseWare Consortium defines OpenCourse-Ware (OCW) as "…free and open digital publication of high quality university-level educational materials. These materials are organized as courses and often include course planning materials and evaluation tools as well as thematic content" (OCW Consortium, 2010).

OCW is a relatively new technology, reaching its ten year mark at the time of this writing in 2011. Originally launched by the Massachusetts Institute of Technology (MIT) in 2001 with content for 1600 courses (Abelson, 2007) today's OCW Consortium has a membership of hundreds of universities and other organizations offering thousands of courses (OpenCourseWare Consortium, 2010). MIT's OCW community alone has grown to over ten million users (Edudemic, 2011). There are clearly large numbers of people posting and accessing material through this new medium.

From the perspective of digital educational resource deployment OCW/OER may be the fastest-growing component of the online educational community. While it is still a young technology sources in the literature see great potential for OCW/OER to influence education in the future. Taylor (2007) makes the following prediction:

*…the OCW movement has the opportunity to expand its vision and operations to enable the OCW learners to have access to academic support, to have the opportunity to be assessed and to have the potential to gain credit towards recognized qualifications awarded by a credible accreditation agency (p. 3).*

Duderstadt (2008) sees open technologies, including OCW/OER as the base for building truly global universities and that the future combination of technologies could yield, "…the linking together of billions of people with limitless access to knowledge and learning tools enabled by a rapidly evolving scaffolding of cyberinfra-

structure; which increases in power one-hundred to one-thousand-fold every decade" (Duderstadt, 2009, p. 31). What deployment could be larger than one to a global audience?

## What OCW/OER Offers

With this framework for deployment defined the question becomes how OCW/OER can benefit digital educational resource deployment. If the goal of a digital educational resource deployment project is to reach the largest possible audience then OCW/OER is the best opportunity available today. By definition, these resources become globally available.

There may be some question as to how becoming a part of the OCW/OER movement differs from just publicly posting material on a website. From a technical perspective there is very little difference; these resources are linked from a publicly accessible site and the files are stored on a server. The difference becomes apparent when the resources are searched for, found, and used. The ultimate value of any educational resource is limited by whether or not people actually use it. For any web-based resource the question today is increasingly one of how an interested user finds the tool.

Subject-matter searches on almost any topic on any search engine return thousands, if not millions, of results. For a user who has a general idea of what kind of topic they need but do not know to go to a particular institution for that material trying to find a public site just posting material can be nearly impossible. So, how does a content provider make their OCW/OER project useful, useful meaning found and utilized?

Participation in organized collections of OCW/OER resources such as the OCW Consortium can make materials easily accessible. There are also many prominent universities who have followed the MIT example and launched their own branded OCW consortiums for the institution. Participation in such organized efforts gives providers of OCW/OER materials better opportunities for interested users to find and access the materials.

As the OCW/OER movement progresses there will also be opportunities for content providers to standardize the format of their delivery. Standardization is often a key component in the development of any technical service, as has been demonstrated throughout the personal computing revolution in the past thirty or more years. Standards for the creation of software, of web content, and in education of ancillary materials to be compatible with LMS products have all driven wider adaptation of such resources.

While there does not appear to be a single standard yet set one was released in 2009 by the Center for Social Media at American University, the Code of Best Practices in Fair Use for Open-CourseWare (Park, 2009). There is no way at the time of this writing to know what parameters will develop as the accepted standard for OCW distribution, if indeed there is a single standard and not multiple competing standards, but the very existence of this set of best practices indicates that standardization is a future point of emphasis for the practitioner community. If such standardization is accomplished then utilization of OCW/OER will become much faster and easier for a larger audience.

## Application

With OCW/OER growing in popularity and more and more resources being disseminated with this technology the question becomes how the educational community is using this new resource. The most obvious use of these resources is for an individual learner; someone with an interest in a subject can access the materials and learn independently. While this is a valuable use of the resources it is also the most limited in scope. The reach and impact of OCW/OER is much larger when these resources are used as the base for the development of new educational experiences. In such a situation instructors are the first to access the materials and then utilize them to build experiences for their students.

While OCW can be useful to students its primary use is as a tool to support course development (Koohang & Harmon, 2007). A 2004 survey of educators using MIT's OCW found that 57% used OCW for course or curriculum development and 47% have adopted elements of MIT materials for use in their classrooms (Marguiles, 2004). If OCW materials are being used for course development and are being incorporated into classroom activities the question becomes how to take OCW/OER materials and turn them into a course for delivery.

Building a course from an OCW/OER foundation is actually quite similar to designing any other course. Goals are set, materials are selected, activities are designed, and the overall product is assessed before offering it to a learning community. Rennie and Mason (2010) have broken the process of transforming OCW/OER resources into courses down into a five step process:

1. Identify the main generic headings for course content (key topics for discussion and learning).
2. Search for relevant resources that can be re-used for these headings.
3. Write 'wrap-around' materials that contextualize and support the learning resources.
4. Add your new materials to the common pool (if required).
5. Select a format for sharing (a wiki, etc).

With these steps in mind it is easier to see how deploying digital educational resources through OCW/OER can reach a broad audience and impact many people around the world. By developing and deploying digital educational resources through OCW/OER a single scholar, or group of scholars, can provide the foundation for countless future learning environments. Through this open content movement anyone with an interest in the materials can freely access the works and make use of them in their own environments.

In the long-term OCW/OER have the potential to greatly impact education worldwide. Some of the projections in the literature see great hopes for what these resources can accomplish. Taylor (2007) projects that:

*...the OCW movement has the opportunity to expand its vision and operations to enable the OCW learners to have access to academic support, to have the opportunity to be assessed and to have the potential to gain credit towards recognized qualifications awarded by a credible accreditation agency (p. 3).*

More encompassing is the view forwarded by Duderstadt (2008), "Open source, open content, open learning, and other 'open' technologies become the scaffolding on which to build truly global universities..." (Duderstadt, 2008, p. 11). In 2009 Duderstadt went even further, forwarding the idea that the combination of OCW, emerging technologies, and other social and educational factors could, in the future, yield, "...the linking together of billions of people with limitless access to knowledge and learning tools enabled by a rapidly evolving scaffolding of cyberinfrastructure; which increases in power one-hundred to one-thousand-fold every decade" (p. 31).

OCW/OER is still too young a technology to predict where it will go or how long it will take to get there but it displays enormous potential. Its potential reach combined with the ease of use of the technology make OCW/OER potentially the biggest future force in digital education.

## SOCIAL NETWORKING AND EDUCATION

The rating website mostpopularwebsites.net regularly updates their list of the most popular websites. On Friday, July 15, 2011 Facebook was #2, YouTube #3 and Twitter #9. Google held the #1 position, but the important point is that three of the top ten positions were held by major social networking sites. Not only do these sites provide free opportunities for educators to post and disseminate information but they also have the valuable property of being places that students are already going.

As more and more information goes online the threat of overload is a very real one. For every new service requiring a login there is an increased likelihood that a user will forgo using some particular service as the total volume of sites to check and login credentials to remember becomes too much. With this in mind perhaps one of the best ways to engage student in digital educational content is to put that content in places where the students are, versus adding another location for them to review.

To begin, there is the question of what constitutes a social network. Boyd and Ellison (2007) identify social network sites as online services that allow users to do three specific things: "(1) construct a public or semi-public profile within a bounded system, (2) articulate a list of other users with whom they share a connection, and (3) view and traverse their list of connections and those made by others within the system" (p 2). While Facebook is nearly synonymous with the term social networking there are many other services that meet this standard. Any online service that provides users with the opportunity to create a profile and interact with others constitutes a social network application. Thus, content-based services like YouTube and Picasa can be social networks.

From the perspective of digital educational resource deployment YouTube, Picasa, Google Docs and similar services can be very valuable. There are certainly other services available but these are market leaders and are also accessible through a single sign-on via a Google account. Each service offers unique features but there are some core similarities.

All of these services offer multiple levels of security settings for who can view, comment on, and in some cases edit uploaded material. Material can be set to be viewable by invitation only or open for anyone on the Internet to access. This provides content creators with great flexibility for how broadly they want their material to be disseminated. Instructors can also build virtual communities with these settings, dividing content viewers among classes or discussion groups. The material posted in these environments can also be embedded in or directly linked from LMS environments or websites. Sharing the content in this way places the material on the site where learners are viewing other material but the burden for storage of the media remains on the Google servers, thus conserving individual or institutional resources.

As individual elements these different services each offer unique opportunities for digital resource sharing. YouTube is primarily for video files, Picasa for still images, and Google Docs for office documents such as word processing files, spreadsheets, and presentations. Some different possibilities for using each of these services will be explored.

Digital video sharing is the most obvious application of YouTube's availability. This is an important tool and YouTube materials can be embedded on web pages and used in other ways to make them as accessible as possible. There are more opportunities, however, than just posting video files. Many different types of materials can be converted to a video format and video formatted

files can be uploaded to YouTube. Many popular screen capture applications offer the option of rendering the final product as a video file. This gives instructors the opportunity to post a recorded lecture with accompanying presentation materials as a video file through YouTube. Technical tutorials and other types of material also fall into this category.

While YouTube is intended for video sharing it is possible to use the service as a sharing site for audio. All that is necessary is to record audio along with some type of image and save that combination as a single video file. This method can be seen in many of the music files that are uploaded to YouTube and can be adopted as a means for posting podcast audio to YouTube.

If still images are the media that needs to be shared Picasa can provide many of the same types of services as YouTube only for still instead of moving digital images. Groups can be set up, invitations can be sent, and Picasa images, albums, and slideshows can be embedded in other websites. For images that are uploaded to Picasa comments can be attached by the originator and comments from users can either be allowed or disallowed depending on the preference of the instructor. Although Picasa is primarily a photo sharing site any digital image can be uploaded and shared, so photos, maps, diagrams, or any other type of information captured as a still image can be effectively distributed through the service.

Google Docs provide a similar, but different opportunity for the sharing of digital media. Files uploaded to or created in Google Docs can be secured and shared online, made available for download, or, because they are documents instead of media works, they can be shared for collaborative editing. This provides a wide range of options to the media creator and can provide unique peer learning opportunities to participants.

There are also many opportunities to use more traditionally recognized social media such as Twitter and Facebook for sharing digital educational resources, and these may in fact be connected to work with other media sharing sites. Twitter has many fewer options with which to work than Facebook, but there are some unique advantages to working inside of a 140 character limit.

Twitter can be connected to a wide variety of outlets via RSS feeds, mobile apps, and other plug-ins in addition to its native web presence. This means that a Twitter feed dedicated to a particular subject can be present inside of an LMS, sent to invited participants, or open for anyone online to follow. The 140 character limit on posts forces users to be brief in their postings, which is an excellent format for quick updates or short descriptions of other items of interest.

If the post is used to direct readers to some other item of interest, most likely posted on another site, a URL can be included in the post allowing users to click on the post and move directly to the resource. This brings up an interesting challenge in the Twitter environment, that being how to post a meaningful description and a URL inside of 140 characters when so many URLs are so large. To optimize the limited space inside of a Twitter post a URL shortening service, such as the free TinyURL service, is very valuable. This allows a user to quickly and easily take a long URL and convert it to a much shorter link, which makes posting to Twitter and other sites much easier. As one simple example the author input a URL of 100 characters and TinyURL output a new URL of only 26 characters.

In addition to distributing information Twitter gives users an opportunity to pass along and refer to information. If a user finds a particular post interesting and wants to share the information they can post the information to their own feed via a retweet (RT). Users can also link to interesting feeds they reference in their own posts using the hash tag (#). These tools not only allow users to pass along and reference interesting materials but can provide the originators of material a helpful tool to reference and forward relevant information from related sources.

While Twitter can quickly direct users to interesting resources Facebook can be a multi-faceted home to many different resources while at the same time providing extensive interactive opportunities for users. A Facebook account dedicated to a particular cause or subject, most likely in the form of a group, can be used to organize users, create a forum for discussion, announcements, and communication, and also share many forms of digital media including photos, audio, and video. Links can be easily posted and Facebook can even be linked with Twitter to create a more integrated online presence. A twitter feed can be linked to Facebook status so that Twitter posts are automatically repeated in the Facebook environment.

Beyond these well-known Facebook capabilities there is also an opportunity to conduct synchronous meetings inside Facebook. Open-Meetings, mentioned earlier in connection to Moodle, is freely available as an app in Facebook. This provides users with all the features of a tele-conferencing system without any cost, without installing a client on their system, and without adding yet another logon to their list of sites. Like other features of social networking OpenMeetings can provide expanded opportunities by placing resources in an environment where students are already working.

Many other social networking sites exist, far more than can be covered in this discussion, but Facebook and Twitter are, at the time of this writing, the most dominant players in the market. Interestingly, during the writing of this chapter Google launched a test of a new social network, Google+. As the new Google service is still an invitation-only test service there is no way to know whether or not it will become an influential part of the social network market but it will be interesting to see how it develops in the future.

## SOLUTIONS AND RECOMMENDATIONS

Deployment of digital educational resources is too complex a topic to solve with just a single solution, but there are strategies that institutions can employ to help their products reach an audience. As is the case with any technology integration project the organization must first assess what it is that they need to accomplish and work from that point to develop an overall technology application strategy. The focus of the recommendations in this chapter is to develop a plan for strategic technology deployment.

From the business practice of management information systems (MIS) comes the perspective that an organization's strategy should drive the selection of technology, but the technology should not drive the strategy of the organization. This holds true for educational organizations as well as corporate interests. With this in mind, the first thing an organization needs to accomplish when preparing to deploy digital educational resources is to identify and clearly communicate their strategy. While this may seem to be a simple step for many organizations it is not.

Organizational strategy is not as clear as just stating that the purpose of the organization is to deliver educational materials. The groups targeted as consumers of the materials, the type of learning environment supported by the materials, and the form of the materials themselves all contribute to what an organization needs to do. Other factors, such as the levels of organizational resources, the abilities of available faculty and staff, and the demands of the learners also contribute to creating the overall deployment environment that will be served by the organizational strategy.

With an established strategy an organization can begin to move towards properly utilizing open source technologies for their resource deployment. First, matches between the materials to be deployed and compatible technologies can be identified. After possible technologies are identified for use they can be compared against the strategic needs of the organization. This will allow the organization to identify the best tools available to use in their particular situation.

Once the right set of tools has been identified the organization can then move towards implementation. At this stage materials are actually mated with technologies and then posted in a live environment. Very importantly, testing follows implementation. Any digital deployment of materials is a complicated process and has many different opportunities for problems. Before giving learners access to a system the providers need to be sure that the system will work properly. Following the testing process the systems, once repaired if necessary, can be released for use by the learners.

After deployment the process does not end. Evaluation and assessment of the system will continue for as long as it is in use. Whether content needs to updated, software versions change, compatibility issues arise with a new browser or new device, or some other aspect of the system's deployment changes there will be changes. Because of this a system cannot be left as a static environment. Continual assessment will be necessary to ensure that the system continues to serve the needs of the organization and of the learners.

These recommendations are broad but deliberately so. Because no two environments are exactly the same there can be no set formula for how to best use open source technologies for educational resource deployment. The overall approach to such activities, however, can be outlined and recommended for organizations to follow. By doing so, they will have a roadmap by which to pursue successful projects.

## FUTURE TRENDS

Open technologies are popular and growing. As more services move towards the cloud computing environment there are good opportunities for such technologies to find even bigger audiences.

Such movement may be accompanied by the global growth of online and distance education opportunities, fueled in no small part by the OCW/OER movement.

While there is no way to know with certainty what will happen in the future one can reasonably project continuing expansion of digital media content and connectivity. What these connections will look like may be one of the biggest changes that can be expected. Already computing is moving to more mobile devices and shifting the way that users of information access and use media.

This mobile shift is already visible in many of the world's emerging markets and growing economies. In order to bring connectivity to as many people as quickly as possible many of these markets skipped wired infrastructure and moved directly to wireless services for phone and data provision. This shift can be seen in leading economies as well, with more people of all ages, and particularly those in the younger generations, working more and more frequently on mobile devices.

In the future the trend of working on mobile devices will force a redesign of how media of all types, including digital educational resources, is delivered. Support for small screen interfaces, multiple operating systems, and a shift to mobile-focused apps from computer-centric software applications will all push new developments in delivery systems. What this means for educational providers is that media will have to be developed from its inception with a focus on mobile delivery. This will mean shifts in tools and shifts in philosophy for development.

Coupled with the shift in content delivery will be a trend towards more synchronous interchanges around the media. While asynchronous communications have long been a standard in much of the online educational environment mobile computing may shift this trend in the future. While asynchronous communications will likely remain a component of online learning environments the ubiquitous access provided through mobile devices will enable learners to be more active in live discussions. This will put digital educational resources in an arena of live exchange versus display and asynchronous posting.

Another trend that will impact digital educational resources in the future is the multinational expansion of digital information access. As education becomes more accessible there will be more cultures and more languages entering the discussion. Long-term technologies may develop that provide reasonably accurate, synchronous translation to enable learners from different languages to engage with the learning materials in a digital environment.

## CONCLUSION

Digital educational resources are a growing part of educational experiences today. In order to capitalize on the opportunities offered by such resources the right tools must be in place to reach learners. The goal of this chapter is to further the conversation about how to build and use a toolbox for digital educational resource deployment.

By exploring available free and open source technologies educational resource providers can find high quality alternatives to commercial services. This practice will not only allow dependable provision of resources to learners but also free financial resources for other investments. Overall, the entire educational environment can be improved through the proper application of free and open source technologies in digital media deployment.

# REFERENCES

Abelson, H. (2007). The creation of OpenCourse-Ware at MIT. *Journal of Science Education and Technology, 17*(2).

Aydin, C., & Tirkes, G. (2010). Open source learning management systems in e-learning and Moodle. *IEEE EDUCON Education Engineering 2010 – The Future of Global Learning Engineering Education* (pp. 593- 600).

Bessen, J. (2005). *Open source software: Free provision of a complex public good.* Retrieved July 22, 2011, from http://www.researchoninnovation.org/opensrc.pdf

Boyd, D., & Ellison, N. (2007). Social network sites: Definition, history, and scholarship. *Journal of Computer-Mediated Communication, 13*(11).

Bretthauer, D. (2002). Open source software: A history. *Information Technology and Libraries, 21*(1), 3–11.

Duderstadt, J. (2008). Higher education in the 21st century: Global imperatives, regional challenges, national responsibilities and emerging opportunities. In Weber, L. E., & Duderstadt, J. J. (Eds.), *The globalization of higher education.*

Duderstadt, J. (2009). *Current global trends in higher education and research: Their impact on Europe.* Speech presented at Universitat Wien, Vienna, Austria.

Edudemic. (2011). *Are you one of the 10 million people using MIT's OpenCourseWare?* Edudemic: Connecting Education & Technology. Retrieved January 20, 2011, from http://edudemic.com/2011/01/10-million-mit/.

Fitzgerald, B. (2006). The transformation of open source software. *Management Information Systems Quarterly, 30*(3), 587–598.

Hylen, J. (2005). *Open educational resources: Opportunities and challenges.* OECD-CERI. Retrieved December 17, 2010 from http://www.oecd.org/dataoecd/1/49/35733548.doc

Koohang, A., & Harman, K. (2007). Advancing sustainability of open educational resources. *Issues in Informing Science and Information Technology, 4*, 535–544.

Margulies, A.H. (2004). A new model for open sharing: Massachusetts Institute of Technology's OpenCourseWare initiative makes a difference. *PLoS Biology, 2*(8), 1071–1073. doi:10.1371/journal.pbio.0020200

OpenCourseWare Consortium. (2010). *What is OpenCourseWare?* Retrieved December 15, 2010 from: http://www.ocwconsortium.org/aboutus/whatisocw

Park, J. (2009). *Code of best practices in fair use for OpenCourseWare.* Creative Commons. Retrieved July 15, 2011, from https://creativecommons.org/weblog/entry/18550

Paudel, B., Harlalka, J., & Shrestha, J. (2010). Open technologies and developing economies. *Proceedings for the CAN IT Conference, 2010.*

Rennie, F., & Mason, R. (2010). Designing higher education courses using open educational resources. In Khine, M. S., & Saleh, I. M. (Eds.), *New science of learning: Cognition, computers and collaboration in education.* Springer. doi:10.1007/978-1-4419-5716-0_13

Sampson, B. (2008). *Open source LMS – 10 Alternatives to Moodle.* Retrieved July 6, 2011, from http://barrysampson.com/2009/04/open-source-lms-10-alternatives-to-moodle/

Taylor, J. (2007). OpenCourseWare futures: Creating a parallel universe. *E-Journal of Instructional Science and Technology, 10*(1). Retrieved 4/25/11 from: http://citeseerx.ist.psu.edu/viewdoc/download?doi=10.1.1.110.555&rep=rep1&type=pdf

Tong, T. (2004). *Free/open source software in education.* UNDP-APDIP 2004.

Wang, H., Blue, J., & Plourde, M. (2010). Community source software in higher education. *IT Professional, 12*(6), 31–37. doi:10.1109/MITP.2010.120

Whalen, T., & Wright, D. (1999). Methodology for cost-benefit analysis of web-based tele-learning: Case Study of the Bell Online Institute. *American Journal of Distance Education, 13*(1), 25–43. doi:10.1080/08923649909527012

## KEY TERMS AND DEFINITIONS

**Free and Open Source Software (FOSS):** Software applications available for use at no charge to the user.

**Open Educational Resources (OER):** "…digitised materials offered freely and openly for educators, students and self-learners to use and re-use for teaching, learning and research" (Hylen, 2005, p. 1).

**OpenCourseWare (OCW):** "…free and open digital publication of high quality university-level educational materials. These materials are organized as courses and often include course planning materials and evaluation tools as well as thematic content" (OCW Consortium, 2010).

# Chapter 8
# Building Open-Source Resources for Online Learning in a Higher Education Environment

**Shalin Hai-Jew**
*Kansas State University, USA*

## ABSTRACT

*Faculty, administrators, and staff at institutions of higher education are singularly well poised to create open-source digital learning contents. Creating open-source digital learning contents seems to fit with a university's mission and the education paradigm of sharing knowledge and training up others to move a domain field forward. Indeed, they have contributed to many open-source endeavors. While individual open-source development endeavors may require a relatively light investment by colleges and universities, the work of building open-source resources involves significant planning in order to support the endeavor in an organized way on a campus. This chapter introduces some of the known challenges and methods to building open-source resources for online learning in the higher education environment in the US.*

## INTRODUCTION

In a university environment, the faculty, administrators, and staff seem especially well-poised to create open-source resources for online learning. After all, many are working in the cutting-edge expressions of their respective fields; many are engaged in online learning with live learners, and most have some motivations in the higher education reward structure to create open-source learning contents (as part of their social contribution and publicity related to academic work—for tenure and reputation). And indeed, some faculty and staff have contributed to the open-source venues and distribution channels. Some universities have open-courseware endeavors to collect

DOI: 10.4018/978-1-4666-2205-0.ch008

faculty work; prepare the contents by removing proprietary video, images, and articles; and publish the curriculums in zipped format for open use. Repositories (digital collections) and referatories (collections of site links with metadata) host a variety of open-source learning objects. Many academic journals and electronic book (e-book) publications are hosted by open-source publishers (or hybrid commercial / open-source ones). Open-source encyclopedias offer direct access to various open-source digital goods. Video, slideshow, image, and other content-type sharing sites enable open-source content creators to share their creations.

Open-source licensing tools (so-called public and viral licenses) are used in search engines along with the substantive words of the search for released objects. Open-source contents are harnessed for massive open online courses (MOOCs) which involve a range of learners who share their co-learning with each other and take responsibility for their own and others' learning. Some faculty and staff host their own sites with open-source downloadable contents. Universities have released open-source learning / course management systems, repository software, open-source publishing software, game authoring tools, and a variety of apps.

The cost-benefit considerations for open-source are affected by a range of considerations. Universities often consider such publications positive for public relations. The acts of sharing contents with learners everywhere resonate well with new-generation learners because of their culture of Web 2.0 sharing and ideals (Oreg & Nov, 2008). For others, publishing broadly to benefit the world assuages some of the guilt of those who live and work in relatively wealthier countries; it's part of the new *noblesse oblige* where "privilege entails to responsibility". Leaders in work places may affect the workplace culture towards open-source sharing by tying material rewards to open-source content creation.

There may be purely selfish considerations for open-source publishing and distribution for many. Those who contribute open-source work *gratis* on the front end may benefit from heightened workplace credibility in terms of longer-term benefits. J. Lerner, P.A. Pathak, and J. Tirole (2006) note:

Economic theory suggests that long-term incentives are stronger under three conditions: 1) the more visible the performance to the relevant audience (peers, labor market, and venture capital community); 2) the higher the impact of effort on performance; 3) the more informative the performance about talent... (p. 114).

Strategic complementarities may mean that high performance in the open-source arena may translate to future job opportunities, constructive collaborations, and other positional goods in the work place like increased social status. Some are calling for contributions to open-source projects to be considered scholarly contributions that are listed in performance reviews (Hafer & Kirkpatrick, 2009). Publicity from such endeavors may also lead to positive chatter.

The nature of digital learning objects also militates against excessive protectionism. After all, all informational contents will date out. Various learning objects will be supplanted by those with more updated information or better designs or higher usability. In many cases, the usefulness of an information object is only for a time.

While traditionalist proprietary approaches emphasize protectionism of all intellectual property (IP), the truth is that not all IP has direct financial value. C. Anderson (2009) suggests that the economy itself has shifted with a new price on numerous goods: free. He carries the argument of how knowledge and experiential digital objects are essentially non-rivalous digital goods, with the major investment occurring only with the first object, and the virtually zero cost of replicability across multiple platforms and online spaces. Multiple uses by multiple individuals can be achieved without much in the way of cost. M.A.

Lemley (2004) suggests that free-riding is not an accurate term to describe the uses of others' digital contents in the sense that there are "positive externalities" to the larger society from such sharing, not negative ones. This feature of digital resources enables broad sharing without added incurred costs. In the ensuing decades after free and open software development became popular in the environment, this construct has made its way into higher education and found strong proponents. Another challenge involves the sense of a loss of control of the digital contents, but those who work in the field are aware of how easily contents may be downloaded and shared. The sense of traditional control over contents is illusory at best. In higher education, the acculturation into open-source continues through the present. Many in leadership positions are starting to make the business case for going open-source. There have been some high-profile grant-funded projects that have indicated interest in open-source approaches from government agencies as well as private and public foundations. (Note that "open-access" is not the same as "open-source." Open-access is about the findability and discoverability of relevant sources online, and these concerns relate to how learning objects are labeled with metadata and made machine-aware of their contents and locations.)

Learning objects that are created in an institution of higher education, based on university or college policies, may be owned by its creator (in the way that publications belong to faculty and staff). If these are created properly, they may have long-term open-source value. Some IP is co-owned between the developer and the university. These are often research discoveries that are discovered in university-owned or sponsored laboratories. Other types of research and development (R&D), which may be exploited for funding streams, will likely involve at least partial ownership interests by the university or college. There have been more commercial and non-profit open-source endeavors for the creation and distribution of open-source objects because of complementarities: consider the creation of free apps to run on hardware devices. Because the apps help sell the devices, companies that make and sell the devices encourage app development through grants and other incentives.

## The Adoption of Open-Source Contents

Adopting open-source contents from outside apparently involves fewer barriers. Many institutions of higher education today use open-source software and information as a matter-of-course. The learning curves for how to use such resources are low, and the work comes for faculty to learn how to integrate the resources in the teaching and learning and the technologists to integrate the new software or middleware. There will be other adjustments, too, in terms of how educators conceptualize information—because the created digital learning objects by others will likely be framed somewhat differently. Some open-source learning objects may come with assessments that may or may not fit a learning circumstance, and others may be without assessments. The formality or informality of the learning object may differ, or the tone of the contents may lack a fit to a learning situation.

Little exists in the educational research literature about programmatic adoptions of open-source resources in a wholesale way at institutions of higher learning in the West. Certainly, there may be risks in the adoption of open-source, such as software that may be unsustainable. Perhaps some open-source software products may have serious security flaws that may be exploitable because of the transparency (Rice, 2008; Hunt, Aiken, Fähndrich, Hawblitzel, Hodson, Larus, Levi, Steensgaard, Tarditi, & Wobber, 2007). One software products are one-offs instead of an ever-improving sequence of software products. The investments in training technologists to use various software programs will be an expense.

Even more hours are needed to develop individuals into effective software developers. There are opportunity costs for an organization to pursue open-source adoption. The expense is even higher to contribute.

Some content developers who contribute to the open-source community started out as consumers of the open-source goods. In the sharing culture of higher education, there is a need for individuals to give back. However, the free rider "collective action" hurdle (the phenomena of people using open-source but not contributing contents) is not a non-trivial one because it's often easier to use the work of others ' labors than to build one's own. In multiple studies of open-source communities, a few star contributors contribute the majority of the work, and the rest free-ride. A power law curve describes these communities of a few high-level contributors and then the steep exponential drop-off of contributors and the rest of the others acting as consumers. Such an imbalance in approach means that developers experience fatigue, and many average short but intense stints of development before dropping out. In one large-scale open-source software development project, developers only apparently average a lifespan of four months on-site.

Having a supportive community is important in open-source development. Social ties often help bring individuals into these communities, and such supports give them resilience in facing the challenges of development (often in semi-isolation, outside of workplace contexts).

It may be that an institution of higher education has to achieve a certain level of maturity and have some degree of excess capacity before being able to contribute to the open-source realm. The community itself has to have certain awareness (and the organizational absorptive capacity to integrate new thinking about innovations and open-sourcing of new developed learning objects) and fairly sophisticated skill sets to contribute in a community-sourced way. Nidy and Kwok (2005) proposed a more meritocratic and structured work approach than is typical in open-source projects for higher education participation in open software development in a higher education context.

There are multiple points-of-entry for an institution of higher education into open-source content creation. For most colleges and universities, they are already using open-source software, such as on their servers. They are likely using plenty of freeware and software apps on their desktop computers. Many instructors likely use open-source contents for their teaching. Within an institution of higher education, there are likely virtual communities with peer-to-peer sharing. Some faculty and staff may well have started experimenting with open-source content creation. One common point-of-entry here would be open-source academic publications. As colleagues use various open-source resources, word-of-mouth may be very compelling. Figure 1, "Various Points of Entry to Open-Source Content Creation" highlights this dynamic.

Getting to the point of considering creating open-source contents is only a first step. After the initial expression of interest, there are some steps to take to actualize the work of creating open-source contents. The following section addresses the substructure dependencies that are required to actualize the work.

## Establishing Need for the Resource

Early work involves an environmental scan to see what open-source contents already exist in the particular domain field. Some domain fields already have some fairly comprehensive collections of open-source resources. Many others maybe have an occasional digital learning object, and still others have none at all. In a sense, there is the first-mover advantage for digital content creators to share works early on because they are able to define the field. On the other hand, first-movers may easily be trumped by second- and third-movers who trump the earlier contents with improved contents, usability interfaces, and

*Figure 1. Various points of entry to open-source content creation*

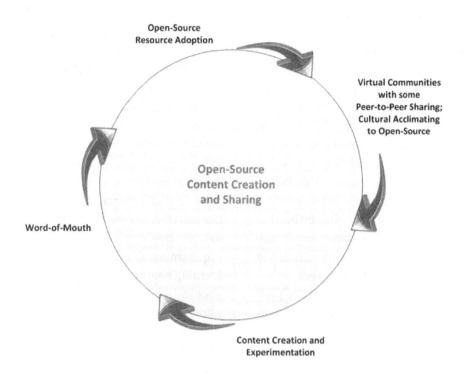

other aspects. Digital content creators generally aim to make their site the destination site for a particular resource. The crowd-sourcing of the Internet users will determine the amount of play that a particular resource gets. Works that do not gain a following will merely reside on the Internet and maybe be used as part of The Long Tail that C. Anderson described, in terms of being in the realm of niche users.

Another aspect of the environmental scan must analyze the potential public need for the particular resource. In other words, who are the potential users of the particular resource? If there is no demand-pull for the digital information or learning experience, then the item may be created, but there will likely be limitations to the supply-push demand created by the mere existence of a digital learning resource. Basic research into the technological adoption model has shown that there has to be a lot of work reaching out to a potential population of users in order to convert individuals

into technology users and to get an installed base to uphold usage of the open-source resources. Once it is clear who the potential users may be, it will be important to conduct some market research to fine-tune the sense of what users want and how to tailor contents that would appeal to them.

## An Enabling Workplace Substructure

For a university or college to begin being able to create open-source contents, it is important that the faculty and staff not only have the initial inspiration and will to follow-through. Some authors suggest that the adoption of open-source may enhance the acceptance and adoption of change (what they term "raging incrementalism") (Georgas, Gorlick, & Taylor, 2005). They need to see the business case for pursuing open-source as both a consumer and a developer. They also need a talented set of individuals on the campus willing to work as part of the development team.

This team will need access to the often-expensive equipment, software, and other resources to create the digital learning objects. They will need fairly sophisticated training in pedagogical design. They will need the political cover to pursue the open-source work. They will need legal cover to release the digital learning objects into the open environment. Intellectual property (IP) policies at campuses may claim some shared rights to some intellectual property, particularly for works that have potential financial implications. All members of a development team (and those they videotape) will need clarity about what rights they own, what they don't own, and what going "open-source" may mean. These understandings have to be codified in the contracts that accompany the work.

To motivate employees, a percentage of their job descriptions may involve working on open-source projects. It may be that in creating digital learning objects, subject matter experts (SMEs) and instructional designers (IDs) will version a part of the work for open-source usage. B. Xu and D. R. Jones (2010) point out the importance of volunteer participation in open-source projects based on social identification with a group, a sense of obligation to contribute, and a sense of cognitive and affective trust with those involved with the group, and shared goals (based on the similarity-attraction paradigm).

The production environments for such digital learning objects may vary from those of non-academia-based open-source developers who are using shared online workspaces to coordinate and share the work. In higher education, the open-source development of learning objects and code may well be in various types of distributed virtual environments, such as the desktop spaces and server spaces of respective employees. Or they may be individual and private laptops that content developers use for their open-source development work. The nature of the production environments may affect the quality of the work and the limits of collaborative interactivity. There are some shared work spaces and repositories for open-source development of educational contents (Meneely, Williams, & Gehringer, 2008), but how widely these are used is in question.

## Building to Established Standards

Open-source digital learning objects have to meet established standards in order to be relevant and usable. Informationally, they need to be accurate to the domain field in terms of established knowledge. They have to be labeled with correct metadata that is human and machine readable. The contents have to be legally and cleanly acquired, and contents have to meet the intellectual property requirements of the various contexts in which the learning contexts will be deployed. Such objects should also be widely accessible—with images alt-texted, videos transcribed, and live events live-captioned. To have learning value, the learning objects must follow applicable pedagogical theories and applications; some may adhere to certain well-known models like the Cisco Systems Reusable Learning Object model. In terms of pedagogical values, it is critical to create learning objects that are dynamic, creative, complex, and serendipitous; currently, much of what is being built is static and non-engaging. These objects have to be built in technologically sophisticated ways, so that they are able to be stored, played, sequenced, tracked, and used on a variety of socio-technical systems. Standards bodies that define various criteria for digital artifacts are continually evolving their guidelines, and it's critical that those who would create such learning objects stay atop the standards.

The design and development teams would also do well to maintain tight in-house standards, such as keeping records of the development work and the raw files—because the records may be used to show the evolution and original ownership of the objects, and the raw files may be re-usable in other contexts. Most work places have in-house workplace policies for the work; they have methods for decision-making and sign-offs. Creating such processes and procedures may be helpful to a workplace that is co-creating open-source digital learning objects.

Once a digital learning object has gone through thorough in-house vetting (alpha testing) from the academic department, the college, and the university, it may go through a level of public user testing (beta-testing), and then it may be ready for prime time? For open-source self-publishing, a work may be uploaded at any time. However, a majority of open-source repositories and referatories are gated, with editorial gatekeepers who offer peer review. Many are curated spaces, with invited works and all others subjected to a kind of blind (or non-blind) reviews.

Just because a work has been accepted into an open-source repository or referatory does not mean that the digital learning object has achieved its final state. Many open-source contents are editable, so the contents may be integrated culturally, linguistically, pedagogically, or put into different contexts. Ideally, digital learning objects should be "stateless" in terms of the cultural context, so they can be reformulated for uses in a variety of settings. Some objects may be versioned to K-12. Others may be versioned to targeted learners from different cultures or language backgrounds, for example.

Some open-source developers will use legal and digital rights management (DRM) means to lock-down learning objects that have particularly sensitive contents that they think may be misapplied if used in other contexts. It is important for the development team to decide the nuances of the open-source release for all contents.

Open-source digital learning objects are in competition with other objects to define particular chunks of learning. Browsers and search engines show clearly which works are dominant in terms of being end-destinations for those who would like to study particular subject matter. The drop-off rate of use is exponential after the top few sites have been explored. The wisdom of the crowds suggests that the larger public will make a judg-

ment call on materials that are available in the public domain. Indeed, the survival and usage of open-source digital learning objects depends on the user base in a symbiotic relationship. Users also provide information to content developers: they serve as testers, and their feedback is critical to improving the current and future work. Learning objects should evolve and enhance over time, and user feedback in participatory design may be one way of connecting with the user base. Self-publishing may mean easy access for content creators, but that does not guarantee any wider usage or click-throughs.

Universities and colleges may find commercial and non-profit entities with whom they may partner for the creation of open-source learning. The efficiencies of online learning have brought many government entities, companies, and organizations to practice online learning—and many have curriculums which may be created for multi-uses. For faculty, working with colleagues from other fields may be beneficial not only for their own professional development but may help link academia with other realms of professional learning.

Finally, open-source projects require sufficient documentation to ensure content quality and clearer understandings of those inheriting the code (Dagenals & Robillard, 2010). Such documentation may also create a sense of institutional memory.

## Learning from Experience

K. Vignare and G.H. Shelle described how their university (Michigan State University) moved to develop open educational programs in a comprehensive and methodical way. The administrators evaluated the institutional capacity for taking open-source development of contents on with the existing staff and with funding by various grant-funding agencies. The university created pilot projects in open-source development to consciously learn from their efforts. They worked with a variety of researchers from various fields and provided support so these subject matter experts (SMEs) could develop, license, publish, and distribute their open-source contents. In this presentation, they explained that the development process involved three basic steps: content development, licensure of the content, and the publishing and distribution of the content. The SMEs that they worked with hailed from all over the world, so they worked on efficient technological ways to achieve effective video lecture captures. The staff shared media release forms to ensure that they were following the privacy laws in the various locales. To avoid copyright challenges, they replaced third-party, copyrighted objects with similar ones that were open-source, or they recreated the object themselves with unique expressions but the same essential learning meaning as the former object. If there was something that the SMEs found critical to use, the de3velopment team would remove the copyrighted object and annotate the work for the informational value. They strove to include the accurate metadata to represent the open-source contents.

They worked with their IT department to set up the necessary databases and other structures to host their contents. Technologically, they strove to create interoperable, interchangeable, and portable digital learning contents. They worked to make sure that the open-source resources were findable and discoverable, so that they would be used. They made sure that staff members on campus were supported in their search for open educational resources.

They aligned with partners globally to ensure an installed virtual adopter community / user base for their open-source digital learning objects and learning programs. This would ensure feedback loops for open-source content improvements over time and longer-term sustainability. This user base would also provide the populations from which other creators, content remixers, and instructors would add innovations to the open-source contents. These two presenters suggested that the field would benefit from more uniform practices in open-source content development and efforts to make digital contents more findable. They observed that novices and experts have varied experiences in terms of finding digital learning contents, and improved systems procedures would help close that gap.

Vignare and Shelle suggested that the ability to share is fundamental to education, and open-source endeavors are about building on ideas and sharing—not giving them away. They exhorted: "Be generous." That said, the team apparently use a license that disallows derivative works to protect the integrity of the information.

Finally, Vignare and Shelle emphasized the importance of justifying the value of open-source contents to administrators. This meant using objective metrics to show the usage of the learning objects that were created. Grant funders needed similar metrics. Their university apparently also collaborated successfully with corporations on open-source learning curriculums built to particular standards for training global employees.

## Maintaining an Audience of Adopter Communities

Building to a much wider potential audience than closed classrooms and more proprietary spaces offers a much different context. Having a diverse public audience means that learners will come at a work with highly variant backgrounds, and it would be important to help learners know what is necessary in terms of antecedent knowledge. While some responses to works may be muted, other works may trigger broad and surprising responses. (Some universities that promote open-source publication protect their faculty subject matter experts from being contacted about the open-source materials they're sharing, in order to protect their work days.)

## SOLUTIONS AND RECOMMENDATIONS

Public universities and colleges are beholden to many: tax payers, the larger publics, the learners, and future generations. They are governed by objectives, and they have to justify all expenditures. They also need to use their restricted resources in careful ways. To decide whether a school should pursue open-source development of contents, it will be important to analyze possible risks and benefits to going open-source (see Table 1). Are there gains for the university in terms of professional development for the employees? Are there efforts with side effects that may result in open-source learning objects? Are there ways to streamline work to take align with what is already being done?

## Measuring Impact and Return on Investment (ROI)

Institutions of higher education have to use their resources with care. Budgets are tight, and the needs are many for a campus's instructors, researchers, and students. This means that any open-source endeavors have to show clear return on investment (ROI). While the hope is that open-source endeavors will enhance university reputations and brand identities in public and electronic spaces, these varied returns on investment have to be observable and measureable to aid the administrative decision-makers. The respect for peers and peer production in higher education may ease the adoption of open-source digital learning objects. Another way of measuring return on investment involves the improving talent sets of the

*Table 1. Risks and benefits of adopting open-source development of contents*

| Category of Investment | Risks | Benefits |
|---|---|---|
| **Human Resources**<br>Staff time<br>Administrative time | Star faculty reputation<br>Staff reputation<br>Political strife<br>Cultural dissonances<br>Protectionism<br>The idealisms of the age | University reputation<br>Star faculty<br>Staff reputation<br>Professional development<br>Publications for the faculty and staff<br>Opportunities for professional networking and collaborations around digital learning objects<br>Easier collaboration with colleagues<br>Sunk costs for similar work already |
| **Technological Substructure**<br>Technology and equipment<br>Platforms for learning object delivery | Cooption of digital contents | Free platforms<br>Built communities of users<br>Wider dissemination of contents<br>Increased faculty brand and name recognition |
| **Marketing and Public Relations**<br>Attracting positive attention<br>Driving traffic<br>Analytics | Unclear information channels<br>Lack of clarity about measures | Positive public relations<br>Positive impressions |
| **Quality Contributions**<br>Quality standards in technology<br>Quality standards in information<br>Quality standards in domain practices<br>Quality standards in legal requirements (IP and accessibility)<br>Quality standards in pedagogical approaches | Poor quality<br>Rush to publication<br>Usurpation of digital rights<br>Uses of materials by competitors who can out-maneuver the originating university or college<br>Challenges of content "clearing" | Peer review<br>Peer review experiences<br>Improved in-house practices<br>De facto release<br>Appeal to public |
| **Pedagogical Value**<br>Learning value | Revision and editing ("modding") to different standards than the original developing team<br>Usurpation for unintended purposes | A wider range of technological usage |

individuals in the institution who have acquired new skills and enhanced public work reputations with their open-source work. The openness of the processes along with the open-sourced resources provides many opportunities for learning by reverse engineering (indirectly) and by design and development (directly).

## Drivers Toward Open-Source in Higher Education

Various drivers are pushing this turn towards open-source. Economic drivers include the fast diminishing funding of public universities and colleges by various states and the need to fend for the institution through grants, alumni, and other funding streams. The severe financial pressures do not look like they will diminish anytime soon, and the costs of developing open-source contents are not minor. Culturally, many of the traditional aged college students and their peers have grown up with a globalist world view. The concepts and practices of open-source resonate with them. Further, the connectivity and affordances of the Internet and WWW enable distributed collaboration, design, and development—as well as the distribution of the spoils of this co-labor. And further, administrators, faculty, and staff have a shared interest in open-courseware and open-source digital learning objects. Lastly, publishing in open-source venues raises the institution of higher education's profile and enhances public relations. For schools that want to win market share in a particular work area, they can benefit from a first-mover advantage by posting solid digital learning objects or sequences of learning in certain niche domain fields. C. Bonk (2011) suggests that much of the world's knowledge may be covered with about 20 dominant websites per knowledge domain, and the competitive advantage in being at the top of the various search engines is clear. For the subject matter experts and content developers, this is a potentially positive situation.

## FUTURE RESEARCH DIRECTIONS

Very little research exists about open-source and community-source development in higher education in the educational literature. As more universities, programs, and individuals take part, their experiences may help inform others about ways to enhance the work.

It will also help to know what the competitive environment is like for the creation of digital learning objects (DLOs) in an open-source and community-sourced context as compared to the commercial proprietary content development firms.

In terms of research, it will help to continue researching how open-source communities develop and evolve, particularly in a higher education context. It will help to know how this work may be incentivized, and further, how to bring new content developers into the fold.

Other strategies for creating program-level endeavors in open-source content development may enhance practices in this realm. Research into the design, development, and maintenance of the socio-technical spaces that enhance such collaborations would enhance this work as well.

Mixed organizational endeavors would provide other channels for research—particularly public-private partnerships in open-source content development.

## CONCLUSION

Open-source has played a role in higher education for the past decade. It has resulted in some very usable resources for the development of online learning. The open-source ethos is very much a part of the younger generations. Whether higher education fully adopts open-source will depend on practitioners today and their attitudes towards sharing their work openly with others. It will also depend on the decisions of administrators as they peruse the open-source landscape and decide whether they want to take part, and if so how and where. Certain institutions of higher education may be able to carve out specialist niches for the development of certain contents.

## REFERENCES

Anderson, C. (2009). *Free: The future of a radical price*. New York, NY: HarperCollins.

Bonk, C. (2011, September 28). *Stretching the edges of technology-enhanced teaching: From tinkering to tottering to totally extreme learning*. The 6th Annual Axio Learning Community Conference: Innovations in Education & Technology Conference 2011. Kansas State University.

Dagenais, B., & Robillard, M. P. (2010). Creating and evolving developer documentation: Understanding the decisions of open source contributors. In the *Proceedings of FSE – 18*, Santa Fe, New Mexico (pp. 127 – 136).

Georgas, J. C., Gorlick, M. M., & Taylor, R. N. (2005). Raging incrementalism: Harnessing change with open-source software. *Proceedings of the Fifth Workshop on Open Source Application Spaces*, (pp. 1–6).

Hafer, L., & Kirkpatrick, A. E. (2009). Assessing open source software as a scholarly contribution. *Communications of the ACM, 52*(12), 126–129. doi:10.1145/1610252.1610285

Hunt, G., Aiken, M., Fähndrich, M., Hawblitzel, C., Hodson, O., & Larus, J. … Wobber, T. (2007). Sealing OS processes to improve dependability and safety. *EuroSys '07,* Lisbon, Portugal, (pp. 341–354).

Lemley, M. A. (2004). *Property, intellectual property, and free riding*. Social Science Research Network Electronic Paper Collection Working Paper No. 291. Retrieved from http://ssrn.com/abstract=582602

Lerner, J., Pathak, P. A., & Tirole, J. (2006). The dynamics of open-source contributors. *The Roots of Innovation, 96*(2), 114–118.

Meneely, A., Williams, L., & Gehringer, E. F. (2008). ROSE: A repository of education-friendly open-source projects. In the *Proceedings of ITiCSE '08*, (pp. 7 – 11). Madrid, Spain: ACM.

Nidy, D. R., & Kwok, F. (2005). Community source development: An emerging model with new opportunities. In the *Proceedings of CHI 2005,* (pp. 1697 – 1700). Portland, OR: ACM.

Oreg, S., & Nov, O. (2008). Exploring motivations for contributing to open source initiatives: The roles of contribution context and personal values. *Computers in Human Behavior, 24*, 2055–2073. doi:10.1016/j.chb.2007.09.007

Rice, D. (2008). *Geekonomics: The real cost of insecure software*. Boston, MA: Pearson Education.

Vignare, K., & Shelle, G. H. (2011, July 11). *Developing open educational programs: Moving beyond the course approach*. (Pre-conference). 4th Annual International Symposium: Emerging Technologies for Online Learning: San Jose, California. Sloan Consortium and MERLOT.

Xu, B., & Jones, D. R. (2010). Volunteers' participation in open source software development: A study from the social-relational perspective. *The Data Base for Advances in Information Systems, 41*(3), 69–84. doi:10.1145/1851175.1851180

## KEY TERMS AND DEFINITIONS

**Attribution:** The act of giving credit for a work; citing as the originator.

**Creative Commons Licensure:** An open-source licensure protocol that releases certain rights to users on multiple levels—in a machine-readable, legal, and human-understandable way.

**Derivative:** Derived or originating from another entity or object.

**Distribution:** The dissemination of objects to recipients.

**Installed Base:** The number of people using a particular technology.

**Metadata:** Information about information.

**Non-Commercial:** Not for profit; not engaged in commerce.

**Open-Source:** A description of software that is available for free with code that is public and able to be copied, modified, and distributed.

**Proprietary:** Legally protected and controlled as intellectual property.

**Referatory:** A publishing repository which points to links of various resources on the Internet.

**Remix:** The release to recombine elements of a digital object.

**Repository:** A database of digital artifacts.

**Template:** A pattern; a defined format.

## APPENDIX

## SOFTCHALK CLOUD REPOSITORY Q&A

## Interviewee Sue Polyson Evans, CEO and Co-Founder of SoftChalk, LLC

## What is The Softchalk Cloud Repository?

SoftChalk Cloud is an e-learning content authoring platform, where educators can easily create, manage and share rich and engaging online learning content. One aspect of the platform is a free, public, Open Education Resource (OER) repository where educator/authors can share learning content that is licensed under a creative commons license (refer to Figure 2).

The SoftChalk Cloud public repository content is created and contributed by the SoftChalk community of users. The SoftChalk content varies in its complexity and may be a single interactive learning activity, or a group of related quiz questions, or a multi-page web lesson, or an entire eCourse (comprised of a group of web lessons delivered as a larger content unit). The public repository content, which includes several thousand content items and is growing daily, covers a wide range of subject areas and academic levels.

The repository provides a search tool so that site users can search based on keyword, subject category, education level, or content type. So, for example, it is possible to search for the keyword "linguist" in the subject category of "Humanities", with education level "Undergraduate", and content type of "Lessons and Courses". The site also offers easy access to "Recently Shared" content and "Highest Rated" content.

All of the content that is shared in the free, OER repository was created using the SoftChalk authoring products (which are licensed and generally available for a fee). However, the freely available repository

*Figure 2. SoftChalk Cloud home page*

content can be used by anyone by simply linking to the permalink url associated with each content item, or by using the provided "embed" code to embed the content into a web page. SoftChalk licensed products are not needed to obtain or use the links and embed codes. A good analogy that is familiar to many is YouTube. Just as anyone can go to the YouTube site and view, link to, or embed YouTube videos, so can anyone go to the SoftChalk Cloud site and view, link to, or embed SoftChalk OER learning content. So to see how the SoftChalk Cloud repository works, imagine YouTube, but instead of video content, envision learning content that could be a web lesson, an interactive crossword puzzle, a sorting activity, a group of quiz questions, or an entire eCourse.

To contribute content to the SoftChalk Cloud site, one must purchase a subscription-based account on the site. SoftChalk Cloud subscribers have the added ability to make copies of OER-shared content in order to modify or repurpose it for their own use based on Creative Commons licensing. Subscribers may also download content from the repository for re-use on their own web site or in a learning management system. There are other benefits to the subscription-based account which include the ability to create and host private, (non-public) learning content, and to track student score result data for that content.

## How Does this Repository Work?

Anyone can access and search the repository, by simply pointing their web browser to softchalkcloud.com. All content found on the public site is, by default, licensed for use under a creative commons "by" license – which means that the content author is allowing others to freely copy, distribute and transmit the work, or to remix the work as long as attribution is given to the original author of the work. (Note that the author can provide limits to re-using their content by choosing other Creative Commons licensing.)

When a SoftChalk Cloud visitor finds a content item of interest, they simply click on that item to see a "preview" of the item. Scrolling down the page, they will also see a "Hyperlink (Permalink)" and the "Embed" code for the item. The Permalink means that even if that content item is updated by its author, the content link is permanent and will not change. The Permalink works just like a standard web page hyperlink – it can be emailed to others, or can be linked to from any other web page. The "Embed" code allows others to actually place the SoftChalk Cloud content inside of another webpage.

Contributors to the site must create an account on SoftChalk Cloud. Accounts are subscription-based for a fee, although there is a 30-day free trial available. Once logged into the site, SoftChalk Cloud users will find services that allow them to create new content, and modify existing content. Subscribers may search the repository, find an item of interest, and then copy that item to their own personal area. The copied content may then be used as-is, or opened in the SoftChalk authoring tools and modified and mashed-up into a new content item.

SoftChalk content is designed to be very modular, so that individual content elements can be used by themselves, or combined with other content elements to form more complex learning content.

When SoftChalk Cloud subscribers create content, they can specify whether the content item is public or "personal". Content that is made public is automatically assigned the Creative Commons "by" license. Content that is kept "personal" is not shared in the public repository and is not automatically assigned a Creative Commons license. Access to "personal" content is limited to those with whom the content owner shares the access url. In addition, the content owner may establish authentication rules for access to their personal content. So, for example, it is possible to require entry of a password, or username and password prior to gaining access to a particular content item.

## What Items Does the SoftChalk Cloud Repository Contain?

SoftChalk content is, by design, very modular. This means it is easy to take individual SoftChalk content items and "mash" them together, as well as "take them apart". It is easy to create and re-use individual learning components which can be used in combination or standalone. The SoftChalk Cloud repository contains individual learning activities, groups of quiz questions, multi-page web-lessons, and eCourses (comprised of a group of web lessons). SoftChalk supports the creation of all the standard quiz question types (true/false, multiple, choice, multiple answer, short answer, essay, etc.) SoftChalk also supports the creation of 22 different interactives – including HotSpot Image Quizzes, Crossword Puzzles, Jigsaw Puzzles, Drag and Drop Image Labeling, Interactive Timeline, Flash Cards, etc. Figures 3, 4, and 5 show a few examples of SoftChalk content created with *SoftChalk Create* and found in *SoftChalk Cloud*.

The SoftChalk interactives and quiz questions can be combined with text, images, media (video, and audio) and web widgets to create multi-page web lessons of endless variety. SoftChalk Cloud can also include digital content of essentially any type (e.g., text, video, sound, image, PowerPoint, PDF) (refer to Figure 6).

*Figure 3. Sorting activity - One of over twenty Interactives available with SoftChalk (drag image to appropriate state box)*

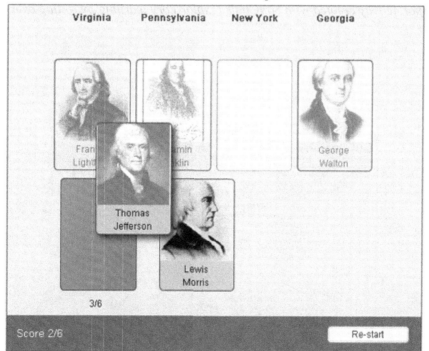

*Figure 4. First page of a SoftChalk created lesson(rollover of text shows textpopper feature)*

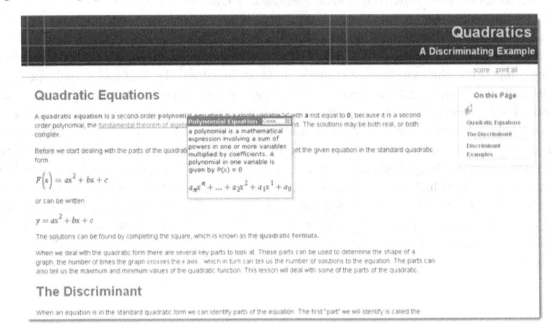

*Figure 5. Hot Spot Activity created with SoftChalk (exploratory learning by rolling over image)*

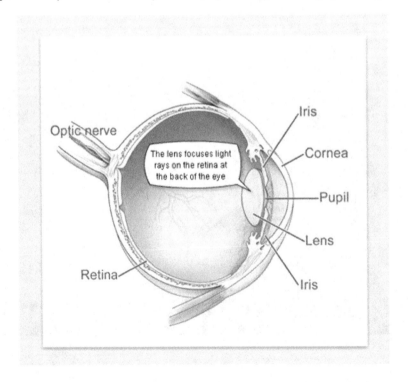

*Figure 6. SoftChalk Create (the authoring tool – showing the development of a math lesson)*

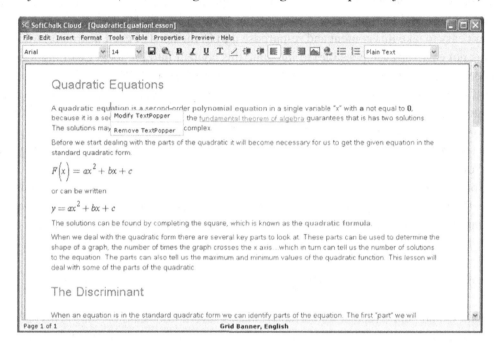

## What Was the Thinking behind the Creation of this Repository?

The SoftChalk Cloud repository serves several objectives. Primarily it was intended to be a large digital repository with quality OER material that could be shared by the SoftChalk and global education communities. New SoftChalk users are often looking for examples of what can be done with the SoftChalk software. We felt that there were no better examples than the actual content developed by SoftChalk educators. Consequently, one of the best uses of the site is as a "getting started" resource for new SoftChalk users – to give them great examples and ideas for the kind of content they can create. Because the content on the site is of such high quality, often educators are able to find content elements that they can repurpose or use as is. SoftChalk is all about making it easy for educators – so providing a way that each educator doesn't have to "reinvent the wheel" is also a purpose for the repository. Lastly, we wanted a way to draw others to our products – there is no better advertisement for SoftChalk than the rich repository of content developed by educators. And those who visit the repository can easily sign up for and try the 30-day free trial of SoftChalk Cloud, which allows them to try their hand at creating content for themselves. Any content they create during the free-trial period can be shared in the repository, or saved locally for reuse on their own website, or in their own learning management system.

## How Does your Company Envision the Usage of this Repository in K-12 and Higher Education?

Much of the content being delivered in today's online learning classrooms may be digital, but it is neither "rich" or engaging. It often lacks interactivity, rich media, and sound instructional design. Educators, who are always pressed for time, need better and easier ways to create, organize, manage and reuse their learning content. Today's students are demanding more interactive and engaging content, while studies are demonstrating that students engaged with content results in better learning outcomes. And while it may be possible to find learning resources available from a variety of online content repositories, it typically isn't easy to take this content and re-purpose it to fit the need of each instructor. Additionally, it typically it is not easy (or even possible) to integrate this content into the local Learning Management System (LMS) or track student score result data related into the local LMS.

The SoftChalk Cloud repository and platform provide an easy solution to address these critical issues. Educators can find content in the repository to use as is, or take their own copy of the content to repurpose for their specific needs. The SoftChalk Cloud platform also provides the ability to package or link that content into the LMS so that student score results can be tracked either into the LMS gradebook, or into the SoftChalk Cloud ScoreCenter.

It is also possible to establish an branded instance of the SoftChalk Cloud for an individual institution. In this case, the institution can create their own private repository for use among its member schools. Or an institution can create a repository that can share content similar to the way that the SoftChalk Cloud repository works.

## In Terms of the Adoption of this Repository, What Have you Seen so far?

The SoftChalk Cloud public repository currently houses several thousand content items submitted by members of the global SoftChalk user community. The site currently also has several thousand member accounts, and is growing daily.

## What Are Incentives for those who Participate in this Repository?

SoftChalk Cloud provides unlimited "free" hosting space for all content that is made available in the public repository by content developers. Visitors to the site may search the site and then "use" the content by obtaining the link or embed code for any content item. This access if provided at no charge, and no SoftChalk Cloud account, or SoftChalk purchase is required for this level of usage. A 30-day free trial of the full SoftChalk Cloud platform is also available, and during the free-trial period.

An additional incentive is our annual Lesson Challenge competition. SoftChalk provides cash awards for the best lessons and eCourses developed by our clients. The content is juried by a panel of external-educators (often past Lesson Challenge winners) and the winning content is available on our websites.

## How Are you Working to Create a Community of Developers around this Repository?

The SoftChalk Cloud repository includes a variety of community-building features. For example, each Cloud member can upload a photo, and maintain a profile on the site. Additionally, each public repository content item can be "rated" using a star rating system, and comments can be posted. This enables educators to share information with the community about their "favorites" on the site and to ask question or share comments about how they intend to use the learning content on the site. In addition, and perhaps more importantly, SoftChalk subscribers can collaboratively edit and build SoftChalk content via the SoftChalk Cloud!

SoftChalk's global community includes clients from both English and non-English speaking countries. We will continue to build, through these international clients, content in the many foreign languages that SoftChalk enables.

## Do you Have Non-Profit Partners in this Endeavor?

SoftChalk is a partner with MERLOT, a leading OER repository, as well as a member of the IMS Global Learning Consortium, a standards body focused on making learning objects interoperable. SoftChalk's Media Search Tool includes several OER communities such as the Orange Grove, National Science Digital Library, Wikipedia, Connexions, IntraLibrary, College Open Textbooks, Equella and others. These relationships are part of our mission to make it easy for educators to search for, find, and integrate rich media into content they create with SoftChalk's authoring tool.

## Is it Difficult to Encourage the Uses of the Creative Commons License Release on these Various Learning Objects? How Protective of their Work Are Content Developers?

Content that is made "public" in SoftChalk Cloud is, by default, assigned a Creative Commons license. Thus, all content found in the SoftChalk Cloud repository is licensed such that it can be copied, and derivatives made. If a SoftChalk Cloud user does not wish to share their content under the Creative Commons license, they may keep that content "personal" and thus they retain more control over who has access to the content and for what purpose (to view, to modify, to copy, etc.) "Personal" content is not made available to the community-at-large via the repository. To date about half the content in SoftChalk Cloud is public and available through Creative Commons licensing.

## How Publicly Available is this Resource?

Content in SoftChalk Cloud is fully free to use, although a subscription account is required to contribute content. Visitors may search and view content in the repository by visiting www.softchalkcloud.com. All those interested in creating or contributing content may register for a the 30-day free trial account for full access to the features of SoftChalk Cloud.

## You Partner with Non-Profit Repositories like the Multimedia Educational Resource for Learning and Online Teaching (MERLOT). What Are Some of the Benefits of Such Alliances? Do you View Each Other as Competitors? Or do you All Tend to be Fairly Collegial?

SoftChalk maintains a number of partnering relationships, MERLOT among them. SoftChalk is being used at a number of the large MERLOT institutions such as the California State University, the Tennessee system, and others. Although MERLOT does offer a simple content building application and a repository of information about open content, the value proposition and market for that product is such that there is no sense of competition. Rather, MERLOT and SoftChalk see each other as partners, making investments in the broadest availability of educational materials. For SoftChalk subscribers that wish to publish their content to MERLOT, they can simultaneously publish to MERLOT and to SoftChalk Cloud; this is especially important since MERLOT Is a referatory and requires an external web presence for content published to it

## What Are Some of the Most Popular Learning Objects in your Repository? Why do you Think they Are so Popular?

SoftChalk Cloud has a voluntary rating system by which all content can be rated by members of the SoftChalk Cloud community. There is a wide variety of content in the Cloud repository and the ratings usually show a diverse set of "winners". The winners recently have been a combination of SoftChalk created lesson, eCourses and individual learning activities. They range from history (WW II), to language studies (spelling), to math sorting activities.

## How do you Control for Educational Quality in Terms of the Digital Learning Objects?

SoftChalk does not monitor or control the educational quality of the content contributed to the Cloud repository. The community, itself, has some ability to monitor the content. For example, inappropriate content can be flagged by any site visitor. Content that is flagged as inappropriate is then evaluated by SoftChalk staff. In the event that there are issues with a content item, SoftChalk staff may contact the owner to address issues, or remove the content if necessary.

## What do you See as the Role of Open-Source in Online Learning?

Open Source can mean a few different things. For those focused on affordability, open source means the opportunity to use educational materials at no cost. For those focused on choice, open source has broadened the range of market participants by removing the need to handle commerce transactions. Open source leadership from elite organizations such as MIT has made contributing material less risky and more of an acceptable strategy for others. For those focused on community, open source has developed a model and best practices to put the structures in place for collaboration. The SoftChalk Cloud repository and content authoring platform is positioned to help support all of these efforts – by providing access to free educational resource content; by making it easy for educators to create high quality eLearning content that can supplement and/or replace commercial content; and by supporting the development of a community for developing and sharing content.

## How do you See this Repository Evolving in the Future?

SoftChalk hopes to see the steady contribution rate continue for SoftChalk Cloud. Future enhancements will be targeted to community-building. So, for example, a future enhancement we are considering is the ability to "follow" a SoftChalk Cloud contributor. That way, if you like the content developed by a particular contributor, you can easily track when that content is revised or when additional content is contributed by that developer.

## Why is the "Cloud" the Way to go?

Because the SoftChalk repository is built in the "cloud", this means that users can access from home, the office, or on-the-road. And no matter where they are or which computer they are at, they always have access to the tools and files needed to create and manage content. The SoftChalk Cloud also provides an easy way to link a single content item into multiple delivery platforms. So, for example, a single SoftChalk Cloud item can be linked into the Learning Management System course and gradebook of multiple courses and multiple LMSs, all at the same time. When the instructor needs to update their content, it is done in one place (the SoftChalk Cloud), and all linked courses are updated simultaneously. This provides much greater management efficiency than creating a copy of each content item for each course.

## What is the Proportion of Open-Source to Closed-Source Contents in your Repository?

Currently, of the several thousand content items on SoftChalk Cloud, approximately half of the items are in the public repository as OER material and half are "private".

# Chapter 9
# Open Source for Higher Conventional and Open Education in India

**Ramesh C. Sharma**
*Indira Gandhi National Open University, India*

## ABSTRACT

*Distance Education in India has come a long way since the launch of correspondence courses in 1962 at the Delhi University. There have been many changes over the period of time, and thus, a transition was observed from print based correspondence courses to media supported distance education. With the advent of technology, expansion of telephone network, and lowering of tariff, there has been expansion of e-learning services, web based education, and mobile learning. Currently there are around 600 conventional (face-to-face) universities in India serving around 1.2 billion students. Starting with one Open University in 1982, now we have 15 open universities. There are single mode and dual mode distance education institutions. These provide instructions from print based to technology enabled means. All these developments transformed the teaching learning. Many of the institutions followed Open Educational Resources and Open Source movement. Reasons are varied for adopting open source. With the purpose to reduce the costs on software development, freedom to improve the software and freedom to redistribute to help neighbours has made individuals, institutions, and governments support open source. In this chapter, the author examines some of the initiatives of Open Source in the field of higher, open and distance education in India.*

DOI: 10.4018/978-1-4666-2205-0.ch009

## 1. INTRODUCTION

India is the largest democracy in the world and population-wise stands next to China with more than 1.2 billion population. Indian education system is very big and has witnessed tremendous growth. After attaining independence in 1947, the government paid special attention to the educational provisions. From 18 universities in 1947 and 496 colleges catering to about one hundred and fifty thousand students, now in 2012 we have more than 600 universities and around 30,000 colleges in all parts of the country. There are different types of universities in India: central (established by Act of Parliament); State Universities (established by a local legislative assembly act); Deemed Universities (established under section 3 of the UGC Act); and Private Universities (approved by UGC). These universities differ in some aspects like subvention by the government, status, service conditions of its staff, governance etc. Private Universities have their own funding mechanisms while Central and State Universities are provided grants by Central or State governments respectively. Deemed universities are institutions of higher learning and research, which may not be full fledged university, in the sense that Central and State universities have colleges affiliated to them for providing educational avenues to the learners. The University Grants Commission (UGC) of India, which is an apex body in terms of governance and funding to the higher education (non-technical) allowed the status of deemed and private university to the institutions fulfilling laid down criteria and quality measures who have their own funding resources. On the basis of kind of program and courses offered, India have traditional universities, technical universities, open universities and other research and development based educational institutions. With the purpose to further boost the higher education sector, the Prime Minister of India appointed National Knowledge Commission (NKC) in 2005 to suggest strategies,

the road map, action plan and possible response for India to emerge as knowledge super power. The National Knowledge Commission (http://www.knowledgecommission.gov.in/) mandated to transform knowledge landscape of the country, focused on five key areas of knowledge paradigm—access to knowledge, knowledge concepts, knowledge creation, knowledge application and development of better knowledge services. Governmental and non-governmental agencies have taken adequate steps and the entry of foreign universities has also given a new dimension to the sector in terms of faculty access, international curriculum and new career pathways. However such initiatives require huge financial resources for implementation which becomes a difficult task in the times of global recession.

## 2. TRANSITION TO AND GROWTH OF HIGHER AND OPEN EDUCATION

After independence, the government of India prepared Five Year Plans for the development of the nation and thus planners made a reference to the alternative systems of education outside the formal system in the First Five Year Plan (1951-56) with the purpose to address the growing demand for higher education. Instructions through radio talks and printed course material were promoted, although the pace was slow till 1961. It was mostly during the Third Five Year Plan (1961-67) distance education was given a serious thought due to ever increasing pressure to provide more educational opportunities. The Third Five Year Plan (1961-67) proposed, *'...in addition to the provision in the plan for expansion for facilities for higher education, proposal for evening colleges, correspondence courses and award for external degrees are at present under consideration'* (GOI, 1961:589). To achieve this objective, a committee was set up by the Central Advisory Board of Education, highest education policy making body in India, (CABE) to suggest strategies for introducing correspondence education. After deliberations, the CABE Committee recommended:

*A correspondence course should be a step designed to expand and equalize educational opportunity, as it aimed at providing additional opportunities for several thousand students who wished to continue their education and the persons who had been denied these facilities and were in full-time employment or were for other reasons prevented from availing themselves of the facilities at college (GOI, 1963: 3-4).*

As an initial experiment, University of Delhi launched correspondence courses in 1962 through its School of Correspondence Courses where the instructions were primarily print based and lesson notes were delivered by post. The courses were basically limited to social sciences and humanities. This experiment was a success and thus the Education Commission (1964-66) recommended that at least one-third students in higher education should be offered education through distance mode in twenty years (GoI, 1966). Such encouragement paved the way for formal distance education in the country and thus in 1982 the first open university of India was established as Andhra Pradesh Open University at Hyderabad (now renamed as Dr. Bhim Rao Ambedkar Open University). The open university system was so successful that a need for a national level open university was felt. The correspondence course system gave way to distance mode of education and distance education started gaining respect. In 1985, Indira Gandhi National Open University was established by an Act of Parliament with jurisdiction all over the country and to act as apex institute for open and distance education.

The correspondence courses were primarily print based and lessons were delivered by post to the learner's address. Since there was lack of personal interaction between the learner and the teacher, they were looked upon as second rate courses although when started in 1962 afterwards they gained popularity as they provided a means to thousands of people to attain and enhance their educational qualifications. To overcome this limitation, multimedia in the form of radio, television, audio cassettes, video cassettes etc were introduced along with some sort of personal contact with the teacher. Here the instructions were imparted at a distance (of time and space between the learner and teacher), hence called as distance education. India has been one of the best example of show casing the success of open and distance education model, even when she has large number of traditional face-to-face universities. In the initial phases (late 90s) DE was still looked upon with suspicion by the employers and they used to prefer students certified under formal educational system. However the success of Indira Gandhi National Open University and then establishment of other State Open Universities helped change the perception of masses and employers, making IGNOU a Mega Open University (Daniel, 1998) where he defined a mega-university as a distance-teaching institution with over 100,000 active students in degree-level courses. There are certain critical success factors for distance education system in India: inexpensive education, open and flexible entry eligibility, own pace of learning, wide variety of courses offered, vast network of learner support centres across the country, even abroad, ICT enabled instructional delivery and a boon for those special groups who hitherto could not have access to education like housewives, jail inmates, tribal members, and the physically challenged, etc.

Table 1 shows the institutional growth of open and distance education in the period 1962 – 2012.

Starting with one Open University in 1982, they have grown to 15 in 2012 open universities. They are listed in Appendix at the end of the chapter.

*Table 1. Institutional growth of distance education*

| Year | Open University | CCIs | Remarks |
|------|-----------------|------|---------|
| 1962-1981 | 0 | 34 | Correspondence era |
| 1982-1985 | 2 | 04 | Transition to open era |
| 1986-2000 | 7 | 32 | Consolidation of open era |
| 2001-2012 | 6 | 80 | Expansion of ODL system and march towards on-line education, OER, and mobile learning |
| **Total** | **15** | **150** | |

## 3. HIGHER AND OPEN EDUCATION AND TECHNOLOGY

In the initial stages, it was more of a face to face contact of the learner with the teacher. Later on technology in the form of radio, television, audio and video cassettes were introduced to extend the outreach of distance education programmes. Subsequently, computers made inroads into the system and thus were being used for academic and administrative purposes. Along with universities in other countries (Bates, 2008; Paul and Brindley, 2008), India also jumped to take advantage of the advent of Internet in 1996 and thus universities switched to networked learning (Sharma, 1999 and 2001, Mishra and Sharma, 2005). Internet being a powerful medium for collaboration and communication in education, it offers a global open platform for information storage, display and communication and integrates text, graphics, audio and video with communication tools such as email, bulletin-boards and chat-rooms to promote synchronous and asynchronous one to one, one to many and many to many interaction / conferencing. Like elsewhere, in India too, e-Learning has gained momentum and thus many higher education (traditional and open distance) systems are offering courses via Internet (Sharma and Mishra, 2007).

Global trends also concur the benefits e-learning in education like it increases the access to vast knowledge base; enhancement in student learning through improved interaction; suits to various pedagogical models; offers flexibility for learners to study anytime, anywhere without any incongruence; allows collaboration amongst faculty and researchers from all over the globe; offers easy and fast updating of content (Bates, 2001, 2008; Evans & Haase, 2001; Collins, 2002; Shea, Pickett & Pelz, 2003; Smith & Rupp, 2004; Rovai & Jordan, 2004; Oakley, 2004; Vaughan & MacVicar, 2004; Homan & Macpherson, 2005; Haughey, Evans & Murphy, 2008). Kawatra & Singh (2006) opine that "on-line distance education system carries more learning advantages than the print based or face to face learning systems."

## 4. OPEN SOURCE INITIATIVES IN INDIAN UNIVERSITIES

As has been introduced in this volume elsewhere, open source software is software developed and released with the source code with limited or no restrictions. Some of the best known examples are Linux operating system (http://www.linux.org/), Firefox browser (http://www.mozilla.org/en-US/firefox/new/), Open Office suite (http://www.openoffice.org/), Moodle Learning Management System (http://moodle.org/) etc. This characteristic of open source made it popular in India in general and in educational institutions.

With reference to India, it seems the biggest endorsement can be said to come from the former President A.P.J. Abdul Kalam, popularly famous as "the missile man of India", a noted scientist. While speaking at the International Institute of Information Technology at Pune IT Park, India, Dr Kalam said, "In India, open source code software will have to come and stay in a big way for the benefit of the people. Open source software needs

139

to be built for further spread of IT and the impact it would have on society" (Financial Express, 2003). While speaking at the inauguration of the three-day National Convention for Academics and Research on 'Computing freedom for technology, education and research,' organised by the Free Software Movement of India (FSMI), a national coalition of regional free software movements, Dr. Kalam urged upon scientists, researchers and academics to go in for the 'open source philosophy' in their respective fields, and contribute towards building 'open source networks' that can help pool talent, research and know-how from around the world (The Hindu, 2010). He believes that such a platform would lead to searching scientific solutions to problems, particularly those being faced in developing countries. Intrigued by non-availability of potable water for masses, he once commented, "Why don't Free Software movements come together to create a network of experts to work on providing free drinking water?" He had further observed, "The most unfortunate thing is that India still seems to believe in proprietary solutions. Further spread of IT, which is influencing the daily life of individuals, would have a devastating effect on the lives of society due to any small shift in the business practice involving these proprietary solutions. It is precisely for these reasons open-source software needs to be built, which would be cost-effective for the entire society. In India, open-source code software will have to come and stay in a big way for the benefit of our billion people." (Becker, 2003).

As explained in introductory chapters of this book, open source software programs are the choice of many due to availability of source code for modification, affordability and variety of choices, making them suitable for institutions after modifying as per their needs. There are other factors too contributing to this success. The high cost of proprietary software programs either for its purchase or maintenance prohibit many to procure them. People advocated for freedom for the production, distribution, modification and use of software. This Free/Open Source Software (FOSS) movement was supported by government departments and faculty and students alike because it lead to lowering of costs, increasing cost of ownership, enhancing creativity and productivity and emergence of new software solutions and products. Main focus of development and research was on Operating Systems, Data Bases, Web Servers, Data Base Servers, Internet & Web Technologies, Programming Languages, applications for computers, mobile, and GPRS etc.

To give a proper direction to FOSS, Department of Information Technology, the government of India, C-DAC (Centre for Development of Advance Computing) Chennai and Anna University, Chennai initiated a project called the National Resource Centre for FOSS (NRCFOSS-AU) in March 2005. Funded by the Department Of Information Technology, the government of India, this project focuses on two objectives: helping to bridge the digital divide (ii) strengthening India's Software and IT industry. During the first phase (2005-2009) C-DAC Chennai and Anna University had these two achievements:

- Development and Promotion of an Indian version of Linux Distribution named BOSS (Bharat Operating System Software) based on the Debian distribution (C-DAC Chennai), particularly for governmental and e-governance applications.
- Introduction of FOSS Elective Courses and Lab. Classes into the curricula of UG Engineering Programs (CSE/IT/MCA) in the country, along with Teacher Training, Text Book preparation, Student project support etc.

Later on a FOSS-based CSE Degree Program was also developed with the purpose to create skill sets for FOSS among the students. (for more details on FOSS Competency Certification Programmes please go to http://certificate.nrcfoss. au-kbc.org.in/home/)

Another best example of the backing of the Governments for FOSS is the establishment of Institute of Open Technology and Applications (IOTA) in 2007 as an autonomous body by the West Bengal government with subvention from Department of Information Technology. Its genesis lies in promotion of FOSS in government and academia. IOTA was mandated with the purpose of "getting the support infrastructure for FOSS/OSS adoption" in all Government departments and educational institutions in West Bengal state of India, with support from Sun Microsystems India and Red Hat India. Its success was felt via FOSS/OSS seeking more attention, books publications, organisation of training programmes and seminars on FOSS, e-Governance and adoption.

Lets learn about some of the open source initiatives adopted for teaching, learning or training by Indian Universities.

## Open Source Initiative at IGNOU

IGNOU now stands as the largest open university serving over 4 million students in India and 36 other countries through 21 Schools of Studies and a network of 67 regional centres, around 3,000 learner support centres and 67 overseas centres. Starting with 2 programmes and around 4400 learners in 1987, it currently offers about 490 certificate, diploma, degree and doctoral programmes (IGNOU, 2011).

## IGNOU-IBM Academia-Industry Collaboration

IBM and IGNOU have partnered to offer a unique opportunity to learn and work on Open Source projects leading to development of industry vertical domain skills and open source software skills in the IT education and training sector. These would be online IT courses available through an online education platform iCOS (Innovatio Centre for Open Standards). iCOS is a novel creation of IBM and CL Infotech Pvt Ltd. This is an online program and platform to promote Open Standards and Open Source Software skill building. Students taking up this innovative program are benefited as it increases chances of employability in the industry.

Under this collaboration the following programmes are envisage to be offered.

## Certificate Programme in Open Source Software (COS)

The Certificate Programme in Open Source Software, is a six month programme aimed at transforming the learners into web application developers. This certificate programme provides the basic theoretical and practical skills required by an individual to get professional competencies in some of the important free and open source software technologies. Though the course is based on the open source software, the principles learnt and the most of the elements of the languages and tools learned are applicable to the other frameworks as well.

## Programme Structure

The programme is comprised of four courses, and a project course of roughly equal duration and each of them carrying 4 credits.

*   **MITI-001:** Computer, Internet and FOSS (4 Credits)
*   **MITI-002:** Programming and Software Development (4 Credits)
*   **MITI-003:** Database Concepts and Applications (4 Credits)
*   **MITI-004:** Web Application Development (4 Credits)
*   **MITP-005:** Project Course (4 Credits)

## Delivery Model

It is an online program and will be delivered through The Innovation Centre for Open Standards (iCOS) – an online platform developed by IBM. Further, an online asynchronous academic support will also be provided by the IBM for the students through this platform. The Interactive Online Course Guide (IOCG) developed by IG-NOU will be used to provide basic details about the programme.

- **Theory Sessions:** One discussion session will be conducted for each course at the study centre. This session will be conducted at the end of each course to summarise the learning.
- **Practical Sessions:** Student's are expected to have access to a Computer and Internet to do the programme. However, in case a student wants services from the study centre then s/he needs to pay for use of computer facility of the study centre as per IGNOU norms.

A CD containing necessary software will be given to the students.

## Other Future Open Source Programs under IGNOU - IBM Partnership

1. Diploma in Open Source Software & Industry Vertical Domain Open Standards

This shall be a 12 months program and would focus on (includes COS modules):

- Introduction to Open Standards, including their Governance
- Open Standards for Enterprise Applications
- Introduction to industry vertical Open Standards
- Healthcare Vertical & Project
- Retail Vertical & Project
- Insurance Vertical & Project

2. Advanced Diploma in Industry Vertical Domain Open Standards (Healthcare/Retail/Insurance)

This would be a 18 months program and would deal with contents (includes the COS and Open Standards Course Modules):

- Data Modelling Refresher: RDBMS Fundamentals - Database
- Database Connectivity, Database Access, Report Generation
- Web Application Development with OSS -(Eclipse, Apps Server)
- iCOS (Innovation Centre for Open Standards) - Intensive Project Days
- Industry Vertical track Selection & Project Scenarios.

## Project Ekalavya

Project ekalavya (http://ekalavya.it.iitb.ac.in/) is an Open Source Knowledge Initiative launched by the Affordable Solutions Laboratory (ASL), Kanwal Rekhi School of Information Technology (KReSIT), IIT Bombay. It offers an interactive platform for the creation, absorption, dissemination and usage of knowledge to those who do not have access to resources, have less experience, exposure and skills. Such people they are although talented, however do not have access to qualified guidance. This project derives its name from the famous self-taught archer 'Ekalavya' from Indian mythology who wanted to learn archery but did not have access to a guru (teacher) and thus learnt archery by observing a teacher teaching other students from a distance. This project offers a unique platform for communication in the form of free exchange of knowledge and ideas, by placing all the relevant material in the Open Source. One of the idea behind this project is to have collaborative communities where knowledge seekers are provided access to givers and thus serving the society. This involves using IT at all levels of education. The channel of communication between seeker and giver is established via discussion forums, mail, news, and announcements etc.

Project ekalavya has been supported by some of the reputable industries like EMC, Infosys, Intel, PSPL, Red Hat, TCS (Tata Consultancy Services), and VIA Technologies. Professional associations, such as, CSI (Computer Society of India) and NASSCOM (National Association of Software and Services Companies) have also expressed their concern for support and contribution. DGF (Development Gateway Foundation) and TIFAC (Technology Information, Forecasting and Assessment Council) are also providing direct support to Project ekalavya.

## Programmes under Project Ekalavya

Project ekalavya has several programmes, such as eGURU, eOUTREACH and eCONTENT.

- The eGURU programme is designed to provide e-guidance and mentorship to needy students of B.E., M.C.A. and M.Sc. (CS/ IT/ Electronics) programmes, in completing their final year projects and challenging them for bringing out innovative technical solutions to various real life problems. For example, the Red Hat Scholarship in partnership with Red Hat, selects the best projects for a monetary prize entitled 'Lord of the Code.' The successful completed projects under eGURU are released under Open Source.
- The eOUTREACH programme builds a bank of high quality Open Source contents, in the form of digital audio/ video and text contents of specialized lectures and workshops. The Open Source software and documentation created or composed under this programme, are made available to the students, teachers and professionals. The OSCAR (Open Source Courseware Animations Repository) scheme under the eOUTREACH programme is in the form of a large repository of interactive animations for teaching various concepts and technologies.

- The eCONTENT programme provides access to Open Source digital contents in Indian languages through translation and new writings, addressing education at all levels.

## Beneficiaries of Project Ekalavya

- **Students**: Studying in final year B.E., M.C.A. and M.Sc. (CS/ IT/ Electronics).
- **Expert Volunteers:** Faculty members, research scholars or Industry professionals, who are willing to devote two hours a week of their free time can register as expert volunteers.
- **Educational Institutions:** Those institutions who do not have adequate and experienced faculty to guide the talented students studying in their colleges, eGURU provides online guidance and mentoring for their students.
- **Industry:** The industry provides the services of expert volunteers, and also ideas for project proposals. Students are encourage to work on real life problems so that they can come up with viable and innovative solutions. The industry is benefitted by the services of such young talent, as well as to usable Open Source software.

## EasyNow

While developing content, we sometimes need to integrate several tools. Not only has this, even to deal with administrative functions at various levels such integration become a necessity. Such integration may result in higher programme cost and non-access to all required resources. Teachers while developing content may not have time and resources to master all ICT tools required for their course content, before narrowing one some special tool. Easy Now comes handy in such situations.

EasyNow is a virtual campus initiative developed by Commonwealth Educational and Media centre for Asia (CEMCA), India. It comprises of easily available open source ICT tools which are easy to learn and use by the content developers to produce quality materials suitable for Open and Distance Learning on the World Wide Web. With the help of EasyNow, we can capture delivered lessons through open source ICT tools and then offer them in various form for target group. We can integrate a media mix like text, audio and video tools that allows for low cost production and easy upload by the developers (refer to Figure 1). The educational material thus captured can be delivered by various formats (collectively called as "Multiple Modes" of delivery). The key ones are:

- Print Media Delivery as HTMLs/PDFs/ODL/ Magnify
- Audio Media Delivery:as mp3 or .wma files
- Video/Audio Media Delivery as .wmv files

Basically there are four stages in EasyNow:

1. Source
2. Capture
3. Preparation/Mapping
4. Delivery

In source we plan of what the source of content would be, for example, recording the lesson being taught by a teacher in a classroom or demonstrating some presentation.

Capture involves getting content, for example, obtaining paper copy or making an audio of the speech by the teacher or video making of the lesson being taught.

Preparation involves like creating a book from printed material, or podcast from the audio captured, or video content burned on a CD or DVD, or streaming video for Internet.

Delivery involves output mode of the content created in above steps. For example, hard copy content can be distributed in the form a book or handouts, audio can be distributed on a CD or

*Figure 1. Lesson on environment via EasyNow*

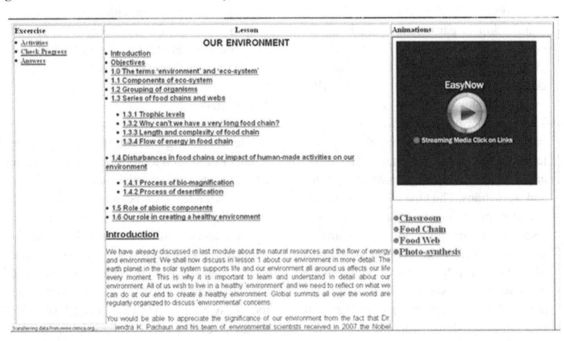

video can be distributed on a DVD or via Internet or uploading on YouTube (see Figure 2).

## Benefits of EASYNOW

- Classroom lessons can be converted into multimedia lessons.
- Such multimedia lessons are suitable in Open Distance Learning system.

## E-Granthalaya

e-Granthalaya (http://egranthalaya.nic.in/Default. aspx) is a library automation software developed by National Informatics Centre, Department of Information Technology, Ministry of Communications and Information Technology, Government of India. With the help of this software the libraries can automate in-house activities as well as user services. e-Granthalaya can be implemented either in stand-alone or in client-server mode.

## A-VIEW (Amrita Virtual Interactive e-Learning World)

A-VIEW (Amrita Virtual Interactive e-Learning World, http://aview.amrita.ac.in/aview-class-room) *an open source software*, is an award winning indigenously built multi-modal, multimedia e-learning platform that provides an immersive e-learning experience that is almost as good as a real classroom experience developed by Amrita e-Learning Research Lab. This lab is a part of Amrita Vishwa Vidhyapeetham, one of the fastest growing institutions of higher learning in India and address the most pressing issue of higher education in India – the shortage of highly qualified teachers (refer to Figure 3).

A-VIEW is part of Talk to a Teacher program coordinated by IIT Bombay and funded by the Ministry of Human Resource Development (MHRD) under the Indian Government's National Mission for Education using Information and Communication Technology (NME-ICT) along with various other projects in Virtual Labs,

*Figure 2. EasyNow*

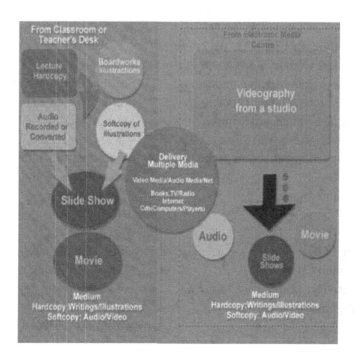

*Figure 3. A-View*

Haptics and Natural Language Processing. A-VIEW is now deployed at several IITs, NITs and other leading educational institutions across the nation. The author has very recently used A-View at the "One-day National Seminar on ICT Integration in Higher Education" conducted by SNDT Women's University, Mumbai on June 25, 2012 where two of the presenters were from USA and Indonesia with participants from Mumbai, India.

It has audio and video interaction, document sharing, desktop sharing and whiteboard features. It allows one to one interaction between the moderator and the student logged into the same class (see Figures 4 and 5).

Minimum system requirements:
For student node:

- **RAM:** Minimum 2 GB
- **Processor:** Minimum Core 2 Duo
- **Internet Connectivity:** Minimum 1 Mbps upload and 1 Mbps download

Required audio and video equipment:

1. WebCamera
2. Headphone with Mic

Other requirements:

- If you are using the campus network connection, then port number – 80 and RTMP protocol has to be opened
- Do not use any video conferencing software when A-VIEW is running, this may have some video device sharing issue between A-VIEW and other software.

A-VIEW Features:

- Click settings, select your Camera as the USB video device and microphone as the connected audio device and then save it.
- Click start, now the video and audio streaming starts.

*Figure 4. Presentation via A-View*

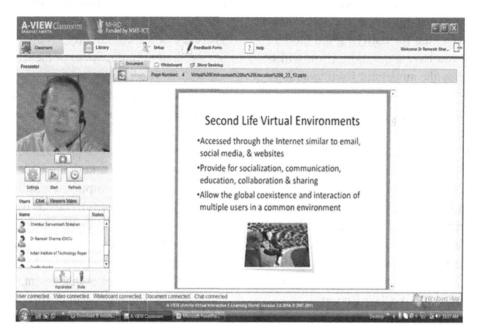

*Figure 5. Multimedia Presentation via A-View*

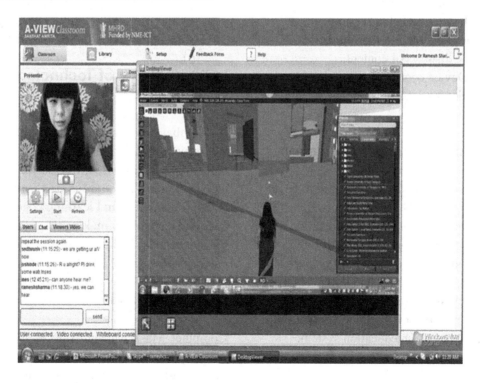

- You can chat through the chat tab.
- Click handraise option at the left bottom of the users tab for notifying the moderator that you have a question. (You will be selected by the moderator for interaction)

## A-VIEW Classroom

Through A-VIEW Classroom framework a teacher is able to create an effective and interactive social er environment for E-Learning. The teacher or presenter can teach in a live interactive mode to various geographical locations via its user friendly video conferencing software. This is also being treated as the Knowledge Cafe where students discuss /chat about the lecture after the live class.

Features of A-VIEW Class Room:

- Live and recorded can be delivered effectively.
- Supports varying bandwidths to multiple devices for delivery of lectures.
- Multiple teacher and student interaction through video and chat sessions.
- Easy desktop and file sharing facility.
- Multiple displays of content.
- Multi-Device compatible whiteboard.
- Handraise option for students to interact with teacher.

## OSS by Not-for-Profit Organisation

There are cases where OSS was found to be advocated even by not-for-profit organisations like Shiksha India Trust. This Trust in association with Red Hat Inc and the Confederation of Indian Industry's (CII's) are developing educational content based on Open Source tools and initiatives to be distributed across the country free of cost with the objective of making software and content more affordable to the Indian education system.

## Open Source Communities

There are some community groups working on open source in India. Some of them are:

- **The Indian Linux Project:** The Indian Linux project is open source and licensed under the GNU General Public License. The members work on I/O modules, development of fonts, kernel enablement, word translation etc. http://www.indlinux.org/.
- **Anjuta DevStudio:** GNOME Integrated Development Environment: Anjuta DevStudio is a versatile software development studio pertaining to development of tools for project management, application wizard, interactive debugger, source editor, version control, GUI designer, profiler etc. http://projects.gnome.org/anjuta/index.html.
- **Google Summer of Code:** Google Summer of Code (GSoC) community works on writing code for various open source projects. (http://code.google.com/opensource/gsoc/2008/faqs.html).

## Indian Institute of Technology Bombay (IITB)

IIT Bombay has a project OSCAR (Open Source Courseware Animations Repository) acting as a repository of web-based, interactive animations and simulations. These are used as learning objects (LOs) for teaching and learning concepts in science and technology making them quite suitable for independent learning and distance education environments.

## Computer Masti

Computer Masti (means 'fun' in Hindi) is the collaborative project of IIT Bombay and InOpen Technologies to teach computer science in schools.

Here emphasis is on concepts using FOSS applications like Edubuntu operating system and Open Source educational applications (e.g. Tux Paint) and games (e.g. GCompris, ChildsPlay, Tux Math etc). Under this project books prepared are released under Creative Commons, license, freely downloadable at the website http://www.cse.iitb.ac.in/~sri/ssrvm The e-books developed are available in 8 Indian languages and 2 foreign languages used by nearly 35000 students in a year and have been downloaded in more than 120 countries.

## OSS for Library and Information Management

Indian university libraries are using OSS to a great extent and here is a representative list. The details of these applications are avoided for brevity of space.

- **CDS/ISIS for Windows**: Available freely from the UNESCO website.
- **CERN**: An integrated digital library management system.
- **DSpace**: Used to store, manage and distribute the collections in digital format.
- **EPrints**: Distributed base of the repository software systems.
- **Fedora**: Flexible Extensible Digital Object and Repository Architecture (FEDORA) can be used to develop institutional repositories and other interoperable web-based digital libraries.
- **Ganesha**: Ganesha Digital Library (GDL) allows sharing of knowledge and its simultaneous access.
- **Greenstone**: Used for creating, building, managing and distributing digital library collections.
- **KOHA**: Open Source Integrated Library Management System.

- **NewGenLib**: An Integrated Library Management System, freely available as an open source.

## 5. DISCUSSION

Open Source movement has become an integral part of India Economy and software development. Communities, individuals, industry, academia and governments are doing their bit to promote OSS. With ever expanding network of Internet and mobile technology, the demand for OSS is increasing, being reduced funding at universities for procurement of propriety software. Various state governments have implemented OSS for e-governance catering to land records, treasury, legal documentation, birth and death registrations etc. However, it seems there is no specific legislation in India covering OSS, albeit it is gaining popularity.

In November 2010, the Department of Information Technology under the Ministry of Communications & Information Technology, Government of India effected a Policy on Open Standards for e-Governance for the purpose of having a consistent, standardized and reliable implementation of e-Governance solutions. The Policy provides a framework for the selection of Standards to facilitate interoperability between systems developed by multiple agencies. It provides organizations the flexibility to select different hardware and software for implementing cost-effective e-Governance solutions. It, therefore, promotes technology choice, and avoids vendor lock-in. It aims for reliable long-term accessibility to public documents and information in Indian context (the government of India, 2010).

Rajan (2006) who is the Principal Adviser of CII expressed his concerns: "India has the second largest education system in the world, and there is an urgent need to modernise it by using information technology. We therefore developed content that we could offer free to educational institutions. Open source can serve as a tool for modernising India, hence we are happy to work with Red Hat to deploy our content and open source software for Indian educational institutions. The CII-Shiksha content for teaching in schools is based on the open source concept. We will let capable and motivated teachers to creatively modify the content and give a distinct flavour to suit local conditions and use it for teaching in other languages." India's growing student enrolments has put great demands on the educational providers. We need to think of newer ways, rethink curricula, faculties competencies and possible partnerships with research companies. This push must lead to creation of new tools, technologies, strategies and opportunities. India is a country of vast cultural differences and languages, all integrated into one unity. The OSS developed and implemented by Indian researchers can be beneficial to the communities in the regions where provisions are scarce. Rural India suffers from lack of educational infrastructure and non-availability of quality teachers. With increasing Internet bandwidth, Govt can plan to link villages and make available OSS via digital means. The Indian government has, as a policy, decided to adopt OSS tools or technologies for e-governance. For ourselves (and others) to learn from such experiences, there is a critical need to document such efforts for the benefit of decision-makers, institutions, governmental and non-governmental agencies and individual developers. Its quite pertinent to understand what works and what fails and what impact such strategies will have on policy planning, making, and implementation. Increased efforts may be put in for capacity-building and training towards OSS. May be there is call for a paradigm shift in the way OS is designed and delivered. We may also have to have a relook at our teamwork and collaborative practices (an underlying principal for OSS development).

FOSS/OSS in India, like elsewhere, is not free from certain challenges. Adequate support for maintenance and troubleshooting for OSS is one of them. In some Indian Universities, OpenOffice suite were installed to cut the costs down for purchase of software, however users soon switched back to propriety software either due to lack of training or support or being not updated enough about converting one format to other.

The issue of providing their product free of cost to others is another challenge which everybody may not be ready to, especially those who make livelihood out of this. Intellectual property is still a problem in India. Readiness on the part of government to bridge the urban/rural divide by introducing appropriate policies would be a welcome step.

## 6. CONCLUSION

Open Source movement can be of immense benefit for distance education system in India. Already DE system has established its credibility and all major educational institutions now offer their courses via distance or e-learning mechanisms. Different Indian Institutes of Technology and Indian Institute of Science (Bangaluru) are already involved in development and delivery of open courseware. National Programme on Technology Enhanced Learning (NPTEL) is the funded project of the Ministry of Human Resource Development, the government of India. NPTEL has been mandated to enhance the quality of Engineering education by offering free online courseware in the form of online Web and Video courses in Engineering, Science and humanities streams (http://nptel. iitm.ac.in/). There is a great potential to learn from India's experiments with the application of FOSS/OSSs in education. The above cited examples indicate that open source software are being developed and used for different purposes. There are some Learning Management Systems like Moodle or Joomla which are being extensively used in educational institutions. Many universities are using Open Office Suite for office document processing work. OSS provides an interface that makes it easy for people to create their own applications. Although the use of open source is on the rise and there are online community groups in India which offer support and guidance in case someone is facing some difficulty, however there are some challenges. IGNOU sometimes back installed Open Office suite on its machines but the users were finding difficulty in converting the format of the documents and thus later on almost all switched back to propriety software programs! Technical support is a big issue. There are reports about open source being unreliable and non-availability of regular updates. In some cases the initial installation costs could be high. Barring such limitations, educational institutions in India at all levels of education and be it formal or open distance mode, are sure progressing towards open source.

# REFERENCES

Bates, T. (2001). *National strategies for e-learning in post-secondary education and training*. Paris, France: UNESCO, IIEP.

Bates, T. (2008). Transforming distance education through new technologies. In Evans, T., Haughey, M., & Murphy, D. (Eds.), *International handbook of distance education*. Emerald.

Becker, D. (2003). *India leader advocates open source*. Retrieved from http://news.cnet.com/India-leader-advocates-open-source/2100-1016_3-1011255.html

Collins, G. R. (2002). Case study: A satellite-based internet learning system for the hospitality industry. *Online Journal of Distance Learning Administration*, *5*(4).

Daniel, J. S. (1998). *Mega-universities and knowledge media: Technology strategies for higher education*. Kogan Page.

Evans, J. R., & Haase, I. M. (2001). On-line business education in the twenty-first century: An analysis of potential target markets. *Internet Research: Networking Applications and Policy*, *11*(3), 246–260. doi:10.1108/10662240110396432

Financial Express. (2003). *Go for open source code, Kalam tells IT industry*. Retrieved from http://www.financialexpress.com/news/go-for-open-source-code-kalam-tells-it-industry/75949/

Govt of India. (2010). *Policy on open standards for e-governance*. New Delhi, India: Department of Information Technology: Ministry of Communications & Information Technology.

Govt. of India (1961). *Third five-year plan*, (p. 589). New Delhi, India: Planning Commission, Govt. of India.

Govt. of India. (1963). *Expert committee report on correspondence courses*, (pp. 3-4). New Delhi, India: Ministry of Education. Govt. of India. (1966). *Report of the education commission*. New Delhi, India: Ministry of Education, Government of India.

Haughey, M., Evans, T., & Murphy, D. (2008). Introduction: From correspondence education to virtual learning environments. In Evans, T., Haughey, M., & Murphy, D. (Eds.), *International handbook of distance education* (pp. 1–24). Emerald.

Homan, G., & Macpherson, A. (2005). E-learning in corporate universities. *Journal of European Industrial Training*, *29*(1), 75–90. doi:10.1108/03090590510576226

IGNOU. (2011). *Profile*. New Delhi, India: Author.

Indian Institute of Technology Bombay (IITB). (n.d.). *Project OSCAR*. Retrieved from http://oscar.iitb.ac.in/aboutOscar.do

Kawatra, P. S., & Singh, N. K. (2006). E-learning in LIS education in India. In C. Khoo, D. Singh, & A.S. Chaudhry (Eds.), *Proceedings of the Asia-Pacific Conference on Library & Information Education & Practice 2006* (A-LIEP 2006), Singapore, 3-6 April 2006 (pp. 605-611). Singapore: School of Communication & Information, Nanyang Technological University.

Mishra, S., & Sharma, R. C. (2005, March 14-20). Development of e-learning in India. *University News, 43*(11), 9 – 15.

*National Knowledge Commission.* (2005). Retrieved from http://www.knowledgecommission.gov.in/

Oakley, B. (2004). The value of online learning: Perspectives from the University of Illinois at Springfield. *Journal of Asynchronous Learning Networks, 8*(3), 22–31.

Paul, R. H., & Bringley, J. E. (2008). New technologies, new learners and new challenges: Leading our universities in times of change. In Evans, T., Haughey, M., & Murphy, D. (Eds.), *International handbook of distance education* (pp. 435–452). Emerald.

Rajan, Y. S. (2006). *Red Hat and CII's education initiative.* Retrieved from http://www.express-computeronline.com/20060116/market04.shtml

Rovai, A. P., & Jordan, H. M. (2004). Blended learning and sense of community: A comparative analysis with traditional and fully online graduate courses. *International Review of Research in Open and Distance Learning, 5*(2).

Sharma, R. (2001). Online delivery of programmes: A case study of Indira Gandhi National Open University (IGNOU). *International Review of Research in Open and Distance Learning, 1*(2). Retrieved from http://www.irrodl.org/index.php/irrodl/rt/printerFriendly/18/356

Sharma, R., & Mishra, S. (2007). *Cases on global e-learning practices: Successes and pitfalls* (pp. 1-372). doi:10.4018/978-1-59904-340-1

Sharma, R. C. (1999). Networked distance education in India. *Indian Journal of Open Learning, 8*(2), 147–156.

Shea, P. J., Pickett, A. M., & Plez, W. E. (2003). A follow-up investigation of "teaching presence" in The SUNY Learning Network. *Journal of Asynchronous Learning Networks, 7*(2), 61–80.

Smith, A. D., & Rupp, W. T. (2004). Managerial implications of computer-based online/face-to-face business education: A case study. *Online Information Review, 28*(2), 100–109. doi:10.1108/14684520410531682

The Hindu. (2010). *Embrace open source philosophy, Kalam tells scientists, researchers.* Retrieved from http://www.thehindu.com/news/cities/Hyderabad/article956890.ece

Vaughan, K., & MacVicar, A. (2004). Employees' pre-implementation attitudes and perceptions to e-learning: A banking case study analysis. *Journal of European Industrial Training, 28*(5), 400–413. doi:10.1108/03090590410533080

## APPENDIX

## NATIONAL OPEN UNIVERSITY

Indira Gandhi National Open University (IGNOU): http://www.ignou.ac.in

## STATE OPEN UNIVERSITIES

Dr. B.R.Ambedkar Open University, Hyderabad: http://www.braou.ac.in/
Dr. Babasaheb Ambedkar Open University, Ahmedabad, Gujarat: http://www.baou.edu.in/
The Global Open University, Nagaland: http://nagaland.net.in/
Karnataka State Open University, Mysore, Karnataka: http://www.ksoumysore.edu.in/
Krishanakant Handique State Open University, Guwahati, Assam: http://www.kkhsou.in/
M.P.Bhoj(Open) University, Bhopal: http://www.bhojvirtualuniversity.com/
Nalanda Open University, Patna, Bihar: http://www.nalandaopenuniversity.com/
Netaji Subhas Open University, Kolkata, WB: http://www.wbnsou.ac.in
Pt. Sunderlal Sharma (Open) University, Bilaspur, Chattisgarh: http://www.pssou.ac.in/
Tamil Nadu Open University, Chennai, Tamil Nadu: http://www.tnou.ac.in/
U.P.Rajarshi Tandon Open University, Allahabad, UP: http://www.uprtouallahabad.org.in
Uttarakhand Open University, Haldwani, Uttarakhand: http://www.uou.ac.in/
Vardhaman Mahaveer Open University, Kota, Rajasthan: http://www.vmou.ac.in/
Yashwantrao Chavan Maharshtra Open University, Nasik, Maharashtra: http://www.ycmou.com/

# Section 3
# Open Source in the Wide World

# Chapter 10

# Measuring Language Learners' Speaking Proficiency in a Second Language Using Economical Digital Tools

**Peter B. Swanson**
*Georgia State University, USA*

## ABSTRACT

*Rising costs, combined with an increasing lack of flexibility of commercial course management technology tools such as uLearn and Blackboard, have prompted educators to consider other options. New advances in free and open source software, webware, and hardware are becoming attractive alternatives for educators and school systems due to decreased funding. These innovative digital tools hold promise to help educators overcome a variety of impediments to teaching and learning in the 21st century such as fostering student motivation. In the context of second/foreign language learning, the author seeks to present various technologies to P-16 educators that can be used for student oral language assessment. The author provides an overview of the obstacles language teachers must overcome in order to teach more effectively, as well as a synopsis of various options with which language instructors may not be familiar. Afterwards, findings from empirical research comparing the use of digital technology for the measurement of student speaking proficiency to the more conventional face-to-face method are presented. Student and instructor perceptions of using free and open source software are discussed, and the chapter concludes with a discussion of challenges that can appear when changes in assessment methods take place as well as avenues for future research.*

DOI: 10.4018/978-1-4666-2205-0.ch010

# INTRODUCTION

Creating and nurturing student motivation to acquire a new language can be a challenging endeavor, particularly when instructors must overcome a myriad of obstacles that tend to decrease instructional time in the classroom. Institutional hindrances such as large classes, complex work schedules, and perceptions that teachers lack voice in the creation of school policy can serve to complicate daily instructional practices (Futernick, 2007). Furthermore, the high stakes testing requirements inherent in *No Child Left Behind* have become overwhelming to many teachers as they lose valuable instructional time due to working around testing schedules and administering the exams (Zellmer, Frontier, & Pheifer, 2006) that have nothing to do with the teaching of a new language. Moreover, classroom time and academic focus can be compromised by sports and other extracurricular activities (Goldman, 1991).

While teachers regardless of discipline must cope with such impediments to teaching and learning, new strategies to take advantage of every minute in the classroom for instructional purposes need to be identified in order to enhance student achievement. In the context of second/foreign language (S/FL) teaching, instructors face these same challenges while struggling with a second quandary, the array of methods in which proficiency can be assessed. Swanson, Early, and Baumann (2011) find that at its core, S/FL instruction in the communicative classroom is dedicated to the ideals and the practice of developing second-language proficiency as conceptualized by the American Council on the Teaching of Foreign Language's (ACTFL) three modes of communication: the Interpersonal, the Interpretive, and the Presentational (National Standards in Foreign Language Education Project, 2006). Formerly conceptualized as the four skills (reading, writing, listening, and speaking), the three modes of communication

are three parts of a common goal, communication, rather than placing focus on any one isolated skill. While proficiency in listening reading, and writing are measured typically through objective testing methods such as multiple choice and true/false items, the assessment of students' ability to speak in the target language has continually presented numerous challenges, which include the development of useful and flexible rubrics (Foster, Tonkyn, & Wigglesworth, 2000) and the time expended in individual learner assessment (Flewelling, 2002).

Furthermore, unlike reading and writing assessments, oral assessments which are traditionally conducted in the classroom during instructional time, fail to leave an assessment artifact that is archivable in nature. Such a lack of what can constitute a body of evidence toward language proficiency hinders overall performance evaluation because such an artifact could be used to measure similarities and/or differences in learner progress towards proficiency goals. Additionally, the artifact can materially support assessment outcomes, and can be presented as concrete evidence of linguistic and cultural proficiency to stakeholders and third-party program evaluators or accreditation bodies. In an effort to address these concerns, language laboratories have been transformed to accommodate digital recordings that can facilitate whole-class concurrent, archival recordings (Flewelling, 2002; Gilgen, 2004). Such advances in the teaching and learning of languages have spawned a body of research centered on the multiple uses of emerging technologies and their potential uses within the context of oral proficiency and assessment (Chan, 2003; Kvavik, 2005; Volle, 2005; Zhao, 2005). This chapter is guided by my research with several colleagues on the integration of digital tools for oral language assessment (Early & Swanson, 2008; Swanson & Early, 2008; Swanson, Early, & Baumann, 2011; Swanson & Schlig, 2010).

## BACKGROUND

While younger teachers are more likely to have grown up in a technology-rich environment, and therefore may be more comfortable integrating technology in the classroom, many of these novice educators suffer the same problem as their veteran counterparts — a lack of time and resources to develop technologically rich lessons (Pierson & Cozart, 2005; Early & Swanson, 2008). Additionally, teachers tend to teach the way that they were taught (Ball, 1990; Vrasidas & McIsaac, 2007, Wright, Wilson, Gordon, & Stallworth, 2002). Even with an abundance of available software, hardware, freeware, and webware, research continues to reiterate Cuban's (2001) finding that school systems have not been restructured fully to support the integration of technology for instruction (Park & Ertmer, 2008). Owing to a variety of issues such as student security and privacy, school districts tend to restrict teacher and student access to a plethora of technologically rich learning opportunities for students and teachers such as blogs, *YouTube*, and even *TeacherTube*. Furthermore, it is commonplace for teachers to lack administrative privileges to install free or open-source software on their classroom computers (Swanson, Early, & Baumann, 2011).

For S/FL teachers, such constraints to use the latest emerging technology for instructional and assessment purposes compels teachers to rely on traditional face-to-face assessment methods, which reduces instructional time dramatically. For example, if a Spanish teacher has 32 students in a class, which is commonplace in public schools in the United States of America, the S/FL teacher could easily spend approximately two minutes per student listening to and evaluating speaking performance on an assessment task. Such a procedure easily consumes at least one hour of instructional time if the teacher does not have to deal with disruptions caused by students who are not being assessed at the moment.

In addition to reducing instructional time, face-to-face oral language assessment can be a source of performance anxiety for language learners (Early & Swanson, 2008; Swanson, Early, & Baumann, 2011). Performance anxiety, the feeling of un-easiness, worry, nervousness and apprehension experienced by non-native speakers when learning or using the target language, is theoretically linked to learners' affective filter and may cause an adverse result during performance assessment. According to Krashen, (1981), the affective filter explains the emotional variables associated with the success or failure of acquiring a second language. The relative basis of the affective filter can either facilitate or hinder language production in a second language. When the learner's affective filter is high, he or she may experience stress, anxiety, and lack of self-confidence that may inhibit success in acquiring a second language. Conversely, a low affective filter facilitates risk-taking behavior with regard to practicing and learning a second language. Therefore, for language learning to take place, the learner needs to be in a state of anxiety-free relaxation (Schinke-Llano & Vicars, 1993). The effects of S/FL learning anxiety have been evidenced in the S/FL classroom for decades, showing that perceptions of anxiety are a strong indicator of academic success (Buttaro, 2009; Carroll, 1963; Chastain, 1975; Gardner, Smythe, Clement, & Gliksman, 1976; McIntyre & Gardner, 1991; Mishra & Sharma, 2005; Naimon, Fröhlich, Stern, & Todesco, 1978; Oller, Baca, & Vigil, 1977; Sharma & Mishra, 2007).

Recent research on the relationship between anxiety and oral performance in the target language indicates that students encounter the most stress when being assessed face-to-face by the instructor (Woodrow, 2006). Other major stressors were performing in front of the class and talking to native speakers. Such findings led Woodrow to recommend that S/FL teachers consider oral language assessment outside the classroom because out-of-class tasks can utilize more rich linguistic resources available to learners.

Over the course of the past 20 years, the emergence of Computer-Assisted Language Learning (CALL) combined with new ideas about language teaching have helped transform S/FL from a teacher-centered or textbook-centered instructional practice to a student-centered approach (Hai-Peng & Deng, 2007). Popular teaching methodologies such as constructivism (Piaget, 1973) and socioculturalism (Vygotsky, 1978) work well with CALL. Both advocate for teachers as facilitators of learning by giving students control over what they do, how fast they do it, and time to find and correct their own mistakes, which results in a transformation of the learning process. Combined with Communicative Language Teaching, an approach to the teaching of S/FL that emphasizes interaction as both the means and the goal of learning a language, these approaches promote linguistic and cultural fluency over accuracy so that language learners take risks and build confidence to use the target language in more student-centered activities. Such notions of interaction have been linked to increased output, a decreased sense of the affective variables, and improved quality of communication (Schinke-Llano & Vicars, 1993; Stepp-Greany, 2002).

By integrating elements of CALL into a constructivist and sociocultural perspective to teaching languages with communication as its goal, there are a number of benefits for students. For example, students participating in a Local Area Network writing project showed positive attitudes about learning in that setting because the network not only represented a low-anxiety situation, they also they expressed that they felt more control than in a traditional classroom (Beauvois, 1998). Additionally, interactive visual media clearly have a unique instructional capability for topics that involve social situations or problem solving (Nunan, 1999), which can provide cultural knowledge not found in the typical S/FL classroom. And when combined with the internet, channels can be created whereby language learners can obtain a vast amount of human experience enabling them to participate in a global community. Such learning opportunities can extend students personal views, thoughts, and experiences as well as teaching them to interact in the real situations found in the target language culture. By integrating CALL, students can take a more active role in the classroom and become the creators not just the receivers of knowledge in a nonlinear fashion facilitating the development of critical thinking skills (Hartman et al., 1995; Lai & Kritsonis, 2006).

In the wake of the obstacles to teaching and learning with which S/FL teachers are confronted continually, I will present a variety of technology tools (software, webware, and portable hardware) that can be used in the S/FL classroom for oral language assessment in an effort to decrease student performance anxiety and increase instructional time. Afterward, I will summarize research using digital voice recording systems that are available to S/FL teachers and their students in the context of oral language proficiency. Then, I discuss some of the issues to consider when using digital voice recording technology for measuring student oral language proficiency before I present some avenues for future research.

## Available Digital Tools

Beginning in 2001, the *No Child Left Behind Act* began to marginalize S/FL instruction because it prioritized instruction in and the allocation of resources to the core areas of science, mathematics, and reading, thus resulting in a narrowing of the curriculum (Rosenbusch, 2005; Rosenbusch & Jensen, 2004; Swanson, 2010). Later, in 2008, the global economic crisis had detrimental effects on schools and those areas not part of the core tested areas. School systems reacted by slashing budgets and decreasing funding allotments. However, due to the STEM (Science, Technology, Engineering, and Mathematics) initiative, funds were available for a variety of purposes such as to update outdated language labs and media centers. Schools used funds to hire instructional technologists in order to introduce teachers to the latest technological advances in personal digital technology as well as hardware and software resources. Of these resources, free and open source software, webware, and inexpensive portable hardware became appealing to school systems struggling with budget issues.

For the S/FL teachers, these new developments hold the potential to allow interested language instructors to use digital technology for oral proficiency measurement. While many tools are available for these purposes, I begin by briefly outlining two free and open source software options that are free of spyware, adware, or license limitations, which do not dominate computer processing and storage resources. Afterward, I will present four webware applications followed by three commonly used portable hardware devices.

## Software

## Windows Sound Recorder

All computers that use the *Windows* operating system are already equipped with the *Windows Sound Recorder*™. Accessible via the Start Menu by clicking on *Programs > Accessories > Entertainment > Sound Recorder*, this recorder allows users to record audio for a maximum of 60 seconds. However, users can extend the 60 second default by referring to various web pages (e.g., Microsoft, PC World) in order to learn how to extend the maximum recording time for *Windows XP* as well as older operating systems. The interface is simple to use; however, the only file format available with the Sound Recorder is the *.wav* format. Nevertheless, users do not have to download an additional file encoder to use this recorder.

## Freecorder

The *Freecorder Toolbar*© < http://applian.com/asktoolbar/>, created by Applian Technologies, is a free video and audio recorder. It uses high quality sound recording technology that includes

a *Google*-based search menu. *Freecorder 4* can be used for a variety of applications such as a song recorder, an internet radio recorder, an audio extractor from videos, and a sound recorder from the computer's microphone. Once downloaded (8.3 MB), the software installs as a tool bar. With a simple mouse click, users can record, stop, pause, and play audio. The interface for each of these functions is straightforward. As the recording process begins, sound is displayed graphically in the form of sound waves. Audio files can be recorded and saved in either the popular *mp3* format or as a *wmv* file. Because the software uses the computer's internal microphone, or an external microphone plugged into the computer, sounds that are detected by the microphone are recorded. In essence, if it can be heard on the computer's speakers, *Freecorder* can record it.

Additionally, *Freecorder* has the capability to separate sounds from individual applications and eliminate background noises. It also eliminates silence at the beginning and end of the recording. Recordings begin when audio is first detected and recording ends when the audio stops. Unlike many other sound recorder software packages, *Freecorder* supports all *Windows* systems. However, Mac users can install Parallels and Windows in order to run *Freecorder*, which can be accessed easily from the Applian Technologies webpage. Overall, *Freecorder* is easy to use and has an intuitive interface, which is of consideration with younger users and less technologically-savvy individuals.

## NanoGong

Developed at the Hong Kong University of Science and Technology, *NanoGong* (http://gong.ust.hk/nanogong/) is a free and open source recording option that can be used to record, playback and save voice recordings. Unlike other free standing audio recording platforms, *NanoGong* is an applet, a small application that performs a specific task that runs within the scope of a larger program.

That is, it can be set within a webpage. It does not require a complicated setup procedure and users only need a simple webpage in order to use it.

An advantage of *NanoGong* is that users can manipulate the speed of the playback by increasing or decreasing the speed of the playback without changing it. Although originally designed to function in the Windows environment, it has been expanded to function on Mac and Linux machines. *NanoGong* was developed using Java technology so users' computers must be equipped with Java in order to use it. However, a drawback of *Nano-Gong* is that it uses only two types of audio format (*Speex* and *IMA ADPCM*) unlike other recording devices and platforms that use the common *mp3* file format. Nonetheless, the *IMA ADPCM* format is part of the .*wav* audio file form, and it can be played by most music software platforms.

An interesting application for *NanoGong* is found when users combine its functionality within *Moodle* (http://moodle.org/) as an integrated component in this course management system. *NanoGong* is compatible with most *Moodle* versions including version 1.9.11. At the time of this publication, it is being tested with *Moodle 2.0*. According to *NanoGong's* website, it can also be used with other course management systems such as *Blackboard* and *Sakai*.

## Audacity

Mazzoni and Dannenberg (2000) designed the *Audacity* recording and editing software as an open source recorder available to the public with relaxed or non-existent intellectual property restrictions <http://audacity.sourceforge.net/>. The software is distributed under the terms of the GNU General Public License and the registered trademark of Dominic Mazzoni. It is available free to users in several platforms (Windows, Mac and Linux/Unix). While *Audacity 1.2.6* (2.1MB) is the main release of the software, it is not supported at present in Windows Vista and Windows 7. Users

running Windows 7, Windows Vista and Mac OS X 10.6/10.7 should use the beta version, *Audacity 1.3.13* (13.8 MB). *Audacity's* creators note that the beta version is a work in progress, and that it is not available yet with complete documentation or translations into world languages. However, version *1.2.6* is considered a stable release, is complete and is fully documented. The creators mention on the website that both *Audacity 1.2.6* and the beta version can be installed on the same machine. Nevertheless, *Audacity's* creators are continually enhancing the software and users are encouraged to check for modifications and innovations periodically.

Once downloaded, users will find its buttons and interface intuitive with relatively sophisticated editing capabilities built into the software. *Audacity* is versatile software that can be used for multiple purposes such as converting audio files from cassette tapes and vinyl records into digital recordings or CDs as well as simply recording one's voice. It can also be used to edit a variety of audio file types (e.g., w*av, .mp3, and Ogg Vorbis,*). Users can cut, copy, and splice sounds together, and even change the speed or pitch of a recording. By default, audio files are recorded in the .*wav* format. However, if an .*mp3* audio file is desired, users can download the *LAME™ MP3 Encoder* from the aforementioned website. *Audacity* does not distribute *mp3* encoders, but a link is provided on *Audacity's* website to a third-party site where the *LAME* encoder can be downloaded at no charge. If audio file size is a consideration, it is recommended that users save audio files as mp3 files because the file format requires less storage space than other audio formats.

## Webware

Webware are classified as online applications of software that do not require downloads and installation of software on individual computers. These digital tools are made available on any computer with an online connection. Webware have the advantage of non-dependence on a particular computer operating system, making them accessible to all platforms: Windows, Mac, and even Linux.

## Odeo

One popular free webware option for voice recording and immediate podcasting is Arturo and Rupert's (2006) *Odeo* <www.odeo.com>. Odeo offers an impressive *mp3* player that functions in web pages. After instructors create an online account, a button can be placed on the instructor's website by copying a line of HTML text and pasting it on a class website. When students click on the button, they can record their voice, and the recording is sent directly to a designated email address. I recommend that instructors create a separate email account with a service that allows for large file storage, as audio files can be quite large.

## Vocaroo

Designed as a completely web-enabled recording service, *Vocaroo* <www.vocaroo.com> offers users an exceptionally simple web interface. Students can record their voice from any computer with a microphone and then send the recording to an instructor's email address. An advantage to using *Vocaroo* is that instructors can designate different email addresses for different classes in order to easily manage student work. Additionally, *Vocaroo* offers an embeddable widget that teachers can insert easily into a class website or blog. However, teachers do not have an audio file to archive as a part of a body of evidence of student performance because the recordings remain on *Vocaroo* servers. Once a recording is made, teachers receive an email with a link to the student's recording.

## VoiceThread

Another webware option is *VoiceThread* (Papell, & Muth, 2007), a free service that allows users to use text and voice using a simple web interface available from www.voicethread.com. Group conversations can be collected and shared without installing any software. *VoiceThread* is a collaborative, multimedia slide show that can serve as a repository of images, documents, and even videos. It allows users to navigate slides and make comments in five different ways: voice (with a computer microphone or telephone), text, audio file, or video via a webcam. Recordings can be saved and played offline. Teachers can store student work on computers, burn them to DVDs, or download them for use on an mp3 player or mobile phone. However, *VoiceThread* charges a fee for downloading files.

Instructors can upload an image or video and post it for students to view. Once the image is posted, a link is generated that can be shared via email or posted on a website or blog. Educators can then use these images as visual prompts for the speaking assessments, utilizing both the text and the recorded comment for instructions for students to hear. Students may then record their voices using the same simple interface and these audible comments are saved on the site. I caution instructors to note that students will be able to hear the comments of the other students in the class, which may make this tool more suitable for formative assessments than for high-stakes summative assessments. The creators of *VoiceThread* are aware of the possibilities for this tool in the education market, and as a result they provide additional services geared to teachers for minor subscription charges. The K-12 products are available along with downloadable instruction sheets for teachers from the educational side of the *VoiceThread* webpage <ed.voicethread.com>.

## gCast™

Developed for podcast production for bloggers by phone, *gCast* <www.gcast.com> is a free-to-use web service with basic features. In order for educators to use its most useful features, teachers must pay an annual subscription cost ($99 US). While categorized as a web tool, *gCast* has a unique advantage over the other web tools in that a computer is not needed to voice record. In order to utilize *gCast*, instructors first create a *gCast* account. After creating an account, a *gCast* web page is created for the instructor. A PIN number is assigned to the account, and then instructors may distribute a toll-free telephone number provided by *gCast*. Students may then be given an access code. Users simply dial the toll free number (there is also an international option), follow the voice prompts, and record. Recordings are archived on an established web account. Again, I urge instructors to create separate accounts for individual classes in order to organize student recordings.

Using any telephone, prevalent mobile technology among today's student population, students can call into the *gCast* account, record their responses, review them, re-record if necessary, and then submit the recording using simple commands. In order to review the recordings, the instructor can logon the *gCast* account and listen to the students' recordings. Due to the sophistication of today's telephone microphone technology, the clarity and quality of recordings is remarkable. The primary advantage for this system of recording is that it does not make presumptions regarding student access to digital technology; any student with access to a telephone can record their voice. However, one unfortunate disadvantage of *gCast* is that the filenames as they appear on the account website do not indicate the name of the caller. Thus, it becomes necessary for students to state their names at some point during the recording.

## Portable Hardware Devices

The explosion of digital music technology has led to many outcomes such as the decline in prices for personal, portable devices and the increased number of such devices. While the large capacity *iPod*® remains among the digital elite, there are many mp3 recorders with built-in microphones at low prices depending upon the features and the storage size of the unit. The *SanDisk Sansa Clip* ($39) is a basic 2GB mp3 player and voice recorder with push-button recording and an integrated microphone (SanDisk, 2011). Although the quality of the recording has a distinctly mechanical tone to it, the articulation is clear and comprehensible.

A comparable technology is the 4GB *Creative Zen Style M100* mp3 player ($39). As well as serving as a full-functioning mp3 player, it contains a voice recorder that accommodates multiple audio formats such as mp3, WMA, Audible 4, and AAX. It also has a micro SD card slot that allows users an additional 32GB of storage space (Creative, 2011). Using a digital menu, the recording process is rather simple where one selects "microphone" from a list of resources on the main menu.

Finally, the *Sanako* mp3 recorder is at the upper end of the price range for personal, portable hardware devices ($120). Although it only has 512 MB of storage capacity, this recorder, specifically designed for language learners and teachers, has the advantage of a dual track recording system, in which the student can record their voice while concurrently listening to a teacher-track (Sanako, 2011). This recorder was primarily planned for use with *Sanako Lab 100* systems in order to provide students with a handy and convenient way of saving and using audio material. The recorder increases opportunities for question and answer assessments or simulated, asynchronous "interviews". The recording quality is excellent; however, its recording process is not intuitive and significant training or detailed user guides may need to be provided to the students in order for them to use the recorder.

## MOVING AWAY FROM TRADITIONAL ASSESSMENT METHODS

Beginning in 2006, the Provost requested that the Department of Modern and Classical Languages at Georgia State University determine a method to assess student proficiency in foreign languages at the introductory level of language learning. The mandate coincided with faculty member interest in replacing traditional face-to-face speaking assessments with digital recordings in order to increase valuable instructional and preparation time. Thus, as one of the Foreign Language Methods professors who had developed a class on integrating technology into instruction, I collaborated with a doctoral student enrolled in the instructional technology program and the professor in charge of the lower division Spanish courses. In addition to our objective of finding a technology tool that would help instructors increase precious instructional and preparation time, we sought to identify technology tools that would be easy-to-use and not increase student performance anxiety as theoretically described by Krashen's (1981) Affective Filter hypothesis. Additionally, we sought to find technologies that would assist students in creating digital portfolios to showcase student progress during the language learning process.

### Pilot Study

University faculty members were accustomed to using the *uLearn* course management platform, and the system was equipped with the *Wimba®* voice recorder (Wimba, 2008). This web-based voice recorder was embedded in the *uLearn* system where students could access the recorder either in the language lab on-campus or from the internet away from campus. With a recording system already in place, we decided to conduct a pilot study of 128 students enrolled in first- and second-semester Spanish ($n = 61$) and Japanese ($n = 67$) courses during the 2006-2007 academic year participated (Early & Swanson, 2008). The research sample was ideal because included a wide range of traditional and nontraditional undergraduate students whose age ranged from 18 to 52 years of age ($M = 23$). Students had a minimum of two oral language assessments during the semester, one at the third week and another at the thirteenth week of the semester. Instructors were taught how to use the *Wimba* system and instructions on how to use the system were published for students and placed on *uLearn* as a resource.

Classes met two or three times per week for a total of three instructional hours and each instructor conducted both traditional in-class speaking assessments and digital voice-recorded assessments. Data analysis provided several interesting findings. First, students and instructors alike favored the digital recording method for speaking assessments. Students reported feeling more self-conscious and anxious when being assessed in-class in front of the instructor and their peers. Students also reported higher levels of affective filter due to peer presence during the assessment process. Additionally, the students felt that their responses in the target language were less authentic and less creative when assessed face-to-face in class.

However, when assessed using voice recordings, the students felt more relaxed. They reported that their responses in the target language were more thorough, and they felt that they could notice oral improvement. Additionally, the students felt more in control of their success in the target language, and they reported that they preferred recording their answers for oral language assessment. Interviews with their instructors confirmed the students' perceptions and offered insight into the process. Instructors viewed the traditional face-to-face in-class method time consuming, which led to student disengagement. The instructors noticed immediately how much instructional time is lost when conducting face-to-face speaking assessments. Furthermore, the instructors remarked that the traditional method of oral language assessment does not allow for a second opinion of a student's grade. They noted that they liked having an artifact of student progress that could be used to re-evaluate student proficiency with an outside reviewer listening to the student's recording and using the same objective scoring rubric.

Moreover, the instructors mentioned that evaluation of student progress could take place at unconventional times; they did not have to evaluate student performance immediately in the classroom. They could listen to the recording several times before concluding the assessment process. Additionally, they found that students could record their responses to instructors' questions at times/places convenient for students. By doing so, the length of student response to questions was longer and many times more accurate when using the voice-recording software. Furthermore, the instructors commented that the rate of success on assignments increased when students were allowed to record their responses outside of class rather than having only one opportunity to respond during in-class assessments. To that end, students said that they often practiced for about an hour before making a final recording to turn in for evaluation. Finally, the instructors stated that they preferred the idea of digital recordings for oral language assessment because it encouraged students to practice and study before submitting work for instructor evaluation. The online assessments given during the semester were formative assessments and provided students with valuable information in order to improve future performances.

## Large-Scale Investigation

After learning about the results from this pilot study, the department wanted to investigate the use of digital recordings on a much larger scale. In 2007, Carmen Schlig and I decided to examine undergraduates' ($N = 1180$) oral language proficiency at the introductory- level of the Spanish courses because it was the language with the larg-

est student enrollment. Instead of searching for other digital recording options, the *Wimba*® voice recorder was used again. The curriculum for Spanish 1001, as well as the curriculum for the other languages taught in the department, was grounded in national standards (National Standards in Foreign Language Education Project, 2006).

Framed by Vygotsky's (1978) zone of proximal development and Long's (1996) Interaction Hypothesis, the researchers trained the 13 instructors who taught multiple sections of the Spanish 1001 course over the course of two consecutive semesters on campus to guard against errors in validity and reliability. Student speaking proficiency was measured at three different periods during the semester (week 3, 8, and 14). The research focused on assessing student speaking ability on five factors: pronunciation, task completion, fluidity of response, linguistic structure, and content. Instructors were trained how to give precise, constructive feedback using various methods to note errors in the five variables of interest. The researchers encouraged instructors to give as much written feedback as possible to help the students improve their speaking proficiency. Additionally, the researchers requested that the instructors note common errors made by students, discuss those in class the following day, and continue to design activities to help students overcome such errors. A total of 2,343 instances of corrective feedback were given over the course of the study.

Statistically significant differences were found for pronunciation, linguistic structure, and content using paired sample t-tests. Additionally, a high degree of inter-rater reliability was reported. Findings from the data suggested that pronunciation, linguistic structure, and content of the speaking assessment task can be improved by systematic interaction using formative feedback in the classroom setting and summative feedback collected from out-of-class recordings of language assessment tasks. Additionally, it was noted that the majority of the students (82%) reported that they liked using digital recording for oral language assessments. The notion of being able to review their answers before submitting them for review was popular with the students as well.

From the instructors' perspective, an increase in the accuracy of evaluation and the accuracy of student response appeared to improve. Additionally, the instructors reported less time assessing student speaking proficiency using the digital recordings and more accuracy of student performance because student work could be reviewed by other instructors to verify instructor accuracy when determining student proficiency. Moreover, instructors noticed that by giving students feedback on a digital file, students could then listen to their recordings for specific areas for improvement. As noted by one of the instructors, "I think the process is helping both of us to improve (instructors in the evaluation process and students in speaking ability)" (Swanson & Schlig, 2010, p. 25). The researchers noted that for many of the students, this was the first time they had the opportunity to listen to themselves speaking in Spanish. Additionally, it appeared that students' affective filters were lowered by implementing mandatory oral assessments as part of the curriculum.

While both studies indicated that the use of digital recordings for oral language assessment should be seriously considered for use in all modern language programs, it was noted that many instructors and students did not favor using the *Wimba* system for three reasons. First, both groups mentioned that the interface was too basic. While it contains a timer and the necessary buttons to record, pause, play, and stop, users noted that many times there is a short delay before recording starts. Second, the lack of a save option forces users to listen to the recording and choose to either record a new answer or save and submit their response for instructor evaluation. Third, conversations with students and instructors indicated that many had experience using other digital recording platforms, and it was strongly suggested that the department

consider exploring free and open source software options. To that end, it was decided to investigate other technology tools.

## Exploring Emerging Technologies

Our investigation into other technology began by reviewing the literature on available tools for oral language assessment, which quickly uncovered that there was a dearth of research on the topic. Further investigation showed that many universities and colleges relied on costly technologies created for multimedia language laboratories such as the *Sanako*© and *Sony*© systems. Therefore, we began to identify inexpensive software, webware, and hardware solutions that were described in detail earlier in this chapter. After much research and testing of the aforementioned digital tools, the instructors and students stated that they preferred *Audacity* for multiple reasons. They found its interface intuitive, and they found many of its features appealing (see Figure 1). They liked the graphic display of their voices, the level meters to control volume before, during, and after recording, its ability to create different file formats, in particular, the popular *mp3* format, and its editing ability for users to cut, copy, paste, and delete portions of recordings.

Additionally, they mentioned the usefulness of *Audacity's* ability to slow the tempo of the recording so that students could listen for specific purposes. For example, the Japanese and Chinese instructors found this feature particularly useful when teaching students to listen for case markers and word boundaries. Those teaching French, German, Portuguese, and Spanish found this feature appealing to teach listening and speaking in terms of unit ideas, which is consistent with best practices (Cervantes & Gainer, 1992; Griffiths, 1992)

Furthermore, the ability to record multiple tracks on the same recording was attractive for the instructors. In the French classes, instructors could record a series of questions allowing enough

*Figure 1. Audacity Interface (Audacity® software is copyright©1999-2011 Audacity Team. The name Audacity® is a registered trademark of Dominic Mazzoni. Used with permission.)*

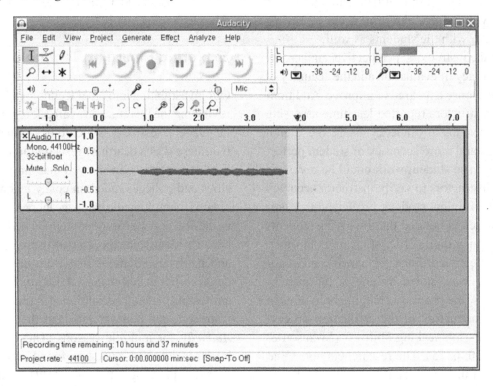

*dead* time for student responses. Then, students could open the file, listen to the questions, and provide answers on a separate track. Then, the file would be saved as one file with questions and responses on it. Overall, it appeared that *Audacity* was the preferred option to explore for oral language assessment.

## Testing Audacity's Usefulness for Oral Language Assessment

While our research on using digital technology for speaking assessments was focused at the undergraduate level, we decided to conduct two more studies using *Audacity* as the digital platform for speaking assessments (Swanson, Early, & Baumann, 2011). The first project broadened the existing work by studying both middle school students' perceptions ($N = 76$) and their teacher's perceptions of using voice recording technology

for out-of-class speaking assessments from a mixed methods approach using data from surveys and interviews. The second study used a qualitative research design to gain understanding about using voice recording technology for out-of-class speaking assessments with a group of eight undergraduate students studying Japanese with their instructors. First, students were asked to place in rank order of importance to them the four skills of language learning (listening, reading, speaking, and writing). Afterward, using a 7-point Likert scale survey, students in both studies were asked to rate their agreement on a scale from 1 (*Strongly Disagree*) to 7 (*Strongly Agree*) on 13 questions centered on three areas of interest: accuracy using the target language, student anxiety, and student grades on assignments. Two additional statements were added to gauge student creativity and ease of use of *Audacity*. Finally, students were asked if they liked using voice recordings for oral language assessment, the students' preference to traditional or digital oral language assessments. The instructors were interviewed in order to understand their perceptions of using *Audacity* as a resource for oral language assessment.

## Student Perceptions

Data analysis from both studies revealed several interesting findings. First, students rated learning how to speak and to listen to people speaking in the target language higher than learning to read and write the language. That is, students were interested in learning how to use the target for oral/aural communicative purposes. Next, related to the three areas of interest, the majority of the students (82%) indicated that their recorded responses outside of class were an accurate representation of their speaking ability in the target language. Additionally, almost all of the students (92%) stated that their responses using digital voice recordings were more accurate than their responses given during in-class speaking assessments and that the use of the digital technology helped improve their ability to communicate orally in the target language. Interviews with students confirmed these findings where most of those interviewed mentioned without being asked about it that it was helpful to listen to their recordings in order to identify errors (e.g., in pronunciation).

In terms of enhancing or diminishing performance anxiety as theoretically conceptualized in the Affective Filter Hypothesis, only one student found her performance anxiety increase when having to record responses for out-of-class oral assignments. Her anxiety was found to be more related to using unfamiliar technology than having to speak in the target language for assessment purposes. The remainder of the students expressed a lower sense of performance anxiety when using *Audacity* for out-of-class speaking assignments because they did not have to speak in front of their classmates, which was found to

be a tremendous source of anxiety for students regardless of educational level.

When asked about improvements in grade using the two methods of assessments, student opinion was divided. More than half of the students felt that their grades on out-of-class speaking assessments were better than those conducted in-class because they had the ability to submit their best work for evaluation. That is, they could record and listen to their responses. If they were dissatisfied with the outcome, they could delete it and then re-record responses as many times as they wanted until they were ready to turn in their best work. Most students (82%) remarked that they re-record their responses more than once with more than a quarter of the students (29%) reporting having spent almost an hour recording a final version of their response.

In terms of measuring differences in student creativity and ease of use, most (81%) did feel that their voice recordings were more creative than responses they would give during an in-class assessment. Additionally, all of the students expressed that *Audacity* was easy to use. They remarked that the interface was intuitive. They found its features easy to locate and they found the Help menu useful. On the whole, the students overwhelmingly concluded that they preferred using digital voice recording for speaking assessments to traditional in-class assessments.

## Instructor Perceptions

Interviews with instructors indicated that the traditional method of oral language assessment was at a disadvantage when compared to using digital recording technology. They noted that in addition to increasing student performance anxiety, the in-class assessments also tended to decrease the likelihood of students using newly-learned grammatical structures. They noted that in class, students tended to be more cautious with their responses and less willing to experiment in the target language. Furthermore, during the in-class assessments, there tended to be more instances of classroom management problems because all of the students were not engaged in the assessment activity. Also, the instructors noted that in-class assessments are fleeting. That is, once the students' responses are given, there is no mechanism to listen to the response a second time, which allowed for possible inaccuracies during the evaluation process. Finally, they noted that due to an increased level of anxiety, students tended to prepare a statement in written form instead of speaking without a script.

However, when the students used *Audacity* to record answers to teacher-created language tasks, the instructors noted various outcomes. First and foremost, they noted that student performance anxiety was much lower because they did not have to perform in front of peers. It appeared that the possibility of peers being able to make judgment about classmates' performance on assessments was a source of increased angst, which is consistent with the literature (Woodrow, 2006). Additionally, student responses appeared to be more animated during the out-of-class assessments. Second, they immediately noticed how much extra time they had during class for instructional purposes. Several of the instructors had estimated that each in-class speaking assessment could consume at least one class meeting. In addition to having more instructional time, it was noted that instructors could evaluate student performance much quicker and more accurately. They did not have to deal with classroom management issues and they could listen to student responses more than once at unconventional times and locations (e.g., at home in the evening). Third, instructors noticed that students tended to complete the language assessment tasks better when recording and the responses also tended to include newly-learned grammatical structures and vocabulary, which the instructors noted tended to lead to an increased sense of control over one's success during assessment. Such findings were due to providing students multiple opportunities for success according to the

instructors. Interestingly, they noted that improvements in linguistic accuracy and improvements in course grades were not observed. However, such findings could be due to the timeframe needed for novice-level language learners to progress to an intermediate level of speaking proficiency on the ACTFL (2012) rating scale.

Next, the instructors found the ability to have a digital artifact of student learning very useful for several purposes. It can serve as a mechanism to measure student progress during language learning. The Japanese instructors noted that many times students become discouraged because they feel they are not progressing adequately. By having recordings at different points throughout the semester, they can play the recordings to students to show linguistic improvements. Such opportunities provide students with not only the ability to note progress in the language; it also can help increase student awareness of errors, which can encourage self-correction. Additionally, the recordings can be used to increase the reliability of assessment whereby multiple instructors can evaluate student performance using objective rubrics. Moreover, the recordings can be archived as part of a body of evidence for institution accreditation purposes.

## Posed Challenges

While instructors and students alike appeared to welcome the notion of continuing to use *Audacity* for speaking assessments, multiple challenges can arise when replacing in-class assessments with out-of-class assessments. First, there is an issue of the digital divide. There is a gap between individuals at different socio-economic levels with regard to opportunities to access information via the internet and communications technologies for an array of activities. Care needs to be taken to assure that all students have access to technology in order to complete such out-of-class assignments. While such shortcomings can be overcome to a large extent by working with media center personnel to download and install *Audacity* and the *LAME* encoder on student workstations, instructors need to make sure all students have the knowledge and the ability to access the technology.

Second, with respect to the equipment, costs related to out-of-class oral language assessments can increase if students do not treat school recording equipment properly. Since the first study in 2006, damage was reported to language lab equipment, in particular the headsets that have earphones and a microphone. Although headsets can be purchased relatively cheaply, the replacement cost can become a serious issue over time. At present, students attending language labs in the aforementioned studies must now check out headsets and return them in proper working order.

Three more issues can emerge when working with large numbers of faculty members. First, arriving at agreement on the technology to implement for non-traditional speaking assessments can become problematic. Due to the increased presence of innovative Apple products in recent years, Microsoft's market share has declined (Halfacree, 2009; Hodgin, 2009), and Mac users may opt for *GarageBand*®, a recording software application developed by Apple. Therefore, it is important to remain focused on the objectives in order to determine an appropriate technology tool. Second, large-scale training sessions to use *Audacity* can prove to be challenging due to instructor inflexibility and complex work schedules. The third involves the paradigm shift from traditional face-to-face assessment to out-of-class assessments. Our research has shown us that less tech-savvy instructors may need special attention to help them embrace a new method of assessment. It is recommended that time and patience be given liberally to all instructors in order for them to learn how to use *Audacity* and then teach their students how to use it effectively. Research indicates that there is a dearth of research on the time needed to form a habit, and therefore, it is difficult to predict how long it would take for instructors to become accustomed to and to form a habit of using digital

technology for oral language assessment (Lally, van Jaarsveld, Potts, & Wardle, 2009).

A final issue can arise if funds have already been allocated for expensive, and possibly outdated, language lab systems. Such was the case when we first set out to measure student speaking proficiency with the undergraduates enrolled in classes in the first two semesters of Spanish. Instructors were interested in pursuing other technologies while administrators felt it was important to use existent technology. Therefore, I advocate conducting comparative research to determine which technology platform will best serve instructors and students alike.

## FUTURE RESEARCH DIRECTIONS

*Audacity's* use in the S/FL language classroom appears even more promising given the recent economic turmoil that began in late 2007, especially in K-12 classrooms. The Great Recession as it has come to be called (Wessel, 2010) caused manifold problems in educational systems worldwide and further research of using free and open source software like *Audacity* is called for. While federal, state, and local policies have been designed to distribute education funds equitably, research indicates that these policies systematically provide more money to higher-income students and wealthier schools. However, at every level of government, policymakers allocate more resources to students who have more resources, and less to those who have less (Carey & Roza, 2008). Therefore, it would be insightful to test the benefits and effectiveness of using *Audacity* in school districts that are suffering from disproportionate funding.

Additionally, it would be interesting to explore using *Audacity* for out-of-class speaking assessments in an elementary school context. For decades linguists have professed that S/FL language learning should occur during the early years of development because younger individuals tend to demonstrate lower levels of performance anxiety (Brown; 2007; Dulay & Burt, 1977; Krashen, 1981, 1982; Omaggio Hadley, 2001). Such research may lead to understandings that could assist adolescents and adults lower affective barriers, which in turn may lead to improved language learning.

Additionally, from an interdisciplinary perspective, research focused on using digital voice recordings in other content areas such as history, science, and the arts would be valuable. It would be interesting to investigate how *Audacity* could be implemented in other curricula to improve student learning. Finally, studying remediation strategies to help students suffering from writing disabilities such as dyslexia using digital voice software such as *Audacity* might reveal unconventional methods to support student learning. Research indicates that computer system remediation is beneficial for students with disabilities such as dyslexia (Draffan, Evans, & Blenkhorn, 2007), and such research is supported by the American Academy of Pediatrics and the American Association for Pediatric Ophthalmology (Bowan, 2002).

## CONCLUSION

Engaging students continues to be a challenge for novice and veteran teachers alike, especially when instructors face a multitude of impediments to learning that tend to decrease instructional time in the classroom. It is crucial that teachers in all disciplines develop new strategies to take advantage of every minute in the classroom for instructional purposes in order to improve student achievement in today's high stakes testing environment. For S/FL teachers, classroom time is lost when assessing students using the traditional face-to-face method. Teaching languages from a communicative approach as set forth by ACTFL combined with the integration of computer assisted technology appears to hold promise for instructors as well

as language learners. Advances in the teaching and learning of languages have led to research highlighting a myriad of emerging technologies for use in the measurement of student speaking proficiency and assessment (Early & Swanson, 2008; Kvavik, 2005; Swanson & Schlig, 2010; Swanson, Early, & Baumann, 2011; Volle, 2005; Zhao, 2005).

In this chapter, I have outlined various software, webware, and hardware technologies for oral language assessment purposes. While each has its advantages and disadvantages, instructors need to spend time determining appropriate objectives and outcomes for its use. In our research, *Audacity* has been shown to be a viable and useful tool for students and instructors. The program downloads and installs very quickly. Its interface is intuitive and becoming acquainted with its features only takes a few minutes. Research has shown that by using *Audacity* for out-of-class speaking assessments, student performance anxiety appears to decrease as students become more confident in their abilities to use the target language. Instructors have noted many benefits of using *Audacity* ranging from an increase in instructional time to less time spent evaluating student performance.

While it can be argued that students using voice recording software out-of-class may choose to write a script and then read it aloud instead of presenting a spontaneous answer, our research has noted that instructors can tell when students are reading instead of providing unrehearsed responses. Nevertheless, I advocate for using *Audacity* for formative but not summative evaluation. Our research indicates that students tend to use the out-of-class assessments as a means to experiment and improve linguistic ability. That said, it is important to remind instructors of the digital divide and that some students may not have access to technology outside of the educational setting. Therefore, instructors should assess student access to technology before implementing out-of-class assessments.

Clearly, the integration of the internet into daily life and the increase in the rate of emerging technologies have helped shape the educational landscape for almost two decades. Such changes have presented numerous opportunities as well as challenges for instructors. The technology tools presented earlier serve as examples of the technology available today. Findings from our research indicate that the use of digital technology for oral language assessment is a viable and preferable option. Future research and the development of new technologies available to language teachers will expand upon our research.

## NOTE

Audacity® software is copyright©1999-2011 Audacity Team. The name Audacity® is a registered trademark of Dominic Mazzoni.

## REFERENCES

American Council on the Teaching of Foreign Languages. (2012). *ACTFL proficiency guidelines -- Speaking*. Alexandria, VA: Author.

Arturo, R., & Rupert, E. (2006). *Odeo* [software]. New York, NY: Sonic Mountain.

Ball, D. L. (1990). The mathematical understandings that prospective teachers bring to teacher education. *The Elementary School Journal, 90*(4), 449–466. doi:10.1086/461626

Beauvois, M. (1998). Conversations in slow motion: Computer-mediated communication in the foreign language classroom. *Canadian Modern Language Review, 54*(2), 198–217. doi:10.3138/cmlr.54.2.198

Bowan, M. D. (2002). Learning disabilities, dyslexia, and vision: A rebuttal, literature review, and commentary. *Optometry (St. Louis, Mo.), 73*(9), 553–575.

Brown, H. D. (2007). *Principles of language learning and teaching* (5th ed.). Englewood Cliffs, NJ: Prentice Hall Regents, Buttaro, L. (2009). Language, learning, and the achievement gap: The influence of classroom practices and conversation on performance. *Language and Learning Journal, 4*(1). Retrieved from http://ojs.gc.cuny.edu/index.php/lljournal/article/view/458/547

Carey, K., & Roza, M. (2008). *School funding's tragic flaw*. Seattle, WA: Center on Reinventing Public Education.

Carroll, J. (1963). The prediction of success in intensive foreign language training. In Glazer, R. (Ed.), *Training research and education* (pp. 87–136). Pittsburgh, PA: University of Pittsburgh Press.

Cervantes, R., & Gainer, G. (1992). The effects of semantic simplification and repetition on listening comprehension. *TESOL Quarterly, 26*(4), 767–770. doi:10.2307/3586886

Chan, M. (2003). Technology and the teaching of oral skills. *CATESOL Journal, 15*, 51–57.

Chastain, K. (1975). Affective and ability factors in second language learning. *Language Learning, 25*, 153–161. doi:10.1111/j.1467-1770.1975.tb00115.x

Creative. (2011). *Creative store*. Retrieved from http://us.store.creative.com/category/ 68709286741/1/ZEN-Style-M100. htm?gclid=CP_uj6qq66wCFZGx7Qod9xCcKA

Cuban, L. (2001). *Oversold & underused: Computers in the classroom*. Cambridge, MA: Harvard University Press.

Draffan, E. A., Evans, G., & Blenkhorn, P. (2007). Use of assistive technology by students with dyslexia in post-secondary education. *Disability and Rehabilitation. Assistive Technology, 2*(2), 105–116. doi:10.1080/17483100601178492

Dulay, H., & Burt, M. (1977). Remarks on creativity in language acquisition. In Burt, M., Dulay, H., & Finnochiaro, M. (Eds.), *Viewpoints on English as a second language* (pp. 95–126). New York, NY: Regents.

Early, P., & Swanson, P. (2008). Technology for oral assessment: Recapturing valuable classroom time. In Cherry, C. M., & Wilkerson, C. (Eds.), *Dimension* (pp. 39–48). Valdosta, GA: SCOLT Publications.

Flewelling, J. (2002). From language lab to multimedia lab: Oral language assessment in the new millennium. In C. M. Cherry (Ed.), *Dimension: Proceedings of the Southern Conference on Language Teaching,* (pp. 33-42). Valdosta, GA: SCOLT Publications.

Foster, P., Tonkyn, A., & Wigglesworth, G. (2000). Measuring spoken language: A unit for all reasons. *Applied Linguistics, 21,* 354–375. doi:10.1093/applin/21.3.354

Futernick, K. (2007, October). Study examines why teachers quit and what can be done. *District Administration, 43*(10), 16.

Gardner, R., Smythe, P., Clement, R., & Gliksman, L. (1976). Second-language learning: A social-psychological perspective. *Canadian Modern Language Review, 32,* 198–213.

Gilgen, R. G. (2004, April 22). *Creating a mobile language learning environment.* Presentation presented at the Educause Midwest Regional Conference, Chicago, IL.

Goldman, J. P. (1991). Balancing school sports and academics. *Education Digest, 56*(8), 67–71.

Griffiths, R. (1992). Speech rate and listening comprehension: Further evidence of the relationship. *TESOL Quarterly, 26*(2), 385–390. doi:10.2307/3587015

Hai-Peng, H., & Deng, L. (2007). Vocabulary acquisition in multimedia environment. *US-China Foreign Language, 5*(8), 55–59.

Halfacree, G. (2009, November 2). Windows loses market share to Mac os. *Bit-Tec.* Retrieved from http://www.bit-tech.net/news/bits/2009/11/02/windows-loses-market-share-to-mac-os/1

Hartman, K., Neuwirth, C., Kiesler, S., Sproull, L., Cochran, C., Palmquist, M., & Zabrow, D. (1995). Patterns of social interaction and learning to write: Some effects of network technologies. In Berge, Z., & Collins, M. (Eds.), *Computer-mediated communication and the online classroom* (pp. 47–78). Creskill, NJ: Hampton Press, Inc. doi:10.1177/0741088391008001005

Hodgin, R. C. (2009). Windows losing market share fast to Mac and linux. *TG Daily.* Retrieved from http://www.tgdaily.com/software-features/41291-report-windows-losing-market-share-fast-to-mac-and-linux

Krashen, S. D. (1981). *Second language acquisition and second language learning.* Oxford, UK: Pergamon.

Krashen, S. D. (1982). *Principles and practice in second language acquisition.* Oxford, UK: Pergamon.

Kvavik, R. B. (2005). Convenience, communication, and control: How students use technology. In D. G. Oblinger & J. L. Oblinger (Eds.), *Educating the Net generation* (pp. 7.1-7.20). Boulder, CO: Educause. Retrieved from http://www.educause.edu/educatingthenetgen

Lai, C. C., & Kritsonis, W. A. (2006). The advantages and disadvantages of computer technology in second language acquisition. *National Journal for Publishing and Mentoring Doctoral Student Research, 3*(1), 1–6.

Lally, P., van Jaarsveld, C. H. M., Potts, H. W. W., & Wardle, J. (2009). How habits are formed: Modelling habit formation in the real world. *European Journal of Social Psychology, 40*(6), 998–1009. doi:10.1002/ejsp.674

Long, M. (1996). The role of the linguistic environment in second language acquisition. In Ritchie, W., & Bhatia, T. (Eds.), *Handbook of second language acquisition* (pp. 413–468). San Diego, CA: Academic Press. doi:10.1016/B978-012589042-7/50015-3

Mazzoni, D., & Dannenberg, R. (2000). *Audacity* [software]. Pittsburg, PA: Carnegie Mellon University.

Mishra, S., & Sharma, R. C. (2005). *Interactive multimedia in education and training*. Hershey, PA: IGI Global.

Naimon, N., Fröhlich, M., Stern, D., & Todesco, A. (1978). *The good language learner*. Toronto, Canada: Ontario Institute for Studies in Education.

National Standards in Foreign Language Education Project. (2006). *Standards for foreign language learning in the 21st century*. Lawrence, KS: Allen Press, Inc.

Nunan, D. (1999). *Second language teaching & learning*. Boston, MA: Heinle & Heinle.

Oller, J. W. Jr, Baca, L., & Vigil, F. (1977). Attitudes and attained proficiency in ESL: A sociolinguistic study of Mexican-Americans in the southwest. *TESOL Quarterly, 11*, 173–183. doi:10.2307/3585453

Omaggio Hadley, A. (2001). *Teaching language in context* (3rd ed.). Boston, MA: Heinle & Heinle.

Papell, B., & Muth, S. (2007). *VoiceThread* [webware]. Chapel Hill, NC: University of North Carolina.

Park, S. H., & Ertmer, P. A. (2008). Examining barriers in technology-enhanced problem-based learning: Using a performance support systems approach. *British Journal of Educational Technology, 39*(4), 631–643. doi:10.1111/j.1467-8535.2008.00858.x

Piaget, J. (1973). *To understand is to invent*. New York, NY: Grossman.

Pierson, M. E., & Cozart, A. (2005). Case studies of future teachers: Learning to teach with technology. *Journal of Computing in Teacher Education, 21*(2), 59–63.

Rosenbusch, M. H. (2005). The No Child Left Behind Act and teaching and learning languages in the U.S. schools. *Modern Language Journal, 89*, 250–261.

Rosenbusch, M. H., & Jensen, J. (2004). Status of foreign language programs in NECTFL states. *NECTFL Review, 56*, 26–37.

Sanako. (2011). *Sanako mp3 recorder*. Retrieved from http://www.sanako.com/Products/Product_container/SANAKO_MP3_Recorder.iw3

SanDisk. (2011). *Sansa clip + mp3 player*. Retrieved from http://www.sandisk.com/products/sansa-music-and-video-players/sandisk-sansa-clipplus-mp3-player

Schinke-Llano, L., & Vicars, R. (1993). The affective filter and negotiated interaction: Do our language activities provide for both? *Modern Language Journal, 77*(3), 325–329. doi:10.1111/j.1540-4781.1993.tb01979.x

Sharma, R. C., & Mishra, S. (2007). *Cases on global e-learning practices: Successes and pitfalls*. Hershey, PA: IGI Global.

Stepp-Greany, J. (2002). Student perceptions on language learning in a technological environment: Implications for the new millennium. *Language Learning & Technology, 6*(1), 165–180.

Swanson, P. (2010). Teacher efficacy and attrition: Helping students at the introductory levels of language instruction appears critical. *Hispania, 93*(2), 305–321.

Swanson, P., & Early, P. (2008). Digital recordings and assessment: An alternative for measuring oral proficiency. In A. Moeller, J. Theiler, & S. Betta (Eds.), *CSCTFL report* (pp. 129-143). Eau Claire, WI: Central States Conference on the Teaching of Foreign Languages.

Swanson, P., Early, P. N., & Baumann, Q. (2011). What audacity! Decreasing student anxiety while increasing instructional time. In Özkan Czerkawski, B. (Ed.), *Free and open source software for e-learning: Issues, successes and challenges* (pp. 168–186). Hershey, PA: IGI Global.

Swanson, P., & Schlig, C. (2010). Improving second language speaking proficiency via interactional feedback. *International Journal of Adult Vocational Education and Technology, 1*(4), 17–30. doi:10.4018/javet.2010100102

Volle, L. (2005). Analyzing oral skills in voice e-mail and online interviews. *Language Learning & Technology, 9*(3), 146–163. Retrieved from http://llt.msu.edu/vol9num3/volle/

Vrasidas, C., & McIsaac, M. S. (2007). Integrating technology in teaching and teacher education: Implications for policy and curriculum reform. *Education Media International*. Retrieved from http://vrasidas.com/wp-content/uploads/2007/07/integrateemi.pdf

Vygotsky, L. S. (1978). *Mind in society*. Cambridge, MA: Harvard University Press.

Wessel, D. (2010, April 8). Did 'great recession' live up to the name? *The Wall Street Journal*. Retrieved from http://online.wsj.com/article/SB10001424052702303591204575169693166352882.html

Wimba. (2008). *Wimba Voice*. Retrieved from http://www.wimba.com/products/wimbavoice/

Woodrow, L. (2006). Anxiety and speaking English as a second language. *RELC Journal, 37*(3), 308–328. doi:10.1177/0033688206071315

Wright, V. H., Wilson, E. K., Gordon, W., & Stallworth, J. B. (2002). Master technology teacher: A partnership between preservice and inservice teachers and Teacher Educators. *Contemporary Issues in Technology & Teacher Education, 2*(3). Retrieved from http://www.citejournal.org/vol2/iss3/currentpractice/article1.cfm

Zellmer, M. B., Frontier, A., & Pheifer, D. (2006, November). What are NCLB's instructional costs? *Educational Leadership, 64*(3), 43–46.

Zhao, Y. (2005). The future of research in technology and second language education. In Zhao, Y. (Ed.), *Research in technology and second language learning: Developments and directions* (pp. 445–457). Greenwich, CT: Information Age Publishing, Inc.

## KEY TERMS AND DEFINITIONS

**Affective Filter Hypothesis:** The theoretical screen that captures the relationship between second language learners and the input needed to acquire a second language. If the filter is high, input is being blocked by affective variables. Conversely, if the filter is low, more input can be received. Teaching and learning environments with low levels of anxiety are postulated to be more conducive to language learning.

**American Council on the Teaching of Foreign Languages:** An United States of America organization whose mission is to improve and expand the teaching and learning of all languages at all levels of instruction. Commonly referred to by its acronym, ACTFL serves as a membership organization for thousands of foreign language teachers and administrators as well as individuals serving in governmental and industrial capacities.

**Instructional Time:** The amount of time teachers have during class to conduct learning activities.

**MP3 Files:** A digital audio recording file format that compresses the size of the file for storage purposes.

**Oral Language Assessment:** The manner in which individuals or groups of language learners are evaluated in terms of their speaking ability.

**Performance Anxiety:** A state of nervousness and apprehension when an individual performs a task before an audience.

**Second/Foreign Language:** For the purposes of this chapter, whether an individual is part of a language program termed as *foreign language*, *immersion*, or even *second language*, the teachers and their students are collectively grouped as S/FL teachers and students because they share the same educational goal, learning a new language.

**Traditional Method of Oral Language Assessment:** Instructors assigning language performance tasks in class and then listening to and evaluating student speaking performance.

# Chapter 11
# Open Source Educational Initiatives to Improve Awareness of Rabies Prevention

**Peter Costa**
*Global Alliance for Rabies Control, USA*

**Deborah J. Briggs**
*Global Alliance for Rabies Control, USA*

## ABSTRACT

*Rabies is the deadliest infectious disease known to humans and animals and yet is almost always pre-ventable even after an exposure has occurred. The lack of educational awareness is a major reason why over 55,000 people die of the disease every year. The Global Alliance for Rabies Control, in association with international partners in the field of public health, initiated new educational initiatives aimed at increasing global awareness for those living at daily risk of exposure to rabies. Three of the open source educational initiatives are described in this chapter, including: World Rabies Day; the establishment of a freely accessible scientifically accurate education bank; and hosting global webinars that connect public health experts interested in reducing the burden of rabies in their regions.*

## INTRODUCTION

Most readers of this chapter will have a specific image of fear and horror in their mind when they hear the word "rabies" and yet few people truly understand the actual disease itself including how they might be exposed to the virus causing rabies and what the current recommendations are

in the event that they were exposed. Increasing awareness on these two issues could save tens of thousands of lives as a lack of true understanding of how rabies viruses are transmitted and how the disease can be prevented are the root causes of almost every human rabies death. Added to the lack of awareness about disease transmission and prevention is the fact that the majority of human

DOI: 10.4018/978-1-4666-2205-0.ch011

rabies deaths occur in populations belonging to the lower socio-economic group where access to resources, including education and anti-rabies biologicals, are limited or non-existent (WHO, 2010). Finally, an evaluation of the highest incidence of disease per age group reveals that at least 50% of all rabies deaths occur in children under the age of 15 indicating that children are not aware of what rabies is, how they could be exposed to infection, and what to do if they were exposed (Rupprecht et al., 2008).

Rabies is in fact, a neglected viral zoonotic disease that is almost always transmitted from an infected mammal to a human (WHO, 2011; Wilde, Briggs, Meslin, Hemachudha, & Sitprija, 2003). Rabies has the highest case fatality rate of any disease known to infect humans and animals (Rupprecht, 2004; Rupprecht et al., 2008). There have been very few patients that have survived rabies because, once clinical signs are evident, the disease progresses rapidly and almost every patient will succumb to the disease within a few days. The World Health Organization (WHO) reports that there are at least 55,000 human deaths every year, thus one person dies of this horrific disease every 10 minutes (WHO, 2010). There are a number of different types, or variants, of rabies viruses circulating in the world and each rabies virus variant tends to be transmitted within one species of animal although 'spillover' of viral infection to other species can and does occur. In fact, it is the spillover of disease to humans that result in human fatalities. Human to human transmission of rabies is extremely rare and has only been laboratory confirmed to have occurred occasionally through organ transplantation although anecdotal transmission of rabies was reported through human bites (Dietzschold & Koprowski, 2004; Fekadu et al., 1996; Lapierre & Tiberghien, 2005). The majority of human rabies deaths, approximately 99% of all estimated global deaths, occur in Africa and Asia after being exposed to (usually through a bite) a rabid dog (WHO, 2005, 2010). Rabies viruses circulate on every continent

in the world, with the exception of Antarctica, resulting in over 3.3 billion people living at risk of contracting the disease.

In North America, the circulation of canine rabies virus variants was eliminated through mass dog vaccination programs initially launched in the 1950's. However, different rabies virus variants continue to circulate within the wildlife population and unvaccinated pets, including dogs and cats, can become infected through exposure to infected wild animals. In the US, between 0 – 6 human rabies deaths are reported annually. Most of these deaths occurred after being exposed to an infected bat for which the patient did not seek prompt medical treatment (Gibbons, Holman, Mosberg, & Rupprecht, 2002; Messenger, Smith, Orciari, Yager, & Rupprecht, 2003).

Despite the extremely high fatality rate of rabies, this disease is almost 100% preventable. Rabies, unlike many other infectious diseases, can be prevented even after an exposure to the infectious agent has occurred. Post-exposure prophylaxis (PEP) consists of washing the wound where rabies virus may have entered, and then administering anti-rabies biologicals to the patient, including vaccine and immunoglobulin (WHO, 2010). In over three decades since modern cell culture rabies vaccines (CCVs) were developed, there have only been a handful of patients that have died of rabies after having received appropriate PEP thus confirming that prompt treatment after exposure could save thousands of lives (Deshmukh, Damle, Bajaj, Bhakre, & Patil, 2011; Hemachudha et al., 1999; Shantavasinkul et al., 2010). Since rabies is preventable and no one would willingly chose to die of rabies if they knew how to prevent the disease, the fact is that the lack of educational awareness on all levels of society is one of the major reasons why humans still die of this disease.

This chapter will outline the role of open source educational awareness in the prevention and control of rabies throughout the world, focusing on three specific initiatives that have used different educational platforms to promote rabies awareness and have resulted in sending rabies prevention messages to over 182 million people in over 150 countries in the past five years. These initiatives include: World Rabies Day; Global Rabies Webinars; and Open Access Rabies Education Bank.

## BACKGROUND

Preventing rabies includes three basic steps: Avoiding exposure to infected animal; receiving protective immunization prior to an exposure; and/or receiving prompt PEP after an exposure has occurred (WHO, 2010, 2011). It is irrelevant as to what species of animal was involved in the exposure nor does it matter in what country the patient was exposed, the information about how to prevent rabies is scientifically identical. To avoid being exposed, humans should stay away from wild animals that may be infected with rabies, keep their pets up to date on their rabies vaccination, and understand how to avoid being bitten through treating their pets respectfully and practicing responsible pet ownership. Rabies prevention for people whose vocation puts them at increased risk of exposure to rabies should include administration of preventative immunization, or pre-exposure vaccination (PrEP) (Manning et al., 2008; WHO, 2005). This group of individuals would include veterinarians and their assistants, scientists and technicians working in rabies laboratories or in rabies vaccine production facilities, and children and other populations living in remote regions where access to rabies biologicals is difficult or not possible. Finally rabies prevention in persons exposed to rabies includes prompt wound washing and administration of anti-rabies biologicals including rabies immune globulin (RIG) and a series of rabies vaccination over two to four weeks (Manning et al., 2008; Rupprecht et al., 2010; WHO, 2005). Without prompt wound care and administration of anti-rabies biologicals, there is a high risk that exposed patients will die of rabies.

Transmitting the information about how to prevent rabies in every country across the world where rabies is endemic may seem like a daunting task, especially considering the number of different languages and various cultures involved. However, digital technology is a powerful communication tool that can provide open source access to information to communities in almost every region and when utilized correctly will deliver live-saving educational materials to those that need them. The implementation of digital technology on a global scale to improve awareness about rabies prevention and control through community based action was initiated by the Global Alliance for Rabies Control (GARC) in 2007. It began by bringing major stakeholders together to develop a strategic plan to improve awareness, followed by the selection of one specific day per year when everyone living at risk of rabies could conduct activities in their own regions to improve awareness. The date agreed upon, September 28th, was designated as "World Rabies Day" (WRD). WRD was launched as a day when all populations across the world living at risk of infection could conduct a multitude of awareness activities, based on their own culturally acceptable messaging, to highlight the ongoing tragedy of rabies and how to prevent infection (Burns, 2009); WRD, 2012).

Outdated or misinformation about how to prevent rabies is not unusual, especially in resource-poor countries where public health professionals responsible for rabies prevention and control do not have the financial resources to travel to international conferences or WHO reference laboratories to learn about new recommendations, diagnostics, surveillance techniques, reduced vaccination protocols etc. (Lapierre & Tiberghien, 2005; Mai le et al., 2010; Rupprecht et al., 2008; Zhang, Zhang, & Yin, 2008). In order to help alleviate this situation, GARC coordinated a series of open access webinars where oral presentations were conducted in 'real time' followed by an opportunity for listeners around the world to ask the speaker questions (GARC, 2012). This was the first time that local public health experts involved in rabies prevention activities, previously hampered from relating information about their own region by the cost of travel or lack of access, could provide information about the rabies situation in their own country to listeners tuning into the webinar from around the world. The only cost incurred to presenters and listeners was their own travel cost to reach a local internet connection, and their time to listen to the presentation.

One of the foremost obstacles for individuals wishing to improve educational awareness in their own country was free access to medically correct informational. Although there was a significant amount of educational material produced by reliable sources in different languages across the world, the fact that there was no central access point made it extremely difficult for individuals to find the educational material that they needed. To alleviate this situation, GARC developed a website where copyright-free educational material could be uploaded and retrieved as needed.

## ISSUES, CONTROVERSIES, PROBLEMS

### Previous Situation

Over the past two decades, a regional rabies prevention and control program overseen by the Pan American Health Organization (PAHO) in collaboration with experts from the Centers for Disease Control and Prevention (CDC) in Atlanta Georgia USA has been underway in Latin America (A. Belotto, Leanes, Schneider, Tamayo, & Correa, 2005; Schneider et al., 2005). PAHO has driven the regional approach by bringing together public health ministries to work together on a regional strategy (A. J. Belotto, 2004). With most Latin American countries complying with the steps outlined in the regional plan, canine rabies control has been greatly reduced throughout the continent although a few countries continue to face chal-

lenges including Haiti and Bolivia. However, in Africa and Asia, no regional approach to rabies prevention and control exists, rabies prevention is not a priority and therefore, canine rabies continues to take a heavy toll on human lives. The inability to implement a regional plan in Africa and Asia could be a result of many factors including the existence of multiple languages and the wide variety of cultures present in the regions. In Latin America, there are fewer major languages to contend with although the problem of providing messaging sensitive to some indigenous populations continues to be a challenge.

In general, prior to the global educational initiatives initiated by GARC, the approach from international public health agencies in Africa and Asia has been to use a "top down" approach where recommendations were developed and passed along to the national governments to implement. When countries have many other diseases to contend with and have limited budgets for public health, financially investing in rabies prevention is often low on the priority list of countries combating HIV, tuberculosis, childhood infectious diseases, poor sanitation, etc. Clearly, the rabies prevention and control recommendations developed by the experts at the international level continue to be important in the overall development of regional and national rabies control strategies. However, understanding how to implement these recommendations at a local level, where citizens live at daily risk of exposure to rabies, required a new strategy.

### Outdated Information and Attitudes

Going global with innovative programs to improve rabies awareness had some initial controversial issues and an array of different types of oppositions to overcome. A quick review of history reveals that the disease of rabies has been with mankind since antiquity and has had an impressive past. For example, rabies was the third disease in history (after smallpox and chicken cholera) for which a vaccine was produced (Wu, Smith, & Rupprecht, 2011). It was Louis Pasteur and his colleagues that finally developed a means by which people exposed to the disease could be saved thus rabies and Louis Pasteur are inextricably linked (Teigen, 2012; Vignal, 1886). In fact, the contribution of Pasteur to rabies prevention is immortalized forever in the beautiful mosaic work depicting a rabid dog on the wall of his crypt beneath what was his home and is now part of the Pasteur Institute in Paris France. The achievements that Louis Pasteur and his colleagues made regarding the development of a rabies vaccine that included multiple injections of a crude preparation into the abdomen to save lives, is so famous that most people do not realize that modern human rabies vaccines are administered into the upper arm, similarly to other modern vaccines. Additionally, the rabies vaccine developed by Louis Pasteur and his colleagues in 1885 was always administered *after* an exposure occurred, as PEP, and was never administered *before* an exposure occurred as a preventative measure, as PrEP. This historical precedent has in fact hampered the extended use of PrEP as one of the valuable tools for governments to use to prevent rabies in populations living in high risk areas with no access to vaccines, or in children the population at highest risk of dog bites and rabies. Changing the attitude of medical professionals to promote the use of PrEP as a means to save human lives was a challenge.

## Building Partnerships

Rabies is a zoonotic disease, meaning that rabies virus circulates within one or more animal species and is almost always transmitted from an infected animal to a human. Human to human transmission rarely ever occurs. Thus human rabies could be greatly reduced or eliminated totally if rabies was eliminated from circulating within animals, the source of human infection. Since dogs are the main source of infection currently causing more than 99% of all human rabies, mass vaccination of

dogs would eliminate 99% of the present number of human deaths. The complicated issue to overcome is that the responsibility for monitoring and enforcing dog rabies control is not clearly established in most resource poor countries. Since rabies is not a notifiable disease in most countries in Africa and Asia and few diagnostic laboratories exist, rabid dogs and dog bites often go unreported and not treated. There is a disconnection between animal health institutions responsible for animal health issues and human health institutions responsible for purchasing and administering PEP to prevent human rabies. There are other ministries that also need to be involved in rabies prevention and control, including the legislative branch, responsible for passing and enforcing laws regarding rabies prevention; waste control, responsible for reducing the amount of garbage and food sources available to dogs; finance departments, required to fund rabies prevention projects; etc. Bringing diverse groups together to discuss common issues of importance and how interrelated programs could save money and lives is not easy and required innovative strategies to overcome obvious communication problems. Bringing the global stakeholders together to work toward common solutions presented a unique opportunity to utilize the time, talent and treasure of various individuals and groups in the field of rabies prevention and control. However, initially it was a challenge to find common 'talking points' and to agree on an overarching strategy that was not biased toward one particular stakeholder.

## Logistics

To physically go to every locality, or even to visit one location in each country to promote rabies prevention and control is a daunting task, and the cost and time required to undertake such a mission is not feasible. Additionally, translating rabies educational messages into each language required to reach people living at risk of dying of rabies in different countries (keeping in mind the need to be sensitive to the local culture) using the expertise of a small team that did not comprehend more than five languages between them was not possible. Therefore, GARC needed to develop a different strategy in order to make the educational messages about rabies prevention freely available to the millions of people that needed them to save their lives. An additional logistic challenge was that of how to conduct real-time webinars aimed at connecting people living in every time zone around the world and having access to different types of internet connections.

## SOLUTIONS AND RECOMMENDATIONS

### World Rabies Day

In 2007, World Rabies Day (WRD) was coordinated by GARC and supported by numerous international partners with the single mission of increasing global awareness about rabies and its prevention because all stakeholders agreed that by increasing awareness about rabies, lives could be saved. It was understood that one of the most important reasons why people continue to die from rabies is because they are not properly informed about what constitutes an exposure to rabies and what they need to do after an exposure has occurred. Additionally, lingering challenges as old as the disease itself continued to hinder the implementation of effective prevention measures including linguistic, religious and cultural barriers, pervasiveness of traditional and ineffective therapeutic practices by local healers and generational inheritance of false local myths, inaccuracies and superstitions. WRD was launched as a health communications campaign and has been the single largest and most successful rabies awareness effort ever conducted. The WRD Campaign is a unique example of a fully functioning One Health effort and has been included as one of the 'annual awareness events' on the United Nation's

calendar of international observances (United Nations, 2012). WRD has involved collaboration by and between every leading human and animal health organization in the world including the World Health Organization, World Organization for Animal Health (OIE), Food and Agricultural Organization of the United Nations (FAO), Centers for Disease Control and Prevention (CDC), and numerous other governmental, private, nonprofit and charitable organization partners. WRD has united all of these organizations towards the common goal of human rabies prevention through improved educational initiatives including eliminating rabies at the source of infection.

By inviting everyone across the world to join in the fight against rabies, WRD has helped restart previously abandoned rabies control programs, build new organizational and societal partnerships and strengthen existing collaborative efforts in nations that formerly thought nothing could be done to stop rabies. Much of what has been accomplished through WRD is attributed to the incorporation of health communications to a field that was vastly dominated by scientists and researchers. Increasingly recognized as a necessary element to improve public health, health communications is critical for people's accessibility and exposure to health information and their resultant ability to make positive health behavior changes (US DHHS, 2003). With the single mission of educating everyone, and especially young people about rabies, WRD sought to convert the endless amounts of relatively stagnant technical data about rabies into freely downloadable, dynamic and intuitive information for lay person utilization. As a grassroots movement needing to quickly surmount numerous and varying behavioral, cultural, demographic and physical barriers to health behavior change, WRD focused on leveraging electronic communications through its own websites and through websites of multi-national partners to reach its target audience members. Sign-ups to the WRD website led to the creation of a global rabies network allowing for instant global communication to more than half a million people in a moment's notice. Additionally, with a focus on 'One Health', WRD eyed intersectoral collaboration from its inception and focused heavily on collaborative engagement by Ministries of Health, Agriculture and Education. This approach not only led to increased participation but illustrated to the world that rabies was a disease that everyone could work together to prevent and the support and dedication of numerous governmental sectors in a single effort signified a united front against a disease of both humans and animals.

The momentum created by WRD has increased the number of global participants involved in improving educational awareness at all levels of society. In the five years since the campaign was launched, 182 million people in 150 countries have received educational messages about how to prevent rabies and close to 8 million animals have been vaccinated against rabies.

Multi-national resolutions to observe WRD each year have been implemented by organizations such as the Association for Southeast Asian Nations (ASEAN), World Organization for Animal Health (OIE) and Rabies Expert Bureaus in Africa, Asia and the Middle East (AfroREB, AREB and MEEREB respectively); recognizing WRD as an opportunity for member countries to pool resources, share expertise and work together in a common concerted effort. WRD has revitalized national programs in numerous countries (Cleaveland, 2010) Governments that had previously abandoned national rabies control efforts are now focusing on understanding the rabies situation in their own countries by self-identifying core capacity deficiencies and requesting technical support and training in areas such as pathology, diagnosis, surveillance, post exposure prophylaxis and communications. New animal vaccination programs have also emerged and with renewed vigor in nations such as Haiti, catalyzed by a mass donation of 500,000 doses of animal vaccine from Brazil in honor of WRD (Schneider et al., 2008) and in Mozambique where previous to WRD it

was forbidden to vaccinate dogs as local folklore told that a vaccinated dog was not a good watch dog. World Rabies Day has been instrumental in helping to dispel such myths and make the case for renewed efforts towards controlling rabies in dogs. In absence of WRD, it is unknown how long local customs and beliefs would have endured resulting in additional human deaths, all due to the lack of correct information. Finally, it is worth mentioning the influx of new and novel partnerships that have been established to help address the need for rabies education. Organizations once separated by now seemingly trivial constraints such as geography or health specialty are now beginning to see the added benefits of working together. One such example is the multi-agency collaborative poster outreach initiative to Africa for WRD; involving participation by seven organizations on three continents and delivering more than 30,000 posters to 22 African nations. Posters were made available in numerous sizes, languages and formats and in many African villages serve as the only means for rabies education (Figure 1).

## Education Bank of Materials

A major focus of World Rabies Day is to increase free access to scientifically accurate rabies prevention educational materials to as many people as possible. For decades, the information to prevent rabies has been understood at higher organizational levels but has not necessarily reached individuals 'on the ground' who are often most at risk and least informed. This has led to the chronic misinterpretation and delivery of erroneous rabies prevention information by ill-informed citizens; conceivably contributing to needless human deaths. Often times materials are simply not in the appropriate language, are culturally or pictorially inaccurate, are inaccessible or limited in their distribution, or may otherwise be rendered unavailable due to funding or copyright constraints. To increase access to educational materials about rabies, an education resource library was constructed and

*Figure 1. African posters distributed by the Global Alliance for Rabies Control and its partners including the Centers for Disease Control and Prevention, the Food and Agricultural Organization, University of Pretoria, Washington State University, and Veterinarians without Borders*

embedded within the WRD website. The WRD website (www.worldrabiesday.org) serves as the campaign's communication hub and has been visited by nearly half a million visitors from over 210 countries and territories since 2007. Since the educational messages to prevent rabies are basically the same all over the world and with so many countries and cultures working individually to control rabies locally, the campaign focused not on working with every community separately but rather to serve as a point source for accurate information and guidance on what material is freely available and helping to create new materials as needed (Wunner et al., 2010). Rabies educational materials, including the WRD logo have been translated into over 40 languages and placed in the public domain.

Educational materials continue to be the most sought after resource on and subsequently the most visited section of the WRD website. Site visitor data is collected through the implementation of an analytics program. Website analytics uses unique internet provider addresses to track visitors coming to the WRD website in a non-identifiable manner. Statistics collected include but are not limited to: pages viewed, length of visit, and keywords

and referring sites leading visitors to a particular webpage. In addition to providing insight into who is visiting the WRD website, analytics, perhaps more importantly, allow for a greater understanding of who is not visiting the website and thus provides an opportunity to compare and contrast those populations with their overall risk of rabies exposure. For example, by looking at website analytics from China (Figure 2), it is clear to see that web visitors from western China are nearly non-existent. Given that rabies is one of the top three most important infectious diseases in China, one would expect visitation to the WRD website, even from poorer, more rural areas of China. To better understand where additional rabies educational efforts may be needed, a physical map of China could be compared to the website analytics visitor map to help define locations for enhanced, targeted rabies education efforts.

## Global Webinars

More than half of the world's population lives at daily risk to rabies (WHOa, 2011). In order to reach these individuals en masse, health educators need to move beyond traditional approaches

*Figure 2. Web visitors to www.worldrabiesday.org originating in China, 2007-2011*

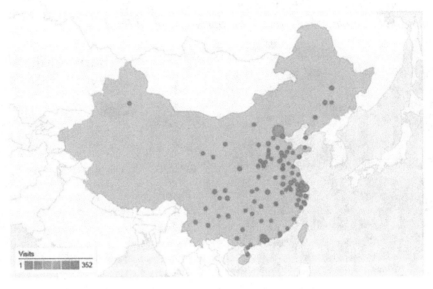

This country/territory sent 5,804 visits via 543 cities

to public health education and begin to leverage electronic communication facilities. Webinars, or web seminars, have evolved over the last decade as an open source solution to educate nearly limitless numbers of people and to reach populations traditionally unable to access accurate and culturally correct health information in a timely manner. Placing information online, for example, on a website, has significantly increased access and helped educate more people but is a static process requiring health information seeking behavior. Therefore, if someone is not actively looking for health information online, the resource may likely be un-utilized or under-utilized and therefore rendered ineffective. Clearly there is a need to not only develop and place information on the world-wide-web but also to actively promote and incentivize its availability.

Historically, online education programs developed for distance learning opportunities at colleges and universities targeted busy students with demanding schedules that wanted to advance their skills and training but were not able to attend traditional, time-fixed classroom learning environments. The provision of online courses offered an

alternative for students to learn and earn course credits in a self-study, self-paced manner. Akin to other great digital discoveries during the last decade, the use of this technology gained immediate popularity. Recently, these online platforms for information dissemination have evolved beyond academia and have been embraced by additional sectors, becoming the most cost effective tool for interacting with customers (Monaghan, 2009). For example, private for-profit companies now advertise their products and services via monthly webinar offerings and public health institutions are marketing healthy behavior by hosting regularly scheduled programs on various topics such as diet and nutrition, preventing occupational injuries, cancer prevention and infectious diseases just to name a few. For many public health professionals, participation in webinars offers the opportunity to learn about a variety of new subjects while gaining continuing education credits without having to leave the workspace.

Given the extreme need for rabies education and the fact that most of the population at risk cannot afford to attend expensive international conferences, GARC began experimenting with ways to best leverage its ever growing online community. Realizing that internet communications through WRD had clearly led to a sea change in the delivery of rabies information, planning began to implement a freely accessible worldwide rabies webinar. In 2010, in observance of WRD, GARC and CDC coordinated the first intercontinental rabies webinar. The motivation behind the webinar was simply to provide information about rabies to as many people as possible over the internet and at no cost to attendees. As a young non-profit organization, GARC was not positioned to host a physical conference. So in line with its mission to educate the world about rabies, GARC leveraged its global network of advocates and available webinar technology to deliver open source rabies education en masse. Instead of hefty registration fees and travel considerations, webinar participation from anywhere in the world required only a computer with an internet connection. After downloading the webinar software and logging in to the online meeting, individuals across the world were instantly connected with rabies subject matter experts in real time.

Similar to a traditional in-person conference, much advance planning is necessary to successfully execute a webinar. Considerations include content, speakers, technology, timing and promotion (Monaghan, 2009). For a global webinar, it is also vital to consider speakers' familiarity (or lack thereof) with the webinar platform, who will facilitate and moderate the webinar and how, when and by whom the webinar will be advertised across different communities, cultures and languages. Similar to any health intervention, formative evaluation measures should also be considered at the outset of webinar planning to assess both the process and impact of the webinar meeting amongst facilitators, speakers and attendees. Similar to traditional meetings in any physical space, the first task is to set a date for the planned webinar. The first intercontinental rabies webinar coordinated in 2010 was held on World Rabies Day (September 28) as GARC's contribution to

the annual observance. However, upon evaluation it was discovered that many individuals could not participate in the webinar because they were involved in their own local WRD events. Unlike most traditional meetings, however, webinar meetings can be recorded, depending on the software and technology used. Therefore, those who were unable to attend the live broadcast were still able to listen and learn from the archived recording.

After receiving numerous accolades from the 2010 webinar, GARC and CDC decided to organize and host a second webinar in September 2011 to be conducted over two days with more speakers and timed one week prior to WRD so that more people could attend. Two separate webinars were coordinated over 16 hours at times convenient for each respective target audience to participate. The first webinar ran overnight (Eastern, US) to accommodate participation from the far-East. Speaker assignments were also aligned by location and time zones. For example, at the outset of the webinar, speakers joined from Australia, Philippines and Japan. As the webinar progressed, speakers joined from India, Nepal, Ghana and the UK, slowly moving westward over an eight hour period until finally reaching the last presenter, located in the United States. Timing of message delivery is a vital component to effective health communications. In order to successfully execute a global webinar, particularly when targeting rabies-vulnerable populations in Asia and Africa, precise timing must be considered for the webinar organizers and speakers but most importantly for the anticipated attendees. When handled correctly, appropriate and precise webinar timing, especially during a time of heightened awareness such as WRD, will result in capturing a much larger portion of the intended target audience. (Table 1).

Though run entirely via internet, an open source webinar resulting in a positive experience for end users requires the focused support and constant attention of numerous organizers working synchronously to ensure seamless speaker and participant coordination, facilitation and moderation

*Table 1. Example of the calculation of the most appropriate timing for a rabies webinar targeting the Eastern Hemisphere. Taken from the World Rabies Day Webinar, Sept. 21, 2011*

|  | New York, United States | Maputo, Mozambique | Istanbul, Turkey | Bangalore, India | Manila, Philippines | Sydney, Australia |
|---|---|---|---|---|---|---|
| Start Time | 0000 | 0600 | 0700 | 0930 | 1200 | 1400 |
| End Time | 0800 | 1400 | 1500 | 1730 | 2000 | 2200 |

and technical functionality. Given the virtual nature of webinars, organizers can opt to be located in the same physical space or connected to the webinar system remotely yet working cooperatively side-by-side in cyber space. The global webinars run by GARC and CDC for example were coordinated by US organizers located 1000 miles apart (Scranton, Pennsylvania and Atlanta, Georgia) from each other. Throughout the webinar, organizers stayed in constant communication via phone, email and text message and also by using the private chat option available within the webinar system. This communication is vital, for example to make sure speakers that are in-line to present are logged into the webinar system, their audio is working and that they are available and ready in advance of their assigned time.

During the webinar, questions continually come into the chat window and require dedicated support staff for timely response. Question and answer sessions that allow live voice broadcast by participants with audio input devices also require a great deal of coordination. Participants' microphones must be manually 'opened' by the webinar staff and they must be congenially addressed and informed that they may now ask their question. Once their question is finished, their microphone may have to be re-muted by the webinar organizers to limit any background noise whilst the speaker is responding to their question. Facilitators must also be cognizant of time constraints and help keep presentations and question and answer sessions 'on time'. Moderation may be required if conflicts arise between speakers and listeners

and must be handled delicately given that hundreds to thousands of logged-in participants are also listening. During webinars, technical issues among participants and those attempting to join the webinar are not uncommon. Dedicated staff support is required to handle these inquiries as webinar organizers cannot take their attention away from the running webinar to assist others. Complete contact information for accessing technical support and guidance on how to handle the most common technical issues should be addressed by the lead organizer at the beginning of each webinar and also provided ahead of time as part of the webinar registration information.

It is well known that many people are hesitant to engage in domains of which they are not knowledgeable. Webinars are still a relatively new concept to most people, especially speakers who are used to conducting presentations to and gathering non verbal cues from a live audience. Webinar organizers must take into account that many speakers will not have any knowledge about how to present information for or log into a webinar and may be slightly intimidated about the idea of participating. For this purpose, a trial run of the webinar should be conducted with each speaker prior to the actual on-line presentation. This process not only familiarizes the speakers with the process but enables organizers to simultaneously conduct an internet connectivity test and an audio test of the speakers' equipment to ensure his/her voice is projecting clear and uninterrupted. Generally once the test run is complete, speakers are much more confident about their ability to participate as a presenter during a webinar. It should also be noted that while webinars offer tremendous access to teaching and learning opportunities in a more time and cost effective manner by harnessing the power of the internet, there are limitations and consequences to such dependence. First, not everyone has access to the internet nor may they have a reliable electrical connection and although the digital divide is becoming narrower with internet access being upheld as a basic human right in many countries (Meredith, 2010) and technological advancements such as the proliferation of web enabled smart phones, those without internet will not be accessible by webinars. Given their dependence on technology, the most significant downfall of webinars is their reliance upon electricity and the risk of power failures and internet connectivity.

## FUTURE TRENDS

Though rabies largely remains a neglected disease, the field of rabies has evolved dramatically as a whole over the past five years. The founding of the non-profit Global Alliance for Rabies Control and its flagship initiative World Rabies Day has most certainly brought new attention to an old disease. The concept of tackling rabies using a 'One Health' approach has prominently and rightfully re-emerged, giving rise to new organizations, initiatives and opportunities for partnerships and fundraising. Multi-national resolutions have been enacted, giving way to aspirations of 'rabies-free' status amongst border-sharing endemic regions through the incorporation of planned mass animal vaccination campaigns and novel information and education programs. Perhaps most important, communities are now taking ownership of addressing local rabies issues using effective and sustainable strategies. Building on this momentum moving forward, the following future trends in rabies prevention and control are expected.

## 'One Health' Approach

Rabies is a disease that circulates in animals but can be transmitted to humans. It is therefore imperative to control rabies in animals that tend to expose humans to the disease (Zinsstag, 2007), most notably the domestic dog. It has become increasing clear in many countries that organizational responsibilities to manage dog populations, including licensure and rabies vaccination, bite confinement and exposure quarantine/euthanasia are undefined or unenforced and oftentimes unfunded. For example, Ministries of Health are accountable for human health and are not necessarily mandated to focus on animal health. Similarly, Ministries of Agriculture are less focused on human health and may see little value in tending to dogs as they are generally not viewed as a commercially viable consumer product. The end result is that the well-being of dogs slips between the cracks. In most countries, there is no one single entity mandated by legislation to ensure dogs are vaccinated against rabies (Lembo et al., 2011). Hence dogs continue to roam, reproduce unchecked, remain unvaccinated and ultimately expose humans to rabies. Future rabies prevention efforts will involve horizontal integration of numerous stakeholders and subject matter experts from both the human and animal sectors.

## Targeted Webinars

The global webinars held during 2010 and 2011 have shown great promise in effectively delivering accurate and credible rabies prevention information to the masses, reaching more than 600,000 listeners in 83 countries. Post webinar evaluations indicating that 98% of respondents would attend a future webinar illustrates the great interest in webinars as an open source technology, particularly for rabies education, and have resulted in numerous requests for topic and or country specific webinars. Health communications increasingly need to meet intended audiences at their level of technology (Rimal et al., 2009) and webinars are a time efficient and cost effective way for any type of organization to reach its target audiences. Given that so many nations are in need of rabies education and it is simply not feasible to visit every one of them in a timely manner, the webinar provides an alternative to participating in person whilst allowing for audio and video integration alongside a presentation for a more personal experience for the end user. Future efforts through use of webinar technology for rabies education will include training on laboratory methods, surveillance techniques and communications training. These fundamental elements can be delivered to countries in need via internet, in real time and by subject matter experts, providing a unique opportunity for individuals across the world to learn from renowned rabies experts.

## Rabies Educators

Although the messages to prevent rabies are the same all over the world and the concepts are fairly straightforward, there are very few people dedicated to delivering rabies prevention messages to communities living at daily risk. Currently, the Global Alliance for Rabies Control fields numerous inquiries on a daily basis that arrive by web, email, phone or text message. Most originate in Asia and each question is unique. However despite efforts to date the wrong information about how to prevent rabies is still prominent in communities around the world as has been described previously in this chapter. Clearly given the number of visitors to the WRD website and listeners on the global webinars there is a desire for further rabies education opportunities. Future efforts for rabies education therefore will include the development of a rabies educator training program to increase knowledge and country capacity for rabies prevention. The Rabies Educator Certificate training program is envisioned to be delivered via webinar and cover all principles of rabies prevention over two days, culminating in an online assessment and awarding

of a certificate to those successfully achieving a passing grade. The Rabies Educator Certificate program is predicted to help increase and play a vital role in the sustainability of local rabies efforts in countries still battling canine rabies.

## CONCLUSION

Over the past seven years, GARC, a registered not-for-profit organization has changed the face of rabies by leveraging open source technology and dramatically increasing the number of people that have received life-saving educational messages about how to prevent contracting the disease. GARC was the first global not-for-profit organization focusing solely on preventing rabies in humans and animals and began by bringing all stakeholders together to work on finding new solutions to improve rabies control. Initially, there was little funding available for promoting rabies prevention and therefore GARC utilized the strengths of its partners, both public and private, to deliver educational materials where they were needed. Additionally, GARC built a web-based education bank that was freely accessible to those that needed information. GARC requested and received donated educational material from public health experts working in over 50 countries around the world. The website soon became the foremost site for anyone seeking rabies educational information and receives approximately 10,000 visitors every month. WRD was promoted by all international public health organizations and member countries of WHO and OIE were encouraged to participate in WRD activities. WRD continues to gain momentum and after five years, over 182 million people have been educated about how to prevent rabies and close to 8 million animals have been vaccinated against the disease.

Overcoming obstacles including translating educational materials into multiple languages was approached by initially turning the situation around and providing simple messages in very few languages, mainly English, and encouraging individuals to translate the material as needed and then provide the translation back to GARC for posting on the website. Additionally, material that was already available in different languages was invited to be posted on the GARC for free access to others.

Encouraging rabies experts and other stakeholders to work together was initially difficult due to the perception of competition for funding and research etc. However, by providing a neutral venue for meetings and discussing commonalities among experts in the field, progress was quickly made and stakeholders began to work jointly on new projects that were freely available and beneficial to all. For example, a *Blueprint for Canine Rabies Control and Human Rabies Prevention* (www.rabiesblueprint.com) was organized and developed by public and private entities and has served as a global template for those wishing to develop strategies to tackle the issue of human rabies prevention and dog rabies control (Lembo, 2012). Modern communication methods, including web-based tools, enabled GARC and its partners to overcome logistic problems including personnel living in different continents with varying time zones.

Changing attitudes about the approach to improving educational awareness was tackled by involving experienced educators in development of new curricular material focused particularly on children, the most vulnerable population at risk of exposure to rabies. In the Philippines, for example, the Ministry of Education was involved as a partner in the initial strategic meetings to develop new strategies to reduce the burden of human rabies. Workshops were hosted for teachers to produce new curriculum materials where rabies information was incorporated into various subjects including English, mathematics, and science.

New web-based communication tools were used to provide public health experts, organiza-

tions and individuals with freely accessible and accurate educational material and the WRD campaign provided the platform for everyone living at risk of rabies to join together on one day to highlight rabies prevention activities. After five years of WRD, more than 500,000 visitors have logged onto the websites hosted by GARC to review rabies educational information and download the material that they need to improve awareness in their own countries.

Empowering communities to take responsibility for their own rabies prevention activities was one of the biggest accomplishments of WRD activities and the establishment of the free education bank. By providing these materials to 'local champions', they were able to educate their own villages. Individual stories from countries around the world were hosted on the GARC websites and published in the GARC Newsletters. Thus local champions were honored for the educational initiatives that they were conducting and were often emulated in other localities as examples of how to improve awareness and save lives.

The success of the GARC indicates that by empowering communities to take responsibility for improving their own rabies prevention educational programs and by utilizing free-access web-based educational tools, millions of people can be protected against the most deadly disease known to mankind.

# REFERENCES

Belotto, A., Leanes, L. F., Schneider, M. C., Tamayo, H., & Correa, E. (2005). Overview of rabies in the Americas. *Virus Research, 111*(1), 5–12. doi:10.1016/j.virusres.2005.03.006

Belotto, A. J. (2004). The Pan American Health Organization (PAHO) role in the control of rabies in Latin America. *Developments in biologicals, 119*, 213–216.

Burns, K. (2009). World Rabies Day promotes prevention of deadly disease. *Journal of the American Veterinary Medical Association, 235*(6), 651–652.

Cleaveland, S., Costa, P., Lembo, T., & Briggs, D. (2010). Catalysing action against rabies. *The Veterinary Record, 167*(11), 422–423. doi:10.1136/vr.c4775

Deshmukh, D. G., Damle, A. S., Bajaj, J. K., Bhakre, J. B., & Patil, N. S. (2011). Fatal rabies despite post-exposure prophylaxis. *Indian Journal of Medical Microbiology, 29*(2), 178–180. doi:10.4103/0255-0857.81786

Dietzschold, B., & Koprowski, H. (2004). Rabies transmission from organ transplants in the USA. *Lancet, 364*(9435), 648–649. doi:10.1016/S0140-6736(04)16912-2

Fekadu, M., Endeshaw, T., Alemu, W., Bogale, Y., Teshager, T., & Olson, J. G. (1996). Possible human-to-human transmission of rabies in Ethiopia. *Ethiopian Medical Journal, 34*(2), 123–127.

GARC. (2008). *World Rabies Day 2007 encourages rabies control in Haiti.* Retrieved April 10, 2012 from http://www.rabiescontrol.net/assets/files/resources/newsletters/ARCnewsletter6.pdf

GARC. (2012). *World Rabies Day webinar.* Retrieved April 9, 2012, from http://www.rabiescontrol.net/news/news-archive/world-rabies-day-webinar-a-huge-success.html

Gibbons, R. V., Holman, R. C., Mosberg, S. R., & Rupprecht, C. E. (2002). Knowledge of bat rabies and human exposure among United States cavers. *Emerging Infectious Diseases, 8*(5), 532–534. doi:10.3201/eid0805.010290

Hemachudha, T., Mitrabhakdi, E., Wilde, H., Vejabhuti, A., Siripataravanit, S., & Kingnate, D. (1999). Additional reports of failure to respond to treatment after rabies exposure in Thailand. *Clinical Infectious Diseases, 28*(1), 143–144. doi:10.1086/517179

Lapierre, V., & Tiberghien, P. (2005). Transmission of rabies from an organ donor. *The New England Journal of Medicine, 352*(24), 2552, author reply 2552.

Lembo, T., Attlan, M., Bourhy, H., Cleaveland, S., Costa, P., & de Balogh, K. …Briggs, D. J. (2011). Renewed global partnerships and redesigned roadmaps for rabies prevention and control. *Veterinary Medicine International.* doi:doi:10.4061/2011/923149

Mai le, T. P., Dung, L. P., Tho, N. T., Quyet, N. T., Than, P. D., Mai, N. D., ... Nasca, P. C. (2010). Community knowledge, attitudes, and practices toward rabies prevention in North Vietnam. *International Quarterly of Community Health Education, 31*(1), 21–31. doi:10.2190/IQ.31.1.c

Manning, S. E., Rupprecht, C. E., Fishbein, D., Hanlon, C. A., Lumlertdacha, B., & Guerra, M. (2008). Human rabies prevention--United States, 2008: Recommendations of the Advisory Committee on Immunization Practices. *MMWR. Recommendations and Reports, 57*(RR-3), 1–28.

Meredith, L. (2010, Jan 28). U.S. considers 'internet access for all'. *Livescience.* Retrieved April 10, 2012, from www.livescience.com

Messenger, S. L., Smith, J. S., Orciari, L. A., Yager, P. A., & Rupprecht, C. E. (2003). Emerging pattern of rabies deaths and increased viral infectivity. *Emerging Infectious Diseases, 9*(2), 151–154. doi:10.3201/eid0902.020083

Monaghan, A. (2009, July/August). Winning webinars. *Pharmaceutical Marketing Europe.* Retrieved April 10, 2012, from http://www.wellshealthcare.com/resources/20090526%20PME%20JulyAug%20article%20as%20published.pdf

Rupprecht, C. E. (2004). A tale of two worlds: Public health management decisions in human rabies prevention. *Clinical Infectious Diseases, 39*(2), 281–283. doi:10.1086/421563

Rupprecht, C. E., Barrett, J., Briggs, D., Cliquet, F., Fooks, A. R., & Lumlertdacha, B. (2008). Can rabies be eradicated? *Developmental Biology, 131*, 95–121.

Rupprecht, C. E., Briggs, D., Brown, C. M., Franka, R., Katz, S. L., & Kerr, H. D. (2010). Use of a reduced (4-dose) vaccine schedule for postexposure prophylaxis to prevent human rabies: recommendations of the advisory committee on immunization practices. *MMWR. Recommendations and Reports, 59*(RR-2), 1–9.

Schneider, M. C., Belotto, A., Ade, M. P., Leanes, L. F., Correa, E., & Tamayo, H. (2005). Epidemiologic situation of human rabies in Latin America in 2004. *Epidemiological Bulletin, 26*(1), 2–4.

Shantavasinkul, P., Tantawichien, T., Wacharapluesadee, S., Jeamanukoolkit, A., Udomchaisakul, P., & Chattranukulchai, P. (2010). Failure of rabies postexposure prophylaxis in patients presenting with unusual manifestations. *Clinical Infectious Diseases, 50*(1), 77–79. doi:10.1086/649873

Teigen, P. M. (2012). The global history of rabies and the historian's gaze: An essay review. *Journal of the History of Medicine and Allied Sciences, 75*(1). doi:doi:10.1093/jhmas/jrr075

United Nations. (2012). *United Nations observances*. Retrieved April 10, 2012, from http://www.un.org/en/events/observances/days.shtml

U.S. Department of Health and Human Services. (2010). *Healthy People 2010: With understanding and improving health and objectives for improving health*, 2 Vols., 2nd ed. Washington, DC: U.S. Government Printing Office, November 2000.

Vignal, M. W. (1886). Report on M, Pasteur's researches on rabies and the treatment of hydrophobia by preventive inoculation. *British Medical Journal, 1*(1322), 809–811. doi:10.1136/bmj.1.1322.809

WHO. (2005). WHO expert consultation on rabies: First report. *Technical Report Series, 931,* (pp. 121).

WHO. (2010). Rabies vaccines: WHO position paper--recommendations. *Vaccine, 28*(44), 7140–7142. doi:10.1016/j.vaccine.2010.08.082

WHO. (2011). *The immunological basis for immunization series: Rabies* (pp. 1–23). Geneva, Switzerland: WHO.

WHO. (2011a). *Rabies fact sheet*, no 99. Retrieved from http://www.who.int/mediacentre/factsheets/fs099/en/

Wilde, H., Briggs, D. J., Meslin, F. X., Hemachudha, T., & Sitprija, V. (2003). Rabies update for travel medicine advisors. *Clinical Infectious Diseases, 37*(1), 96–100. doi:10.1086/375605

Wu, X., Smith, T. G., & Rupprecht, C. E. (2011). From brain passage to cell adaptation: The road of human rabies vaccine development. *Expert Review of Vaccines, 10*(11), 1597–1608. doi:10.1586/erv.11.140

Wunner, W. H., & Briggs, D. J. (2010). Rabies in the 21st century. *Plos Neglected Tropical Disease, 4*(3), e591. doi:10.1371/journal.pntd.0000591

Zhang, Y., Zhang, Z. L., & Yin, J. Y. (2008). Evaluation on the knowledge of rabies through health education programs among the residents in Tianjin, 2007. *Zhonghua Liu Xing Bing Xue Za Zhi, 29*(7), 744.

## KEY TERMS AND DEFINITIONS

**AfroREB:** African rabies expert bureau.

**AREB:** Asian expert rabies bureau.

**ASEAN:** Association for Southeast Asian Nations.

**CDC:** Centers for Disease Control and Prevention.

**FAO:** Food and agricultural organization.

**GARC:** Global Alliance for Rabies Control.

**MEEREB:** Middle East rabies expert bureau.

**OIE:** World animal health organization.

**PAHO:** Pan American Health Organization; a branch of the World Health Organization.

**PEP:** Post-exposure vaccination after being exposed to rabies.

**PrEP:** Pre-exposure vaccination for prevention of rabies prior to an exposure.

**RIG:** Rabies immune globulin; administered into and around the wound site after exposure to provide passive immune treatment that will help to inactivate rabies virus deposited in a wound after exposure.

**WHO:** World Health Organization.

**WRD:** World Rabies Day September 28th.

# Chapter 12
# The Web 2.0 Mandate for a Transition from Webmaster to Wiki Master

**Roger W. McHaney**
*Kansas State University, USA*

## ABSTRACT

*This chapter focuses on the how the advent of Web 2.0 has influenced the role of webmaster and given rise to the wiki master. In section 1, the author provides an overview of the role of webmaster and how a Web 2.0 mindset began to exert an influence on the duties of this individual. The section concludes with the rise of collaborative Web technologies, specifically Wikis. Section 2 describes the evolution of the wiki master and provides a distinction from its predecessor. The specific roles of a wiki master are described in detail here. Section 3 provides a case study-type overview of the wiki master at ELATEwiki. org. Section 4 provides more detail by looking a typical day in the life of the wiki master at ELATEwiki. Conclusive remarks are provided in the final section of this chapter.*

## INTRODUCTION

When the Internet first emerged as a world-wide communication network, no one envisioned the social media revolution that would follow. Among the first steps along this path were the development and acceptance of technologies and protocols that permitted the creation of the World Wide Web (Berners-Lee, 1992). The idea of websites quickly captured the general public's enthusiastic attention and all forms of information began to appear in easy-to-access online formats. Web sites were informational in this environment and comprised a collection of linked pages usually containing text and images. Later, videos and digital assets such as flash animation were added to the mix. These

DOI: 10.4018/978-1-4666-2205-0.ch012

websites were hosted on one or more web servers which were sometimes tied to database systems or application servers, and were accessible through Internet addresses known as Uniform Resource Locators (URLs). The collective whole of public websites became known as the World Wide Web.

From a technical perspective, web pages are documents constructed according to governing specifications known as Hypertext Markup Language (W3C, 2009) that permit a wide variety of software developers to create systems that work according to the same rules. This means web pages created anywhere by anyone, as long as they conform to the standards, will work on all compliant browsers and computer systems. Web pages are distributed and accessed using the Hypertext Transfer Protocol (HTTP), which means a web browser acts as a *client*, requesting a page a user wishes to view. The pages are stored on a networked computer running a program that responds to client requests. So, the computer hosting a website functions as a *server*. Technically speaking, the client submits an HTTP *request* and the server responds by searching through stored content and returns a response message which generally contains the requested content. The transmission of requested web pages can use encryption (HTTPS) to provide higher levels of security and privacy. Once the transmitted, material is received by the client application, usually a web browser, that will interpret the HTML markup language instructions and render the page into a human visible form that appears on the display terminal. The arriving material may also take the form of other digital artifacts that result in animation, video, or audio outputs.

It stands to reason that the process of creating, maintaining, updating, protecting, and monitoring web pages takes skill and acquired expertise. In fact, many IT professionals specialize in these areas and often use titles such as web analyst, web developer, web administrator, or webmaster to represent their roles. Of these, the concept of webmaster is most relevant to this article.

## Webmaster Concepts

Generally, a webmaster is the person responsible for the oversight of one or more websites. A webmaster may have responsibility for the web server hardware and software, site organization, storage hardware and software, security, controls, navigation design, spam filters, day-to-day operations, site design and redesign, web page creation and updates, maintenance of a public presence, visitor comment response, site reputation, advertising placement, user rights, and traffic analysis. For some websites, webmasters must also be experts in secure payment processing and the prevention of system intruders and attacks. Webmasters must have a wide range of knowledge and need the ability to recognize when specialists are needed for particular task accomplishments (TechTarget, 2008).

In smaller organizations or for specific websites, the webmaster may have responsibility for technical implementation. In larger organizations with greater levels of resources, the webmaster may be viewed more as a manager. In these scenarios, the webmaster may use online media and other software systems to oversee operations such as product marketing, sales, order entry and fulfillment, and publicity.

## Advent of Web 2.0

As Internet-based software and hardware systems become more sophisticated, powerful, and faster, more applications became viable. A variety of new web sites began to use this platform for real time communication, collaborative content development, and social interaction. The ability to connect to the Internet moved from the work place to the private sector and this promoted the integration of technology into everyday lives. The term, *Web 2.0,* is used to describe using Internet technologies in a different way. Web 2.0 doesn't refer to a technical update of underlying software and hardware but rather to changes in the way the web is being used by businesses, universities and society in general. In general, Web 2.0 can be viewed as comprising five major, interrelated components: social computing, social media, filtering/recommendations, content sharing, and Web applications (McHaney, 2011).

In general, Web 2.0 concepts move the inherent social nature of humans onto new digital platforms. Social computing is based on the premise that people are profoundly communal and have a need to interact using voice, gesture, and written language. Not only do people seek social outlets, they rely on social clues in decision making, planning, and communication. Social computing supports a variety of interaction in digital environments by making it possible for users to supply, aggregate, filter, and consume information in various forms. New computing paradigms are emerging to support what people want to do (McHaney, 2011). It was against this backdrop that web sites controlled by webmasters gave rise to sites, called Wikis, formed with the idea of interactive, social creation of content (Lamb, 2004; Leuf and Cunningham, 2001).

## Wikis

Wikis unleash the collaborative power of the Web by enabling like-minded people to develop a website filled with co-developed, informative content (Wagner, 2004). A wiki provides a many-to-many environment where users can co-create and edit Web pages using browsers from their current location provided it is connected to the Internet (Cummings, 2008; Richardson, 2009). Like most websites, Wikis support images, audio files, video clips, text, hyperlinks, and other Web page features. Wikis can be open or carefully controlled to give editing privileges to specific users (Sherifudeen, 2005).

The term wiki, based on the Hawaiian word for *fast,* originated with Ward Cunningham who conceived of using collaborative web technology to co-create a shared repository of software design knowledge. In his opinion, the material needed to be accessible to those using it and for it to be changeable by anyone with a vested interest in its success. In other words, those who would share in the long term benefit of having this co-created, tacit knowledge maintained, needed to be empowered as editors. He felt important knowledge was lost and reinvented over and over in his software development group. In response, Cunningham developed a Wiki called the *Portland Pattern Repository* so certain lessons-learned could be captured and communicated. This approach became recognized in software development circles as a synergistic example of Web 2.0 in practice (Leuf and Cunningham, 2001; McHaney, 2011). Cunningham's Wiki gave control to those who would directly benefit from accurate and useful information. The idea caught the public's imagination and soon spread to many organizations and groups (Bishop, 2004; Deursen and Visser, 2002; Fernando, 2005).

Foremost in the wiki world is *Wikipedia*, a web-based, free-content, collaborative encyclopedia anyone can edit. It was founded by Jimmy Wales and Larry Sanger in 2001. They wanted to "create and distribute a multilingual free encyclopedia of the highest quality to every single person on the planet in his or her own language (Wikipedia, 2008)." Wikipedia has demonstrated that group-created knowledge repositories are a viable method of codifying, maintaining, improving, and collecting information. It has more than 3.7 million articles in English, 15 million users, and 260 languages. Further, Wikipedia promotes democratization of the web by allowing a group of users to create and edit a web page.

Due to the popularity of Wikipedia and the emergence of a great number of both private and public wikis, this technology has become a primary example of a viable Web 2.0 application. This class of web site has matured from general use as a means to enable mass collaborative authoring to much more. Most wikis now provide features that enable users to create and edit content, develop topic or subject areas, link pages, and cross reference material. Wikis are flexible and can display dynamic web content with add-ins such as video, audio, PowerPoint slides, PDF documents, flash animations, and other artifacts. Mature wikis have become long-term knowledge repositories and have been successfully used in private, personal, corporate and educational settings (Hai-Jew, 2008; Hai-Jew and McHaney, 2010; McHaney, 2009; Phillipson, 2008).

Wikis have been used as the basis for learning communities (Gilbert, Chen and Sabol, 2008). Specialty add-ins permit Wikis to be set up with user rights, ranging from open, public access to restricted, private access. Most wiki pages are primarily text-based although multimedia extensions are available. When a page is edited, it displays as text with embedded formatting options. Depending on the wiki software being used, these can be hypertext-based or use a specific scripting language such as Mediawiki created for wiki development. As users make changes to a wiki page, the changes are tracked and a history record is created. This enables vandalism and inaccuracies to be "backed out" easily. Over time, revision histories are created and the latest version of a page is displayed as the current text (Hai-Jew and McHaney, 2010; McHaney 2009). Like traditional web sites, wikis must be designed, managed, maintained, and updated (Klobas, 2006, pp. 215-216).

As mentioned earlier, traditional websites generally have a webmaster that oversees site operation. The equivalent role for wikis is wiki master. Like a webmaster, wiki masters often are tasked with responsibilities for overseeing the operations of the site. However, the duties of the wiki master have evolved in a different direction based on the collaborative nature of the technology being used. Generally, traditional websites acquire their content through the efforts of key individuals or hired writers. Wikis are a Web 2.0 technology, collaboratively populated with content by a variety of people with varying writing skills

and different knowledge levels. This means that in addition to administrative duties, a wiki master must also possess the ability to oversee collaboration, assess accuracy of posted material, and add/modify content.

A primary criticism of wiki use revolves around the ease with which inaccurate information can be added to the site. For instance, Wikipedia has been criticized for its potential to include incorrect information and for furthering commercial and political causes (Black, 2008). In these instances, it becomes the responsibility of the wiki master take both corrective and preventative action. The next section looks into the intricacies of being a wiki master (Adler and Alfaro, 2006).

## WIKI MASTER 101

To say a wiki master is a glorified webmaster is a misstatement. While the two roles have emerged from similar motivations, the technology differences between general websites and wikis have resulted in sharp distinctions. This section provides an in-depth look at various roles a wiki master is expected to fill in a variety of areas. These roles will be broken into *Platform* and *Content* areas.

### Platform Roles

Wiki masters will need to be *software specialists* with knowledge regarding wiki systems. While online providers of wiki systems (e.g. pbworks, wikidot) have software conventions for use of their systems, most wikis currently require the wiki master to have a working knowledge of Mediawiki, a popular web-based wiki software application, used by Wikipedia and other leading wikis. Mediawiki is open source software developed by the Wikimedia Foundation, based the PHP programming language and a backend database (Wikipedia, 2011a). Software knowledge required to be a wiki master comprises several areas. First, most wiki software systems are highly customizable. For instance, Mediawiki has more than 700 configuration settings and more than 1,600 extensions that permit a wiki master to enable or disable various features (Mediawiki, 2011). Additionally, most wiki masters will need to develop software solutions to support user community needs. Open source wiki software gives a wide range of capability in this regard.

Initially, the wiki master may function as an *outsourcing specialist* and be involved in an organizational decision regarding whether a server and wiki software implementation should be onsite or if a wiki should be implemented on a third party web site such as PBworks or Wikidot. For smaller organizations, or individual academic users, it makes sense to develop a wiki application on a third party website. The advantages of this approach mean that hardware issues are removed from the wiki master's portfolio of duties. Likewise, many security, backup and recovery, spam, software system updates, and other tasks are managed by the third-party provider.

Particularly in smaller wiki implementations, a wiki master also might have *hardware specialist* duties. This means the wiki master could be involved in hardware selection, purchase, update, maintenance and operation. Generally, hardware systems designed as web server platforms also are recommended for wiki sites. If hardware is maintained onsite, the wiki master might have additional duties that include maintenance, upgrades, hardware monitoring, and security.

If dealing with software and hardware, a wiki master may also function as a *system maintenance supervisor*. Maintenance in a wiki takes several forms. First, if the wiki is locally hosted, software upgrades, patches, and versions must be researched, obtained, and installed. Uploaded contents must be maintained whether the wiki is local or hosted by a third-party. At an operational level, this means, removing outdated images, videos, links, and so forth. Many contributors to a wiki will upload multiple versions of digital artifacts and then abandon them as they change site content. While it would be nice to imagine

contributors would remove outdated material, this seldom occurs. Even when an image is not visible on a page, it is still held in the Wiki's library. In Mediawiki-based implementations, a special page is available (called Special:UnusedImages) to list all unused files. This image list can be periodically checked and removed to conserve space and help track spam entries.

In a more general sense, the wiki master must act as an *operations manager* and ensure the wiki remains online and operating. Hardware crashes, software crashes, spam or other malicious attacks, lapse of domain name registrations, and server changes can all result in a wiki going off line. The operations manager must be aware of the wiki's status and take action as needed.

Many times, a wiki's operating status will be linked to security breaches and this means a wiki master must be a *security specialist*. Most wikis are developed using the basic premise that they are open for contributions. This philosophy, however, does not ensure everyone who does contribute has the same motivation. In other words, vandalism, spam, trolling, and other issues can become major problems (The Computer Language Company, 2011). Depending on the size and structure of a wiki, intentional vandalism or even unintentional errors may go unnoticed for long periods of time. Added to this is the difficulty of various wiki conventions and systems (Maciak, 2008). The wiki master must spend a portion of his or her time reviewing changes to the wiki and then take corrective action to undo any problematic entries (Sutton, 2006). Historically, wiki masters tend to be non-confrontational and rather than provoke retaliatory responses, use subtle methods to protect the wiki, its users, and its informational integrity from injurious actions. ELATEwiki for instance, uses the concept of a wiki keeper rather than a wiki master to emphasize this soft security approach (Meatballwiki, 2011).

Many wikis follow a philosophy of nonviolence (in the cyber sense) and work to create architectural structures as defenses. These defenses are meant to keep people from attacking the site and to limit damage when attacks do happen. These structures have to tread the fine line between offering protection to the wiki and preventing legitimate users from being unnecessarily constrained. A basic premise of many wikis' security approaches is to gradually ramp up action as the trolling and spam entries become more troublesome.

One approach taken by some wikis has been to make "undoing damage" easy by offering rollback features. Bots and specialty pages on a wiki can be used to review changes and identify potentially troubling entries. Often, vandals will attempt to avoid detection by making very subtle changes that are difficult to detect. Other strategies by vandals include deleting pages or deleting page contents.

For many wikis, ignoring vandalism is not an option because contributor time is wasted and inaccurate information can ruin the reputation of the wiki. Ill intentions can be countered by requiring a user login, no longer accepting particular tags in wikiscript, and the use of blacklist add-ins that prevent particular IP addresses or userIDs from making edits or new entries. Unfortunately, requiring a login lowers the desire for participation and makes it more difficult and less anonymous for a user to contribute (Mohan, 2005).

## Content

In addition to operational concerns, a wiki master's role is most frequently associated with responsibility for managing the content of the site. This often entails both organizing the material and ensuring it is accurate and consistent in a variety of ways.

The wiki master must function as an *overall site designer*. This means envisioning a starting point for the wiki that permits it to gently evolve into a community that meets the needs of its users. One method of accomplishing this is to create an ontology or macro-structure to categorize and hold the wiki's initial contents (Hai-Jew and McHaney, 2010). "Ontologies are unambiguous representations of concepts, relationships between concepts (such as a hierarchy), ontologically sig-

nificant individuals, and axioms (Hepp, Siorpaes, & Bachlechner, 2007, p. 55)." A primary reason to develop ontology relates to user friendliness. If a wiki has too loose of a structure, users will not understand or be motivated to contribute. On the other hand, if the ontology is too rigid, users may find the wiki does not meet their expectations for content collaboration. An initial ontology can be created in Mediawiki through the use of descriptive tags, category titles, and hyperlinks to portal pages using prominent titles. To support ontology, design can also extend to template development. Templates are essentially a series of pre-developed page structures pre-loaded with category tags to make a user's addition to the content easier and to increase productivity while lowering the learning curve (Hai-Jew and McHaney, 2011).

In addition to defining an initial ontology which needs to be supported with tags and templates, the wiki master must design a look and feel for the wiki's pages as *page designer*. A wiki generally provides a consistent view for users and this is often accomplished by encouraging contributors to use a common interface that is available in the form of a skin or palette of colors and preloaded images.

As a wiki-based community grows, diversity of views will emerge. This is an inherent feature of wikis and is generally desirable. The wiki master will have to deal with this as a *content management supervisor*. As more users add their voices, a more natural ontology should emerge as defined by participants using the site. Occasionally, the wiki master will need to view the terms being used as tags and update the overall ontology. This means updating and modifying tags so they have both a "conceptual consistency" and a "syntactic consistency" over time (Hepp, Siorpaes, and Bachlechner, 2007, p. 55). Additionally, the wiki master may need to group tags and add templates, update page designs, and create additional cross-referencing capability. Links may need to be added to key pages. It is important to ensure minor spelling and word use differences do not result in particular portions of content becoming orphaned with regard to the larger classification scheme (Hai-Jew and McHaney, 2010).

Wiki masters must also be *content specialists* and have a general understanding of the material being posted on their site. Material must be vetted for accuracy, timeliness and relevancy to the site. Although site users will provide this service, the wiki master must also become involved with site content issues. Much of a wiki master's time, particularly in small wikis, will be spent as a *content editor*. As new content is added by users, the style, wording, and appearance may not be consistent with the rest of the site or it may be substandard. When this occurs, the wiki master first hopes other users interested in that topic might take on the editors' roles. However, if this doesn't happen, then the wiki master becomes responsible for making edits. Depending on the quality of contributed material, this could result in a substantial time commitment.

One of the most difficult duties of the wiki master is to continually seek out new and updated content for a wiki as an *acquisitions specialist*. Once established and added to search engines, a wiki will receive a great deal of 'reader' traffic. A more difficult task is to create enough interest so users will take time from their busy schedules to write for the wiki. This might mean specifically asking content experts to submit material, it might involve acquiring information as classroom research assignments, or it might mean advertising among the community that stands to benefit from the wiki's existence.

Finally, the wiki master must be a *conflict resolution specialist*. In is inevitable that wiki content will result in conflict. This phenomenon has been studied by researchers who state: "[conflict resolution] will increasingly play an important role in Wikipedia. To address these challenges, there exists a need to identify and understand the process that generates these conflicts and coordination needs." (Suh, Chi, Pendleton and Kittur, 2007). Suh, et al. go on to introduce a

"model for understanding user disagreements in Wikipedia articles. This model relies on users' editing history and the relationships between user edits, especially revisions that void previous edits, known as reverts." In a related article, these same authors state that: "[a]s Wikipedia continues to grow, the potential for conflict and the need for consensus building and coordination increase as well." (Kittur, Suh, Pendleton, and Chi, 2007). They examine the growth of "non-direct work and [describe] the development of tools to characterize and identify conflict and coordination costs in Wikipedia." So in other words, a wiki master will find conflict in terms of definitions, ideas, and appropriateness of topics in a collaborative environment and have to resolve these issues. Although Suh, et al.'s work involved Wikipedia, it is applicable to all wiki applications.

The use of talk pages on wikis has been designed to specifically provide space where conflicting views can be discussed and resolved without resorting to "back and forth" changes and edits to a page (Kittur, Suh, Pendleton, and Chi, 2007; Kittur, Suh and Chi, 2009). Some sources call extreme cases of reverting pages and engaging in disputes over editing, *edit wars*. According to Wikipedia which experiences frequent edit wars (Wikipedia, 2011b), these situations can also occur as users repetitively revert a page to the version they favor. Some wiki software allows an administrator to stop edit wars by locking a page from further editing until a decision has been made on what version of the page would be most appropriate (Black, Delaney and Fitzgerald, 2007, p. 245).

## CASE STUDY: ELATEWIKI.ORG

The following case study provides insight into the activities, responsibilities, and time constraints of the wiki master (called a wiki keeper) at ELATEwiki.org.

*Figure 1. ELATEwiki homepage location*

## ELATEwiki Overview

Kansas State University publicly released ELATEwiki, the Electronic Learning and Teaching Exchange in 2009. ELATEwiki was developed to facilitate the creation and documentation of innovative teaching approaches used by individuals and organizations interested in advancing the use of technology in both classroom teaching and distance learning. This synergistic exchange hosts a wealth of freely available information categorized and organized into course issue, tool, student, and instructor related topics. It is useful to teachers, scholars, students, and administrators seeking to understand the higher education landscape (Augar, Raitman and Zhou, 2004). ELATEwiki is a small wiki in comparison to Wikipedia. As of August of 2011, this site had approximately 700 pages and 600 registered users, some of which were registered specifically with the intent of adding spam pages to the site. ELATEwiki can be found at http://ELATEwiki.org (McHaney R., 2009). See Figure 1.

## Wiki Master History at ELATEwiki

In many wikis, particularly small ones, the wiki master is may be responsible for the entire web site operation. ELATEwiki was conceptualized and developed by a small team. The development effort included brainstorming potential contents and developing an identity as well as look and feel for the Website (McHaney, 2009). The implementation team, which comprised K-State faculty members, instructional designers, distance learning administrators, and technology special-

ists, discussed various naming options and after numerous suggestions determined ELATEwiki (an acronym for Electronic Learning and Teaching Exchange) was suitable, memorable, and available as a domain name. In general, K-State's Distance Education Leadership group "recognized a need to better support e-learning faculty members. Geographically dispersed faculty members often 'reinvented the wheel' and had no clear way of acquiring knowledge of successful practices employed by colleagues. Although several on-campus teaching exchanges existed, it became apparent additional resources were required for teachers without easy campus access." (McHaney, 2010). The domain was secured by K-State and registered for use as ELATEwiki.org. A K-State graphic artist was hired to develop prototype logos to brand the site. The implementation team selected the logo shown in Figure 2.

Simultaneously, the team researched various wiki software and hardware configurations. The team evaluated and compared commercial wiki farms to K-State's servers being used to house open-source wiki software. Server load, multimedia content inclusions and future capabilities were all considered. Access privileges for the site were debated (e.g. whether the site should be

*Figure 2. ELATEwiki logo*

*Figure 3. Site content example at ELATEwiki*

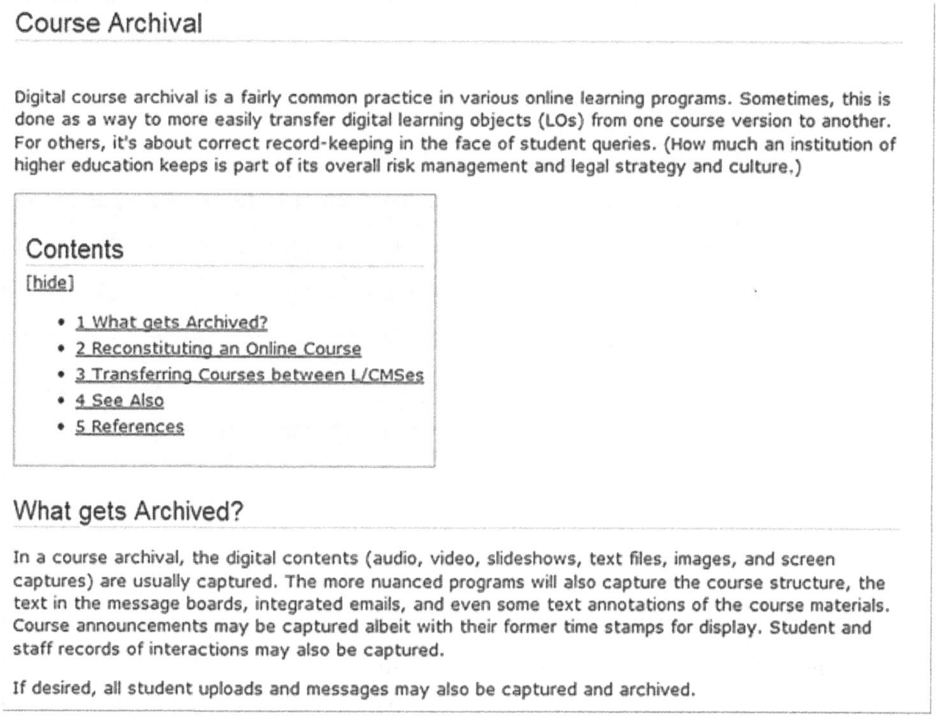

## Course Archival

Digital course archival is a fairly common practice in various online learning programs. Sometimes, this is done as a way to more easily transfer digital learning objects (LOs) from one course version to another. For others, it's about correct record-keeping in the face of student queries. (How much an institution of higher education keeps is part of its overall risk management and legal strategy and culture.)

### Contents
[hide]

- 1 What gets Archived?
- 2 Reconstituting an Online Course
- 3 Transferring Courses between L/CMSes
- 4 See Also
- 5 References

## What gets Archived?

In a course archival, the digital contents (audio, video, slideshows, text files, images, and screen captures) are usually captured. The more nuanced programs will also capture the course structure, the text in the message boards, integrated emails, and even some text annotations of the course materials. Course announcements may be captured albeit with their former time stamps for display. Student and staff records of interactions may also be captured.

If desired, all student uploads and messages may also be captured and archived.

private, public or a mix). Control and quality were researched and the team determined Mediawiki, the open-source wiki technology that underlies Wikipedia would be used on K-State servers. "The software was installed by K-State's Office of Mediated Education (OME) on a K-State server with a clustered environment having two nodes (to ensure a higher level of uptime). The server was prepared by pre-loading PHP 5.2.8 and MySQL database software. Version 1.13.3 of Mediawiki software was loaded and configured." (McHaney 2010). A member of the OME office was given wiki master privileges with the intention of becoming a system software and hardware expert for the site.

Implementation continued with the team deciding to move ahead with the construction of the wiki. A faculty member wiki master was selected and assigned necessary privileges in the installed instance of Mediawiki. The new wiki master worked with the technical lead to select a color

pallet and Media wiki template. An instructional designer was also given privileges on the site and began creating content for the site (See Figure 3).

*Figure 4. ELATEwiki ontology*

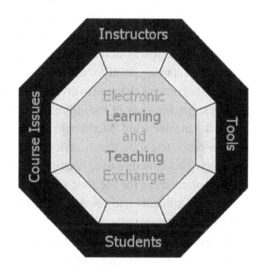

*Figure 5. Foursquare entry categorized as 'tool' with tags*

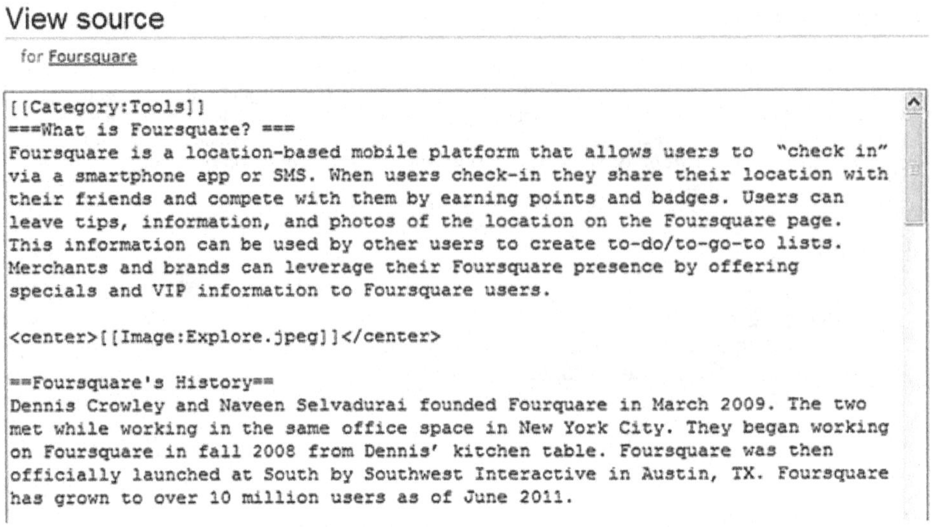

## View source

for Foursquare

```
[[Category:Tools]]
===What is Foursquare? ===
Foursquare is a location-based mobile platform that allows users to  "check in"
via a smartphone app or SMS. When users check-in they share their location with
their friends and compete with them by earning points and badges. Users can
leave tips, information, and photos of the location on the Foursquare page.
This information can be used by other users to create to-do/to-go-to lists.
Merchants and brands can leverage their Foursquare presence by offering
specials and VIP information to Foursquare users.

<center>[[Image:Explore.jpeg]]</center>

==Foursquare's History==
Dennis Crowley and Naveen Selvadurai founded Fourquare in March 2009. The two
met while working in the same office space in New York City. They began working
on Foursquare in fall 2008 from Dennis' kitchen table. Foursquare was then
officially launched at South by Southwest Interactive in Austin, TX. Foursquare
has grown to over 10 million users as of June 2011.
```

The wiki master together with the implementation team determined a Web 2.0 worldview would be used. This open and collaborative approach would ensure contributors that their material would remain accessible by others and would facilitate sharing intellectual resources. This approach was put into place with a Creative Commons license.

An ontology for ELATEwiki was developed to make the process of contributing material easier and to help organize content for users. The initial ontology at ELATEwiki was discussed by the team and implemented by the wiki master in the form of templates, graphic design and navigation menus/hyperlinks. It was determined the initial ontology was a starting point for users and could be expanded as contents changed over time. Figure 4 provides a graphic view of the initial ontology.

The wiki master used Mediawiki software features in order to create the infrastructure for the ontology. This structure used Mediawiki tags to create content areas for the four sections: instructors, tools, students, and course issues. These tags allow the structure to be displayed in special pages according to classification. In addition, one page of content can be tagged with multiple cat-egories giving added flexibility to the site. Figure 5 illustrates the concept of tags

The categories were made more visible when the wiki master placed hyperlink entries on

*Figure 6. Navigation bar category links*

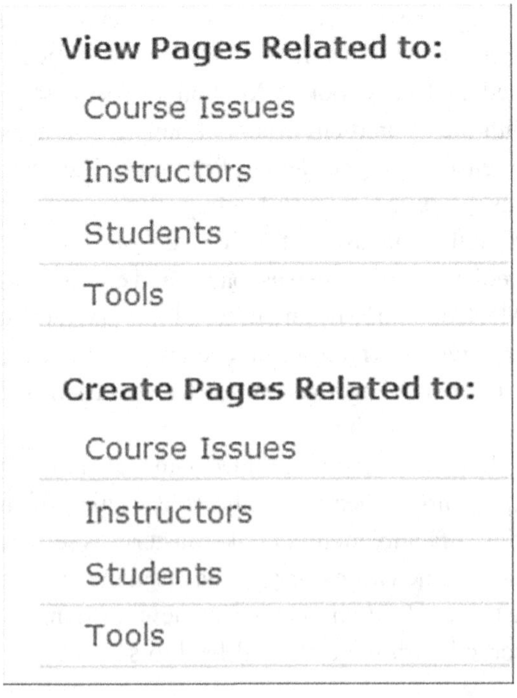

### View Pages Related to:

Course Issues

Instructors

Students

Tools

### Create Pages Related to:

Course Issues

Instructors

Students

Tools

*Figure 7. Template on ELATEwiki*

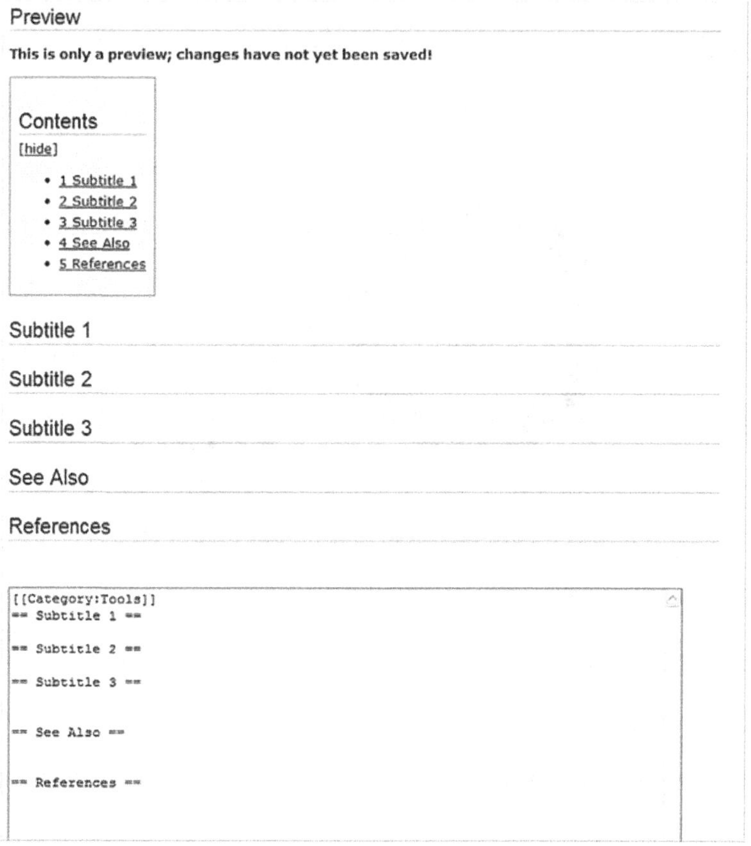

*Figure 8. Subset of tags on ELATEwiki*

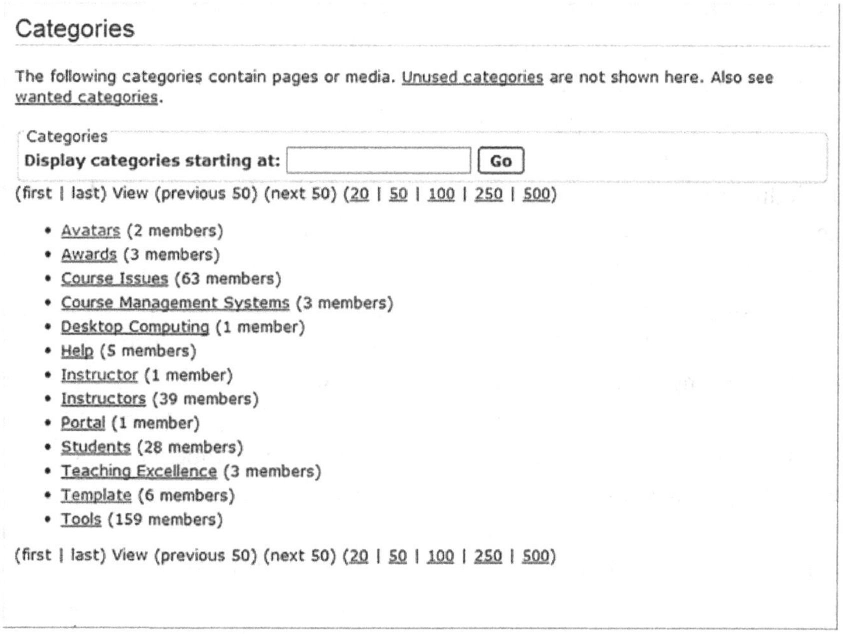

*Figure 9. Main page of ELATEwiki*

ELATEwiki's main page navigation bar. Figure 6 illustrates.

The *Create Page* hyperlinks on the main navigation page open new page templates pre-configured with the appropriate tags matching the site's initial ontology. These templates essentially are Mediawiki wikitext pages preloaded with wiki tags that facilitate content entry and reduce technical complexity. This approach ensures a reduced learning curve for the contributors and a reduction of editing for the wiki master. As more experience was gained, the templates were updated to prevent coding errors. Figure 7 illustrates a template in its preview mode.

The wiki also allows users to add their own tags through Mediawiki coding. Figure 8 illustrates a subset of the tags used on the site. The wiki master must review these tags and ensure they are used on the correct pages and that untagged pages are updated. On occasion, similar tags must be combined and inappropriate tags removed from the wiki.

With the ontology and templates in place, the wiki master developed other features to ensure users could effectively interact with the site. First, the 'Main Page' sidebar was organized then developed with wikitext. Other wikitext features were developed to automate new page creation and to provide an overall view of all topics (McHaney 2010). ELATEwiki's main page was developed as shown in Figure 9.

## Wiki Master Role in Launching ELATEwiki

Once the site was prepared for use, a multi-phase strategy was used to launch ELATEwiki (McHaney 2010). The site was seeded with articles, primarily developed by an instructional designer and students. This was done to ensure potential users found value upon their first visit. Several articles were added to each category and developed in a way that would provide an example for future contributions. Various features of the

*Figure 10. Help page example from ELATEwiki*

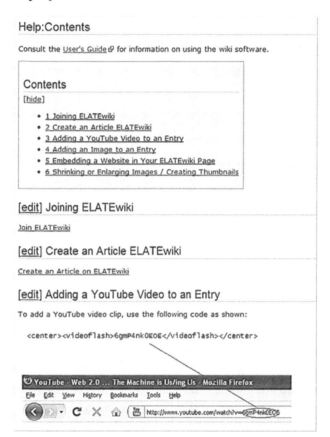

site included video use, images, tagging, and page links were put into articles by the wiki master as examples. Help pages were created and posted to the wiki (see Figure 10)

An instructional design specialist worked with a university attorney to develop a legal disclaimer for the site and its use (Black, Delaney and Fitzgerald, 2007). Shortly after this, the wiki master invited *"a select group of on-campus e-*

*Figure 11. RECAPTCHA Plug-in*

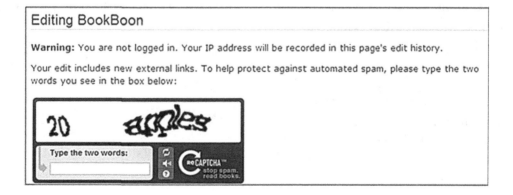

*Figure 12. ConfirmEdit extension*

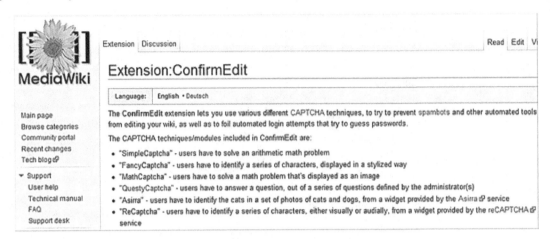

learning experts to stress test the wiki and to create further content (McHaney, 2010)." Several problems were uncovered and enhancements suggested. The wiki master implemented these and the site was generally declared ready for public use by the implementation team.

The public launch was initiated by the wiki master and a wider community of users was contacted through email, posted notices, submissions to web search engines, flyers at conferences, and publicity articles in news media.

## ELATEwiki Overview

In a small wiki such ELATEwiki, two large challenges are overarching. First, the site must have oversight. Even with an active community of contributors and readers, a wiki master must keep his or her eyes on the Web site and its pages, tags, content, and so forth. Second, a wiki master must attempt to find ways to keep readers returning and ensure a fresh supply of new content and updates. In a small wiki, the later is probably the most challenging aspect of the wiki master job. And in ELATEwiki it remains somewhat frustrating and disappointing at times.

Oversight involves both corrective and preventive action on the part of the ELATEwiki wiki master. Conceptually, a wiki is intended to attract

users to form a community that maintains the integrity and quality of the site. This does not always happen as easily, particularly in smaller wikis. This means wiki master's oversight is required to ensure the contents remain fundamentally sound. This is particularly important in the instance of ELATEwiki because it is being used by students and educators. The ELATEwiki implementation team believed direct oversight would be needed, in part, due to the relatively small founding group and in part due to the importance of maintaining academically sound contents (McHaney, 2010). In terms of preventive action, the wiki master implemented several tools with the help of the technical team. Among these were the RECAPTCHA plug-in for MediaWiki to eliminate vandalism which became nearly unmanageable as the site gained popularity (See Figure 11). Later, as spam bots gained the capability to overcome the RECAPTCHA plug-in, the approach was changed

*Figure 13. Numeric ConfirmEdit Captchas*

14 - 9

Answer : [          ] [ Submit ]

*Figure 14. ImageMagick*

| Screenshot | [show] |
|---|---|
| Developer(s) | ImageMagick Studio LLC |
| Stable release | 6.7.1-9 / 21 August 2011; 7 days ago |
| Written in | C |
| Operating system | Cross-platform |
| Type | Image manipulation |
| License | Apache 2.0 License ⮺ |
| Website | imagemagick.org ⮺ |

to the Mediawiki ConfirmEdit extension (See Figure 12).

Like RECAPTCHA, ConfirmEdit uses simple tests to ensure the visitor is human before creating an account or engaging in particular types of edits like adding external links. ConfirmEdit gives the option of using image captchas or simple math problems (see Figure 13). Currently ELATEwiki is using math problems to ensure maximum accessibility within the constrained environment. These simple addition or subtraction problems make it more difficult for a bot to perform automated edits. ConfirmEdit allows other options to be set. For instance, sysops and other registered users are not asked to confirm their edits. Regis-

tered users can be asked to confirm only if external links are added or riskier edits are entered. Other options are also available.

Certain bots and spam programs can overwhelm ConfirmEdit and finally ELATEwiki got to the point where edits had to be restricted to confirmed users. This meant the user had to register and supply a valid email address. This was not a preferred solution since many wiki contributors would like to remain anonymous. ELATEwiki had gotten to the point where nearly 500 spam entries and edits were occurring in a 24 hour period. It became impractical for the wiki master to roll these back constantly. ELATEwiki will be updated in the future to remove the confirmed email restriction but only after new protective strategies become available (UMassWiki, 2011).

Another preventative action added to ELATEwiki was the SpamBlacklist extension. This extension analyzes potential changes to the wiki and compares those with a list of known URLs that have a history of association with spam. SpamBlacklist uses Wikimedia's blacklist which is updated periodically as new spam sites and techniques become known. In addition, a local blacklist can be created and used to stop spam specific to the current site.

Another preventative tool added to ELATEwiki was the ImageMagick extension which automatically generates thumbnail images and allows image scaling and resizing. This extension was added because a number of pages had images that didn't fit well or were too large and pushed the text into difficult-to-read configurations. The addition of this tool allowed users to adjust the size of their images and removed much of the burden from the wiki master. See Figure 14.

The final prevention put into place was branding the wiki master as a wiki keeper. The idea was to create a subtle presence, not a combative one that would incite spammers and create an environment that vandals would enjoy destroying. The concept of a wiki keeper is that of a care taker

*Figure 15. Special Stats*

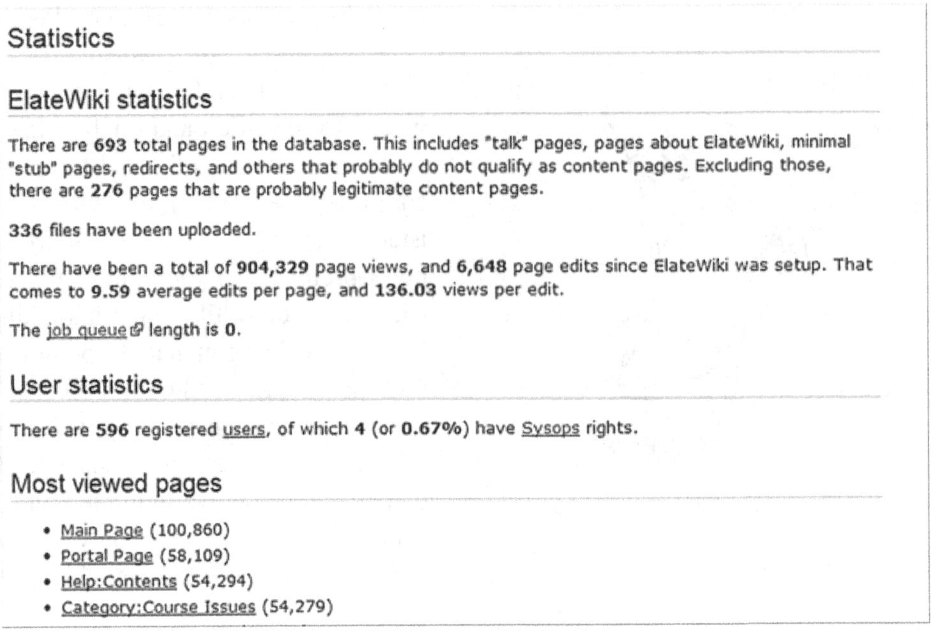

## Statistics

### ElateWiki statistics

There are **693** total pages in the database. This includes "talk" pages, pages about ElateWiki, minimal "stub" pages, redirects, and others that probably do not qualify as content pages. Excluding those, there are **276** pages that are probably legitimate content pages.

**336** files have been uploaded.

There have been a total of **904,329** page views, and **6,648** page edits since ElateWiki was setup. That comes to **9.59** average edits per page, and **136.03** views per edit.

The job queue length is **0**.

### User statistics

There are **596** registered users, of which **4** (or **0.67%**) have Sysops rights.

### Most viewed pages

- Main Page (100,860)
- Portal Page (58,109)
- Help:Contents (54,294)
- Category:Course Issues (54,279)

and not a 'master' or 'ruler.' The care taker approach is consistent with the idea that ELATEwiki is a communal web site and belongs to everyone who wishes to read its contents, edit/update, or contribute their knowledge. Together with a Creative Commons license and wiki keeper concept for oversight, it was believed many problems would be prevented. We feel this approach has accomplished this goal.

## A DAY IN THE LIFE OF ELATEwiki's WIKI KEEPER

We believe wikis have a bright future in Higher Education (Parker & Chao, 2007) and will enable information to be freely exchanged using the world view espoused in Juha Suoranta and Tere Veden's book *Wikiworld* (2010). This being said, sometimes, the larger purpose becomes obscured in the daily minutia encountered by the wiki master. The following paragraphs provide a glimpse into a day in the life of a wiki master. In ELATEwiki's instance, this is the wiki keeper.

## Wiki Master Life

On a typical day, after fortifying myself with tea and granola bars, my duties as wiki keeper begin. First, I type www.elatewiki.org into my browser at home to ensure the Web site is up and running. There have only been a couple occasions where I have been greeted by a crashed site, and in those instances, I contacted the technical project lead and he quickly restarted the system.

After ensuring the system is operational, I log into ELATEwiki as ProfRogerMc, the official wiki keeper. I check the number of hits on the site by visiting the statistics special page, (http://elatewiki.org/index.php/Special:Statistics as shown in Figure 15). It can be accessed by following links from the main page. If I see a vastly increased number of hits or no new hits, then I may investigate individual page counts in more detail.

If all is well, next I go to the recent changes link from the main page. I typically evaluate recent changes by viewing the entries being edited by wiki contributors and, particularly if new pages are indicated (see Figure 16), I will visit those

*Figure 16. New pages indicated by 'N'*

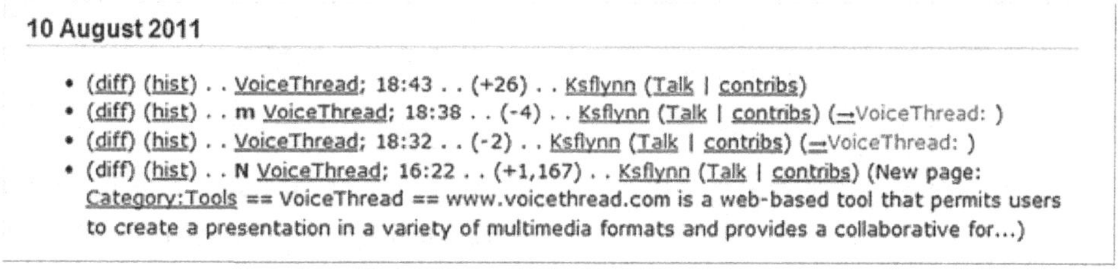

**10 August 2011**

- (diff) (hist) . . VoiceThread; 18:43 . . (+26) . . Ksflynn (Talk | contribs)
- (diff) (hist) . . m VoiceThread; 18:38 . . (-4) . . Ksflynn (Talk | contribs) (→VoiceThread: )
- (diff) (hist) . . VoiceThread; 18:32 . . (-2) . . Ksflynn (Talk | contribs) (→VoiceThread: )
- (diff) (hist) . . **N** VoiceThread; 16:22 . . (+1,167) . . Ksflynn (Talk | contribs) (New page: Category:Tools == VoiceThread == www.voicethread.com is a web-based tool that permits users to create a presentation in a variety of multimedia formats and provides a collaborative for...)

and occasionally enhance the entries or correct small issues I notice.

Occasionally new entries may contain spam content. The number of these spam entries or other vandal issues vary each day. On some mornings, I have discovered hundreds of spam entries. On other mornings, there would be none. In general, the spam falls into several categories at ELATEwiki. One category of changes is what I call *malicious damage*. I am not sure if this is done for fun by hackers or if it is being done systematically to determine how quickly the changes are undone so the perpetrators know how likely more substantial changes will be left alone. The second category of changes is *posting advertising pages*. To the individuals involved in this damage, the wiki represents free server space where they can post material for themselves or their clients. This is probably the most common type of damage done to the wiki and may be done by individuals or through the use of automated programs. The SpamBlacklist helps prevent these entries in the long run but on any given day new entries might come from new IP locations and userIDs. The next type of damage being done is called *embedded links*. The hacker will add links to reference lists, into article bodies, and in other locations to link back to their sites or their clients' sites. The motivation here is to raise their search engine ranks and by having more links back to their site from established locations, they can help achieve their goal. Similar to embedded links, some vandals will embed keywords. Like adding links, keywords are used to help raise the search

*Figure 17. Spam entries*

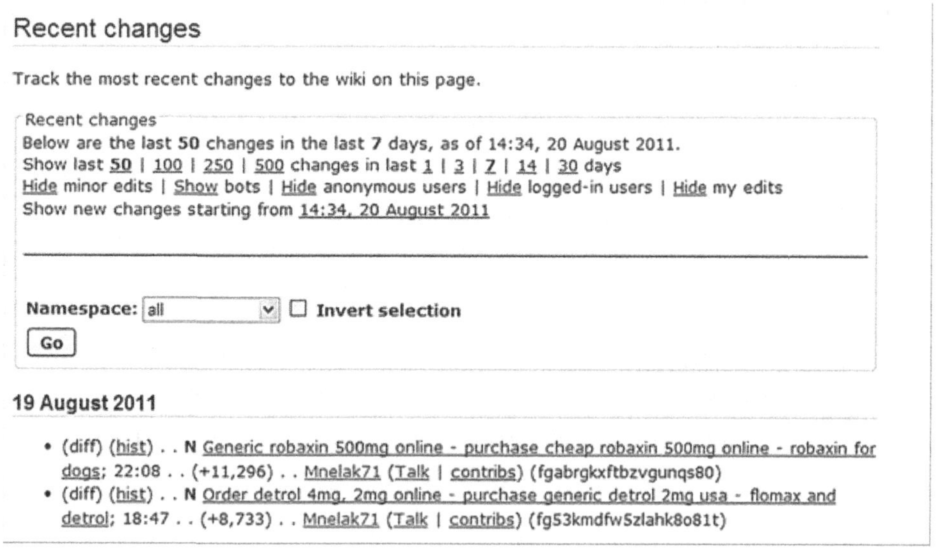

## Recent changes

Track the most recent changes to the wiki on this page.

Recent changes
Below are the last **50** changes in the last **7** days, as of 14:34, 20 August 2011.
Show last **50** | 100 | 250 | 500 changes in last 1 | 3 | **7** | 14 | 30 days
Hide minor edits | Show bots | Hide anonymous users | Hide logged-in users | Hide my edits
Show new changes starting from 14:34, 20 August 2011

Namespace: all    ☐ Invert selection
Go

**19 August 2011**

- (diff) (hist) . . **N** Generic robaxin 500mg online - purchase cheap robaxin 500mg online - robaxin for dogs; 22:08 . . (+11,296) . . Mnelak71 (Talk | contribs) (fgabrgkxftbzvgunqs80)
- (diff) (hist) . . **N** Order detrol 4mg, 2mg online - purchase generic detrol 2mg usa - flomax and detrol; 18:47 . . (+8,733) . . Mnelak71 (Talk | contribs) (fg53kmdfw5zlahk8o81t)

*Table 1. ELATEwiki spam categories*

| Category | Description |
|---|---|
| Malicious Damage | Done to test the water and determine response time for wiki repair |
| Posting Advertising Pages | Take advantage of free web server space and provide awareness of products or services |
| Embedding Links | Raise ranking in search engines |
| Embedding Keywords | Raise ranking in search engines and provide awareness of products or services |

engine awareness of particular sites. Both embedded links and keywords may be added by a bots or by individual hackers (Table 1).

After evaluating the daily vandalism to the site, I take corrective action. Depending on the entry type and amount of damage, different actions may be taken. On the day, this article was written, the spam entries found in Figure 17 were discovered. Both of these entries were created by an individual or bot that was able to register as an ELATEwiki user and then create the advertising pages.

Two corrective actions were taken to eliminate these entries. First, I visited a maintenance report provided by Mediawiki called uncategorized pages (http://elatewiki.org/index.php/ Special:UncategorizedPages). This report provides a list of all pages that have been entered into the wiki but are not included in the underlying ontology of topics. Sometimes, pages displayed here need to be appropriately tagged but generally are pages created outside the scope intended for ELATEwiki. This means these are spam entries. As can be seen in Figure 18, nine uncategorized pages have been added to the wiki. I visited the pages (Figure 19) and their history (Figure 20) and discovered they were added through the use of two userIDs, Arcanesong79 and Mnelak71. These user IDs were blocked (see Figures 21 and 22).

The pages were deleted from the wiki. Next I visit the maintenance report for unused files (http://elatewiki.org/index.php/Special:UnusedImages) to determine if images or other files were uploaded to support the pages that were just deleted. Figures 23 and 24 illustrate. These files are deleted from the wiki and their contributors (if different from previous ones) are blocked.

*Figure 18. Nine uncategorized pages*

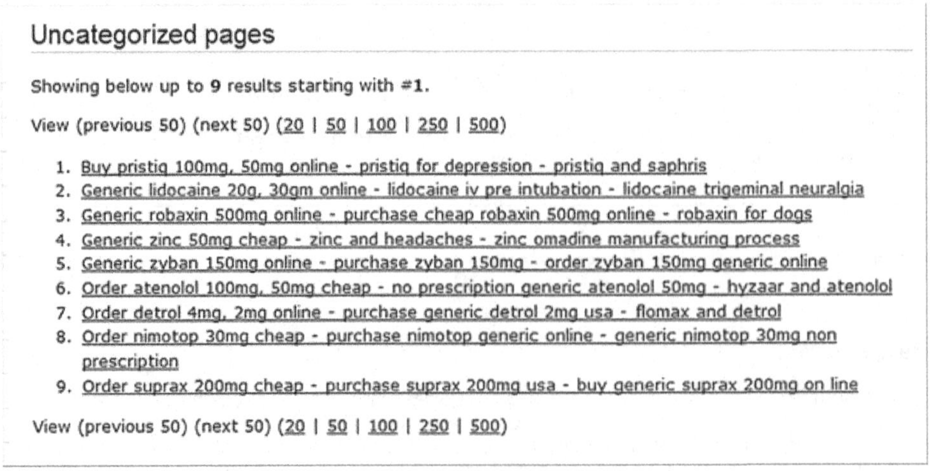

Uncategorized pages

Showing below up to **9** results starting with #**1.**

View (previous 50) (next 50) (20 | 50 | 100 | 250 | 500)

1. Buy pristiq 100mg, 50mg online - pristiq for depression - pristiq and saphris
2. Generic lidocaine 20g, 30gm online - lidocaine iv pre intubation - lidocaine trigeminal neuralgia
3. Generic robaxin 500mg online - purchase cheap robaxin 500mg online - robaxin for dogs
4. Generic zinc 50mg cheap - zinc and headaches - zinc omadine manufacturing process
5. Generic zyban 150mg online - purchase zyban 150mg - order zyban 150mg generic online
6. Order atenolol 100mg, 50mg cheap - no prescription generic atenolol 50mg - hyzaar and atenolol
7. Order detrol 4mg, 2mg online - purchase generic detrol 2mg usa - flomax and detrol
8. Order nimotop 30mg cheap - purchase nimotop generic online - generic nimotop 30mg non prescription
9. Order suprax 200mg cheap - purchase suprax 200mg usa - buy generic suprax 200mg on line

View (previous 50) (next 50) (20 | 50 | 100 | 250 | 500)

*Figure 19. View of spam page*

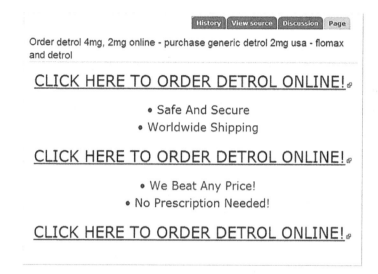

*Figure 20. View of spam page history*

## Other Occasional Wiki Master Duties

As wiki keeper, I get occasional emails from system users. These have ranged from questions about use and contributions to requesting the removal from the list of registered users. A typical week might result in a few emails.

Depending on the material being posted, particularly regarding spam and vandalism, I might spend time researching the Mediawiki site for available upgrades and new information. The technical lead for ELATEwiki might be consulted and new scripts installed on the server. Currently, the website is being upgraded to include image-maps. See Figure 25.

Other occasional duties include publicity for the site. As wiki keeper, I develop presentations, informational emails and flyers, and articles to promote the use of ELATEwiki. This is a fun part of the job because I meet and interact with very

*Figure 21. UserID associated with spam*

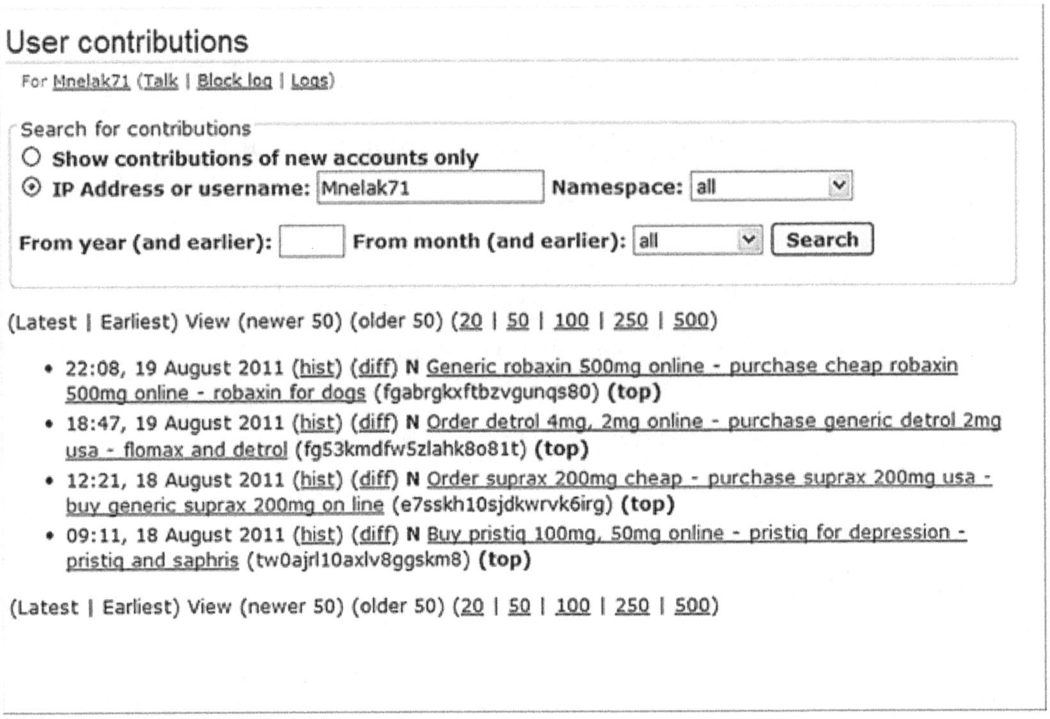

## User contributions

For Mnelak71 (Talk | Block log | Logs)

Search for contributions
○ **Show contributions of new accounts only**
⊙ **IP Address or username:** Mnelak71    **Namespace:** all

**From year (and earlier):** [    ]    **From month (and earlier):** all    [ **Search** ]

(Latest | Earliest) View (newer 50) (older 50) (20 | 50 | 100 | 250 | 500)

- 22:08, 19 August 2011 (hist) (diff) **N** Generic robaxin 500mg online - purchase cheap robaxin 500mg online - robaxin for dogs (fgabrgkxftbzvgunqs80) **(top)**
- 18:47, 19 August 2011 (hist) (diff) **N** Order detrol 4mg, 2mg online - purchase generic detrol 2mg usa - flomax and detrol (fg53kmdfw5zlahk8o81t) **(top)**
- 12:21, 18 August 2011 (hist) (diff) **N** Order suprax 200mg cheap - purchase suprax 200mg usa - buy generic suprax 200mg on line (e7sskh10sjdkwrvk6irg) **(top)**
- 09:11, 18 August 2011 (hist) (diff) **N** Buy pristiq 100mg, 50mg online - pristiq for depression - pristiq and saphris (tw0ajrl10axlv8ggskm8) **(top)**

(Latest | Earliest) View (newer 50) (older 50) (20 | 50 | 100 | 250 | 500)

*Figure 22. Block UserID*

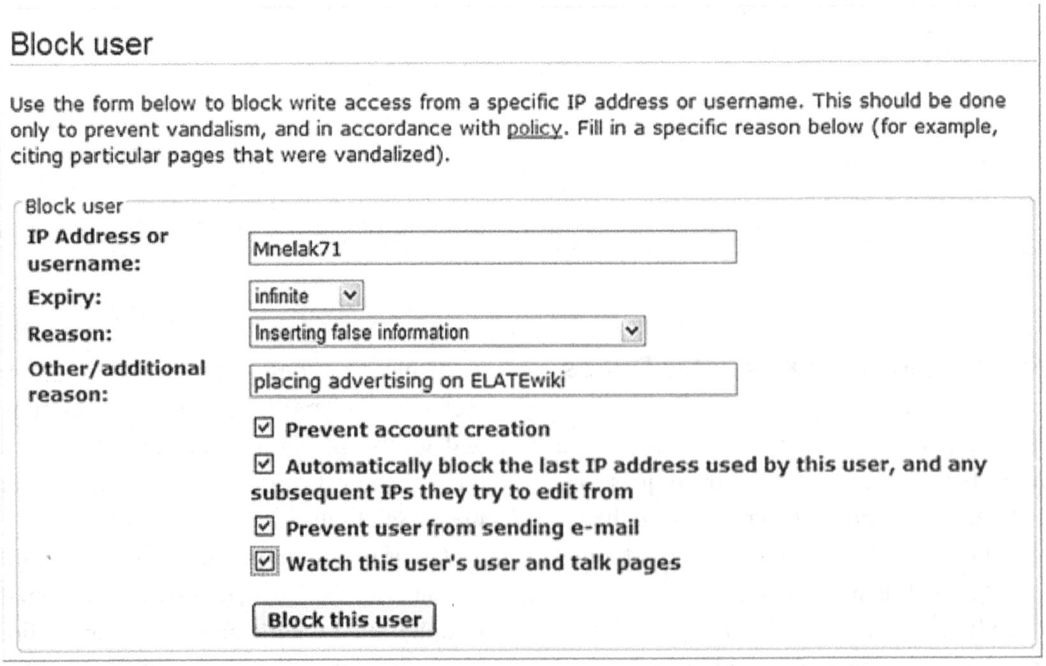

## Block user

Use the form below to block write access from a specific IP address or username. This should be done only to prevent vandalism, and in accordance with policy. Fill in a specific reason below (for example, citing particular pages that were vandalized).

Block user
**IP Address or username:** Mnelak71

**Expiry:** infinite

**Reason:** Inserting false information

**Other/additional reason:** placing advertising on ELATEwiki

☑ **Prevent account creation**

☑ **Automatically block the last IP address used by this user, and any subsequent IPs they try to edit from**

☑ **Prevent user from sending e-mail**

☑ **Watch this user's user and talk pages**

[ **Block this user** ]

*Figure 23. Unused images*

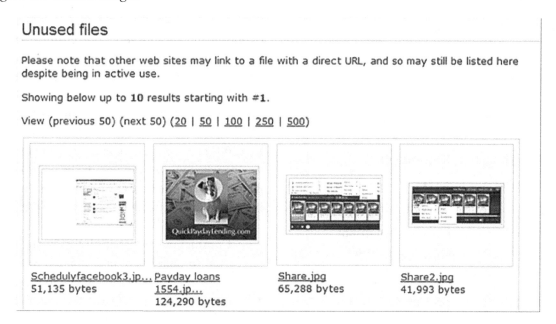

*Figure 24. Deleting unused files*

*Figure 25. Imagemaps extension*

| MediaWiki extensions manual - list | |
|---|---|
| **ImageMap** | |
| **Release status: stable** | |
| Implementation | Tag |
| Description | HTML image maps |
| Author(s) | Tim Starling[™] |
| MediaWiki | 1.11+ |
| License | Any OSI approved license |
| Download | Download snapshot |
| | Subversion [Help] |
| | Browse source code |
| | View code changes |
| Example | Children's encyclopedia |
| Hooks used | [Expand] |
| check usage *(experimental)* | |
| Bugs: list open  list all  report | |

interesting, motivated people. Currently a project to enable *English as a Second Language* students to collaboratively develop documents is being added to the site.

## CONCLUSION

The Internet and its applications have provided the platform necessary for the development of wide scale collaborative documents that capture the knowledge of many users. Specifically, wikis have enabled communities of interest to develop and co-create valuable information repositories in collective fashion. The evolution and expansion of the webmaster into collaborative, Web 2.0 spaces have resulted in the wiki master. The wiki master is meant to be a subtle, organizing presence that

unobtrusively enables a wiki's community to function at a higher level, maintaining an awareness of outside threats with support to ensure minimal internal mistakes and problems. This article has demonstrated how a wiki master approaches the complex, emerging environment and seeks to fill this evolving role. Two experts in open source environments, Eric Sheppard (2009) and Gwai Lo (2009) provide insight and advice worth following when viewed through the lens of the wiki master's eyes. The Five C's for a successful wiki implementation include (Sheppard, 2009):

- **Completeness:** Cover all topics that users need to understand and create a thorough piece of documentation and help files.
- **Correctness:** The instructions and explanations should be 100% correct. Usability testing provides an appropriate mechanism.
- **Clarity:** Use proper formatting and language so the readers can understand the documentation.
- **Convenience:** Provide easy to understand organization--the user should not have to search for his or her solution. It should be easily available.
- **Consistency:** The document should follow the same layout, the language should be in one voice, and the style should be uniform.

Gwai Lo adds (Lo, 2006):

- **Check Your Ego at the Door:** The wiki should be an environment of open and welcoming communicators. You are just as useful to the discussion and success of the document as your fellow collaborators. Be respectful.
- **Don't be Territorial**: This isn't just YOUR document. It belongs to everyone. Your ideas may simply not connect well with your fellow contributors.
- **Collaboration means Someone knows More than You:** Welcome the input and

ideas of others. You never know how much you'll learn or how useful those ideas can be.

These words of wisdom set the stage for productive, online collaboration and make it possible for the collective wisdom of many to far surpass anything a single individual can accomplish.

## ACKNOWLEDGMENT

This research was funded by the Kansas State University College of Business Dean's Office.

## REFERENCES

W3C. (2009). *Standards*. W3C Consortium. Retrieved from http://www.w3.org/standards

Adler, B. T., & Alfaro, L. (2006). *A content-driven reputation system for the Wikipedia.* Technical Report ucsc-crl-06-18, School of Engineering, University of California, Santa Cruz, 2006. Retrieved from http://works.bepress.com/luca_de_alfaro/3

Augar, N., Raitman, R., & Zhou, W. (2004). Teaching and learning online with wikis. In R. Atkinson, C. McBeath, D. Jonas-Dwyer, & R. Phillips (Eds.), *Beyond the Comfort Zone: Proceedings of the 21st ASCILITE Conference* (pp. 95-104). Perth, 5-8 December. Retrieved from http://www.ascilite.org.au/conferences/perth04/procs/augar.html

Berners-Lee, T. J. (1992). The world-wide web. *Computer Networks and ISDN Systems, 25*(4-5), 454–459. doi:10.1016/0169-7552(92)90039-S

Bishop, T. (2004, January 26). *Microsoft Notebook: Wiki pioneer planted the seed and watched it grow.* Retrieved from http://www.seattlepi.com/business/158020_msftnotebook26.html

Black, E. (2008). Wikipedia and academic peer review: Wikipedia as a recognised medium for scholarly publication? *Online Information Review, 32*(1), 73–88. doi:10.1108/14684520810865994

Black, P., Delaney, H., & Fitzgerald, B. (2007). Legal issues for wikis: The challenge of user-generated and peer-produced knowledge Content and Culture. *European Law Journal, 14,* 245–282.

Cummings, R. E. (2008). What was a wiki and why do I care? A short and usable history of wikis. In Cummings, R. E., & Barton, M. (Eds.), *Wiki writing: Collaborative learning in the college classroom* (pp. 1–18). Ann Arbor, MI: University of Michigan Press.

Deursen, A. V., & Visser, E. (2002). The reengineering wiki. In *Proceedings 6th European Conference on Software Maintenance and Reengineering* (CSMR), IEEE Computer Society, (pp. 217-220).

*ELATEwiki Home Page.* (2011). Retrieved from http://www.ELATEwiki.org

Fernando, P. (2005). Wiki: New way to collaborate. *Communication World, 22*(3), 8–19.

Gilbert, D., Chen, H. L., & Sabol, J. (2008). Building learning communities with wikis. In Cummings, R. E., & Barton, M. (Eds.), *Wiki writing: Collaborative learning in the college classroom* (pp. 1–18). Ann Arbor, MI: University of Michigan Press.

Hai-Jew, S. (2008). Developing a distance learning faculty wiki. *SIDLIT Conference Proceedings.* Paper 4. Retrieved from http://scholarspace.jccc.edu/sidlit/4

Hai-Jew, S., & McHaney, R. W. (2010). ELATEwiki: Evolving an e-learning faculty wiki. In Luppicini, R., & Haghi, A. K. (Eds.), *Cases on digital technologies in higher education: Issues and challenges* (pp. 1–23). doi:10.4018/978-1-61520-869-2.ch001

Hepp, M., Siorpaes, K., & Bachlechner, D. (2007, September). Harvesting Wiki consensus: Using Wikipedia entries for knowledge management. *IEEE Internet Computing, Special Issue on Semantic Knowledge Management,* 54–65.

Kittur, A., Suh, B., & Chi, E. H. (2009). What's in Wikipedia? Mapping topics and conflict using socially annotated category structure. *27th Annual CHI Conference on Human Factors in Computing Systems (CHI),* April 4-9, Boston MA.

Kittur, A., Suh, B., Pendleton, B. A., & Chi, E. H. (2007). He says, she says: Conflict and coordination in Wikipedia. *25th Annual ACM Conference on Human Factors in Computing Systems (CHI 2007),* April 28 - May 3, San Jose, CA (pp. 453-462). New York, NY: ACM.

Klobas, J. (2006). *Wikis: Tools for information work and collaboration.* Oxford, UK: Chandos Publishing.

Lamb, B. (2004). Wide open spaces: Wikis ready or not. *EDUCAUSE Review, 39*(5). Retrieved from http://www.educause.edu/EDUCAUSE+Review/EDUCAUSEReviewMagazineVolume39/WideOpenSpacesWikisReadyorNot/157925

Leuf, B., & Cunningham, W. (2001). *The Wiki way: Quick collaboration on the Web.* Boston, MA: Addison-Wesley.

Lo, G. (2006, October 27). Documentation in the open source world. *Notes on the Free Software and Open Source Symposium.* Retrieved from http://justagwailo.com/filter/2006/10/27/open-source-world

Lo, G. (2009, November). Free and open source documentation. *Just a Gwai Lo.* Retrieved from http://justagwailo.com/fsoss-documentation

Maciak, L. (2008, June 18). The problem with Wikis. *Terminally Incoherent.* Retrieved from http://www.terminally-incoherent.com/blog/2008/06/18/the-problem-with-wikis/

McHaney, R. W. (2009, November 4). Implementation of ELATEwiki. *EDUCAUSE Quarterly, 32*(4). Retrieved from http://www.educause.edu/EDUCAUSE+Quarterly/EDUCAUSEQuarterlyMagazineVolum/ImplementationofELATEwiki/192968

McHaney, R. W. (2011). *The new digital shoreline: How Web 2.0 and millennials are revolutionizing higher education.* Stylus Publishing.

Meatballwiki. (2011). *Softsecurity.* Retrieved from http://meatballwiki.org/wiki/SoftSecurity

Mediawiki. (2011, February 7). *Category:MediaWiki configuration settings.* MediaWiki. Retrieved from http://www.mediawiki.org/wiki/Category:MediaWiki_configuration_settings

*MediaWiki.org.* (2011). Retrieved from http://www.mediawiki.org/wiki/MediaWiki.

Mohan, R. (2005, December). The problem with Wikis. *CircleID.* Retrieved from http://www.circleid.com/posts/the_problem_with_wikis/

Parker, K. R., & Chao, J. T. (2007). Wiki as a teaching tool. *Interdisciplinary Journal of Knowledge and Learning Objects, 3,* 57–72.

Phillipson, M. (2008). Wikis in the classroom: A taxonomy. In Cummings, R. E., & Barton, M. (Eds.), *Wiki writing: Collaborative learning in the college classroom* (pp. 19–43). Ann Arbor, MI: University of Michigan Press.

Richardson, W. (2009). *Blogs, wikis, podcasts, and other powerful web tools for classrooms* (2nd ed.). Thousand Oaks, CA: Corwin Press.

Sheppard, E. (2009, November 21). Wikis for end-user document. *Useful Tips when Open Sourcing.* Retrieved from http://wikis4userdoc.intodit.com/page/useful-tips-when-open-sourcing

Sherifudeen, M. (2005). *Wiki using ASP.NET.* Master's Thesis, Kansas State University.

Suh, B., Chi, E. H., Pendleton, B. A., & Kittur, A. (2007). Us vs. them: Understanding social dynamics in Wikipedia with revert graph visualizations. *IEEE Symposium on Visual Analytics Science and Technology (VAST '07)*, October 30 - November 3, Sacramento, CA, (pp. 163-170). Piscataway, NJ: IEEE.

Suoranta, J., & Veden, T. (2010). *Wikiworld.* London, UK: PlutoPress.

Sutton, A. (2006, September). Stop using wikis as documentation. *Symphonious.* Retrieved from http://www.symphonious.net/2006/09/02/stop-using-wikis-as-documentation/

TechTarget. (2008). *Webmaster.* Retrieved from http://whatis.techtarget.com/definition/0,sid9_gci213349,00.html

The Computer Language Company. (2011). Definition of: Trolling. *PCMAG.COM.* Retrieved from http://www.pcmag.com/encyclopedia_term/0,2542,t=trolling&i=53181,00.asp

UMassWiki. (2011). *UMassWiki: Blocking spam in MediaWiki.* Retrieved from http://www.umass-wiki.com/wiki/UMassWiki:Blocking_Spam_In_Mediawiki

Wagner, C. (2004). Wiki: A technology for conversational knowledge management and group collaboration. *Communications of the Association for Information Systems, 13*, 265–289.

Wikipedia. (2008, December 3). *Wikipedia.* Retrieved from Wikipedia.org: http://en.wikipedia.org

Wikipedia. (2011a). *Mediawiki.* Retrieved from http://en.wikipedia.org/wiki/MediaWiki

Wikipedia. (2011b). *Edit wars.* Retrieved from http://en.wikipedia.org/wiki/Edit_war

## KEY TERMS AND DEFINITIONS

**ConfirmEdit:** Confirmedit is a free, open source software extension for Mediawiki that provides a set of tools to ensure changes to pages are being made by humans and not bots or other automated processes.

**Mediawiki:** MediaWiki is free, open source software for the implementation of wikis. It was originally developed for Wikipedia but has since been implemented for many projects. It is written in PHP.

**Recaptcha:** Recaptcha is a system developed at Carnegie Mellon University that uses images of characters to help verify that site users are not automated processes but real users. This helps protect websites from spam and other problems.

**Web 2.0:** Web 2.0 is a class of applications that enable the Internet to be used for social collaboration. A Web 2.0 site enables users to collaborate using social media while achieving creative goals.

**Webmaster:** A webmaster is the individual responsible for the maintenance and overall operation of a website. The duties of the webmaster often include ensuring website software and hardware are operational, that the website is designed appropriately, that pages and links on the site are up-to-date, that users are managed and given responses, that traffic analysis is conducted and that the site's goals are achieved.

**Wiki:** A Wiki is an instance of special software running on a server that enables users to create and edit Web page content from their Web browser. Wikis were considered to be one of the first true Web 2.0 applications.

**Wiki Keeper:** A wiki keeper is a variant of wiki master that seeks to promote harmony on a wiki and maintain a subtle, cooperative presence to help the community of users achieve their goals in a non-coercive way.

**Wiki Master:** Similar to a webmaster, a wiki master is an individual that oversees the opera-tion of a wiki. In addition to skills possessed by a webmaster, a wiki master must edit collaboratively created content in a subtle and non-obtrusive way.

**Wikimedia:** Wikimedia is the organization responsible for Wikipedia, the Mediawiki software system, and other wiki sites. It is a not-for-profit organization.

# Chapter 13
# Creating Open–Source Interactive Articles for the Wider Publics

**Shalin Hai-Jew**
*Kansas State University, USA*

## ABSTRACT

*A core form of the international sharing of research and analysis is done through articles, both those presented in live conferences and those published in any number of journals. Interactive articles integrate various elements to the basic text: hyperlinks; immersive simulations; electronic games; data sets; knowledge collections; digital photographs; multimedia; integrated wikis and blogs; and other aspects. These value-added pieces that build exploration, experience, and interactivity, are enabled by current authoring tools and Web servers and open-source contents. Enriched articles often encourage return engagements, and their open-source publishing often leads to greater levels of citations and readership. These enable the design of a work for multiple audiences, with opt-in sections for different levels of readers, for example. Interaction enables opportunities for more reflection, recursiveness, and understanding a topic from multiple angles and different levels of abstraction. Interactive articles tend to appear in open-source (or at least open-access) publications online, which enables access by wider reading publics and machine-searchability and often wider citations.*

DOI: 10.4018/978-1-4666-2205-0.ch013

## INTRODUCTION

*Many of us have imagined a world where objects are content-rich, interactive, and provide personalized information. But problems abound: Where does the information about the objects reside? How do we get content to said objects? How do you make sure the content is relevant to the consumer...? How do you empower users so that they can decide what content they wish to experience? -Fred Kitson, HP Laboratories, in "Mobile Media: Making it a Reality" in Q Focus (2005, p. 40)*

The spirit of the present cyber-age is characterized by interactivity and openness: the power of individual customization and choice-making (of selective experiences) in automated spaces; the crowd-sourcing of information by virtual strangers; the sharing of open-source information and digital objects; and the co-creation of digital contents released into the public sphere through copyright releases. This interactivity is a method for enriched engagement with the digital contents for more effective learning.

As a basic unit of analysis, an article is a foundational form of academic exchange through which researchers share their learning with others (and build professional legacies). While different academic publications have various editorial stances and visions, most traditional articles consist of the following elements: a title, an abstract or executive summary (or bulleted points to highlight the main points of the article), an introduction, a literature review, the core research, analysis and discussion of the implications of the research, a conclusion, a references list, and an acknowledgments section. These articles are linear and sequential, with a main focus on text. The guidelines tend to be spelled out clearly, with precise word counts, formal phrasing in the writing, and regimented conventions.

In online spaces, such articles may have hyperlinks to various resources. There may be more imagery (diagrams and photos) because of the nominal cost of electronic publishing. Some images tend to be "above the fold" (a print newspaper term which means higher than the midsection of a broadsheet-sized newspaper, in the section that fits into the newspaper vending box viewing window) in order to attract potential reader attention. Such articles often are linked to a unique identifier known as a digital object identifier (DOI). Electronic versions tend to have more elaborate author biographies and links to author websites.

Interactive articles are a kind of third-generation iteration of academic articles. These contain aspects of the Social Web or Web 2.0 features—such as links to wikis, blogs, and social networking sites. More sophisticated authoring tools and editing software enable the integration of image maps, simple games, mnemonic exercises, digital exploratories, interactive timelines, and interactive videos. Such articles are interactive and immersive. Readers are expected to not only interact with the site but to bring their own insights and talents to interacting with other readers and sharing ideas. Such articles delve into "extreme layering" of reader experiences. Further, such articles now are created to be mobile-friendly ones—to enhance access and consumption of the contents.

This modernist approach enables more competition for modern readers' attention (getting beyond the high barrier of apathy) with an enriched reader experience that is enhanced by interactive multimedia. This also enables the writers to reach out to multiple audiences simultaneously (with both opt-in and opt-out sorts of experiences). This approach is somewhat more edgy. This aligns with some of the new publishing models, such as those that offer rolling deadlines instead of set publishing schedules. Interactive articles are very much a cultural production and an enablement of the confluence of various technologies and social movements.

From a pedagogical perspective, interactive articles enable learning enrichment by encouraging reader reflection and return visits (recursiveness) and a longer article "shelf life". These interactive forms may be applied to e-books and electronic chapters as well. This type of interactive academic writing, though, offers a point of no return to the paper format—which would not be able to mimic the same contents except in a highly abstracted and experientially degraded way.

## MAIN FOCUS OF THE CHAPTER

To understand the early moves towards popularizing interactive articles, it may help to see this emergent article form as a culmination of multiple influences. First, Web 2.0 social connectivity has connected individuals with various backgrounds to congregate around shared interests. Various hacker movements have broken down the barriers between the means of production from the "cathedral" to the "bazaar." Readers are expected to be participatory and contributory to the reading experience. Open-source sharing and publishing has enabled access to rich source materials for use

in the designs of interactive articles. Open-source resource types include images, data, maps, videos, and other resources. And finally, authoring tools and other technologies have enabled the building of interactivity in online articles. The emergence of interactive articles depends on layers of dependencies. Without this confluence of factors, it is hard to imagine that interactive articles would be able to be created or would find a readership base. Figure 1, "Interactive Articles a Product of Their Time," highlights these causative factors that influence the readership, the available resources, and the enabling technologies.

The popularization of multimedia and self-broadcasting and crowd-sourcing of information has meant that formal expertise is under pressure to prove itself with fresh insights. Further, those who would self-identify as experts and publish need to compete with a range of other media for reader attention. The flood of open-source resources lowers the cost of content creation for

*Figure 1. Interactive articles a product of their time*

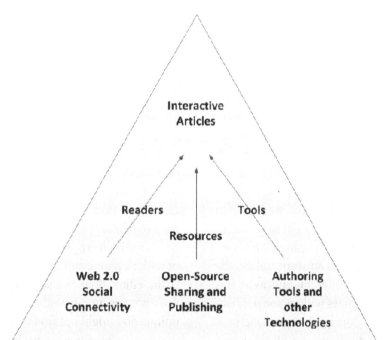

interactive articles because quality materials are available (at least in targeted areas of study). Open-source publishers offer strong platforms for the inclusion of peer-reviewed interactive articles, and their reputations and credibility assure a core user base of readers. Further, open-source publishers often enhance the discoverability of publications—which sometimes means more research citations. Finally, authoring tools simplify the creation of interactivity in an integrative and experiential whole.

This chapter abstracts direct learning from the building of two interactive articles that were peer-reviewed and published in 2011. This describes the steps taken to achieve both articles based on the disparate objectives of each. This then examines some lessons learned in this process and the emerging ethos of these interactive articles. Further, this chapter examines some potential future research questions about this new form of academic article.

## THE DESIGN OF INTERACTIVE ARTICLES

Before an interactive article is even pursued, there is some preliminary work that has to be done to determine whether it is even a good idea to proceed. After all, in an academic environment, there are political risks to pursuing publishing—because of the sense of public eyes on the project and the university. There are political risks if an article is rejected in peer review, and if an article is not accepted within a certain period of time, the contents will age out—no matter how well written or designed the original work might have been.

Creating a research paper requires a high investment in effort, expertise, and time. Often, the project funding does not cover this endeavor. It is assumed that the researchers will pursue publishing on their own time. Going public does increase risk—so it is critical to document all work and

decision-making and to ensure that all materials have been properly vetted for intellectual property and media releases and overall legality.

Another potential challenge may be the tensions with colleagues that may sometimes arise with publication and the sense of competition that that may spark. Ideally, such a project will make a development team stronger, and it will not spark professional jealousies among colleagues who have not worked on the project.

A "showstopper" is anything that may prevent the project from progressing and becoming reality. Some early ones in a political environment may involve a lack of political support. To gauge the environment, it helps to have a general awareness of the objectives of the administrators. It's also critical to check with all potential stakeholders to get their buy-in or permission. If administrators ask for oversight of all the contents, then that is a clear signal to avoid pursuing the project further. That level of professional censorship works counter to the academic freedoms of the principal investigators (PIs) and the rest of the development team. Another showstopper involves the development team. If there are any negative dynamics—such as low trust with the PIs and administrators—then it's not advisable to proceed. If the development team will have to work too far outside of their skill sets to create the contents for the article, that is another warning sign against proceeding. If there are any intellectual property challenges—such as core proprietary non-includable information or a lack of media releases for digital contents—that may be sufficient to stop this endeavor.

One other potential showstopper involves an early query to a publisher. If the team has an idea for a particular publisher with whom there might be a good fit, it is a good idea to send a query email or make a phone call to run the idea by the editor. If the editor does not see a fit with the topic or does not see an interest, and if the topic is fairly unique and might not find a publisher elsewhere, then it may be critical to just hold off on the work.

The core point of creating an article is making sure it finds an audience. If something is written and created but shelved, it will have cost the team in time and effort and in political good will as well. The nuances of whether to proceed or not really belong to the PI. In some domain fields, a solid article with new research information will generally be publishable; in some other domain fields, it may be hard to gauge whether a work will land or not.

Finally, team members may have outsized expectations of what publishing will mean to their respective careers and fortunes. Publishing often involves very minimal effects on a writer's life. As such, it's critical to manage expectations.

The benefits of publishing successfully though may well outweigh any anticipated risks. One benefit involves rallying the development team on an instructional project to use their shared knowledge and skills to share their learning with a broader public. There is always the interest in recruiting students to a particular course or learning sequence. Publishing a peer-reviewed article and acknowledging the grant funders is another way to express gratitude and to hopefully shape the environment for future funding.

## Eight Steps in the Process

There were eight steps that were followed to create the two interactive articles at the heart of this case.

**Step 1:** Inspiration and Vision
**Step 2:** Political Environment
**Step 3:** Available Resources
**Step 4:** Topic Suitability for an Interactive Article
**Step 5:** Planning and Execution
**Step 6:** Alpha and Beta Testing
**Step 7:** Shopping the Digital Manuscript
**Step 8:** Addressing Peer Reviews
**Step 9:** Revision and Launch

The original PI and development team should be enthusiastic about a particular angle of their shared work to motivate them to create the contents for possible publication. The political environment needs to be healthy—in the development team, in the work space, in the larger educational institution, in the potential publishing houses, and even in the larger academic environment. The development team should have access to all the necessary resources to actualize the work. This includes various technologies, digital contents, time, and energy. The topic of the work project should be suitable for an interactive article. If the contents do not fit the medium, then the team may end up with a mix-match of content and form—which will make it very difficult to publish. The team will need to plan and execute the work to achieve the necessary quality within the limited time span. Once the article is drafted and loaded on a test server, it should be put through the paces of alpha and beta testing. The digital manuscript should then be shopped and double-blind peer reviewed by reviewers. If the reviewers suggest a interest in publishing the work, then the dev team will need to respond to the comments of the peer reviewers through revisions and a point-by-point response. Finally, upon initial publisher acceptance, the article is revised and launched.

There are a number of unique contextual circumstances that will affect various steps of the process. However, as an abstraction, the above steps are fairly inclusive. Table 1, "Questions to Consider at Each Step of Creating an Interactive Article" highlights some questions that may be asked at each step.

The table above offers a beginning list of questions that may be considered for individuals and teams interested in creating interactive articles. This is by no means a comprehensive list. The next sections highlight two separate cases of the creation of interactive articles.

*Table 1. Questions to consider at each step of creating an interactive article*

| |
|---|
| **Step 1: Inspiration and Vision**<br>   • What aspects of a real-world project are "proof of concept" and would benefit other instructional designers or developers or those in educational information technology (IT)?<br>     • How original is the idea? Where would this work fit in the context of the academic literature?<br>     • Is there sufficient theory and research to backstop the article?<br>     • Will the ideas translate well to a global audience, or is the approach provincial and localized (and possibly non-transferable)?<br>     • Will there be benefits to the development team to pursue development and possible publishing?<br>     • Will the idea and the execution of that idea get past peer reviewers?<br>     • Is there sufficient glamour to the project to command human attention? |
| **Step 2: Political Environment**<br>   • Does publishing fit with the core values of the organization and its "bottom line" goals? (Note: In an educational institution of higher education, publishing does contribute to future grant funding; skills development of the dev team; recruitment of students for an online course, and the university's public standing and brand identity.)<br>     • Who are the principal investigators (PIs) on the project, and are they open to having an article? Are they comfortable with public space and public exposure?<br>     • Is there tacit or open support from local administrators to pursue this work—even if it's not fully recompensed financially?<br>     • Who are the development team members, and are they willing to join the endeavor?<br>     • Is there a publication with whom one has a trust relationship that might provide publishing opportunities? Sufficient critique feedback and support?<br>     • If there is a human research element, would the institutional review board (IRB) approve? What might be some sticking points—if any? How might those be mitigated? |
| **Step 3: Available Resources**<br>   • What digital contents are available for use from the extant project? Are these readily available and access (labeled with proper naming protocols, in the right digital formats)? What may be repurposed?<br>     • What open-source contents are available for possible use? Generally available proprietary contents (through linkage or iFraming)?<br>     • What new materials have to be made from scratch?<br>     • Are there sufficient software technologies? (photo editing, video editing, drafting, screen captures, lecture capture, authoring tools, and others?) Hardware or equipment? (SCLB7 is one of the tools used to bring the pieces together into a coherent whole.)<br>   • Is there access to a local test Web server?<br>   • Is there sufficient time and energy to create the work and go to press on deadline? (There's a reputational cost to trying and failing.)<br>   • Are all the dependencies (human good will, technological, political, content, and others) present to enable a successful collaboration?<br>   • If there are potential showstoppers, are they able to be mitigated? |
| **Step 4: Topic Suitability for an Interactive Article**<br>   • Is the general or target audience interest in the topic?<br>   • Is there an inherent structure to the information to create automated coherence (without a direct human mediator)? Is it possible to design an article where each piece has a purpose (with explanations and automations)?<br>   • Does the topic have current relevance? Will it have some classic enduring value even in Internet time?<br>   • Does the topic allow smooth integration of multiple skill sets and contributor voices?<br>   • Is there a practical way of framing the contents—such as about problem-solving, conflict resolution, discovery, or other?<br>   • Will it be possible to mitigate for potential negative learning? |
| **Step 5: Planning and Execution**<br>   • Are there clear understood standards for the article (usually drawn from the project stylebook)?<br>   • Are there ways to draft out a structure—through the definition of organizational principles, storyboarding, scripting, and roughs?<br>   • Does the team have access to all the relevant digital resources? Does it have the wherewithal and resources to create necessary digital contents?<br>   • How is the article drafted for sequencing and interactivity? The social connectivity?<br>   • Does the team agree on who the primary author is? The corresponding author? The contributors list?<br>   • What editing and revision standards need to be applied to make sure that all the pieces of the article align? |
| **Step 6: Alpha and Beta Testing**<br>   • Is there a clear structure for reader navigation of the article? Are there multiple navigational options?<br>   • Are there sufficient contents to comprehensively convey the information necessary?<br>   • Are there various types of interactive elements to engage the human senses (while being accessible)?<br>   • Is the tone consistent and suited to the contents? Is the tone suited to the target publication(s)?<br>   • Will the contents be playable on various platforms?<br>   • Is there sufficient academic research to back-stop the article?<br>   • Is the article built to in-domain-field standards? Academic? Professional? Accessibility? Technological? Metadata labeling?<br>   • Does the article connect with readers and the general public? What works? What doesn't? Why? |

*continued on following page*

*Table 1. Continued*

| Step 7: Shopping the Digital Manuscript |
|---|
| • Which publisher has been queried about the digital manuscript, and what have they said? |
| • Are there known alignments with a publisher's objectives? Target audiences? Forthcoming issue themes? |
| • Is the publisher an open-source or proprietary publisher? Is there a fit between the development team and the form of publisher? |
| • What are the technological capabilities of the target publisher (in terms of hosting rich media and microsites and social IT tools)? |
| • What is the reputation of the publisher in the academic community? Would that reputation enhance the team and university? |
| • What sort of editorial support does the publisher offer to the writers who publish with them? |
| **Step 8: Addressing Peer Reviews** |
| • What have the responses been from the peer reviewers? |
| • If there is a conditional acceptance or outright acceptance, how may the team respond to the suggestions for improvement in measurable and observable ways? What sort of written response will they offer to the peer reviewers and editors? |
| • Are the changes within the purview of the team's ambitions for the article? |
| **Step 9: Revision and Launch** |
| • How may the manuscript be revised for improved navigability? Readability and clarity? Aesthetics? Interactivity? Fun? |
| • Who should be acknowledged in the "thanks"? |
| • If materials were launched on a test server, when should that be deleted in order to promote "single sourcing"? (without Web crawlers and spiders mapping to the old site) |
| • What sort of publicity and outreach plan should be followed up with? |
| • Are there benefits to the original PIs and project? If so, how may the dev team promote that benefit? |

## CASE 1: THE PARTICIPATORY DESIGN OF A (TODAY AND) FUTURE DIGITAL ENTOMOLOGY LAB

"The Participatory Design of a (Today and) Future Digital Entomology Lab" by Shalin Hai-Jew

http://www.educause.edu/ EDUCAUSE+Quarterly/EDUCAUSEQuarterlyMagazineVolum/TheParticipatoryDesignofa-Today/236669

The original inspiration for "The Participatory Design…" came from the reading of a book about the dearth of digital online laboratories to augment the learning in fully online science courses in the US. When the opportunity arose to pursue internal grant funds to build a digital lab, the author worked with the faculty member to write the grant and won a small amount of funding to purchase a specialized camera with the capability of capturing macro images (with the subjects close-in to the lens). A further ambition was to spark a discourse about the apparent American reluctance to pursue the building of digital labs in simulation to replace physical labs or wetlabs for a variety of online courses.

Then, an unexpected challenge in the execution of the project brought a further reason for writing about this endeavor. The promise of a developer by the sponsoring department did not materialize. This meant that there was not the talent to code unique tools to develop the actual digital entomology lab features—only the capture of macro images. The high-end detailed images were hosted on a very static site (hosted by the Kansas State University Department of Entomology) which lacked even a basic search function. These images provided a small sense of digital tangibles in terms of what might be done with a digital lab, but as executed, there were severe limits.

It was hoped that an article could showcase the originality of laying the groundwork for such a lab and to possibly fund-raise additional moneys to build a next iteration of this digital entomology lab. This was a more ambitious endeavor—because it would require readers to visualize the work that occurred and then possibilities for the future iterations of the digital lab. The article would have to inform readers and prime them to offer fresh ideas. It would also have to reach out to create a kind of empathy—for a sense of shared endeavor. Figure 2, "A Screenshot of the Top-Level of 'The Participatory Design…' Interactive and Open-Source Article" shows what the published article looks like.

The article was built in layers. At the top layer, it was important to use some design elements to capture potential reader attention "above the fold." The images of insects shown from various angles on a grid background aimed to fulfill that purpose.

Readers could use an iFrame to navigate to the actual digital entomology lab to explore the meta-data-ed images. Figure 3, "An iFrame of the K-State Department of Entomology Website" shows a screenshot of the iFrame. Note the scrollbar to the right of the navigable website. As much as was possible, it was important to strive for transparency—so all assertions with backed up with evidence.

The top level of the article had embedded a link to a microsite. Earlier, the publishers had tried to use an iFrame to contain the microsite, but that was too constraining of the various interactive activities and objects. The limits of the screen real estate meant that a new pop-up window would be a preferable choice. Figure 4, "A Microsite within the Article that Leads to Exploratory Spaces" shows what that interface looks like. The microsite itself has a clear outline structure to help users navigate. Readers may navigate sequentially page-by-page, or they may pick their way through the contents. Return users should be able to pinpoint exactly where they want to go.

First, it was important to help readers understand the history of the endeavor. A photo album was created that showed the physical entomology lab and the tools within it, then the need for a digital version. The core function of the lab is to

*Figure 2. A screenshot of the top-level of "the participatory design…" interactive and open-source article*

*Figure 3. An iFrame of the K-State Department of Entomology website*

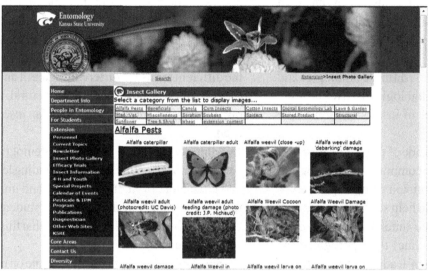

*Figure 4. A microsite within the article that leads to exploratory spaces*

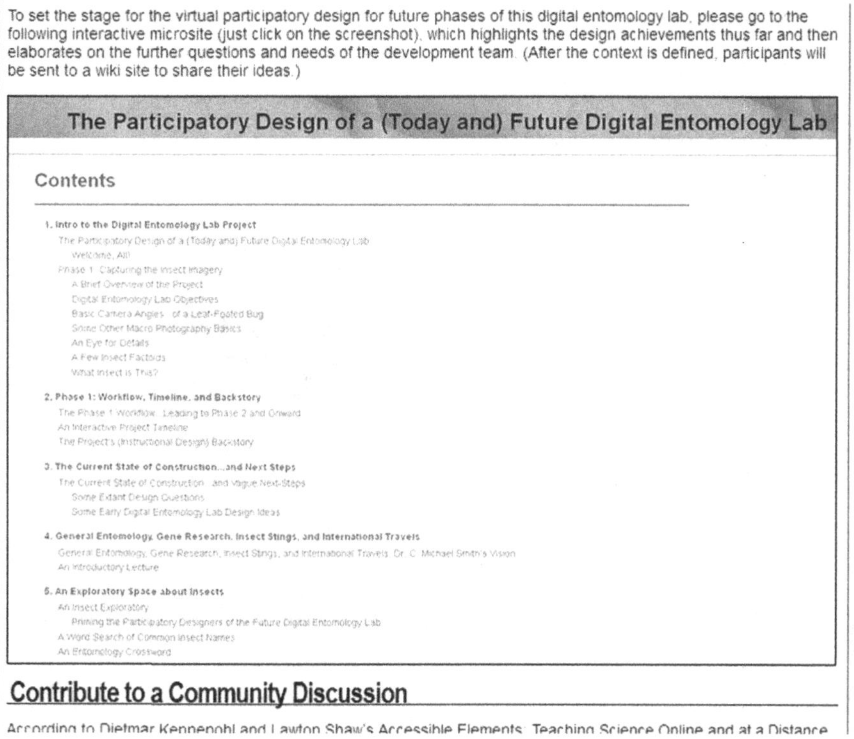

help students study for morphology (form) and function of these various insects and to help them begin to differentiate these insects by physical features into types. The photo album included photos of the PI and the student photographer hired to capture the images. There were also screenshots of the photo editing technologies and desktop publishing technologies used to show the high-resolution images of insects from multiple directions (Figure 5).

Once that groundwork of project history was laid, it was important to communicate the progress made on the current version of the digital entomology lab. This would help set a design context. To that end, there were timelines (including an interactive digital timeline) that spotlighted the work achieved and then leading into the future with optimal work that could be done then (if funded). There as an audio file (and transcript) from the instructional designer point-of-view. Figure 6, "A 2D Timeline Describing the Project's Progress" shows the work timeline. The interactive timeline included images with captions placed on a timeline.

There was an interactive insect exploratory where people could engage with terminology (in crossword puzzles, word finds, and digital flashcards). They could put together digital jigsaw puzzles. They could look at a close-up high-resolution image of an insect. They could practice the different terms for different angles of an insect (lateral, anterior, posterior, dorsal, ventral, and so on). One open-source image map of an insect was used.

Multiple audience members' demographics were visualized for this article—including learners and instructors from other colleges and universities, professionals in the field, and students and educators from K-12. The hope was that this work would include the large publics.

Some of the contents were available on mobile devices given that the site was also put out in HTML5. Delivering multimedia on mobile devices poses various challenges, with a variety of devices with different screen sizes, memory capabilities and processing power (Pellan & Concolato, 2008). For an experience to play coherently, there should not be frame drops in video captures or latency

*Figure 5. A photo album activity that highlights the history of the project*

*Figure 6. A 2D timeline describing the project's progress*

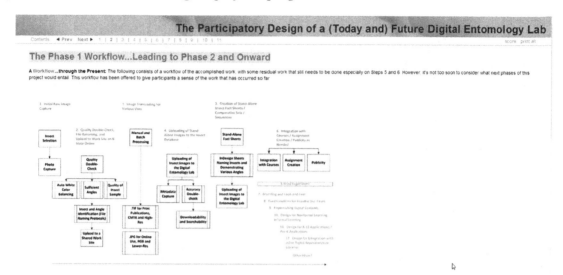

in user interactions with a simulation or game or interaction or image download. Flash objects, though, were not playable on iPads. Figure 7, "An Interactive Mobile Activity for Pinning a Virtual Insect" offers a sense of what happens to

insects prior to the close-in photo captures. This activity was a mobile version of a more in-depth online version.

Figure 8, "One of the Multiple Digital Jigsaw Puzzles from Multiple Points of View" helps

*Figure 7. An interactive mobile activity for pinning a virtual insect*

*Figure 8. One of the multiple digital jigsaw puzzles from multiple points of view*

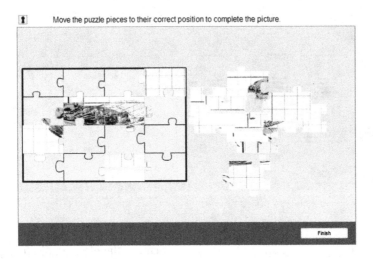

Mystery Insect #1

The following is a 16-piece digital jigsaw puzzle of a "mystery" insect. Drag each piece of the puzzle to the proper location, and drop it there.

Move the puzzle pieces to their correct position to complete the picture.

Finish

Mystery Solved! You have put together a cicada. Bravo!

readers to focus on form and structure while solving a digital jigsaw. This spotlights a type of attention to form. If entomology was a more commonly encountered topic, this amount of priming through opt-in activities would have been less.

The terminology of a field is an important aspect to the learning. In that spirit, there were multiple activities that practiced different types of terminologies for the learners. Figure 9, "An Entomology Crossword Puzzle" focused on particular insect parts and functions. Anytime the activity was restarted, the computer would output another form of the crossword, and the definitions would be remixed.

Figure 10, "A Digital Flashcard Activity for the Practice of Insect Morphological Terms" offered an ability to customize vocabulary lists for practice. Users may choose to have the definitions displayed alone, or the words displayed alone, too.

Readers who enjoy word searches may learn the new terms by interacting with a digital word search. Figure 11, "An Adaptive Digital Word Search for Insect Names" showcases this activity. This activity also reconstitutes itself in a different way every time it is refreshed.

Dr. C. Michael Smith, an entomology professor, offered a lecture, a 44-step dichotomous key for "keying" different types of insects, and a Q&A in which he talked about his work in entomology. There was a conscious effort to humanize the principal investigator (PI) and how he came to work in entomology. He spoke about his travels. He also introduced some of his research, based on genetics.

With all these contents to prime potential participatory designers to consider different design issues, the readers were then sent to a page on the E-Learning and Teaching Exchange (ELATEwiki) site to share their ideas based on targeted design questions (which were set up in the main text of

*Figure 9. An entomology crossword puzzle*

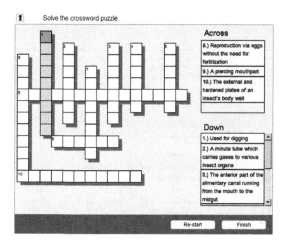

*Figure 10. A digital flashcard activity for the practice of insect morphological terms*

*Figure 11. An adaptive digital word search for insect names*

the article). Because such a solicitation of information (as "crowd-sourcing") may have had human implications, this work was put through the institutional review board (IRB) to ensure that it would pass muster among professionals. Figure 12, "An Invitation to a Specially Designed Wiki Page to Post Shared Ideas" shows the invitation.

A repeated image was moved to the wiki page. Further, the design questions raised by the original article were echoed again. Figure 13, "The Uses of a MediaWiki Page to Collect Reader Insights (on the ELATEwiki)" shows what that page looked like.

While it was hoped that a small group would offer some ideas, even though the article had been up for a full quarter, no comments were posted. The author received some emails with commentary, but there were no serious endeavors to try to help in the design of future versions of the digital entomology lab.

## CASE 2: CREATING A GLOBAL HEALTH COURSE AND GAME

"Creating an Online Global Health Course and Game" by Brent A. Anders, Deborah J. Briggs, Shalin Hai-Jew, Zachary J. Caby, and Mary Werick

http://www.educause.edu/ EDUCAUSE+Quarterly/EDUCAUSEQuarterlyMagazineVolum/CreatinganOnlineGlobalHealthCo/242682

The original inspiration for "Creating a Global Health Course and Game" was really to push the proof-of-concept of whether the development team at K-State could create a basic game around an engaging idea: the idea of showcasing a global health expert who is on the constant move from country-to-country, and who is being pursued by an intrepid reporter. The idea of focusing on the travel was to represent an actual reality of much of the work of global health, but also to make a

*Figure 12. An invitation to a specially designed wiki page to post shared ideas*

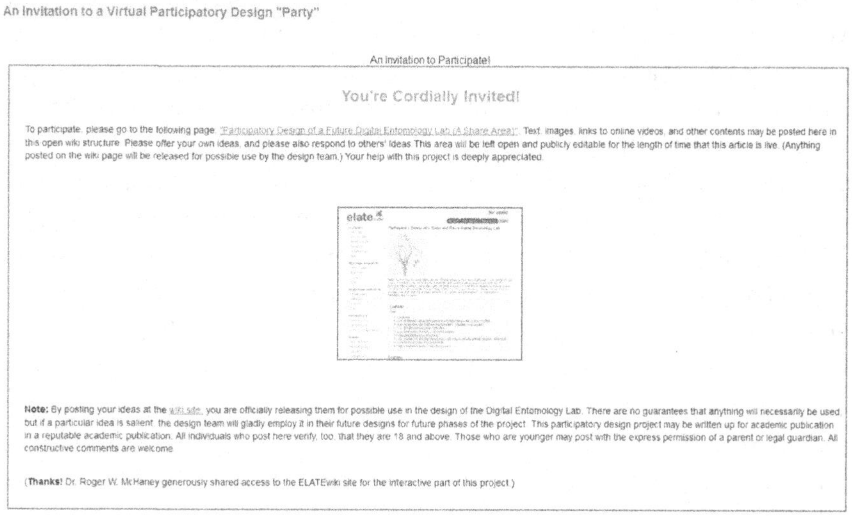

*Figure 13. The uses of a MediaWiki page to collect reader insights (on the ELATEwiki)*

send-up or play on the popular game from the 1980s (the similarity ends there). A further motivation may have been a little more prosaic. The development team had worked hard over multiple years to build a trust-filled and productive working relationship with Dr. Deborah J. Briggs, a global health expert and rabies prevention specialist, who lived in Europe and would only see the team for short periods of time (during brief visits stateside). The online course build had come to an end, and there was still enthusiasm and energy. There was the hope that the work would continue for a little longer. Further, there was hope that an article might bring positive attention to the article and attract potential students. Figure 14, "A Screenshot of the Top-Level of 'Creating an Online Global Health...' Interactive and Open-Source Article" shows a top-level screenshot of the actual article.

If telepresence of the instructor is a critical piece in an online course to encourage student participation, in an interactive article, it was critical to show the power of the individual. Plenty of research into human cognition has shown that people tend to respond to others and to stories (Kahneman, 2011)—much more so than to the abstractions of statistics or microbial pathogens and faraway lands. People also respond to entertainment and a sense of humor and fun. These insights into how humans learn informed the design. These realities emphasized the importance of showcasing Dr. Briggs' personality (and her alter ego, the fictgional Dr. Salus 'Dynamica' Mundi). Figure 15, "The Design of Social Pres-

*Figure 14. A screenshot of the top-level of "creating an online global health..." interactive and open-source article*

*Figure 15. The design of social presence to encourage learner interactivity with the professor*

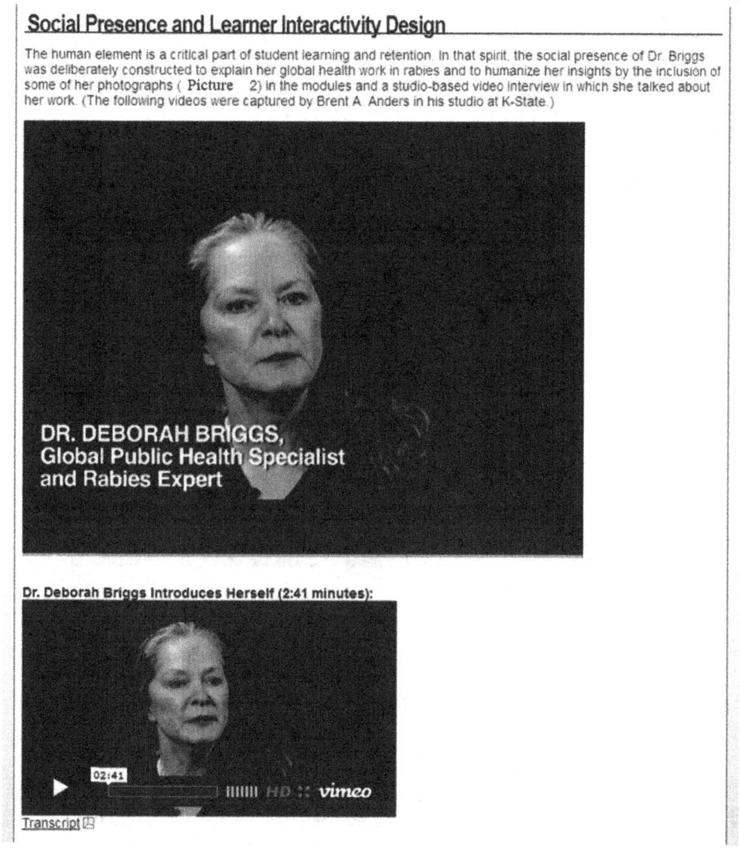

ence to Encourage Learner Interactivity with the Professor" shows links to videos of Dr. Briggs talking about the work of global health. These videos were hosted on the video-sharing site, Vimeo™.

Two microsites were built into this interactive article. One was a from-life view of Dr. Brigg's work as director of the Global Alliance for Rabies Control (GARC). Her work has taken her around the world many times. She wrote a sidebar about rabies to share an expert, research-based, and scientific view of rabies and some strategies for rabies prevention. She shared photos from her global travels, which were built into digital photo albums that were carefully captioned. This sidebar includes an open-source chloropleth map of rabies prevalence around the world from the World Health Organization. An open-source time-zones map was also used to convey both the concept of time zones and the organizing structure of the photo albums. Figure 16, "Link to a Rabies Sidebar with Maps and International Photo Albums of Rabies Prevention Endeavors" was based on a screenshot from the photo album on "Fighting Rabies in Egypt."

Arguably, the highlight of the article was the global health game, titled "Where in the World is Dr. Salus 'Dynamica' Mundi?" The original game inspiration came from the author, who also sketched out the scenarios and wrote the main contents. Brent A. Anders wrote some video scripts and shot the video of Dr. Briggs ("Dr. Mundi") and Mary Werick ("Nina Novus") on green screen. The game artifice based on travel, geography and public health. Figure 17, "The Link to the "Where in the World is Dr. Salus 'Dynamica' Mundi?" Game (Image Created by Brent A. Anders)" captures some of the spirit of the game.

*Figure 16. Link to a rabies sidebar with maps and international photo albums of rabies prevention endeavors*

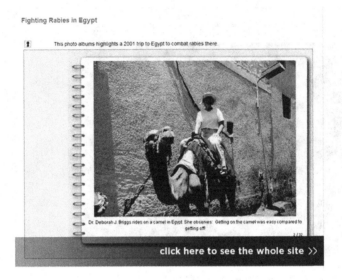

*Figure 17. The link to the "Where in the World is Dr. Salus 'Dynamica' Mundi?" game (image created by Brent A. Anders)*

The multi-scenario game may be seen at the top-level of the microsite. At the end of the game, there is a culminating interview between the fictional reporter Nina Novus and Dr. Mundi. Figure 18, "A Top-Level Screenshot of a Multi-Scenario Game" includes a multi-page game-debriefing at the end which explains the game design—the embedded global health principles and the actual flowchart of the game play.

Brent A. Anders and his videography team used music and background to showcase the various locations where Nina Novus traveled in pursuit of Dr. Mundi, famous globetrotter. The game elements were humorous and also evoked conventions of the field. The game was clearly sectioned off from the non-fictional parts of the article because of the need to protect Dr. Deborah J. Brigg's continuing work from the fun of the game design. Figure 19, "Reporter Nina Novus Reports from Japan (from the Game)" shows a screenshot from one of the reportage trips. (And no, Dr. Mundi was not in Japan in that scenario.)

Anders created a state-of-the-art video to explain the magic of green-screening (chromakeying) to create various illusions. He and his team only had about an hour and a bit to capture Dr. Deborah J. Briggs as Dr. Mundi, so he had to be inventive. Members of his staff appeared in some of the scenes as various characters. One of the walk-ons (Dr. Jodi Freifeld) had her wardrobe

*Figure 18. A top-level screenshot of a multi-scenario game*

**Where in the World is Dr. Salus "Dynamica" Mundi?**
(A Global Public Health Game)

Contents

**1. Where...The International--The First Sighting**
Where in the World is Dr. Salus "Dynamica" Mundi?
Game Section Introduction
Game Instructions:
Where in the World is Dr. Salus "Dynamica" Mundi?
The International: The First Sighting
The Importance of International Conferences for Global Health

**2. Where...Pharmaceutical Success**
Where in the World is Dr. Salus "Dynamica" Mundi?
Pharmaceutical Success
International Pharmaceutical Companies and their Impact on Vaccinating the Needy

**3. Where... The Clean Water Village**
Where in the World is Dr. Salus "Dynamica" Mundi?
The Clean Water Village

**4. Where... Refugee Camp Readiness**
Where in the World is Dr. Salus "Dynamica" Mundi?
Refugee Camp Readiness
Understanding Refugee Camps and their Dynamics

**5. Where... A Diagnostic Lab**
Where in the World is Dr. Salus "Dynamica" Mundi?
A Diagnostic Lab

**6. Where...Finally, the Interview!**
Dr. Salus "Dynamica" Mundi: Traveling around the World for Global Public Health

**7. The Brief Global Health Backstory of this Game**
The Brief Global Health Backstory of the Game
Early Game Design Thoughts
Takeaway Concepts

**8. The Game: Goals, Creation, and Assessment (A Case Study)**
The Game: Goals, Creation, and Assessment
A Case Study Explanation of the "Where in the World is Dr. Salus 'Dynamica' Mundi" Higher Education Game
Onwards... and Contact Information
Acknowledgments and Thanks

return to top

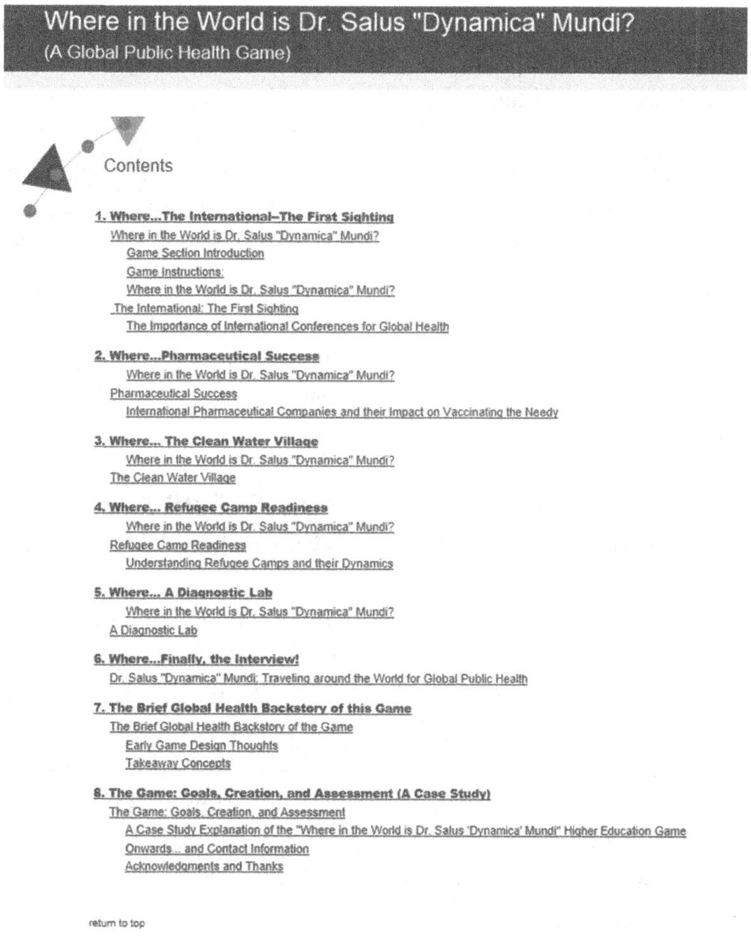

*Figure 19. Reporter Nina Novus reports from Japan (from the game)*

borrowed by the entire female crew of actors because she brought an armload of fashionable clothes. Figure 20, "Brent A. Anders Explains the Videography and Game Design Work" illuminates some of the visual tricks of green-screening—combined with creative videography.

This interactive article really showcased how various members of a team must collaborate effectively with their various skill sets to actualize an ambitious interactive article plan.

## A Preliminary Ethos of Interactive Articles

In reflecting on these two interactive article-building experiences, the author considered some aspects of the new ethos of interactive articles. These values stem from Web 2.0 and open-source endeavors, which inform the work. Interactive articles are transparent and richly explanatory. They draw from the social ideals of open-source sharing. They tap into multiple perceptual channels and tend towards universal-access accessibility. Ideally, these would have multi-directional communications and on-going collaborations especially post-production between authors and readers. The roles of authors would change to

be facilitators and learners; the roles of readers would change to be co-creators and critics (in a constructive sense). A deep participatory ethos pervades so much of Web 2.0, and translating some of that good will into interactive articles would be positive. Such articles tend to be less formal than traditional academic ones, and these may even be on occasion playful. Finally, such endeavors also tap into the pro-environment or green movement—with re-use of open-source digital objects and keeping it all electronic and non-paper.

## SOLUTIONS AND RECOMMENDATIONS

Given the newness of this sort of project, there were quite a few fresh insights. As stated earlier, it is critical to review the context to make sure that pursuing the writing of an interactive article makes sense politically and resource-wise. Once that commitment is made, it is important to work through the steps and to ask the right questions and to get the right answers along the way.

The work of building an interactive article as a follow-on to an instructional design project is

*Figure 20. Brent A. Anders explains the videography and game design work*

helped only minimally by the contents that were created for the project. The in-depth knowledge of the work is critical for the successful writing of the article, but the article itself requires plenty of new digital objects that require plenty of additional work—even if open-source digital objects are used.

The writing, creation, and revision work are highly iterative. With so many moving parts in an interactive article, it helps to have many sets of eyes on a project in order to catch mistakes. Further, content developers / authors may expect to easily use a dozen different software programs to author, create, edit and revise the various elements that are collated for a coherent interactive article.

Most organizations do not want to host microsites—not the end destination publishers, not the host universities of the development team. Hosting into perpetuity is a serious responsibility. (The author finally ended up hosting the microsites on the SoftChalk CONNECT repository in a generous trade deal with the software maker.) What this reluctance to host means is that such interactive articles will tend to reside in the cloud on various

servers. For resilience, the authors should have test servers to host the contents themselves on the off-chance a video sharing site or commercial repository fails to maintain their servers. However, it may be that a reality of digital publishing today is that many resources will be hosted in different locations with only some contents packaged at the publisher.

Another observation is that each reader of an online article is hard-earned. Some traditionalist readers who expect text-heavy and paper-based articles and well designed transitions may find the presentation of interactive articles difficult. The attentional space for most readers is so competitive that it's hard to win reader attention, and it's even more difficult elicit participatory contributions. For information to be salient, it has to capture reader attention and then engage them for a time—and optimally connect some of the new learning to some of their prior experiences.

While interactive articles may feasibly continuously evolve, common practice is to freeze an article once it is live. It's possible for a top-level of an article to be frozen by the publisher but to have access to the microsites even when an article has been published and has gone live. Whether a team decides to do so may depend on the context and the changes that are desired. The basic ethics are to "freeze" the microsites as well once an article has gone live.

The emergence of interactive articles may mean changing roles for authors and for readers. If there are more exchanges of responsibilities and collaborations in this "community" of writers and readers, then it is very possible that the additional roles of co-creators and facilitators and others will be added on to all.

## FUTURE RESEARCH DIRECTIONS

Future research may well focus on new evolutions of this form of electronic or digital article. New technologies and innovative practices, evolutions in publisher / writer / content developer / reader visions, and the proliferation of ever greater amounts of open-source contents will affect how these forms evolve.

Other research may focus on whether such forms are more or less efficacious for learning, more or less inclusive of a virtual readership, and more or less informative.

It may help to research what types of interactivity are most effective for certain types of learning and engagement. After all, interactivity is addressed in a range of ways in the research literature and also in the lived environment.

Interactive articles may be used in a variety of ways. They have been used here to possibly solicit funds, to elicit design ideas from a crowd-sourcing virtual community, to share ideas about global public health, and to share entertainment. It is likely that other types of interactive articles will have a wide range of other motivations and purposes for the authors. Researchers may want to evaluate how effective these forms are for the specific aim of the development team.

## CONCLUSION

This chapter is a very early on in terms of addressing a new form for which there are only a few live examples in public spaces. Putting interactivity on a site is not particularly innovative, but fitting a range of interactivity in academic articles for various objectives is becoming a little more cutting edge—because this goes beyond videos and simple hyperlinking. The inclusion of participatory technologies like wikis, the building of exploratory spaces, the inclusion of holistic games, and such endeavors push the edges of this phenomena. It is possible that interactive articles may strike a chord and be here to stay.

## ACKNOWLEDGMENT

Thanks to Steve Saltzberg of SoftChalk for encouraging discussion of the concept of interactive articles. This chapter evolved from a webinar "Building Interactive Articles for Peer-Reviewed Journals with SoftChalk" (Feb. 22, 2012) presented in the SoftChalk Innovators webinar series. Thanks also to the principal investigators (PIs) and colleagues in the interactive article projects. As is widely expressed, little actual work happens as a product of a sole innovator phenomena. Rather, we all work in teams and as members of a larger community to actualize a project.

## REFERENCES

Anders, B. A., Briggs, D. J., Hai-Jew, S., Caby, Z., & Werick, M. (2011). Creating an online global health course and game. *Educause Quarterly.* Retrieved from http://www.educause.edu/EDUCAUSE+Quarterly/EDUCAUSEQuarterlyMagazineVolum/CreatinganOnlineGlobalHealthCo/242682

Hai-Jew, S. (2011). Participatory design of a (today and) future digital entomology lab. *Educause Quarterly*. Retrieved from http://www.educause.edu/EDUCAUSE+Quarterly/EDUCAUSEQuarterlyMagazineVolum/TheParticipatoryDesignofaToday/236669

Kahneman, D. (2011). *Thinking, fast and slow*. New York, NY: Farrar, Straus and Giroux.

Pellan, B., & Concolato, C. (2008). Adaptation of scalable multimedia documents. In the *Proceedings of DocEng '08:* São Paulo, Brazil (pp. 32–41).

## KEY TERMS AND DEFINITIONS

**Above the Fold:** A term which refers to the section higher than the midsection of a broadsheet-sized newspaper, in the section that fits into the newspaper vending box viewing window (and which is therefore broadly viewable by passersby).

**Alpha Testing:** In-house testing of a site for the meeting of various standards.

**Artifice:** A clever or inventive illusion.

**Authoring Tool:** A software tool that enables the creation of digital contents.

**Beta Testing:** The inclusion of the general public or people from outside the organization to get a sense of how a particular article or website or learning object might be received.

**Cloud:** The delivery of software services and digital contents from remote servers (termed "the cloud" in a colloquial sense).

**Conventions:** A typical methodology for how to achieve particular aims.

**iFrame:** A method of displaying a website within a website, with the featured site fully navigable.

**Immersion:** The high-engagement of humans in 3D virtual spaces.

**Interactive Article:** An electronic article which is hosted on a Web server and which is designed to offer readers various interactive experiences to enhance the learning.

**Interactivity:** The ability to engage in depth with automated digital objects; the decision-making of human users on a website; rich inter-communications between people.

**Microsite:** A small and targeted website that is often part of a larger website.

**Mobile-Friendly:** The capability for an object to be read and/or experienced on a mobile device.

**Navigation:** The way in which individuals move through a particular website.

**Participatory Design:** The work of a virtual and distributed team to co-design a shared object.

**Peer Review:** The provision of critical feedback about an article by a colleague in a profession (often in a double-blind situation).

**Recursion:** The act of going back over something again.

**Repository:** An electronic collection of contents.

**Showstopper:** A fundamental weakness or challenge that will prevent a project from moving forward.

**Test Server:** A Web server (a computer) which publishes authored contents on a website in a human-readable way.

# Chapter 14

# Creating a Video Based Educational Game:
## A How-To Guide

**Brent A. Anders**
*Kansas State University, USA*

## ABSTRACT

*Although the subject of educational games has become a massive area of study, this chapter will present a small overview of what an instructor/facilitator should know and comprehend so as to start to put together an educational game. Through understanding of the components, structure, and utilization of various resources (such as open-source materials), the creation of an educational game is achievable to all.*

## CHAPTER OBJECTIVES

- Define the meaning of an educational game
- Describe the "why" in using an educational game as well as pedagogical explanations of game use within the educational realm
- How to identify what an instructor really wants/needs the educational game to do (accomplish)
- Understanding the structure and game-play of an educational game
- Utilization of video within an educational game
- How to put all the components of an educational game together
- Assessment and effects of an educational game

## INTRODUCTION

The development of educational games has been noted as an important trend by the Educause sponsored Horizon Report: "Game-based learning is poised to see greater use within the next two to three years...Game-playing itself may be used to develop decision-making and problem-solving abilities, as well as leadership skills, or educational content embedded into games can teach students as they play." (Wieder, 2011). As this new educational technique continues to gain popularity, more is being understood as to exactly what an educational game is and what goes in to making one.

DOI: 10.4018/978-1-4666-2205-0.ch014

## What is an Educational Game?

The question "what exactly is an educational game," is both a simple and complex inquiry to answer. Jane McGonigal, author of the often-sited book "*Reality Is Broken: Why Games Make Us Better and How They Can Change the World*," said it well when she stated, "There's something essentially unique about the way games structure experience" (McGonigal, 2011, ch. 1). Many view games as simply a diversion or something to do for fun. Yet many more are seeing the power of games when utilized to enhance education. In Raph Koster's famous book "*A Theory of Fun*," he states "Games are puzzles to solve…[in which] the stakes are lower" (Koster, 2005, p. 34) Another author, Marc Prensky, states "Digital Game-Based Learning is precisely about fun and engagement, and the coming together of serious learning and interactive entertainment into a newly emerging and highly exciting medium" (Prensky, 2001, p. 5). The simple answer is that an educational game is a means to harness the power of "fun" so as to motivate and educate through engagement.

There are many different types of games ranging from the simple crossword/word-find puzzle (free example: http://www.puzzle-maker.com) to the fully immersive 3D world multiplayer games: World of Warcraft (http://us.battle.net/wow/en), Minecraft (http://www.minecraft.net; older version available for free), etc. Use of a certain type of game and complexity of the game depends on what an instructor wants to do, the budget available for the game, how an instructor plans to do it, and why an instructor wants to use a game for education.

## WHY USE A GAME?

### Pedagogical Explanations

Marc Prensk's reference to J.C. Herz's book "Joystick Nation" states "It is becoming clear that one reason we are not more successful at educating our children and workforce, despite no lack of effort on our part, is because we are working hard to educate a new generation in old ways, using tools that have ceased to be effective" (Prensky, 2001, p. 7). Using games is an old tool that has become new through the use of computer enhancement.

Although there are many pedagogical theories on how to best implement games for learning, it is important to first understand the underlying principles of why using a game is beneficial for the student learner. The Education Arcade of MIT (Massachusetts Institute of Technology) explains that for both children and adults, the act of play is the exercising of freedom that spans five different axes:

1.  **The Freedom to Fail:** To do things during play that might look like failure to others, but allows the student/learner/player to learn from failure.
2.  **The Freedom to Experiment:** The ability to find new uses and new ways of doing things.
3.  **The Freedom to Fashion Identities:** The ability to try on different roles and identities to gain perspective.
4.  **The Freedom of Effort:** To choose how much intensity and vigore one wants to commit to any given task.
5.  **The Freedom of Interpretation:** The player will continue to learn about the game while also learning through the game at the same time. The individual freedom means that players perceptions and experiences may not be the same, learners may not have learned the same things through the same game (Klopfer, Osterweil, & Salen, 2009).

This knowledge is important in that the more an educational game correlates with the five freedoms of play, the more "fun" it will be and thereby enhance the chances of a successful educational game.

Fun is an important component, but not the only important factor. "...the fun factor is not the magic bullet in educational game design. The promise of educational games is to engage and motivate players, " (Kiili, 2004, p. 14). The trifecta of a great game and education in general is that of: fun, engagement, and motivation. The greatest detriment to learning is when the content or presentation is boring/dry/overly technical. Incorporating the trifecta components will make the learning experience positive and memorable.

A new question arises in how can an instructor achieve fun, engagement and motivation. The fact that an instructor is using a game is at least a start. Telling students that there will be a game to play generally sparks interest/motivation in most learners. The key is to maintain and continue to enhance this motivation by expressing the games importance and ensuring that all understand the merits of the game, and directly telling students why they should play the game (example: it will help you to understand this, you will get to see this, you'll know what it's like to...). Relevancy for many students is very important. Explaining a learning component's relevancy/importance for both the short term and long term will provide great dividends in motivating students/players. The use of games for education has been proven through research to enhance student motivation and offer additional educational benefits (Ibrahim R. & Jaafar A. 2009).

The fun component comes from the presentation of the game itself. "...attention has to be paid also to the creation of an engaging storyline, appropriate graphics and sounds..." (Kiili, 2004, p. 20). All the little components are actually really important. Sound effects, visuals, stylistic choices all work to make the immersive story that much more believable (even if the story is complete fantasy). An easy way to understand this is to think of a good movie. It was good because it had a good "engaging" story that was enhanced by sound effects, visual effects, etc. These components are just as important for an educational

game. Additionally the game-play affects the fun one experiences while playing the game. Game-play deals with how the student/learner/player engages with and is engaged by the actual game.

The engagement portion is a critical part of an educational game in that this is where the advanced critical thinking occurs. This critical thinking is derived from posing questions (forcing them to make a decision) to the student as well as through providing feedback to the student (student must process the feedback information and chose what to do next). The feedback itself can range from the complex (ex. detailed information on what went wrong and why) to the simple (ex. stating that this was the wrong answer and that they should try a different solution). This is a pedagogical/learning theory choice that the game designer (and/or instructor) must fully think about in that it will affect the game-play as well as what and how the player learns; "...some games even incorporated multiple learning theories depending on the game genres and game content" (Ibrahim, R. & Jaafar, A. 2009, p. 294).

## Identifying What You Want the Game to Do

In order to identify what you want your game to do (instructional components) you need to firmly identify what your learning outcomes are to be. After the learning outcomes are identified they are broken down (chunking) into more manageable enabling learning objectives. The game is then structured around exposing/teaching the enabling learning objectives so as to attain the identified learning outcomes by the conclusion of the game.

## Example: Where in the World is Dr. Salus Dynamica Mundi

In 2011 an educational team from Kansas State University consisting of Dr. Shalin Hai-Jew, Dr. Debra Briggs and myself, set about the task of creating an education game (*Where in the World* is *Dr. Salus "Dynamica" Mundi*), that would seek to expose students to what it was like to be a global public health practitioner (Figure 1). The key learning outcomes identified by the instructor and instructional designer were:

A. For students to understand the true global nature of international public health
B. The need to utilize and understand a wide range of communications technologies
C. The cultural/political/interpersonal aspect of international public health

From these three learning outcomes, enabling learning objectives were derived:

A. Students understand global nature of international public health
   1. Students are exposed to different countries
   2. Students are exposed to the issues of frequent travel
   3. Students are exposed to different languages
B. Need to utilize/understand wide range of comm. Technologies

   1. Students exposed to various text based communication technologies: journal article, LinkedIn post, Tweet
   2. Students exposed to various audio/video communication technologies: cellphone video, Facebook video, YouTube video
C. Cultural/political/interpersonal aspect of international public health
   1. Student exposed to cultural difference between countries/peoples
   2. Student exposed to different personal one-on-one interactions dealing with public health

## Structure and Game-Play

As stated earlier there are different types of games ranging from simple to very complex, a choice needs to be made as to what type of game(s) to use and in what way. One can try and identify different types of games such as: adventure games, first person shooter games, simulations, massively multiplayer online role playing games (MMORPGs), simple puzzle games, strategy games, racing games, physics games, general shooting games, fighting games, flying games, sports games, dress

*Figure 1. Identification of game's instructional components*

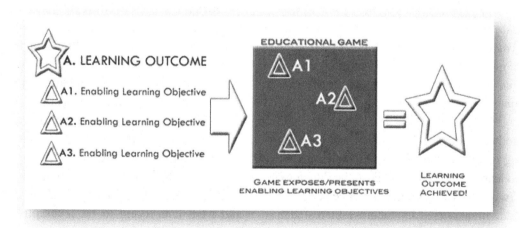

up games, maze games, medieval games, jumping games, guessing games, shape games, logic games, brain games, the list of categories and types goes on and on, so as an instructor there is a lot to choose from.

One approach could be to simply find a game that matches what you are trying to get your students to understand.

As an example, take a Chemistry instructor who is trying to get his/her students to understand the concept of a chain reaction. The instructor could give a quick overview of the concept: "a reaction that results in a product necessary for the continuance of the reaction" (Dictionary.com), and then have students play a game to fully understand the information. In this case a free online game like "Chain Reaction" (http://www.freeonlinegames. com/game/chain-reaction) would help to make the concept more salient. But again, continuing with the trifecta components already described (fun, engagement, and motivation) the game can be enhanced/maximized, as an example:

*Alright class, I now want you to go through this game (colorful game with cool sounds = fun component) for the next 5 to 10 minutes and experience the chain reaction. In understanding this concept it will help you when you apply it in the lab later this week with real chemicals (relevancy = enhanced motivation). You'll see that you can cause small reactions or large reactions based off of your actions (engagement). I have been authorized by the president of United States to let you out 5 minutes early (motivation) if we can all get a reaction of over 300! Your country and your schoolmates are counting on you (fun component)!*

Another quite novel approach is to use an existing game, but modified so as to address the desired learning outcome. While at the Educause (http://www.educause.edu) conference in 2011, I attended a breakout session for those interested in games for education. While there someone talked about the great success they had in using a game to help with comprehension of a foreign language. The instructor identified a game that all students in the class liked and had access to (in this case a commercial first person shooter game). She then modified the game so that all the clues and additional in-game instructions were in the foreign language being taught. In order to succeed in the game one needed to quickly be able to understand the clues and instructions. Hints such as "additional weapons, ammo, or health are available in this area," or "an enemy is hiding over here," were shown/said and had to be "actioned" within seconds or the result could be lost opportunity or an unexpected engagement. Students already liked the commercial game (fun and engaging) and were motivated to fully understand the foreign language so as to be able to understand the game's hints. Additionally the instructor gave extra credit (additional motivation) for advancing or simply time spent within the game.

In the previously stated Kansas State University's *Where in the World is Dr. Salus "Dynamica" Mundi* example we chose to completely create our own educational game and use a choose-your-own adventure (direction) type of game-play. The overall "story" was that the student-player would be trying to help a news reporter catch up to Dr. Mundi (global public health practitioner) so as to conduct an interview. Dr. Mundi was constantly on the move so it was a difficult task to accomplish. The idea was to present information to the student-player (accomplished via text, audio, video) as to the possible location of Dr. Mundi and then have the student chose where to go next. It seems simple enough but there was a lot of information in that there were many scenarios (location/situations) and a lot of choices. A game-play flow map was created so as to better perceive how the game would be structured (refer to Figure 2).

As noted there are many different approaches, so it is important to fully think about the game and what it is trying to be accomplished. Ted Castronova, a telecommunications professor at

*Figure 2. Game-play map from educational game developed by Kansas State University*

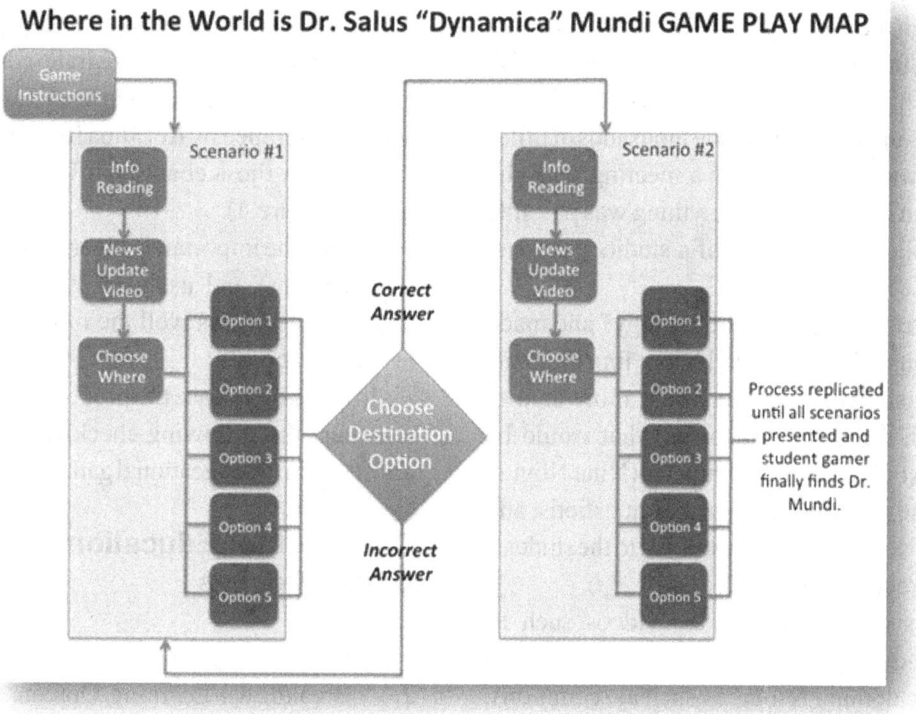

Indiana University Bloomington, social scientist and researcher of economies of synthetic (virtual) worlds, offers five tips for game making:

1.  **Don't Be Overly Ambitious:** Small steps are good; don't build a world when all you need is a town.
2.  **Go Low Tech:** Text games, mobile games, etc. all offer different opportunities. One doesn't necessary need a 3D virtual environment to have a successful educational game.
3.  **Think About Your Audience:** Think about what they are expecting, do testing, get plenty of feedback and keep the game fun.
4.  **Get a Full-Time Staff:** The more dedicated professional staff you have to help you build the game, the better.

5.  **Concede Screw-ups:** If something doesn't work don't continue to use it. Learn from the problem and move on (Wired Magazine: [Baker, 2008]).

## Video Component

The *Where in the World is Dr. Salus "Dynamica" Mundi* educational game used videos throughout its implementation for several different reasons. Still images were first considered but the instructor requested that more excitement and energy be infused into the game. The addition of audio was then introduced. This improved the energy a bit, but did little for the excitement. Animation was considered but that would have required more time and specific talents that where not available (not to mention beyond the budget). In the end the most cost effective solution, that still addressed all of the client's needs, was the use of live-action video.

Through the use of live-action video and green screen technology, we were able to accomplish pretty much any type of scenario needed. Whether it was news update from a plane thousands of miles up on its way to Europe, or a meeting with the mayor of an Indian village, anything was possible through video (and the use of a studio and some special effects) (see Figure 3).

This greatly enhanced the "energy" and made going through the game much more fun. Students who were shown the game where motivated to go through the game just to see what would be shown next. The reporter character (Nina Novus) of the game provided clues, asked questions, and gave feedback while directly talking to the student-player (direct engagement).

Various components of the videos such as background images and some sounds came from free public domain resources such as: commons. wikimedia.org/wiki, morguefile.com, and roy-altyfreemucic.com/free-music-resources.html.

## PUTTING IT ALL TOGETHER, THE HOW

An educational model that clearly presents the components needed to integrate education into games is that of the Educational Games Design Model developed by Rosalina Ibrahim and Azizah Jaafar from the Kebangsaan University of Malaysia (Figure 4).

Notice the importance given to fun, interaction (engagement) and usability when dealing with the game design as well the motivational aspect in the pedagogy.

In an effort to ease the process of "putting it all together" the following checklist was created to assist you in the educational game creation process:

### Checklist for Educational Game Process

1. Identify Learning Outcomes
2. Breakdown Learning Outcomes into manageable Enabling Learning Objectives
3. Create a story framework for the game

*Figure 3. Green screen examples from educational game developed by Kansas State University*

*Figure 4. Educational games design model (Ibrahim R. & Jaafar A. 2009)*

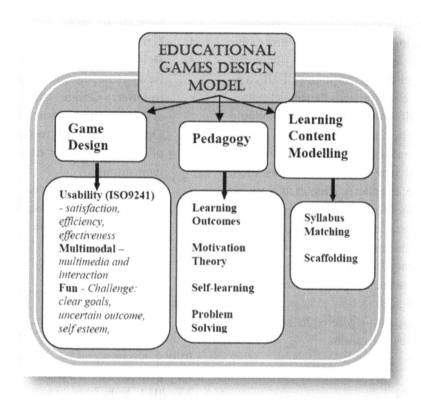

4.  Choose game type and implementation technique (choose your own adventure, 3D immersive world, other, etc.)
5.  Identify Engagement Mechanisms (challenges) so as to address/present enabling learning objectives
6.  Create Game (ensure trifecta components are utilized)
7.  Review Game: testing, gamer feedback
8.  Improve Game
9.  Utilize Educational Game
10. Conduct Game Assessment

## ASSESSMENT AND EFFECTS

Assessment of the effectiveness of the educational game's ability to help students learn is needed but can be somewhat complicated to fully attain. De-

pending on what exactly the game was supposed to do will require the assessment to be geared to try and capture its impact. Pre and post tests of the information to be learned is an option. For more advanced educational games, a student-player's ability to progress (or score highly) through the game could be used as a rubric for mastery of content learning. Additionally with advanced games, other components of the game-play could be captured for possible use as a rubric (game play duration, challenge engagements, redoing of levels/scenarios, techniques used to advanced, use of in-game tutorials or help functions, etc.) Other possibilities include reflective surveys, internal game quizzes, and control groups.

Generally the best technique would be to utilize different assessment agents so as to get a more complete view of what students learned. In addition to obvious (and easier to measure) educational items such as content learned and time needed to achieve learning outcome, other components could be assessed such as motivation to continue learning the material, long-term retention of materials learned, application of content mastered in novel/diverse settings, self-efficacy, and changes in feelings towards the subject matter. These additionally assessed components would give an even better understanding of what the educational game actually provided to the students.

An advanced idea dealing with assessment would be to use a properly structured game as the assessment tool for previously taught course material. An educational game could be organized so that a student would have to use prior knowledge (learned through the course) so as to properly complete the game. This would present interesting ideas such as how to actually assign a grading scheme but is offered as an idea for educational games utilization.

## CONCLUSION

Creating an educational game is a big task but it can be accomplished through study, analysis, organization and proper implementation. Important components to remember are the trifecta of a good game (and education in general): fun, engagement, and motivation. Additionally, other factors of the game such as learning outcome, enabling learning objectives, game story-line, game style, use of video, game complexity and modes of assessment must be considered so as to attain the greatest student-player experience and educational outcome.

Time and costs allocations for an educational game will vary based off of subject matter, game complexity, method of distribution and availability of resources. Costs for the game's creation can be minimized through the use of public domain and open source materials such as those already listed as well as:

- **ORGE:** Game-engine (www.ogre3d.org)
- **Irrlicht:** Game-engine (www.irrlicht.sourceforge.net)
- **Grit:** Game-engine (www.gritengine.com)
- **Delta 3D:** Gaming and simulation engine (www.delta3d.org)
- **Sploder:** Online game creator (www.sploder.com/free-game-creator.php)
- **Open Game Art:** Free game music, sound effects, are artwork resource (www.opengameart.org)
- **VideoLan Movie Creator:** Video editing software (www.videolan.org/vlmc)
- **Blender:** 3D animation software (www.blender.org)

## REFERENCES

Baker, C. (2008, March 24). Trying to design a truly entertaining game can defeat even a certified genius. *Wired Magazine*. Retrieved April 13, 2012, from http://www.wired.com/gaming/gamingreviews/magazine/16-04/pl_games

Kiili, K. (2004). Digital game-based learning: Towards an experiential gaming model. *The Internet and Higher Education, 8,* 13-14. Retrieved April 9, 2012, from http://www.google.com/url?sa=t&rct=j&q=&esrc=s&source=web&cd=1&ved=0CC0QFjAA&url=http%3A%2F%2Fwww.sciencedirect.com%2Fscience%2Farticle%2Fpii%2F-S1096751604000776&ei=BASHT9abIMWa8AGBhpzACA&usg=AFQjCNFWffP-xZqdfbX9xbvT__VCR6Rf1w&sig2=6UCBPKoFdtBqt2fjNJ3nDg

Klopfer, E., Osterweil, S., & Salen, K. (2009). Moving learning games forward: Obstacles, opportunities & openness. *The Education Arcade*. Retrieved April 12, 2012, from http://education.mit.edu/papers/MovingLearningGamesForward_EdArcade.pdf

Koster, R. (2005). *A theory of fun for game design.* Scottsdale, AZ: Paraglyph Press, Inc.

McGonigal, J. (2011). *Reality is broken: Why games make us better and how they can change the world.* New York, NY: Penguin Press HC.

Prensky, M. (2001). The digital game-based learning revolution. In M. Prensky (Ed.), *Digital game-based learning.* Saint Paul, MN: Paragon House. Retrieved April 11, 2012, from http://courses.ceit. metu.edu.tr/ceit420/week2/Prensky-Ch1-Digital-Game-Based-Learning.pdf

Roslina, I., & Jaafar, A. (2009). *Educational games (EG) design framework: Combination of game design, pedagogy and content modeling.* 2009 International Conference on Electrical Engineering and Informatics. Selangor, Malaysia. Retrieved April 12, 2012, from http://ieeexplore.ieee.org/stamp/stamp.jsp?tp=&arnumber=5254771

Wieder, B. (2011, February 11). 6 top tech trends on the horizon for higher education. *The Chronicle of Higher Education.* Retrieved April 10, 2012, from http://chronicle.com/blogs/wiredcampus/6-top-tech-trends-on-the-horizon-for-education/29581

# Section 4
# Developing the User "Installed Base" for Open Source Resources

# Chapter 15

# Creating Open Source Lecture Materials:
## A Guide to Trends, Technologies, and Approaches in the Information Sciences

**William H. Hsu**
*Kansas State University, USA*

## ABSTRACT

*This chapter surveys recent and continuing trends in software tools for preparation of open courseware, in particular audiovisual lecture materials, documentaries and tutorials, and derivative materials. It begins by presenting a catalog of tools ranging from open source wikis and custom content management systems to desktop video production. Next, it reviews techniques for preparation of lecture materials consisting of five specific learning technologies: animation of concepts and problem solutions; explanation of code; video walkthroughs of system documentation; software demonstrations; and creation of materials for instructor preparation and technology transfer. Accompanying the description of each technology and the review of its state of practice is a discussion of the goals and assessment criteria for deployed courseware that uses those tools and techniques. Holistic uses of these technologies are then analyzed via case studies in three domains: artificial intelligence, computer graphics, and enterprise information systems. An exploration of technology transfer to college and university-level instructors in the information sciences then follows. Finally, effective practices for encouraging adoption and dissemination of lecture materials are then surveyed, starting with comprehensive, well-established open courseware projects that adapt pre-existing content and continuing through recent large-scale online courses aimed at audiences of tens to hundreds of thousands.*

DOI: 10.4018/978-1-4666-2205-0.ch015

# 1. TRENDS IN OPEN COURSEWARE FOR INFORMATION SCIENCES

## 1.1 Tools

This section provides a brief history of open educational resources (OER) for the information sciences, followed by a taxonomic survey of OER development tools.

### 1.1.1 Brief History

Open educational resources (OER) for the information sciences date back to the early decades of the field, beginning with the development of *PLATO (Programmed Logic for Automated Teaching Operations)*, the first computer-assisted instruction (CAI) system, at the University of Illinois. (Van Meer, 2003; PLATO History Foundation, 2011) The first version of *PLATO*, implemented on the ILLIAC I *circa* 1960, included what is now termed lessonware and was funded jointly by the U.S. Army, Navy, and Air Force. Meanwhile, by the late 1960s, video lecture consortia such as the Stanford Honors Co-op were delivering proprietary closed-circuit television content to corporate sponsors (House & Price, 2009). The 1970s brought a wave of intelligent tutoring systems (Carbonell, 1970; Sleeman & Brown, 1982; Iiyoshi & Kumar, 2008). By the 1980s, cable-access distance learning and extension courseware had begun to be distributed using precursors of open source licenses, culminating in the founding of the Free Software Foundation in 1985 and the first releases of the Berkeley Standard Distribution (BSD) License (1988), GNU General Public License (1989), Open Content License (1998), and Creative Commons License (2001). (Free Software Foundation, 2012) Abelson, a founder of the Massachusetts Institute of Technology OpenCourseWare (MIT OCW) initiative (Abelson, The Creation of OpenCourseWare at MIT, 2007; Attwood, 2009) and founding member of Creative Commons (Creative Commons Corpora-

tion, 2011), had been distributing *Structure and Interpretation of Computer Programs*, a leading introductory textbook in computer science, online. With the advent of MIT OCW, video lectures prepared for the MIT/Hewlett-Packard consortium (House & Price, 2009) as early as 1986 were made available (Abelson, 2005).

### 1.1.2 Technologies for Producing Open Source Software

When discussing "open source tools," professionals and students in science, technology, engineering, and mathematics (STEM) fields often refer only to *open source software* (DiBona, Ockman, & Stone, 1999; Raymond, 1999; Open Source Initiative, 2006)[1] rather than the more general concept of *open content* (Wiley, 2011) as coined by David Wiley in 1998 (Wikipedia, 2012). The means of production are diverse for both forms of creative work, with free redistribution and access being the unifying characteristic. For open source software, however, the chief production technologies are software engineering tools: integrated development environments; content management systems; and version control systems, also known as "source code control systems."

Integrated development environments (IDEs) are suites of development applications consisting of source code editors, compilers (and/or interpreters), and build/execution controls, plus optional components such as build utilities, interfaces to version control systems, visual code layout and refactoring tools, and interactive code inspection and debugging tools. (D'Anjou, Fairbrother, Kehn, Kellerman, & McCarthy, 2005; Nourie, 2005) They range from the proprietary (*e.g.*, Microsoft *Visual Studio* and Apple *Xcode*) to open source (*e.g.*, *Eclipse* and Oracle *NetBeans*). The range of available IDEs depends foremost on the programming languages to be supported and secondarily on the development platform, comprising the computer architecture, operating system, and compilers or interpreters. For ease of use, efficiency, and portability, many open source developers use simple editors, version control, and compilation tools to augment or replace full-featured IDE s when their full power is not required.

A content management system (CMS) is a collection of procedures (implemented manually or computationally) for organizing and carrying out work flow in a collaborative environment. (Depow, 2003; Mauthe & Thomas, 2004) Specific CMSes may be implemented as web services or using other software as a service (SaaS) architectures, or as standalone applications such as most wikis. Both types of CMSes occur in both proprietary and open source varieties. Schaffert *et al.* (2006) describe *semantic wikis*, which capture information on the deep relational structure between pages and provide this information to agents and services beyond mere linking. These are referred to as *semantic wikis*, after the Semantic Web, or Web 3.0. Moreover, both enterprise and public wikis may be used for distance learning and distribution of lecture materials, but in academic institutions and consortia, enterprise wikis are the more common type. The most popular enterprise wikis are the Wikimedia Foundation's *MediaWiki*, *Tiki Wiki CMS Groupware*, and *TWiki*. (Wikipedia, 2012)

A version control system, also called a source code control system or revision control system, is a specific type of software configuration management system designed for the curation and archival of collaboratively created content, including but not limited to program source code. The dominant version control systems in use at present are the client-server systems *Subversion* (SVN), *Concurrent Version Systems* (CVS), and *Git*. Because of their predominance within the open source community, and the existence of popular hosting services such as *GitHub*, which supports *Git*, and *SourceForge*, which supports a number of collaborative version control systems, SVN, CVS, and Git have retained their preeminence in social development contexts such as authoring of open source software and open content.

## 1.1.3 Current and Emerging Technologies for Producing Other Open Content

Other forms of open content (Wiley, 2011) have included databases and data acquisition resources such as the *OpenMind Initiative* (Stork, 1999; Singh, et al., 2002; Chklovski & Gil, 2005), a collaborative framework for producing large data sets, domain knowledge bases, and ontologies for commonsense reasoning and machine learning. Open courseware itself is an instance of open content, often excerpted and reused with "some rights reserved" as per the Creative Commons License (Creative Commons Corporation, 2011).

Current software tools for preparation of open courseware, especially audiovisual lecture materials, documentaries and tutorials, and derivative materials, focus on production of notes, slides, audio (traditional "podcasting"), and videos (including "webcasting"). Numerous office suites providing functionality similar to *Microsoft Office* are distributed under purportedly free software licenses. The best-known and most popular of these at present is Apache *OpenOffice* (Apache Software Foundation, 2011), originally released by Sun Microsystems and briefly by Oracle Corporation. (Wikipedia, 2012) Most office suites provide native file formats for lecture slides with animations and for non-interactive reading material, and support exporting of content to static formats such as text and PDF. True open source packages for video production include *Blender* (Blender Foundation, 2012) and *VirtualDub* (Lee, 2012), whereas some proprietary software is freeware or shareware when used under a noncommercial license. *Fraps* (Beepa, 2012), a popular video capture utility used to make recordings of software demonstrations and machinima-based animations (Lowood & Nitsche, 2011), is one such example.

## 1.2 Computing and Information Science Disciplines

The list of content production tools given in the previous section is representative rather than comprehensive, but it covers a majority of basic content types by category and format. To understand the potential impact of these tools when used in tandem, a brief review of the state of the field in computing and information sciences is provided here.

Computing science incorporates theoretical computer science and its applications to STEM disciplines, comprising the field generally known as "computational science" or scientific computing, whose branches include industrial applications (technical computing), analysis of data (statistical computing), applied numerical analysis, *etc.* Meanwhile, the very broad interdisciplinary field *of information science overlaps* with computer science, but also includes aspects of the theory and practice of information processing, management, and retrieval that that are not purely computational, as they incorporate aspects of mathematics, cognitive science, linguistics, library science, and social sciences. Subsuming computational science and engineering *and* information sciences is the even broader academic field of informatics – a term for the "[study of the] structure, algorithms, behavior, and interactions of natural and artificial systems that store, process, access and communicate information." (Wikipedia, 2012) This definition underscores a subtle but important distinction: the systems need not be computational, so that informatics is generally distinct from computer science and information technology.

Educational issues often reported among in the above fields include low comprehension and retention rates among undergraduate students. Loidl, Mühlbacher, and Schauer (2005) and Stephenson, Gal-Ezer, Haberman, and Verno (2005) discuss prominent unmet needs in the pedagogy of informatics and computer science, and put forth the hypothesis that student performance below expectations across information science curricula are due to a lack of comprehensible preparatory material at the high school and early university level. desJardins and Littman (2010) documented a materials-oriented remediation plan for issues identified by instructors and students, along with data demonstrating positive student outcomes. These materials have been made publicly available (Littman, 2007; Rutgers University, 2012) and provide several of the motivating examples of production, evaluation, and dissemination techniques in Section 3 of this article.

## 2. TRADEOFFS

Both open source tools for content production, and open content itself, represent tradeoffs when compared to closed source analogues. Advocates of open content and open source software cite lower cost, accessibility, and community quality assurance while advocates of commercial and other proprietary tools cite provider services, functional features, and ease of adoption, maintenance, and support. Understanding this tradeoff presents a challenging economics problem because of fundamental differences in the means of production, motivating rewards for labor, and underlying forms of capital involved. (Lerner & Tirole, 2002; Lerner & Tirole, 2004) This is especially true in domains such as computer graphics, where content and content development tools are conflated due to both of them being used directly by instructors and students.

As part of a 2007 interview of CEO Dean Drako of Barracuda Networks[2], *CNet* columnist Matt Asay reported on a survey conducted by Barracuda of 228 of their enterprise customers who were asked to list one or more advantages of commercial software *versus* open source software. (Asay, 2007)

## 2.1 Claimed Advantages for Commercial Off-The-Shelf (COTS) Tools

The top three specific advantages of commercial software over open source software cited by Barracuda Networks customers were: vendor professional services (cited by 65%), ease of adoption (47%), and automated updates (41%). These were followed by six additional specific advantages, for a total of nine: reduced IT support (35%), best product functionality (28%), security (23%), code quality (17%), intellectual property protection (7%), and price (3%). (Asay, 2007)

Comparative benefits of commercial software cited (as disadvantages of open source software) in an article first compiled in 2004 by the Canadian Internet Policy and Public Interest Clinic (CIPPIC) were: "liability for intellectual property infringement," a "guarantee of quality or fitness," and "licensing" issues. (Kerr & Bornfreund, 2007) While liability, accountability, and warranties of quality or fitness are cited as advantages by COTS proponents, some open source consultants and vendors such as GBDirect, Ltd. have noted that both proprietary and open source licenses "typically disclaim all liabilities and warranties, including such basic warranties as merchantability and fitness for purpose." (GBDirect, 2004) 17% of customers surveyed by Barracuda cited "quality" as one of nine specific COTS advantages, though this survey did not list "warranty" as a separate response. (Asay, 2007)

## 2.2 Claimed Advantages for Open Source Tools

According to the 2007 Barracuda customer survey discussed above, the top three specific advantages of open source software over commercial software were price (cited by 80%), access to source code (57%), and community code review (41%). These were followed by six additional specific advantages, for a total of nine: bug fix turnaround

(18%), security (15%), code quality (15%), best product functionality (15%), ease of adoption (10%), and intellectual property protection (5%). (Asay, 2007) Of these desiderata, the last four were also cited as advantages of commercial software in the same survey, with commercial software receiving a higher percentage of citation in these categories: 17% *vs.* 15% for code quality; 28% *vs.* 15% for best product functionality; 47% *vs.* 10% for ease of adoption; and 7% *vs.* 5% for intellectual property protection. These responses were from the same pool of customers, who were asked to list advantages of commercial software over open source software **and** *vice versa.*

Kerr and Bornfreund (2007) cite "four inherent advantages [of open source software] over proprietary software": (1) lower cost; (2) access to source code, allowing the user community to "detect and fix programming bugs" and providing for greater customizability and freedom in scheduling updates; (3) security through transparency; and (4) reduced vendor "lock in." Similarly, 435 respondents to the 2009 Future of Open Source survey at the InfoWorld Open Source Business Conference gave the "top four factors that make open source software attractive" as: (1) lower cost; (2) security, (3) no vendor "lock in," and (4) better quality. (Guseva, 2009) In an earlier survey of firms, Dedrick and West (2003) reported lower cost, third-party expertise availability, risk tolerance, and "trial basis" as adoption factors. Other researchers have elaborated on the nature of "free" user-to-user assistance as a part of the open source model, a consideration that is often relevant to educators seeking accessible resources. (Bonaccorsi & Rossi Lamastra, 2003; Lakhani & Hippel, 2003; Singh, Twidale, & Rathi, 2006)

Open source developers have long cited rationales for open source as a *business* model, especially lower production costs amortized over individuals, large user communities, and reliability through transparency. (DiBona, Ockman, & Stone, 1999; Hars & Ou, 2001; Krishnamurthy, 2002; Carmichael & Honour, 2002; O'Hara & Kay,

2003; Ye & Kishida, 2003; Downes, 2007) von Krogh and Spaeth (2007) note that significant consequences of these properties are that they result in a high influx of developers, perceived market tension with proprietary software publishers, and a paradigm shift in perceptions of intellectual property, as also noted by Fitzgerald (2006).

The causal attribution of specific problems experienced by users of open source tools, whether to instability, a dearth of documentation, production quality, software maintenance, or deficiencies in content, is difficult to further attribute to economic factors of production. These include labor, materials, means, and various forms of organizational, intellectual, and social capital that are technically complex. At present, they are infeasible to quantify because of a lack of controls or baselines for comparing the production platforms of free software *versus* commercial software.

## 3. TECHNIQUES FOR LECTURE MATERIAL PREPARATION

Next, the article continues with a review of techniques for preparation of lecture materials consisting of five specific learning technologies: animation of concepts and problem solutions; explanation of code; video walkthroughs of system documentation; software demonstrations; and creation of materials for instructor preparation and technology transfer. These technologies are presented first in terms of a motivating pedagogical principle and then in terms of means, choices, and costs associated with their implementation. Accompanying the description of each technology and the review of its state of practice is a discussion of the goals and assessment criteria for deployed courseware that uses those tools and techniques. This technical survey concludes with examples and recommendations from the relevant literature on education and outreach.

## 3.1 Production Techniques

Effective production of open educational content involves materials design, planning and development of a syllabus that will incorporate the content, and – due to the open nature of the content – deliberate planning for reusability by other instructors and content developers. In this section, we focus on development of syllabi for video lectures, along with the requisite preparation of materials.

Interactive materials design consists of mapping from teaching objectives to concrete lesson plans with corresponding educational media, including text, audiovisual components, and software. A fundamental requirement and common first step of materials design is to adapt and integrate text, some of which may be recaptured from hard copy and some of which may have been prepared for electronic distribution (*e.g.*, as digital textbooks or documents). Office suites such as those mentioned in Section 1.1.3 facilitate repurposing of content (Obrenovic, Starcevic, & Selic, 2004; Verbert, GaSvevic, Jovanovic, & Duval, 2005). *Content repurposing*, the adaptation of existing information from various media to serve a new use case (Hossain, Rahman, & El-Saddik, 2004; Obrenovic, Starcevic, & Selic, 2004; Duffy, 2008), can be achieved through methods that include format conversion (including screen captures), embedding of images and video, hypertext linking of documents, and porting of software. Some user interface and web components are designed for portability and reuse; these components range from widgets to frameworks and whole graphical user interfaces (GUIs), particularly in educational software toolkits. Finally, at the most basic technical level of reuse is source code, which may be provided purely for functionality (*e.g.*, as part of a component library) to support educational programming, or together with documentation, as a teaching material in its own right (*e.g.*, example code to illustrate algorithms).

Video lecture syllabus planning begins with formulating a lesson plan that incorporates source material. This provides a key goal of content repurposing in the materials design phase: to excerpt or adapt text and multimedia from previously formatted documents: PDF, *PowerPoint*, *etc.* (Poindexter & Heck, 1999) Potential value added by this step includes retention of formatting (including layout and mathematical typesetting); adaptation to an interactive medium, such as interactive animation; and subsequent capture of preprogrammed or planned interactions, such as software demonstrations and problem solving traces, on video. (Evans & Fan, 2002; Duffy, 2008) A large segment of the videos of this nature distributed via *YouTube* are produced using popular video capture utilities, including the free utility *FRAPS* (Beepa, 2011). Finally, the integrated video lecture must be recorded and produced. Many educational videos are produced using feature-intensive third-party screen recording software such as *Tegrity* or *Camtasia* (Prabaker, Bergman, & Castelli, 2006; Gaspar & Langevin, 2007).

Finally, planning for reusability involves several considerations. First, regularly offered courses typically require a minimum frequency of turnover in order to maintain the freshness of the information, and the instructor's currency and familiarity with it. This frequency depends upon the discipline and the specific domain of the course, and in particular with the speed of new developments. A balance is needed between popularity of modules and materials across many curricula and demand for the material within one course. Second, the time constraints placed on authors of open courseware and content may necessitate triage: correcting obsolete or erroneous material in order of priority. This need is further exacerbated by the challenges inherent in preparing lectures as long as a class period: producing new versions of lectures demands recording and post-production time in addition to the time needed to update old lectures or correct errata. Third, keeping up with demand in academia or industry for timely

and popular topics requires some awareness and responsiveness to student needs. These may be elicited through informal polling ranging from impromptu classroom straw polls to nonscientific open surveys on a course web site, or through more formal surveys or controlled studies. Fourth, courses may need to be tailored for different clientele, such as undergraduate and graduate students, on-campus and distance students, or traditional students and industry professionals (either group of which may be enrolled online). Depending on whom a course is being offered to, demand may arise for additional material or spin-off material for a second course. This type of deliberate reuse carries its own incentives, such as being able to create review notes for a prerequisite course, and its own risks, such as having too much redundancy or a "one size fits all" type of inflexibility in the prepared materials. Fifth, a related kind of reuse is cross-medium: most courses include material from books, written notes, lecture slides, homework, exams, recordings, videos, and open content may span or integrate more than one of these.

## 3.2 Learning Technologies

Several unifying themes recur across learning technologies in information technology: problem-solving traces; learning by watching (Kuniyoshi, Inaba, & Inoue, 1994), apprenticeship learning (Collins, Brown, & Newman, 1987), and learning by doing (Shank, Berman, & Macpherson, 1999); and principled integration and reuse. These are not necessarily specific to open source tools, but as the examples given in this section illustrate, they are quite prevalent among open source technology for the approaches surveyed.

Delivering this type of visualization as open content requires preparation of multimedia in formats that are portable across platforms. Commercial presentation software packages such as Microsoft *PowerPoint* provide such functionality, but to reach the widest audience, many authors now make extensive use of public video sites, particularly *YouTube*. These are frequently accessed by linking offsite (Luo, 2010). Production of multimedia often involves a combination of video technologies. The traditional web approach of linking still accounts for a significant amount of video content delivery. Embedding of videos in course wikis, blogs, and other groupware is becoming prevalent with the advent of Web 2.0 technology, namely, *Asynchronous JavaScript and XML (AJAX)*, where XML stands for *eXtensible Markup Language*. (Lin, Chi, Chang, Cheng, & Huang, 2007; Duffy, 2008; Luo, 2009) Finally, digital compositing using video capture (Beepa, 2011) and 3-D computer-generated animation (CGA) engines such as machinima (Lowood, 2006) provide three-dimensional multimedia production technology that is used in both entertainment and education industries. (Chang, Chiu, & Hung, 2010; Lowood & Nitsche, 2011)

## 3.2.1 Animation of Concepts and Problem Solutions

Animating the process of solving problems in mathematics and programming predates the earliest online educational resources surveyed in Section 1.1.1: Tufte (1997) gives many examples of visual explanations involving paper pop-ups, three-dimensional mechanical displays, and other forms of non-electronic (often manually-operated) displays. With the proliferation of educational supplements specializing in solved problems, a niche has formed for computer visualization of both abstract concepts and problem solutions. (Tufte, 1990; Tufte, 1997; Tufte, 2006)

Early work on systems for computer-assisted instruction (CAI) in mathematics and foreign languages led to the first controlled evaluations (Suppes & Morningstar, 1969). Simulation-based educational software systems were identified as a key trend in CAI by the 1970s, especially in science, technology, engineering, and mathematics (STEM) disciplines. (Chambers & Sprecher, 1980; Rieber, 1990; Mayer & Anderson, 1992;

Pane, Corbett, & John, 1996) Successes in computer-based instructional technologies led to a wide proliferation of CAI applications in the 1980s. These fell into two main branches: drill-and-practice systems and tutoring systems. Kulik and Kulik (1991) identified two other major categories of computer-based instruction systems besides CAI: *computer-managed instruction*[3], including automated grading and critiquing[4]; and *computer-enriched instruction*, comprising some simulations, data generation, and environments for exploring and experimenting with software.

By the early 1990s, algorithm visualization had emerged as its own distinct application area of CAI (Gloor, 1992; Hundhausen, Douglas, & Stasko, 2002; Naps, et al., 2002) This led to the development of recommended practices for interactive visualization that closely mirror and extend principles of information graphic design (Tufte, 1997). Lester *et al.* (1997) reported improved problem solving in a tutoring system with an "animated pedagogical agent" – an effect they attributed to multimodal information delivery, improvements in personalization and contextualization of advice, and improved student motivation due to the use of an anthropomorphic agent. Additional information design principles of animation in educational multimedia have also been guided by cognitive psychology. These include a cognitive design theory developed by Mayer (1999) for facilitating problem-solving transfer, wherein experience in solving one problem generalizes to others. This theory gave rise to seven principles put forth by Mayer and Moreno (2002):

1. "Present animation and narration rather than narration alone" (multimedia)
2. "Present on-screen text near rather than far from corresponding animation" (spatial contiguity)
3. "Present corresponding animation and narration simultaneously rather than successively" (temporal contiguity)

4. "Exclude extraneous words, sounds, and video" (coherence)

5. "Present animation and narration rather than animation and onscreen text" (multimodality)

6. "Present animation and narration rather than animation, narration, and on-screen text" (nonredundancy)

7. "Present words in conversational rather than formal style" (personalization)

Plaisant and Schneiderman (2005) provide the following list of principles for producing recorded demonstrations in cybereducation:

1. "Provide procedural instruction rather than conceptual information."

2. "Keep segments short" (15 - 30 seconds).

3. "Ensure that tasks are clear and simple," using scripted narration of concrete running examples.

4. "Coordinate demonstrations with textual documentation."

5. "Use spoken narration" (as opposed to textual explanations), for greater communication efficiency through multisensory integration.

6. "Be faithful to the actual user interface."

7. "Use highlighting to guide attention," combining sound and visual effects for amplified multisensory effect.

8. "Keep file sizes small" by using on-screen digital recording, optimized data formats, codecs, and compression schemes for the type of multimedia (usually audiovisual) information being delivered.

9. "Strive for universal usability" by developing demonstrations with high portability and accessibility, minimal documentation requirements, and highly intuitive user interfaces.

10. "Ensure user control" by providing ease of navigation through the material, such as by allowing users to resume demonstrations and skip previously-covered parts.

In recent years, numerous controlled studies have been conducted on the effectiveness of animation in CAI in various disciplines. While some have shown that animation of physical and biological processes can improve comprehension of basic science concepts (Thatcher, 2006), findings have been inconclusive in many disciplines, such as medical education (Ruiz, Cook, & Levinson, 2009). Holzinger, Kickmeier-Rust, and Albert (2008) report similar variability in a survey of dynamic media for computer science education, and conclude:

*Dynamic media is only successful in facilitating learning in comparison to traditional static media such as texts or images, when they are able to (1) reduce the cognitive load, which is necessary to comprehend them, (2) serve to generate mental models of a concept and, consequently (3), offer visualizations that correspond to a meaningful mental model.*

Ruiz *et al.* and Holzinger *et al.* report that fielded systems bear out the findings of cognitive psychologists with regards to cognitive load theory: that dynamic visualizations of complex processes, both physiological and algorithmic, can aid in comprehension, but that attentional cueing is needed to focus the viewer's attention on one or a few aspects of the visualized processes (Koning, Tabbers, Rikers, & Paas, 2007; Hasler, Kersten, & Sweller, 2007). This bears out earlier research on mental models, particularly *epistemic fidelity*, a measure of goodness of algorithm visualization that is based on the premise that graphics closely correspond to the mental model of an algorithm that a designer forms and uses. (Hundhausen, Douglas, & Stasko, 2002) Application of these criteria have led to social constructivist design principles for individualized interactive learning using tools for algorithm visualization (Lawrence, Badre, & Stasko, 1994) and ethnographic field studies of how such tools were used in undergraduate classes in computer science. (Hundhausen, 2002;

Stasko, Badre, & Lewis, 1993) For examples of additional learning technologies based on social constructivism, the interested reader is referred to Jonassen, Howland, & Marra (2011).

## 3.2.2 Explanation of Code

A key part of computer science pedagogy centers around learning to produce code (*i.e.*, program) by reading good examples of code that accomplishes certain specified functions. (Raymond D. R., 1991) This approach has its roots in *structured programming*, a paradigm of computer programming that aims at improving the clarity, reliability, and development efficiency of programs by using functions (also known as procedures and subroutines in imperative programming and methods in object-oriented programming), iteration, and block structure. (Dijkstra, Hoare, & Dahl, 1972)

The practice of "learning by reading code" was further advanced by the introduction of *literate programming*, the synthesis of documentation paradigms "suitable for program exposition" and coding paradigms "suitable for program creation." (Knuth, 1984; Van Wyk, 1990; Ramsey, 1994) In addition to establishing a methodology for creating programs with formatted inline documentation together with a "web of abstract objects," Knuth (1984) highlighted the role of documentation in programmer training, which has since been increasingly recognized as an integral component of software education. (Sametinger, 1994) This has led to an art of computer documentation that has garnered its own constructivist theory. (Spinuzzi & Zachry, 2000; Spinuzzi, 2002)

Building upon this practice of literate programming and code review, Linn and Clancy (1992) developed case studies of programming problems and outlined a pedagogical framework for presenting decisions and the rationale for each one. They presented a case study template that combined program specifications, example inputs, diagrams of program traces, pseudocode, analogies depicting the program's desired behavior,

references to more general templates (behavioral supertypes) and those using the template as a behavioral subtype or other design pattern, and debugging notes. In later work surveying several studies of their own and other computer science education researchers, Clancy and Linn (1999) report that problem solving transfer (Mayer, 1999) by means of learning design patterns varies by student background, being very low for novices; is directly proportionate to abstract understanding, generality, and reusability; is enhanced when accompanied by syntax, use case examples, and execution traces. As with algorithm visualization, students still need to learn by doing and interacting. For example, Gaspar and Langevin (2007) note that observing the process of deriving computer programs as solutions to problems, which they call "coding with intention" (as opposed to "cut and paste-oriented programming"), tends to restore a deeper understanding of solution design and synthesis. (Starr, Manaris, & Stalvey, 2008) By contrast, they find that presentation of working code examples alone tends to result in shallower analogical thinking.

Learning to read source code and design documents, like learning to read documentation, is a crucial and foundational skill for students of information technology, including both theoretical computer science and informatics. The organization and documentation of software differs by type – Brooks (1995) classifies software as simple standalone programs, *programming products* (tested, documented, portable, and fielded applications), *programming systems* (application programmer interfaces, libraries, frameworks, modular interfaces, and middleware), and *programming systems products*. Studying solutions by dissection, using concrete examples, specifications, test cases, and formal properties, is recommended for many topics in computer science education, from elementary programming (Deek, Kimmel, & McHugh, 1998; Ben-Ari, Berglund, Booth, & Holmboe, 2004) to computational science and informatics (Stevenson, 1993) to computer security and information security (Yang, 2001). This underscores the importance of open source materials: O'Hara and Kay (2003) advocate the study of open source software in computer science education for its high achievable degree of verifiability. In an annual President's Letter to the Association for Computing Machinery (ACM), Patterson (2006) lists courses that "leverage high-quality examples of the open source movement" as the #1 category of "course I would love to take," while advocating "writing documentation for portions of open source code" as a good way to learn large systems.

### 3.2.3 Walkthroughs of Programming Systems and Products: Documentation and Videos

We have seen how interactive algorithm visualizations and literate programs have been systematically shown to be superior to watching recorded animations and reading source code as flat text, through studies by both educational psychologists and professional societies within information technology. A natural extension of the hypothesis that interactivity yields good mental models for learning programming and problem solving skills is that this benefit also arises from interactive user and developer documentation. Toward this end, studies have been conducted that assess the effectiveness of online documentation (Hertzum & Frøkjær, 1996) and instructional materials in general (Mehlenbacher, 2002; Zhang, Zhao, Zhou, & Nunamaker, 2004). A common conclusion was that usability measures such as readability, ease of interpretation, adaptability to differences in student background and aptitude are all important. (Winslow, 1996)

Programming system and product walkthroughs are a variant of the traditional software walkthrough (Bias, 1991) and *cognitive walkthrough* (Wharton, Rieman, Lewis, & Polson, 1994); they typically fit the definition of a *sociotechnical walkthrough* (Herrmann, Kunau, Loser,

& Menold, 2004; Herrmann, 2009). Following the terminology of Corbi (1989), studies of programming products and systems can be divided into *static analysis* (reading the code) and *dynamic analysis* (running the code). Both yield important and cognitively disparate understandings of a program. A formal understanding of static analysis provides programmers with the tools needed to both analyze and synthesize solutions from specification, by articulating the process of problem decomposition and stepwise refinement down to the most basic problem solving steps. (Soloway, 1986) Dynamic analysis allows the student to think concretely, explore boundary cases, understand, and visualize the performance of programs.

Software walkthroughs are technically considered a form of peer review called *static testing*, as opposed to formal verification by static analysis. They are distinguished from software inspection in that they permit direct alterations to the programming product (whereas software inspections are made relative to a fixed specification) and do not include measurement criteria for the development process or product. (IEEE, 1998) As software walkthroughs are often conducted in person, *via* videoteleconferencing systems, or using groupware, so are programming system and product walkthroughs. Xiao, Chi, and Yang (2007) describe groupware-based software product development, particularly collaborative development using wikis.

The importance of a walkthrough, with students in the role of clients and end users, is that student feedback may be collected and used. In the classroom, this can serve to provide points of clarification (Soloway, 1986) for homework, term projects, and follow-up (independent study) projects. The process of refinement can also facilitate development of supplemental materials such as collections of exercises. (Clancy & Linn, 1999) Walkthroughs can also serve as aids in restructuring courses to balance between basic problem solving and programming tasks, and in outcomes-based assessment of such changes. (Deek, Kimmel, & McHugh, 1998) Finally, they can aid in design of programming systems components that have high variable amounts of code, such as graphical user interfaces that may be reconfigurable with no programming or may require several times the amount of code as is in the original program. (Karat, Campbell, & Fiegel, 1992; Rowley & Rhoades, 1992; Brooks, 1995)

As with case studies of programming problems and source code, the delivery format of peer review matters. The technology exists to produce videos of programs (and of programming systems or products) being used, modified, and evaluated through walkthroughs. This recapitulates the actual practice of peer review at a higher level of fidelity and interactivity than reading evaluation reports. Similar techniques, applied in basic programming education, have yielded better comprehension, basic skill acquisition, and problem solving transfer. (Deek, Kimmel, & McHugh, 1998; Prabaker, Bergman, & Castelli, 2006; Gaspar & Langevin, 2007) Finally, text documentation itself is also subject to walkthrough and inspection-based peer review. (Novick, 2000)

### 3.2.4 Software Demonstrations

In addition to algorithm animation, code inspection, and walkthroughs of code with specifications, documentation, and test cases, there are demonstrations of programming products. With proprietary software, these are usually shrink-wrapped commercial off-the-shelf (COTS) products (Ncube & Maiden, 2000), but with open source educational software, they are usually *local builds* – that is, compiled for (or ported to) a particular platform consisting of a computer architecture and operating system, using a specified compiler version and runtime environment. Live demonstrations usually entail choosing the most popular of these, but recorded demos may be prepared for multiple versions and self-study may involve tasks such as performing platform-specific configuration,

retargeting a compiler, or even porting applications between programming languages.

Getting and using student feedback is a challenge in both traditional campus environments and distance learning environments. Telepresence and archival systems have proven useful for managing the distance e-learning environment. (Baecker, Wolf, & Rankin, 2004; Rankin, Baecker, & Wolf) In addition, tracking student outcomes can be challenging even in a capstone course – more so for a low-level course in an undergraduate curriculum. Liu (2006) presents a pedagogical application of software project demonstrations as both an assessment tool for instructors and a learning tool for student presenters and their peer reviewers.

### 3.2.5 Creation of Materials for Instructors and Technology Transfer

Creation of open educational resources entails selection of development and delivery platforms. These are often selected on the basis of introspective student feedback about understanding of the course material and whether they tend to promote attentional focus. (Anderson, Anderson, & Simon, 2004) Other considerations, however, are instructor usability, reusability, and documentation, which are important not only for prospective adopters of prepared materials but for team-taught courses and those that often change instructors.

Authoring systems (Kearsley, 1982) provide not only content for CAI (and by extension, e-learning), but also tie-ins with the other educational materials surveyed in this section. Both the marketing goals and technology transfer goals of authors are furthered by tools that enable them to support open educational resources. This includes technical support – namely, help systems, documentation, demos, and content management systems, as previously described in this paper. It also includes nontechnical support: responding to resource provision requests and following up. The MIT *DSpace* project (Smith, et al., 2003) is a good example of a materials repository that facilitates open access, particularly public information retrieval functions (search, indexing, and ranking). Each of these forms of support plays a useful role in course promotion and solicitation of adoption of materials by individuals at other institutions.

## 4. CASE STUDIES

Holistic uses of these technologies are then analyzed via case studies in three domains: artificial intelligence, computer graphics, and enterprise information systems. These case studies give an overview of existing materials and practices pertaining to the learning technologies covered. An exploration of technology transfer to college and university-level instructors in the information sciences then follows. This chapter emphasizes courses in computer science, informatics, and computational science and engineering, discussing the presentation of materials that combine mathematical theory, algorithms, software implementations, and data.

### 4.1 Artificial Intelligence

Open educational materials for the upper-division undergraduate-level course *Introduction to Artificial Intelligence* (CIS 530) and the graduate level *Artificial Intelligence* (CIS 730) course at Kansas State University were developed starting in 2004. Over 30 sets of lecture slides were prepared for 42 lectures. These initially consisted primarily of materials written by the authors of the textbook (Russell & Norvig, 2010), but by 2009 nearly all of the running examples in Russell and Norvig's slides had been converted to PowerPoint animations, except for the Bayesian network examples, which were animated using the author's own software.

Figure 1 depicts a manual animation developed from a series of static black-and-white images in the second edition of the textbook. The graph being

search is shown in a separate slide not pictured here. Many similar concepts – intelligent agents, state space search, constraint satisfaction search, game tree search, and logical reasoning – were illustrated and usually animated in similar fashion.

Figure 2 depicts an animation of a concept (computability or decidability of various formal languages related to first-order logic). Because most undergraduate and a few graduate students had not been previously exposed to computability theory in an automata theory course, other than an informal introduction to the halting problem, this elective course provided the first introduction to the topic. Students reported in the first years after this figure was drawn by hand that comprehension and retention were low for this concept. A significant improvement was observed after the preparation of this animation.

Figure 3 depicts an animation of the moralization step prior to triangulation and clique-finding in the junction tree algorithm for exact inference in Bayesian networks. This algorithm is known for being difficult to explain effectively in an introductory course in artificial intelligence or visualize in a lecture format, even a recorded lecture. The *Bayesian Network tools in Java* toolkit (Hsu, Guo, Joehanes, Perry, & Thornton, 2003; Hsu & Barber, 2004) was used to animate the junction tree algorithm, among others.

Both PDF and *PowerPoint* versions were created of all slides; similarly, both PDF and *Word* versions were created of all assignments. All of the lectures in this course were recorded and produced using *Camtasia*, and provided to enrolled students *K-State Online*, a content management system based upon *Axio*, and to the public using an Apache-based public mirror web site.

### 4.2 Computer Graphics

Open educational materials for three computer graphics courses at Kansas State University were developed starting in 2008, and completed in 2011: the upper-division undergraduate-level course *In-*

*Figure 1. Algorithm animation in Kansas State University CIS 530/730 (Artificial Intelligence): A/A\* search*

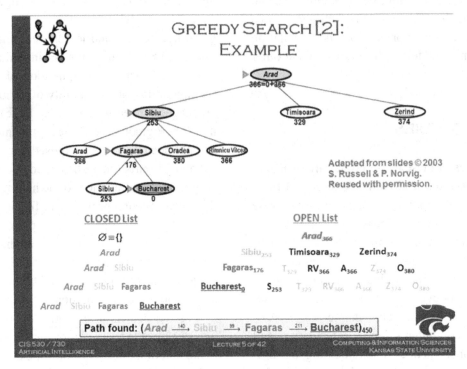

*Figure 2. Concept animation in KSU CIS 530/730 (Artificial Intelligence): computability of formal languages*

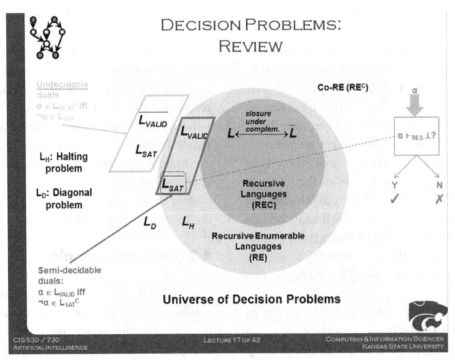

*Figure 3. Algorithm animation and software demonstration in KSU CIS 530/730 (Artificial Intelligence): exact inference in graphical models of probability using the junction tree algorithm*

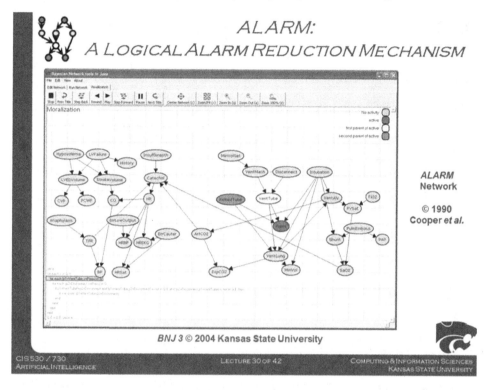

troduction to Computer Graphics and the graduate level *Interactive Computer Graphics*. 35 sets of lecture slides were prepared for 42 lectures, plus slides for background refresher lectures for the undergraduate course and advanced topics for the second graduate course. These initially consisted primarily of materials written by the first author of a past textbook for the course (Foley, van Dam, Feiner, & Hughes, 1991), but by 2011 nearly all of the running examples in Van Dam's slides had been converted to PowerPoint animations, except some computer-generated animations which were cited and adapted from *YouTube*.

Figure 4 depicts a key series of concepts in 3-D rendering: the model view transformation and cumulative transformation matrices that comprise the normalizing transformation for perspective projection. (Eberly, 2006) This slide is accompanied by a voiceover by the instructor explaining each step. It is the culmination of a series of five

lectures on viewing that include several figures and animations, each the basis of a screencast. This synopsis slide is one of several that are prepared for students to use for exam review and as a long-term reference.

Figure 5 depicts inline documentation explaining the function of two toy example shaders: a vertex shader that performs two simple operations and a fragment shader that changes object colors. This is an example of both code explanation (covered in Section 3.2.2) and a third-party programming system walkthrough (covered in 3.2.3).

## 4.3 Enterprise Information Systems

Both the *Database System Concepts* (CIS 560) and *Enterprise Information Systems* (CIS 562) courses at Kansas State University include course modules in relational database management systems (RDBMS), particularly database design approaches

*Figure 4. Explanation of concept in KSU CIS 536/636 and 736 (Computer Graphics): coordinate systems and transformations for 3-D perspective viewing. Based on Eberly (2006) and Foley et al. (1991).*

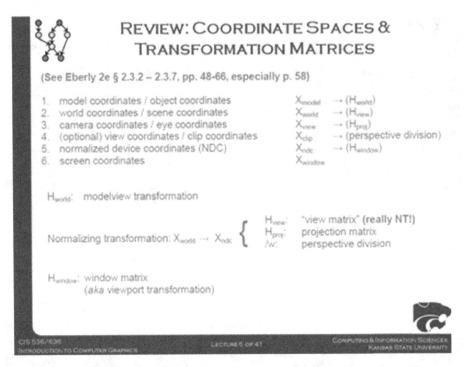

*Figure 5. Explanation of code and multimedia walkthrough in KSU CIS 536/636 and 736 (Computer Graphics): vertex and pixel/fragment shaders in the OpenGL Shading Language*

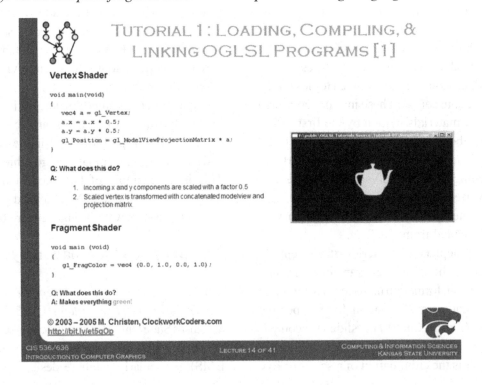

such as entity-relational (E-R) data modeling. One of the challenges in making RDBMS accessible and engaging to undergraduate computer science students is formulating concrete examples of schema design and refactoring without losing the abstract comprehension that students need in order to apply known algorithms for calculating functional dependencies and normalize a data model, analyze existing E-R diagrams to understand what the dependencies entail, synthesize a new model that meets specified criteria, and evaluate alternative designs. (Starr, Manaris, & Stalvey, 2008) Some variability among these concrete examples is necessary: too little and students tend to overfit their mental models to the examples encountered; too much and it becomes difficult to grasp their common features. This leads to the challenge of encouraging students to "design with intention" in RDBMS design and development – a problem analogous to that faced by Gaspar and Langevin (2007) in getting students to "code with intention."

Toward this end, a general-purpose data generator environment was developed in PHP for use in both courses. This data generator takes instances of abstract data types as input. These represent distributions over random variables that are attributes within some relational schema. For example, in an E-R diagram consisting of entities Subscriber and Magazine, and the relationship Subscribes-To, the Gender and Age attributes of Subscriber directly influence Magazine.Genre.

Figure 6 shows a partial code listing with inline documentation describing functions for generating prior and conditional distribution. The comments describe the default number of instances generated (independently, for prior distributions) and the conditional probability function being represented, whether the distribution itself is represented by apportionment of likelihood ("roulette wheel" random sampling) or by a conditional probability table. Code listings such as these, given as background material on programming projects, support

*Figure 6. Reading source code and going through programming system walkthrough in KSU CIS 560 (Database System Concepts) and CIS 562 (Enterprise Information Systems)*

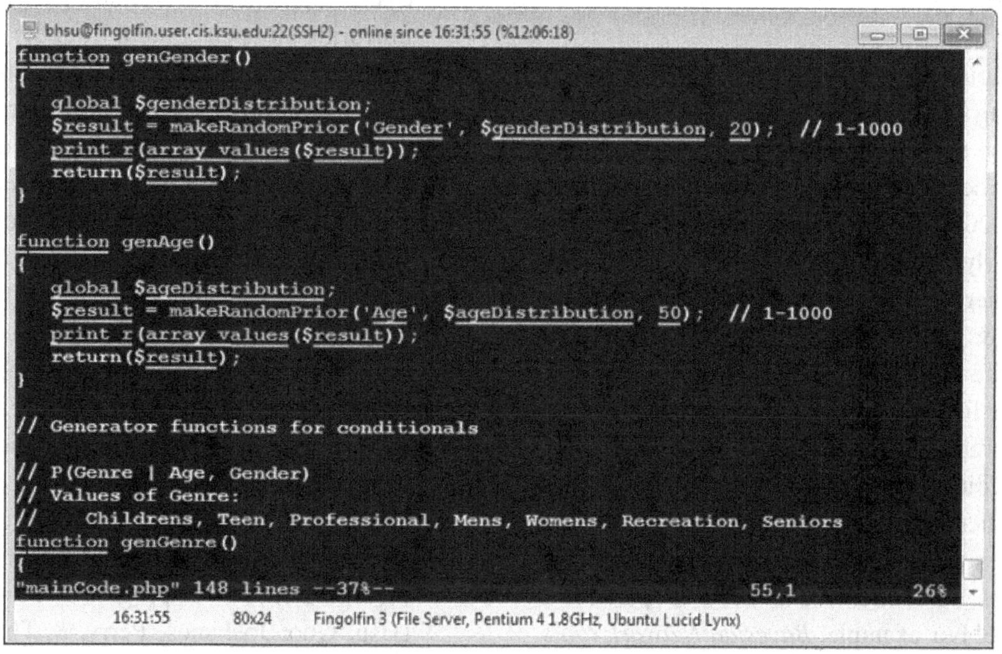

reading of the source code and code explanation (covered in Section 3.2.2) and a walkthrough of a instructor-supplied programming system (covered in 3.2.3). In addition, generation of data is a process that *itself* admits visualization (covered in 3.2.1), if the algorithm being used to perform random sampling is effective and transparent enough. Finally, the reconfigurability of the above programming system makes software demonstrations (such as those discussed in 3.2.4) feasible.

## 5. EFFECTIVE PRACTICES FOR ENCOURAGING ADOPTION AND DISSEMINATION

Finally, we review effective practices for encouraging dissemination and adoption of lecture materials. These include development practices for comprehensive, well-established open courseware projects that adapt pre-existing content, dating back over 25 years or more. More recent large-scale online courses have been aimed at audiences of tens to hundreds of thousands.

### 5.1 Adoption

Encouraging course adoption is often a matter of providing a complete set of materials for a course or course unit. In the three case studies above, these are centered around a textbook – Russell and Norvig (2010) for the artificial intelligence course and Eberly (2006) for the graphics course. However, other textbooks including Foley, van Dam, Feiner, & Hughes (1991) have been used with nearly the same lecture slides, video recordings, and code listings, without significant degradation in comprehension or retention.

In addition to holistic adoption of course materials, there is also the possibility that instructors may use specific resources such as lecture slides, exercises, animations, data sets, or particular software. For example, *Bayesian Network tools in Java* or *BNJ* (Hsu, Guo, Joehanes, Perry, &

Thornton, 2003; Hsu & Barber, 2004), the author's open source software package for inference and learning using graphical models, has several thousand downloads per year and has generated dozens of adoption inquiries, but most users are the silent variety and download *BNJ* to use its format conversion utilities (Hsu, Guo, Joehanes, Perry, & Thornton, 2003) or other similar functions that are available at no cost through packages such as *BNJ*.

### 5.2 Dissemination and Reuse

Lessons learned about dissemination in the techniques and domains surveyed are as follows:

1.  **Open Content Requires (some) Open Access.** Institutional access limits dissemination to students of research collaborators and other instructors. Some consumers of open educational resources – both administrators and students – may prefer this mechanism for dissemination, because of convenient communication features, or perceived security and privacy. However, a public wiki can easily supplement this kind of channel by mirroring all open content from the course.

2.  **Recycle Creative Input from Students and Instructors.** Several generations of the artificial intelligence and graphics courses have yielded term projects that themselves provide data for algorithm animation (Hsu & Barber, 2004); code for review (implementing the algorithms described in Section 4.1); additional examples and documentation for walkthroughs (such as shown in the "instructor-supplied code" in Figure 6 of Section 4.3); standalone applications and demonstrations (Hsu, Cunningham, & Hart, 2008); and modules that are contributed back by third-party developers and can be incorporated into a programming system (Hsu, Guo, Joehanes, Perry, & Thornton, 2003).

3.  **Share across Media.** *The MASSFORGE Project*, whose goal is to develop "the open-source core of a full-featured artificial life and intelligent agents-based multi-character animation system" (Hsu, Cunningham, & Hart, 2008), began in 2005 as a series of independent study projects. Since then, it has produced several demos on YouTube that illustrate aspects of computer-generated animation: particle systems, 3-D rotations, and repurposing of models (land vehicles and spacecraft). Similarly, these videos demonstrate aspects of game artificial intelligence: flocking and herding models, target acquisition, follow-the-leader behavior, and dynamic path finding. The videos, in turn, have been used to help students brainstorm in the instructor's graphics and artificial intelligence courses, and come up with new ideas for projects.

# REFERENCES

Abelson, H. (2005). *6.001 structure and interpretation of computer programs, Spring 2005 - Video lectures*. Retrieved April 17, 2012, from http://ocw.mit.edu/courses/electrical-engineering-and-computer-science/6-001-structure-and-interpretation-of-computer-programs-spring-2005/video-lectures/

Abelson, H. (2007, May). The creation of Open-CourseWare at MIT. *Journal of Science Education and Technology, 17*(2), 164–174. doi:10.1007/s10956-007-9060-8

Anderson, R., Anderson, R., & Simon, B. (2004). Experiences with a tablet PC based lecture presentation system in computer science courses. *SIGCSE '04 Proceedings of the 35th SIGCSE Technical Symposium on Computer Science Education.*

Apache Software Foundation. (2011). *OpenOffice: The free and open productivity suite*. Retrieved from http://www.openoffice.org/

Asay, M. (2007, October 2). *Why choose proprietary software over open source? Survey says!* Retrieved from http://news.cnet.com/8301-13505_3-9789275-16.html

Attwood, R. (2009, September 24). Get it out in the open. *Times Higher Education*. Retrieved April 17, 2012, from http://www.timeshighereducation.co.uk/story.asp?storycode=408300

Baecker, R., Wolf, P., & Rankin, k. (2004). The ePresence interactive webcasting and archiving system: Technology overview and current research issues. *Proceedings of World Conference on E-Learning in Corporate, Government, Healthcare, and Higher Education 2004* (pp. 2532-2537). Washington, DC: World Conference on E-Learning in Corporate, Government, Healthcare, and Higher Education (ELEARN) 2004.

Beepa. (2012). *FRAPS show fps, record video game movies, screen capture software*. Fraps: Real-time video capture & benchmarking. Retrieved from http://www.fraps.com/

Ben-Ari, M., Berglund, A., Booth, S., & Holmboe, C. (2004). What do we mean by theoretically sound research in computer science education? *Proceedings of the 9th Annual SIGCSE Conference on Innovation and Technology in Computer Science Education* (pp. 230-231). Leeds, UK: ACM.

Bias, R. (1991). Interface-walkthroughs: Efficient collaborative testing. *IEEE Software*, (n.d.), 94–95. doi:10.1109/52.84220

Blender Foundation. (2012). *Blender.org home*. Retrieved April 17, 2012, from http://www.blender.org

Bonaccorsi, A., & Rossi Lamastra, C. (2003). Why open source software can succeed. *Research Policy, 32*(7), 1243–1258. doi:10.1016/S0048-7333(03)00051-9

Brooks, F. P. (1995). *The mythical man-month: Essays on software engineering, anniversary edition* (2nd ed.). Boston, MA: Addison-Wesley Professional.

Carbonell, J. R. (1970, December). AI in CAI: An artificial-intelligence approach to computer-assisted instruction. *IEEE Transactions on Man-Machine Systems, 11*(4), 190–202. doi:10.1109/TMMS.1970.299942

Carmichael, P., & Honour, L. (2002). Open source as appropriate technology for global education. *International Journal of Educational Development, 22*(1), 47–53. doi:10.1016/S0738-0593(00)00077-8

Chambers, J. A., & Sprecher, J. W. (1980, June). Computer assisted instruction: Current trends and critical issues. *Communications of the ACM, 23*(6), 332–342. doi:10.1145/358876.358881

Chang, M. Y., Chiu, C.-M., & Hung, S.-S. (2010). A machinima-like 3D animation production system. *10th WSEAS International Conference on Systems Theory and Scientific Computation* (pp. 208-217). Taipei, Taiwan: WSEAS Press.

Chklovski, T., & Gil, Y. (2005). An analysis of knowledge collected from volunteer contributors. *Proceedings of the 20th National Conference on Artificial Intelligence (AAAI 2005)* (pp. 564-571). Menlo Park, CA: AAAI Press / The MIT Press.

Clancy, M. J., & Linn, M. C. (1999). Patterns and pedagogy. *Proceedings of the 30th SIGCSE Technical Symposium on Computer Science Education* (pp. 37-42). New York, NY: ACM Press.

Collins, A., Brown, J. S., & Newman, S. E. (1987). *Cognitive apprenticeship: Teaching the craft of reading, writing, and mathematics*. Champaign, IL: University of Illinois at Urbana-Champaign.

Corbi, T. A. (1989). Program understanding: Challenge for the 1990s. *IBM Systems Journal, 28*(2), 294–306. doi:10.1147/sj.282.0294

Creative Commons Corporation. (2011). *History - Creative commons*. Retrieved April 17, 2012, from http://creativecommons.org/about/history

D'Anjou, J., Fairbrother, S., Kehn, D., Kellerman, J., & McCarthy, P. (2005). *The Java developer's guide to Eclipse* (2nd ed.). Boston, MA: Addison-Wesley.

Dedrick, J., & West, J. (2003). Why firms adopt open source platforms: A grounded theory of innovation and standards adoption. In J. L. King, & K. Lyytinen (Ed.), *MIS Quarterly Special Issue - Workshop on Standard Making: A Critical Research Frontier for Information Systems*, (pp. 236-257).

Deek, F. P., Kimmel, H., & McHugh, J. A. (1998). Pedagogical changes in the delivery of the first-course in computer science: Problem solving, then programming. *Journal of Engineering Education, 87*, 313–320.

Depow, J. (2003). Open source software: Two learning management systems. *International Review of Research in Open and Distance Learning, 4*(2). Retrieved April 15, 2012, from http://www.irrodl.org/index.php/irrodl/article/view/135/215

desJardins, M., & Littman, M. (2010). Broadening student enthusiasm for computer science with a great insights course. In G. Lewandowski, S. A. Wolfman, T. J. Cortina, & E. L. Walker (Eds.), *Proceedings of the 41st ACM Technical Symposium on Computer Science Education (SIGCSE 2010)* (pp. 157-161). New York, NY: ACM Press.

DiBona, C., Ockman, S., & Stone, M. (1999). *Open sources: Voices from the open source revolution.* Sebastopol, CA: O'Reilly Media. Retrieved from http://oreilly.com/openbook/opensources/book/

Dijkstra, E. W., Hoare, C. A., & Dahl, O.-J. (1972). Structured programming: *Vol. A. P.I.C. Studies in Data Processing, No. 8.* Waltham, MA: Academic Press.

Downes, S. (2007). Models for sustainable open educational resources. *Interdisciplinary Journal of Knowledge and Learning Objects, 3,* 29–44.

Duffy, P. (2008). Engaging the YouTube Google-eyed generation: Strategies for using Web 2.0 in teaching and learning. *Strategies.* (n.d), 119–130.

Eberly, D. H. (2006). *3D game engine design, 2nd edition: A practical approach to real-time computer graphics.* San Francisco, CA: Morgan Kaufmann.

Edwards, S. H. (2003). Rethinking computer science education from a test-first perspective. *Companion of the 18th Annual ACM SIGPLAN Conference on Object-Oriented Programming, Systems, Languages, and Applications* (pp. 148-155). New York, NY: ACM.

Fitzgerald, B. (2006). The transformation of open source software. *Management Information Systems Quarterly, 30*(3), 587–598.

Foley, J. D., Dam, A. v., Feiner, S. K., & Hughes, J. F. (1991). *Computer graphics: Principles and practice in C* (2nd ed.). Reading, MA: Addison-Wesley.

Free Software Foundation. (2012, February 22). *Various licenses and comments about them.* The GNU Operating System. Retrieved April 17, 2012, from http://www.gnu.org/licenses/license-list.html

Gaspar, A., & Langevin, S. (2007). Restoring "coding with intention" in introductory programming courses. *Proceedings of the 8th Conference on Information Technology Education* (pp. 91-98). New York, NY: ACM Press.

GBDirect. (2004). *Benefits of using open source software.* Open Source Software, Free Software and Software Libre. Retrieved April 17, 2012, from http://open-source.gbdirect.co.uk/migration/benefit.html

Gloor, P. A. (1992). AACE-algorithm animation for computer science education. *Proceedings IEEE Workshop on Visual Languages 1992,* (pp. 25-31). Cambridge, MA.

Guseva, I. (2009). *Bad economy is good for open source.* CMS Wire. Retrieved April 17, 2012, from http://www.cmswire.com/cms/web-cms/bad-economy-is-good-for-open-source-004187.php

Hars, A., & Ou, S. (2001). Working for free? – Motivations of participating in open source projects. *Proceedings of the 34th Hawaii International Conference on System Sciences.*

Hasler, B. S., Kersten, B., & Sweller, J. (2007). Learner control, cognitive load and instructional animation. *Applied Cognitive Psychology, 21*(6), 713–729. doi:10.1002/acp.1345

Herrmann, T. (2009). Systems design with the socio-technical walkthrough. In Whitworth, B., & de Moor, A. (Eds.), *Handbook of research on socio-technical design and social networking systems.* doi:10.4018/978-1-60566-264-0.ch023

Herrmann, T., Kunau, G., Loser, K.-U., & Menold, N. (2004). Socio-technical walkthrough: Designing technology along work processes. *Proceedings of the 8th Conference on Participatory Design: Artful Integration: Interweaving Media, Materials and Practices* (pp. 132-141). New York, NY: ACM Press.

Hertzum, M., & Frøkjær, E. (1996). Browsing and querying in online documentation: A study of user interfaces and the interaction process. *ACM Transactions on Computer-Human Interaction, 3*(2), 136–161. doi:10.1145/230562.230570

Holzinger, A., Kickmeier-Rust, M., & Albert, D. (2008). Dynamic media in computer science education: Content complexity and learning performance: Is less more? *Journal of Educational Technology & Society, 11*(1), 279–290.

Hossain, M. S., Rahman, M. A., & El-Saddik, A. (2004). A framework for repurposing multimedia content. *Canadian Conference on Electrical and Computer Engineering*, (pp. 971-974).

House, C. H., & Price, R. L. (2009). The secret sauce. In House, C. H., & Price, R. L. (Eds.), *The HP phenomenon: Innovation and business transformation* (pp. 216–256). Stanford, CA: Stanford University Press.

Hsu, W. H., & Barber, J. (2004, July 28). *Retrieved from Bayesian Network tools in Java* (BNJ). Retrieved from http://bnj.sourceforge.net/

Hsu, W. H., Cunningham, D., & Hart, J. (2008, August 6). *The MASSFORGE project community: An intelligent agent-based multi-character animation project.* Retrieved April 17, 2012, from LiveJournal: http://massforge.livejournal.com/

Hsu, W. H., Guo, H., Joehanes, R., Perry, B. B., & Thornton, J. A. (2003, November 5). *Bayesian network tools in Java v2.* SourceForge.net. Retrieved from http://sourceforge.net/project/shownotes.php?release_id=195787

Hundhausen, C. D. (2002). Integrating algorithm visualization technology into an undergraduate algorithms course: Ethnographic studies of a social constructivist approach. *Computers & Education, 39*(3), 237–260. doi:10.1016/S0360-1315(02)00044-1

Hundhausen, C. D., Douglas, S. A., & Stasko, J. T. (2002). A meta-study of algorithm visualization effectiveness. *Journal of Visual Languages and Computing, 13*(3), 259–290. doi:10.1006/jvlc.2002.0237

IEEE. (1998). *IEEE standard for software reviews.* New York, NY: Institute of Electrical and Electronics Engineers (IEEE Std. 1028-1997).

Iiyoshi, T., & Kumar, V. (2008). *Opening up education: The collective advancement of education through open technology, open content, and open knowledge.* Cambridge, MA: The MIT Press.

Jonassen, D. H., Howland, J. L., & Marra, R. M. (2011). *Meaningful learning with technology.* Boston, MA: Pearson Education.

Karat, C.-M., Campbell, R., & Fiegel, T. (1992). Comparison of empirical testing and walkthrough methods in user interface evaluation. In P. Bauersfeld, J. Bennett, & G. Lynch (Ed.), *Conference on Human Factors in Computing Systems (CHI 1992)* (pp. 397-404). New York, NY: ACM Press.

Kearsley, G. (1982). Authoring systems in computer based education. *Communications of the ACM, 25*(7), 429–437. doi:10.1145/358557.358569

Kerr, I. M., & Bornfreund, M. (2007, June 2). *Open source software.* Canadian Internet Policy and Public Interest Clinic (CIPPIC). Retrieved April 17, 2012, from http://www.cippic.ca/open-source/

Knuth, D. E. (1984). Literate programming. *The Computer Journal, 27*(2), 97–111. doi:10.1093/comjnl/27.2.97

Koning, B. B., Tabbers, H. K., Rikers, R. M., & Paas, F. (2007). Attention cueing as a means to enhance learning from an animation. *Applied Cognitive Psychology, 21*(6), 731–746. doi:10.1002/acp.1346

Krishnamurthy, S. (2002). Cave or community? An empirical examination of 100 mature open source projects. *First Monday, 7*(6). Retrieved April 15, 2012, from http://firstmonday.org/htbin/cgiwrap/bin/ojs/index.php/fm/article/view/1477/1392

Kulik, C.-L. C., & Kulik, J. A. (1991). Effectiveness of computer-based instruction: An updated analysis. *Computers in Human Behavior, 7*(1-2), 75–94. doi:10.1016/0747-5632(91)90030-5

Kuniyoshi, Y., Inaba, M., & Inoue, H. (1994). Learning by watching: Extracting reusable task knowledge from visual observation of human performance. *IEEE Transactions on Robotics and Automation, 10*(6), 799–822. doi:10.1109/70.338535

Lakhani, K., & Hippel, E. V. (2003). How open source software works: "free" user-to-user assistance. *Research Policy, 32*(7), 923–943. doi:10.1016/S0048-7333(02)00095-1

Lawrence, A. W., Badre, A. M., & Stasko, J. T. (1994). Empirically evaluating the use of animations to teach algorithms. *Proceedings of the 1994 IEEE Symposium on Visual Languages*, (pp. 48-54).

Lee, A. (2012, April 16). *Virtualdub.org: Proof that I had too much free time in college.* Retrieved April 17, 2012, from http://www.virtualdub.org/

Lerner, J., & Tirole, J. (2002, June). Some simple economics of open source. *The Journal of Industrial Economics, 50*(2), 197–234. doi:10.1111/1467-6451.00174

Lerner, J., & Tirole, J. (2004). *The economics of technolgy sharing: Open source and beyond - NBER Working Paper No. 10956.* Cambridge, MA: National Bureau of Economic Research.

Lester, J. C., Converse, S. A., Stone, B. A., Kahler, S. E., & Barlow, S. T. (1997). Animated pedagogical agents and problem-solving effectiveness: A large-scale empirical evaluation. *Proceedings of Eighth World Conference on Artificial Intelligence in Education*, (pp. 23-30).

Lin, Y.-T., Chi, Y.-C., Chang, L.-C., Cheng, S.-C., & Huang, Y.-M. (2007). Web 2.0 synchronous learning environment using AJAX. *Proceedings of the 9th IEEE International Symposium on Multimedia* (pp. 453-458). New York, NY: IEEE Press.

Linn, M. C., & Clancy, M. J. (1992, March). The case for case studies of programming problems. *Communications of the ACM, 35*(3), 121–132. doi:10.1145/131295.131301

Littman, M. (2007). *Computer scientist Michael Littman shares his videos on computer science, artificial intelligence, and family.* Retrieved April 17, 2012, from http://www.youtube.com/user/mlittman

Liu, C. (2006). Software project demonstrations as not only an assessment tool but also a learning tool. *Proceedings of the 37th SIGCSE Technical Symposium on Computer Science Education (SIGCSE 2006)*, (pp. 423-427).

Loidl, S., Mühlbacher, J., & Schauer, H. (2005). Preparatory knowledge: Propaedeutic in informatics. In R. T. Mittermeir (Ed.), *From Computer Literacy to Informatics Fundamentals: International Conference on Informatics in Secondary Schools – Evolution and Perspectives, LNCS 3422* (pp. 104-115). Heidelberg, Germany: Springer.

Lowood, H. (2006). High-performance play: The making of machinima. *Journal of Media Practice, 7*(1), 25–42. doi:10.1386/jmpr.7.1.25/1

Lowood, H., & Nitsche, M. (2011). *The machinima reader.* Cambridge, MA: The MIT Press.

Luo, L. (2009). Web 2.0 integration in information literacy instruction: An overview. *Journal of Academic Librarianship, 36*(1), 32–40. doi:10.1016/j.acalib.2009.11.004

Mauthe, A., & Thomas, P. (2004). *Professional content management systems: Handling digital media assets.* West Sussex, UK: John Wiley and Sons. doi:10.1002/0470855444

Mayer, R. E. (1999). Multimedia aids to problem-solving transfer. *International Journal of Educational Research, 31,* 611–623. doi:10.1016/S0883-0355(99)00027-0

Mayer, R. E., & Anderson, R. B. (1992). The instructive animation: Helping students build connections between words and pictures in multimedia learning. *Journal of Educational Psychology, 84*(4), 444–452. doi:10.1037/0022-0663.84.4.444

Mayer, R. E., & Moreno, R. (2002). Animation as an aid to multimedia learning. *Educational Psychology Review, 14*(1), 87–99. doi:10.1023/A:1013184611077

Mehlenbacher, B. (2002). Assessing the usability of on-line instructional materials. *New Directions for Teaching and Learning, 91,* 91–98. doi:10.1002/tl.71

Naps, T. L., Rößling, G., Almstrum, V., Dann, W., Fleischer, R., Hundhausen, C., & Velázquez-Iturbide, J. Á. (2002). *Exploring the role of visualization and engagement in computer science education. Working group reports from ITiCSE on Innovation and technology in computer science education* (pp. 131–152). New York, NY: ACM.

Ncube, C., & Maiden, N. (2000). *COTS software selection: The need to make tradeoffs between system requirements, architectures and COTS/Components.* ACM SIGSOFT COTS Workshop: Continuing Collaborations for Successful COTS Development. New York, NY: ACM Press.

Nourie, D. (2005, March 24). *Getting started with an integrated development environment (IDE).* Oracle Sun Developer Network. Retrieved April 17, 2012, from http://java.sun.com/developer/technicalArticles/tools/intro.html

Novick, D. G. (2000). Testing documentation with "low-tech" simulation. In S. B. Jones, B. W. Moeller, M. Priestley, & B. Long (Eds.), *Proceedings of IEEE Professional Communication Society International Professional Communication Conference and Proceedings of the 18th Annual ACM International Conference on Computer Documentation: Technology & Teamwork* (pp. 55-68). New York, NY: IEEE Press.

O'Hara, K. J., & Kay, J. S. (2003). Open source software and computer science education. *Journal of Computing Sciences in Colleges, 18*(3), 1–7.

Obrenovic, Z., Starcevic, D., & Selic, B. (2004). A model-driven approach to content repurposing. *IEEE MultiMedia, 11*(1), 62–71. doi:10.1109/MMUL.2004.1261109

Open Source Initiative. (2006). *The open source definition (annotated), version 1.9.* (B. Perens, & K. Coar, Eds.). Open Source Initiative. Retrieved April 17, 2012, from http://www.opensource.org/osd.html

Pane, J. F., Corbett, A. T., & John, B. E. (1996). Assessing dynamics in computer-based instruction. In M. J. Tauber (Ed.), *Conference on Human Factors in Computing Systems: Common Ground* (pp. 197-204). New York, NY: ACM Press.

Patterson, D. A. (2006). Computer science education in the 21st century. *Communications of the ACM, 49*(3), 27–30. doi:10.1145/1118178.1118212

Plaisant, C., & Shneiderman, B. (2005). Show me! Guidelines for producing recorded demonstrations. *2005 IEEE Symposium on Visual Languages and Human-Centric Computing* (pp. 171-178). IEEE.

PLATO History Foundation. (2011, March 22). *PLATO history: Remembering the future*. Retrieved April 17, 2012, from http://www.plato-history.org/.

Poindexter, S. E., & Heck, B. S. (1999). Using the web in your courses: What can you do? What should you do? *IEEE Control Systems*, February, 83-92.

Prabaker, M., Bergman, L., & Castelli, V. (2006). An evaluation of using programming by demonstration and guided walkthrough techniques for authoring and utilizing documentation. In R. E. Grinter, T. Rodden, P. M. Aoki, E. Cutrell, R. Jeffries, & G. M. Olson (Eds.), *Proceedings of the 2006 Conference on Human Factors in Computing Systems (CHI 2006)* (pp. 241-250). New York, NY: ACM Press.

Ramsey, N. (1994, September). Literate programming simplified. *IEEE Software, 11*(5), 97–105. doi:10.1109/52.311070

Rankin, K., Baecker, R., & Wolf, P. (2004). ePresence: An open source interactive webcasting and archiving system for elearning. *Proceedings of E-Learn 2004.*

Raymond, D. R. (1991). Reading source code. *Proceedings of the 1991 Conference of the Centre for Advanced Studies on Collaborative Research, CASCON '91.*

Raymond, E. S. (1999). *The cathedral and the bazaar*. Sebastopl, CA: O'Reilly Media.

Rieber, L. P. (1990). Animation in computer-based instruction. *Educational Technology Research and Development, 38*(1), 77–86. doi:10.1007/BF02298250

Rößling, G., Malmi, L., Clancy, M., Joy, M., Kerren, A., & Korhonen, A. (2008, December). Enhancing Learning management systems to better support computer science education. *SIGCSE Bulletin, 40*(4), 1.

Rowley, D. E., & Rhoades, D. G. (1992). The cognitive jogthrough: A fast-paced user interface evaluation procedure. In P. Bauersfeld, J. Bennett, & G. Lynch (Ed.), *Conference on Human Factors in Computing Systems (CHI 1992)* (pp. 389-395). New York, NY: ACM Press.

Ruiz, J. G., Cook, D. A., & Levinson, A. J. (2009). Computer animations in medical education: A critical literature review. *Medical Education, 43*(9), 838–846. doi:10.1111/j.1365-2923.2009.03429.x

Russell, S. J., & Norvig, P. O. (2010). *Artificial intelligence: A modern approach*. Boston, MA: Pearson.

Rutgers University. (2012). *Rutgers.edu*. Retrieved April 17, 2012, from http://www.youtube.com/user/rutgers

Sametinger, J. (1994). The role of documentation in programmer training. In Woodman, M. (Ed.), *Programming languages: Experiences and practice*. Chapman & Hall.

Schaffert, S., Bischof, D., Bürger, T., Gruber, A., Hilzensauer, W., & Schaffert, S. (2006). Learning with semantic wikis. *Proceedings of the First Workshop on Semantic Wikis – From Wiki To Semantics (SemWiki 2006)*, Budva, Montenegro. Retrieved April 17, 2012, from http://www.schaffert.eu/wp-content/uploads/Schaffert06_SemWikiLearning.pdf

Shank, R. C., Berman, T. R., & Macpherson, K. A. (1999). Learning by doing. In Reigeluth, C. M. (Ed.), *Instructional-design theories and models: A new paradigm of instructional theory (Vol. II,* pp. 161–181). Mahwah, NJ: Lawrence Erlbaum Associates.

Singh, P., Lin, T., Mueller, E. T., Lim, G., Perkins, T., & Zhu, W. L. (2002). Open mind common sense: Knowledge acquisition from the general public. In R. Meersman, Z. Tari, & M. Papazoglu (Eds.), *Proceedings of On the Move to Meaningful Internet Systems 2002: Confederated International Conferences CoopIS, DOA, and ODBASE 2002, LNCS 2519*, (pp. 1223-1237). Heidelberg, Germany: Springer.

Singh, V., Twidale, M. B., & Rathi, D. (2006). Open source technical support: A look at peer help-giving. *Proceedings of the 39th Hawaii International Conference on System Sciences.*

Sleeman, D., & Brown, J. S. (1982). Introduction: Intelligent tutoring systems. In Sleeman, D., & Brown, J. S. (Eds.), *Intelligent tutoring systems* (pp. 1–10). Orlando, FL: Academic Press.

Smith, M., Barton, M., Bass, M., Branschofsky, M., McClellan, G., Stuve, D., & Walker, J. H. (2003). *DSpace: An open source dynamic digital repository*. Corporation for National Research Initiatives.

Soloway, E. (1986, September). Learning to program = learning to construct mechanisms and explanations. *Communications of the ACM, 29*(9), 850–858. doi:10.1145/6592.6594

Spinuzzi, C. (2002). Modeling genre ecologies. In K. Haramundanis, & M. Priestley (Eds.), *Proceedings of the 20th Annual International Conference on Documentation (SIGDOC 2002)*, (pp. 200-207).

Spinuzzi, C., & Zachry, M. (2000, August). Genre ecologies: An open-system approach to understanding and constructing documentation. *ACM Journal of Computer Documentation, 24*(3), 169–181. doi:10.1145/344599.344646

Starr, C. W., Manaris, B., & Stalvey, R. H. (2008). Bloom's taxonomy revisited: Specifying assessable learning objectives in computer science. *Proceedings of the 39th SIGCSE Technical Symposium on Computer Science Education* (pp. 261-265). New York, NY, USA: ACM Press.

Stasko, J., Badre, A., & Lewis, C. (1993). Do algorithm animations assist learning? An empirical study and analysis. *INTERACT, 93*, 24–29.

Stephenson, C., Gal-Ezer, J., Haberman, B., & Verno, A. (2005). *The new educational imperative: Improving high school - Final report of the CSTA Task Force*. New York, NY: Computer Science Teachers Association, Association for Computing Machinery.

Stevenson, D. E. (1993). Science, computational science and computer science: At a crossroads. In S. C. Kwasny, & J. F. Buck (Eds.), *Proceedings of the 1993 ACM Conference on Computer Science (CSC 1993)* (pp. 7-14). New York, NY: ACM Press.

Stork, D. G. (1999, May/June). The open mind initiative. *IEEE Intelligent Systems and their Applications, 14*(3), 16-20.

Suppes, P., & Morningstar, M. (1969, October 17). Computer-assisted instruction. *Science, 166*, 343–350. doi:10.1126/science.166.3903.343

Thatcher, J. D. (2006). Computer animation and improved student comprehension. *The Journal of the American Osteopathic Association, 106*(1), 9–14.

Tufte, E. R. (1990). *Envisioning information*. Cheshire, CT: Graphics Press.

Tufte, E. R. (1997). *Visual explanations: Images and quantities, evidence and narrative*. Cheshire, CT: Graphics Press. doi:10.1063/1.168637

Tufte, E. R. (2006). *Beautiful evidence*. Cheshire, CT: Graphics Press.

Van Meer, E. (2003). PLATO: From computer-based education to corporate social responsibility. *Iterations: An Interdisciplinary Journal of Software History, 2*, 1-22. Retrieved April 17, 2012, from http://www.cbi.umn.edu/iterations/vanmeer.html

Van Wyk, C. J. (1990, March). Literate programming: An assessment. *Communications of the ACM, 33*(3), 361, 365.

Verbert, K. GaSvevic, D., Jovanovic, J., & Duval, E. (2005). Ontology-based learning content repurposing. *Special interest tracks and posters of the 14th International Conference on World Wide Web* (pp. 1140-1141). Chiba, Japan: ACM.

von Krogh, G., & Spaeth, S. (2007). The open source software phenomenon: Characteristics that promote research. *The Journal of Strategic Information Systems, 16*(3), 236–253. doi:10.1016/j.jsis.2007.06.001

Wharton, C., Rieman, J., Lewis, C., & Polson, P. (1994). The cognitive walkthrough method: A practitioner's guide. In J. Nielsen, & R. L. (Eds.), *Usability inspection methods* (pp. 105-140). New York, NY: Wiley.

Wikipedia. (2012, April 16). *Content management system*. Retrieved April 17, 2012, from http://en.wikipedia.org/wiki/Content_management_system

Wikipedia. (2012, April 17). *Informatics (academic field)*. Retrieved from http://en.wikipedia.org/wiki/Informatics_(academic_field)

Wikipedia. (2012, March 12). *Open content*. Retrieved April 17, 2012, from http://en.wikipedia.org/wiki/Open_content

Wikipedia. (2012, April 13). *OpenOffice.org*. Retrieved from http://en.wikipedia.org/wiki/OpenOffice.org

Wiley, D. (Ed.). (2011). *Defining the "open" in open content*. Retrieved April 17, 2012, from http://www.opencontent.org/definition/

Winslow, L. E. (1996). Programming pedagogy --A psychological overview. *ACM Special Interest Group on Computer Science Education Bulletin*, 17-22.

Xiao, W., Chi, C., & Yang, M. (2007). On-line collaborative software development via Wiki. *Proceedings of the 2007 International Symposium on Wikis* (pp. 177-183). New York, NY: ACM Press.

Yang, A. T. (2001). Computer security and impact on computer scienc eeducation. *Proceedings of the Sixth Annual CCSC Northeastern Conference on The Journal of Computing in Small Colleges* (pp. 233-246). Middlebury, VT: Consortium for Computing Sciences in Colleges.

Ye, Y., & Kishida, K. (2003). Toward an understanding of the motivation of open source software developers. *Proceedings of the 25th International Conference on Software Engineering*, (pp. 419-429).

Zhang, D., Zhao, J. L., Zhou, L., & Nunamaker, J. F. (2004). Can e-learning replace classroom learning? *Communications of the ACM, 47*(5), 75–79. doi:10.1145/986213.986216

## ENDNOTES

[1] The first edition of DiBona, Ockman, & Stone (1999) is available as an e-book from http://oreilly.com/openbook/opensources/book/.

[2] Barracuda Networks, Inc. is a company providing "security, networking and storage

solutions based on network appliances and cloud services" ("Barracuda Networks," Wikipedia, 2012)

[3] Rößling *et al.* (2008) provide a representative survey of contemporary computer-managed instruction systems.

[4] Automated grading and test case generation systems for basic programming courses are also studied by Edwards (2003), who notes that they tend to elicit a cultural shift from *ad hoc* debugging styles to more principled and systematic ones.

# Chapter 16
# Aligning Practice and Philosophy:
## Opening up Options for School Leaders

**Kathryn Moyle**
*Charles Darwin University, Australia*

## ABSTRACT

*The educational use of digital technologies such as mobile devices, computers, and the Internet are progressively replacing pens, books, and the physical spaces known as libraries. Both online synchronous and asynchronous learning modes are emerging as part of the learning styles used with children physically attending schools. Consequently schools and school districts deploy various sorts of software applications to meet the range of teaching, learning, and management functions they perform. As leaders of schools, principals have heightened responsibilities concerning the philosophical directions of schools, as well as aligning the uses of technologies across all facets of their organizations. Set against the backdrop of Australian experiences, this chapter sets out to canvas some of the less considered factors that ought to be taken into account when schools select software applications. Gaining congruence between school philosophies and the technologies used, often-time means open source software ought to be a preferable solution to closed, proprietary software. This argument is justified from pedagogical and management perspectives. Furthermore, it is argued that making informed decisions before adopting the use of a particular technology requires that school leaders understand the educational and technical demands of that technology, and also have a socially-critical understanding of technologies in education and in society more generally. Finally, it is argued that if school principals are willing to consider open source software solutions, the options for teaching and learning with technologies and the strategies for managing the infrastructure of the school in robust and cost effective ways, opens up.*

DOI: 10.4018/978-1-4666-2205-0.ch016

## INTRODUCTION: CONTEXTS AND CHOICES

In Australia there are 3,541,836 students attending 9468 schools (Australian Bureau of Statistics (ABS), 2011a; 2010). These students have access to computers both at home and at school. In 2010-11, broadband was accessed by nearly three-quarters (73%) of all households in Australia, and 92% of all households had ordinary Internet access (ABS, 2011b). As a result of a major rollout of computers in secondary schools since 2008, there are in excess of 780,000 computers in Australian secondary schools (Department of Education, Employment and Workplaces Relations (DEEWR) 2011; Garrett, 2011). Some of these computers run open source software but most use proprietary operating systems and software applications (Australian Government Department of Finance and Deregulation Australian Government Information Management Office, 2009; Catto, 2011).

Here 'open source software' refers to software that is freely available to anyone wishing to access and use it. There are different types of licenses that guide the use of the various open source software applications and operating systems (cf Joint Information Systems Committee (JISC), 2011), but some of the most important license requirements of open source software are the free redistribution of the software, unrestricted access to the source code, and the ability to change or modify the software and other derived works that may be distributed under the same licensing conditions (JISC, 2011). The ability to copy and redistribute open source software without any license limitations is one of its most attractive characteristics for schools where the implications of copyright can be severe (Moyle, 2006). Proprietary and commercial software in comparison, is produced to create a profit for its developers, and usually the source code is closed to redistribution through copyright restrictions (JISC, 2011).

Australian school education policies promote technologies as foundational for success in all learning areas. The *Melbourne Declaration on Educational Goals for Young Australians*, which was endorsed by all Australian Ministers of Education in 2008 states that students as a result of attending school will gain:

> *... the essential skills in literacy and numeracy and [be] creative and productive users of technology, especially ICT [information and communication technologies] (Ministerial Council Education, Early Child Development and Youth Affairs (MCEEDYA), 2008, p. 8).*

The use of many technologies used in schools is mediated through screen interfaces. Computing and mobile technologies provide opportunities for students to develop their literacy and interpersonal skills by communicating via the Internet with their teachers and peers, both nearby and around the world. Educational discourses can cover topics of various depths of sophistication, using different functionality. The Internet, for example, provides teachers and students with opportunities to share, view, discuss and learn about each other's work. Students can contribute their creations to public showcases and online events, or to collaborate on joint projects (Childnet International, 2008). Teachers and school principals can form online communities of practice around topics of interest (Bond, 2004; Duncan-Howell, 2007).

Research by the United States (US) national education nonprofit group *Project Tomorrow* suggests that over the past few years, interest in online learning has grown in popularity amongst students, educators, parents and policymakers (Project Tomorrow, 2011). This research shows that in 2010, compared with 2008, five times as many parents reported that they would incorporate online classes into their vision of the 'ultimate school' (Project Tomorrow, 2011). The characteristics of online learning reported as being attractive include self-study online courses, teacher-led online classes as well as blended or hybrid learning environments at school (Project Tomorrow, 2011). Like schools around the world, Australian schools are starting to adopt online learning modes as part of the classroom teaching and learning styles they use. These developments mean school principals have to demonstrate leadership in making decisions about which technologies to use.

## Some Choices

Schools are places where choices are made about the hardware and software to be used by and with children and staff. These choices not only reflect the educational requirements and purposes to which those computing technologies are to be put, but also reflect the philosophical priorities of those who, in leadership and management are directing those choices. Determining the answers to these choices requires asking: how will the technologies be used; what learnings are best fostered with which technologies; where should the technologies be located; who is responsible for the technologies; and which companies (if any) should be commissioned to provide services, hardware and/or software? Too often technologies are seen as artifacts that have emerged from thin air, or have somehow been imposed. This view positions the school leader as an observer without control, rather than recognizing that school leaders have choices about which hardware, software and services they can use.

To illustrate the choices facing school leaders, imagine you are considering the deployment of an online learning platform in your school. Making choices about which software to adopt requires reflection upon the types of learning that is to be fostered and valued, and on the ways in which these values can be achieved across the school. Just as the physical architecture of schools is reflective of the implicit beliefs about what is valued in school education, so too the information technologies (IT) infrastructure of a school is symbolic of the values the school holds dear.

School buildings of the 19th and 20th century can be seen as reflective of the culture and types of teaching and learning that were valued at that time (Hargreaves, 1994). So too in 21st century schools, the IT infrastructures and the ways in which learning about technologies are fostered, can be 'read' to see the values they reflect.

Deploying technologies in schools inevitably brings with it the private IT market. Educators from across a range of disciplines argue that the multi-national companies have too great an influence on the policies, priorities and content of schooling (cf Apple 2004; 2001; Beder, 2009). Unlike the intentions of most schools, markets create powerful relationships based on dominance, submissiveness and control (Marginson, 1997). In addition, links are drawn between countries' economic competitiveness, and the knowledge, skills and capabilities of their people, including their capacity to use technologies, and to innovate. These themes are tightly woven together by policy-makers, economists and multinational companies (cf Porter & Schwab, 2008). What results are policy intersections that focus on the education and training systems of a country (Moyle 2010). But there can be tensions that arise from such close interfaces between the socializing and educating roles of schools, and the legitimate profit motive of many IT companies. One way to offset this tension however, is to use robust open source software. Open source applications are free of license costs and generally not made to make a profit. The removal of financial issues are ones that often confine the choices in many schools, and so accessing open source software, without the costs of proprietary licenses therefore provides schools with broader options of software use.

However, open source software and associated open education approaches are not simply about money. The processes underpinning these approaches are based on philosophies that are more potent than the force of finances. The models of co-creation developed through open source communities when applied to technology issues in school education, provide benefits available to all by promoting values consistent with those in school education and minimizing social, political and economic barriers (Bosco, 2010). But for school leaders and school systems, the choices can be complex. It can be mind-boggling to try to make choices that balance an understanding of the symbiotic relationships between education theories, fit for purpose, technology functionality, technical support, and upfront and ongoing costs. This chapter aims to unpack some of these issues.

## School Leadership, Policies, and Decision-Making

Schools principals are leaders within their school communities. They are the people to whom parents, teachers and students look for guidance. Australian research (Moyle, 2006) suggests that school principals see themselves as 'leading' not just 'supporting' the integration of technologies into classroom practices. A participant in this 2006 study stated:

*Leadership in schools is very important: if there is none, then the school can't effectively manage an ICT [information and communication technologies] program. If there is no leadership with ICT, teachers are not able to fully integrate ICT and as a result the kids and their learning suffer. If teachers don't feel comfortable teaching ICT then they will not teach with it (Moyle, 2006, p11).*

As such, school leaders and particularly school principals, have heightened responsibilities about aligning the uses of technologies in their schools: not only to ensure there is 'fit for purpose' with the respective technological and education demands of the school community, but also to ensure that the work across all facets of the school, including technology deployments are conducted in ways that are consistent with individual school philosophies.

School leadership then, involves being able to make choices. School principals hold a special place in schools as they are often the 'barometer check' on the various external pressures and forces placed on schools. To be able weigh up options and to make well considered judgments it is argued here, requires that school leaders be able to identify and question the 'taken-for-granted' assumptions about schools, and the infrastructure they house. To do so requires school leaders have a socially-critical understanding of place of technologies in school education.

Furthermore, school principals sit at the point of intersection between external policies about schools, and the work that is undertaken within their schools. What is published in policies and what is taught in schools, symbolically and practically captures what is of value to a school as well as to society at any given time. School policies around the world promote key themes that focus upon students' academic achievements, economic prosperity, and the development of students' generic capabilities such as literacy, numeracy, problem-solving, innovation and creativity, often through the use of technologies (cf Australian Government, 2009; Organisation for Economic Co-operation and Development (OECD), 2009; Partnerships for 21st century skills, 2009; Porter & Schwab 2008). Australian education policies are highly consistent with comparable OECD countries' policies (Moyle, 2010). Australian policies promote pedagogies where students are to learn how to use technologies to access information and turn it into knowledge applicable to their own circumstances (cf MCEECDYA, 2008).

But while school policies promote generic capabilities that deserve active, inquiry-based learning to be fostered, a challenge for schools seems to be how to ensure students are engaged and extended in their learning. Surveys by *Project Tomorrow* in the US point to a digital disconnect between what happens in schools and what happens in the home. These national surveys report that students 'power down' at school and 'power up' at home (Project Tomorrow, 2006). Students consistently report they use technologies in passive ways at school and enjoy the challenges of their chosen online activities at home (Project Tomorrow 2009). Indeed, tens of the thousands of US students report that the end of their school day they go home and use collaborative Web 2.0 tools like social networking, participate in online software development projects, and play virtual games (Project Tomorrow, 2011). At home, if students want, they can 'lift the hood' on the internal workings of open source software applications, examine them and test them out. Students use activities such as these to both educate and entertain themselves.

Furthermore, mobile learning devices are emerging as the new communication tools of students. The United Nations Educational, Scientific and Cultural Organization (UNESCO), for example, is hosting several mobile learning projects to foster school education (UNESCO, 2012). Mobile devices include laptops, net books, iPads, iPod Touch and smart cell phones (Johnson, Adams & Haywood 2011). A range of open source applications are being developed that can be used by school students on their mobile phones. Examples include *tweetero*, which is an open source *Twitter* client for mobile phones (Melton, 2012). *Rhomobile* is a cross-platform open source mobile application framework that enables the development of mobile applications for use on all smartphone phone operating systems (http://www.rhomobile.com/). And *Core Plot* is an open source graphing framework that provides the capacity to use 2D visualization data with Apple technologies such as *Core Animation* and *Core Data* (see http://code.google.com/p/core-plot/).

Students' patterns of behavior in both developed and developing nations, is seeing changes to the balance between formal learning at school and informal learning at home, and to the devices they choose to use. These changes present challenges for school leaders and policy makers about the value and meaning of the education they provide. If school leaders understand the educational and technical functions of the technology however, as well as have a socially-critical understanding of technologies, options for adopting the use of a particular technology does open up.

## BACKGROUND: SCHOOL EDUCATION AND THEORIES OF EDUCATION

Over the past several decades, there has been much conversation about how schools fail their students (cf Alliance for Excellent Education, 2009; Balfanz & Legters, 2004; National Science Teachers Association, 2006; Vockell, 1993). Changes to the ways classroom activities are conducted, have regularly been demanded. In the 21st century, the Internet provides the access point to people and education resources never previously imaged. Furthermore, open source software development models offer approaches to promoting collaborative learning approaches using the Internet. Indeed, one of the strengths of open source software to school education is that the philosophies that underpin these software development projects are consistent with key theories of education that promote constructivist, constructionist, active learning and other related approaches to teaching and learning (cf Bruner, 1961; Dewey 1916; Papert, 1980; Papert & Harel, 1991; Vygotsky, 1962). A brief overview of the prominent theories of education from the past century that have currency today, and the principles underpinning open source software development models are discussed shortly. The purpose of this section is to provide a background to the forthcoming discussion about the pedagogical and school management reasons why principals and policy makers should consider the use of open source software in their schools.

## Education Theories of Learning

In the first half of the 20th century, the influential US philosopher John Dewey promoted educational methods that fostered students' inquiry and experimentation as ways of learning. He argued that students learnt better if they had ownership over their own learning. Dewey also consistently argued that since education and learning involve interactive social processes, schools therefore, are social institutions (Dewey, 1916). Subsequently, Dewey (1929) reiterated that students should learn by doing; that is learning through practical activities and applications of the concepts or ideas being taught. But while Dewey's theories about education have been influential, it seems that schools in Western countries around the world have struggled to meaningfully apply his theories to teaching and learning in schools (Stuckart & Glanz, 2010; Weiss, DeFalco & Weiss, 2005). Nonetheless, Dewey's theories have underpinned much subsequent thinking about how to include technologies into the teaching and learning undertaken in schools.

In the 1970's Illich argued that the provision of education should be 'deschooled' and organized to provide students with access to the resources they require; where students freely and voluntarily share their skills and ideas; and that those sharing common interests could work together (Illich, 1971). He proposed the replacement of the often didactic teaching approaches used in schools, with 'curiosity-based learning' where students are encouraged to observe, imitate, investigate and use trial and error, to help them learn. Illich's (1971) ideas about how students should access education and the styles of learning they should undertake are increasingly possible through the use of computing and mobile technologies linked to the Internet.

In response to perceived inadequacies of teaching in schools, the concepts of inquiry-based learning (cf Bruner, 1990; 1986; 1961) and authentic learning (cf Herrington & Oliver, 2000; Lombardi

& Oblinger 2007; Newmann, Marks & Gamoran, 1996) emerged in the later half of the 20th century, based on the earlier work of Dewey. These theories are based on the theory of constructivism (Bruner, 1962; Vygotsky, 1962). Constructivism is based on the proposition that people create knowledge, meaning and understanding from the interactions that occur between their experiences and their ideas (cf Bruner, 1961; Vygotsky, 1978). Constructivist approaches to teaching and learning are student centered, where learning is promoted using active constructive processes. These theories now underpin concepts of personalized learning through the use of the Internet (Centre for Educational Research and Innovation (CERI), 2006).

Other student-centered pedagogies have been proposed by Seymour Papert, who developed the theory of constructionism, based on the concepts of experimentation (Piaget, 1962) and constructivism in education (Bruner, 1961). Papert uses the term 'constructionism' to refer to the way people create mental models or concepts in order to understand the world around them: that is 'learning by making' (Papert & Harel, 1991). Papert drew on Piaget's theories to inform his work on developing the programming language 'Logo' (Logo Foundation, 2011). Papert attempted to merge theories of learning according to Piaget with educational computer-based technologies (Papert, 1980). His aim was to improve the quality of learning by school students. Against this backdrop of educators and others theorizing about how students best learn, in 1994, Hargreaves nonetheless claimed that much teaching and learning in British schools is "… still artificial, contrived and formalised…" (p11). Similarly, in 2012, writers and education researchers continue to bemoan the perceived failure of schools to engage students in their learning (cf Faubert, 2012).

To be successful, schools have to draw on the best ideas available to them. Deliberately or not, open source software and open education approaches employ a range of approaches that are consistent with educators' and philosophers' views about education including 'learning by doing' (cf Dewey, 1929; Papert & Harel 1991; Resnick, 2008); inquiry and active based learning (cf Bruner, 1990; 1986; 1961); and the use of communities of practice approaches, where students work as a team on a common project by sharing skills and ideas (cf Wenger, 2006). Indeed, in the 21st century, the Internet provides the access point to education resources that Illich was proposing. In addition, open source software development models offer insights into how to promote collaborative learning approaches using the Internet that are consistent with key educational theories of the 20th and 21st centuries.

## MAIN FOCUS OF THE CHAPTER

Congruence between the philosophies and the technologies used within schools means that school communities receive consistent messages about what is of value to particular schools. To gain congruence between educational philosophies and the practices of schools, can mean that open source software is a preferable solution to closed, proprietary software. This view is justified here from pedagogical and school management perspectives. Learning how open source software projects are undertaken collectively through online communities, can assist school leaders and policy makers to understand how online communities can function effectively to achieve tangible outcomes, and to evaluate whether certain open source software applications have a place in their schools' IT portfolios.

To develop an understanding of the processes and outcomes of software developments, it is fundamental to understand that both open source and closed proprietary software are created by people. Indeed it is important to recognise that the creation and use of software is both a social process as well as a technical one. Understanding and accepting that software development is a social phenomenon, can assist school leaders

and policy makers to understand how different software licenses work, and how various types of software helpdesk support services can be made available freely over the Internet. Furthermore, if school leaders understand the design processes of open source software developments projects, they can provide opportunities for teachers and students to learn about how the processes of software development and application work in practice. That is, there can be pedagogical benefits to using open source software for teaching and learning purposes in schools, as well as providing suitable, robust administrative infrastructure software. As such, a brief overview of how open source software projects operate is outlined here.

## Open Source Software Projects

Members of open source software projects share beliefs and values about the nature of how software is developed and made accessible to others. Consistent with prominent 20th and 21st century education theories, open source software projects promote collaborative effort through team work to achieve the desired goals the project teams set themselves. Software creation involves writing programs that make the software work. Programming requires the use of a language, known as programming languages. Like other languages, programming can be taught in schools. The programming language of software provides 'software authors' with the tools to write the commands that make different types of software enable various technologies to work (Raymond, 2001). In the case of open source software, programmers collaborate by communicating using the Internet to develop the software, often through online mailing lists. The quality of their work is judged by their peers around the world (Weber, 2004).

Open source software projects are conducted on the basis of contributing to the public good through online networked activities (Bessen, 2006). In the case of open source software, the respective processes of development, creation, deployment and maintenance of the software are undertaken by interested and skilled volunteers, or by employees of companies supporting open source software projects. In comparison to open source software, the development of proprietary software is often undertaken in secret (Raymond, 2001). As such, rather than the centralized approach for software development used by proprietary vendors, a devolved model of product development is used for creating, testing, deploying and maintaining open source software (Raymond, 2001).

It is a common view of those working on open source software projects, that the capacity to rewrite and redistribute a software's source code gives users control over their technologies. This view is positioned in contrast to vendors of proprietary software who limit their customers by restricting access to their software code, and thereby positioning users as passive consumers of technologies. Open source software projects have cultures that encourage code sharing and peer-review of the works created (Elliot & Scacchi, 2003). There is a shared belief that software should be freely redistributable, both in terms of an absence of license costs, and freely redistributable in terms of being able to share the software with others without infringing copyright requirements (Weber, 2004). Among open source software communities it is considered a good thing that the software can be modified to suit the social and cultural requirements to which the software is to be put (Elliot & Scacchi, 2003). These shared beliefs justify the contribution of considerable collective effort, and it is the right to copy being left in place that is one of the most beneficial characteristics of open source software to schools.

To handle the development work, open source software projects adopt collaborative governance models, where the successful projects usually have clear rules for how the members contribute to that project (JISC, 2012). These projects generally have a leader; commonly one of the most skilled programmers in the group. Open source software project leaders recognize the skills of those work-

ing on their projects and are accountable to the members of that group (Nalley, 2011). They lead communities of developers who work in cyberspace to create their software. Only those people with programming knowledge, recognized as being sufficiently skilled by their peers, are allowed to directly work on the programming of the software. Whether someone is sufficiently skilled or not to write the programs for open source software is determined by the group working on that open source software development project (cf Ubuntu, 2012). Recognition of the skill of programmers occurs through their peers reviewing each other's software programming. That is, individual programmers develop a track record of programming success through peer review that occurs over the Internet and through testing the quality of their software in various settings (cf Apache Software Foundation, 2012). Others can participate in the development processes by testing and debugging software, writing user documentation, and helping others use the software. These processes of open source software development, serve to illustrate how creative activities such as making software can occur collaboratively in online environments. Educators will recognize how these approaches to project management and software development mirror valued pedagogical approaches.

## Pedagogical

To look at open source software development from an education perspective, there is congruence between the philosophies underpinning open source software development and the theories that underpin school education. Like software development, a high quality 21st century education depends upon encouraging students to discuss their learning with other students, to network and communicate with each other, and to share their ideas and solutions to the problems they are trying to individually and collectively solve. With the inclusion of technologies in teaching and learning in schools however, a challenge for teachers is how to move students from users and consumers of technologies to creators and producers. Here two approaches are discussed: collaborating online to achieve a common goal; and learning to program.

## Collaborating Online

Teachers often aim to build students' capacity to be innovative and creative with technologies (Moyle, 2010). Two key educational approaches that support this capacity-building are using audiences of students' work to provide meaningful and credible feedback to students; and for the students to be able to model their learning on that of others.

Learning through the use of open technologies and posting their completed and in-progress work to the Internet, provides students with audiences who can give feedback to improve the outcomes they achieve from their learning. The Internet also provides a platform through which students can view the source code of software applications developed by others. The work undertaken at the *Lifelong Kindergarten* located in Massachusetts Institute of Technology (MIT) Media Lab provides good examples of how the Internet can be used to enable young people to create interactive stories, games and animations, and to share their creations with others on the Internet (Resnick, 2007).

The aim of the *Lifelong Kindergarten* is to enable children to grow up learning how to design, create, and express themselves, including with the use of technologies. Much of this activity occurs through young people participating in projects such as *Scratch* or learning with Lego's programmable bricks. In all the activities promoted through the *Lifelong Kindergarten,* young people are encouraged to create interactive stories, games, animations, and simulations, and to share their creations with one another online (*Lifelong Kindergarten,* 2012*)*.

Some of the key pedagogical benefits provided through the open approaches used by *Lifelong Kindergarten* are that the Internet affords students with a ready-made audience for the stories, games

and animations they develop. Their audiences comprise other children as well as adults. Offering other children the opportunity to provide feedback to their peers, is also a highly educative experience in itself. By commenting on postings and contributing to group efforts to further develop and improve the software creations posted, builds students' confidence as well as their literacy and programming skills.

## Learning to Program

Another benefit of using open source software is that it provides opportunities for students at a young age to learn how to program a computer. As outlined earlier, source code is the language of programmers. It is a language that can begin to be taught at primary school (cf Lin, Yen, Yang & Chen, 2005). Many educators however, see computer programming as a narrow, technical activity, that only a small part of the student population should learn. Here this view is challenged. It is argued that if children can learn to speak other languages then they also have the capacity to learn the language of computer programming. Indeed, Seymour Papert argued that children could 'learn by doing' using the computer language Logo, as he explained to a Japanese audience in the 1980's.

Let me give you some examples: children in a school in California, the Gardner Academy, in a project called Project MindStorms, the children made a calendar. And this is the work of a fourth-grade child who programmed the computer to make this shape, thinking of squares and triangles and how to fit them together. And because she had to explain all that to the computer, writing programs in LOGO, she was really using mathematics to make something which she liked, which was even commercially valuable because they sold this calendar and got money to improve their project (Papert, n.d., part 1).

While the use of open source code enables students to learn the programming language required to move and change around pieces of code in order to solve problems or to fix bugs in the software, some school leaders and policy makers can be reticent about seeing these skills taught in schools. Sometimes the process of moving code around is inaccurately referred to as 'hacking' (Himanen 2001). There is a stigma to 'hacking', so school leaders can be forgiven for shying away from activities that the ill-informed can construe as illegal or subversive. The term 'hacking' however, sits in contrast to digital vandalism, which tends to be referred to as 'hacking' but more correctly should be referred to as 'cracking' (Raymond 2001). Comparing the difference in approaches to the management of source code however, can be edifying for a school leader.

In comparison to open source software code, the source code of proprietary off-the-shelf products is often closed, cannot be directly viewed, and is not open to re-writing unless it is 'cracked', or in some cases, where the consumer pays a fee to the company. But for some, the placement of restrictions on the access and changing of software source code is problematic both from technical and ideological points of view. Indeed for students so inclined, closed software presents a temptation and a challenge: they ask, can the code be accessed and viewed? The challenges for students of seeing something forbidden however, means they subsequently recognise, as Young states:

*...legally restricting access to knowledge of the infrastructure [source code] that our society increasingly relies on (via the propriety binary-only software licences our industry historically has used) results in less freedom and slower innovation (Young 2001: x).*

Yet on the other hand, well selected open source software provides opportunities for curious school students with their able teachers to look at how the software works and how it has been programmed. Rather than closing down learning, there is the capacity through the use of open source software, for opening it up.

## Managing Educational Technologies

Just as open source software has provided commercial organizations with options for the management of their back of office functions, so too open source software can be used to support learning at school. Open source software can be used to enable online teaching and learning activities; address license and copyright issues; and provide robust technical infrastructure.

## Using Open Source Software to Support Learning

Schools can use open source operating systems such as *Linux*, *Free BSD* and *Debian* as well using open networking standards to enable interoperability. Schools can support their teaching and learning through the use of open source software systems learning management systems (eg *Moodle, OLAT* and *ATutor*), library systems (eg *Koha, OpenBibio* and *BiblioteQ*), and open source software for specific discipline-based teaching and learning purposes (eg *EduForge portal*).

But the extent of software used in schools can generate managerial and logistical complexities due to the various license agreements and technical requirements many proprietary applications carry. The proprietary 'back office' software systems often used by schools to support learning can also be expensive. There are however, alternative software systems that can be used to replace the back office systems used in schools. Consolidated descriptions of open source back office systems are provided on several reputable websites and portals such as *OSS Watch* (JISC, 2011). The blog *Tech Analyser* (2011) provides comparisons between common proprietary software and suggests alternative open source software, such as *GIMP* for *Photoshop* and *OpenOffice* for *Microsoft Office*.

Although schools have to manage multiple versions of software, cloud technologies may go some way to alleviating the use of numerous applications. The *New Media Consortium* for example, suggests that particularly for data warehousing and email, the use of cloud computing by schools is a rapidly emerging trend (Johnson, Adams & Haywood, 2011). But in Australia schools are generally risk-adverse places, particularly so with the provision of access to the Internet (Moyle, 2009), and so the entre by schools into cloud computing is occurring in a very careful and considered way. Similarly, in the US schools are proceeding carefully with cloud technologies, however, there are some US schools who are working together with industry providers to create private clouds. *The Learning Curve*, a not-for-profit educational consortium of 40 Massachusetts school districts, is working with *IMG Software* and the *EMC* Corporation to provide cloud computing options on shared servers that integrate the various districts' proprietary data management tools (Johnson, Adams & Haywood, 2011). The open source software learning management system, *Moodle* is a part of this Massachusetts initiative (The Learning Curve Consortium, 2012).

Another thorny management issue for schools that can be addressed with the use of open source software is the problem of copyright. School principals are often concerned about activities such as illegal copying of software and restricted replication of the materials used in schools. In Australian schools, most software used is proprietary and so school software is generally locked down to avoid students and others tampering with it and to avoid copyright infringements. In an Australian study investigating school leaders views of their roles supporting teaching and learning with technologies (Moyle, 2006), digital copyright requirements were identified as working against enthusiastic teachers wanting to include digital content in their lessons. The concerns expressed focused upon the costs associated with replicating multiple copies of software applications for students and their families, replicating websites in teaching and learning activities, and the management implications arising from the processes of enforcement required within their school to avoid the piracy of software. Since open source software licenses leave the right to copy in place, issues of potential copyright infringements through software piracy can be removed or at least minimalized.

## Robust Infrastructure and Technical Support

With the widespread use of digital technologies in schools, the necessity of technical support to be available either within or associated with schools, has emerged (Moyle, 2010; 2004). The deployment of software for use by school staff and students has to run faultlessly and without downtime (Gartner 2012). There is less research in the schools sector about the implications of downtime than for commercial enterprises, but just as is the case for businesses, data loss and computer downtime have serious implications for schools. Risk identification and management of IT systems is new area of responsibility for schools. As such, school leaders and policy makers now have to understand the relationships that exist between software deployments and other related products and services to ensure there is seamless access by students and staff without downtimes to the software provided in schools.

The successful deployment and maintenance of all software requires training. Indeed, where schools or school systems deploy significant proprietary software deployments, ongoing access to trained technical staff is often essential. School leaders face a choice of either building the capacity of their workforce to handle the technical requirements or to buy in the expertise. IT technical support also requires taking into account the ease of access to 'just in time' technical support. Schools in Australia tend to engage software companies to provide specialist technical support to schools for their products. This level of support is often seen to be required to ensure the IT infrastructure of a school does not crash. But this type of technical support comes at a cost to the school, and often without any explicit skills transfer strategy between the company and the teachers.

The level of access to technical support required in Australian schools is in part essential due to the extent or scale of the deployments in schools and across school districts. This necessity for software-specific trained staff however, feeds the continuing dominance of the major software companies. Indeed, it feeds hegemonic relationships (Gramsci, 1971). Such hegemonic relationships are maintained due to unquestioned dependencies between the company and the school that are initiated and then maintained (Moyle, 2003). To ensure a workable IT infrastructure requires technical assistance, and hence accessing support for the software deployed is 'common sense', and the longer the 'common sense' is maintained, the less palatable it is to question or change the arrangements. And this is how schools and school systems get locked into ongoing contract relationships with large multinational software companies.

An alternative for school leaders is to choose to invest in the capacity building of their staff, and to choose open source software that includes help desk support through user groups. These helpdesks are available from the Internet or from companies established to provide technical support to those seeking to deploy open source software in their organization. It has to be acknowledged however, that to access such online support does requires that the school has a suitably capable technical officer to get value from the support that is available online.

## Scaling Up

Open source software can also assist in enabling the scaling-up of technologies use in schools. For example, research from Ireland suggests that open source software offers an efficient and value for money opportunity for schools interested in building their use of technologies. In their study, Anderson, Galvin, Gardner, Mitchell, Moyle & McMorrough (2011) found that scalability of their technology deployments were more achievable with open source rather than proprietary software.

The reason for this finding was due to the low cost, open and collaborative nature of open source software. In comparison to open source software, deploying comparable proprietary software was seen to incur substantial costs and thereby reduce the scalability of technologies in the Irish schools concerned. Also arising from this study was the development of a planned move away from proprietary products and applications. Trials of Linux commenced in selected Irish schools in the academic year 2008/09. By mid-2009 all stakeholders had agreed that Linux would be introduced (Anderson et al, 2011).

To summarize then, for school leaders and policy makers to make choices about which technologies to be used in their schools involves understanding the relationships between education theories and the philosophies underpinning software development. Issues that have to be addressed include the educational purposes for using technologies; the fit for educational purpose the selected technologies offer; the functionality of the technologies; the technical support required and the costs involved in the deployment of the technologies. Using open source software is one of the ways of gaining congruence between school philosophies and the technologies used in schools. This argument has been justified from pedagogical and school management perspectives.

## FUTURE RESEARCH DIRECTIONS

This chapter has examined some of the issues school leaders have concerning their choices of the technologies that are to be deployed in their schools. This discussion however, has not been exhaustive. There are many avenues for future research concerning the role and use of open source software in school education. The whole field is under-researched. The *2011 Horizon Report K-12 Edition* (Johnson, Adams & Haywood, 2011) however, does provide some insights into the breadth and depth of avenues for future potential research. The options discussed here though have been limited to some key, urgent avenues for future research.

While arguing that open source software can address some of the problems that arise from the deployment of technologies in schools, it has also been argued that understanding how open source software communities function is critical to school leaders' work. But there is little research about the technology requirements of schools and how they can be met with open source software compared with software that is available off-the-shelf. Furthermore, there is little research about how open source software and the role of schools intersects. It has also been argued that making informed decisions about the adoption of a particular technology requires that school leaders understand the educational and technical functions of that technology. But again, there is little research about the role of school principals and how they can develop socially-critical understandings about the technologies they use in their schools.

This chapter has also discussed how using online projects can assist students to network with each other, by connecting with their peers either in their own or in different schools. These processes can enrich the curricula and increase the transfer of generic and disciplined-based knowledge and skills. The place of open source software in assisting these networks however, is under-researched. Teachers and school leaders would benefit from examples of how to use open source software to foster student-centered approaches to teaching and learning. These examples could include illustrations of how open source software developments can be used as ready-made projects in which students and teachers can participate. Research is required to determine the types of skills required by students to meaningfully engage in a range of online open education and open source software projects.

Linked to students learning is the concept of 'assessment'. Students require feedback to their work so that they can develop and grow. A report released by Grunwald Associates in 2010, outlines how open source software can provide cost-effective platforms for the conduct of student assessments. Further research is required however, to build on this work and to provide examples of how these platforms can efficiently be used to the benefit of schools.

Finally, to engage in open source software communities requires a level of technical knowledge. Some argue that the ability to participate in an open source community requires higher technical skills than those required to simply maintain the operation of software. This claim however, ought to be investigated and suitable training programs developed that are aimed specifically at in-school technical officers. Such programs could be used to not only build the knowledge and skills of school based officers but to also afford opportunities for building the confidence within a school to look at a broader set of options for software than that provided through proprietary software.

## CONCLUSION

School leaders create the conditions to enable students' learning, teachers' professional learning, and to establish and maintain management strategies to enable the core business of schools to be delivered. This chapter set out to canvas some of the less considered factors that ought to be taken into account when schools select software applications. To do so, this chapter started from the view that being clear about beliefs and the assumptions that underpin teaching and learning including with technologies and of technology acquisition, enables school leaders to achieve consistency and congruence between the educational goals of their schools and the procurement approaches used. In addition, it has been argued that having congruence between the philosophy and values underpinning teaching and learning and teaching and learning with technologies can be achieved through the use of open source software.

Aligning practices and philosophy concerning the place of technologies in schools however, presents challenges for many school leaders. To address these challenges it has been argued that school principals should understand the contexts within which the hardware, software and services they wish to use in their schools, have been developed. It has further been argued that developing this understanding can assist school leaders to adopt consistent strategies appropriate for deploying software and hardware within their schools.

It has been argued too that software is the artifact of people collaborating either in secret or in public to create that software. Understanding that software is an outcome of social processes can assist school leaders to make informed decisions about which software is suitable for a given school context. That is, understanding how software has been created can inform whether it is the right fit for purpose and can be supported.

The principles that underpin the functioning of the communities that develop open source software can be of benefit to schools. Open source communities are communities of experts and learners who assist each other in the processes of continuous improvement of both the software they are collectively developing, and of the skills of the people involved. As such, open source communities have purposes and functions in relation to the development, deployment and maintenance of software that can be educative in themselves. These models can be easily viewed and lesson can be learnt from them.

This chapter has also outlined some current theories of education and their associated learning approaches, and the models of open source software development. It has been shown that the implementation of key education theories are akin to the software development models used by open source projects. Indeed it has been argued that the models of co-creation used in open source communities provides benefits when applied to technology issues in school education. Underpinning the arguments promoting the educational use of open source software are the values which are consistent between open source software communities and theories underpinning exemplary educational practices about active and inquiry based learning. Such learning activities require young people to work in teams with others in their class and over the Internet. In such circumstances, students are actively engaged in their learning with others.

Finally, in this chapter it has been argued that understanding how open source software project communities work can assist school leaders to gain alignment between their philosophies and practices. This position has been put because when school leaders are weighing up both the options for teaching and learning with technologies, and the strategies for managing the infrastructure of the schools, they should consider open source software solutions in their deliberations. If school leaders adopt this approach then a wider range of highly effective options for learning and administration become available. As such, aligning practice and philosophy opens up options for school leaders and their school communities.

# REFERENCES

Alliance for Excellence Education. (2009). *Fact sheet: High school dropouts in America*. Alliance for Excellence Education. Retrieved 12 February, 2012, from http://www.all4ed.org/files/GraduationRates_FactSheet.pdf

Anderson, J., Galvin, C., Gardner, J., Mitchell, S., Moyle, K., & McMorrough, A. (2011). *Valuing education technology in schools in Ireland: North and South*. Standing Conference on Teacher Education, North and South (SCoTENS)

Apache Software Foundation. (2012). *How the ASF works*. Apache Software Foundation. Retrieved 12 March, 2012, from http://www.apache.org/foundation/how-it-works.html#meritocracy

Apple, M. (2001). *Educating the 'right' way: Markets, standards, God and inequality*. New York, NY: RoutledgeFalmer Press.

Apple, M. (2004). *Ideology and curriculum*. New York, NY: RoutledgeFalmer.

Australian Bureau of Statistics (ABS). (2010). Schools. *Schools, Australia, 2010 - 4221.0*. Retrieved 3 February, 2012, from http://www.abs.gov.au/ausstats/abs@.nsf/lookup/4221.0Main+Features32010?OpenDocument

Australian Bureau of Statistics (ABS). (2011a). Commentary on student numbers. *Schools, Australia, 2011 - 4221.0*. Retrieved 3 February, 2012, from http://www.abs.gov.au/ausstats/abs@.nsf/mf/4221.0

Australian Bureau of Statistics (ABS). (2011b). Main findings. *Household Use of Information Technology, Australia, 2010-11- 8146.0*. Retrieved 3 February, 2012, from http://www.abs.gov.au/ausstats/abs@.nsf/Latestproducts/8146.0Media%20Release12010-11?opendocument&tabname=Summary&prodno=8146.0&issue=2010-11&num=&view=

Australian Government. (2009). *The productivity agenda: Education, skills, training, science and innovation*. Responding to the Australia 2020 Summit. Canberra, Commonwealth of Australia. Retrieved 10 February, 2012, from http://www.australia2020.gov.au/docs/government_response/2020_summit_response_full.pdf

Australian Government, Department of Finance and Deregulation, Australian Government Information Management Office. (2009). *Guide to open source software for Australian Government*. Canberra, Australian Government. Retrieved 10 February, 2012, from http://www.finance.gov.au/publications/guide-to-open-source-software/introduction.html

Balfanz, R., & Legters, N. (2004). *Locating the dropout crisis: Which high schools produce the nation's dropouts? Where are they located? Who attends them?* Baltimore, MD: John Hopkins University Center for Social Organization of Schools.

Beder, S. (2009). *This little kiddy went to market: The corporate capture of childhood*. Sydney, Australia: UNSW Press.

Bessen, J. (2006). Open source software: Free provision of complex public goods. In Bitzer, J., & Schroeder, P. (Eds.), *The economics of open source software development*. Amsterdam, The Netherlands: Elsevier, B.V.

Bond, P. (2004). Communities of practice and complexity: Conversation and culture. *Organisations and People, 11*(4), 1–7.

Bosco, J. (2010). Forward. In Moyle, K. (Ed.), *Building innovation: Learning with technologies, Australia Education Review*. Melbourne, Australia: Australian Council for Educational Research Bruner, J. (1990). Acts of meaning. Cambridge, MA: Harvard University Press.

Bruner, J. (1961). The act of discovery. *Harvard Educational Review, 31*(1), 21–32.

Bruner, J. (1962). *The process of education*. Cambridge, MA: Harvard University Press.

Bruner, J. (1986). *Actual minds, possible worlds*. Cambridge, MA: Harvard University Press.

Catto, B. (2011). *Open source software and the Australian government*. Open Source Developers Conference, Canberra 18th November 2011, Australian Government Information Management Office, Department of Finance and Deregulation. Retrieved 19 February, 2012, from http://agimo.govspace.gov.au/files/2011/12/Open-Source-Software-and-the-Australian-Government-Speech-Transcript.pdf

Centre for Educational Research and Innovation (CERI). (2006). *Personalising education. Organisation for Economic Cooperation and Development*. Paris: OECD.

Childnet International. (2008). *Young people and social networking services: A Childnet International research report*. USA: Childnet. Retrieved 3 February, 2012, from http://www.digizen.org/downloads/fullReport.pdf

Department of Education. Employment and Workplace Relations (DEEWR). (2011). National secondary computer fund. *Digital Education Revolution*, Retrieved 3 February, 2012, from http://www.deewr.gov.au/Schooling/DigitalEducationRevolution/ComputerFund/Pages/NationalSecondarySchoolComputerFundOverview.aspx

Dewey, J. (1916). *Democracy and education. An introduction to the philosophy of education.* Macmillan.

Dewey, J. (1929). *Experience and nature* (2nd ed.). Open Court Publishing Company.

Duncan-Howell, J. (2007). *Online communities of practice and their role in the professional development of teachers.* PhD thesis, Queensland University of Technology.

Elliot, M., & Scacchi, W. (2003). *Free software: A case study of software development in a virtual organizational culture.* ISR Technical Report #UCI-ISR-03-6. Retrieved 12 March, 2012, from http://www.isr.uci.edu/tech_reports/UCI-ISR-03-6.pdf

Faubert, B. (2012). *A literature review of school practices to overcome school failure.* Organisation of Economic and Cultural Development (OECD) Education Working Papers, No. 68, OECD Publishing. Retrieved 15 February, 2012, from http://dx.doi.org/10.1787/5k9flcwwv9tk-en

Garrett, P. (2011). *Digital education revolution transforming Australian classrooms.* Minister's Media Centre, Education, Employment and Workplace Relations portfolio. Retrieved 3 February, 2012, from http://ministers.deewr.gov.au/garrett/digital-education-revolution-transforming-australian-classrooms

Gartner. (2012). *K-12 total cost of ownership tool.* Gartner. Retrieved 15 February, 2012, from http://k12tco.gartner.com/home/default.aspx

Gramsci, A. (1971). *Selections from the prison notebooks.* London, UK: Lawrence and Wishart.

Grunwald., & Associates, L. L. C. (2010). *A platform for Internet-based assessment. A report on Education leaders' perceptions of online testing in an open source environment.* Grunwald and Associates LLC. Retrieved 15 February, 2012, from http://grunwald.com/pdfs/Grunwald_Open_Source_Public_Report_v3.pdf

Hargreaves, D. (1994). *The mosaic of learning: Schools and teachers for the new century.* London, UK: Demos.

Herrington, J., & Oliver, R. (2000). An instructional design framework for authentic learning environments. *Educational Technology Research and Development, 48*(3), 23–48.

Himanen, P. (2001). *The hacker ethic and the spirit of the information age.* Great Britain: Secker & Warburg.

Illich, I. (1971). *Deschooling society.* Retrieved 3 February, 2012, from http://ournature.org/~novembre/illich/1970_deschooling.html

Johnson, L., Adams, S., & Haywood, K. (2011). *The NMC horizon report: 2011 K-12 edition.* Austin, TX: The New Media Consortium.

Johnson, L., Smith, R., Willis, H., Levine, A., & Haywood, K. (2011). *The 2011 horizon report.* Austin, TX: The New Media Consortium.

Joint Information Systems Committee (JISC). (2011). What is open source software. *OSS Watch.* University of Oxford. Retrieved 15 February, 2012, from http://www.oss-watch.ac.uk/resources/softwareexamples.xml

Joint Information Systems Committee (JISC). (2012). Governance models. *OSS Watch.* University of Oxford. Retrieved 12 March, 2012, from http://www.oss-watch.ac.uk/resources/governanceModels.xml

Lifelong Kindergarten. (2012). *Lifelong Kindergarten.* MIT Media Lab, Massachusetts Institute of Technology. Retrieved 29 February, 2012, from http://llk.media.mit.edu/projects.php

Lin, J., Yen, L., Yang, M., & Chen, C. (2005). Teaching computer programming in elementary schools: A pilot study. *National Educational Computing Conference 2005,* Philadelphia. Retrieved 20 February, 2012, from http://www.stagecast.com/pdf/research/Lin_NECC2005_Paper_RP.pdf

Logo Foundation. (2011). *What is Logo?* Logo Foundation. Retrieved 15 February, 2012, from http://el.media.mit.edu/logo-foundation/logo/index.html

Lombardi, M. with Oblinger, D. (Eds.). (2007). *Authentic learning for the 21st century: An overview.* Educause. Retrieved 15 February, 2012, from http://net.educause.edu/ir/library/pdf/ELI3009.pdf

Marginson, S. (1997). *Markets in education.* Sydney, Australia: Allen & Unwin.

Melton, F. (2012). *Open source handbook.* Retrieved 12 March, 2012, from http://www.open-sourcehandbook.com/?s=index

Ministerial Council Education, Early Child Development and Youth Affairs (MCEEDYA). (2008). *Melbourne declaration on educational goals for young Australians.* Melbourne, Australia: Author. Retrieved 15 February, 2012, from http://www.mceecdya.edu.au/verve/_resources/National_Declaration_on_the_Educational_Goals_for_Young_Australians.pdf

Moyle, K. (2003). New secularism: Reorienting the private order of digital technologies. In Reid, A., & Thomson, P. (Eds.), *Rethinking public education: Towards a public curriculum.* Brisbane, Australia: Australian Curriculum Studies Association.

Moyle, K. (2004). *What place does open source software have in Australian and New Zealand schools' and jurisdictions' ICT portfolios? Total cost of ownership and open source software.* Research paper, Canberra, Ministerial Council Education, Early Child Development and Youth Affairs (MCEEDYA). Retrieved 3 February, 2012, from http://www.mceecdya.edu.au/verve/_resources/total_cost_op.pdf

Moyle, K. (2006). *Leadership and learning with ICT: Voices from the profession.* Canberra, Australia: Teaching Australia, Australian Institute for Teaching and School Leadership.

Moyle, K. (2009). *Varying approaches to internet safety: The role of filters in schools.* Washington, DC: CoSN. Retrieved from http://www.cosn.org/Portals/7/docs/Web%202.0/Varying%20Approaches%20to%20Internet%20Safety.pdf

Moyle, K. (2010). *Building innovation, learning with technologies.* Australian Education Review, Australian Council for Educational Research (ACER). Retrieved 3 February, 2012, from http://research.acer.edu.au/aer/10

Nalley, D. (2011). Leadership in open source communities. *Opensource.com.* Retrieved 12 February, 2012, from http://opensource.com/business/11/2/leadership-open-source-communities

National Science Teachers Association (NSTA). (2006). *Report: 1.2 million students fail to graduate high school.* NSTA. Retrieved 12 February, 2012, from http://www.nsta.org/publications/news/story.aspx?id=52205

Newmann, F., Marks, H., & Gamoran, A. (1996). Authentic pedagogy and student performance. *American Journal of Education, 104*, 280–312.

Organisation for Economic Co-operation and Development (OECD). (2009). *Education today: The OECD perspective*. Paris, France: OECD. Retrieved 10 February, 2012, from http://www.oecd-bookshop.org/oecd/get-it.asp?REF=9609021E. PDF&TYPE=browse

Papert, S. (1980). *Mindstorms: Children, computers, and powerful ideas*. Basic Books.

Papert, S. (n.d.). Part 1, teaching vs learning. *Instructionism vs Constructivism*. Retrieved 10 February, 2012, from http://www.papert.org/articles/const_inst/const_inst1.html

Papert, S. (n.d.) Part 5, conclusion. *Instructionism vs Constructivism*. Retrieved 10 February, 2012, from http://www.papert.org/articles/const_inst/const_inst5.html

Papert, S., & Harel, I. (Eds.). (1991). *Constructionism: Research reports and essays 1985–1990. The Epistemology and Learning Research Group, the Media Lab, Massachusetts Institute of Technology*. Norwood, NJ: Ablex Pub. Corp.

Partnership for 21st Century Skills. (2009). *Framework for 21st century learning*. Partnership for 21st Century Skills. Retrieved 10 February, 2012, from http://www.21stcenturyskills.org/index.php?Itemid=120&id=254&option=com_content&task=view

Piaget, J. (1962). *Play, dreams and imitation in childhood*. New York, NY: Norton.

Porter, M., & Schwab, K. (2008). *Global competitiveness report 2008–2009*. Geneva, Switzerland: World Economic Forum. Retrieved 10 February, 2012, from http://www.weforum.org/pdf/GCR08/GCR08.pdf

Project Tomorrow. (2006). K-12 student national findings. *Speak Up Reports*. Project Tomorrow, California. Retrieved 3 February, 2012, from http://www.tomorrow.org/docs/Speak%20Up%202006%20National%20Snapshot_K-12%20Students.pdf

Project Tomorrow. (2009). *Media release, 24 March 2009*. CA: Project Tomorrow. Retrieved 3 February, 2012, from http://www.tomorrow.org/speakup/pdfs/PT%20releaseFINAL.pdf

Project Tomorrow. (2011). *The new 3 E's of education: Enabled, engaged and empowered how today's students are leveraging emerging technologies for learning*. Project Tomorrow, California. Retrieved 3 February, 2012, from http://www.tomorrow.org/speakup/pdfs/SU10_3EofEducation(Students).pdf

Raymond, E. (2001). *The cathedral and the bazaar. Musings on Linux and open source code by an accidental revolutionary* (2nd ed.). O'Reilly.

Resnick, M. (2007). Sowing the seeds for a more creative society. *Learning and Leading with Technology*, (pp. 18–22). International Society for Technology in Education (ISTE). Retrieved 13 February, 2012, from http://web.media.mit.edu/~mres/papers/Learning-Leading-final.pdf

Resnick, M. (2008). *Falling in love with Seymour's ideas*. American Educational Research Association (AERA) Annual Conference. New York, NY: AERA. Retrieved 13 February, 2012, from http://web.media.mit.edu/~mres/papers/AERA-seymour-final.pdf

Stuckart, D. W., & Glanz, J. (2010). *Revisiting Dewey: Best practices for educating the whole child today*. Rowman and Littlefield Publishing Group Tech Analyser. (2011). Open source alternative to commercial software. *Tech Analyser*. Retrieved 18 February, 2012, from http://tech-analyser.blogspot.com.au/2011/10/open-source-alternative-to-commercial.html

The Learning Curve Consortium. (2011). *Home.* The Learning Curve Consortium Worldwide Inc. Retrieved 18 February, 2012, from http://www. thelearningcurve.org/?q=content/complete-cost-effective-elearning-solution

Ubuntu. (2012). About Ubuntu governance. *Ubuntu.* Retrieved 12 March, 2012, from http://www. ubuntu.com/project/about-ubuntu/governance

United Nations Educational, Scientific and Cultural Organization (UNESCO). (2012). *Mobile learning.* UNESCO. Retrieved 12 March, 2012, from http://www.unesco.org/new/en/unesco/ themes/icts/m4ed/

Vockell, E. (1993). Why schools fail and what we can do about it. *Clearing House (Menasha, Wis.)*, *66*(4), 200–205.

Vygotsky, L. S. (1962). *Thought and language.* Cambridge, MA: Massachusetts Institute of Technology Press.

Vygotsky, L. S. (1978). *Mind and society: The development of higher mental processes.* Cambridge, MA: Harvard University Press.

Weber, S. (2004). *The success of open source.* Cambridge, MA: Harvard University Press.

Weiss, S. G., DeFalco, A. A., & Weiss, E. M. (2005). *Progressive = permissive? Not according to John Dewey...Subjects matter!* Retrieved 10 February, 2012, from http://www.usca.edu/ essays/vol142005/defalco.pdf

Wenger, E. (2006). *Communities of practice: A brief introduction.* Retrieved 10 February, 2012, from http://www.ewenger.com/theory/

Young, B. (2001). Forward. In Raymond, E. (Ed.), *The cathedral and the bazaar. Musings on Linux and open source code by an accidental revolutionary* (2nd ed.). O'Reilly.

# Chapter 17
# Selectively Employing Open-Source Resources for Online Learning

**Shalin Hai-Jew**
*Kansas State University, USA*

## ABSTRACT

*Those who work in instructional technologies and design have long been turning to the usages of open-source resources (learning/course management systems, software tools and apps, authoring tools, digital learning objects, simulations, games, and virtual spaces) for online learning—for many reasons—their easy availability (through download), the often-free price-tag, the popularity of open-source resources among learners, and the savings in terms of development (not maintenance) costs. This chapter examines the selective adoption of open-source resources for online learning and the practical considerations that inform this decision.*

## INTRODUCTION

*Under certain technological circumstances, practically feasible opportunities for action are distributed in such a pattern that they are amenable to execution by a class of approaches to organizing production that rely on sharing. These are typified by (1) radical decentralization of the capacity to contribute to effective action and the authority to decide on the contribution and (2) reliance on social information flows, organizational approaches, and motivation structures, rather than on prices or commands, to motivate and direct productive contributions. - Yochai Benkler (2004, p. 331)*

Institutions of higher education have benefited from the idealistic streak in Web 2.0 that has enabled widespread open-source sharing of digital contents. Human goodwill and ingenuity have enabled the creation of a number of open-source and generally free resources based on what J.L. Zittrain calls the "generative Internet" (2006). While open-source software creation has existed for decades and had powerful proponents, and Open Courseware (OCW) and Open Educational Resources (OER) movements have also had well-known individuals promoting their success, open-source contents have simply been elicited through the creation of various socio-technical

DOI: 10.4018/978-1-4666-2205-0.ch017

spaces. These spaces have enabled peer-to-peer sharing (of images, audio, video, slideshows, games, code modifications, and other digital elements); the easy downloading of open-source software tested for malware; the structural open-sources software for knowledge management; the crowd-sourcing to know the popularity and validity of certain open-source software; and the enablement of virtual communities to coalesce around certain digital tools and resources.

While open-source software, on the surface, may seem like an easy choice, those in the field have advised paying attention to the hidden costs of the adoption of some open-source tools. The integration of open-source tools in mission-critical endeavors at a university or college may be an issue of concern unless a software has been thoroughly vetted. Such software could include learning / course management systems; digital repositories, and knowledge management software. The risks of open-adoption may be of many sorts: investment, development, coordination, motivation, control, security, governance, and culture risk (Arakji & Lang, 2007, 37 – 38). The shape and manifestation of the risk will vary depending on the institution of higher education, the context, and the technologies. This chapter explores the adoption of open-source resources for online learning and the practical considerations that may go into this decision.

## BACKGROUND

Commercial and proprietary corporations have gone to open-source resources as a "commercial engineering force-multiplier and important option for avoiding significant software development costs" (Hubbard, 2004, p. 25). In recent years, research has found that K-12 institutions are responding to open-source digital resources, with cost-savings as a central motivation (Waters, 2010). In higher education, too, the adoption of open-source resources for teaching and learning

has been gaining traction, particularly over the past three years (van Rooij, 2011). While it is said that the ideological positioning of an organization affects whether it adopts open-source software (Ven & Verelst, 2008), many are finding the use of open-source resources strategic and practical, with saving on software licensing fees and learning object development costs.

## The Many Cultures of Higher Education

Higher education accommodates a range of diverse cultures as it integrates a variety of diverse fields and thinkers from around the world. While it requires core knowledge that are necessary for global citizenship, it also enables high levels of specialization particularly at the graduate levels. The learning is not just about helping the learners find meaningful and rewarding lifelong work but about developing them as fully actualized human beings who are sufficiently confident to explore their world (think study abroad programs) and contribute to it. The focus of higher education is to share learning and to include diverse voices and variant points-of-view. A strong streak of altruism may be found in higher education—with plenty of mentored service learning endeavors. Open-source contributions by learners are many, and many maintain the liberal assumption of peer-to-peer sharing in the exchanges of digital resources. Learners have taken readily to using open-source resources.

For administrators, the authorizing environment may be somewhat more constrained. Any system-level adoption of mission critical technologies has to support the school's policies or rules of engagement. Any adopted technologies have to be secure and ensure learner privacy. Technologies have to support intellectual property rights. They have to provide accessibility mitigations to be inclusive of various learners. They have to interact well with other technological systems. They have to function effectively on the equipment substructure. Budget-wise, such technologies have to evaluated for the total cost of ownership because schools have to consider the requisite technical expertise, the trainings, the costs of moving data, transition costs (if a solution does not work), the many dependencies in a technology system, and the other changes that are required to make a larger system work. With the options of outsourcing certain functionalities, going to the cloud, or partnerships, many universities and colleges are finding that in-house tool creations are more expensive and less efficient than other options. Top-down decision-making is critical for enterprise and system-wide opens-source adoptions, and these decisions are highly informed by the relevant technologists on campus (and / or advising the campus).

Gallego, Luna, and Bueno (2008) suggest that potential users have an important input in the open-source technology adoption decision. The software quality, system capabilities, social influence, and software flexibility all affect the perceived usefulness and perceived ease-of-use of the resource—which affects both the intention to use and usage behaviors. These authors conducted research using a questionnaire to create a path diagram (a relational diagram showing relationships between entities, represented as circles or nodes) of the various interaction effects of such impressions on open-source adoption. The researchers designed part of their research based on the Technology Acceptance Model (TAM) (Davis, 1989).

In a study of the motivational factors affecting individual adoption of open-source software, some researchers found that amotivation affects non-adopters of open-source technologies; further, "identified regulation" is the major extrinsic motivation affecting adoption for adopters. Lastly, they found that "intrinsic motivation to accomplish and capacity beliefs amotivation do not significantly affect adoption extent and adoption intention respectively" (Li, Tan, Xu, & Teo, 2011, p. 76), which suggests structural factors external to decision-makers about open-source software may have an outsized impact on open-source technology adoptions.

At college, department, program, and individual levels, the adoption of open-source resources often involves smaller or simpler integrations. These decisions are based on their own subcultures, leadership considerations and choices, and social-based enthusiasms. These localized adoptions may include the uses of open-source software for wikis or blogs or knowledge management systems, learning objects, hosted solutions on other sites, learning / course management systems (L/CMSes), software packages, and other resources. The makers of open-source digital resources strive to offer strings-free usage, and the flexibility of no long-term commitments (except structural ones and the costs of making a change) makes open-source an attractive option.

Research into technological adoption and diffusion points to the "absorptive capacity" of an organization to assimilate new information for productivity gains and innovations. The capability for organizational learning depends in part on the institution's prior knowledge, diversity of backgrounds, potential for absorptive capacity, and then its actual realized absorptive capacity (to translate the learning into actual production). Every university or college has its own political ecosystem that allows for innovation or which squelches it.

For organizations considering adoption of open-source resources, there are a number of adoption barriers: knowledge barriers, legacy integration (to technology systems), "forking" (a lack of interoperability between open-source software and other applications), sunk costs or prior investments in proprietary software, and technological immaturity in open-source products (resulting, for example, in less user support oftentimes than for some proprietary products) (Nagy, Yassin, & Bhattacherjee, 2010, p. 149). Such challenges require workplace efforts at mitigating these barriers.

Finally, each institution has its own unique mix of top-down or bottom-up adoptions of open-source software, resources, and contents based on the various subcultures, leadership, technological capabilities, and learners and stakeholders. Using open-source resources is the most common participation method in virtual open-source communities. Moving deeper into the heart of the open-source community, though, requires complex skill sets.

## Joining the Larger Open-Source Community

At the most common user level, users use the resources in an unengaged or passive way. A more engaging level of interaction may involve contributing funds to an open-source endeavor. Many remain virtually anonymous to the open-source community. A higher level of user engagement involves providing feedback about the resource to improve the product. Such users may make comments about the functionality. They may have suggestions for the user interface.

In an "onion" diagram (circles within circles) representing the distributed social structure of a general open source software development project, the distributed organization begins with an outer ring of Passive Users and Observers, Active Users, then Developers, Project Managers, Community Managers, and Core Developers (Jensen & Scacchi, 2007). Such structures tend to be meritocracies based on what each of the members will contribute to the larger whole. The open-source community leaders support, encourage, and enable the participation of various members in different roles based on their expressed interests and skill sets. There may be calls for certain roles—in quality assurance, code development, project community management, software testing, code documentation, marketing, website maintenance, and others. Role migrations occur through consensus among group members for the advancement of others. Many such organizations use technology tracking to see what various members have contributed.

While volunteering is generally open, getting into the governance structure usually is done through an earned rank or appointment. There is variance in organizational structure depending on the large-scale software project, but a common sequence has been end user, developer, committee, and then administrative hierarchy.

For those working in higher education, the cost-benefit equation about having staff members participate in open-source communities often depends on pragmatics: What can the institution of higher education gain from this participation? Will the staff member acquire new skills and maintain current ones? Will the school benefit from the investment in the open-source resource? Will the word-of-mouth from the school's participation benefit its brand identity and broader reputation? (Such questions focus on an enterprise-level adoption vs. piecemeal uses of stand-alone digital learning objects.)

## Quality Concerns

Often, the state-of-the-art is defined by commercial practitioners in the field. Open-source volunteer development may result in some types of pathologies. Some pathologies (resource limitations, developer perspectives, working methods and sequences, focuses on software functionality over usability) in open-source development circles may result in poorer software usability, excess complexity, and feature bloat (Nichols & Twidale, 2002). As challenges with open-source software came to the fore, there have been various endeavors to mitigate these challenges. New software application frameworks have built-in tools for security oversight and formatting consistency. To address some of the collective action challenges, there are more tools to incentivize individual and group contributions with certain extrinsic rewards.

Many early open-source codes lacked usability expertise, which meant a difficult user experience. Bach, DeLine, and Carroll (2009) have resorted to making an open call for designers to enhance the user interface design for open-source software products and have proposed a basic process to consider user interface design issues. According to the research literature, many open-source projects also lacked sufficient annotation of the task and codes—which are necessary for both future work and institutional memory.

Another concern relates to the security of open-source software. While E.S. Raymond, author of "The Cathedral and the Bazaar," famously observed that the more eyes there are on a code, the more "shallow" the bugs are, many have still expressed concerns over open-source software's vulnerabilities (Rice, 2008). Others suggest that while more may be aware of software bugs, open-source projects may be patched in a slower way than for proprietary software products.

An empirical study examined the contrasts between the patching (update) behavior of both proprietary and open-source vendors and the severity of un-patched vulnerabilities for both groups. Significantly, they found no significant difference between the entities: "The empirical results have shown that open source and closed source software do not significantly differ in terms of the severity of vulnerabilities, the type of development of vulnerability disclosure over time, and vendors' patching behavior" (Schryen, 2011, p. 140). The author found that the policies of the particular vendors affected patching behaviors.

Other challenges have been the potential threats of the disappearance of the resource or its morphing into a different form. In the same way that businesses have a fairly high failure rate (said to be 80% in five years), whether a product is firm-based or part of an open-source social production model, there is always some risk of product discontinuance and a requirement to protect data and other investments into that technology. The long-term sustainability and viability of some open-source projects depend on the size of the installed base of users and of funders (whether corporate, private, individual, or other).

## MAIN FOCUS OF THE CHAPTER

To over-generalize and simplify the types of open-source resources available for online learning, one may generalize to three different types of open-source resources: structural, tool, and content-based resources.

1.  "Structural" resources may be a learning/course management system (L/CMS), a wiki, a blog, a repository, or a referatory. These host contents. They ingest information and deliver the data back out to users through a Web interface. These may be used as collaborative work spaces. They may be used to structure and represent information in knowledge spaces. These provide a user interface with back-end functionalities.

2.  "Tool" resources provide various types of functionalities. Microblogs offer real-time sharing of short text messaging. Mobile applications help learners have real-time space and location awareness. Other tools help collate information from the Web. Some provide audio or video editing. Others are authoring tools that enable the creation of 3D or 2D images. Some are open-source communications tools that offer free voice over IP; other tools offer multi-channel communications for web conferencing. Others offer data storage in the cloud. Others offer automated translation services. Others are web browsers. Others aid in the maintenance of computer systems. Essentially, various open-source Web tools provide different functionalities.

3.  Open-source "content" resources vary widely. Many have only broad and general tie-ins to higher education—such as unclassified images, audio snippets, slideshows, and videos—linked to peer-to-peer sharing sites. Others that are more closely designed to be actual digital learning objects offer a

patchwork of resources, with some objects that are stand-alone and others that offer a sequence of learning (like open courseware) or at least a more immersive learning experience.

What considerations go into whether an open-source resource is adopted for online learning in higher education? Table 1 offers insights to some of the on-ground considerations. These are phrased from a point-of-view of an individual because oftentimes these decisions are made by the subject matter expert (SME) or faculty member. However, these ideas apply as easily to committees that are in a position to make such decisions.

## Solutions and Recommendations

While the potential market for open-source resources in higher education is still in its infancy, it may not be too early to make some tentative suggestions.

## A Catalog of Resources

If there is truly to be cost-savings from the development of open-source resources, there have to be smoother mechanisms to help professionals be aware of what open-source resources exist—so that the proverbial wheel is not reinvented. Further, there should be greater efficiencies for the sharing of learning objects between institutions of higher education—without the traditionalist protectionism around learning materials. While there are referatories and patchworks of federated schools sharing open educational resources, a comprehensive clearinghouse of such resources would be helpful. So much information and so many resources are still in the wild, in uncatalogued spaces.

## Digital Learning Object (DLO) Design Standards

Standards for the development of digital learning objects need to be better defined. Currently, there are many different types of solutions possible to engineer a learning object with defined learning objectives. It may be helpful to have more models for what these learning objects may look like and even the development of templates for different learning needs. Technological standards, too, are constantly evolving, and having a clear and up-to-date definition would be helpful. This is not to squelch creativity or innovation but to ensure basic quality standards of such digital learning objects.

## Funding and Support; Practical Alliances

Grants that help schools collaborate around creating open-source digital learning objects seem rare. Further, many such objects are created as a byproduct of extant courses and curriculums, and many are dating out. If more solid sequences of learning may be created professionally, tested for efficacy, and supported, the open-source realm for online learning in higher education may progress more methodically and effectively. Further, if there may be more formal partnerships between various partnership institutions—where such alliances make interdisciplinary sense—this could also further enhance an open-source approach.

Finally, a number of online resources are open-access, which enhance the findability and discoverability of many sources, but these are not open-source resources with generous copyright releases. Oftentimes, open-access learning sequences are free for informal and non-formal learning but involve a cost if tutoring or formal crediting is involved. This area may be fruitful to explore for possibilities of releasing some of the contents into the open-source realm to extend the usability of the resources for many others.

*Table 1. Adoptability considerations in considering open-source resources for online learning in higher education*

| Issue for Consideration | Practical Questions |
| --- | --- |
| **No Strings Attached** | Are there any commitments to using this open-source resource? Will I have to give away information? Will I have to accept advertising? Will I have to compromise my privacy? Will I have to renew my membership or get permissions annually or over a regular period of time? Will adoption of a learning resource lead to other future commitments to that resource or to follow-on resources that may be undesirable or expensive? |
| **Informational Value** | Is the information (or code) up-to-date and valid? Is the resource original or derivative? (Are there substitutes for this resource? What do the competing resources look like?) Is the information aligned with the extant paradigms in the field? Is there sufficient nuance to accurately represent the contents? |
| **Pedagogical Neutrality** | Do the resources offer pedagogical neutrality or a wide degree of freedom for adopting faculty and subject matter experts (SMEs) to apply their own approaches and understandings and conceptual models? |
| **A Part or a Whole / Sufficiency or Insufficiency or Excess** | Will I have to accept more than the portion that I need? Or on the contrary, is there sufficient mass of information and learning experiences to justify adoption of the early parts of a curriculum? |
| **Editability for Localization and Customization (Access to Raw and / or Base Files)** | Will I have access to the raw and editable underlying files to a learning object? If I don't, will I be able to build a curricular context around the adopted materials to mitigate the contents? Will I be able to localize and customize the learning? Are the resources updatable to the future? (Local control is critical in online learning—for branding but also for academic freedoms.) |
| **The Time Factor** | Will the open-source resource be transient or permanent at least into the near-term? |
| **Cost Factors** | What are hidden costs to using this resource? Will we need local technological expertise? Will we need server space? Will we need development work? What are continuing costs into the future? Will this resource go obsolete in the near-future and require some future-proofing work? What are the expected costs to adopt the open-source resource, and if needed, what are the expected costs of porting resources away from the open-source resource? Is this resource going to be a productivity enhancement, or will be an expensive endeavor? |
| **Stability** | Is the resource sufficiently stable into the near-term? If it is hosted, is it hosted with a stable digital object identifier (DOI)? Is the sponsoring organization or company or university / college sufficiently reputable to protect its resources? |
| **Social Adoptability** | How well will the targeted learners accept this resource? What is the anticipated learning curve for understanding and using this resource? How well will technical and non-technical users use this resource? How much documentation is there for supporting users? What sorts of helpdesk support is available from the makers of the open-source resource? |
| **Source Credibility** | How credible is the source? Does the source have political or other motives that may taint the open-source resources for online learning? Are there potential implied partnerships that the university or college should avoid? Is there any question about the credibility of the subject matter expertise behind the learning objects? |
| **Clean and Legal Builds (with appropriate open-source licensing)** | Is the resource clean in terms of intellectual property? Are all rights appropriately represented, and are all copyright laws followed? Is the proper open-source licensing applied? |
| **Accessibility** | Is the work accessible, according to applicable laws and policies? Is the work machine-readable? |
| **Accurate Metadata** | Do the learning resources have sufficient documentation of their provenance and origins? Is there clear provenance of the source? (If images are used, it is clear under what conditions those images were taken? In what location? Is what is depicted accurately labeled?) |
| **Technological Interoperability** | Do the resources interoperate on the various systems that it may be housed in—such as L/CMSes, repositories, and websites? |
| **The Political Context** | Will the resources be will well used in the local political context? |

## FUTURE RESEARCH DIRECTIONS

Research into the uses of open-source resources in online learning in higher education may shed light on other considerations than the ones mentioned here. Particularly, research may be done on technologist concerns with open-source adoptions. Those who would design open-source digital learning objects would benefit from explorations of how to design for the greatest versatility. Researchers may offer case studies in their open-source adoption experiences or their partnerships in creating open-source resources. Researchers may explore methods for assimilating and localizing adopted open-source technologies into learning situations. It may help to have a thorough categorization and cataloguing of open-source resources for online learning. And finally, for developers of open-source contents, it would help to know how to design socio-technical spaces that are more effective for the co-development of digital learning objects and technologies.

## CONCLUSION

This chapter has shown that there are a range of considerations for the adoption of open-source resources to support online learning in higher education. This early work suggests certain design approaches for the creation of open-source technologies, tools, and digital learning objects, to make them useful for others.

## REFERENCES

Arakji, R. Y., & Lang, K. R. (2007). The virtual cathedral and the virtual bazaar. *The Data Base for Advances in Information Systems, 38*(4), 32–39. doi:10.1145/1314234.1314242

Bach, P. M., DeLine, R., & Carroll, J. M. (2009). Designers wanted: Participation and the user experience in open source software development. In the *Proceedings of CHI 2009: Software Developers and Programmers* (pp. 985– 994). Boston, MA: Association of Computing Machines.

Benkler, Y. (2004). Sharing nicely: On shareable goods and the emergence of sharing as a modality of economic production. *The Yale Law Journal, 114*(2), 273–358. doi:10.2307/4135731

Gallego, M. D., Luna, P., & Bueno, S. (2008). User acceptance model of open source software. *Computers in Human Behavior, 24*, 2199–2216. doi:10.1016/j.chb.2007.10.006

Hubbard, J. (2004). *Open source to the core* (pp. 25 – 31). Retrieved from www.acmqueue.com

Jensen, C., & Scacchi, W. (2007). Role migration and advancement processes in OSSD projects: A comparative case study. In the *Proceedings of the 29th International Conference on Software Engineering*.

Li, Y., Tan, C.-H., Xu, H., & Teo, H.-H. (2011). Open source software adoption: Motivations of adopters and amotivations of non-adopters. *The Data Base for Advances in Information Systems, 42*(2), 76–94. doi:10.1145/1989098.1989103

Nagy, D., Yassin, A. M., & Bhattacherjee, A. (2010). Organizational adoption of open source software: Barriers and remedies. *Communications of the ACM, 53*(3), 148–151. doi:10.1145/1666420.1666457

Nichols, D. M., & Twidale, M. B. (2002). *Usability and open source software*. The University of Waikato, Department of Computer Science, Working Paper Series. ISSN 1170-487X

Nichols, D. M., & Twidale, M. B. (2006). *Usability processes in open source projects* (pp. 1–20). Wiley Online Library.

Rice, D. (2008). *Geekonomics: The real cost of insecure software*. Boston, MA: Pearson Education.

Schryen, G. (2011). Is open source security a myth? What does vulnerability and patch data say? *Communications of the ACM, 54*(5), 130–140. doi:10.1145/1941487.1941516

van Rooij, S. W. (2011). Higher education sub-cultures and open source adoption. *Computers & Education, 57*, 1171–1183. doi:10.1016/j.compedu.2011.01.006

Ven, K., & Verelst, J. (2008). The impact of ideology on the organizational adoption of open source software. *Journal of Database Management, 19*(2), 58–72. doi:10.4018/jdm.2008040103

Waters, J. K. (2010). Prepare for impact. *T.H.E. Journal, 37*(5), 20–25.

Zittrain, J. L. (2006). The generative Internet. *Harvard Law Review, 119*(7), 1974–2040.

## KEY TERMS AND DEFINITIONS

**Accessibility:** The state of being versioned in multiple ways so as to be usable by people with visual acuity, auditory acuity, symbolic processing, or other challenges.

**Adoption:** To take on or assume.

**Culture:** A system of shared values and practices.

**Dependency:** A requirement.

**Downloadable:** Able to be transferred or copied from a website and onto a computer.

**Freeware:** Software distributed without cost.

**Generative:** Producing, creating.

**Legacy System or Code:** A technological system inherited from the past.

**Licensure:** The act of granting under license or legal contract.

**Online Learning:** Distance learning.

**Open-Source:** Released into the public domain with defined usages through licensure.

**Patching:** The act of sending out an update on an existing software to correct errors and to protect against security incursions by malware.

**Path Diagram:** A 2D visual representation of relationships between entities (represented as nodes).

**Proprietary:** Controlled as an (intellectual) property.

**Provenance:** Origins; a place of origin.

**Role Migration:** The changing of roles within a particular community.

**Sub-Culture:** A system of shared values and practices among a particular group within a society.

**Technology Acceptance Model (TAM):** An information systems theory that suggests that technology is or is not accepted based on perceived usefulness and ease-of-use.

**Usability:** The capability of being used.

**User Interface Design:** A designed input and interactive surface for people to interact with a computer.

**Vendor:** A commercial company that sells a particular product.

**Versioning:** The outputting of various forms of a digital learning object for different learning contexts or target learners.

**Virtual Team:** A geographically distributed group of individuals who are collaborating around a particular shared work or development endeavor.

# Compilation of References

Abelson, H. (2005). *6.001 structure and interpretation of computer programs, Spring 2005 - Video lectures.* Retrieved April 17, 2012, from http://ocw.mit.edu/courses/electrical-engineering-and-computer-science/6-001-structure-and-interpretation-of-computer-programs-spring-2005/video-lectures/

Abelson, H. (2007). The creation of OpenCourseWare at MIT. *Journal of Science Education and Technology, 17*(2).

Abelson, H. (2007, May). The creation of OpenCourse-Ware at MIT. *Journal of Science Education and Technology, 17*(2), 164–174. doi:10.1007/s10956-007-9060-8

Ackerman, B., & Zellner, K. S. (2012). *Integrating external open courseware into degreed programs: Assessing costs, benefits, and strategies.* Washington, DC: University Leadership Council, Education Advisory Board.

Adler, B. T., & Alfaro, L. (2006). *A content-driven reputation system for the Wikipedia.* Technical Report ucsc-crl-06-18, School of Engineering, University of California, Santa Cruz, 2006. Retrieved from http://works.bepress.com/luca_de_alfaro/3

Adler, P. S., & Kwon, S. (2002). Social capital: Prospects for a new concept. *Academy of Management Review, 27*, 17–40.

Alliance for Excellence Education. (2009). *Fact sheet: High school dropouts in America.* Alliance for Excellence Education. Retrieved 12 February, 2012, from http://www.all4ed.org/files/GraduationRates_FactSheet.pdf

American Council on the Teaching of Foreign Languages. (2012). *ACTFL proficiency guidelines -- Speaking.* Alexandria, VA: Author.

Anders, B. A., Briggs, D. J., Hai-Jew, S., Caby, Z., & Werick, M. (2011). Creating an online global health course and game. *Educause Quarterly.* Retrieved from http://www.educause.edu/EDUCAUSE+Quarterly/EDUCAUSEQuarterlyMagazineVolum/CreatinganOnlineGlobalHealthCo/242682

Anderson, J., Galvin, C., Gardner, J., Mitchell, S., Moyle, K., & McMorrough, A. (2011). *Valuing education technology in schools in Ireland: North and South.* Standing Conference on Teacher Education, North and South (SCoTENS)

Anderson, R., Anderson, R., & Simon, B. (2004). Experiences with a tablet PC based lecture presentation system in computer science courses. *SIGCSE '04 Proceedings of the 35th SIGCSE Technical Symposium on Computer Science Education.*

Anderson, C. (2009). *Free: The future of a radical price.* New York, NY: HarperCollins.

Anderson, E., & Dongbin, K. (2006). Increasing the success of minority students in science and technology. In *The unfinished agenda: Ensuring success for students of color, Mo. 4.* Washington, DC: American Council on Education.

Andreev, P., Feller, J., Finnegan, P., & Moretz, J. (2010). *Conceptualizing the commons-based peer production of software: An activity theoretic analysis.*

Angelsen, A. (1993). *Individual choice under uncertainty.* Working paper. Bergen, Norway: Chr. Michelsen Institute: Development Studies and Human Rights.

Antelman, K. (2004). Do open-access articles have a greater research impact? *College & Research Libraries, 65*(5), 372 – 382. Retrieved September 9, 2011, from http://crl.acrl.org/content/65/5/372

Apache Software Foundation. (2011). *OpenOffice: The free and open productivity suite.* Retrieved from http://www.openoffice.org/

Apache Software Foundation. (2012). *How the ASF works.* Apache Software Foundation. Retrieved 12 March, 2012, from http://www.apache.org/foundation/how-it-works.html#meritocracy

Apple, M. (2001). *Educating the 'right' way: Markets, standards, God and inequality.* New York, NY: RoutledgeFalmer Press.

Apple, M. (2004). *Ideology and curriculum.* New York, NY: RoutledgeFalmer.

Arakji, R. Y., & Lang, K. R. (2007). The virtual cathedral and the virtual bazaar. *The Data Base for Advances in Information Systems, 38*(4), 32–39. doi:10.1145/1314234.1314242

Arturo, R., & Rupert, E. (2006). *Odeo* [software]. New York, NY: Sonic Mountain.

Asay, M. (2007, October 2). *Why choose proprietary software over open source? Survey says!* Retrieved from http://news.cnet.com/8301-13505_3-9789275-16.html

Attwood, R. (2009, September 24). Get it out in the open. *Times Higher Education.* Retrieved April 17, 2012, from http://www.timeshighereducation.co.uk/story.asp?storycode=408300

Augar, N., Raitman, R., & Zhou, W. (2004). Teaching and learning online with wikis. In R. Atkinson, C. McBeath, D. Jonas-Dwyer, & R. Phillips (Eds.), *Beyond the Comfort Zone: Proceedings of the 21st ASCILITE Conference* (pp. 95-104). Perth, 5-8 December. Retrieved from http://www.ascilite.org.au/conferences/perth04/procs/augar.html

Auguste, B. G., Cota, A., Jayaram, K., & Laboissière, M. (2010). *Winning by degrees: The strategies of highly productive higher-education institutions.* Washington, DC: McKinsey and Company.

Australian Bureau of Statistics (ABS). (2010). Schools. *Schools, Australia, 2010 - 4221.0.* Retrieved 3 February, 2012, from http://www.abs.gov.au/ausstats/abs@.nsf/lookup/4221.0Main+Features32010?OpenDocument

Australian Bureau of Statistics (ABS). (2011). Commentary on student numbers. *Schools, Australia, 2011 - 4221.0.* Retrieved 3 February, 2012, from http://www.abs.gov.au/ausstats/abs@.nsf/mf/4221.0

Australian Bureau of Statistics (ABS). (2011). Main findings. *Household Use of Information Technology, Australia, 2010-11- 8146.0.* Retrieved 3 February, 2012, from http://www.abs.gov.au/ausstats/abs@.nsf/Latestproducts/8146.0Media%20Release12010-11?opendocument&tabname=Summary&prodno=8146.0&issue=2010-11&num=&view=

Australian Government, Department of Finance and Deregulation, Australian Government Information Management Office. (2009). *Guide to open source software for Australian Government.* Canberra, Australian Government. Retrieved 10 February, 2012, from http://www.finance.gov.au/publications/guide-to-open-source-software/introduction.html

Australian Government. (2009). *The productivity agenda: Education, skills, training, science and innovation.* Responding to the Australia 2020 Summit. Canberra, Commonwealth of Australia. Retrieved 10 February, 2012, from http://www.australia2020.gov.au/docs/government_response/2020_summit_response_full.pdf

Aydin, C., & Tirkes, G. (2010). Open source learning management systems in e-learning and Moodle. *IEEE EDUCON Education Engineering 2010 – The Future of Global Learning Engineering Education* (pp. 593- 600).

Bach, P. M., DeLine, R., & Carroll, J. M. (2009). Designers wanted: Participation and the user experience in open source software development. In the *Proceedings of CHI 2009: Software Developers and Programmers* (pp. 985–994). Boston, MA: Association of Computing Machines.

Baecker, R., Wolf, P., & Rankin, k. (2004). The ePresence interactive webcasting and archiving system: Technology overview and current research issues. *Proceedings of World Conference on E-Learning in Corporate, Government, Healthcare, and Higher Education 2004* (pp. 2532-2537). Washington, DC: World Conference on E-Learning in Corporate, Government, Healthcare, and Higher Education (ELEARN) 2004.

Baker, C. (2008, March 24). Trying to design a truly entertaining game can defeat even a certified genius. *Wired Magazine*. Retrieved April 13, 2012, from http://www.wired.com/gaming/gamingreviews/magazine/16-04/pl_games

Baldwin, C. Y., & Clark, K. B. (2006). The architecture of participation: Does code architecture mitigate free riding in the open source development model? *Management Science, 52*(7), 1116–1127. doi:10.1287/mnsc.1060.0546

Balfanz, R., & Legters, N. (2004). *Locating the dropout crisis: Which high schools produce the nation's dropouts? Where are they located? Who attends them?* Baltimore, MD: John Hopkins University Center for Social Organization of Schools.

Ball, D. L. (1990). The mathematical understandings that prospective teachers bring to teacher education. *The Elementary School Journal, 90*(4), 449–466. doi:10.1086/461626

Bates, T. (2001). *National strategies for e-learning in post-secondary education and training.* Paris, France: UNESCO, IIEP.

Bates, T. (2008). Transforming distance education through new technologies. In Evans, T., Haughey, M., & Murphy, D. (Eds.), *International handbook of distance education.* Emerald.

Beauvois, M. (1998). Conversations in slow motion: Computer-mediated communication in the foreign language classroom. *Canadian Modern Language Review, 54*(2), 198–217. doi:10.3138/cmlr.54.2.198

Becker, D. (2003). *India leader advocates open source.* Retrieved from http://news.cnet.com/India-leader-advocates-open-source/2100-1016_3-1011255.html

Beder, S. (2009). *This little kiddy went to market: The corporate capture of childhood.* Sydney, Australia: UNSW Press.

Beepa. (2012). *FRAPS show fps, record video game movies, screen capture software.* Fraps: Real-time video capture & benchmarking. Retrieved from http://www.fraps.com/

Belotto, A. J. (2004). The Pan American Health Organization (PAHO) role in the control of rabies in Latin America. [Review]. *Developments in biologicals, 119*, 213–216.

Belotto, A., Leanes, L. F., Schneider, M. C., Tamayo, H., & Correa, E. (2005). Overview of rabies in the Americas. [Review]. *Virus Research, 111*(1), 5–12. doi:10.1016/j.virusres.2005.03.006

Ben-Ari, M., Berglund, A., Booth, S., & Holmboe, C. (2004). What do we mean by theoretically sound research in computer science education? *Proceedings of the 9th Annual SIGCSE Conference on Innovation and Technology in Computer Science Education* (pp. 230-231). Leeds, UK: ACM.

Benkler, Y. (2004). Sharing nicely: On shareable goods and the emergence of sharing as a modality of economic production. *The Yale Law Journal, 114*(2), 273–358. doi:10.2307/4135731

Benkler, Y., & Nissenbaum, H. (2006). Commons based peer production and virtue. *Journal of Political Philosophy, 14*(4), 394–419. doi:10.1111/j.1467-9760.2006.00235.x

Bergquist, W., & Pawlak, K. (2007). *Engaging the six cultures of the academy.* San Francisco, CA: Jossey-Bass.

*Berlin Declaration on Open Access to Knowledge in the Sciences and Humanities.* (2003). Retrieved from http://oa.mpg.de/openaccess-berlin/berlindeclaration.html

Berners-Lee, T. J. (1992). The world-wide web. *Computer Networks and ISDN Systems, 25*(4-5), 454–459. doi:10.1016/0169-7552(92)90039-S

Bessen, J. (2005). *Open source software: Free provision of a complex public good.* Retrieved July 22, 2011, from http://www.researchoninnovation.org/opensrc.pdf

Bessen, J. (2006). Open source software: Free provision of complex public goods. In Bitzer, J., & Schroeder, P. (Eds.), *The economics of open source software development*. Amsterdam, The Netherlands: Elsevier, B.V.

Bias, R. (1991). Interface-walkthroughs: Efficient collaborative testing. *IEEE Software*, (n.d.), 94–95. doi:10.1109/52.84220

Bishop, T. (2004, January 26). *Microsoft Notebook: Wiki pioneer planted the seed and watched it grow*. Retrieved from http://www.seattlepi.com/business/158020_msft-notebook26.html

Black, E. (2008). Wikipedia and academic peer review: Wikipedia as a recognised medium for scholarly publication? *Online Information Review*, *32*(1), 73–88. doi:10.1108/14684520810865994

Black, P., Delaney, H., & Fitzgerald, B. (2007). Legal issues for wikis: The challenge of user-generated and peer-produced knowledge Content and Culture. *European Law Journal*, *14*, 245–282.

Blender Foundation. (2012). *Blender.org home*. Retrieved April 17, 2012, from http://www.blender.org

Bonaccorsi, A., & Rossi Lamastra, C. (2003). Why open source software can succeed. *Research Policy*, *32*(7), 1243–1258. doi:10.1016/S0048-7333(03)00051-9

Bond, P. (2004). Communities of practice and complexity: Conversation and culture. *Organisations and People*, *11*(4), 1–7.

Bonk, C. (2011, September 28). *Stretching the edges of technology-enhanced teaching: From tinkering to tottering to totally extreme learning*. The 6th Annual Axio Learning Community Conference: Innovations in Education & Technology Conference 2011. Kansas State University.

Boranić, M. (1979). Silent information. *Journal of Medical Ethics*, *5*, 80–82. doi:10.1136/jme.5.2.80

Bosco, J. (2010). Forward. In Moyle, K. (Ed.), *Building innovation: Learning with technologies, Australia Education Review*. Melbourne, Australia: Australian Council for Educational Research Bruner, J. (1990). Acts of meaning. Cambridge, MA: Harvard University Press.

Bowan, M. D. (2002). Learning disabilities, dyslexia, and vision: A rebuttal, literature review, and commentary. *Optometry (St. Louis, Mo.)*, *73*(9), 553–575.

Boyd, D., & Ellison, N. (2007). Social network sites: Definition, history, and scholarship. *Journal of Computer-Mediated Communication*, *13*(11).

Bretthauer, D. (2002). Open source software: A history. *Information Technology and Libraries*, *21*(1), 3–11.

Brooks, F. P. (1995). *The mythical man-month: Essays on software engineering, anniversary edition* (2nd ed.). Boston, MA: Addison-Wesley Professional.

Brown, H. D. (2007). *Principles of language learning and teaching* (5th ed.). Englewood Cliffs, NJ: Prentice Hall Regents, Buttaro, L. (2009). Language, learning, and the achievement gap: The influence of classroom practices and conversation on performance. *Language and Learning Journal*, *4*(1). Retrieved from http://ojs.gc.cuny.edu/index.php/lljournal/article/view/458/547

Brown, J. S., & Adler, R. P. (2008, January). February). Minds on fire: Open education, the Long Tail, and Learning 2.0. *EDUCAUSE Review*, *43*(1).

Bruner, J. (1961). The act of discovery. *Harvard Educational Review*, *31*(1), 21–32.

Bruner, J. (1962). *The process of education*. Cambridge, MA: Harvard University Press.

Bruner, J. (1986). *Actual minds, possible worlds*. Cambridge, MA: Harvard University Press.

Burns, K. (2009). World Rabies Day promotes prevention of deadly disease. [News]. *Journal of the American Veterinary Medical Association*, *235*(6), 651–652.

Carbonell, J. R. (1970, December). AI in CAI: An artificial-intelligence approach to computer-assisted instruction. *IEEE Transactions on Man-Machine Systems*, *11*(4), 190–202. doi:10.1109/TMMS.1970.299942

Carey, K., & Roza, M. (2008). *School funding's tragic flaw*. Seattle, WA: Center on Reinventing Public Education.

Carmichael, P., & Honour, L. (2002). Open source as appropriate technology for global education. *International Journal of Educational Development*, *22*(1), 47–53. doi:10.1016/S0738-0593(00)00077-8

Carroll, J. (1963). The prediction of success in intensive foreign language training. In Glazer, R. (Ed.), *Training research and education* (pp. 87–136). Pittsburgh, PA: University of Pittsburgh Press.

Casado, M., Watson, G., & McKeown, N. (2005). Reconfigurable networking hardware: A classroom tool. In *13th Symposium on High Performance Interconnects (HOTI'05)* (pp.151-157).

Catto, B. (2011). *Open source software and the Australian government*. Open Source Developers Conference, Canberra 18th November 2011, Australian Government Information Management Office, Department of Finance and Deregulation. Retrieved 19 February, 2012, from http://agimo.govspace.gov.au/files/2011/12/Open-Source-Software-and-the-Australian-Government-Speech-Transcript.pdf

Centre for Educational Research and Innovation (CERI). (2006). *Personalising education. Organisation for Economic Cooperation and Development*. Paris: OECD.

Cervantes, R., & Gainer, G. (1992). The effects of semantic simplification and repetition on listening comprehension. *TESOL Quarterly, 26*(4), 767–770. doi:10.2307/3586886

Chambers, J. A., & Sprecher, J. W. (1980, June). Computer assisted instruction: Current trends and critical issues. *Communications of the ACM, 23*(6), 332–342. doi:10.1145/358876.358881

Chang, M. Y., Chiu, C.-M., & Hung, S.-S. (2010). A machinima-like 3D animation production system. *10th WSEAS International Conference on Systems Theory and Scientific Computation* (pp. 208-217). Taipei, Taiwan: WSEAS Press.

Chan, L., & Costa, S. (2005). Participation in the global knowledge commons: Challenges and opportunities for research dissemination in developing countries. *New Library World, 106*(3/4), 141–163. doi:10.1108/03074800510587354

Chan, M. (2003). Technology and the teaching of oral skills. *CATESOL Journal, 15*, 51–57.

Chao, L. (2011). Development of virtual computer lab with public cloud. In P. Kommers, J. P. Zhang, T. Issa, & P. Isaias (Eds.), *Proceedings of IADIS International Conference on Internet Technologies & Society 2011* (pp. 217-220). Shanghai, China.

Chao, L. (2009). *Utilizing open source tools for online teaching and learning: Applying Linux technologies*. Hershey, PA: IGI Publishing. doi:10.4018/978-1-60566-376-0

Chastain, K. (1975). Affective and ability factors in second language learning. *Language Learning, 25*, 153–161. doi:10.1111/j.1467-1770.1975.tb00115.x

Chen, P. Y., & Forman, C. (2006). Compatibility in an environment with open standards. *Management Information Systems Quarterly*, (n.d), 30.

Childnet International. (2008). *Young people and social networking services: A Childnet International research report*. USA: Childnet. Retrieved 3 February, 2012, from http://www.digizen.org/downloads/fullReport.pdf

Chklovski, T., & Gil, Y. (2005). An analysis of knowledge collected from volunteer contributors. *Proceedings of the 20th National Conference on Artificial Intelligence (AAAI 2005)* (pp. 564-571). Menlo Park, CA: AAAI Press /The MIT Press.

Choi, C. J., Kim, S. W., & Yu, S. (2009). Global ethics of collective internet governance: Intrinsic motivation and open source software. *Journal of Business Ethics, 90*, 523–531. doi:10.1007/s10551-009-0057-5

Christensen, C. M. (1997). *The innovator's dilemma: When new technologies cause great firms to fail*. Harvard Business Press.

Chu, H. (2006). *OpenLDAP 2.4 highlights features of the upcoming release*. Retrieved October 30, 2011, from http://www.openldap.org/pub/hyc/LDAPcon2007.pdf

Citrix Systems. (2009). *Xen*. Retrieved December 15, 2011, from http://www.xen.org

Clancy, M. J., & Linn, M. C. (1999). Patterns and pedagogy. *Proceedings of the 30th SIGCSE Technical Symposium on Computer Science Education* (pp. 37-42). New York, NY: ACM Press.

Cleaveland, S., Costa, P., Lembo, T., & Briggs, D. (2010). Catalysing action against rabies. *The Veterinary Record, 167*(11), 422–423. doi:10.1136/vr.c4775

Cockerill, M. J., & Knols, B. G. J. (2008). Open access to research for the developing world. *Issues in Science and Technology, 24*(2), 65–69.

Collins, A., Brown, J. S., & Newman, S. E. (1987). *Cognitive apprenticeship: Teaching the craft of reading, writing, and mathematics*. Champaign, IL: University of Illinois at Urbana-Champaign.

Collins, G. R. (2002). Case study: A satellite-based internet learning system for the hospitality industry. *Online Journal of Distance Learning Administration, 5*(4).

Commons, O. E. R. (2012). *About OER Commons*. Retrieved from http://www.oercommons.org

Corbesero, S. (2006). Rapid and inexpensive lab deployment using open source software. *Journal of Computing Sciences in Colleges, 22*(2), 228–234.

Corbi, T. A. (1989). Program understanding: Challenge for the 1990s. *IBM Systems Journal, 28*(2), 294–306. doi:10.1147/sj.282.0294

Cordova, D. (2010, June 10). *Diversity as an educational imperative for the 21st century*. Association for Professional Administrators of CSTEP and STEP. Retrieved December 12, 2011, from http://www.apacs.org/events/DCordovaKNPresentation2010.pdf

Correia, E., & Watson, R. (2006). VMware as a practical learning tool. In Sarkar, N. (Ed.), *Tools for teaching computer networking and hardware concepts* (pp. 338–354). Hershey, PA: Idea Group Inc.doi:10.4018/978-1-59140-735-5.ch018

Cottey, A. (2009). Open science - An outline. Retrieved July 27, 2011, from http://www.uea.ac.uk/~c013/open_science/open_science.html

Creative Commons Corporation. (2011). *History - Creative commons*. Retrieved April 17, 2012, from http://creativecommons.org/about/history

Creative Commons. (2003). *Creative Commons license*.

Creative. (2011). *Creative store*. Retrieved from http://us.store.creative.com/category/68709286741/1/ZEN-Style-M100.htm?gclid=CP_uj6qq66wCFGx7Qod9x-CcKA

Cuban, L. (2001). *Oversold & underused: Computers in the classroom*. Cambridge, MA: Harvard University Press.

Cummings, R. E. (2008). What was a wiki and why do I care? A short and usable history of wikis. In Cummings, R. E., & Barton, M. (Eds.), *Wiki writing: Collaborative learning in the college classroom* (pp. 1–18). Ann Arbor, MI: University of Michigan Press.

Dagenais, B., & Robillard, M. P. (2010). Creating and evolving developer documentation: Understanding the decisions of open source contributors. In the *Proceedings of FSE – 18,* Santa Fe, New Mexico (pp. 127 – 136).

Daniel, J. S. (1998). *Mega-universities and knowledge media: Technology strategies for higher education*. Kogan Page.

Daniel, J., Kanwar, A., & Uvalic-Trumbic, S. (2006). A tectonic shift in global higher education. *Change: The Magazine of Higher Learning, 38*(4), 16–23. doi:10.3200/CHNG.38.4.16-23

D'Anjou, J., Fairbrother, S., Kehn, D., Kellerman, J., & McCarthy, P. (2005). *The Java developer's guide to Eclipse* (2nd ed.). Boston, MA: Addison-Wesley.

Dedrick, J., & West, J. (2003). Why firms adopt open source platforms: A grounded theory of innovation and standards adoption. In J. L. King, & K. Lyytinen (Ed.), *MIS Quarterly Special Issue - Workshop on Standard Making: A Critical Research Frontier for Information Systems,* (pp. 236-257).

Deek, F. P., Kimmel, H., & McHugh, J. A. (1998). Pedagogical changes in the delivery of the first-course in computer science: Problem solving, then programming. *Journal of Engineering Education, 87,* 313–320.

Department of Education. Employment and Workplace Relations (DEEWR). (2011). National secondary computer fund. *Digital Education Revolution*, Retrieved 3 February, 2012, from http://www.deewr.gov.au/Schooling/DigitalEducationRevolution/ComputerFund/Pages/NationalSecondarySchoolComputerFundOverview.aspx

Depow, J. (2003). Open source software: Two learning management systems. *International Review of Research in Open and Distance Learning, 4*(2). Retrieved April 15, 2012, from http://www.irrodl.org/index.php/irrodl/article/view/135/215

Deshmukh, D. G., Damle, A. S., Bajaj, J. K., Bhakre, J. B., & Patil, N. S. (2011). Fatal rabies despite post-exposure prophylaxis. [Case Reports]. *Indian Journal of Medical Microbiology, 29*(2), 178–180. doi:10.4103/0255-0857.81786

desJardins, M., & Littman, M. (2010). Broadening student enthusiasm for computer science with a great insights course. In G. Lewandowski, S. A. Wolfman, T. J. Cortina, & E. L. Walker (Eds.), *Proceedings of the 41st ACM Technical Symposium on Computer Science Education (SIGCSE 2010)* (pp. 157-161). New York, NY: ACM Press.

Deursen, A. V., & Visser, E. (2002). The reengineering wiki. In *Proceedings 6th European Conference on Software Maintenance and Reengineering* (CSMR), IEEE Computer Society, (pp. 217-220).

Dewey, J. (1916). *Democracy and education. An introduction to the philosophy of education.* Macmillan.

Dewey, J. (1929). *Experience and nature* (2nd ed.). Open Court Publishing Company.

Dewey, J., & Dewey, E. (1962). *Schools of tomorrow.* New York, NY: E.P. Dutton. (Original work published 1915)

DiBona, C., Ockman, S., & Stone, M. (1999). *Open sources: Voices from the open source revolution.* Sebastopol, CA: O'Reilly Media. Retrieved from http://oreilly.com/openbook/opensources/book/

Dick, W. O., Carey, L., & Carey, J. O. (2004). *Systematic design of instruction* (6th ed.). Upper Saddle River, NJ: Allyn & Bacon.

Dietzschold, B., & Koprowski, H. (2004). Rabies transmission from organ transplants in the USA. *Lancet, 364*(9435), 648–649. doi:10.1016/S0140-6736(04)16912-2

Dijkstra, E. W., Hoare, C. A., & Dahl, O.-J. (1972). Structured programming: *Vol. A. P.I.C. Studies in Data Processing, No. 8.* Waltham, MA: Academic Press.

Dixit, A., Skeath, S., & Reiley, D. (2009). Games of strategy, 3rd ed. New York, NY: W. W. Norton & Company. 704.

Donnellan, B., Fitzgerald, B., Lake, B., & Sturdy, J. (2005). Implementing an open source knowledge base. *IEEE Software, 22*(6), 92–95. doi:10.1109/MS.2005.155

Downes, S. (2007). Models for sustainable open educational resources. *Interdisciplinary Journal of Knowledge and Learning Objects, 3,* 29–44.

Draffan, E. A., Evans, G., & Blenkhorn, P. (2007). Use of assistive technology by students with dyslexia in post-secondary education. *Disability and Rehabilitation. Assistive Technology, 2*(2), 105–116. doi:10.1080/17483100601178492

Duderstadt, J. (2009). *Current global trends in higher education and research: Their impact on Europe.* Speech presented at Universitat Wien, Vienna, Austria.

Duderstadt, J. (2008). Higher education in the 21st century: Global imperatives, regional challenges, national responsibilities and emerging opportunities. In Weber, L. E., & Duderstadt, J. J. (Eds.), *The globalization of higher education.*

Duffy, P. (2008). Engaging the YouTube Google-eyed generation: Strategies for using Web 2.0 in teaching and learning. *Strategies.* (n.d), 119–130.

Dulay, H., & Burt, M. (1977). Remarks on creativity in language acquisition. In Burt, M., Dulay, H., & Finnochiaro, M. (Eds.), *Viewpoints on English as a second language* (pp. 95–126). New York, NY: Regents.

Duncan-Howell, J. (2007). *Online communities of practice and their role in the professional development of teachers.* PhD thesis, Queensland University of Technology.

Eamon, W. (1994). *Science and the secrets of nature.* Princeton, NJ: Princeton University Press.

Early, P., & Swanson, P. (2008). Technology for oral assessment: Recapturing valuable classroom time. In Cherry, C. M., & Wilkerson, C. (Eds.), *Dimension* (pp. 39–48). Valdosta, GA: SCOLT Publications.

Eberly, D. H. (2006). *3D game engine design, 2nd edition: A practical approach to real-time computer graphics.* San Francisco, CA: Morgan Kaufmann.

Edudemic. (2011). *Are you one of the 10 million people using MIT's OpenCourseWare?* Edudemic: Connecting Education & Technology. Retrieved January 20, 2011, from http://edudemic.com/2011/01/10-million-mit/.

Edwards, S. H. (2003). Rethinking computer science education from a test-first perspective. *Companion of the 18th Annual ACM SIGPLAN Conference on Object-Oriented Programming, Systems, Languages, and Applications* (pp. 148-155). New York, NY: ACM.

*ELATEwiki Home Page.* (2011). Retrieved from http://www.ELATEwiki.org

Elliot, M., & Scacchi, W. (2003). *Free software: A case study of software development in a virtual organizational culture.* ISR Technical Report #UCI-ISR-03-6. Retrieved 12 March, 2012, from http://www.isr.uci.edu/tech_reports/UCI-ISR-03-6.pdf

Evans, J. R., & Haase, I. M. (2001). On-line business education in the twenty-first century: An analysis of potential target markets. *Internet Research: Networking Applications and Policy, 11*(3), 246–260. doi:10.1108/10662240110396432

Faubert, B. (2012). *A literature review of school practices to overcome school failure.* Organisation of Economic and Cultural Development (OECD) Education Working Papers, No. 68, OECD Publishing. Retrieved 15 February, 2012, from http://dx.doi.org/10.1787/5k9flcwwv9tk-en

Fekadu, M., Endeshaw, T., Alemu, W., Bogale, Y., Teshager, T., & Olson, J. G. (1996). Possible human-to-human transmission of rabies in Ethiopia. [Case Reports]. *Ethiopian Medical Journal, 34*(2), 123–127.

Fernando, P. (2005). Wiki: New way to collaborate. *Communication World, 22*(3), 8–19.

Financial Express. (2003). *Go for open source code, Kalam tells IT industry.* Retrieved from http://www.financialexpress.com/news/go-for-open-source-code-kalam-tells-it-industry/75949/

Fitzgerald, B. (2006). The transformation of open source software. *Management Information Systems Quarterly, 30*(3), 587–598.

Flewelling, J. (2002). From language lab to multimedia lab: Oral language assessment in the new millennium. In C. M. Cherry (Ed.), *Dimension: Proceedings of the Southern Conference on Language Teaching,* (pp. 33-42). Valdosta, GA: SCOLT Publications.

Foley, J. D., Dam, A. v., Feiner, S. K., & Hughes, J. F. (1991). *Computer graphics: Principles and practice in C* (2nd ed.). Reading, MA: Addison-Wesley.

Foon, R. (2009, November 23rd). Obama highlights science education. *Boston Globe.* Retrieved December 20, 2011, from http://www.boston.com/news/politics/politicalintelligence/2009/11/obama_highlight_4.html

Fosfuri, A., Giarratana, M. S., & Luzzi, A. (2008). The penguin has entered the building: The commercialization of open source software products. *Organization Science, 192*, 292–378. doi:10.1287/orsc.1070.0321

Foster, P., Tonkyn, A., & Wigglesworth, G. (2000). Measuring spoken language: A unit for all reasons. *Applied Linguistics, 21*, 354–375. doi:10.1093/applin/21.3.354

Franke, S. (2005). *Measurement of social capital reference document for public policy research, development, and education.* Ottawa, Canada: Government of Canada.

Free Software Foundation. (2012, February 22). *Various licenses and comments about them.* The GNU Operating System. Retrieved April 17, 2012, from http://www.gnu.org/licenses/license-list.html

Freeman, R. E. (1984). *Strategic management: A stakeholder approach.* Boston, MA: Pitman.

Friedman, T. (2005). *The world is flat.* New York, NY: Farrar, Straus and Giroux.

FSF. (2011). *Free Software Foundation.* Retrieved June 21, 2011, from http://www.fsf.org/

Futernick, K. (2007, October). Study examines why teachers quit and what can be done. *District Administration, 43*(10), 16.

Gallego, M. D., Luna, P., & Bueno, S. (2008). User acceptance model of open source software. [ScienceDirect.]. *Computers in Human Behavior, 24*, 2199–2216. doi:10.1016/j.chb.2007.10.006

GARC. (2008). *World Rabies Day 2007 encourages rabies control in Haiti*. Retrieved April 10, 2012 from http://www.rabiescontrol.net/assets/files/resources/newsletters/ARCnewsletter6.pdf

GARC. (2012). *World Rabies Day webinar*. Retrieved April 9, 2012, from http://www.rabiescontrol.net/news/news-archive/world-rabies-day-webinar-a-huge-success.html

Gardner, R., Smythe, P., Clement, R., & Gliksman, L. (1976). Second-language learning: A social-psychological perspective. *Canadian Modern Language Review, 32*, 198–213.

Garrett, P. (2011). *Digital education revolution transforming Australian classrooms*. Minister's Media Centre, Education, Employment and Workplace Relations portfolio. Retrieved 3 February, 2012, from http://ministers.deewr.gov.au/garrett/digital-education-revolution-transforming-australian-classrooms

Gartner. (2012). *K-12 total cost of ownership tool*. Gartner. Retrieved 15 February, 2012, from http://k12tco.gartner.com/home/default.aspx

Gaspar, A., & Langevin, S. (2007). Restoring "coding with intention" in introductory programming courses. *Proceedings of the 8th Conference on Information Technology Education* (pp. 91-98). New York, NY: ACM Press.

GBDirect. (2004). *Benefits of using open source software*. Open Source Software, Free Software and Software Libre. Retrieved April 17, 2012, from http://open-source.gbdirect.co.uk/migration/benefit.html

Georgas, J. C., Gorlick, M. M., & Taylor, R. N. (2005). Raging incrementalism: Harnessing change with open-source software. *Proceedings of the Fifth Workshop on Open Source Application Spaces,* (pp. 1–6).

Gerdes, J., & Tilley, S. (2007). A conceptual overview of the virtual networking laboratory. In *SIGITE'07* (pp. 75-82).

Gibbons, R. V., Holman, R. C., Mosberg, S. R., & Rupprecht, C. E. (2002). Knowledge of bat rabies and human exposure among United States cavers. *Emerging Infectious Diseases, 8*(5), 532–534. doi:10.3201/eid0805.010290

Gilbert, D., Chen, H. L., & Sabol, J. (2008). Building learning communities with wikis. In Cummings, R. E., & Barton, M. (Eds.), *Wiki writing: Collaborative learning in the college classroom* (pp. 1–18). Ann Arbor, MI: University of Michigan Press.

Gilgen, R. G. (2004, April 22). *Creating a mobile language learning environment*. Presentation presented at the Educause Midwest Regional Conference, Chicago, IL.

Gloor, P. A. (1992). AACE-algorithm animation for computer science education. *Proceedings IEEE Workshop on Visual Languages 1992,* (pp. 25-31). Cambridge, MA.

Goldman, J. P. (1991). Balancing school sports and academics. *Education Digest, 56*(8), 67–71.

Govt of India. (2010). *Policy on open standards for e-governance*. New Delhi, India: Department of Information Technology: Ministry of Communications & Information Technology.

Govt. of India (1961). *Third five-year plan,* (p. 589). New Delhi, India: Planning Commission, Govt. of India.

Govt. of India. (1963). *Expert committee report on correspondence courses,* (pp. 3-4). New Delhi, India: Ministry of Education. Govt. of India. (1966). *Report of the education commission*. New Delhi, India: Ministry of Education, Government of India.

Goyal, R., Lai, S., Jain, R., & Durresi, A. (1998). Laboratories for data communications and computer networks. In *1998 FIE Conference* (pp. 1113-1119).

Gramsci, A. (1971). *Selections from the prison notebooks*. London, UK: Lawrence and Wishart.

Griffiths, R. (1992). Speech rate and listening comprehension: Further evidence of the relationship. *TESOL Quarterly, 26*(2), 385–390. doi:10.2307/3587015

Grunwald., & Associates, L. L. C. (2010). *A platform for Internet-based assessment. A report on Education leaders' perceptions of online testing in an open source environment*. Grunwald and Associates LLC. Retrieved 15 February, 2012, from http://grunwald.com/pdfs/Grunwald_Open_Source_Public_Report_v3.pdf

Guseva, I. (2009). *Bad economy is good for open source.* CMS Wire. Retrieved April 17, 2012, from http://www. cmswire.com/cms/web-cms/bad-economy-is-good-for-open-source-004187.php

Hafer, L., & Kirkpatrick, A. E. (2009). Assessing open source software as a scholarly contribution. *Communications of the ACM, 52*(12), 126–129. doi:10.1145/1610252.1610285

Hahn, J., Moon, J. Y., & Zhang, C. (2006). Impact of social ties on open source project team formation. In Damiani, E., Fitzgerald, B., Scacchi, W., Scotto, M., & Succi, G. (Eds.), *Open source systems* (pp. 307–317). Boston, MA: Springer. doi:10.1007/0-387-34226-5_31

Hai-Jew, S. (2008). Developing a distance learning faculty wiki. *SIDLIT Conference Proceedings.* Paper 4. Retrieved from http://scholarspace.jccc.edu/sidlit/4

Hai-Jew, S. (2011). Participatory design of a (today and) future digital entomology lab. *Educause Quarterly.* Retrieved from http://www.educause.edu/EDUCAUSE+Quarterly/EDUCAUSEQuarterlyMagazineVolum/TheParticipatoryDesignofaToday/236669

Hai-Jew, S., & McHaney, R. W. (2010). ELATEwiki: Evolving an e-learning faculty wiki. In Luppicini, R., & Haghi, A. K. (Eds.), *Cases on digital technologies in higher education: Issues and challenges* (pp. 1–23). doi:10.4018/978-1-61520-869-2.ch001

Hai-Peng, H., & Deng, L. (2007). Vocabulary acquisition in multimedia environment. *US-China Foreign Language, 5*(8), 55–59.

Halfacree, G. (2009, November 2). Windows loses market share to Mac os. *Bit-Tec.* Retrieved from http://www.bit-tech.net/news/bits/2009/11/02/windows-loses-market-share-to-mac-os/1

Hann, I.-H., Roberts, J., Slaughter, S., & Fielding, R. (2004). An empirical analysis of economic returns to open source participation. *2004 Annual Meeting of the American Economic Association, San Diego, "Economics of Open Source Software"* (pp. 1–39).

Hargreaves, D. (1994). *The mosaic of learning: Schools and teachers for the new century.* London, UK: Demos.

Harhoff, D., & Henkel, J., & von Hippel. (2003). Profiting from voluntary information spillovers: How users benefit by freely revealing their innovations. *Research Policy, 32*, 1753–1769. doi:10.1016/S0048-7333(03)00061-1

Harris-Perry, M. (2011). *Sister citizen: Shame, stereotype, and racism in America.* New Haven, CT: Yale University Press.

Hars, A., & Ou, S. (2001). Working for free? – Motivations of participating in open source projects. *Proceedings of the 34th Hawaii International Conference on System Sciences.*

Hartman, K., Neuwirth, C., Kiesler, S., Sproull, L., Cochran, C., Palmquist, M., & Zabrow, D. (1995). Patterns of social interaction and learning to write: Some effects of network technologies. In Berge, Z., & Collins, M. (Eds.), *Computer-mediated communication and the online classroom* (pp. 47–78). Creskill, NJ: Hampton Press, Inc. doi:10.1177/0741088391008001005

Hasler, B. S., Kersten, B., & Sweller, J. (2007). Learner control, cognitive load and instructional animation. *Applied Cognitive Psychology, 21*(6), 713–729. doi:10.1002/acp.1345

Haughey, M., Evans, T., & Murphy, D. (2008). Introduction: From correspondence education to virtual learning environments. In Evans, T., Haughey, M., & Murphy, D. (Eds.), *International handbook of distance education* (pp. 1–24). Emerald.

Hemachudha, T., Mitrabhakdi, E., Wilde, H., Vejabhuti, A., Siripataravanit, S., & Kingnate, D. (1999). Additional reports of failure to respond to treatment after rabies exposure in Thailand. [Case Reports]. *Clinical Infectious Diseases, 28*(1), 143–144. doi:10.1086/517179

Hepp, M., Siorpaes, K., & Bachlechner, D. (2007, September). Harvesting Wiki consensus: Using Wikipedia entries for knowledge management. *IEEE Internet Computing, Special Issue on Semantic Knowledge Management,* 54–65.

Herrington, J., & Oliver, R. (2000). An instructional design framework for authentic learning environments. *Educational Technology Research and Development, 48*(3), 23–48.

Herrmann, T., Kunau, G., Loser, K.-U., & Menold, N. (2004). Socio-technical walkthrough: Designing technology along work processes. *Proceedings of the 8th Conference on Participatory Design: Artful Integration: Interweaving Media, Materials and Practices* (pp. 132-141). New York, NY: ACM Press.

Herrmann, T. (2009). Systems design with the socio-technical walkthrough. In Whitworth, B., & de Moor, A. (Eds.), *Handbook of research on socio-technical design and social networking systems*. doi:10.4018/978-1-60566-264-0.ch023

Hertzum, M., & Frøkjær, E. (1996). Browsing and querying in online documentation: A study of user interfaces and the interaction process. *ACM Transactions on Computer-Human Interaction, 3*(2), 136–161. doi:10.1145/230562.230570

Hilton, J., Wiley, D., Stein, J., & Johnson, A. (2010). The four R's of openness and ALMS analysis frameworks for open educational resources. *Open Learning: The Journal of Open and Distance Learning, 25*(1), 37–44. doi:10.1080/02680510903482132

Himanen, P. (2001). *The hacker ethic and the spirit of the information age*. Great Britain: Secker & Warburg.

Hoagland, D., Brewer, S. D., & Hoogendyk, T. A. (2002). *Linux in higher education: Two applications that improve student learning*. Paper presented at the Massachusetts Education Computing Conference (MECC), West Barnstable, MA.

Hodgin, R. C. (2009). Windows losing market share fast to Mac and linux. *TG Daily*. Retrieved from http://www.tgdaily.com/software-features/41291-report-windows-losing-market-share-fast-to-mac-and-linux

Holzinger, A., Kickmeier-Rust, M., & Albert, D. (2008). Dynamic media in computer science education: Content complexity and learning performance: Is less more? *Journal of Educational Technology & Society, 11*(1), 279–290.

Homan, G., & Macpherson, A. (2005). E-learning in corporate universities. *Journal of European Industrial Training, 29*(1), 75–90. doi:10.1108/03090590510576226

Honebein, P. (1996). Seven goals for the designing of Constructivist Learning environments. In Wilson, B. (Ed.), *Constructivists learning environments* (pp. 11–24). New Jersey: Educational Technology Publications.

Hossain, M. S., Rahman, M. A., & El-Saddik, A. (2004). A framework for repurposing multimedia content. *Canadian Conference on Electrical and Computer Engineering*, (pp. 971-974).

House, C. H., & Price, R. L. (2009). The secret sauce. In House, C. H., & Price, R. L. (Eds.), *The HP phenonenon: Innovation and business transformation* (pp. 216–256). Stanford, CA: Stanford University Press.

Hsu, W. H., & Barber, J. (2004, July 28). *Retrieved from Bayesian Network tools in Java* (BNJ). Retrieved from http://bnj.sourceforge.net

Hsu, W. H., Cunningham, D., & Hart, J. (2008, August 6). *The MASSFORGE project community: An intelligent agent-based multi-character animation project*. Retrieved April 17, 2012, from LiveJournal: http://massforge.livejournal.com/

Hsu, W. H., Guo, H., Joehanes, R., Perry, B. B., & Thornton, J. A. (2003, November 5). *Bayesian network tools in Java v2*. SourceForge.net. Retrieved from http://sourceforge.net/project/shownotes.php?release_id=195787

Hubbard, J. (2004). *Open source to the core* (pp. 25 – 31). Retrieved from www.acmqueue.com

Hundhausen, C. D. (2002). Integrating algorithm visualization technology into an undergraduate algorithms course: Ethnographic studies of a social constructivist approach. *Computers & Education, 39*(3), 237–260. doi:10.1016/S0360-1315(02)00044-1

Hundhausen, C. D., Douglas, S. A., & Stasko, J. T. (2002). A meta-study of algorithm visualization effectiveness. *Journal of Visual Languages and Computing, 13*(3), 259–290. doi:10.1006/jvlc.2002.0237

Hunt, G., Aiken, M., Fähndrich, M., Hawblitzel, C., Hodson, O., & Larus, J. … Wobber, T. (2007). Sealing OS processes to improve dependability and safety. *EuroSys '07*, Lisbon, Portugal, (pp. 341–354).

Hylen, J. (2005). *Open educational resources: Opportunities and challenges.* OECD-CERI. Retrieved December 17, 2010 from http://www.oecd.org/dataoecd/1/49/35733548.doc

IEEE. (1998). *IEEE standard for software reviews.* New York, NY: Institute of Electrical and Electronics Engineers (IEEE Std. 1028-1997).

IEEE/ACM. (2008). *IT 2008, Curriculum guidelines for undergraduate degree programs in information technology* (Final Draft). Retrieved January 16, 2009, from http://www.acm.org//education/curricula/IT2008%20Curriculum.pdf

IGNOU. (2011). *Profile.* New Delhi, India: Author.

Iiyoshi, T., & Kumar, V. (2008). *Opening up education: The collective advancement of education through open technology, open content, and open knowledge.* Cambridge, MA: The MIT Press.

Illich, I. (1971). *Deschooling society.* Retrieved 3 February, 2012, from http://ournature.org/~novembre/illich/1970_deschooling.html

Indian Institute of Technology Bombay (IITB). (n.d.). *Project OSCAR.* Retrieved from http://oscar.iitb.ac.in/aboutOscar.do

Jackiewicz, T. (2004). *Deploying OpenLDAP.* New York, NY: Apress.

Jensen, C., & Scacchi, W. (2007). Role migration and advancement processes in OSSD projects: A comparative case study. In the *Proceedings of the 29th International Conference on Software Engineering.*

Johnson, L., Adams, S., & Haywood, K. (2011). *The NMC horizon report: 2011 K-12 edition.* Austin, TX: The New Media Consortium.

Johnson, L., Levine, A., Smith, R., & Stone, S. (2010). *The 2010 horizon report.* Austin, TX: New Media Consortium.

Johnson, L., Smith, R., Willis, H., Levine, A., & Haywood, K. (2011). *The 2011 horizon report.* Austin, TX: The New Media Consortium.

Joint Information Systems Committee (JISC). (2011). What is open source software. *OSS Watch.* University of Oxford. Retrieved 15 February, 2012, from http://www.oss-watch.ac.uk/resources/softwareexamples.xml

Joint Information Systems Committee (JISC). (2012). Governance models. *OSS Watch.* University of Oxford. Retrieved 12 March, 2012, from http://www.oss-watch.ac.uk/resources/governanceModels.xml

Jonassen, D. H., Howland, J. L., & Marra, R. M. (2011). *Meaningful learning with technology.* Boston, MA: Pearson Education.

Kahneman, D. (2011). *Thinking, fast and slow.* New York, NY: Farrar, Straus and Giroux.

Kallinikos, J. (2009). *Panel: Regulation and governance in commons-based peer (social) production.*

Kandori, M., Mailath, G. J., & Rob, R. (1993). Learning, mutation, and long run equilibria in games. *Econometrics, 61*(1), 29–56. doi:10.2307/2951777

Kapadia, N. H. (1999). *On the design of a demand-based network computing system: The Purdue network computing hubs.* PhD thesis, School of Electrical and Computer Engineering, Purdue University.

Karat, C.-M., Campbell, R., & Fiegel, T. (1992). Comparison of empirical testing and walkthrough methods in user interface evaluation. In P. Bauersfeld, J. Bennett, & G. Lynch (Ed.), *Conference on Human Factors in Computing Systems (CHI 1992)* (pp. 397-404). New York, NY: ACM Press.

Kawatra, P. S., & Singh, N. K. (2006). E-learning in LIS education in India. In C. Khoo, D. Singh, & A.S. Chaudhry (Eds.), *Proceedings of the Asia-Pacific Conference on Library & Information Education & Practice 2006* (A-LIEP 2006), Singapore, 3-6 April 2006 (pp. 605-611). Singapore: School of Communication & Information, Nanyang Technological University.

Kearsley, G. (1982). Authoring systems in computer based education. *Communications of the ACM, 25*(7), 429–437. doi:10.1145/358557.358569

Kelty, C. (2008). *Two bits. The cultural significance of free software.* Durham, NC: Duke University Press.

Kerr, I. M., & Bornfreund, M. (2007, June 2). *Open source software*. Canadian Internet Policy and Public Interest Clinic (CIPPIC). Retrieved April 17, 2012, from http://www.cippic.ca/open-source/

Kiili, K. (2004). Digital game-based learning: Towards an experiential gaming model. *The Internet and Higher Education, 8,* 13-14. Retrieved April 9, 2012, from http://www.google.com/url?sa=t&rct=j&q=&esrc=s&source=web&cd=1&ved=0CC0QFjAA&url=http%3A%2F%2Fwww.sciencedirect.com%2Fscience%2Farticle%2Fpii%2F-S1096751604000776&ei=BASHT9abIMWa8AGBhpzACA&usg=AFQjCNFWffP-xZqdfbX9xbvT__VCR6Rflw&sig2=6UCBPKoFdtBqt2fjNJ3nDg

Kittur, A., Suh, B., & Chi, E. H. (2009). What's in Wikipedia? Mapping topics and conflict using socially annotated category structure. *27th Annual CHI Conference on Human Factors in Computing Systems (CHI),* April 4-9, Boston MA.

Kittur, A., Suh, B., Pendleton, B. A., & Chi, E. H. (2007). He says, she says: Conflict and coordination in Wikipedia. *25th Annual ACM Conference on Human Factors in Computing Systems (CHI 2007),* April 28 - May 3, San Jose, CA (pp. 453-462). New York, NY: ACM.

Klobas, J. (2006). *Wikis: Tools for information work and collaboration*. Oxford, UK: Chandos Publishing.

Klopfer, E., Osterweil, S., & Salen, K. (2009). Moving learning games forward: Obstacles, opportunities & openness. *The Education Arcade*. Retrieved April 12, 2012, from http://education.mit.edu/papers/MovingLearningGamesForward_EdArcade.pdf

Kneale, B., Horta, A. Y., & Box, L. (2004). Velnet: Virtual environment for learning networking. In *Proceedings of the Sixth Conference on Australasian Computing Education, Vol. 30* (pp. 161-169).

Knuth, D. E. (1984). Literate programming. *The Computer Journal, 27*(2), 97–111. doi:10.1093/comjnl/27.2.97

Koch, S. (2007). Exploring the effects of coordination and communication tools on the efficiency of open source projects using data envelopment analysis. In Feller, J., Fitzgerald, B., Scacchi, W., & Stilitti, A. (Eds.), *Open source development, adoption and innovation* (pp. 97–108). Boston, MA: Springer. doi:10.1007/978-0-387-72486-7_8

Koning, B. B., Tabbers, H. K., Rikers, R. M., & Paas, F. (2007). Attention cueing as a means to enhance learning from an animation. *Applied Cognitive Psychology, 21*(6), 731–746. doi:10.1002/acp.1346

Koohang, A., & Harman, K. (2007). Advancing sustainability of open educational resources. *Issues in Informing Science and Information Technology, 4,* 535–544.

Koster, R. (2005). *A theory of fun for game design*. Scottsdale, AZ: Paraglyph Press, Inc.

Krashen, S. D. (1981). *Second language acquisition and second language learning*. Oxford, UK: Pergamon.

Krashen, S. D. (1982). *Principles and practice in second language acquisition*. Oxford, UK: Pergamon.

Krechmer, K. (2005). *The meaning of open standards*.

Krishnamurthy, S. (2002). Cave or community? An empirical examination of 100 mature open source projects. *First Monday, 7*(6). Retrieved April 15, 2012, from http://firstmonday.org/htbin/cgiwrap/bin/ojs/index.php/fm/article/view/1477/1392

Kuhn, T. S. (1962). *The structure of scientific revolutions*. Chicago, IL: University of Chicago Press.

Kulik, C.-L. C., & Kulik, J. A. (1991). Effectiveness of computer-based instruction: An updated analysis. *Computers in Human Behavior, 7*(1-2), 75–94. doi:10.1016/0747-5632(91)90030-5

Kuniyoshi, Y., Inaba, M., & Inoue, H. (1994). Learning by watching: Extracting reusable task knowledge from visual observation of human performance. *IEEE Transactions on Robotics and Automation, 10*(6), 799–822. doi:10.1109/70.338535

Kvavik, R. B. (2005). Convenience, communication, and control: How students use technology. In D. G. Oblinger & J. L. Oblinger (Eds.), *Educating the Net generation* (pp. 7.1-7.20). Boulder, CO: Educause. Retrieved from http://www.educause.edu/educatingthenetgen

Lai, C. C., & Kritsonis, W. A. (2006). The advantages and disadvantages of computer technology in second language acquisition. *National Journal for Publishing and Mentoring Doctoral Student Research, 3*(1), 1–6.

Lakhani, K., & Hippel, E. V. (2003). How open source software works: "free" user-to-user assistance. *Research Policy, 32*(7), 923–943. doi:10.1016/S0048-7333(02)00095-1

Lally, P., van Jaarsveld, C. H. M., Potts, H. W. W., & Wardle, J. (2009). How habits are formed: Modelling habit formation in the real world. *European Journal of Social Psychology, 40*(6), 998–1009. doi:10.1002/ejsp.674

Lamb, B. (2004). Wide open spaces: Wikis ready or not. *EDUCAUSE Review, 39*(5). Retrieved from http://www.educause.edu/EDUCAUSE+Review/EDUCAUSEReviewMagazineVolume39/WideOpenSpacesWikisReady-orNot/157925

Lapierre, V., & Tiberghien, P. (2005). Transmission of rabies from an organ donor. [Comment Letter]. *The New England Journal of Medicine, 352*(24), 2552, author reply 2552.

Lawrence, A. W., Badre, A. M., & Stasko, J. T. (1994). Empirically evaluating the use of animations to teach algorithms. *Proceedings of the 1994 IEEE Symposium on Visual Languages*, (pp. 48-54).

Lee, A. (2012, April 16). *Virtualdub.org: Proof that I had too much free time in college.* Retrieved April 17, 2012, from http://www.virtualdub.org/

Lembo, T., Attlan, M., Bourhy, H., Cleaveland, S., Costa, P., & de Balogh, K. …Briggs, D. J. (2011). Renewed global partnerships and redesigned roadmaps for rabies prevention and control. *Veterinary Medicine International.* doi:doi:10.4061/2011/923149

Lemley, M. A. (2004). *Property, intellectual property, and free riding.* Social Science Research Network Electronic Paper Collection Working Paper No. 291. Retrieved from http://ssrn.com/abstract=582602

Lemley, M. A. (2008). *Are universities patent trolls?* (pp. 611 – 631). Retrieved September 10, 2011, from http://law.fordham.edu/publications/article.ihtml?pubID=200&id=2732

Lerner, J., & Tirole, J. (2000). *The simple economics of open source.* Harvard Business School. Retrieved September 2, 2011, from http://www.people.hbs.edu/jlerner/simple.pdf

Lerner, J., & Tirole, J. (2004). *The economics of technolgy sharing: Open source and beyond - NBER Working Paper No. 10956.* Cambridge, MA: National Bureau of Economic Research.

Lerner, J., & Tirole, J. (2005). The scope of open source licensing. *The Journal of Law, Economics, & Organization, 19*(2). Retrieved October 5, 2011, from http://jleo.oxfordjournals.org/content/21/1/20.full.pdf+html

Lerner, J., Pathak, P. A., & Tirole, J. (2006). The dynamics of open-source contributors. *The Roots of Innovation, 96*(2), 114–118.

Lerner, J., & Tirole, J. (2002, June). Some simple economics of open source. *The Journal of Industrial Economics, 50*(2), 197–234. doi:10.1111/1467-6451.00174

Lerner, J., & Tirole, J. (2005). The economics of technology sharing: Open source and beyond. *The Journal of Economic Perspectives, 19*(2), 99–120. doi:10.1257/0895330054048678

Lester, J. C., Converse, S. A., Stone, B. A., Kahler, S. E., & Barlow, S. T. (1997). Animated pedagogical agents and problem-solving effectiveness: A large-scale empirical evaluation. *Proceedings of Eighth World Conference on Artificial Intelligence in Education*, (pp. 23-30).

Leuf, B., & Cunningham, W. (2001). *The Wiki way: Quick collaboration on the Web.* Boston, MA: Addison-Wesley.

Lewis, T. (1999, February). The open source acid test. *IEEE Computer: Binary Critic,* 124 – 127.

Lifelong Kindergarten. (2012). *Lifelong Kindergarten.* MIT Media Lab, Massachusetts Institute of Technology. Retrieved 29 February, 2012, from http://llk.media.mit.edu/projects.php

Lin, J., Yen, L., Yang, M., & Chen, C. (2005). Teaching computer programming in elementary schools: A pilot study. *National Educational Computing Conference 2005,* Philadelphia. Retrieved 20 February, 2012, from http://www.stagecast.com/pdf/research/Lin_NECC2005_Paper_RP.pdf

Lin, Y.-T., Chi, Y.-C., Chang, L.-C., Cheng, S.-C., & Huang, Y.-M. (2007). Web 2.0 synchronous learning environment using AJAX. *Proceedings of the 9th IEEE International Symposium on Multimedia* (pp. 453-458). New York, NY: IEEE Press.

Linn, M. C., & Clancy, M. J. (1992, March). The case for case studies of programming problems. *Communications of the ACM, 35*(3), 121–132. doi:10.1145/131295.131301

Littman, M. (2007). *Computer scientist Michael Littman shares his videos on computer science, artificial intelligence, and family.* Retrieved April 17, 2012, from http://www.youtube.com/user/mlittman

Liu, C. (2006). Software project demonstrations as not only an assessment tool but also a learning tool. *Proceedings of the 37th SIGCSE Technical Symposium on Computer Science Education (SIGCSE 2006)*, (pp. 423-427).

Liu, Y. (2010). Social media tools as a learning resource. *Journal of Educational Technology Development and Exchange, 3*(1), 101–114.

Li, Y., Tan, C.-H., Xu, H., & Teo, H.-H. (2011). Open source software adoption: Motivations of adopters and amotivations of non-adopters. *The Data Base for Advances in Information Systems, 42*(2), 76–94. doi:10.1145/1989098.1989103

Lo, G. (2006, October 27). Documentation in the open source world. *Notes on the Free Software and Open Source Symposium.* Retrieved from http://justagwailo.com/filter/2006/10/27/open-source-world

Lo, G. (2009, November). Free and open source documentation. *Just a Gwai Lo.* Retrieved from http://justagwailo.com/fsoss-documentation

Logo Foundation. (2011). *What is Logo?* Logo Foundation. Retrieved 15 February, 2012, from http://el.media.mit.edu/logo-foundation/logo/index.html

Loidl, S., Mühlbacher, J., & Schauer, H. (2005). Preparatory knowledge: Propaedeutic in informatics. In R. T. Mittermeir (Ed.), *From Computer Literacy to Informatics Fundamentals: International Conference on Informatics in Secondary Schools – Evolution and Perspectives, LNCS 3422* (pp. 104-115). Heidelberg, Germany: Springer.

Lombardi, M. with Oblinger, D. (Eds.). (2007). *Authentic learning for the 21st century: An overview.* Educause. Retrieved 15 February, 2012, from http://net.educause.edu/ir/library/pdf/ELI3009.pdf

Long, M. (1996). The role of the linguistic environment in second language acquisition. In Ritchie, W., & Bhatia, T. (Eds.), *Handbook of second language acquisition* (pp. 413–468). San Diego, CA: Academic Press. doi:10.1016/B978-012589042-7/50015-3

Lowood, H. (2006). High-performance play: The making of machinima. *Journal of Media Practice, 7*(1), 25–42. doi:10.1386/jmpr.7.1.25/1

Lowood, H., & Nitsche, M. (2011). *The machinima reader.* Cambridge, MA: The MIT Press.

Luo, L. (2009). Web 2.0 integration in information literacy instruction: An overview. *Journal of Academic Librarianship, 36*(1), 32–40. doi:10.1016/j.acalib.2009.11.004

Maak, T. (2007). Responsible leadership, stakeholder engagement, and the emergence of social capital. *Journal of Business Ethics, 74*, 329–343. doi:10.1007/s10551-007-9510-5

Machina, M. J. (1987). Choice under uncertainty: Problems solved and unsolved. *The Journal of Economic Perspectives, 1*(1), 121–154.

Maciak, L. (2008, June 18). The problem with Wikis. *Terminally Incoherent.* Retrieved from http://www.terminally-incoherent.com/blog/2008/06/18/the-problem-with-wikis/

Mahmod, M., Yusof, S. A. M., & Dahalin, Z. M. (2010). Women contributions to open source software innovation: A social constructivist perspective. 2010 International Symposium on Information Technology, (pp. 1433–1438).

Mai le, T. P., Dung, L. P., Tho, N. T., Quyet, N. T., Than, P. D., Mai, N. D., ... Nasca, P. C. (2010). Community knowledge, attitudes, and practices toward rabies prevention in North Vietnam. *International Quarterly of Community Health Education, 31*(1), 21–31. doi:10.2190/IQ.31.1.c

Maikish, A. (2006). Moodle: A free, easy, and constructivist online learning tool. *Technology and Schools, 13*(3), 24–28.

Manning, S. E., Rupprecht, C. E., Fishbein, D., Hanlon, C. A., Lumlertdacha, B., & Guerra, M. (2008). Human rabies prevention--United States, 2008: Recommendations of the Advisory Committee on Immunization Practices. [Practice Guideline]. *MMWR. Recommendations and Reports, 57*(RR-3), 1–28.

Marginson, S. (1997). *Markets in education*. Sydney, Australia: Allen & Unwin.

Margulies, A.H. (2004). A new model for open sharing: Massachusetts Institute of Technology's OpenCourse-Ware initiative makes a difference. *PLoS Biology, 2*(8), 1071–1073. doi:10.1371/journal.pbio.0020200

Mauthe, A., & Thomas, P. (2004). *Professional content management systems: Handling digital media assets*. West Sussex, UK: John Wiley and Sons. doi:10.1002/0470855444

Maxwell, S. (2000). *Red Hat Linux network management tools*. New York, NY: McGraw-Hill.

Mayer, R. E. (1999). Multimedia aids to problem-solving transfer. *International Journal of Educational Research, 31*, 611–623. doi:10.1016/S0883-0355(99)00027-0

Mayer, R. E., & Anderson, R. B. (1992). The instructive animation: Helping students build connections between words and pictures in multimedia learning. *Journal of Educational Psychology, 84*(4), 444–452. doi:10.1037/0022-0663.84.4.444

Mayer, R. E., & Moreno, R. (2002). Animation as an aid to multimedia learning. *Educational Psychology Review, 14*(1), 87–99. doi:10.1023/A:1013184611077

Mazzoni, D., & Dannenberg, R. (2000). *Audacity* [software]. Pittsburg, PA: Carnegie Mellon University.

McAndrew, A. (2008). Teaching cryptography with open-source software. *Special Interest Group Computer Science Education, 40*(1), 325–330.

McGonigal, J. (2011). *Reality is broken: Why games make us better and how they can change the world*. New York, NY: Penguin Press HC.

McHaney, R. W. (2009, November 4). Implementation of ELATEwiki. *EDUCAUSE Quarterly, 32*(4). Retrieved from http://www.educause.edu/EDUCAUSE+Quarterly/EDUCAUSEQuarterlyMagazineVolum/Implementation-ofELATEwiki/192968

McHaney, R. W. (2011). *The new digital shoreline: How Web 2.0 and millennials are revolutionizing higher education*. Stylus Publishing.

McHugh, J. (2005). The Firefox explosion. *Wired, 13*(02), 92(7).

Meatballwiki. (2011). *Softsecurity*. Retrieved from http://meatballwiki.org/wiki/SoftSecurity

Mediawiki. (2011, February 7). *Category:MediaWiki configuration settings*. MediaWiki. Retrieved from http://www.mediawiki.org/wiki/Category:MediaWiki_configuration_settings

*MediaWiki.org*. (2011). Retrieved from http://www.mediawiki.org/wiki/MediaWiki.

Mehlenbacher, B. (2002). Assessing the usability of online instructional materials. *New Directions for Teaching and Learning, 91*, 91–98. doi:10.1002/tl.71

Meiklejohn, A. (1932). *The experimental college*. New York, NY: Harper and Brothers.

Melton, F. (2012). *Open source handbook*. Retrieved 12 March, 2012, from http://www.opensourcehandbook.com/?s=index

Meneely, A., Williams, L., & Gehringer, E. F. (2008). ROSE: A repository of education-friendly open-source projects. In the *Proceedings of ITiCSE '08*, (pp. 7 – 11). Madrid, Spain: ACM.

Meredith, L. (2010, Jan 28). U.S. considers 'internet access for all'. *Livescience*. Retrieved April 10, 2012, from www.livescience.com

Messenger, S. L., Smith, J. S., Orciari, L. A., Yager, P. A., & Rupprecht, C. E. (2003). Emerging pattern of rabies deaths and increased viral infectivity. [Research Support, Non-U.S. Gov't Research Support, U.S. Gov't, P.H.S.]. *Emerging Infectious Diseases, 9*(2), 151–154. doi:10.3201/eid0902.020083

Microsoft. (2009). *Virtualization*. Retrieved December 6, 2011, from http://www.microsoft.com/virtualization/default.mspx

Ministerial Council Education, Early Child Development and Youth Affairs (MCEEDYA). (2008). *Melbourne declaration on educational goals for young Australians*. Melbourne, Australia: Author. Retrieved 15 February, 2012, from http://www.mceecdya.edu.au/verve/_resources/National_Declaration_on_the_Educational_Goals_for_Young_Australians.pdf

Mishra, S., & Sharma, R. C. (2005, March 14-20). Development of e-learning in India. *University News, 43*(11), 9 – 15.

Mishra, S., & Sharma, R. C. (2005). *Interactive multimedia in education and training*. Hershey, PA: IGI Global.

Mohan, R. (2005, December). The problem with Wikis. *CircleID*. Retrieved from http://www.circleid.com/posts/the_problem_with_wikis/

Monaghan, A. (2009, July/August). Winning webinars. *Pharmaceutical Marketing Europe*. Retrieved April 10, 2012, from http://www.wellshealthcare.com/resources/20090526%20PME%20JulyAug%20article%20as%20published.pdf

Mooney, P., Corcoran, P., & Winstanley, A. (2010). *The effects of crowdsourcing on quality in OpenStreetMap*. Retrieved August 2, 2011, from http://na-srv-1dv.nuim.ie/stratag/index.php

Morning, A. (2008). Reconstructing race in science and society: Biology textbooks: 1952-2002. *American Journal of Sociology, 114*, S106–137. doi:10.1086/592206

Morrow, J. D. (1994). *Game theory for political scientists*. Princeton, NJ: Princeton University Press.

Moyle, K. (2004). *What place does open source software have in Australian and New Zealand schools' and jurisdictions' ICT portfolios? Total cost of ownership and open source software*. Research paper, Canberra, Ministerial Council Education, Early Child Development and Youth Affairs (MCEEDYA). Retrieved 3 February, 2012, from http://www.mceecdya.edu.au/verve/_resources/total_cost_op.pdf

Moyle, K. (2009). *Varying approaches to internet safety: The role of filters in schools*. Washington, DC: CoSN. Retrieved from http://www.cosn.org/Portals/7/docs/Web%202.0/Varying%20Approaches%20to%20Internet%20Safety.pdf

Moyle, K. (2010). *Building innovation, learning with technologies*. Australian Education Review, Australian Council for Educational Research (ACER). Retrieved 3 February, 2012, from http://research.acer.edu.au/aer/10

Moyle, K. (2003). New secularism: Reorienting the private order of digital technologies. In Reid, A., & Thomson, P. (Eds.), *Rethinking public education: Towards a public curriculum*. Brisbane, Australia: Australian Curriculum Studies Association.

Moyle, K. (2006). *Leadership and learning with ICT: Voices from the profession*. Canberra, Australia: Teaching Australia, Australian Institute for Teaching and School Leadership.

Mozilla. (2011). *Mozilla Thunderbird*. Retrieved July 12, 2011, from http://www.mozilla.org/en-US/thunderbird/

Nagios. (2011). *Nagios*. Retrieved November 30, 2011, from http://www.nagios.org

Nagy, D., Yassin, A. M., & Bhattacherjee, A. (2010). Organizational adoption of open source software: Barriers and remedies. *Communications of the ACM, 53*(3), 148–151. doi:10.1145/1666420.1666457

Naimon, N., Fröhlich, M., Stern, D., & Todesco, A. (1978). *The good language learner*. Toronto, Canada: Ontario Institute for Studies in Education.

Nalley, D. (2011). Leadership in open source communities. *Opensource.com*. Retrieved 12 February, 2012, from http://opensource.com/business/11/2/leadership-open-source-communities

Naps, T. L., Rößling, G., Almstrum, V., Dann, W., Fleischer, R., Hundhausen, C., & Velázquez-Iturbide, J. Á. (2002). *Exploring the role of visualization and engagement in computer science education. Working group reports from ITiCSE on Innovation and technology in computer science education* (pp. 131–152). New York, NY: ACM.

*National Knowledge Commission*. (2005). Retrieved from http://www.knowledgecommission.gov.in/

National Science Teachers Association (NSTA). (2006). *Report: 1.2 million students fail to graduate high school*. NSTA. Retrieved 12 February, 2012, from http://www.nsta.org/publications/news/story.aspx?id=52205

National Standards in Foreign Language Education Project. (2006). *Standards for foreign language learning in the 21st century*. Lawrence, KS: Allen Press, Inc.

Ncube, C., & Maiden, N. (2000). *COTS software selection: The need to make tradeoffs between system requirements, architectures and COTS/Components*. ACM SIGSOFT COTS Workshop: Continuing Collaborations for Successful COTS Development. New York, NY: ACM Press.

Nessus. (2011). *Tenable network security*. Retrieved November 30, 2011, from http://www.nessus.org/nessus

Newmann, F., Marks, H., & Gamoran, A. (1996). Authentic pedagogy and student performance. *American Journal of Education, 104*, 280–312.

Nichols, D. M., & Twidale, M. B. (2002). *Usability and open source software*. The University of Waikato, Department of Computer Science, Working Paper Series. ISSN 1170-487X

Nichols, D. M., & Twidale, M. B. (2006). *Usability processes in open source projects* (pp. 1–20). Wiley Online Library.

Nidy, D. R., & Kwok, F. (2005). Community source development: An emerging model with new opportunities. In the *Proceedings of CHI 2005*, (pp. 1697 – 1700). Portland, OR: ACM.

Nourie, D. (2005, March 24). *Getting started with an integrated development environment (IDE)*. Oracle Sun Developer Network. Retrieved April 17, 2012, from http://java.sun.com/developer/technicalArticles/tools/intro.html

Novick, D. G. (2000). Testing documentation with "low-tech" simulation. In S. B. Jones, B. W. Moeller, M. Priestley, & B. Long (Eds.), *Proceedings of IEEE Professional Communication Society International Professional Communication Conference and Proceedings of the 18th Annual ACM International Conference on Computer Documentation: Technology & Teamwork* (pp. 55-68). New York, NY: IEEE Press.

Nov, O., & Kuk, G. (2008). Open source content contributors' response to free-riding: The effect of personality and context. *Computers in Human Behavior, 24*, 2848–2861. doi:10.1016/j.chb.2008.04.009

Nunan, D. (1999). *Second language teaching & learning*. Boston, MA: Heinle & Heinle.

Oakley, B. (2004). The value of online learning: Perspectives from the University of Illinois at Springfield. *Journal of Asynchronous Learning Networks, 8*(3), 22–31.

Obrenovic, Z., Starcevic, D., & Selic, B. (2004). A model-driven approach to content repurposing. *IEEE MultiMedia, 11*(1), 62–71. doi:10.1109/MMUL.2004.1261109

O'Hara, K. J., & Kay, J. S. (2003). Open source software and computer science education. *Journal of Computing Sciences in Colleges, 18*(3), 1–7.

Olifer, N., & Olifer, V. (2006). *Computer networks: Principles, technologies and protocols for network design*. San Francisco, CA: John Wiley & Sons.

Oller, J. W. Jr, Baca, L., & Vigil, F. (1977). Attitudes and attained proficiency in ESL: A sociolinguistic study of Mexican-Americans in the southwest. *TESOL Quarterly, 11*, 173–183. doi:10.2307/3585453

Omaggio Hadley, A. (2001). *Teaching language in context* (3rd ed.). Boston, MA: Heinle & Heinle.

Open Source Initiative. (2006). *The open source definition (annotated), version 1.9*. (B. Perens, & K. Coar, Eds.). Open Source Initiative. Retrieved April 17, 2012, from http://www.opensource.org/osd.html

OpenCourseWare Consortium. (2010). *What is OpenCourseWare?* Retrieved December 15, 2010 from: http://www.ocwconsortium.org/aboutus/whatisocw

OpenCourseWare Consortium. (2012). *Consortium members*. Retrieved from http://www. ocwconsortium.org/members/consortium-members.html

OpenStreetMap Foundation. (2011). *OSMF-OpenStreetMap Foundation website*. Retrieved from http://www. osmfoundation.org/wiki/Main_Page

Oreg, S., & Nov, O. (2008). Exploring motivations for contributing to open source initiatives: The roles of contribution context and personal values. *Computers in Human Behavior, 24*, 2055–2073. doi:10.1016/j.chb.2007.09.007

Organisation for Economic Co-operation and Development (OECD). (2009). *Education today: The OECD perspective*. Paris, France: OECD. Retrieved 10 February, 2012, from http://www.oecdbookshop.org/oecd/get-it.asp?REF=9609021E.PDF&TYPE=browse

OSI. (2011). *Open Source Initiative portal.* Retrieved from http://www.opensource.org/

Pane, J. F., Corbett, A. T., & John, B. E. (1996). Assessing dynamics in computer-based instruction. In M. J. Tauber (Ed.), *Conference on Human Factors in Computing Systems: Common Ground* (pp. 197-204). New York, NY: ACM Press.

Papell, B., & Muth, S. (2007). *VoiceThread* [webware]. Chapel Hill, NC: University of North Carolina.

Papert, S. (n.d.) Part 5, conclusion. *Instructionism vs Constructivism.* Retrieved 10 February, 2012, from http://www.papert.org/articles/const_inst/const_inst5.html

Papert, S. (n.d.). Part 1, teaching vs learning. *Instructionism vs Constructivism.* Retrieved 10 February, 2012, from http://www.papert.org/articles/const_inst/const_inst1.html

Papert, S. (1980). *Mindstorms: Children, computers, and powerful ideas.* Basic Books.

Papert, S., & Harel, I. (Eds.). (1991). *Constructionism: Research reports and essays 1985 – 1990. The Epistemology and Learning Research Group, the Media Lab, Massachusetts Institute of Technology.* Norwood, NJ: Ablex Pub. Corp.

Park, J. (2009). *Code of best practices in fair use for OpenCourseWare.* Creative Commons. Retrieved July 15, 2011, from https://creativecommons.org/weblog/entry/18550

Parker, K. R., & Chao, J. T. (2007). Wiki as a teaching tool. *Interdisciplinary Journal of Knowledge and Learning Objects, 3,* 57–72.

Park, S. H., & Ertmer, P. A. (2008). Examining barriers in technology-enhanced problem-based learning: Using a performance support systems approach. *British Journal of Educational Technology, 39*(4), 631–643. doi:10.1111/j.1467-8535.2008.00858.x

Partnership for 21st Century Skills. (2009). *Framework for 21st century learning.* Partnership for 21st Century Skills. Retrieved 10 February, 2012, from http://www.21stcenturyskills.org/index.php?Itemid=120&id=254&option=com_content&task=view

Patel, H., Pettitt, M., & Wilson, J. R. (2011). Factors of collaborative working: A framework for a collaboration model. *Applied Ergonomics, 43*(1).

Patterson, D. A. (2006). Computer science education in the 21st century. *Communications of the ACM, 49*(3), 27–30. doi:10.1145/1118178.1118212

Paudel, B., Harlalka, J., & Shrestha, J. (2010). Open technologies and developing economies. *Proceedings for the CAN IT Conference, 2010.*

Paul, R. H., & Bringley, J. E. (2008). New technologies, new learners and new challenges: Leading our universities in times of change. In Evans, T., Haughey, M., & Murphy, D. (Eds.), *International handbook of distance education* (pp. 435–452). Emerald.

Pellan, B., & Concolato, C. (2008). Adaptation of scalable multimedia documents. In the *Proceedings of DocEng '08:* São Paulo, Brazil (pp. 32 – 41).

Penrod, J. I., & Harbor, A. F. (2000). Designing and implementing a learning organization-oriented information technology planning and management process. In Petrides, L. A. (Ed.), *Case studies on information technology in higher education: Implications for policy and practice* (pp. 7–19). Hershey, PA: IGI Publishing. doi:10.4018/978-1-878289-74-2.ch001

Perkins, D. N. (2001, May). Technology meets constructivism: Do they make a marriage? *Educational Technology,* (n.d), 18–23.

Phillipson, M. (2008). Wikis in the classroom: A taxonomy. In Cummings, R. E., & Barton, M. (Eds.), *Wiki writing: Collaborative learning in the college classroom* (pp. 19–43). Ann Arbor, MI: University of Michigan Press.

Piaget, J. (1962). *Play, dreams and imitation in childhood.* New York, NY: Norton.

Piaget, J. (1973). *To understand is to invent.* New York, NY: Grossman.

Pierson, M. E., & Cozart, A. (2005). Case studies of future teachers: Learning to teach with technology. *Journal of Computing in Teacher Education, 21*(2), 59–63.

Plaisant, C., & Shneiderman, B. (2005). Show me! Guidelines for producing recorded demonstrations. *2005 IEEE Symposium on Visual Languages and Human-Centric Computing* (pp. 171-178). IEEE.

PLATO History Foundation. (2011, March 22). *PLATO history: Remembering the future.* Retrieved April 17, 2012, from http://www.platohistory.org/.

Poindexter, S. E., & Heck, B. S. (1999). Using the web in your courses: What can you do? What should you do? *IEEE Control Systems*, February, 83-92.

Polanski, A. (2007). Is the general public licence (sic) a rational choice? *The Journal of Industrial Economics*, *66*(4), 691–714. doi:10.1111/j.1467-6451.2007.00326.x

Porter, M., & Schwab, K. (2008). *Global competitiveness report 2008–2009.* Geneva, Switzerland: World Economic Forum. Retrieved 10 February, 2012, from http://www.weforum.org/pdf/GCR08/GCR08.pdf

Prabaker, M., Bergman, L., & Castelli, V. (2006). An evaluation of using programming by demonstration and guided walkthrough techniques for authoring and utilizing documentation. In R. E. Grinter, T. Rodden, P. M. Aoki, E. Cutrell, R. Jeffries, & G. M. Olson (Eds.), *Proceedings of the 2006 Conference on Human Factors in Computing Systems (CHI 2006)* (pp. 241-250). New York, NY: ACM Press.

Prensky, M. (2001). The digital game-based learning revolution. In M. Prensky (Ed.), *Digital game-based learning.* Saint Paul, MN: Paragon House. Retrieved April 11, 2012, from http://courses.ceit.metu.edu.tr/ceit420/week2/Prensky-Ch1-Digital-Game-Based-Learning.pdf

Preston, D. S. (Ed.). (2004). *Virtual learning and higher education.* New York, NY: Rodopi.

Project Tomorrow. (2006). K-12 student national findings. *Speak Up Reports.* Project Tomorrow, California. Retrieved 3 February, 2012, from http://www.tomorrow.org/docs/Speak%20Up%202006%20National%20Snapshot_K-12%20Students.pdf

Project Tomorrow. (2009). *Media release, 24 March 2009.* CA: Project Tomorrow. Retrieved 3 February, 2012, from http://www.tomorrow.org/speakup/pdfs/PT%20releaseFINAL.pdf

Project Tomorrow. (2011). *The new 3 E's of education: Enabled, engaged and empowered how today's students are leveraging emerging technologies for learning.* Project Tomorrow, California. Retrieved 3 February, 2012, from http://www.tomorrow.org/speakup/pdfs/SU10_3EofEducation(Students).pdf

Quint-Rapoport, M. (2010). *Open source in higher education: A situational analysis of the open journal systems software project.* Doctoral dissertation, Toronto, Canada, University of Graduate Department of Theory and Policy Studies in Education University of Toronto.

Rajan, Y. S. (2006). *Red Hat and CII's education initiative.* Retrieved from http://www.expresscomputeronline.com/20060116/market04.shtml

Ramsey, N. (1994, September). Literate programming simplified. *IEEE Software*, *11*(5), 97–105. doi:10.1109/52.311070

Rankin, K., Baecker, R., & Wolf, P. (2004). ePresence: An open source interactive webcasting and archiving system for elearning. *Proceedings of E-Learn 2004.*

Raymond, D. R. (1991). Reading source code. *Proceedings of the 1991 Conference of the Centre for Advanced Studies on Collaborative Research, CASCON '91.*

Raymond, E. S. (2003). The cathedral and the bazaar. *First Monday*, 1-45. Retrieved December 28, 2010, from http://131.193.153.231/www/issues/issue3_3/aymond/index.html

Raymond, E. (2001). *The cathedral and the bazaar: Musings on Linux and open source code by an accidental revolutionary* (2nd ed.). O'Reilly.

Raymond, E. S. (1999). *The cathedral and the bazaar.* New York, NY: O'Reilly Media, Inc.

Rennie, F., & Mason, R. (2010). Designing higher education courses using open educational resources. In Khine, M. S., & Saleh, I. M. (Eds.), *New science of learning: Cognition, computers and collaboration in education.* Springer. doi:10.1007/978-1-4419-5716-0_13

Resnick, M. (2007). Sowing the seeds for a more creative society. *Learning and Leading with Technology*, (pp. 18–22). International Society for Technology in Education (ISTE). Retrieved 13 February, 2012, from http://web.media.mit.edu/~mres/papers/Learning-Leading-final.pdf

Resnick, M. (2008). *Falling in love with Seymour's ideas.* American Educational Research Association (AERA) Annual Conference. New York, NY: AERA. Retrieved 13 February, 2012, from http://web.media.mit.edu/~mres/papers/AERA-seymour-final.pdf

Rice, D. (2008). *Geekonomics: The real cost of insecure software.* Boston, MA: Pearson Education.

Richardson, W. (2009). *Blogs, wikis, podcasts, and other powerful web tools for classrooms* (2nd ed.). Thousand Oaks, CA: Corwin Press.

Rieber, L. P. (1990). Animation in computer-based instruction. *Educational Technology Research and Development, 38*(1), 77–86. doi:10.1007/BF02298250

Riesco, N. B., & Navón, J. C. (2006). Enterprise applications: Taking the open source option seriously. In Avison, D., Elliott, S., Krogstie, J., & Pries-Heje, J. (Eds.), *The past and future of information systems: 1976 – 2006 and beyond* (pp. 107–118). Boston, MA: Springer.

Rosenbusch, M. H. (2005). The No Child Left Behind Act and teaching and learning languages in the U.S. schools. *Modern Language Journal, 89*, 250–261.

Rosenbusch, M. H., & Jensen, J. (2004). Status of foreign language programs in NECTFL states. *NECTFL Review, 56*, 26–37.

Roslina, I., & Jaafar, A. (2009). *Educational games (EG) design framework: Combination of game design, pedagogy and content modeling.* 2009 International Conference on Electrical Engineering and Informatics. Selangor, Malaysia. Retrieved April 12, 2012, from http://ieeexplore.ieee.org/stamp/stamp.jsp?tp=&arnumber=5254771

Rößling, G., Malmi, L., Clancy, M., Joy, M., Kerren, A., & Korhonen, A. (2008, December). Enhancing Learning management systems to better support computer science education. *SIGCSE Bulletin, 40*(4), 1.

Rovai, A. P., & Jordan, H. M. (2004). Blended learning and sense of community: A comparative analysis with traditional and fully online graduate courses. *International Review of Research in Open and Distance Learning, 5*(2).

Rowley, D. E., & Rhoades, D. G. (1992). The cognitive jogthrough: A fast-paced user interface evaluation procedure. In P. Bauersfeld, J. Bennett, & G. Lynch (Ed.), *Conference on Human Factors in Computing Systems (CHI 1992)* (pp. 389-395). New York, NY: ACM Press.

Ruiz, J. G., Cook, D. A., & Levinson, A. J. (2009). Computer animations in medical education: A critical literature review. *Medical Education, 43*(9), 838–846. doi:10.1111/j.1365-2923.2009.03429.x

Rupprecht, C. E. (2004). A tale of two worlds: Public health management decisions in human rabies prevention. [Comment Editorial]. *Clinical Infectious Diseases, 39*(2), 281–283. doi:10.1086/421563

Rupprecht, C. E., Barrett, J., Briggs, D., Cliquet, F., Fooks, A. R., & Lumlertdacha, B. (2008). Can rabies be eradicated? [Review]. *Developmental Biology, 131*, 95–121.

Rupprecht, C. E., Briggs, D., Brown, C. M., Franka, R., Katz, S. L., & Kerr, H. D. (2010). Use of a reduced (4-dose) vaccine schedule for postexposure prophylaxis to prevent human rabies: recommendations of the advisory committee on immunization practices. [Guideline]. *MMWR. Recommendations and Reports, 59*(RR-2), 1–9.

Russell, S. J., & Norvig, P. O. (2010). *Artificial intelligence: A modern approach.* Boston, MA: Pearson.

Rutgers University. (2012). *Rutgers.edu.* Retrieved April 17, 2012, from http://www.youtube.com/user/rutgers

Saint-Paul, G. (2003). Growth effects of non-proprietary innovation. *Journal of the European Economic Association: Papers and Proceedings, 1*(2-3), 429–439. doi:10.1162/154247603322391062

Sametinger, J. (1994). The role of documentation in programmer training. In Woodman, M. (Ed.), *Programming languages: Experiences and practice.* Chapman & Hall.

Sampson, B. (2008). *Open source LMS – 10 Alternatives to Moodle.* Retrieved July 6, 2011, from http://barrysampson.com/2009/04/open-source-lms-10-alternatives-to-moodle/

Sanako. (2011). *Sanako mp3 recorder.* Retrieved from http://www.sanako.com/Products/Product_container/SANAKO_MP3_Recorder.iw3

Schaffert, S., Bischof, D., Bürger, T., Gruber, A., Hilzensauer, W., & Schaffert, S. (2006). Learning with semantic wikis. *Proceedings of the First Workshop on Semantic Wikis – From Wiki To Semantics (SemWiki 2006)*, Budva, Montenegro. Retrieved April 17, 2012, from http://www.schaffert.eu/wp-content/uploads/Schaffert06_SemWikiLearning.pdf

Schinke-Llano, L., & Vicars, R. (1993). The affective filter and negotiated interaction: Do our language activities provide for both? *Modern Language Journal, 77*(3), 325–329. doi:10.1111/j.1540-4781.1993.tb01979.x

Schneider, M. C., Belotto, A., Ade, M. P., Leanes, L. F., Correa, E., & Tamayo, H. (2005). Epidemiologic situation of human rabies in Latin America in 2004. *Epidemiological Bulletin, 26*(1), 2–4.

Schroeder, U., & Spannagel, C. (2006). Supporting the active learning process. *International Journal on E-Learning, 5*(2), 245–264.

Schryen, G. (2011). Is open source security a myth? What does vulnerability and patch data say? *Communications of the ACM, 54*(5), 130–140. doi:10.1145/1941487.1941516

Shank, R. C., Berman, T. R., & Macpherson, K. A. (1999). Learning by doing. In Reigeluth, C. M. (Ed.), *Instructional-design theories and models: A new paradigm of instructional theory* (Vol. II, pp. 161–181). Mahwah, NJ: Lawrence Erlbaum Associates.

Shantavasinkul, P., Tantawichien, T., Wacharapluesadee, S., Jeamanukoolkit, A., Udomchaisakul, P., & Chattranukulchai, P. (2010). Failure of rabies postexposure prophylaxis in patients presenting with unusual manifestations. [Case Reports Research Support, Non-U.S. Gov't]. *Clinical Infectious Diseases, 50*(1), 77–79. doi:10.1086/649873

Sharma, R., & Mishra, S. (2007). *Cases on global e-learning practices: Successes and pitfalls* (pp. 1-372). doi:10.4018/978-1-59904-340-1

Sharma, R. (2001). Online delivery of programmes: A case study of Indira Gandhi National Open University (IGNOU). *International Review of Research in Open and Distance Learning, 1*(2). Retrieved from http://www.irrodl.org/index.php/irrodl/rt/printerFriendly/18/356

Sharma, R. C. (1999). Networked distance education in India. *Indian Journal of Open Learning, 8*(2), 147–156.

Sharma, R. C., & Mishra, S. (2007). *Cases on global e-learning practices: Successes and pitfalls*. Hershey, PA: IGI Global.

Shea, P. J., Pickett, A. M., & Plez, W. E. (2003). A follow-up investigation of "teaching presence" in The SUNY Learning Network. *Journal of Asynchronous Learning Networks, 7*(2), 61–80.

Sheppard, E. (2009, November 21). Wikis for end-user document. *Useful Tips when Open Sourcing*. Retrieved from http://wikis4userdoc.intodit.com/page/useful-tips-when-open-sourcing

Sherifudeen, M. (2005). *Wiki using ASP.NET*. Master's Thesis, Kansas State University.

Shibuya, B., & Tamai, T. (2009). Understanding the process of participating in open source communities. *Proceedings of FLOSS '09*, Vancouver, Canada, IEEE, (pp. 1 – 6).

Siegfried, T. (2006). *A beautiful math: John Nash, game theory, and the modern quest for a code of nature* (p. 213). Washington, DC: Joseph Henry Press.

Singh, P., Lin, T., Mueller, E. T., Lim, G., Perkins, T., & Zhu, W. L. (2002). Open mind common sense: Knowledge acquisition from the general public. In R. Meersman, Z. Tari, & M. Papazoglu (Eds.), *Proceedings of On the Move to Meaningful Internet Systems 2002: Confederated International Conferences CoopIS, DOA, and ODBASE 2002, LNCS 2519*, (pp. 1223-1237). Heidelberg, Germany: Springer.

Singh, V., Twidale, M. B., & Rathi, D. (2006). Open source technical support: A look at peer help-giving. *Proceedings of the 39th Hawaii International Conference on System Sciences.*

Sleeman, D., & Brown, J. S. (1982). Introduction: Intelligent tutoring systems. In Sleeman, D., & Brown, J. S. (Eds.), *Intelligent tutoring systems* (pp. 1–10). Orlando, FL: Academic Press.

Smith, A. D., & Rupp, W. T. (2004). Managerial implications of computer-based online/face-to-face business education: A case study. *Online Information Review, 28*(2), 100–109. doi:10.1108/14684520410531682

Smith, D. E., & Nair, R. (2005). The architecture of virtual machines. [IEEE Computer Society]. *Computer, 38*(5), 32–38. doi:10.1109/MC.2005.173

Smith, M. S. (2009). Open educational. *Science, 323*, 89–93. doi:10.1126/science.1168018

Smith, M., Barton, M., Bass, M., Branschofsky, M., McClellan, G., Stuve, D., & Walker, J. H. (2003). *DSpace: An open source dynamic digital repository*. Corporation for National Research Initiatives.

Soloway, E. (1986, September). Learning to program = learning to construct mechanisms and explanations. *Communications of the ACM, 29*(9), 850–858. doi:10.1145/6592.6594

Spinuzzi, C. (2002). Modeling genre ecologies. In K. Haramundanis, & M. Priestley (Eds.), *Proceedings of the 20th Annual International Conference on Documentation (SIGDOC 2002)*, (pp. 200-207).

Spinuzzi, C., & Zachry, M. (2000, August). Genre ecologies: An open-system approach to understanding and constructing documentation. *ACM Journal of Computer Documentation, 24*(3), 169–181. doi:10.1145/344599.344646

Stallman, R. (1986). What is the Free Software Foundation? *GNU's (GNUs Not Unix). Bulletin, 1*(1), 7–8.

Stallman, R. M. (2004). *GNU general public license*. Free Software Foundation, Inc.

Staring, K., & Titlestad, O. H. (2008). *Development as a free software: Extending commons based peer production to the south.*

Starr, C. W., Manaris, B., & Stalvey, R. H. (2008). Bloom's taxonomy revisited: Specifying assessable learning objectives in computer science. *Proceedings of the 39th SIGCSE Technical Symposium on Computer Science Education* (pp. 261-265). New York, NY, USA: ACM Press.

Stasko, J., Badre, A., & Lewis, C. (1993). Do algorithm animations assist learning? An empirical study and analysis. *INTERACT, 93*, 24–29.

Stephenson, C., Gal-Ezer, J., Haberman, B., & Verno, A. (2005). *The new educational imperative: Improving high school - Final report of the CSTA Task Force*. New York, NY: Computer Science Teachers Association, Association for Computing Machinery.

Stepp-Greany, J. (2002). Student perceptions on language learning in a technological environment: Implications for the new millennium. *Language Learning & Technology, 6*(1), 165–180.

Stevenson, D. E. (1993). Science, computational science and computer science: At a crossroads. In S. C. Kwasny, & J. F. Buck (Eds.), *Proceedings of the 1993 ACM Conference on Computer Science (CSC 1993)* (pp. 7-14). New York, NY: ACM Press.

Stork, D. G. (1999, May/June). The open mind initiative. *IEEE Intelligent Systems and their Applications, 14*(3), 16-20.

Stuckart, D. W., & Glanz, J. (2010). *Revisiting Dewey: Best practices for educating the whole child today.* Rowman and Littlefield Publishing Group Tech Analyser. (2011). Open source alternative to commercial software. *Tech Analyser.* Retrieved 18 February, 2012, from http://tech-analyser.blogspot.com.au/2011/10/open-source-alternative-to-commercial.html

Sue, D. W., Arrendondo, P., & McDavis, R. J. (1992). Multicultural competencies/standards: A call to the profession. *Journal of Counseling and Development, 70*(4), 477–486. doi:10.1002/j.1556-6676.1992.tb01642.x

Sue, D. W., Carter, R. T., Casas, J. M., Fouad, N. A., Ivey, A. E., & Jensen, M. (1998). *Multicultural counseling competencies: Individual and organizational development.* Thousand Oaks, CA: Sage.

Sue, D. W., & Sue, D. (2008). *Counseling the culturally diverse: Theory and practice* (5th ed.). Hoboken, NJ: Wiley.

Sue, D. W., & Torino, G. C. (2005). Racial-cultural competence: Awareness, knowledge, and skills. In Carter, R. T. (Ed.), *Handbook of racial-cultural psychology and counseling* (pp. 3–18). Hoboken, NJ: Wiley.

Suh, B., Chi, E. H., Pendleton, B. A., & Kittur, A. (2007). Us vs. them: Understanding social dynamics in Wikipedia with revert graph visualizations. *IEEE Symposium on Visual Analytics Science and Technology (VAST '07)*, October 30 - November 3, Sacramento, CA, (pp. 163-170). Piscataway, NJ: IEEE.

Suoranta, J., & Veden, T. (2010). *Wikiworld*. London, UK: PlutoPress.

Suppes, P., & Morningstar, M. (1969, October 17). Computer-assisted instruction. *Science, 166*, 343–350. doi:10.1126/science.166.3903.343

Sutton, A. (2006, September). Stop using wikis as documentation. *Symphonious*. Retrieved from http://www.symphonious.net/2006/09/02/stop-using-wikis-as-documentation/

Swanson, P., & Early, P. (2008). Digital recordings and assessment: An alternative for measuring oral proficiency. In A. Moeller, J. Theiler, & S. Betta (Eds.), *CSCTFL report* (pp. 129-143). Eau Claire, WI: Central States Conference on the Teaching of Foreign Languages.

Swanson, P. (2010). Teacher efficacy and attrition: Helping students at the introductory levels of language instruction appears critical. *Hispania, 93*(2), 305–321.

Swanson, P., Early, P. N., & Baumann, Q. (2011). What audacity! Decreasing student anxiety while increasing instructional time. In Özkan Czerkawski, B. (Ed.), *Free and open source software for e-learning: Issues, successes and challenges* (pp. 168–186). Hershey, PA: IGI Global.

Swanson, P., & Schlig, C. (2010). Improving second language speaking proficiency via interactional feedback. *International Journal of Adult Vocational Education and Technology, 1*(4), 17–30. doi:10.4018/javet.2010100102

Taleb, N. N. (2010). *The black swan: The impact of the highly improbable*. New York, NY: Random House. (Original work published 2007)

Taylor, J. (2007). OpenCourseWare futures: Creating a parallel universe. *E-Journal of Instructional Science and Technology, 10*(1). Retrieved 4/25/11 from: http://citeseerx.ist.psu.edu/viewdoc/download?doi=10.1.1.110.555&rep=rep1&type=pdf

Teare, D., & Paquet, C. (2005). *Campus network design fundamentals*. Indianapolis, IN: Cisco Press.

Technology acceptance model. (n.d.). *Wikipedia*. Retrieved July 10, 2011, from http://en.wikipedia.org/wiki/Technology_acceptance_model

TechTarget. (2008). *Webmaster*. Retrieved from http://whatis.techtarget.com/definition/0,sid9_gci213349,00.html

Teigen, P. M. (2012). The global history of rabies and the historian's gaze: An essay review. *Journal of the History of Medicine and Allied Sciences, 75*(1). doi:doi:10.1093/jhmas/jrr075

Thatcher, J. D. (2006). Computer animation and improved student comprehension. *The Journal of the American Osteopathic Association, 106*(1), 9–14.

The Computer Language Company. (2011). Definition of: Trolling. *PCMAG.COM*. Retrieved from http://www.pcmag.com/encyclopedia_term/0,2542,t=trolling&i=53181,00.asp

The Hindu. (2010). *Embrace open source philosophy, Kalam tells scientists, researchers*. Retrieved from http://www.thehindu.com/news/cities/Hyderabad/article956890.ece

The Learning Curve Consortium. (2011). *Home*. The Learning Curve Consortium Worldwide Inc. Retrieved 18 February, 2012, from http://www.thelearningcurve.org/?q=content/complete-cost-effective-elearning-solution

Tierney, W. (1988). Organizational culture in higher education. *The Journal of Higher Education, 59*, 2–21. doi:10.2307/1981868

Tong, T. (2004). *Free/open source software in education*. UNDP-APDIP 2004.

Tsiavos, P., & Whitley, E. (2010). *Open sourcing regulation: The development of the Creative Commons licenses as a form of commons based peer production*.

Tufte, E. R. (1990). *Envisioning information*. Cheshire, CT: Graphics Press.

Tufte, E. R. (1997). *Visual explanations: Images and quantities, evidence and narrative*. Cheshire, CT: Graphics Press. doi:10.1063/1.168637

Tufte, E. R. (2006). *Beautiful evidence*. Cheshire, CT: Graphics Press.

U.S. Census Bureau. (2001). *Population profile of the United States*. Retrieved January 2, 2012, from http://www.census.gov/population/www/pop-profile/natproj.html

U.S. Department of Health and Human Services. (2010). *Healthy People 2010: With understanding and improving health and objectives for improving health,* 2 Vols., 2nd ed. Washington, DC: U.S. Government Printing Office, November 2000.

Ubuntu. (2012). About Ubuntu governance. *Ubuntu.* Retrieved 12 March, 2012, from http://www.ubuntu.com/project/about-ubuntu/governance

UMassWiki. (2011). *UMassWiki: Blocking spam in MediaWiki.* Retrieved from http://www.umasswiki.com/wiki/UMassWiki:Blocking_Spam_In_Mediawiki

UNESCO. (2002). *Forum on the impact of open courseware for higher education in developing countries: Final report.* Retrieved from http://wcet.info/resources/publications/unescofinalreport.pdf

United Nations Educational, Scientific and Cultural Organization (UNESCO). (2012). *Mobile learning.* UNESCO. Retrieved 12 March, 2012, from http://www.unesco.org/new/en/unesco/themes/icts/m4ed/

United Nations. (2012). *United Nations observances.* Retrieved April 10, 2012, from http://www.un.org/en/events/observances/days.shtml

University of Birmingham. (2009). *Developing a virtual teaching and learning centre for problem based learning.* Retrieved August 1, 2009, from http://www.education.bham.ac.uk/research/projects1/pbl/index.shtml

Uys, P. (2001). Networked educational management: Transforming educational management in a networked institute. In C. Montgomerie & J. Viteli (Eds.), *Proceedings of World Conference on Educational Multimedia, Hypermedia and Telecommunications 2001* (pp. 1917-1923). Chesapeake, VA: AACE.

Van Meer, E. (2003). PLATO: From computer-based education to corporate social responsibility. *Iterations: An Interdisciplinary Journal of Software History, 2,* 1-22. Retrieved April 17, 2012, from http://www.cbi.umn.edu/iterations/vanmeer.html

van Rooij, S. W. (2011). Higher education sub-cultures and open source adoption. *Computers & Education, 57,* 1171–1183. doi:10.1016/j.compedu.2011.01.006

Van Wyk, C. J. (1990, March). Literate programming: An assessment. *Communications of the ACM, 33*(3), 361, 365.

Vaughan, K., & MacVicar, A. (2004). Employees' pre-implementation attitudes and perceptions to e-learning: A banking case study analysis. *Journal of European Industrial Training, 28*(5), 400–413. doi:10.1108/03090590410533080

Ven, K., & Verelst, J. (2008). The impact of ideology on the organizational adoption of open source software. *Journal of Database Management, 19*(2), 58–72. doi:10.4018/jdm.2008040103

Verbert, K. GaSvevic, D., Jovanovic, J., & Duval, E. (2005). Ontology-based learning content repurposing. *Special interest tracks and posters of the 14th International Conference on World Wide Web* (pp. 1140-1141). Chiba, Japan: ACM.

Vignal, M. W. (1886). Report on M, Pasteur's researches on rabies and the treatment of hydrophobia by preventive inoculation. *British Medical Journal, 1*(1322), 809–811. doi:10.1136/bmj.1.1322.809

Vignare, K., & Shelle, G. H. (2011, July 11). *Developing open educational programs: Moving beyond the course approach.* (Pre-conference). 4th Annual International Symposium: Emerging Technologies for Online Learning: San Jose, California. Sloan Consortium and MERLOT.

VMWare. (2009). *VMWare.* Retrieved December 6, 2011, from http://www.vmware.com

Vockell, E. (1993). Why schools fail and what we can do about it. *Clearing House (Menasha, Wis.), 66*(4), 200–205.

Volle, L. (2005). Analyzing oral skills in voice e-mail and online interviews. *Language Learning & Technology, 9*(3), 146–163. Retrieved from http://llt.msu.edu/vol9num3/volle/

von Krogh, G., & Spaeth, S. (2007). The open source software phenomenon: Characteristics that promote research. *The Journal of Strategic Information Systems, 16*(3), 236–253. doi:10.1016/j.jsis.2007.06.001

Vrasidas, C., & McIsaac, M. S. (2007). Integrating technology in teaching and teacher education: Implications for policy and curriculum reform. *Education Media International.* Retrieved from http://vrasidas.com/wp-content/uploads/2007/07/integrateemi.pdf

Vygotsky, L. S. (1962). *Thought and language.* Cambridge, MA: Massachusetts Institute of Technology Press.

Vygotsky, L. S. (1978). *Mind and society: The development of higher mental processes.* Cambridge, MA: Harvard University Press.

W3C. (2009). *Standards.* W3C Consortium. Retrieved from http://www.w3.org/standards

Wagner, C. (2004). Wiki: A technology for conversational knowledge management and group collaboration. *Communications of the Association for Information Systems, 13,* 265–289.

Wang, H., Blue, J., & Plourde, M. (2010). Community source software in higher education. *IT Professional, 12*(6), 31–37. doi:10.1109/MITP.2010.120

Waters, J. K. (2010). Prepare for impact. *T.H.E. Journal, 37*(5), 20–25.

Weber, S. (2004). *The success of open source.* Cambridge, MA: Harvard University Press.

Weiss, S. G., DeFalco, A. A., & Weiss, E. M. (2005). *Progressive = permissive? Not according to John Dewey... Subjects matter!* Retrieved 10 February, 2012, from http://www.usca.edu/essays/vol142005/defalco.pdf

Weller, M. (2007). The open source option. In *Virtual learning environments* (pp. 96–110). London, UK: Routledge.

Wenger, E. (2006). *Communities of practice: A brief introduction.* Retrieved 10 February, 2012, from http://www.ewenger.com/theory/

Wessa, P. (2009). How reproducible research leads to non-rote learning within socially constructivist statistics education. *Electronic Journal of e-Learning, 7*(2), 173-182.

Wessel, D. (2010, April 8). Did 'great recession' live up to the name? *The Wall Street Journal.* Retrieved from http://online.wsj.com/article/SB100014240527023035 91204575169693166352882.html

Whalen, T., & Wright, D. (1999). Methodology for cost-benefit analysis of web-based tele-learning: Case Study of the Bell Online Institute. *American Journal of Distance Education, 13*(1), 25–43. doi:10.1080/08923649909527012

Wharton, C., Rieman, J., Lewis, C., & Polson, P. (1994). The cognitive walkthrough method: A practitioner's guide. In J. Nielsen, & R. L. (Eds.), *Usability inspection methods* (pp. 105-140). New York, NY: Wiley.

WHO. (2005). WHO expert consultation on rabies: First report. *Technical Report Series, 931,* (pp. 121).

WHO. (2010). Rabies vaccines: WHO position paper-recommendations. *Vaccine, 28*(44), 7140–7142. doi:10.1016/j.vaccine.2010.08.082

WHO. (2011). *The immunological basis for immunization series: Rabies* (pp. 1–23). Geneva, Switzerland: WHO.

WHO. (2011). *Rabies fact sheet,* no 99. Retrieved from http://www.who.int/mediacentre/factsheets/fs099/en/

Wieder, B. (2011, February 11). 6 top tech trends on the horizon for higher education. *The Chronicle of Higher Education.* Retrieved April 10, 2012, from http://chronicle.com/blogs/wiredcampus/6-top-tech-trends-on-the-horizon-for-education/29581

Wikipedia. (2008, December 3). *Wikipedia.* Retrieved from Wikipedia.org: http://en.wikipedia.org

Wikipedia. (2011). *Mediawiki.* Retrieved from http://en.wikipedia.org/wiki/MediaWiki

Wikipedia. (2011). *Edit wars.* Retrieved from http://en.wikipedia.org/wiki/Edit_war

Wikipedia. (2012, April 13). *OpenOffice.org.* Retrieved from http://en.wikipedia.org/wiki/OpenOffice.org

Wikipedia. (2012, April 16). *Content management system.* Retrieved April 17, 2012, from http://en.wikipedia.org/wiki/Content_management_system

Wikipedia. (2012, April 17). *Informatics (academic field).* Retrieved from http://en.wikipedia.org/wiki/Informatics_(academic_field)

Wikipedia. (2012, March 12). *Open content.* Retrieved April 17, 2012, from http://en.wikipedia.org/wiki/Open_content

Wilde, H., Briggs, D. J., Meslin, F. X., Hemachudha, T., & Sitprija, V. (2003). Rabies update for travel medicine advisors. *Clinical Infectious Diseases*, *37*(1), 96–100. doi:10.1086/375605

Wiley, D. (2007). *On the sustainability of open educational resource initiatives in higher education*, (pp. 1–21). Paper commissioned by the OECD's Centre for Educational Research and Innovation (CERI).

Wiley, D. (Ed.). (2011). *Defining the "open" in open content*. Retrieved April 17, 2012, from http://www.opencontent.org/definition/

Willinsky, J. (2003). The nine flavours of open access scholarly publishing. *E-Medicine*, *49*(3), 263–267.

Wimba. (2008). *Wimba Voice*. Retrieved from http://www.wimba.com/products/wimbavoice/

Winslow, L. E. (1996). Programming pedagogy -- A psychological overview. *ACM Special Interest Group on Computer Science Education Bulletin*, 17-22.

Wireshark. (2011). *The world's foremost network protocol analyzer*. Retrieved November 30, 2011, from http://www.wireshark.org

Witkin, H. A., Moore, C. A., Goodenough, D. R., & Cox, P. W. (1977). Field-dependent and field-independent cognitive styles and their educational implications. *Review of Educational Research*, *47*(1), 1–64. Retrieved from http://www.jstor.org/stable/1169967

Woodrow, L. (2006). Anxiety and speaking English as a second language. *RELC Journal*, *37*(3), 308–328. doi:10.1177/0033688206071315

Wright, J., Carpin, S., Cerpa, A., & Gavilan, G. (2007). *An open source teaching and learning facility for computer science and engineering education* (pp. 368–373). FECS.

Wright, V. H., Wilson, E. K., Gordon, W., & Stallworth, J. B. (2002). Master technology teacher: A partnership between preservice and inservice teachers and Teacher Educators. *Contemporary Issues in Technology & Teacher Education*, *2*(3). Retrieved from http://www.citejournal.org/vol2/iss3/currentpractice/article1.cfm

Wunner, W. H., & Briggs, D. J. (2010). Rabies in the 21$^{st}$ century. [Research Support, U.S. Gov't, P.H.S.]. *Plos Neglected Tropical Disease*, *4*(3), e591. doi:10.1371/journal.pntd.0000591

Wu, X., Smith, T. G., & Rupprecht, C. E. (2011). From brain passage to cell adaptation: The road of human rabies vaccine development. [Historical Article Review]. *Expert Review of Vaccines*, *10*(11), 1597–1608. doi:10.1586/erv.11.140

Xen. (2011). *Xen Cloud Platform project*. Retrieved November 30, 2011, from http://xen.org/products/cloudxen.html

Xiao, W., Chi, C., & Yang, M. (2007). On-line collaborative software development via Wiki. *Proceedings of the 2007 International Symposium on Wikis* (pp. 177-183). New York, NY: ACM Press.

Xu, B., & Jones, D. R. (2010). Volunteers' participation in open source software development: A study from the social-relational perspective. *The Data Base for Advances in Information Systems*, *41*(3), 69–84. doi:10.1145/1851175.1851180

Yang, A. T. (2001). Computer security and impact on computer scienc eeducation. *Proceedings of the Sixth Annual CCSC Northeastern Conference on The Journal of Computing in Small Colleges* (pp. 233-246). Middlebury, VT: Consortium for Computing Sciences in Colleges.

Ye, Y., & Kishida, K. (2003). Toward an understanding of the motivation of open source software developers. *Proceedings of the 25th International Conference on Software Engineering*, (pp. 419-429).

Young, B. (2001). Forward. In Raymond, E. (Ed.), *The cathedral and the bazaar. Musings on Linux and open source code by an accidental revolutionary* (2nd ed.). O'Reilly.

Zellmer, M. B., Frontier, A., & Pheifer, D. (2006, November). What are NCLB's instructional costs? *Educational Leadership*, *64*(3), 43–46.

Zhang, D., Zhao, J. L., Zhou, L., & Nunamaker, J. F. (2004). Can e-learning replace classroom learning? *Communications of the ACM, 47*(5), 75–79. doi:10.1145/986213.986216

Zhang, Y., Zhang, Z. L., & Yin, J. Y. (2008). Evaluation on the knowledge of rabies through health education programs among the residents in Tianjin, 2007. *Zhonghua Liu Xing Bing Xue Za Zhi, 29*(7), 744.

Zhao, Y. (2005). The future of research in technology and second language education. In Zhao, Y. (Ed.), *Research in technology and second language learning: Developments and directions* (pp. 445–457). Greenwich, CT: Information Age Publishing, Inc.

Zittrain, J. L. (2006). The generative Internet. *Harvard Law Review, 119*(7), 1974–2040.

# About the Contributors

**Shalin Hai-Jew**, Instructional Designer at K-State and Instructor for WashingtonOnline, has worked in higher education for many years as a tenured professor. She has BAs in English and Psychology and an MA in English, from the University of Washington, where she was an Early Entrant at 15 (through the Hal and Nancy Robinson Center for Young Scholars) and a Hugh Paradise Scholar. She has an Ed.D. in Educational Leadership / Public Administration from Seattle University (2005), where she was a Morford Scholar. Her dissertation was about the role of trust in online learning. Dr. Hai-Jew has written several books and edited others related to information technologies. She reviews for a number of educational publications. She was born in Huntsville, Alabama, in the US.

\* \* \*

**Brent A. Anders** is a Senior Electronic Media Coordinator for the Office of Mediated Education at Kansas State University. His work includes: educational media consulting, videography/filmmaking (directing, capturing, editing and final production), live webcasting and web accessibility/usability. Mr. Anders has a Bachelor's degree in Psychology (human computer interaction focus), and a Master's degree in Education with an instructional technology focus. He also serves in the Army National Guard as a Master Sergeant. His military duties include Branch Chief for a military educational institute that teaches a variety of courses and as Chief Instructor for ABIC (Army Basic Instructors Course). Mr. Anders has been in the education field for over 12 years dealing with military training, distance education, educational media, and higher education in general.

**Deborah J. Briggs** is an Adjunct Professor at Kansas State University College of Veterinary Medicine and is the Executive Director of the Global Alliance for Rabies Control, a registered 501c3 organization based in the United States. She is currently serving as an expert on the World Health Organization Expert Committee for rabies. Dr. Briggs has been involved in rabies prevention and control activities for over two decades and continues to work with public and private partners to improve rabies education throughout the world. Dr. Briggs has developed both real-time and on-line courses for graduate students in the field of public health at Kansas State University. Her courses are focused on improving awareness about the components and complexities of global public health. Dr. Briggs and her colleagues developed and launched several new educational initiatives over the past five years to help empower communities to take responsibility for preventing rabies. Dr. Briggs has published numerous articles and book chapters on the subject of rabies and has been an invited speaker to discuss rabies prevention throughout the world.

**Doris Carroll** is Associate Professor within the College of Education at Kansas State University in Manhattan, Kansas, where she teaches and conducts applied research in student affairs practice and higher education administration, with emphasis in diversity, multicultural counseling, distance education, and curriculum development. Dr. Carroll is a well-respected multicultural educator with more than 30 years of clinical practice, teaching, and professional service at four major research universities including the University of Nebraska-Lincoln, University of Texas at Austin, and Georgia State University before her appointment at Kansas State University in 1999. Dr. Carroll has presented national and international papers and presentations related to distance education, college student retention, and multicultural competency, and she is well published in these areas.

**Jason Caudill** holds an MBA and a PhD in Instructional Technology from the University of Tennessee. He has worked as a faculty member in the field of Business teaching primarily Information Systems and Management courses at the undergraduate and Master's level as well as teaching graduate-level Instructional Technology courses in the field of Education. Dr. Caudill's scholarship has centered on issues of technology and online education, particularly relating to issues of management and integration of technology. Most recently Dr. Caudill has been working on issues of the shifting nature of higher education as an industry. This work includes issues of the higher education market and particularly the rising popularity of OpenCourseWare and Open Educational Resources and the shift of those delivery methods into credentialed open learning solutions and Massively Open Online Courses (MOOCs). Outside of work Dr. Caudill is a member of the United States Coast Guard Auxiliary where he serves in operations and also as a member of the national staff. Dr. Caudill enjoys time in the outdoors, working with his hands, and is a sports fan, particularly college football and the UFC.

**Lee Chao** is currently a Professor of Math and Computer Science in the school of Arts and Sciences at University of Houston – Victoria, USA. He received his Ph. D. from the University of Wyoming, USA, and he is certified as Oracle Certified Professional and Microsoft Solution Developer. His current research interests are data analysis and technology-based teaching. Dr. Chao is also the author of over a dozen of research articles in data analysis and math modeling, and books in the development of computer labs and database systems.

**Yolanda Debose Columbus** left a career as a Computer Programmer in 2003 to pursue a career as an educator. While she enjoyed the technical and analytical nature of her job, she craved more people interaction. Since then she completed a Ph.D. in Education Psychology and supported various educators in their efforts to integrate technology and improve their courses. In this work, she has been able to combine her experience with and love of technology with her desire to help and serve educators. She is formally trained as an instructional designer. Her professional work includes developing and providing professional development, managing a help desk, managing a learning management system, and evaluating the quality of courses. She writes: "When I managed a college-supported learning management system we did not advertise or solicit users. Many of our faculty members chose to switch from the university-supported learning management system (LMS) to our college's LMS. During the first year, we supported 20 academic courses and approximately 1700 students. Two years later, we hosted 60+ academic courses, 15 continuing education courses, 4 research projects and 5500+ students. The type of projects I have worked on and the success of this project are based largely on my commitment to engaging stakeholders and building social capital. These experiences have reiterated my commitment to collaboration and communication."

**Peter Costa** serves as the Director of Global Communications for the Global Alliance for Rabies Control and is the Coordinator of the Alliance's flagship initiative, World Rabies Day Campaign, held annually on September 28 in 150 countries. Peter is one of only a few people in the world communicating rabies prevention messages on a global basis. Prior to his position with Alliance, he served as a Health Educator at the North Carolina Division of Public Health. In this role, Peter led the development of community-based health promotion and exposure prevention awareness programs for environmental hazards and directed state-wide educational efforts on environmental emergency response. Peter earned his Master of Public Health degree in Community Health Education from East Stroudsburg University of Pennsylvania and is certified as a Master Health Education Specialist.

**Gladys Palma de Schrynemakers**, Associate Provost at LIU/Brooklyn, directs the Collegiate Science Technology Program (CSTEP) and was Principal Investigator (P.I.) for Predominantly Black Institutions (PBI) Undergraduate STEM Grant, both prepare undergraduate minority and economically disadvantaged students to enter the STEM fields. As the Executive Vice President of APACS, Association of Administrators of CSTEP and STEP, she works closely with over 200 CSTEP/STEP directors and program staff to create a statewide professional development network for diverse students in high school, college/university to enter into STEM and licensed professions. She is the P.I. for the New York State's Smart Scholars Early College High School this program specifically engages groups of students who historically have not had access to college. She Co-Chairs the annual Teaching Narrative Conference at the Brooklyn Campus, an event that focuses on teaching narratives as a form of inquiry about student learning. Dr. Schrynemakers serves as a member of the Leadership Team for Integrative Assessment of the Imagine America Initiative. During her 22-year career with the University, she has secured over 9 million dollars in grants, taught social science research, and published frequently in peer-reviewed venues on theory and practice of constructing knowledge and assessment.

**Sue Polyson Evans** is the CEO and co-Founder of SoftChalk LLC and a pioneer in the e-Learning industry. Beginning in the mid 1990s, Sue was lead developer of one of the first commercially-available learning management systems (LMS) in the world, Web Course in a Box. She was also co-founder and president of madDuck Technologies, which developed and sold Web Course in a Box. After merging madDuck Technologies with e-learning industry giant, Blackboard Inc., Sue remained on board at Blackboard until leaving to found SoftChalk, in 2002. Prior to her experience as an entrepreneur and product developer, Evans held management positions in instructional technology at Virginia Commonwealth University. She has presented and conducted workshops at leading industry conferences, as well as published articles in the areas of e-Learning technology and the use of web technologies for education. Evans holds B.S. and M.A. degrees from Indiana State University.

**William H. Hsu** is an Associate Professor in the Department of Computing and Information Sciences at Kansas State University. He received a B.S. in Mathematical Sciences and Computer Science and an M.S.Eng. in Computer Science from Johns Hopkins University in 1993, and a Ph.D. in Computer

Science from the University of Illinois at Urbana-Champaign in 1998. At the National Center for Supercomputing Applications (NCSA) he was a co-recipient of an Industrial Grand Challenge Award for work on text analytics. His research interests include machine learning and probabilistic reasoning, with applications to information extraction, time series prediction, and data mining, especially link mining and bioinformatics (computational genomics and proteomics). Published applications of his research include spatiotemporal event detection, veterinary epidemiology, analysis of social networks and heterogeneous information networks, text mining, and sentiment analysis. Current work in his lab deals with: topic detection and tracking from news articles and social media; learning, visualizing, and reasoning with models of natural language from large text corpora; and graphical models of probability and utility for information security. Dr. Hsu has published more than 40 refereed conference and journal papers and book chapters, and has over 30 additional publications.

**Dimitris Kavroudakis** is a Geographer working as Researcher in the University of the Aegean, Geography Department. He studied Computer info Systems in the American College of Greece and Geography in The University of the Aegean. He obtained an MSc in GIS from the University of Leeds, UK and holds a PhD in Geography from the University of Sheffield, UK. As a researcher in UCL, University of Sheffield and University of The Aegean, he has been engaged in high quality geographical research which led to a number of scientific publications in the field. Some of his academic interests include GIS, open source, spatial analysis, and social and spatial inequalities. He has been involved in research concerning web GIS, visualization, spatial statistics, EU population inequalities, spatial economics and open source GIS development. He uses new methodologies of understanding space such as Artificial Intelligence and Agent Based Modeling. Aiming to promote new methods in geographical analysis, he supports computational modeling with the use of grid computing. He is a Linux and Open Source supporter and he keeps a blog concerning geography, statistics and open source in www.dimitrisk.gr/blog. Dimitris lives on an island in Greece, enjoys fishing and farming, and he holds a brown belt in Shotokan karate.

**Roger W. McHaney**, Daniel D. Burke Chair for Exceptional Faculty and Professor of Management Information Systems, is an expert on business use of technology and on the ways Web 2.0 and tech-savvy millennials are impacting higher education and learning. He also works developing distance education learning techniques. His work has been published in many top business and education journals. He has written textbooks and developed a variety of instructional material and has lectured internationally in countries such as India, New Zealand, China, the United Kingdom, Italy, Greece, Belgium, and the Netherlands. A K-State faculty member since 1995, McHaney teaches courses in management of information systems, information resources management, software development and enterprise computing. His research areas include: web 2.0 in education and business, technologies used by millennials, discrete event simulation, educational simulation systems, computer-mediated communication systems, SAP, and organizational computing. His ongoing research includes study on how social media is impacting business and education, distance learning techniques, business applications in virtual worlds such as second life and development of online training simulations. McHaney was recognized for his excellence in teaching by being named K-State's 2006-2007 Coffman Chair for University Distinguished Teaching Scholars.

**Kathryn Moyle** lives in Australia, where is the Executive Director of the *Centre for School Leadership, Learning and Development* at Charles Darwin University, in the Northern Territory. She is also an Adjunct Professor at the University of Canberra and an Adjunct Research Fellow at the University of South Australia. Professor Moyle researches and writes about technologies in teaching and learning in school education. This work includes leading government-funded national and international research projects focused on information and communication technologies (ICT) in schools. She has published on the place of technologies in schools from a range of perspectives: students, teachers, school leaders. Over the past decade, her work has included papers about the use of open source software in schools. In 2010 the Australian Council of Education Research published her book: "Building Innovation, Learning with Technologies." Kathryn's current work is examining the place of school leaders in supporting teaching and learning with technologies. Her work takes her to the USA, Europe and Asia.

**Ramesh C. Sharma** is working as Regional Director of Indira Gandhi National Open University (IGNOU), India. He has been involved in the planning, design and development of teaching and learning materials for Indira Gandhi National Open University; M P Bhoj Open University; Vardhman Mahaveer Open University, Rajasthan, and Maharshi Dayanand University, India for over two decades. From July 2009 till June 2011, he was the Director of the Institute of Distance and Continuing Education (IDCE), at University of Guyana, Guyana, South America (on behalf of the Commonwealth Secretariat, United Kingdom). He is the Co-Editor of *Asian Journal of Distance Education* ISSN 1347-9008, (www.ASIAN-JDE.org). In addition, he has been on the Editorial Advisory Board of journals including *International Review of Research in Open and Distance Learning*, online journal published by Athabasca University, Canada, *International Journal of Distance Education Technologies* published by IGI Global, USA; *Indian Journal of Open Learning* published by IGNOU, and *Distance Education* published by the Taylor & Francis Group.

**Peter B. Swanson** is Associate Professor of Spanish and Foreign Language Education at Georgia State University and serves as the Coordinator for the Foreign Language Teacher Education program. He teaches courses on pedagogy, second language acquisition, and technology integration at the undergraduate and graduate levels. Prior to joining the professoriate, Dr. Swanson taught Spanish for 15 years in the Rocky Mountains. While working as a public school educator, his interest in methods to increase student achievement and proficiency in a second language led him to research best practices in the measurement of students' oral/aural proficiency. As a faculty member of the Department of Modern and Classical Languages, he has established a cogent line of research focusing on the integration of technology into instruction as well as foreign language teacher recruitment and retention. He is the author of several books and numerous articles in highly-respected national and international journals.

# Index